THE ART OF ASSEMBLY LANGUAGE

by Randall Hyde

NO STARCH PRESS

San Francisco

THE ART OF ASSEMBLY LANGUAGE. Copyright © 2003 by Randall Hyde.

 Printed on recycled paper in the United States of America

1 2 3 4 5 6 7 8 9 10 – 06 05 04 03

Publisher: William Pollock
Managing Editor: Karol Jurado
Cover and Interior Design: Octopod Studios
Copyeditor: Kenyon Brown
Proofreader: Stephanie Provines
Compositor: Wedobooks

Distributed to the book trade in the United States by Publishers Group West, 1700 Fourth Street, Berkeley, CA 94710; phone: 800-788-3123; fax: 510-658-1834.

Distributed to the book trade in Canada by Jacqueline Gross & Associates, Inc., One Atlantic Avenue, Suite 105, Toronto, Ontario M6K 3E7 Canada; phone: 416-531-6737; fax 416-531- 4259.

For information on translations or book distributors outside the United States, please contact No Starch Press, Inc. directly:

No Starch Press, Inc.
555 De Haro Street, Suite 250, San Francisco, CA 94107
phone: 415-863-9900; fax: 415-863-9950; info@nostarch.com; http://www.nostarch.com

Library of Congress Cataloguing-in-Publication Data

```
Hyde, Randall.
  The art of assembly language / Randall Hyde.
       p. cm.
  ISBN 1-886411-97-2
 1. Assembly language (Computer program language) 2.  Programming languages (Electronic computers)
I. Title.
  QA76.73.A8H97 2003
  005.13'6--dc21
                                                        2003000471
```

THE ART OF
ASSEMBLY LANGUAGE

ACKNOWLEDGMENTS

This book has literally taken over a decade to create. It started out as "How to Program the IBM PC, Using 8088 Assembly Language" way back in 1989. I originally wrote this book for the students in my assembly language course at Cal Poly Pomona and UC Riverside. Over the years, hundreds of students have made small and large contributions (it's amazing how a little extra credit can motivate some students). I've also received thousands of comments via the Internet after placing an early, 16-bit edition of this book on my website at UC Riverside. I owe everyone who has contributed to this effort my gratitude.

I would also like to specifically thank Mary Phillips, who spent several months helping me proofread much of the 16-bit edition upon which I've based this book. Mary is a wonderful person and a great friend.

I also owe a deep debt of gratitude to William Pollock at No Starch Press, who rescued this book from obscurity. He is the one responsible for convincing me to spend some time beating on this book to create a publishable entity from it. I would also like to thank Karol Jurado for shepherding this project from its inception — it's been a long, hard road. Thanks, Karol.

BRIEF CONTENTS

CONTENTS IN DETAIL

1

HELLO, WORLD OF ASSEMBLY LANGUAGE

4

CONSTANTS, VARIABLES, AND DATA TYPES

5

PROCEDURES AND UNITS

6

ARITHMETIC

7

LOW LEVEL CONTROL STRUCTURES

8
FILES

9
ADVANCED ARITHMETIC

10

MACROS AND THE HLA COMPILE TIME LANGUAGE

11

BIT MANIPULATION

12
THE STRING INSTRUCTIONS

13
THE MMX INSTRUCTION SET

14
CLASSES AND OBJECTS

15

MIXED LANGUAGE PROGRAMMING

A
ASCII CHARACTER SET
853

B
THE 80X86 INSTRUCTION SET
857

INDEX
889

1

HELLO, WORLD
OF ASSEMBLY LANGUAGE

1.1 Chapter Overview

This chapter is a "quick-start" chapter that lets you start writing basic assembly language programs as rapidly as possible. This chapter:

- Presents the basic syntax of an HLA (High Level Assembly) program
- Introduces you to the Intel CPU architecture
- Provides a handful of data declarations, machine instructions, and high level control statements
- Describes some utility routines you can call in the HLA Standard Library
- Shows you how to write some simple assembly language programs

By the conclusion of this chapter, you should understand the basic syntax of an HLA program and should understand the prerequisites that are needed to start learning new assembly language features in the chapters that follow.

1.2   The Anatomy of an HLA Program

A typical HLA program takes the form shown in Figure 1-1.

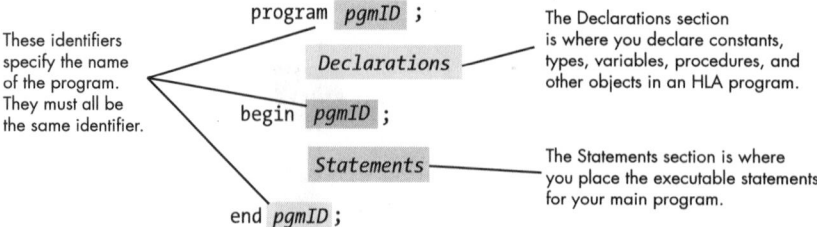

These identifiers specify the name of the program. They must all be the same identifier.

The Declarations section is where you declare constants, types, variables, procedures, and other objects in an HLA program.

The Statements section is where you place the executable statements for your main program.

PROGRAM, BEGIN, and END are HLA reserved words that delineate the program. Note the placement of the semicolons in this program.

Figure 1-1: Basic HLA Program.

pgmID in the template above is a user-defined program identifier. You must pick an appropriate, descriptive name for your program. In particular, *pgmID* would be a horrible choice for any real program. If you are writing programs as part of a course assignment, your instructor will probably give you the name to use for your main program. If you are writing your own HLA program, you will have to choose an appropriate name for your project.

Identifiers in HLA are very similar to identifiers in most high level languages. HLA identifiers may begin with an underscore or an alphabetic character, and may be followed by zero or more alphanumeric or underscore characters. HLA's identifiers are *case neutral.* This means that the identifiers are case sensitive insofar as you must always spell an identifier exactly the same way in your program (even with respect to upper and lower case). However, unlike case-sensitive languages like C/C++, you may not declare two identifiers in the program whose name differs only by alphabetic case.

A traditional first program people write, popularized by Kernighan and Ritchie's *The C Programming Language* is the Hello World program. This program makes an excellent concrete example for someone who is learning a new language. Listing 1-1 presents the HLA Hello World program.

Listing 1-1: The Hello World Program.

```
program helloWorld;
#include( "stdlib.hhf" );

begin helloWorld;

    stdout.put( "Hello, World of Assembly Language", nl );

end helloWorld;
```

The #include statement in this program tells the HLA compiler to include a set of declarations from the *stdlib.hhf* (Standard Library, HLA header file). Among other things, this file contains the declaration of the stdout.put code that this program uses.

The stdout.put statement is the print statement for the HLA language. You use it to write data to the standard output device (generally the console). To anyone familiar with I/O statements in a high level language, it should be obvious that this statement prints the phrase "Hello, World of Assembly Language." The nl appearing at the end of this statement is a constant, also defined in *stdlib.hhf*, that corresponds to the newline sequence.

Note that semicolons follow the program, begin, stdout.put, and end statements.[1] Technically speaking, a semicolon does not follow the #include statement. It is possible to create include files that generate an error if a semicolon follows the #include statement, so you may want to get in the habit of not putting a semicolon here.

The #include is your first introduction to HLA declarations. The #include itself isn't actually a declaration, but it does tell the HLA compiler to substitute the file *stdlib.hhf* in place of the #include directive, thus inserting several declarations at this point in your program. Most HLA programs you will write will need to include one or more of the HLA Standard Library header files (*stdlib.hhf* actually includes all the Standard Library definitions into your program).

Compiling this program produces a *console* application. Running this program in a command window prints the specified string and then control returns back to the command line interpreter (or *shell* in UNIX terminology).

HLA is a free-format language. Therefore, you may split statements across multiple lines if this helps to make your programs more readable. For example, you could write the stdout.put statement in the Hello World program as follows:

```
stdout.put
(
    "Hello, World of Assembly Language",
    nl
);
```

Another item you'll see appearing in sample code throughout this text is that HLA automatically concatenates any adjacent string constants it finds in your source file. Therefore, the statement above is also equivalent to:

```
stdout.put
(
    "Hello, "
    "World of Assembly Language",
    nl
);
```

---

[1] Technically, from a language design point of view, these are not all statements. However, this chapter will not make that distinction.

Indeed, nl (the newline) is really nothing more than a string constant, so (technically) the comma between the nl and the preceding string isn't necessary. You'll often see the above written as:

```
stdout.put( "Hello, World of Assembly Language" nl );
```

Notice the lack of a comma between the string constant and nl; this turns out to be perfectly legal in HLA, though it only applies to certain constants; you may not, in general, drop the comma. A later chapter will explain in detail how this works. This discussion appears here because you'll probably see this "trick" employed by sample code prior to the formal explanation.

1.3 Running Your First HLA Program

The whole purpose of the Hello World program is to provide a simple example by which some who is learning a new programming language can figure out how to use the tools needed to compile and run programs in that language. True, the Hello World program in the previous section helps demonstrate the format and syntax of a simple HLA program, but the real purpose behind a program like Hello World is to learn how to create and run a program from beginning to end. Although the previous section presents the layout of an HLA program, it did not discuss how to edit, compile, and run that program. This section will briefly cover those details.

All of the software you need to compile and run HLA programs can be found on the CD-ROM accompanying this book. The software can also be found at the following web address:

```
http://webster.cs.ucr.edu
```

(Note that the latest version of the software can always be found on Webster, so you might want to visit Webster to get any updates that may have appeared since the production of the CD-ROM; note, however, that all the software appearing in this text works just fine with the software appearing on the CD-ROM.)

This section will not describe how to install and set up the HLA system. Those instructions change over time and any attempt to describe the installation of HLA on these pages would be wasted because such instructions would become obsolete. The *readme.txt* file in the root directory of the CD-ROM is the place to go to learn how to install HLA on your system. From this point forward, this text will assume that you've successfully installed HLA and other necessary tools on your system (those instructions also show you how to compile and run your first program, so we'll skip details from that discussion, as well).

The process of creating, compiling, and running an HLA program is very similar to the process you'd use for a program written in any computer language. The first step is to create or edit your source file using a text editor. HLA is not an "integrated development system" (IDE) that allows you to edit, compile, test and debug, and run your application all from within the same program (like many software development tools). Therefore, you're going to need a text editor in order to create and edit HLA programs.

Windows and Linux both provide a plethora of text editor options. You can even use the text editor provided with other languages' IDEs to create and edit HLA programs (e.g., Visual C++, Borland's Delphi, Borland's Kylix, and similar packages). The only restriction is that HLA expects ASCII text files, so the editor you use must be capable of manipulating text files. Note that under Windows you can always use *notepad.exe* to create HLA programs; under Linux you can use *joe, vi,* or *emacs* if you don't prefer some other editor.

The HLA compiler[2] is a traditional *command line compiler.* This means that you need to run it from a Windows' *command line prompt* or a Linux *shell.* To do so, you'd type something like the following into the compile line prompt or shell window:

```
hla hw.hla
```

This command tells HLA to compile the *hw.hla* (Hello World) program to an executable file. Assuming there are no errors, you can run the resulting program by typing the following command into your command prompt window (Windows):

```
hw
```

or into the shell interpreter window (Linux):

```
./hw
```

If you're having problems getting the program to compile and run properly, please see the HLA installation instructions in the HLA Reference Manual on the accompanying CD-ROM. These instructions describe in great detail how to install, set up, and use HLA.

1.4   Some Basic HLA Data Declarations

HLA provides a wide variety of constant, type, and data declaration statements. Later chapters will cover the declaration section in more detail, but it's important to know how to declare a few simple variables in an HLA program.

HLA predefines several different signed integer types including int8, int16, and int32, corresponding to 8-bit (one byte) signed integers, 16-bit (two byte) signed integers, and 32-bit (four byte) signed integers, respectively.[3] Typical variable declarations occur in the HLA *static variable section.* A typical set of variable declarations takes the form shown in Figure 1-2.

---

[2] Traditionally, programmers have always called translators for assembly languages *assemblers* rather than *compilers*. However, because of HLA's high level features, it is more proper to call HLA a compiler rather than an assembler.

[3] A discussion of bits and bytes will appear in the next chapter if you are unfamiliar with these terms.

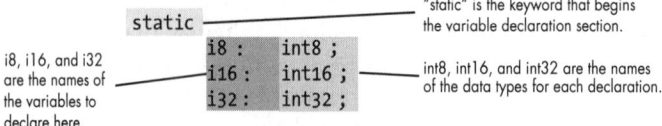

Figure 1-2: Static Variable Declarations.

Those who are familiar with the Pascal language should be comfortable with this declaration syntax. This example demonstrates how to declare three separate integers, i8, i16, and i32. Of course, in a real program you should use variable names that are a little more descriptive. While names like "i8" and "i32" describe the type of the object, they do not describe its purpose. Variable names should describe the purpose of the object.

In the static declaration section, you can also give a variable an initial value that the operating system will assign to the variable when it loads the program into memory. Figure 1-3 provides the syntax for this.

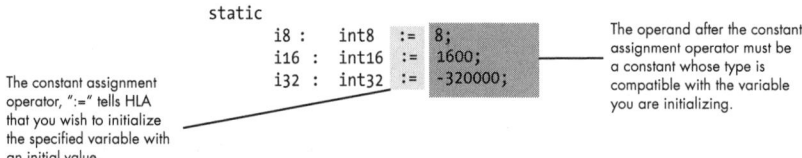

Figure 1-3: Static Variable Initialization.

It is important to realize that the expression following the assignment operator (":=") must be a constant expression. You cannot assign the values of other variables within a static variable declaration.

Those familiar with other high level languages (especially Pascal) should note that you may only declare one variable per statement. That is, HLA does not allow a comma-delimited list of variable names followed by a colon and a type identifier. Each variable declaration consists of a single identifier, a colon, a type ID, and a semicolon.

Listing 1-2 provides a simple HLA program that demonstrates the use of variables within an HLA program.

Listing 1-2: Variable Declaration and Use.

```
Program DemoVars;
#include( "stdlib.hhf" )

static
    InitDemo:       int32 := 5;
    NotInitialized: int32;

begin DemoVars;
```

```
// Display the value of the pre-initialized variable:

stdout.put( "InitDemo's value is ", InitDemo, nl );

// Input an integer value from the user and display that value:

stdout.put( "Enter an integer value: " );
stdin.get( NotInitialized );
stdout.put( "You entered: ", NotInitialized, nl );

end DemoVars;
```

In addition to static variable declarations, this example introduces three new concepts. First, the stdout.put statement allows multiple parameters. If you specify an integer value, stdout.put will convert that value to its string representation on output. The second new feature Listing 1-2 introduces is the stdin.get statement. This statement reads a value from the standard input device (usually the keyboard), converts the value to an integer, and stores the integer value into the NotInitialized variable. Finally, this program also introduces the syntax for (one form of) HLA comments. The HLA compiler ignores all text from the "//" sequence to the end of the current line. Those familiar with Java, C++, and Delphi/Kylix should recognize these comments.

1.5   Boolean Values

HLA and the HLA Standard Library provides limited support for boolean objects. You can declare boolean variables, use boolean literal constants, use boolean variables in boolean expressions, and print the values of boolean variables.

Boolean literal constants consist of the two predefined identifiers true and false. Internally, HLA represents the value true using the numeric value one; HLA represents false using the value zero. Most programs treat zero as false and anything else as true, so HLA's representations for true and false should prove sufficient.

To declare a boolean variable, you use the boolean data type. HLA uses a single byte (the least amount of memory it can allocate) to represent boolean values. The following example demonstrates some typical declarations:

```
static
    BoolVar:     boolean;
    HasClass:    boolean := false;
    IsClear:     boolean := true;
```

As this example demonstrates, you can initialize boolean variables if you desire.

Because boolean variables are byte objects, you can manipulate them using any instructions that operate directly on eight-bit values. Furthermore, as long as you ensure that your boolean variables only contain zero and one (for false and true, respectively), you can use the 80x86 and, or, xor, and not instructions to manipulate these boolean values (we'll describe these instructions a little later in this text).

You can print boolean values by making a call to the stdout.put routine, e.g.,

```
stdout.put( BoolVar )
```

This routine prints the text "true" or "false" depending upon the value of the boolean parameter (zero is false; anything else is true). Note that the HLA Standard Library does not allow you to read boolean values via stdin.get.

1.6 Character Values

HLA lets you declare one-byte ASCII character objects using the char data type. You may initialize character variables with a literal character value by surrounding the character with a pair of apostrophes. The following example demonstrates how to declare and initialize character variables in HLA:

```
static
    c: char;
    LetterA: char := 'A';
```

You can print character variables use the stdout.put routine, and you can read character variables using the stdin.get procedure call.

1.7 An Introduction to the Intel 80x86 CPU Family

Thus far, you've seen a couple of HLA programs that will actually compile and run. However, all the statements appearing in programs to this point have been either data declarations or calls to HLA Standard Library routines. There hasn't been any *real* assembly language. Before we can progress any further and learn some real assembly language, a detour is necessary; for unless you understand the basic structure of the Intel 80x86 CPU family, the machine instructions will make little sense.

The Intel CPU family is generally classified as a *Von Neumann Architecture Machine.* Von Neumann computer systems contain three main building blocks: the *central processing unit* (CPU), *memory,* and *input/output devices* (I/O). These three components are connected together using the *system bus* (consisting of the address, data, and control busses). The block diagram in Figure 1-4 shows this relationship.

The CPU communicates with memory and I/O devices by placing a numeric value on the address bus to select one of the memory locations or I/O device port locations, each of which has a unique binary numeric *address.* Then the CPU, I/O, and memory device pass data between themselves by placing the data on the data bus. The control bus contains signals that determine the direction of the data transfer (to/from memory, and to/from an I/O device).

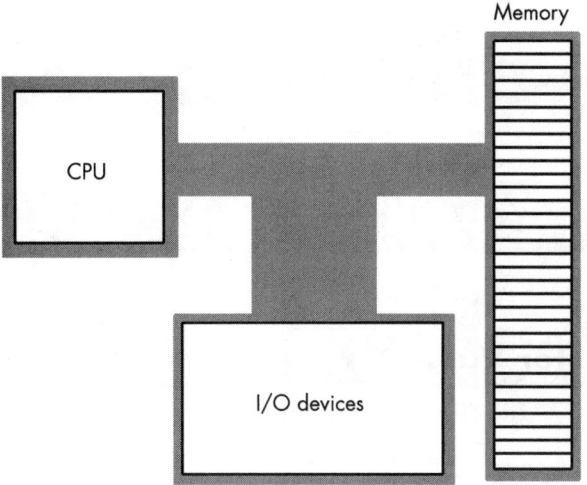

Figure 1-4: Von Neumann Computer System Block Diagram.

Within the CPU the registers is the most prominent feature. The 80x86 CPU registers can be broken down into four categories: general purpose registers, special-purpose application accessible registers, segment registers, and special-purpose kernel mode registers. This text will not consider the last two sets of registers. The segment registers are not used much in modern 32-bit operating systems (e.g., Windows, BeOS, and Linux); because this text is geared around programs written for 32-bit operating systems, there is little need to discuss the segment registers. The special-purpose kernel mode registers are intended for writing operating systems, debuggers, and other system level tools. Such software construction is well beyond the scope of this text, so once again there is little need to discuss the special purpose kernel mode registers.

The 80x86 (Intel family) CPUs provide several general purpose registers for application use. These include eight 32-bit registers that have the following:

EAX, EBX, ECX, EDX, ESI, EDI, EBP, and ESP

The "E" prefix on each name stands for *extended*. This prefix differentiates the 32-bit registers from the eight 16-bit registers that have the following names:

AX, BX, CX, DX, SI, DI, BP, and SP

Finally, the 80x86 CPUs provide eight 8-bit registers that have the following names:

AL, AH, BL, BH, CL, CH, DL, and DH

Unfortunately, these are not all separate registers. That is, the 80x86 does not provide 24 independent registers. Instead, the 80x86 overlays the 32-bit registers with the 16-bit registers, and it overlays the 16-bit registers with the 8-bit registers. Figure 1-5 on the next page shows this relationship.

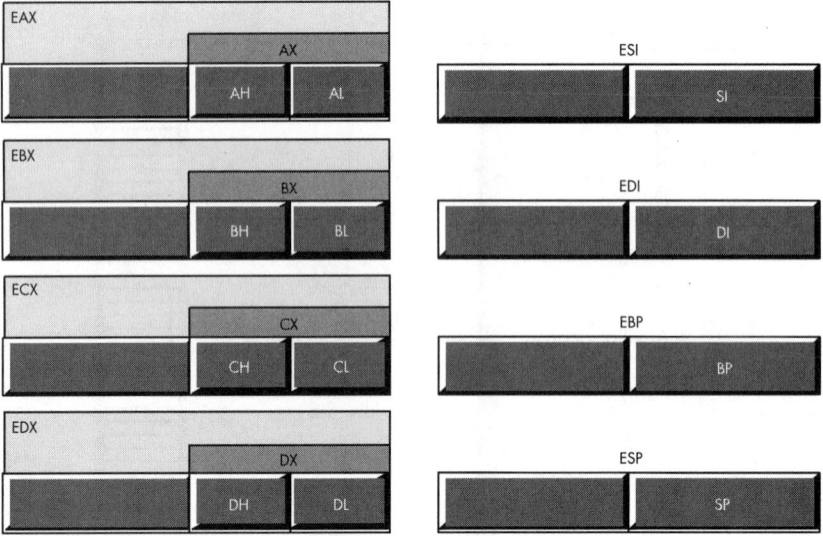

Figure 1-5: 80x86 (Intel CPU) General Purpose Registers.

The most important thing to note about the general purpose registers is that they are not independent. Modifying one register may modify as many as three other registers. For example, modification of the EAX register may very well modify the AL, AH, and AX registers. This fact cannot be overemphasized here. A very common mistake in programs written by beginning assembly language programmers is register value corruption because the programmer did not fully understand the ramifications of Figure 1-5.

The EFLAGS register is a 32-bit register that encapsulates several single-bit boolean (true/false) values. Most of the bits in the EFLAGS register are either reserved for kernel mode (operating system) functions or are of little interest to the application programmer. Eight of these bits (or *flags*) are of interest to application programmers writing assembly language programs. These are the overflow, direction, interrupt disable[4], sign, zero, auxiliary carry, parity, and carry flags. Figure 1-6 shows the layout of the flags within the lower 16 bits of the EFLAGS register.

Of the eight flags that are usable by application programmers, four flags in particular are extremely valuable: the overflow, carry, sign, and zero flags. Collectively, we will call these four flags the *condition codes*.[5] The state of these flags lets you test the result of previous computations. For example, after comparing two values, the condition code flags will tell you if one value is less than, equal to, or greater than a second value.

---

[4] Applications programs cannot modify the interrupt flag, but we'll look at this flag later in this text, hence the discussion of this flag here.

[5] Technically the parity flag is also a condition code, but we will not use that flag in this text.

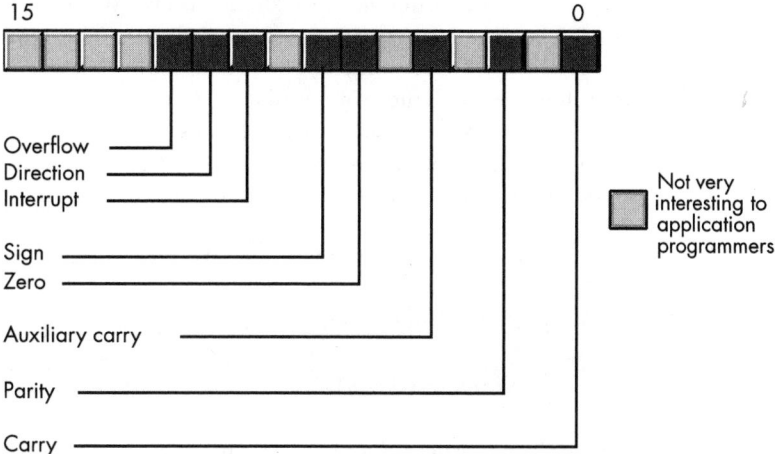

Figure 1-6: Layout of the Flags Register (Lower 16 Bits of EFLAGS).

One important fact that comes as a surprise to those just learning assembly language is that almost all calculations on the 80x86 CPU involve a register. For example, to add two variables together, storing the sum into a third variable, you must load one of the variables into a register, add the second operand to the value in the register, and then store the register away in the destination variable. Registers are a middleman in nearly every calculation. Therefore, registers are very important in 80x86 assembly language programs.

Another thing you should be aware of is that although some registers are referred to as "general purpose" you should not infer that you can use any register for any purpose. The SP/ESP register pair for example, has a very special purpose that effectively prevents you from using it for any other purpose (it's the *stack pointer*). Likewise, the BP/EBP register has a special purpose that limits its usefulness as a general purpose register. All the 80x86 registers have their own special purposes that limit their use in certain contexts. For the time being, you should simply avoid the use of the ESP and EBP registers for generic calculations; also keep in mind that the remaining registers are not completely interchangeable in your programs.

1.7.1 The Memory Subsystem

A typical 80x86 processor running a modern 32-bit OS can access a maximum of 2^{32} different memory locations, or just over four billion bytes. A few years ago, four gigabytes of memory would have seemed like infinity; modern machines, however, are pushing this limit. Nevertheless, because the 80x86 architecture supports a maximum four-gigabyte address space when using a 32-bit operating system like Windows or Linux, the following discussion will assume the four-gigabyte limit.

Of course, the first question you should ask is, "What exactly is a memory location?" The 80x86 supports *byte addressable memory*. Therefore, the basic memory unit is a byte, which is sufficient to hold a single character or a (very) small integer value (we'll talk more about that in the next chapter).

Think of memory as a linear array of bytes. The address of the first byte is zero, and the address of the last byte is 2^{32}-1. For a Pentium processor, the following pseudo-Pascal array declaration is a good approximation of memory:

```
Memory: array [0..4294967295] of byte;
```

C/C++ and Java users might prefer the following syntax:

```
byte Memory[4294967296];
```

To execute the equivalent of the Pascal statement "Memory [125] := 0;" the CPU places the value zero on the data bus, the address 125 on the address bus, and asserts the write line (this generally involves setting that line to zero), as shown in Figure 1-7.

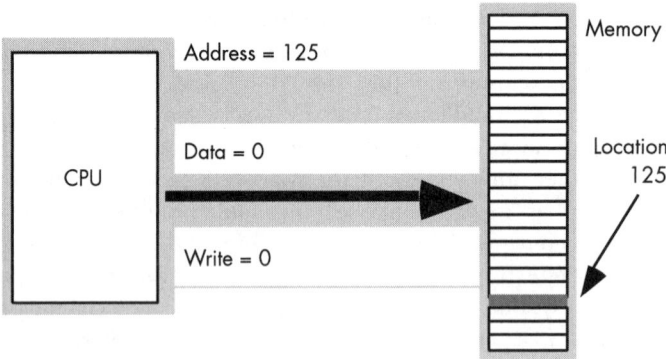

Figure 1-7: Memory Write Operation.

To execute the equivalent of "CPU := Memory [125];" the CPU places the address 125 on the address bus, asserts the read line (because the CPU is reading data from memory), and then reads the resulting data from the data bus (see Figure 1-8).

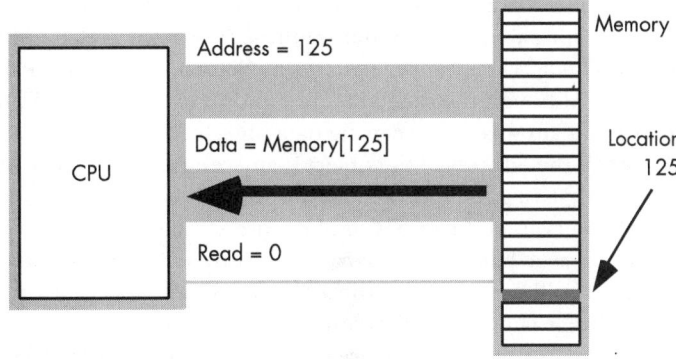

Figure 1-8: Memory Read Operation.

This discussion applies *only* when accessing a single byte in memory. So what happens when the processor accesses a word or a double word? Because memory consists of an array of bytes, how can we possibly deal with values larger than a single byte? Easy, to store larger values the 80x86 uses a sequence of consecutive memory locations. Figure 1-9 shows how the 80x86 stores bytes, words (two bytes), and double words (four bytes) in memory. The memory address of each of these objects is the address of the first byte of each object (i.e., the lowest address).

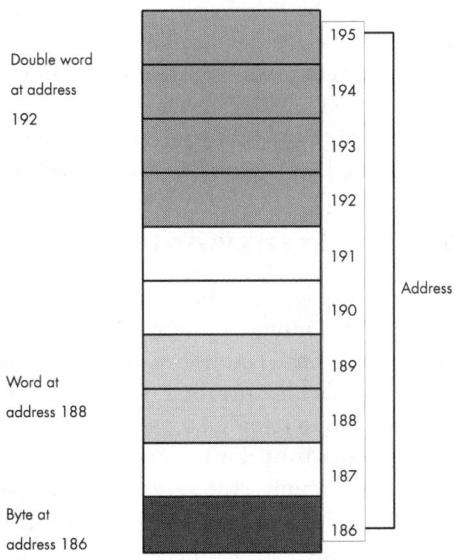

Figure 1-9: Byte, Word, and Double Word Storage in Memory.

Modern 80x86 processors don't actually connect directly to memory. Instead, there is a special memory buffer on the CPU known as the *cache* (pronounced "cash") that acts as a high-speed intermediary between the CPU and main memory. Although the cache handles the details automatically for you, one fact you should know is that accessing data objects in memory is sometimes more efficient if the address of the object is an even multiple of the object's size. Therefore, it's a good idea to *align* four-byte objects (double words) on addresses that are an even multiple of four. Likewise, it's most efficient to align two-byte objects on even addresses. You can efficiently access single-byte objects at any address. You'll see how to set the alignment of memory objects in a later chapter.

Before leaving this discussion of memory objects, it's important to understand the correspondence between memory and HLA variables. One of the nice things about using an assembler/compiler like HLA is that you don't have to worry about numeric memory addresses. All you need to do is declare a variable in HLA and HLA takes care of associating that variable with some unique set of memory addresses. For example, if you have the following declaration section:

```
static
    i8          :int8;
    i16         :int16;
    i32         :int32;
```

HLA will find some unused eight-bit byte in memory and associate it with the i8 variable; it will find a pair of consecutive unused bytes and associate i16 with them; finally, HLA will find four consecutive unused bytes and associate the value of i32 with those four bytes (32 bits). You'll always refer to these variables by their names, you generally don't have to concern yourself with their numeric address. Still, you should be aware that HLA is doing this for you behind your back.

1.8   Some Basic Machine Instructions

The 80x86 CPU family provides just over a hundred to many thousands of different machine instructions, depending on how you define a machine instruction. Even at the low end of the count (greater than 100), it appears as though there are far too many machine instructions to learn in a short period of time. Fortunately, you don't need to know all the machine instructions. In fact, most assembly language programs probably use around 30 different machine instructions.[6] Indeed, you can certainly write several meaningful programs with only a small handful of machine instructions. The purpose of this section is to provide a small handful of machine instructions so you can start writing simple HLA assembly language programs right away.

---

[6] Different programs may use a different set of 30 instructions, but few programs use more than 30 distinct instructions.

Without question, the mov instruction is the most oft-used assembly language statement. In a typical program, anywhere from 25 to 40 percent of the instructions are mov instructions. As its name suggests, this instruction moves data from one location to another.[7] The HLA syntax for this instruction is:

```
mov( source_operand, destination_operand );
```

The *source_operand* can be a register, a memory variable, or a constant. The *destination_operand* may be a register or a memory variable. Technically the 80x86 instruction set does not allow both operands to be memory variables; HLA, however, will automatically translate a mov instruction with two-word or double word memory operands into a pair of instructions that will copy the data from one location to another. In a high level language like Pascal or C/C++, the mov instruction is roughly equivalent to the following assignment statement:

```
destination_operand = source_operand ;
```

Perhaps the major restriction on the mov instruction's operands is that they must both be the same size. That is, you can move data between two byte (eight-bit) objects, between two-word (16-bit) objects, or between two double word (32-bit) objects; you may not, however, mix the sizes of the operands. Table 1-1 lists all the legal combinations for the mov instruction.

Table 1-1: Legal 80x86 MOV Instruction Operands

Source	Destination
Reg_8	Reg_8
Reg_8	Mem_8
Mem_8	Reg_8
constant[1]	Reg_8
constant[1]	Mem_8
Reg_{16}	Reg_{16}
Reg_{16}	Mem_{16}
Mem_{16}	Reg_{16}
constant[1]	Reg_{16}
constant[1]	Mem_{16}
Reg_{32}	Reg_{32}
Reg_{32}	Mem_{32}
Mem_{32}	Reg_{32}
constant[1]	Reg_{32}
constant[1]	Mem_{32}

1. The constant must be small enough to fit in the specified destination operand.

---

[7] Technically, mov actually copies data from one location to another. It does not destroy the original data in the source operand. Perhaps a better name for this instruction should have been copy. Alas, it's too late to change it now.

You should study this table carefully. Most of the general purpose 80x86 instructions use this same syntax. Note that in addition to the forms above, the HLA mov instruction lets you specify two memory operands as the source and destination. However, this special translation that HLA provides only applies to the mov instruction; it does not generalize to the other instructions.

The 80x86 add and sub instructions let you add and subtract two operands. Their syntax is nearly identical to the mov instruction:

```
add( source_operand, destination_operand );
sub( source_operand, destination_operand );
```

The add and sub operands take the same form as the mov instruction.[8] The add instruction does the following:

```
destination_operand = destination_operand + source_operand ;
destination_operand += source_operand;   // For those who prefer C syntax
```

The sub instruction does the calculation:

```
destination_operand = destination_operand - source_operand ;
destination_operand -= source_operand ;   // For C fans.
```

With nothing more than these three instructions, plus the HLA control structures that the next section discusses, you can actually write some sophisticated programs. Listing 1-3 provides a sample HLA program that demonstrates these three instructions.

Listing 1-3: Demonstration of MOV, ADD, and SUB Instructions.

```
program DemoMOVaddSUB;

#include( "stdlib.hhf" )

static
    i8:     int8    := -8;
    i16:    int16   := -16;
    i32:    int32   := -32;

begin DemoMOVaddSUB;

    // First, print the initial values
    // of our variables.

    stdout.put
```

---

[8] Remember, though, that add and sub do not support memory-to-memory operations.

```
(
    nl,
    "Initialized values: i8=", i8,
    ", i16=", i16,
    ", i32=", i32,
    nl
);

// Compute the absolute value of the
// three different variables and
// print the result.
// Note, because all the numbers are
// negative, we have to negate them.
// Using only the MOV, ADD, and SUB
// instruction, we can negate a value
// by subtracting it from zero.

mov( 0, al );    // Compute i8 := -i8;
sub( i8, al );
mov( al, i8 );

mov( 0, ax );    // Compute i16 := -i16;
sub( i16, ax );
mov( ax, i16 );

mov( 0, eax );   // Compute i32 := -i32;
sub( i32, eax );
mov( eax, i32 );

// Display the absolute values:

stdout.put
(
    nl,
    "After negation: i8=", i8,
    ", i16=", i16,
    ", i32=", i32,
    nl
);

// Demonstrate ADD and constant-to-memory
// operations:

add( 32323200, i32 );
stdout.put( nl, "After ADD: i32=", i32, nl );


end DemoMOVaddSUB;
```

1.9   Some Basic HLA Control Structures

The mov, add, and sub instructions, while valuable, aren't sufficient to let you write meaningful programs. You will need to complement these instructions with the ability to make decisions and create loops in your HLA programs before you can write anything other than a trivial program. HLA provides several high level control structures that are very similar to control structures found in high level languages. These include if..then..elseif..else..endif, while..endwhile, repeat..until, and so on. By learning these statements you will be armed and ready to write some real programs.

Before discussing these high level control structures, it's important to point out that these are not real 80x86 assembly language statements. HLA compiles these statements into a sequence of one or more real assembly language statements for you. Later in this text, you'll learn how HLA compiles the statements, and you'll learn how to write pure assembly language code that doesn't use them. However, there is a lot to learn before you get to that point, so we'll stick with these high level language statements for now.

Another important fact to mention is that HLA's high level control structures are *not* as high level as they first appear. The purpose behind HLA's high level control structures is to let you start writing assembly language programs as quickly as possible, not to let you avoid the use of assembly language altogether. You will soon discover that these statements have some severe restrictions associated with them, and you will quickly outgrow their capabilities. This is intentional. Once you reach a certain level of comfort with HLA's high level control structures and decide you need more power than they have to offer, it's time to move on and learn the real 80x86 instructions behind these statements.

The following sections assume that you're familiar with at least one high level language. They present the HLA control statements from that perspective without bothering to explain how you actually use these statements to accomplish something in a program. One prerequisite this text assumes is that you already know how to use these generic control statements in a high level language; you'll use them in HLA programs in an identical manner.

1.9.1   Boolean Expressions in HLA Statements

Several HLA statements require a boolean (true or false) expression to control their execution. Examples include the if, while, and repeat..until statements. The syntax for these boolean expressions represents the greatest limitation of the HLA high level control structures. This is one area where your familiarity with a high level language will work against you: You'll want to use the fancy expressions you use in a high level language, yet HLA only supports some basic forms.

HLA boolean expressions always take the following forms:[9]

```
flag_specification
!flag_specification
```

---

[9] There are a few additional forms that we'll cover in later sctions and later chapters.

```
register
!register
Boolean_variable
!Boolean_variable
mem_reg relop mem_reg_const
register in LowConst..HiConst
register not in LowConst..HiConst
```

A *flag_specification* may be one of the symbols that are described in Table 1-2.

Table 1-2: Symbols for *flag_specification*

Symbol	Meaning	Explanation
@c	Carry	True if the carry is set (1), false if the carry is clear (0).
@nc	No carry	True if the carry is clear (0), false if the carry is set (1).
@z	Zero	True if the zero flag is set, false if it is clear.
@nz	No zero	True if the zero flag is clear, false if it is set.
@o	Overflow	True if the overflow flag is set, false if it is clear.
@no	No overflow	True if the overflow flag is clear, false if it is set.
@s	Sign	True if the sign flag is set, false if it is clear.
@ns	No sign	True if the sign flag is clear, false if it is set.

The use of the flag values in a boolean expression is somewhat advanced. You will begin to see how to use these boolean expression operands in the next chapter.

A register operand can be any of the 8-bit, 16-bit, or 32-bit general purpose registers. The expression evaluates false if the register contains a zero; it evaluates true if the register contains a non-zero value.

If you specify a boolean variable as the expression, the program tests it for zero (false) or non-zero (true). Because HLA uses the values zero and one to represent false and true, respectively, the test works in an intuitive fashion. Note that HLA requires such variables be of type boolean. HLA rejects other data types. If you want to test some other type against zero/not zero, then use the general boolean expression discussed next.

The most general form of an HLA boolean expression has two operands and a relational operator. Table 1-3 lists the legal combinations.

Table 1-3: Legal Boolean Expressions

Left Operand	Relational Operator	Right Operand
Memory variable	= or == <> or !=	Memory variable,
or	< <=	Register,
Register	> >=	or
		Constant

Note that both operands cannot be memory operands. In fact, if you think of the *right operand* as the source operand and the *left operand* as the destination operand, then the two operands must be the same that add and sub allow.

Also like the add and sub instructions, the two operands must be the same size. That is, they must both be byte operands, they must both be word operands, or they must both be double word operands. If the right operand is a constant, its value must be in the range that is compatible with the left operand.

There is one other issue: If the left operand is a register and the right operand is a positive constant or another register, HLA uses an *unsigned* comparison. The next chapter will discuss the ramifications of this; for the time being, do not compare negative values in a register against a constant or another register. You may not get an intuitive result.

The in and not in operators let you test a register to see if it is within a specified range. For example, the expression "EAX in 2000..2099" evaluates true if the value in the EAX register is between 2000 and 2099 (inclusive). The not in (two words) operator checks to see if the value in a register is outside the specified range. For example, "AL not in 'a'..'z'" evaluates true if the character in the AL register is not a lower case alphabetic character.

Here are some examples of legal boolean expressions in HLA:

```
@c
Bool_var
al
ESI
EAX < EBX
EBX > 5
i32 < -2
i8 > 128
al < i8
eax in 1..100
ch not in 'a'..'z'
```

1.9.2   The HLA IF..THEN..ELSEIF..ELSE..ENDIF Statement

The HLA if statement uses the syntax shown in Figure 1-10.

The expressions appearing in an if statement must take one of the forms from the previous section. If the boolean expression is true, the code after the then executes, otherwise control transfers to the next elseif or else clause in the statement.

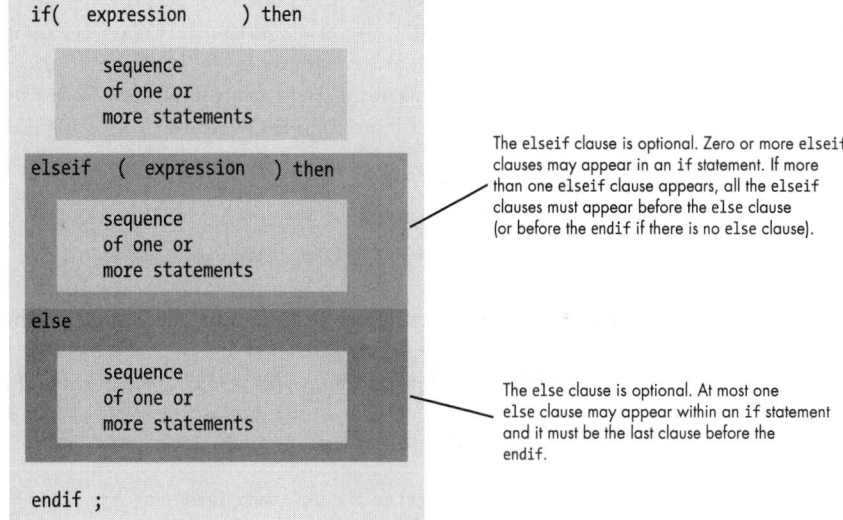

```
if(   expression      ) then

        sequence
        of one or
        more statements

elseif  ( expression   ) then

        sequence
        of one or
        more statements

else

        sequence
        of one or
        more statements

endif ;
```

The elseif clause is optional. Zero or more elseif clauses may appear in an if statement. If more than one elseif clause appears, all the elseif clauses must appear before the else clause (or before the endif if there is no else clause).

The else clause is optional. At most one else clause may appear within an if statement and it must be the last clause before the endif.

Figure 1-10: HLA IF Statement Syntax.

Because the elseif and else clauses are optional, an if statement could take the form of a single if..then clause, followed by a sequence of statements and a closing endif clause. The following is such a statement:

```
if( eax = 0 ) then

    stdout.put( "error: NULL value", nl );

endif;
```

If, during program execution, the expression evaluates true, then the code between the then and the endif executes. If the expression evaluates false, then the program skips over the code between the then and the endif.

Another common form of the if statement has a single else clause. The following is an example of an if statement with an optional else clause:

```
if( eax = 0 ) then

    stdout.put( "error: NULL pointer encountered", nl );

else

    stdout.put( "Pointer is valid", nl );

endif;
```

If the expression evaluates true, the code between the then and the else executes; otherwise the code between the else and the endif clauses executes.

You can create sophisticated decision-making logic by incorporating the elseif clause into an if statement. For example, if the CH register contains a character value, you can select from a menu of items using code like the following:

```
if( ch = 'a' ) then

    stdout.put( "You selected the 'a' menu item", nl );

elseif( ch = 'b' ) then

    stdout.put( "You selected the 'b' menu item", nl );

elseif( ch = 'c' ) then

    stdout.put( "You selected the 'c' menu item", nl );

else

    stdout.put( "Error: illegal menu item selection", nl );

endif;
```

Although this simple example doesn't demonstrate it, HLA does not require an else clause at the end of a sequence of elseif clauses. However, when making multiway decisions, it's always a good idea to provide an else clause just in case an error arises. Even if you think it's impossible for the else clause to execute, just keep in mind that future modifications to the code could void this assertion, so it's a good idea to have error reporting statements in your code.

1.9.3   Conjunction, Disjunction, and Negation in Boolean Expressions

Some obvious omissions in the list of operators in the previous sections are the conjunction (logical AND), disjunction (logical OR), and negation (logical NOT) operators. This section describes their use in boolean expressions (the discussion had to wait until after describing the if statement in order to present realistic examples).

HLA uses the "&&" operator to denote logical AND in a run-time boolean expression. This is a dyadic (two-operand) operator and the two operands must be legal run-time boolean expressions. This operator evaluates true if both operands evaluate to true. Example:

```
if( eax > 0 && ch = 'a' ) then

    mov( eax, ebx );
    mov( ' ', ch );

endif;
```

The two mov statements above execute only if EAX is greater than zero *and* CH is equal to the character 'a'. If either of these conditions is false, then program execution skips over these mov instructions.

Note that the expressions on either side of the "&&" operator may be any legal boolean expression; these expressions don't have to be comparisons using the relational operators. For example, the following are all legal expressions:

```
@z && al in 5..10
al in 'a'..'z' && ebx
boolVar && !eax
```

HLA uses *short-circuit evaluation* when compiling the "&&" operator. If the leftmost operand evaluates false, then the code that HLA generates does not bother evaluating the second operand (because the whole expression must be false at that point). Therefore, in the last expression above, the code will not check EAX against zero if boolVar contains false.

Note that an expression like "eax < 10 && ebx <> eax" is itself a legal boolean expression and, therefore, may appear as the left or right operand of the "&&" operator. Therefore, expressions like the following are perfectly legal:

```
eax < 0 && ebx <> eax && !ecx
```

The "&&" operator is left associative, so the code that HLA generates evaluates the expression above in a left-to-right fashion. If EAX is less than zero, the CPU will not test either of the remaining expressions. Likewise, if EAX is not less than zero but EBX is equal to EAX, this code will not evaluate the third expression because the whole expression is false regardless of ECX's value.

HLA uses the "||" operator to denote disjunction (logical OR) in a run-time boolean expression. Like the "&&" operator, this operator expects two legal runtime boolean expressions as operands. This operator evaluates true if either (or both) operands evaluate true. Like the "&&" operator, the disjunction operator uses short-circuit evaluation. If the left operand evaluates true, then the code that HLA generates doesn't bother to test the value of the second operand. Instead, the code will transfer to the location that handles the situation when the boolean expression evaluates true. Examples of legal expressions using the "||" operator:

```
@z || al = 10
al in 'a'..'z' || ebx
!boolVar || eax
```

As for the "&&" operator, the disjunction operator is left associative so multiple instances of the "||" operator may appear within the same expression. Should this be the case, the code that HLA generates will evaluate the expressions from left to right, e.g.,

```
eax < 0 || ebx <> eax || !ecx
```

The code above executes if either EAX is less than zero, EBX does not equal EAX, or ECX is zero. Note that if the first comparison is true, the code doesn't bother testing the other conditions. Likewise, if the first comparison is false and the second is true, the code doesn't bother checking to see if ECX is zero. The check for ECX equal to zero only occurs if the first two comparisons are false.

If both the conjunction and disjunction operators appear in the same expression then the "&&" operator takes precedence over the "||" operator. Consider the following expression:

```
eax < 0 || ebx <> eax  && !ecx
```

The machine code HLA generates evaluates this as

```
eax < 0 || (ebx <> eax  && !ecx)
```

If EAX is less than zero, then the code HLA generates does not bother to check the remainder of the expression, the entire expression evaluates true. However, if EAX is not less than zero, then both of the following conditions must evaluate true in order for the overall expression to evaluate true.

HLA allows you to use parentheses to surround sub expressions involving "&&" and "||" if you need to adjust the precedence of the operators. Consider the following expression:

```
(eax < 0 || ebx <> eax)  && !ecx
```

For this expression to evaluate true, ECX must contain zero and either EAX must be less than zero or EBX must not equal EAX. Contrast this to the result the expression produces without the parentheses.

HLA uses the "!" operator to denote logical negation. However, the "!" operator may only prefix a register or boolean variable; you may not use it as part of a larger expression (e.g., "!eax < 0"). To achieve the logical negative of an existing boolean expression you must surround that expression with parentheses and prefix the parentheses with the "!" operator, e.g.,

```
!( eax < 0 )
```

This expression evaluates true if EAX is not less than zero.

The logical not operator is primarily useful for surrounding complex expressions involving the conjunction and disjunction operators. While it is occasionally useful for short expressions like the one above, it's usually easier (and more readable) to simply state the logic directly rather than convolute it with the logical not operator.

Note that HLA also provides the "|" and "&" operators, but these are distinct from "||" and "&&" and have completely different meanings. See the HLA reference manual for more details on these (compile time) operators.

1.9.4 The WHILE..ENDWHILE Statement

The while statement uses the basic syntax shown in Figure 1-11.

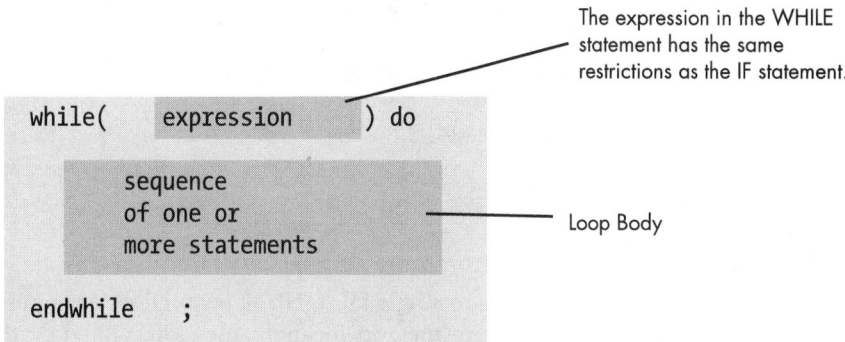

Figure 1-11: HLA WHILE Statement Syntax.

This statement evaluates the boolean expression. If it is false, control immediately transfers to the first statement following the endwhile clause. If the value of the expression is true, then the CPU executes the body of the loop. After the loop body executes, control transfers back to the top of the loop where the while statement retests the loop control expression. This process repeats until the expression evaluates false.

Note that the while loop, like its high level language counterpart, tests for loop termination at the top of the loop. Therefore, it is quite possible that the statements in the body of the loop will not execute (if the expression is false when the code first executes the while statement). Also note that the body of the while loop must, at some point, modify the value of the boolean expression or an infinite loop will result.

Example of an HLA while loop:

```
mov( 0, i );
while( i < 10 ) do

    stdout.put( "i=", i, nl );
    add( 1, i );

endwhile;
```

1.9.5 The FOR..ENDFOR Statement

The HLA for loop takes the following general form:

```
for( Initial_Stmt; Termination_Expression; Post_Body_Statement ) do

    << Loop Body >>

endfor;
```

This is equivalent to the following while statement:

```
Initial_Stmt;
while( Termination_expression ) do

    << loop_body >>

    Post_Body_Statement;



endwhile;
```

Initial_Stmt can be any single HLA/80x86 instruction. Generally this statement initializes a register or memory location (the loop counter) with zero or some other initial value. *Termination_expression* is an HLA boolean expression (same format that while allows). This expression determines whether the loop body executes. The *Post_Body_Statement* executes at the bottom of the loop (as shown in the while example above). This is a single HLA statement. Usually it is an instruction like add that modifies the value of the loop control variable.

The following gives a complete example:

```
for( mov( 0, i ); i < 10; add(1, i )) do

    stdout.put( "i=", i, nl );

endfor;



// The above, rewritten as a while loop, becomes:

mov( 0, i );
while( i < 10 ) do

    stdout.put( "i=", i, nl );

    add( 1, i );

endwhile;
```

1.9.6   The REPEAT..UNTIL Statement

The HLA repeat..until statement uses the syntax shown in Figure 1-12. C/C++/C# and Java users should note that the repeat..until statement is very similar to the do..while statement.

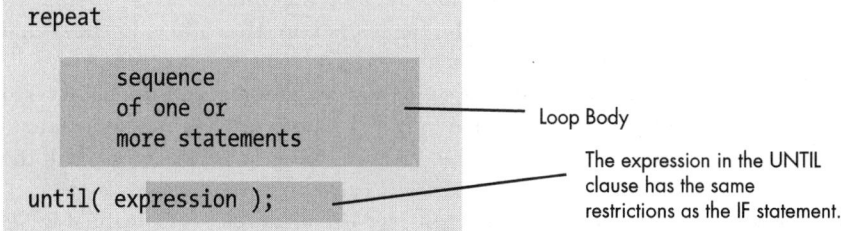

Figure 1-12: HLA REPEAT..UNTIL Statement Syntax.

The HLA repeat..until statement tests for loop termination at the bottom of the loop. Therefore, the statements in the loop body always execute at least once. Upon encountering the until clause, the program will evaluate the expression and repeat the loop if the expression is false[10] (that is, it repeats while false). If the expression evaluates true, the control transfers to the first statement following the until clause.

The following simple example demonstrates the repeat..until statement:

```
mov( 10, ecx );
repeat

    stdout.put( "ecx = ", ecx, nl );
    sub( 1, ecx );

until( ecx = 0 );
```

If the loop body will always execute at least once, then it is usually more efficient to use a repeat..until loop rather than a while loop.

1.9.7   The BREAK and BREAKIF Statements

The break and breakif statements provide the ability to prematurely exit from a loop. Figure 1-13 provides the syntax for these two statements.

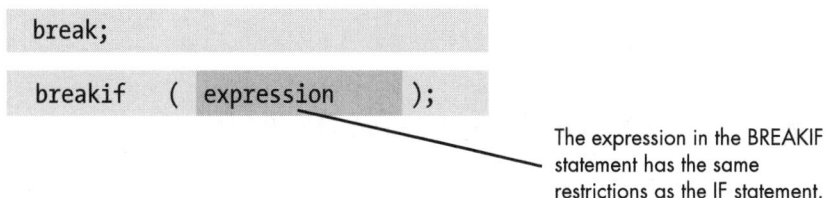

Figure 1-13: HLA BREAK and BREAKIF Syntax.

---

[10] Note that this condition is the opposite of the do..while loop found in C/C++ and Java.

The break statement exits the loop that immediately contains the break; the breakif statement evaluates the boolean expression and exits the containing loop if the expression evaluates true.

Note that the break and breakif statements do not allow you to break out of more than one nested loop. HLA does provide statements that do this, the begin..end block and the exit/exitif statements. Please consult the HLA Reference Manual for more details. HLA also provides the continue/continueif pair that let you repeat a loop body. Again, see the HLA reference manual for more details.

1.9.8   The FOREVER..ENDFOR Statement

Figure 1-14 shows the syntax for the forever statement.

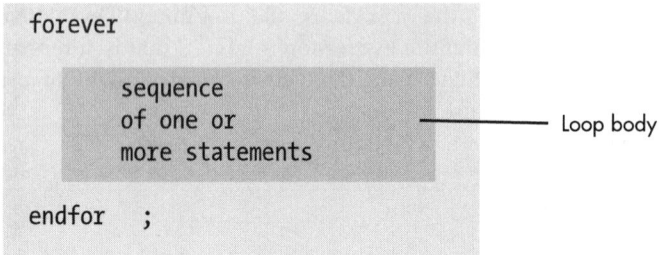

Figure 1-14: HLA FOREVER Loop Syntax.

This statement creates an infinite loop. You may also use the break and breakif statements along with forever..endfor to create a loop that tests for loop termination in the middle of the loop. Indeed, this is probably the most common use of this loop as the following example demonstrates:

```
forever

    stdout.put( "Enter an integer less than 10: " );
    stdin.get( i );
    breakif( i < 10 );
    stdout.put( "The value needs to be less than 10!", nl );

endfor;
```

1.9.9   The TRY..EXCEPTION..ENDTRY Statement

The HLA try..exception..endtry statement provides very powerful *exception handling* capabilities. The syntax for this statement appears in Figure 1-15.

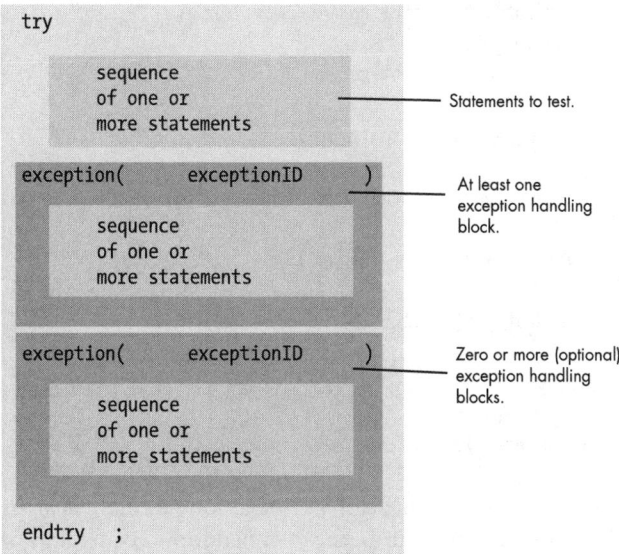

Figure 1-15: HLA TRY..EXCEPTION..ENDTRY Statement Syntax.

The try..endtry statement protects a block of statements during execution. If the statements between the try clause and the first exception clause (the *protected block*), execute without incident, control transfers to the first statement after the endtry immediately after executing the last statement in the protected block. If an error (exception) occurs, then the program interrupts control at the point of the exception (that is, the program *raises* an exception). Each exception has an unsigned integer constant associated with it, known as the exception ID. The *excepts.hhf* header file in the HLA Standard Library predefines several exception IDs, although you may create new ones for your own purposes. When an exception occurs, the system compares the exception ID against the values appearing in each of the exception clauses following the protected code. If the current exception ID matches one of the exception values, control continues with the block of statements immediately following that exception. After the exception handling code completes execution, control transfers to the first statement following the endtry.

If an exception occurs and there is no active try..endtry statement, or the active try..endtry statements do not handle the specific exception, the program will abort with an error message.

The following code fragment demonstrates how to use the try..endtry statement to protect the program from bad user input:

```
repeat

    mov( false, GoodInteger );    // Note: GoodInteger must be a boolean var.
    try
```

```
            stdout.put( "Enter an integer: " );
            stdin.get( i );
            mov( true, GoodInteger );

        exception( ex.ConversionError );

            stdout.put( "Illegal numeric value, please re-enter", nl );

        exception( ex.ValueOutOfRange );

            stdout.put( "Value is out of range, please re-enter", nl );

        endtry;

    until( GoodInteger );
```

The repeat..until loop repeats this code as long as there is an error during input.
Should an exception occur because of bad input, control transfers to the
exception clauses to see if a conversion error (e.g., illegal characters in the
number) or a numeric overflow occurs. If either of these exceptions occur, then
they print the appropriate message and control falls out of the try..endtry
statement and the repeat..until loop repeats because the code will not have set
GoodInteger to true. If a different exception occurs (one that is not handled in this
code), then the program aborts with the specified error message.[11]

Table 1-4 on the following page lists the exceptions provided in the
excepts.hhf header file as this was being written. Please see the *excepts.hhf* header
file provided with HLA for the most current list of exceptions.

Table 1-4: Exceptions Provided in *Excepts.hhf*

Exception	Description
ex.StringOverflow	Attempt to store a string that is too large into a string variable.
ex.StringIndexError	Attempt to access a character that is not present in a string.
ex.ValueOutOfRange	Value is too large for the current operation.
ex.IllegalChar	Operation encountered a character code whose ASCII code is not in the range 0..127.
ex.ConversionError	String-to-numeric conversion operation contains illegal (non-numeric) characters.
ex.BadFileHandle	Program attempted a file access using an invalid file handle value.
ex.FileOpenFailure	Operating system could not open file (file not found).
ex.FileCloseError	Operating system could not close file.
ex.FileWriteError	Error writing data to a file.
ex.FileReadError	Error reading data from a file.
ex.DiskFullError	Attempted to write data to a full disk.
ex.EndOfFile	Program attempted to read beyond the end of file.

---

[11]An experienced programmer may wonder why this code uses a boolean variable rather than a
breakif statement to exit the repeat..until loop. There are some technical reasons for this that you
will learn about later in this text.

Table 1-4: Exceptions Provided in *Excepts.hhf*

Exception	Description
ex.MemoryAllocationFailure	Insufficient system memory for allocation request.
ex.AttemptToDerefNULL	Program attempted to access data indirectly using a NULL pointer.
ex.CannotFreeMemory	Memory free operation failure.
ex.WidthTooBig	Format width for numeric to string conversion was too large.
ex.TooManyCmdLnParms	Command line contains too many arguments for processing by arg.c and arg.v.
ex.ArrayShapeViolation	Attempted operation on two arrays whose dimensions don't match.
ex.ArrayBounds	Attempt to access an element of an array, but the index was out of bounds.
ex.InvalidDate	Attempted date operation with an illegal date.
ex.InvalidDateFormat	Conversion from string to date contains illegal characters.
ex.TimeOverflow	Overflow during time arithmetic.
ex.AssertionFailed	ASSERT statement encountered a failed assertion.
ex.ExecutedAbstract	Attempt to execute an abstract class method.
ex.AccessViolation	Attempt to access an illegal memory location.
ex.Breakpoint	Program executed a breakpoint instruction (INT 3).
ex.SingleStep	Program is operating with the trace flag set.
ex.PrivInstr	Program attempted to execute a kernel-only instruction.
ex.IllegalInstr	Program attempted to execute an illegal machine instruction.
ex.BoundInstr	Bound instruction execution with "out of bounds" value.
ex.IntoInstr	Into instruction execution with the overflow flag set.
ex.DivideError	Program attempted division by zero or other divide error.
ex.fDenormal	Floating point exception (see the chapter on arithmetic).
ex.fDivByZero	Floating point exception (see the chapter on arithmetic).
ex.fInexactResult	Floating point exception (see the chapter on arithmetic).
ex.fInvalidOperation	Floating point exception (see the chapter on arithmetic).
ex.fOverflow	Floating point exception (see the chapter on arithmetic).
ex.fStackCheck	Floating point exception (see the chapter on arithmetic).
ex.fUnderflow	Floating point exception (see the chapter on arithmetic).
ex.InvalidHandle	OS reported an invalid handle for some operation.
ex.StackOverflow	OS reported a stack overflow.

Most of these exceptions occur in situations that are well beyond the scope of this chapter. Their appearance here is strictly for completeness. See the HLA Reference Manual, the HLA Standard Library documentation, and the HLA Standard Library source code for more details concerning these exceptions. The *ex.ConversionError, ex.ValueOutOfRange*, and *ex.StringOverflow* exceptions are the ones you'll most commonly use.

We'll return to the discussion of the try..endtry statement a little bit later in this chapter. First, however, we need to cover a little more material.

1.10   Introduction to the HLA Standard Library

There are two reasons HLA is much easier to learn and use than standard assembly language. The first reason is HLA's high level syntax for declarations and control structures. This leverages your high level language knowledge, allowing you to learn assembly language more efficiently. The other half of the equation is the HLA Standard Library. The HLA Standard Library provides many common, easy-to-use assembly language routines that you can call without having to write this code yourself (or, more importantly, having to learn how to write yourself). This eliminates one of the larger stumbling blocks many people have when learning assembly language: the need for sophisticated I/O and support code in order to write basic statements. Prior to the advent of a standardized assembly language library, it often took considerable study before a new assembly language programmer could do as much as print a string to the display. With the HLA Standard Library, this roadblock is removed and you can concentrate on learning assembly language concepts rather than learning low level I/O details that are specific to a given operating system.

A wide variety of library routines is only part of HLA's support. After all, assembly language libraries have been around for quite some time.[12] HLA's Standard Library complements HLA by providing a high level language interface to these routines. Indeed, the HLA language itself was originally designed specifically to allow the creation of a high level set of library routines. This high level interface, combined with the high level nature of many of the routines in the library packs a surprising amount of power in an easy-to-use package.

The HLA Standard Library consists of several modules organized by category. Table 1-5 lists many of the modules that are available:[13]

Table 1-5: HLA Standard Library Modules

Name	Description
args	Command line parameter parsing support routines.
conv	Various conversions between strings and other values.
cset	Character set functions.
DateTime	Calendar, date, and time functions.
excepts	Exception handling routines.
fileio	File input and output routines.
hla	Special HLA constants and other values.
hll	Implements the high level language switch statement.
Linux	Linux system calls (HLA Linux version only).
math	Extended precision arithmetic, transcendental functions, and other mathematical functions.
memory	Memory allocation, deallocation, and support code.
misctypes	Miscellaneous data types.
patterns	The HLA pattern matching library.
rand	Pseudo-random number generators and support code.

---

[12]E.g., the UCR Standard Library for 80x86 Assembly Language Programmers.

---

[13] Because the HLA Standard Library is expanding, this list is probably out of date. Please see the HLA documentation for a current list of Standard Library modules.

Table 1-5: HLA Standard Library Modules

Name	Description
stdin	User input routines.
stdout	Provides user output and several other support routines.
stdlib	A special include file that links in all HLA Standard Library modules.
strings	HLA's powerful string library.
tables	Table (associative array) support routines.
win32	Constants used in Windows calls (HLA Win32 version, only).
x86	Constants and other items specific to the 80x86 CPU.

Later sections of this text will explain many of these modules in greater detail. This section will concentrate on the most important routines (at least to beginning HLA programmers), the *stdio* library.

1.10.1 Predefined Constants in the STDIO Module

Perhaps the first place to start is with a description of some common constants that the stdio module defines for you. Consider the following (typical) example:

```
stdout.put( "Hello World", nl );
```

The nl appearing at the end of this statement stands for *newline*. The nl identifier is not a special HLA reserved word, nor is it specific to the stdout.put statement. Instead, it's simply a predefined constant that corresponds to the string containing the standard end-of-line sequence (this is a carriage return/line feed pair under Windows or just a line feed under Linux).

In addition to the nl constant, the HLA standard I/O library module defines several other useful character constants, as listed in Table 1-6:

Table 1-6: Character Constants Defined by the HLA Standard I/O Library

Character	Definition
stdio.bell	The ASCII bell character. Beeps the speaker when printed.
stdio.bs	The ASCII backspace character.
stdio.tab	The ASCII tab character.
stdio.lf	The ASCII linefeed character.
stdio.cr	The ASCII carriage return character.

Except for nl, these characters appear in the stdio *namespace*[14] (and, therefore, require the "stdio." prefix). The placement of these ASCII constants within the stdio namespace helps avoid naming conflicts with your own variables. The nl name does not appear within a namespace because you will use it very often and typing stdio.nl would get tiresome very quickly.

---

[14] Namespaces will be the subject of a later chapter.

1.10.2 Standard In and Standard Out

Many of the HLA I/O routines have a stdin or stdout prefix. Technically, this means that the Standard Library defines these names in a namespace. In practice, this prefix suggests where the input is coming from (the standard input device) or going to (the standard output device). By default, the standard input device is the system keyboard. Likewise, the default standard output device is the console display. So, in general, statements that have stdin or stdout prefixes will read and write data on the console device.

When you run a program from the command line window (or shell), you have the option of *redirecting* the standard input and/or standard output devices. A command line parameter of the form ">outfile" redirects the standard output device to the specified file (outfile). A command line parameter of the form "<infile" redirects the standard input so that its data comes from the specified input file (infile). The following examples demonstrate how to use these parameters when running a program named *testpgm* in the command window:[15]

```
testpgm <input.data
testpgm >output.txt
testpgm <in.txt >output.txt
```

1.10.3 The stdout.newln Routine

The stdout.newln procedure prints a newline sequence to the standard output device. This is functionally equivalent to saying "stdout.put(nl);" the call to stdout.newln is sometimes a little more convenient. The following page shows an example:

```
stdout.newln();
```

1.10.4 The stdout.putiX Routines

The stdout.puti8, stdout.puti16, and stdout.puti32 library routines print a single parameter (one byte, two bytes, or four bytes, respectively) as a signed integer value. The parameter may be a constant, a register, or a memory variable, as long as the size of the actual parameter is the same as the size of the formal parameter.

These routines print the value of their specified parameter to the standard output device. These routines will print the value using the minimum number of print positions possible. If the number is negative, these routines will print a leading minus sign. Here are some examples of calls to these routines:

```
stdout.puti8( 123 );
stdout.puti16( dx );
stdout.puti32( i32Var );
```

---

[15] Note for Linux users: Depending on how your system is set up, you may need to type "./" in front of the program's name to actually execute the program, e.g., "./testpgm <input.data".

1.10.5 The stdout.putiXSize Routines

The `stdout.puti8Size`, `stdout.puti16Size`, and `stdout.puti32Size` routines output signed integer values to the standard output, just like the *stdout.putiX* routines. These routines, however, provide more control over the output; they let you specify the (minimum) number of print positions the value will require on output. These routines also let you specify a padding character should the print field be larger than the minimum needed to display the value. These routines require the following parameters:

```
stdout.puti8Size( Value8, width, padchar );
stdout.puti16Size( Value16,width, padchar );
stdout.puti32Size( Value32, width, padchar );
```

The Value^x parameter can be a constant, a register, or a memory location of the specified size. The `width` parameter can be any signed integer constant that is between -256 and +256; this parameter may be a constant, register (32-bit), or memory location (32-bit). The `padchar` parameter should be a single character value.

Like the *stdout.putix* routines, these routines print the specified value as a signed integer constant to the standard output device. These routines, however, let you specified the *field width* for the value. The field width is the minimum number of print positions these routines will use when printing the value. The `width` parameter specifies the minimum field width. If the number would require more print positions (e.g., if you attempt to print "1234" with a field width of two), then these routines will print however many characters are necessary to properly display the value. On the other hand, if the width parameter is greater than the number of character positions required to display the value, then these routines will print some extra padding characters to ensure that the output has at least width character positions. If the width value is negative, the number is left justified in the print field; if the width value is positive, the number is right justified in the print field.

If the absolute value of the `width` parameter is greater than the minimum number of print positions, then these *stdout.putiXSize* routines will print a padding character before or after the number. The `padchar` parameter specifies which character these routines will print. Most of the time you would specify a space as the pad character; for special cases, you might specify some other character. Remember, the `padchar` parameter is a character value; in HLA character constants are surrounded by apostrophes, not quotation marks. You may also specify an 8-bit register as this parameter.

Listing 1-4 provides a short HLA program that demonstrates the use of the `stdout.puti32Size` routine to display a list of values in tabular form.

Listing 1-4: Columnar Output Demonstration Using stdio.Puti32Size.

```
program NumsInColumns;

#include( "stdlib.hhf" )
```

```
var
    i32:    int32;
    ColCnt: int8;

begin NumsInColumns;

    mov( 96, i32 );
    mov( 0, ColCnt );
    while( i32 > 0 ) do

        if( ColCnt = 8 ) then

            stdout.newln();
            mov( 0, ColCnt );

        endif;
        stdout.puti32Size( i32, 5, ' ' );
        sub( 1, i32 );
        add( 1, ColCnt );

    endwhile;
    stdout.newln();

end NumsInColumns;
```

1.10.6   The stdout.put Routine

The stdout.put routine[16] is one of the most flexible output routines in the standard output library module. It combines most of the other output routines into a single, easy to use, procedure.

The generic form for the stdout.put routine is the following:

```
stdout.put( list_of_values_to_output );
```

The stdout.put parameter list consists of one or more constants, registers, or memory variables, each separated by a comma. This routine displays the value associated with each parameter appearing in the list. Because we've already been using this routine throughout this chapter, you've already seen many examples of this routine's basic form. It is worth pointing out that this routine has several additional features not apparent in the examples appearing in this chapter. In particular, each parameter can take one of the following two forms:

```
value
value:width
```

---

[16] *Stdout.put* is actually a macro, not a procedure. The distinction between the two is beyond the scope of this chapter. However, this text will describe their differences a little later.

The value may be any legal constant, register, or memory variable object. In this chapter, you've seen string constants and memory variables appearing in the stdout.put parameter list. These parameters correspond to the first form above. The second parameter form above lets you specify a minimum field width, similar to the *stdout.putiXSize* routines.[17] The program in Listing 1-5 produces the same output as the program in Listing 1-4 previously; however, Listing 1-5 uses stdout.put rather than stdout.puti32Size:

Listing 1-5: Demonstration of stdout.put Field Width Specification.

```
program NumsInColumns2;

#include( "stdlib.hhf" )

var
    i32:     int32;
    ColCnt: int8;

begin NumsInColumns2;

    mov( 96, i32 );
    mov( 0, ColCnt );
    while( i32 > 0 ) do

        if( ColCnt = 8 ) then

            stdout.newln();
            mov( 0, ColCnt );

        endif;
        stdout.put( i32:5 );
        sub( 1, i32 );
        add( 1, ColCnt );

    endwhile;
    stdout.put( nl );

end NumsInColumns2;
```

The stdout.put routine is capable of much more than the few attributes this section describes. This text will introduce those additional capabilities as appropriate.

---

[17] Note that you cannot specify a padding character when using the *stdout.put* routine; the padding character defaults to the space character. If you need to use a different padding character, call the *stdout.putiXSize* routines.

1.10.7 The stdin.getc Routine

The stdin.getc routine reads the next available character from the standard input device's input buffer.[18] It returns this character in the CPU's AL register. The program in Listing 1-6 demonstrates a simple use of this routine.

Listing 1-6: Demonstration of the stdin.getc() Routine.

```
program charInput;

#include( "stdlib.hhf" )

var
    counter: int32;

begin charInput;

    // The following repeats as long as the user
    // confirms the repetition.

    repeat

        // Print out 14 values.

        mov( 14, counter );
        while( counter > 0 ) do

            stdout.put( counter:3 );
            sub( 1, counter );

        endwhile;

        // Wait until the user enters 'y' or 'n'.

        stdout.put( nl, nl, "Do you wish to see it again? (y/n):" );
        forever

            stdin.readLn();
            stdin.getc();
            breakif( al = 'n' );
            breakif( al = 'y' );
            stdout.put( "Error, please enter only 'y' or 'n': " );

        endfor;
        stdout.newln();
```

---

[18] "Buffer" is just a fancy term for an array.

```
        until( al = 'n' );

end charInput;
```

This program uses the stdin.ReadLn routine to force a new line of input from the user. A description of stdin.ReadLn appears just a little later in this chapter.

1.10.8   The stdin.getiX Routines

The stdin.geti8, stdin.geti16, and stdin.geti32 routines read 8-, 16-, and 32-bit signed integer values from the standard input device. These routines return their values in the AL, AX, or EAX register, respectively. They provide the standard mechanism for reading signed integer values from the user in HLA.

Like the stdin.getc routine, these routines read a sequence of characters from the standard input buffer. They begin by skipping over any white space characters (spaces, tabs, and so on) and then convert the following stream of decimal digits (with an optional, leading minus sign) into the corresponding integer. These routines raise an exception (that you can trap with the try..endtry statement) if the input sequence is not a valid integer string or if the user input is too large to fit in the specified integer size. Note that values read by stdin.geti8 must be in the range -128..+127; values read by stdin.geti16 must be in the range -32,768..+32,767; and values read by stdin.geti32 must be in the range -2,147,483,648..+2,147,483,647.

The sample program in Listing 1-7 demonstrates the use of these routines.

Listing 1-7: stdin.getiX Example Code.

```
program intInput;

#include( "stdlib.hhf" )

var
    i8:     int8;
    i16:    int16;
    i32:    int32;

begin intInput;

    // Read integers of varying sizes from the user:

    stdout.put( "Enter a small integer between -128 and +127: " );
    stdin.geti8();
    mov( al, i8 );

    stdout.put( "Enter a small integer between -32768 and +32767: " );
    stdin.geti16();
    mov( ax, i16 );

    stdout.put( "Enter an integer between +/- 2 billion: " );
```

```
    stdin.geti32();
    mov( eax, i32 );


    // Display the input values.

    stdout.put
    (
        nl,
        "Here are the numbers you entered:", nl, nl,
        "Eight-bit integer: ", i8:12, nl,
        "16-bit integer:     ", i16:12, nl,
        "32-bit integer:     ", i32:12, nl
    );



end intInput;
```

You should compile and run this program and test what happens when you enter
a value that is out of range or enter an illegal string of characters.

1.10.9   The stdin.readLn and stdin.flushInput Routines

Whenever you call an input routine like stdin.getc or stdin.geti32, the program
does not necessarily read the value from the user at that moment. Instead, the
HLA Standard Library buffers the input by reading a whole line of text from the
user. Calls to input routines will fetch data from this input buffer until the buffer
is empty. While this buffering scheme is efficient and convenient, sometimes it
can be confusing. Consider the following code sequence:

```
stdout.put( "Enter a small integer between -128 and +127: " );
stdin.geti8();
mov( al, i8 );

stdout.put( "Enter a small integer between -32768 and +32767: " );
stdin.geti16();
mov( ax, i16 );
```

Intuitively, you would expect the program to print the first prompt message, wait
for user input, print the second prompt message, and wait for the second user
input. However, this isn't exactly what happens. For example if you run this code
(from the sample program in the previous section) and enter the text "123 456"
in response to the first prompt, the program will not stop for additional user
input at the second prompt. Instead, it will read the second integer (456) from
the input buffer read during the execution of the stdin.geti16 call.

In general, the stdin routines only read text from the user when the input
buffer is empty. As long as the input buffer contains additional characters, the
input routines will attempt to read their data from the buffer. You may take
advantage of this behavior by writing code sequences such as the following:

```
stdout.put( "Enter two integer values: " );
stdin.geti32();
mov( eax, intval );
stdin.geti32();
mov( eax, AnotherIntVal );
```

This sequence allows the user to enter both values on the same line (separated by one or more white space characters), thus preserving space on the screen. So the input buffer behavior is desirable every now and then. The buffered behavior of the input routines can be counter-intuitive at other times.

Fortunately, the HLA Standard Library provides two routines, stdin.readLn and stdin.flushInput, that let you control the standard input buffer. The stdin.readLn routine discards everything that is in the input buffer and immediately requires the user to enter a new line of text. The stdin.flushInput routine simply discards everything that is in the buffer. The next time an input routine executes, the system will require a new line of input from the user. You would typically call stdin.readLn immediately before some standard input routine; you would normally call stdin.flushInput immediately after a call to a standard input routine.

NOTE *If you are calling* stdin.readLn *and you find that you are having to input your data twice, this is a good indication that you should be calling* stdin.flushInput *rather than* stdin.readLn. *In general, you should always be able to call* stdin.flushInput *to flush the input buffer and read a new line of data on the next input call. The* stdin.readLn *routine is rarely necessary, so you should use* stdin.flushInput *unless you really need to immediately force the input of a new line of text.*

1.10.10   The stdin.get Routine

The stdin.get routine combines many of the standard input routines into a single call, just as the stdout.put combines all of the output routines into a single call. Actually, stdin.get is a bit easier to use than stdout.put because the only parameters to this routine are a list of variable names.

Let's rewrite the example given in the previous section:

```
stdout.put( "Enter two integer values: " );
stdin.geti32();
mov( eax, intval );
stdin.geti32();
mov( eax, AnotherIntVal );
```

Using the stdin.get routine, we could rewrite this code as:

```
stdout.put( "Enter two integer values: " );
stdin.get( intval, AnotherIntVal );
```

As you can see, the stdin.get routine is a little more convenient to use.

Note that stdin.get stores the input values directly into the memory variables you specify in the parameter list; it does not return the values in a register unless you actually specify a register as a parameter. The stdin.get parameters must all be variables or registers.

1.11   Additional Details About TRY..ENDTRY

As you may recall, the try..endtry statement surrounds a block of statements in order to capture any exceptions that occur during the execution of those statements. The system raises exceptions in one of three ways: through a hardware fault (such as a divide-by-zero error), through an operating system generated exception, or through the execution of the HLA raise statement. You can write an exception handler to intercept specific exceptions using the exception clause. The program in Listing 1-8 provides a typical example of the use of this statement.

Listing 1-8: TRY..ENDTRY Example.

```
program testBadInput;
#include( "stdlib.hhf" )

static
    u:      int32;


begin testBadInput;

    try

        stdout.put( "Enter a signed integer:" );
        stdin.get( u );
        stdout.put( "You entered: ", u, nl );

    exception( ex.ConversionError )

        stdout.put( "Your input contained illegal characters" nl );

    exception( ex.ValueOutOfRange )

        stdout.put( "The value was too large" nl );

    endtry;


end testBadInput;
```

HLA refers to the statements between the try clause and the first exception clause as the *protected* statements. If an exception occurs within the protected statements, then the program will scan through each of the exceptions and compare the value of the current exception against the value in the parentheses after each of the exception clauses.[19] This exception value is simply a 32-bit value. The value in the parentheses after each exception clause, therefore, must be a 32-bit value. The HLA *excepts.hhf* header file predefines several exception constants. Other than it would be an incredibly bad style violation, you could substitute the numeric values for the two exception clauses above.

1.11.1 Nesting TRY..ENDTRY Statements

If the program scans through all the exception clauses in a try..endtry statement and does match the current exception value, then the program searches through the exception clauses of a *dynamically nested* try..endtry block in an attempt to find an appropriate exception handler. For example, consider the code in Listing 1-9.

Listing 1-9: Nested TRY..ENDTRY Statements.

```
program testBadInput2;
#include( "stdlib.hhf" )

static
    u:      int32;

begin testBadInput2;

    try

        try

            stdout.put( "Enter a signed integer:" );
            stdin.get( u );
            stdout.put( "You entered: ", u, nl );

          exception( ex.ConversionError )

            stdout.put( "Your input contained illegal characters" nl );

        endtry;

        stdout.put( "Input did not fail due to a value out of range" nl );


      exception( ex.ValueOutOfRange )

        stdout.put( "The value was too large" nl );
```

---

[19] Note that HLA loads this value into the EAX register. So upon entry into an exception clause, EAX contains the exception number.

```
    endtry;

end testBadInput2;
```

In Listing 1-9 one try statement is nested inside another. During the execution of the *stdin.get* statement, if the user enters a value greater than four billion and some change, then stdin.get will raise the *ex.ValueOutOfRange* exception. When the HLA run-time system receives this exception, it first searches through all the exception clauses in the try..endtry statement immediately surrounding the statement that raised the exception (this would be the nested try..endtry in the example above). If the HLA run-time system fails to locate an exception handler for *ex.ValueOutOfRange* then it checks to see if the current try..endtry is nested inside another try..endtry (as is the case in Listing 1-9). If so, the HLA run-time system searches for the appropriate exception clause in the outer try..endtry statement. Within the try..endtry block appearing in Listing 1-9 the program finds an appropriate exception handler, so control transfers to the statements after the "exception(ex.ValueOutOfRange)" clause.

After leaving a try..endtry block, the HLA run-time system no longer considers that block active and will not search through its list of exceptions when the program raises an exception.[20] This allows you to handle the same exception differently in other parts of the program.

If two try..endtry statements handle the same exception, and one of the try..endtry blocks is nested inside the protected section of the other try..endtry statement, and the program raises an exception while executing in the innermost try..endtry sequence, then HLA transfers control directly to the exception handler provided by the innermost try..endtry block. HLA does not automatically transfer control to the exception handler provided by the outer try..endtry sequence.

In the previous example (Listing 1-9) the second try..endtry statement was statically nested inside the enclosing try..endtry statement.[21] As mentioned without comment earlier, if the most recently activated try..endtry statement does not handle a specific exception, the program will search through the exception clauses of any dynamically nesting try..endtry blocks. Dynamic nesting does not require the nested try..endtry block to physically appear within the enclosing try..endtry statement. Instead, control could transfer from inside the enclosing try..endtry protected block to some other point in the program. Execution of a try..endtry statement at that other point dynamically nests the two try statements. Although there are many ways to dynamically nest code, there is one method you are probably familiar with from your high level language experience: the procedure call. Later in this text, when you learn how to write procedures (functions) in assembly language, you should keep in mind that any call to a procedure within the protected section of a try..endtry block can create a dynamically nested try..endtry if the program executes a try..endtry within that procedure.

---

[20] Unless, of course, the program reenters the TRY..ENDTRY block via a loop or other control structure.

[21] "Statically nested" means that one statement is physically nested within another in the source code. When we say one statement is nested within another, this typically means that the statement is statically nested within the other statement.

1.11.2   The UNPROTECTED Clause in a TRY..ENDTRY Statement

Whenever a program executes the try clause, it preserves the current exception environment and sets up the system to transfer control to the exception clauses within that try..endtry statement should an exception occur. If the program successfully completes the execution of a try..endtry protected block, the program restores the original exception environment and control transfers to the first statement beyond the endtry clause. This last step, restoring the execution environment, is very important. If the program skips this step, any future exceptions will transfer control to this try..endtry statement even though the program has already left the try..endtry block. Listing 1-10 demonstrates this problem.

Listing 1-10: Improperly Exiting a TRY..ENDTRY Statement.

```
program testBadInput4;
#include( "stdlib.hhf" )

static
    input:  int32;

begin testBadInput4;

    // This forever loop repeats until the user enters
    // a good integer and the BREAK statement below
    // exits the loop.

    forever

        try

            stdout.put( "Enter an integer value: " );
            stdin.get( input );
            stdout.put( "The first input value was: ", input, nl );
            break;

          exception( ex.ValueOutOfRange )

            stdout.put( "The value was too large, reenter." nl );

          exception( ex.ConversionError )

            stdout.put( "The input contained illegal characters, reenter." nl );

        endtry;

    endfor;

    // Note that the following code is outside the loop and there
    // is no TRY..ENDTRY statement protecting this code.
```

```
        stdout.put( "Enter another number: " );
        stdin.get( input );
        stdout.put( "The new number is: ", input, nl );

end testBadInput4;
```

This example attempts to create a robust input system by putting a loop around the try..endtry statement and forcing the user to reenter the data if the stdin.get routine raises an exception (because of bad input data). While this is a good idea, there is a big problem with this implementation: The break statement immediately exits the forever..endfor loop without first restoring the exception environment. Therefore, when the program executes the second stdin.get statement, at the bottom of the program, the HLA exception handling code still thinks that it's inside the try..endtry block. If an exception occurs, HLA transfers control back into the try..endtry statement looking for an appropriate exception handler. Assuming the exception was ex.ValueOutOfRange or ex.ConversionError, the program in Listing 1-10 will print an appropriate error message *and then force the user to reenter the first value.* This isn't desirable.

Transferring control to the wrong try..endtry exception handlers is only part of the problem. Another big problem with the code in Listing 1-10 has to do with the way HLA preserves and restores the exception environment: specifically, HLA saves the old execution environment information in a special region of memory known as the *stack*. If you exit a try..endtry without restoring the exception environment, this leaves the old execution environment information on the stack, and this extra data could cause your program to malfunction.

Although this discussion makes it quite clear that a program should not exit from a try..endtry statement in the manner that Listing 1-10 uses, it would be nice if you could use a loop around a try..endtry block to force the reentry of bad data as this program attempts to do. To allow for this, HLA's try..endtry statement provides an unprotected section. Consider the code in Listing 1-11.

Listing 1-11: The TRY..ENDTRY UNPROTECTED Section.

```
program testBadInput5;
#include( "stdlib.hhf" )

static
    input:  int32;

begin testBadInput5;

    // This forever loop repeats until the user enters
    // a good integer and the BREAK statement below
    // exits the loop.  Note that the BREAK statement
    // appears in an UNPROTECTED section of the TRY..ENDTRY
    // statement.

    forever
```

```
            try

                stdout.put( "Enter an integer value: " );
                stdin.get( input );
                stdout.put( "The first input value was: ", input, nl );

            unprotected

                break;

            exception( ex.ValueOutOfRange )

                stdout.put( "The value was too large, reenter." nl );

            exception( ex.ConversionError )

                stdout.put( "The input contained illegal characters, reenter." nl );

            endtry;

        endfor;

        // Note that the following code is outside the loop and there
        // is no TRY..ENDTRY statement protecting this code.

        stdout.put( "Enter another number: " );
        stdin.get( input );
        stdout.put( "The new number is: ", input, nl );

end testBadInput5;
```

Whenever the try..endtry statement hits the unprotected clause, it immediately restores the exception environment. As the phrase suggests, the execution of statements in the unprotected section is no longer protected by that try..endtry block (note, however, that any dynamically nesting try..endtry statements will still be active; unprotected only turns off the exception handling of the try..endtry statement containing the unprotected clause). Because the break statement in Listing 1-11 appears inside the unprotected section, it can safely transfer control out of the try..endtry block without "executing" the endtry because the program has already restored the former exception environment.

Note that the unprotected keyword must appear in the try..endtry statement immediately after the protected block. That is, it must precede all exception keywords.

If an exception occurs during the execution of a try..endtry sequence, HLA automatically restores the execution environment. Therefore, you may execute a break statement (or any other instruction that transfers control out of the try..endtry block) within an exception clause.

Because the program restores the exception environment upon encountering an unprotected block or an exception block, an exception that occurs within one of these areas immediately transfers control to the previous (dynamically nesting) active try..endtry sequence. If there is no nesting try..endtry sequence, the program aborts with an appropriate error message.

1.11.3   The ANYEXCEPTION Clause in a TRY..ENDTRY Statement

In a typical situation, you will use a try..endtry statement with a set of exception clauses that will handle all possible exceptions that can occur in the protected section of the try..endtry sequence. Often, it is important to ensure that a try..endtry statement handles all possible exceptions to prevent the program from prematurely aborting due to an unhandled exception. If you have written all the code in the protected section, you will know the exceptions it can raise so you can handle all possible exceptions. However, if you are calling a library routine (especially a third-party library routine), making a OS API call, or otherwise executing code that you have no control over, it may not be possible for you to anticipate all possible exceptions this code could raise (especially when considering past, present, and future versions of the code). If that code raises an exception for which you do not have an exception clause, this could cause your program to fail. Fortunately, HLA's try..endtry statement provides the anyexception clause that will automatically trap any exception the existing exception clauses do not handle.

The anyexception clause is similar to the exception clause except it does not require an exception number parameter (because it handles any exception). If the anyexception clause appears in a try..endtry statement with other exception sections, the anyexception section must be the last exception handler in the try..endtry statement. An anyexception section may be the only exception handler in a try..endtry statement.

If an otherwise unhandled exception transfers control to an anyexception section, the EAX register will contain the exception number. Your code in the anyexception block can test this value to determine the cause of the exception.

1.11.4   Registers and the TRY..ENDTRY Statement

The try..endtry statement preserves about 16 bytes of data whenever you enter a try..endtry statement. Upon leaving the try..endtry block (or hitting the unprotected clause), the program restores the exception environment. As long as no exception occurs, the try..endtry statement does not affect the values of any registers upon entry to or upon exit from the try..endtry statement. However, this claim is not true if an exception occurs during the execution of the protected statements.

Upon entry into an exception clause the EAX register contains the exception number, but values of all other general purpose registers are undefined. Because the operating system may have raised the exception in response to a hardware error (and, therefore, has played around with the registers), you can't even assume that the general purpose registers contain whatever values they happened to contain at the point of the exception. The underlying code that HLA generates for exceptions is subject to change in different versions of the compiler, and certainly it changes across operating systems, so it is never a good idea to experimentally determine what values registers contain in an exception handler and depend upon those values in your code.

Because entry into an exception handler can scramble the register values, you must ensure that you reload important registers if the code following your endtry clause assumes that the registers contain certain values (i.e., values set in the protected section or values set prior to executing the try..endtry statement). Failure to do so will introduce some nasty defects into your program (and these defects may be very intermittent and difficult to detect because exceptions rarely occur and may not always destroy the value in a particular register). The following code fragment provides a typical example of this problem and its solution:

```
static
    sum: int32;

        .
        .
        .

    mov( 0, sum );
    for( mov( 0, ebx ); ebx < 8; inc( ebx )) do

        push( ebx );  // Must preserve EBX in case there is an exception.
        forever
            try

                stdin.geti32();
                unprotected break;

            exception( ex.ConversionError )

                stdout.put( "Illegal input, please reenter value: " );

            endtry;
        endfor;
        pop( ebx );  // Restore EBX's value.
        add( ebx, eax );
        add( eax, sum );

    endfor;
```

Because the HLA exception handling mechanism messes with the registers, and because exception handling is a relatively inefficient process, you should never use the try..endtry statement as a generic control structure (e.g., using it to simulate a switch/case statement by raising an integer exception value and using the exception clauses as the cases to process). Doing so will have a very negative impact on the performance of your program and may introduce subtle defects because exceptions scramble the registers.

For proper operation, the try..endtry statement assumes that you only use the EBP register to point at *activation records* (the chapter on procedures later in this book discusses activation records). By default, HLA programs automatically use

EBP for this purpose; as long as you do not modify the value in EBP, your programs will automatically use EBP to maintain a pointer to the current activation record. If you attempt to use the EBP register as a general purpose register to hold values and compute arithmetic results, HLA's exception handling capabilities will no longer function properly (along with other possible problems). Therefore, you should never use the EBP register as a general purpose register. Of course, this same discussion applies to the ESP register.

1.12 High Level Assembly Language vs. Low Level Assembly

Before concluding this chapter, it's important to remind you that none of the control statements appearing in this chapter are "real" assembly language. The 80x86 CPU does not support machine instructions like if, while, repeat, for, break, breakif, and try. Whenever HLA encounters these statements, it *compiles* them into a sequence of one or more true machine instructions that do the operation as the high level statements you've used. While these statements are convenient to use, and in many cases just as efficient as the sequence of low level machine instructions into which HLA translates them, don't lose sight of the fact that they are not true machine instructions.

The purpose of this text is to teach you low level assembly language programming; these high level control structures are simply a means to that end. Remember, learning the HLA high level control structures allows you to leverage your high level language knowledge early on in the educational process so you don't have to learn everything about assembly language all at once. By using high level control structures that you're already comfortable with, this text can put off the discussion of the actual machine instructions you'd normally use for control flow until much later in the text. By doing so, this text can regulate how much material it presents so, hopefully, you'll find learning assembly language to be much more pleasant. However, you must always remember that these high level control statements are just a pedagogical tool to help you learn assembly language. Though you're free to use them in your assembly programs once you master the real control flow statements, you really must learn the low level control statements if you really want to learn assembly language programming. Since, presumably, that's why you're reading this book, don't allow the high level control structures to become a crutch. When you get to the point where you learn how to really write low level control statements, embrace and use them (exclusively). As you gain experience with the low level control statements and learn their advantages and disadvantages, you'll be in a good position to decide whether a high level or low level code sequence is most appropriate for a given application. However, until you gain considerable experience with the low level control structures, you'll not be able to make an educated decision. Remember, you can't really call yourself an "Assembly Language Programmer" unless you've mastered the low level statements.

Another thing to keep in mind is that the HLA Standard Library functions are not part of the assembly *language*. They're just some convenient functions that have been pre-written for you. Although there is nothing wrong with calling these functions, always remember that they are not machine instructions and that there is nothing special about these routines; as you gain experience writing assembly language code, you can write your own versions of each of these routines (and even write them more efficiently).

If you're learning assembly language because you want to write the most efficient programs possible (either the fastest or the smallest code), you need to understand that you won't achieve this goal completely if you're using high level control statements and making a lot of calls to the HLA Standard Library. HLA's code generator and the HLA Standard Library aren't *horribly* inefficient, but the only true way to write efficient programs in assembly language is to *think* in assembly language. HLA's high level control statements and many of the routines in the HLA Standard Library are great because they let you *avoid* thinking in assembly language. While this is great while you're first leaning assembly, if your ultimate goal is to write efficient code, then you've got to learn to think in assembly language. This text will get you to that point (and does so much more rapidly because it uses HLA's high level features), but don't forget that your ultimate goal is to give up these high level features in favor of low level coding.

1.13   For More Information

This chapter has covered a lot of ground! While you've still got a lot to learn about assembly language programming, this chapter, combined with your knowledge of high level languages, provides just enough information to let you start writing real assembly language programs.

Although this chapter has covered many different topics, the three primary topics of interest are the 80x86 CPU architecture, the syntax for simple HLA programs, and the HLA Standard Library. For additional topics on these subjects, please consult the (unabridged) electronic version of this text, the HLA Reference Manual, and the HLA Standard Library Manual. All three are available on the CD-ROM that accompanies this book.

2

DATA REPRESENTATION

2.1 Chapter Overview

A major stumbling block many beginners encounter when attempting to learn assembly language is the common use of the binary and hexadecimal numbering systems. Many programmers think that hexadecimal (or hex[1]) numbers represent absolute proof that God never intended anyone to work in assembly language. While it is true that hexadecimal numbers are a little different from what you may be used to, their advantages outweigh their disadvantages by a large margin. Therefore, understanding these numbering systems is important because their use simplifies other complex topics including bit operations, signed numeric representation, character codes, and packed data.

This chapter discusses several important concepts including the binary and hexadecimal numbering systems, binary data organization (bits, nibbles, bytes, words, and double words), signed and unsigned numbering systems, arithmetic, logical, shift, and rotate operations on binary values, bit fields, and packed data. This is basic material, and the remainder of this text depends upon your understanding of these concepts. If you are already familiar with these terms from other courses or study, you

---

[1] Hexadecimal is often abbreviated as *hex* even though, technically speaking, hex means base 6, not base 16.

should at least skim this material before proceeding to the next chapter. If you are unfamiliar with this material or only vaguely familiar with it, you should study it carefully before proceeding. *All of the material in this chapter is important!* Do not skip over any material. In addition to the basic material, this chapter also introduces some new HLA statements and HLA Standard Library routines.

2.2   Numbering Systems

Most modern computer systems do not represent numeric values using the decimal system. Instead, they typically use a binary or two's complement numbering system. To understand the limitations of computer arithmetic, you must understand how computers represent numbers.

2.2.1   A Review of the Decimal System

You've been using the decimal (base 10) numbering system for so long that you probably take it for granted. When you see a number like "123," you don't think about the value 123; rather, you generate a mental image of how many items this value represents. In reality, however, the number 123 represents

$$1*10^2 + 2 * 10^1 + 3*10^0$$

or

$$100+20+3$$

In the positional numbering system, each digit appearing to the left of the decimal point represents a value between zero and nine times an increasing power of ten. Digits appearing to the right of the decimal point represent a value between zero and nine times an increasing negative power of ten. For example, the value 123.456 means

$$1*10^2 + 2*10^1 + 3*10^0 + 4*10^{-1} + 5*10^{-2} + 6*10^{-3}$$

or

$$100 + 20 + 3 + 0.4 + 0.05 + 0.006$$

2.2.2   The Binary Numbering System

Most modern computer systems operate using binary logic. The computer represents values using two voltage levels (usually 0v and +2.4..5v). With two such levels we can represent exactly two different values. These could be any two different values, but they typically represent the values zero and one. These two values, coincidentally, correspond to the two digits the binary numbering system uses. Because there is a correspondence between the logic levels used by the 80x86 and the two digits used in the binary numbering system, it should come as no surprise that the PC employs the binary numbering system.

The binary numbering system works just like the decimal numbering system, with two exceptions: binary only allows the digits 0 and 1 (rather than 0..9), and binary uses powers of two rather than powers of ten. Therefore, it is very easy to convert a binary number to decimal. For each "1" in the binary string, add in 2^n where "n" is the zero-based position of the binary digit. For example, the binary value 11001010_2 represents:

$1*27 + 1*26 + 0*25 + 0*24 + 1*23 + 0*22 + 1*21 + 0*20$

=

$128 + 64 + 8 + 2$

=

202_{10}

To convert decimal to binary is slightly more difficult. You must find those powers of two that, when added together, produce the decimal result. One method is to work from a large power of two down to 2^0. Consider the decimal value 1359:

- 2^{10}=1024; 2^{11}=2048. So 1024 is the largest power of two less than 1359. Subtract 1024 from 1359 and begin the binary value on the left with a "1" digit. Binary = "1"; decimal result is 1359 – 1024 = 335.

- The next lower power of two ($2^9 = 512$) is greater than the result from above, so add a "0" to the end of the binary string. Binary = "10"; decimal result is still 335.

- The next lower power of two is 256 (2^8). Subtract this from 335 and add a "1" digit to the end of the binary number. Binary = "101"; decimal result is 79.

- 128 (2^7) is greater than 79, so tack a "0" to the end of the binary string. Binary = "1010"; decimal result remains 79.

- The next lower power of two ($2^6 = 64$) is less than 79, so subtract 64 and append a "1" to the end of the binary string. Binary = "10101"; decimal result is 15.

- 15 is less than the next power of two ($2^5 = 32$) so simply add a "0" to the end of the binary string. Binary = "101010"; decimal result is still 15.

- 16 (2^4) is greater than the remainder so far, so append a "0" to the end of the binary string. Binary = "1010100"; decimal result is 15.

- 2^3 (eight) is less than 15, so stick another "1" digit on the end of the binary string. Binary = "10101001"; decimal result is 7.

- 2^2 is less than seven, so subtract four from seven and append another "1" to the binary string. Binary = "101010011"; decimal result is 3.

- 2^1 is less than three, so append a "1" to the end of the binary string and subtract two from the decimal value. Binary = "1010100111"; decimal result is now 1.

- Finally, the decimal result is 1, which is 2^0, so add a final "1" to the end of the binary string. The final binary result is "10101001111."

If you actually have to convert a decimal number to binary by hand, the algorithm above probably isn't the easiest to master. A simpler solution is the "even/odd - divide by two" algorithm. This algorithm uses the following steps:

- If the number is even, emit a zero. If the number is odd, emit a one.

- Divide the number by two and throw away any fractional component or remainder.

- If the quotient is zero, the algorithm is complete.

- If the quotient is not zero and is odd, insert a "1" before the current string; if the number is even, prefix your binary string with zero.

- Go back to step two above and repeat.

Fortunately, you'll rarely need to convert decimal numbers directly to binary strings, so neither of these algorithms is particularly important in real life.

Binary numbers, although they have little importance in high level languages, appear everywhere in assembly language programs (even if you don't convert between decimal and binary). So you should be somewhat comfortable with them.

2.2.3   Binary Formats

In the purest sense, every binary number contains an infinite number of digits (or *bits* which is short for binary digits). For example, we can represent the number five by any of the following:

---

101   00000101   0000000000101 .. 000000000000101

Any number of leading zero digits may precede the binary number without changing its value.

We will adopt the convention of ignoring any leading zeros if present in a value. For example, 101_2 represents the number five but because the 80x86 typically works with groups of 8 bits, we'll find it much easier to zero extend all binary numbers to some multiple of 4 or 8 bits. Therefore, following this convention, we'd represent the number five as 0101_2 or 00000101_2.

In the United States, most people separate every three digits with a comma to make larger numbers easier to read. For example, 1,023,435,208 is much easier to read and comprehend than 1023435208. We'll adopt a similar convention in this text for binary numbers. We will separate each group of four binary bits with an underscore. For example, we will write the binary value 1010111110110010 as 1010_1111_1011_0010.

We often pack several values together into the same binary number. One form of the 80x86 mov instruction uses the binary encoding 1011 0rrr dddd dddd to pack three items into 16 bits: a five-bit operation code (1_0110), a three-bit register field (rrr), and an 8-bit immediate value (dddd_dddd). For convenience, we'll assign a numeric value to each bit position. We'll number each bit as follows:

1. The rightmost bit in a binary number is bit position zero.

2. Each bit to the left is given the next successive bit number.

An 8-bit binary value uses bits 0..7:

X_7 X_6 X_5 X_4 X_3 X_2 X_1 X_0

A 16-bit binary value uses bit positions 0..15:

X_{15} X_{14} X_{13} X_{12} X_{11} X_{10} X_9 X_8 X_7 X_6 X_5 X_4 X_3 X_2 X_1 X_0

A 32-bit binary value uses bit positions 0..31, and so on.

Bit zero is the *low order* (L.O.) bit (some refer to this as the *least significant bit*). The leftmost bit is typically called the *high order* (H.O.) bit (or the *most significant bit*). We'll refer to the intermediate bits by their respective bit numbers.

2.3   The Hexadecimal Numbering System

A big problem with the binary system is verbosity. To represent the value 202_{10} requires eight binary digits. The decimal version requires only three decimal digits and, thus, represents numbers much more compactly than does the binary numbering system. This fact is not lost on the engineers who design binary computer systems. When dealing with large values, binary numbers quickly become too unwieldy. Unfortunately, the computer thinks in binary, so most of the time it is convenient to use the binary numbering system. Although we can convert between decimal and binary, the conversion is not a trivial task. The hexadecimal (base 16) numbering system solves many of the problems inherent in the binary system. Hexadecimal numbers offer the two features we're looking for: They're very compact, and it's simple to convert them to binary and vice versa. Because of this, most computer systems engineers use the hexadecimal numbering system. Because the radix (base) of a hexadecimal number is 16, each hexadecimal digit to the left of the hexadecimal point represents some value times a successive power of 16. For example, the number 1234_{16} is equal to:

$$1 * 16^3 + 2 * 16^2 + 3 * 16^1 + 4 * 16^0$$

or

$$4096 + 512 + 48 + 4 = 4660_{10}$$

Each hexadecimal digit can represent one of 16 values between 0 and 15_{10}. Because there are only ten decimal digits, we need to invent six additional digits to represent the values in the range $10_{10}..15_{10}$. Rather than create new symbols for these digits, we'll use the letters A..F. The following are all examples of valid hexadecimal numbers:

1234_{16} $DEAD_{16}$ $BEEF_{16}$ $OAFB_{16}$ $FEED_{16}$ $DEAF_{16}$

Because we'll often need to enter hexadecimal numbers into the computer system, we'll need a different mechanism for representing hexadecimal numbers. After all, on most computer systems you cannot enter a subscript to denote the radix of the associated value. We'll adopt the following conventions:

- All hexadecimal values begin with a "$" character, e.g., $123A4.

- All binary values begin with a percent sign ("%").

- Decimal numbers do not have a prefix character.

- If the radix is clear from the context, this book may drop the leading "$" or "%" character.

Examples of valid hexadecimal numbers:

$1234 $DEAD $BEEF $AFB $FEED $DEAF

As you can see, hexadecimal numbers are compact and easy to read. In addition, you can easily convert between hexadecimal and binary. Consider Table 2-1.

Table 2-1: Binary/Hex Conversion

Binary	Hexadecimal
%0000	$0
%0001	$1
%0010	$2
%0011	$3
%0100	$4
%0101	$5
%0110	$6
%0111	$7
%1000	$8
%1001	$9
%1010	$A
%1011	$B
%1100	$C
%1101	$D
%1110	$E
%1111	$F

This table provides all the information you'll ever need to convert any hexa-decimal number into a binary number or vice versa.

To convert a hexadecimal number into a binary number, simply substitute the corresponding 4 bits for each hexadecimal digit in the number. For example, to convert $ABCD into a binary value, simply convert each hexadecimal digit according to the preceding table:

A	B	C	D	Hexadecimal
1010	1011	1100	1101	Binary

To convert a binary number into hexadecimal format is almost as easy. The first step is to pad the binary number with zeros to make sure that there is a multiple of 4 bits in the number. For example, given the binary number 1011001010, the first step would be to add 2 bits to the left of the number so that it contains 12 bits. The converted binary value is 001011001010. The next step is to separate the binary value into groups of 4 bits, e.g., 0010_1100_1010. Finally, look up these binary values in the preceding table and substitute the appropriate hexa-decimal digits, i.e., $2CA. Contrast this with the difficulty of conversion between decimal and binary or decimal and hexadecimal!

Because converting between hexadecimal and binary is an operation you will need to perform over and over again, you should take a few minutes and memo-rize the table. Even if you have a calculator that will do the conversion for you, you'll find manual conversion to be a lot faster and more convenient when con-verting between binary and hex.

2.4   Data Organization

In pure mathematics a value may take an arbitrary number of bits. Computers, on the other hand, generally work with some specific number of bits. Common collections are single bits, groups of 4 bits (called *nibbles*), groups of 8 bits (*bytes*), groups of 16 bits (*words*), groups of 32 bits (*double words* or *dwords*), groups of 64 bits (*quad words* or *qwords*), groups of 128 bits (*long words* or *lwords*), and more. The sizes are not arbitrary. There is a good reason for these particular values. This section will describe the bit groups commonly used on the Intel 80x86 chips.

2.4.1   Bits

The smallest "unit" of data on a binary computer is a single bit. Because a single bit is capable of representing only two different values (typically zero or one) you may get the impression that there are a very small number of items you can rep-resent with a single bit. Not true! There are an infinite number of items you can represent with a single bit.

With a single bit, you can represent any two distinct items. Examples include zero or one, true or false, on or off, male or female, and right or wrong. However, you are *not* limited to representing binary data types (that is, those objects that have only two distinct values). You could use a single bit to represent the num-bers 723 and 1,245. Or perhaps the values 6,254 and 5. You could also use a single bit to represent the colors red and blue. You could even represent two unrelated objects with a single bit. For example, you could represent the color red and the number 3,256 with a single bit. You can represent *any two* different values with a single bit. However, you can represent *only two* different values with a single bit.

To confuse things even more, different bits can represent different things. For example, you could use 1 bit to represent the values zero and one, while an adjacent bit could represent the values true and false. How can you tell by looking at the bits? The answer, of course, is that you can't. But this illustrates the whole idea behind computer data structures: *data is what you define it to be.* If you use a bit to represent a boolean (true/false) value, then that bit (by your definition) represents true or false. For the bit to have any real meaning, you must be consistent. If you're using a bit to represent true or false at one point in your program, you shouldn't use that value to represent red or blue later.

Because most items you'll be trying to model require more than two different values, single bit values aren't the most popular data type you'll use. However, because everything else consists of groups of bits, bits will play an important role in your programs. Of course, there are several data types that require two distinct values, so it would seem that bits are important by themselves. However, you will soon see that individual bits are difficult to manipulate, so we'll often use other data types to represent two-state values.

2.4.2 Nibbles

A *nibble* is a collection of 4 bits. It wouldn't be a particularly interesting data structure except for two items: BCD (*binary coded decimal*) numbers[2] and hexadecimal numbers. It takes 4 bits to represent a single BCD or hexadecimal digit. With a nibble, we can represent up to 16 distinct values because there are 16 unique combinations of a string of 4 bits:

0000
0001
0010
0011
0100
0101
0110
0111
1000
1001
1010
1011
1100
1101
1110
1111

---

[2] Binary coded decimal is a numeric scheme used to represent decimal numbers using 4 bits for each decimal digit.

In the case of hexadecimal numbers, the values 0, 1, 2, 3, 4, 5, 6, 7, 8, 9, A, B, C, D, E, and F are represented with 4 bits. BCD uses ten different digits (0, 1, 2, 3, 4, 5, 6, 7, 8, 9) and requires also 4 bits (because you can only represent eight different values with 3 bits). In fact, any 16 distinct values can be represented with a nibble, though hexadecimal and BCD digits are the primary items we can represent with a single nibble.

2.4.3 Bytes

Without question, the most important data structure used by the 80x86 microprocessor is the byte. A byte consists of 8 bits and is the smallest addressable datum (data item) on the 80x86 microprocessor. Main memory and I/O addresses on the 80x86 are all byte addresses. This means that the smallest item that can be individually accessed by an 80x86 program is an 8-bit value. To access anything smaller requires that you read the byte containing the data and mask out the unwanted bits. The bits in a byte are normally numbered from zero to seven as shown in Figure 2-1.

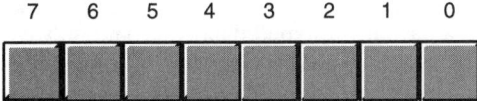

Figure 2-1: Bit Numbering.

Bit 0 is the *low order bit* or *least significant bit*, bit 7 is the *high order bit* or *most significant bit* of the byte. We'll refer to all other bits by their number.

Note that a byte also contains exactly two nibbles (see Figure 2-2).

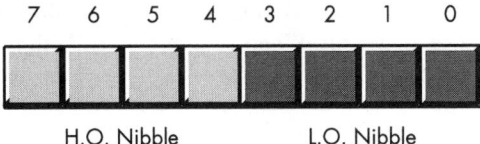

H.O. Nibble   L.O. Nibble

Figure 2-2: The Two Nibbles in a Byte.

Bits 0..3 comprise the *low order nibble*, bits 4..7 form the *high order nibble*. Because a byte contains exactly two nibbles, byte values require two hexadecimal digits.

Because a byte contains 8 bits, it can represent 2^8, or 256, different values. Generally, we'll use a byte to represent numeric values in the range 0..255, signed numbers in the range -128..+127 (see the discussion of signed numbers later in this chapter), ASCII/IBM character codes, and other special data types requiring no more than 256 different values. Many data types have fewer than 256 items so 8 bits is usually sufficient.

Because the 80x86 is a byte addressable machine, it turns out to be more efficient to manipulate a whole byte than an individual bit or nibble. For this reason, most programmers use a whole byte to represent data types that require no more than 256 items, even if fewer than 8 bits would suffice. For example, we'll often represent the boolean values true and false by 00000001_2 and 00000000_2 (respectively).

Probably the most important use for a byte is holding a character value. Characters typed at the keyboard, displayed on the screen, and printed on the printer all have numeric values. To allow it to communicate with the rest of the world, PCs typically use a variant of the *ASCII character set.* There are 128 defined codes in the ASCII character set. PCs typically use the remaining 128 possible values in a byte for extended character codes including European characters, graphic symbols, Greek letters, and math symbols.

Because bytes are the smallest unit of storage in the 80x86 memory space, bytes also happen to be the smallest variable you can create in an HLA program. As you saw in the last chapter, you can declare an 8-bit signed integer variable using the int8 data type. Because int8 objects are signed, you can represent values in the range -128..+127 using an int8 variable. You should only store signed values into int8 variables; if you want to create an arbitrary byte variable, you should use the *byte* data type, as follows:

```
static
        byteVar: byte;
```

The byte data type is a partially untyped data type. The only type information associated with a byte object is its size (one byte). You may store any 8-bit value (small signed integers, small unsigned integers, characters, and so on) into a byte variable. It is up to you to keep track of the type of object you've put into a byte variable.

2.4.4 Words

A word is a group of 16 bits. We'll number the bits in a word starting from zero on up to 15, as Figure 2-3 shows. Like the byte, bit 0 is the low order bit. For words, bit 15 is the high order bit. When referencing the other bits in a word, we'll use their bit position number.

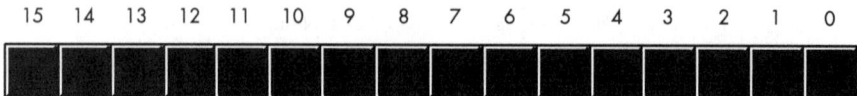

Figure 2-3: Bit Numbers in a Word.

Notice that a word contains exactly two bytes. Bits 0..7 form the low order byte, bits 8..15 form the high order byte (see Figure 2-4).

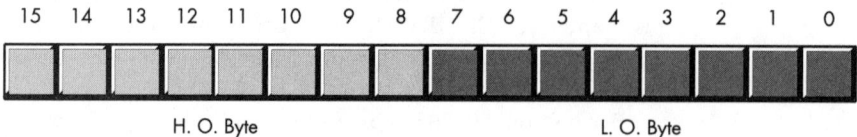

Figure 2-4: The Two Bytes in a Word.

Naturally, a word may be further broken down into four nibbles, as shown in Figure 2-5. Nibble zero is the low order nibble in the word and nibble three is the high order nibble of the word. We'll simply refer to the other two nibbles as "nibble one" or "nibble two."

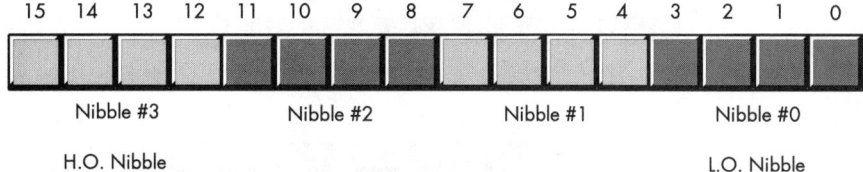

Figure 2-5: Nibbles in a Word.

With 16 bits, you can represent 2^{16} (65,536) different values. These could be the values in the range 0..65,535 or, as is usually the case, the signed values -32,768..+32,767, or any other data type with no more than 65,536 values. The three major uses for words are "short" signed integer values, "short" unsigned integer values, and Unicode characters.

Words can represent integer values in the range 0..65,535 or -32,768..+32,767. Unsigned numeric values are represented by the binary value corresponding to the bits in the word. Signed numeric values use the two's complement form for numeric values. As Unicode characters, words can represent up to 65,536 different characters, allowing the use of non-Roman character sets in a computer program. Unicode is an international standard, like ASCII, that allows computers to process non-Roman characters like Asian, Greek, and Russian characters.

Like bytes, you can also create word variables in an HLA program. Of course, in the last chapter you saw how to create 16-bit signed integer variables using the int16 data type. To create an arbitrary word variable, just use the word data type, as follows:

```
static
        w: word;
```

2.4.5   Double Words

A double word is exactly what its name implies, a pair of words. Therefore, a double word quantity is 32 bits long, as shown in Figure 2-6.

Figure 2-6: Bit Numbers in a Double Word.

Naturally, this double word can be divided into a high order word and a low order word, four different bytes, or eight different nibbles (see Figure 2-7).

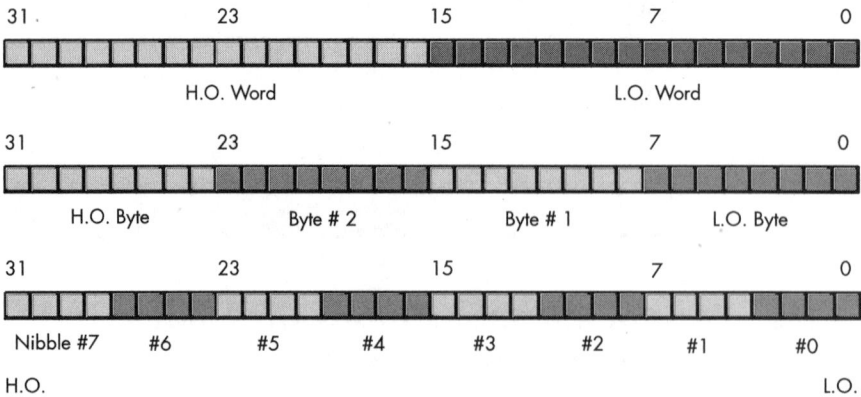

Figure 2-7: Nibbles, Bytes, and Words in a Double Word.

Double words (dwords) can represent all kinds of different things. A common item you will represent with a double word is a 32-bit integer value (that allows unsigned numbers in the range 0..4,294,967,295 or signed numbers in the range -2,147,483,648..+2,147,483,647). 32-bit floating point values also fit into a double word. Another common use for double word objects is to store pointer values.

In the previous chapter, you saw how to create 32-bit signed integer variables using the int32 data type. You can also create an arbitrary double word variable using the dword data type as the following example demonstrates:

```
static
        d: dword;
```

2.4.6   Quad Words and Long Words

Obviously, we can keep on defining larger and larger word sizes. However, the 80x86 only supports certain native sizes, so there is little reason to keep on defining terms for larger and larger objects. Although bytes, words, and double words are the most common sizes you'll find in 80x86 programs, quad word (64-bit) values are also important because certain floating point data types require 64 bits. Likewise, the MMX instruction set of modern 80x86 processors can manipulate 64-bit values. In a similar vein, long word (128-bit) values are also important because the SSE instruction set on later 80x86 processors can manipulate 128-bit values. HLA allows the declaration of 64- and 128-bit values using the qword and lword types, as follows:

```
static
    q    :qword;
    l    :lword;
```

Note that you may also define 64-bit and 128-bit integer values using HLA declarations like the following:

```
static
    i64         :int64;
    i128        :int128;
```

Note, however, that you may not directly manipulate 64-bit and 128-bit integer objects using standard instructions like mov, add, and sub because the standard 80x86 integer registers only process 32 bits at a time. Later in this text, you will see how to manipulate these *extended precision* values.

2.5 Arithmetic Operations on Binary and Hexadecimal Numbers

There are several operations we can perform on binary and hexadecimal numbers. For example, we can add, subtract, multiply, divide, and perform other arithmetic operations. Although you needn't become an expert at it, you should be able to, in a pinch, perform these operations manually using a piece of paper and a pencil. Having just said that you should be able to perform these operations manually, the correct way to perform such arithmetic operations is to have a calculator that does them for you. There are several such calculators on the market; following is a list.

Some manufacturers of hexadecimal calculators (in 2002):

* Casio
* Hewlett-Packard
* Sharp
* Texas Instruments

This list is by no means exhaustive. Other calculator manufacturers probably produce these devices as well. The Hewlett-Packard devices are arguably the best of the bunch. However, they are more expensive than the others. Sharp and Casio produce units that sell for well under $50. If you plan on doing any assembly language programming at all, owning one of these calculators is essential.

To understand why you should spend the money on a calculator, consider the following arithmetic problem:

```
  $9
+ $1
----
```

You're probably tempted to write in the answer "$10" as the solution to this problem. But that is not correct! The correct answer is ten, which is "$A," not 16 which, is "$10." A similar problem exists with the subtraction problem:

```
  $10
- $1
----
```

You're probably tempted to answer "$9" even though the true answer is "$F."
Remember, this problem is asking "what is the difference between sixteen and
1?" The answer, of course, is 15, which is "$F."

Even if the two problems above don't bother you, in a stressful situation your
brain will switch back into decimal mode while you're thinking about something
else and you'll produce the incorrect result. Moral of the story: If you must do an
arithmetic computation using hexadecimal numbers by hand, take your time and
be careful about it. Either that, or convert the numbers to decimal, perform the
operation in decimal, and convert them back to hexadecimal.

2.6   A Note About Numbers vs. Representation

Many people confuse numbers and their representation. A common question
beginning assembly language students ask is, "I've got a binary number in the
EAX register; how do I convert that to a hexadecimal number in the EAX
register?" The answer is, "You don't." Although a strong argument could be made
that numbers in memory or in registers are represented in binary, it's best to view
values in memory or in a register as *abstract numeric quantities*. Strings of symbols
like 128, $80, or %1000_0000 are not different numbers; they are simply dif-
ferent representations for the same abstract quantity that we refer to as "one
hundred twenty-eight." Inside the computer, a number is a number regardless of
representation; the only time representation matters is when you input or output
the value in a human readable form.

Human readable forms of numeric quantities are always strings of characters. To print the value 128 in human readable form, you must convert the
numeric value 128 to the three-character sequence '1' followed by '2' followed by
'8.' This would provide the decimal representation of the numeric quantity. If
you prefer, you could convert the numeric value 128 to the three-character
sequence "$80." It's the same number, but we've converted it to a different
sequence of characters because (presumably) we wanted to view the number
using hexadecimal representation rather than decimal. Likewise, if we want to
see the number in binary, then we must convert this numeric value to a string
containing a one followed by seven zeros.

By default, HLA displays all byte, word, dword, qword, and lword variables
using the hexadecimal numbering system when you display them using the
stdout.put routine. Likewise, HLA's stdout.put routine will display all register values in hex. Consider the program in Listing 2-1 that converts values input as decimal numbers to their hexadecimal equivalents.

Listing 2-1: Decimal to Hexadecimal Conversion Program.

```
program ConvertToHex;
#include( "stdlib.hhf" )
static
    value: int32;

begin ConvertToHex;
```

```
        stdout.put( "Input a decimal value:" );
        stdin.get( value );
        mov( value, eax );
        stdout.put( "The value ", value, " converted to hex is $", eax, nl );

end ConvertToHex;
```

In a similar fashion, the default input base is also hexadecimal for registers and byte, word, dword, qword, or lword variables. The program in Listing 2-2 is the converse of the one in Listing 2-1: It inputs a hexadecimal value and outputs it as decimal.

Listing 2-2: Hexadecimal to Decimal Conversion Program.

```
program ConvertToDecimal;
#include( "stdlib.hhf" )
static
    value: int32;

begin ConvertToDecimal;

    stdout.put( "Input a hexadecimal value: " );
    stdin.get( ebx );
    mov( ebx, value );
    stdout.put( "The value $", ebx, " converted to decimal is ", value, nl );

end ConvertToDecimal;
```

Just because the HLA stdout.put routine chooses decimal as the default output base for int8, int16, and int32 variables doesn't mean that these variables hold "decimal" numbers. Remember, memory and registers hold numeric values, not hexadecimal or decimal values. The stdout.put routine converts these numeric values to strings and prints the resulting strings. The choice of hexadecimal vs. decimal output was a design choice in the HLA language, nothing more. You could very easily modify HLA so that it outputs registers and byte, word, dword, qword, or lword variables as decimal values rather than as hexadecimal. If you need to print the value of a register or byte, word, or dword variable as a decimal value, simply call one of the *putiX* routines to do this. The stdout.puti8 routine will output its parameter as an 8-bit signed integer. Any 8-bit parameter will work. So you could pass an 8-bit register, an int8 variable or a byte variable as the parameter to stdout.puti8 and the result will always be decimal. The stdout.puti16 and stdout.puti32 provide the same capabilities for 16-bit and 32-bit objects. The program in Listing 2-3 demonstrates the decimal conversion program (Listing 2-2) using only the EAX register (i.e., it does not use the variable iValue).

Listing 2-3: Variable-less Hexadecimal to Decimal Converter.

```
program ConvertToDecimal2;
#include( "stdlib.hhf" )
begin ConvertToDecimal2;

    stdout.put( "Input a hexadecimal value: " );
    stdin.get( ebx );
    stdout.put( "The value $", ebx, " converted to decimal is " );
    stdout.puti32( ebx );
    stdout.newln();

end ConvertToDecimal2;
```

Note that HLA's stdin.get routine uses the same default base for input as stdout.put uses for output. That is, if you attempt to read an int8, int16, or int32 variable, the default input base is decimal. If you attempt to read a register or byte, word, dword, qword, or lword variable, the default input base is hexadecimal. If you want to change the default input base to decimal when reading a register or a byte, word, dword, qword, or lword variable, then you can use stdin.geti8, stdin.geti16, stdin.geti32, stdin.geti64, or stdin.geti128.

If you want to go in the opposite direction, that is you want to input or output an int8, int16, int32, int64, or int128 variable as a hexadecimal value, you can call the stdout.putb, stdout.putw, stdout.putd, stdout.putq, stdout.putl stdin.getb, stdin.getw, stdin.getd, stdin.getq, or stdin.getl routines. The stdout.putb, stdout.putw stdout.putd, stdout.putq, and stdout.putl routines write 8-bit, 16-bit, 32-bit, 64-bit, or 128-bit objects as hexadecimal values. The stdin.getb, stdin.getw, stdin.getd, stdin.getq, and stdin.getl routines read 8-, 16-, 32-, 64-, and 128-bit values, respectively; they return their results in the AL, AX, or EAX registers (or in a parameter location for 64-bit and 128-bit values). The program in Listing 2-4 demonstrates the use of a few of these routines:

Listing 2-4: Demonstration of stdin.getd and stdout.putd.

```
program HexIO;

#include( "stdlib.hhf" )

static
    i32: int32;

begin HexIO;

    stdout.put( "Enter a hexadecimal value: " );
    stdin.getd();
    mov( eax, i32 );
    stdout.put( "The value you entered was $" );
```

```
        stdout.putd( i32 );
        stdout.newln();

end HexIO;
```

2.7   Logical Operations on Bits

There are four primary logical operations we'll do with hexadecimal and binary numbers: AND, OR, XOR (exclusive-or), and NOT. Unlike the arithmetic operations, a hexadecimal calculator isn't necessary to perform these operations. It is often easier to do them by hand than to use an electronic device to compute them. The logical AND operation is a dyadic[3] operation (meaning it accepts exactly two operands). These operands are individual binary bits. The AND operation is:

```
        0 and 0 = 0
        0 and 1 = 0
        1 and 0 = 0
        1 and 1 = 1
```

A compact way to represent the logical AND operation is with a truth table. A truth table takes the form shown in Table 2-2.

Table 2-2: AND Truth Table

AND	0	1
0	0	0
1	0	1

This is just like the multiplication tables you've encountered in school. The values in the left column correspond to the leftmost operand of the AND operation. The values in the top row correspond to the rightmost operand of the AND operation. The value located at the intersection of the row and column (for a particular pair of input values) is the result of logically ANDing those two values together.

In English, the logical AND operation is, "If the first operand is one and the second operand is one, the result is one; otherwise the result is zero." We could also state this as "If either or both operands are zero, the result is zero."

One important fact to note about the logical AND operation is that you can use it to force a zero result. If one of the operands is zero, the result is always zero regardless of the other operand. In the truth table above, for example, the row labeled with a zero input contains only zeros and the column labeled with a zero only contains zero results. Conversely, if one operand contains a one, the result is exactly the value of the second operand. These results of the AND operation are very important, particularly when we want to force bits to zero. We will investigate these uses of the logical AND operation in the next section.

---

[3] Many texts call this a binary operation. The term *dyadic* means the same thing and avoids the confusion with the binary numbering system.

The logical OR operation is also a dyadic operation. Its definition is:

```
0 or 0 = 0
0 or 1 = 1
1 or 0 = 1
1 or 1 = 1
```

The truth table for the OR operation takes the form appearing in Table 2-3.

Table 2-3: OR Truth Table

OR	0	1
0	0	1
1	1	1

Colloquially, the logical OR operation is, "If the first operand or the second operand (or both) is one, the result is one; otherwise the result is zero." This is also known as the *inclusive-OR* operation.

If one of the operands to the logical-OR operation is a one, the result is always one regardless of the second operand's value. If one operand is zero, the result is always the value of the second operand. Like the logical AND operation, this is an important side effect of the logical-OR operation that will prove quite useful.

Note that there is a difference between this form of the inclusive logical OR operation and the standard English meaning. Consider the phrase "I am going to the store *or* I am going to the park." Such a statement implies that the speaker is going to the store or to the park but not to both places. Therefore, the English version of logical OR is slightly different than the inclusive-OR operation; indeed, this is the definition of the *exclusive-OR* operation.

The logical XOR (exclusive-or) operation is also a dyadic operation. Its definition follows:

```
0 xor 0 = 0
0 xor 1 = 1
1 xor 0 = 1
1 xor 1 = 0
```

The truth table for the XOR operation takes the form shown in Table 2-4.

Table 2-4: XOR Truth Table

XOR	0	1
0	0	1
1	1	0

In English, the logical XOR operation is, "If the first operand or the second operand, but not both, is one, the result is one; otherwise the result is zero." Note that the exclusive-or operation is closer to the English meaning of the word "or" than is the logical OR operation.

If one of the operands to the logical exclusive-OR operation is a one, the result is always the *inverse* of the other operand; that is, if one operand is one, the result is zero if the other operand is one and the result is one if the other operand is zero. If the first operand contains a zero, then the result is exactly the value of the second operand. This feature lets you selectively invert bits in a bit string.

The logical NOT operation is a monadic operation (meaning it accepts only one operand). It is:

```
NOT 0 = 1
NOT 1 = 0
```

The truth table for the NOT operation appears in Table 2-5.

Table 2-5: NOT Truth Table

NOT	0	1
	1	0

2.8 Logical Operations on Binary Numbers and Bit Strings

The previous section defines the logical functions for single bit operands. Because the 80x86 uses groups of 8, 16, or 32 bits, we need to extend the definition of these functions to deal with more than 2 bits. Logical functions on the 80x86 operate on a *bit-by-bit* (or *bitwise*) basis. Given two values, these functions operate on bit zero producing bit zero of the result. They operate on bit one of the input values producing bit one of the result, and so on. For example, if you want to compute the logical AND of the following two 8-bit numbers, you would perform the logical AND operation on each column independently of the others:

```
%1011_0101
%1110_1110
----------
%1010_0100
```

You may apply this bit-by-bit calculation to the other logical functions as well.

Because we've defined logical operations in terms of binary values, you'll find it much easier to perform logical operations on binary values than on other representations. Therefore, if you want to perform a logical operation on two hexadecimal numbers, you should convert them to binary first. This applies to most of the basic logical operations on binary numbers (e.g., AND, OR, XOR, and so on).

The ability to force bits to zero or one using the logical AND/OR operations and the ability to invert bits using the logical XOR operation is very important when working with strings of bits (e.g., binary numbers). These operations let you selectively manipulate certain bits within some bit string while leaving other bits unaffected. For example, if you have an 8-bit binary value X and you want to guarantee that bits 4..7 contain zeros, you could logically AND the value X with the binary value %0000_1111. This bitwise logical AND operation would force the H.O. 4 bits to zero and pass the L.O. 4 bits of X unchanged. Likewise, you could force the L.O. bit of X to one and invert bit number two of X by logically ORing X with %0000_0001 and logically exclusive-ORing X with %0000_0100, respectively. Using the logical AND, OR, and XOR operations to manipulate bit strings in this fashion is known as *masking* bit strings. We use the term "masking" because we can use certain values (one for AND, zero for OR/XOR) to "mask out" or "mask in" certain bits from the operation when forcing bits to zero, one, or their inverse.

The 80x86 CPUs support four instructions that apply these bitwise logical operations to their operands. The instructions are and, or, xor, and not. The and, or, and xor instructions use the same syntax as the add and sub instructions; that is,

```
and( source, dest );
 or( source, dest );
xor( source, dest );
```

These operands have the same limitations as the add operands. Specifically, the source operand has to be a constant, memory, or register operand and the dest operand must be a memory or register operand. Also, the operands must be the same size and they cannot both be memory operands. These instructions compute the obvious bitwise logical operation via the equation:

```
dest = dest operator source
```

The 80x86 logical not instruction, because it has only a single operand, uses a slightly different syntax. This instruction takes the following form:

```
not( dest );
```

This instruction computes the following result:

```
dest = NOT( dest )
```

The dest operand (for not) must be a register or memory operand. This instruction inverts all the bits in the specified destination operand.

The program in Listing 2-5 inputs two hexadecimal values from the user and calculates their logical AND, OR, XOR, and NOT:

Listing 2-5: AND, OR, XOR, and NOT Example.

```
program LogicalOp;
#include( "stdlib.hhf" )
begin LogicalOp;

    stdout.put( "Input left operand: " );
    stdin.get( eax );
    stdout.put( "Input right operand: " );
    stdin.get( ebx );

    mov( eax, ecx );
    and( ebx, ecx );
    stdout.put( "$", eax, " AND $", ebx, " = $", ecx, nl );

    mov( eax, ecx );
    or( ebx, ecx );
    stdout.put( "$", eax, " OR $", ebx, " = $", ecx, nl );

    mov( eax, ecx );
    xor( ebx, ecx );
    stdout.put( "$", eax, " XOR $", ebx, " = $", ecx, nl );

    mov( eax, ecx );
    not( ecx );
    stdout.put( "NOT $", eax, " = $", ecx, nl );

    mov( ebx, ecx );
    not( ecx );
    stdout.put( "NOT $", ebx, " = $", ecx, nl );

end LogicalOp;
```

2.9   Signed and Unsigned Numbers

Thus far, we've treated binary numbers as unsigned values. The binary number ...00000 represents zero, ...00001 represents one, ...00010 represents two, and so on toward infinity. What about negative numbers? Signed values have been tossed around in previous sections and we've mentioned the two's complement numbering system, but we haven't discussed how to represent negative numbers using the binary numbering system. That is what this section is all about!

To represent signed numbers using the binary numbering system we have to place a restriction on our numbers: they must have a finite and fixed number of bits. For our purposes, we're going to severely limit the number of bits to 8, 16, 32, 64, 128, or some other small number of bits.

With a fixed number of bits we can only represent a certain number of objects. For example, with 8 bits we can only represent 256 different values. Negative values are objects in their own right, just like positive numbers; therefore, we'll have to use some of the 256 different 8-bit values to represent negative numbers. In other words, we've got to use up some of the bit combinations to represent negative numbers. To make things fair, we'll assign half of the possible combinations to the negative values and half to the positive values and zero. So we can represent the negative values -128..-1 and the non-negative values 0..127 with a single 8-bit byte. With a 16-bit word we can represent values in the range -32,768..+32,767. With a 32-bit double word we can represent values in the range -2,147,483,648..+2,147,483,647. In general, with n bits we can represent the signed values in the range -2^{n-1} to $+2^{n-1}-1$.

Okay, so we can represent negative values. Exactly how do we do it? Well, there are many possible ways, but the 80x86 microprocessor uses the two's complement notation. In the two's complement system, the H.O. bit of a number is a *sign bit*. If the H.O. bit is zero, the number is positive; if the H.O. bit is one, the number is negative. Examples:

For 16-bit numbers:

```
$8000 is negative because the H.O. bit is one.
 $100 is positive because the H.O. bit is zero.
$7FFF is positive.
$FFFF is negative.
$FFF ($0FFF) is positive.
```

If the H.O. bit is zero, then the number is positive and uses the standard binary format. If the H.O. bit is one, then the number is negative and uses the two's complement form. To convert a positive number to its negative, two's complement form, you use the following algorithm:

1. Invert all the bits in the number — i.e., apply the logical NOT function.
2. Add one to the inverted result.

For example, to compute the 8-bit equivalent of -5:

```
%0000_0101          Five (in binary).
%1111_1010          Invert all the bits.
%1111_1011          Add one to obtain result.
```

If we take -5 and perform the two's complement operation on it, we get our original value, %0000_0101, back again, just as we expect:

```
%1111_1011          Two's complement for -5.
%0000_0100          Invert all the bits.
%0000_0101          Add one to obtain result (+5).
```

The following examples provide some positive and negative 16-bit signed values:

```
$7FFF: +32767, the largest 16-bit positive number.
$8000: -32768, the smallest 16-bit negative number.
$4000: +16,384.
```

To convert the numbers above to their negative counterpart (i.e., to negate them), do the following:

```
$7FFF:      %0111_1111_1111_1111   +32,767
            %1000_0000_0000_0000   Invert all the bits ($8000)
            %1000_0000_0000_0001   Add one ($8001 or -32,767)

$4000:      %0100_0000_0000_0000   16,384
            %1011_1111_1111_1111   Invert all the bits ($BFFF)
            %1100_0000_0000_0000   Add one ($C000 or -16,384)

$8000:      %1000_0000_0000_0000   -32,768
        %0111_1111_1111_1111   Invert all the bits ($7FFF)
        %1000_0000_0000_0000   Add one (8000h or -32768)
```

$8000 inverted becomes $7FFF. After adding one we obtain $8000! Wait, what's going on here? -(-32,768) is -32,768? Of course not. But the value +32,768 cannot be represented with a 16-bit signed number, so we cannot negate the smallest negative value.

Why bother with such a miserable numbering system? Why not use the H.O. bit as a sign flag, storing the positive equivalent of the number in the remaining bits? The answer lies in the hardware. As it turns out, negating values is the only tedious job. With the two's complement system, most other operations are as easy as the binary system. For example, suppose you were to perform the addition 5+(-5). The result is zero. Consider what happens when we add these two values in the two's complement system:

```
            %   0000_0101
            %   1111_1011
            ------------
          %1_0000_0000
```

We end up with a carry into the ninth bit and all other bits are zero. As it turns out, if we ignore the carry out of the H.O. bit, adding two signed values always produces the correct result when using the two's complement numbering system. This means we can use the same hardware for signed and unsigned addition and subtraction. This wouldn't be the case with some other numbering systems.

Usually, you will not need to perform the two's complement operation by hand. The 80x86 microprocessor provides an instruction, neg (negate), that performs this operation for you. Furthermore, all the hexadecimal calculators will perform this operation by pressing the change sign key (+/- or CHS). Nevertheless, performing a two's complement by hand is easy, and you should know how to do it.

Once again, you should note that the data represented by a set of binary bits depends entirely on the context. The 8-bit binary value %1100_0000 could represent an IBM/ASCII character, it could represent the unsigned decimal value 192, or it could represent the signed decimal value -64. As the programmer, it is your responsibility to define the data's format and then use the data consistently.

The 80x86 negate instruction, neg, uses the same syntax as the not instruction; that is, it takes a single destination operand:

```
neg( dest );
```

This instruction computes "dest = -dest;" and the operand has the same limitations as for not (it must be a memory location or a register). Neg operates on byte-, word-, and dword-sized objects. Of course, because this is a signed integer operation, it only makes sense to operate on signed integer values. The program in Listing 2-6 demonstrates the two's complement operation by using the neg instruction:

Listing 2-6: AND, OR, XOR, and NOT Example.

```
program twosComplement;
#include( "stdlib.hhf" )

static
    PosValue:    int8;
    NegValue:    int8;

begin twosComplement;

    stdout.put( "Enter an integer between 0 and 127: " );
    stdin.get( PosValue );

    stdout.put( nl, "Value in hexadecimal: $" );
    stdout.putb( PosValue );

    mov( PosValue, al );
    not( al );
    stdout.put( nl, "Invert all the bits: $", al, nl );
    add( 1, al );
    stdout.put( "Add one: $", al, nl );
    mov( al, NegValue );
    stdout.put( "Result in decimal: ", NegValue, nl );

    stdout.put
    (
        nl,
        "Now do the same thing with the NEG instruction: ",
        nl
    );
    mov( PosValue, al );
    neg( al );
    mov( al, NegValue );
```

```
        stdout.put( "Hex result = $", al, nl );
        stdout.put( "Decimal result = ", NegValue, nl );


end twosComplement;
```

As you've seen previously, you use the int8, int16, int32, int64, and int128 data types to reserve storage for signed integer variables. You've also seen routines like stdout.puti8 and stdin.geti32 that read and write signed integer values. Because this section has made it abundantly clear that you must differentiate signed and unsigned calculations in your programs, you should probably be asking yourself about now, "How do I declare and use unsigned integer variables?"

The first part of the question, how do you declare unsigned integer variables, is the easiest to answer. You simply use the uns8, uns16, uns32, uns64, and uns128 data types when declaring the variables, for example:

```
static
    u8:         uns8;
    u16:        uns16;
    u32:        uns32;
    u64:        uns64;
    u128:       uns128;
```

As for using these unsigned variables, the HLA Standard Library provides a complementary set of input/output routines for reading and displaying unsigned variables. As you can probably guess, these routines include stdout.putu8, stdout.putu16, stdout.putu32, stdout.putu64, stdout.putu128, stdout.putu8Size, stdout.putu16Size, stdout.putu32Size, stdout.putu64Size, stdout.putu128Size, stdin.getu8, stdin.getu16, stdin.getu32, stdin.getu64, and stdin.getu128. You use these routines just as you would use their signed integer counterparts except, of course, you get to use the full range of the unsigned values with these routines. The source code in Listing 2-7 demonstrates unsigned I/O as well as demonstrating what can happen if you mix signed and unsigned operations in the same calculation.

Listing 2-7: Unsigned I/O.

```
program UnsExample;
#include( "stdlib.hhf" )

static
    UnsValue:   uns16;

begin UnsExample;

    stdout.put( "Enter an integer between 32,768 and 65,535: " );
    stdin.getu16();
    mov( ax, UnsValue );

    stdout.put
```

```
    (
        "You entered ",
        UnsValue,
        ".  If you treat this as a signed integer, it is "
    );
    stdout.puti16( UnsValue );
    stdout.newln();

end UnsExample;
```

2.10 Sign Extension, Zero Extension, Contraction, and Saturation

Because two's complement format integers have a fixed length, a small problem develops. What happens if you need to convert an 8-bit two's complement value to 16 bits? This problem, and its converse (converting a 16-bit value to 8 bits) can be accomplished via *sign extension* and *contraction* operations.

Consider the value -64. The 8-bit two's complement value for this number is $C0. The 16-bit equivalent of this number is $FFC0. Now consider the value +64. The 8- and 16-bit versions of this value are $40 and $0040, respectively. The difference between the 8- and 16-bit numbers can be described by the rule: "If the number is negative, the H.O. byte of the 16-bit number contains $FF; if the number is positive, the H.O. byte of the 16-bit quantity is zero."

To extend a signed value from some number of bits to a greater number of bits is easy, just copy the sign bit into all the additional bits in the new format. For example, to sign extend an 8-bit number to a 16-bit number, simply copy bit 7 of the 8-bit number into bits 8..15 of the 16-bit number. To sign extend a 16-bit number to a double word, simply copy bit 15 into bits 16..31 of the double word.

You must use sign extension when manipulating signed values of varying lengths. Often you'll need to add a byte quantity to a word quantity. You must sign extend the byte quantity to a word before the operation takes place. Other operations (multiplication and division, in particular) may require a sign extension to 32 bits:

Sign Extension:		
8 Bits	16 Bits	32 Bits
$80	$FF80	$FFFF_FF80
$28	$0028	$0000_0028
$9A	$FF9A	$FFFF_FF9A
$7F	$007F	$0000_007F
---	$1020	$0000_1020
---	$8086	$FFFF_8086

To extend an unsigned value to a larger one you must zero extend the value. Zero extension is very easy: Just store a zero into the H.O. byte(s) of the larger operand. For example, to zero extend the 8-bit value $82 to 16 bits you simply add a zero to the H.O. byte yielding $0082.

```
Zero Extension:
8 bits          16 Bits             32 Bits
  $80           $0080               $0000_0080
  $28           $0028               $0000_0028
  $9A           $009A               $0000_009A
  $7F           $007F               $0000_007F
  ---           $1020               $0000_1020
  ---           $8086               $0000_8086
```

The 80x86 provides several instructions that will let you sign or zero extend a smaller number to a larger number. Table 2-6 lists a group of instructions that will sign extend the AL, AX, or EAX register.

Table 2-6: Instructions for Extending AL, AX, and EAX

Instruction	Explanation
cbw();	// Converts the byte in AL to a word in AX via sign extension.
cwd();	// Converts the word in AX to a double word in DX:AX.
cdq();	// Converts the double word in EAX to the quad word in EDX:EAX.
cwde();	// Converts the word in AX to a doubleword in EAX.

Note that the cwd (convert word to double word) instruction does not sign extend the word in AX to the double word in EAX. Instead, it stores the H.O. word of the sign extension into the DX register (the notation "DX:AX" tells you that you have a double word value with DX containing the upper 16 bits and AX containing the lower 16 bits of the value). If you want the sign extension of AX to go into EAX, you should use the cwde (convert word to double word, extended) instruction.

The four instructions above are unusual in the sense that these are the first instructions you've seen that do not have any operands. These instructions' operands are *implied* by the instructions themselves.

Within a few chapters you will discover just how important these instructions are, and why the cwd and cdq instructions involve the DX and EDX registers. However, for simple sign extension operations, these instructions have a few major drawbacks: You do not get to specify the source and destination operands and the operands must be registers.

For general sign extension operations, the 80x86 provides an extension of the mov instruction, movsx (move with sign extension), that copies data and sign extends the data while copying it. The movsx instruction's syntax is very similar to the mov instruction:

```
movsx( source, dest );
```

The big difference in syntax between this instruction and the mov instruction is the fact that the destination operand must be larger than the source operand. That is, if the source operand is a byte, the destination operand must be a word or a double word. Likewise, if the source operand is a word, the destination operand must be a double word. Another difference is that the destination operand has to be a register; the source operand, however, can be a memory location.[4]

To zero extend a value, you can use the movzx instruction. It has the same syntax and restrictions as the movsx instruction. Zero extending certain 8-bit registers (AL, BL, CL, and DL) into their corresponding 16-bit registers is easily accomplished without using movzx by loading the complementary H.O. register (AH, BH, CH, or DH) with zero. Obviously, to zero extend AX into DX:AX or EAX into EDX:EAX, all you need to do is load DX or EDX with zero.[5]

The sample program in Listing 2-8 demonstrates the use of the sign extension instructions.

Listing 2-8: Sign Extension Instructions.

```
program signExtension;
#include( "stdlib.hhf" )

static
    i8:     int8;
    i16:    int16;
    i32:    int32;

begin signExtension;

    stdout.put( "Enter a small negative number: " );
    stdin.get( i8 );

    stdout.put( nl, "Sign extension using CBW and CWDE:", nl, nl );

    mov( i8, al );
    stdout.put( "You entered ", i8, " ($", al, ")", nl );

    cbw();
    mov( ax, i16 );
    stdout.put( "16-bit sign extension: ", i16, " ($", ax, ")", nl );

    cwde();
    mov( eax, i32 );
    stdout.put( "32-bit sign extension: ", i32, " ($", eax, ")", nl );

    stdout.put( nl, "Sign extension using MOVSX:", nl, nl );

    movsx( i8, ax );
    mov( ax, i16 );
    stdout.put( "16-bit sign extension: ", i16, " ($", ax, ")", nl );
```

---

[4] This doesn't turn out to be much of a limitation because sign extension almost always precedes an arithmetic operation that must take place in a register.

---

[5] Zero extending into DX:AX or EDX:EAX is just as necessary as the CWD and CDQ instructions, as you will eventually see.

```
        movsx( i8, eax );
        mov( eax, i32 );
        stdout.put( "32-bit sign extension: ", i32, " ($", eax, ")", nl );

end signExtension;
```

Sign contraction, converting a value with some number of bits to the identical value with a fewer number of bits, is a little more troublesome. Sign extension never fails. Given an *m*-bit signed value you can always convert it to an *n*-bit number (where $n > m$) using sign extension. Unfortunately, given an *n*-bit number, you cannot always convert it to an *m*-bit number if $m < n$. For example, consider the value -448. As a 16-bit signed number, its hexadecimal representation is $FE40. Unfortunately, the magnitude of this number is too large for an 8-bit value, so you cannot sign contract it to 8 bits. This is an example of an overflow condition that occurs upon conversion.

To properly sign contract one value to another, you must look at the H.O. byte(s) that you want to discard. The H.O. bytes you wish to remove must all contain either zero or $FF. If you encounter any other values, you cannot contract it without overflow. Finally, the H.O. bit of your resulting value must match *every* bit you've removed from the number. Examples (16 bits to 8 bits):

```
$FF80 can be sign contracted to $80.
$0040 can be sign contracted to $40.
$FE40 cannot be sign contracted to 8 bits.
$0100 cannot be sign contracted to 8 bits.
```

Another way to reduce the size of an integer is by *saturation*. Saturation is useful in situations where you must convert a larger object to a smaller object, and you're willing to live with possible loss of precision. To convert a value via saturation you simply copy the larger value to the smaller value if it is not outside the range of the smaller object. If the larger value is outside the range of the smaller value, then you *clip* the value by setting it to the largest (or smallest) value within the range of the smaller object.

For example, when converting a 16-bit signed integer to an 8-bit signed integer, if the 16-bit value is in the range -128..+127 you simply copy the L.O. byte of the 16-bit object to the 8-bit object. If the 16-bit signed value is greater than +127, then you clip the value to +127 and store +127 into the 8-bit object. Likewise, if the value is less than -128, you clip the final 8-bit object to -128. Saturation works the same way when clipping 32-bit values to smaller values. If the larger value is outside the range of the smaller value, then you simply set the smaller value to the value closest to the out-of-range value that you can represent with the smaller value.

Obviously, if the larger value is outside the range of the smaller value, then there will be a loss of precision during the conversion. While clipping the value to the limits the smaller object imposes is never desirable, sometimes this is acceptable as the alternative is to raise an exception or otherwise reject the calculation. For many applications, such as audio or video processing, the clipped result is still recognizable, so this is a reasonable conversion to use.

2.11 Shifts and Rotates

Another set of logical operations that apply to bit strings are the *shift* and *rotate* operations. These two categories can be further broken down into *left shifts, left rotates, right shifts,* and *right rotates.* These operations turn out to be extremely useful to assembly language programmers.

The left shift operation moves each bit in a bit string one position to the left (Figure 2-8 provides an example of an 8-bit shift).

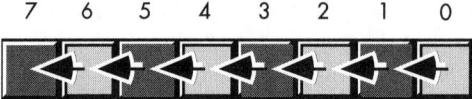

Figure 2-8: Shift Left Operation.

Bit zero moves into bit position one, the previous value in bit position one moves into bit position two, and so on. There are, of course, two questions that naturally arise: "What goes into bit zero?" and "Where does the high order bit wind up?" We'll shift a zero into bit zero and the previous value of the high order bit will become the *carry* out of this operation.

The 80x86 provides a shift left instruction, shl, that performs this useful operation. The syntax for the shl instruction is

---
```
shl( count, dest );
```

The count operand is either CL or a constant in the range 0..n, where *n* is one less than the number of bits in the destination operand (i.e., n=7 for 8-bit operands, n=15 for 16-bit operands, and n=31 for 32-bit operands). The dest operand is a typical destination operand; it can be either a memory location or a register.

When the count operand is the constant one, the shl instruction does the operation shown in Figure 2-9.

Figure 2-9: Shift Left Operation.

In Figure 2-9, the "C" represents the carry flag. That is, the H.O. bit shifted out of the operand moves into the carry flag. Therefore, you can test for overflow after a "shl(1, dest);" instruction by testing the carry flag immediately after executing the instruction (e.g., by using "if(@c) then . . ." or "if(@nc) then . . .").

Intel's literature suggests that the state of the carry flag is undefined if the shift count is a value other than one. Usually, the carry flag contains the last bit shifted out of the destination operand, but Intel doesn't seem to guarantee this.

Note that shifting a value to the left is the same thing as multiplying it by its radix. For example, shifting a decimal number one position to the left (adding a zero to the right of the number) effectively multiplies it by ten (the radix):

```
1234 shl 1 = 12340   (shl 1 means shift one digit position to the left)
```

Because the radix of a binary number is two, shifting it left multiplies it by two. If you shift a binary value to the left twice, you multiply it by two twice (i.e., you multiply it by four). If you shift a binary value to the left three times, you multiply it by eight (2*2*2). In general, if you shift a value to the left n times, you multiply that value by 2^n.

A right shift operation works the same way, except we're moving the data in the opposite direction. For a byte value, bit seven moves into bit 6, bit 6 moves into bit 5, bit 5 moves into bit 4, and so on. During a right shift, we'll move a zero into bit 7, and bit 0 will be the carry-out of the operation (see Figure 2-10).

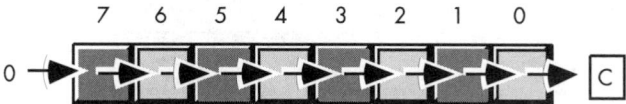

Figure 2-10: Shift Right Operation.

As you would probably expect, the 80x86 provides a shr instruction that will shift the bits to the right in a destination operand. The syntax is the same as the shl instruction except, of course, you specify shr rather than shl:

```
shr( count, dest );
```

This instruction shifts a zero into the H.O. bit of the destination operand; it shifts all the other bits one place to the right (that is, from a higher bit number to a lower bit number). Finally, bit 0 is shifted into the carry flag. If you specify a count of one, the shr instruction does the operation shown in Figure 2-11.

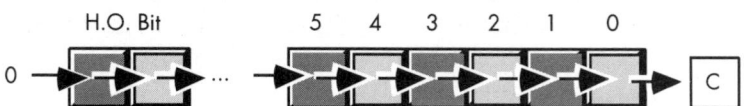

Figure 2-11: Shift Right Operation.

Once again, Intel's documents suggest that shifts of more than one bit leave the carry in an undefined state.

Because a left shift is equivalent to a multiplication by two, it should come as no surprise that a right shift is roughly comparable to a division by two (or, in general, a division by the radix of the number). If you perform n right shifts, you will divide that number by 2^n.

There is one problem with shift rights with respect to division: A shift right is only equivalent to an *unsigned* division by two. For example, if you shift the unsigned representation of 254 ($FE) one place to the right, you get 127 ($7F), exactly what you would expect. However, if you shift the binary representation of -2 ($FE) to the right one position, you get 127 ($7F), which is *not* correct. This problem occurs because we're shifting a zero into bit 7. If bit 7 previously contained a one, we're changing it from a negative to a positive number. Not a good thing when dividing by two.

To use the shift right as a division operator, we must define a third shift operation: arithmetic shift right.[6] An arithmetic shift right works just like the normal shift right operation (a logical shift right) with one exception: instead of shifting a zero into the high order bit, an arithmetic shift right operation copies the high order bit back into itself, that is, during the shift operation it does not modify the high order bit, as Figure 2-12 shows.

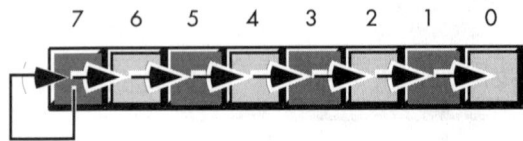

Figure 2-12: Arithmetic Shift Right Operation.

An arithmetic shift right generally produces the result you expect. For example, if you perform the arithmetic shift right operation on -2 ($FE) you get -1 ($FF). Keep one thing in mind about arithmetic shift right, however. This operation always rounds the numbers to the closest integer *that is less than or equal to the actual result.* Based on experiences with high level programming languages and the standard rules of integer truncation, most people assume this means that a division always truncates toward zero. But this simply isn't the case. For example, if you apply the arithmetic shift right operation on -1 ($FF), the result is -1, not zero. Minus one is less than zero, so the arithmetic shift right operation rounds toward -1. This is not a "bug" in the arithmetic shift right operation; it just uses a different (though valid) definition of integer division.

The 80x86 provides an arithmetic shift right instruction, sar (shift arithmetic right). This instruction's syntax is nearly identical to shl and shr. The syntax is

```
sar( count, dest );
```

---

[6] There is no need for an arithmetic shift left. The standard shift left operation works for both signed and unsigned numbers, assuming no overflow occurs.

The usual limitations on the count and destination operands apply. This instruction operates as shown in Figure 2-13 if the count is one.

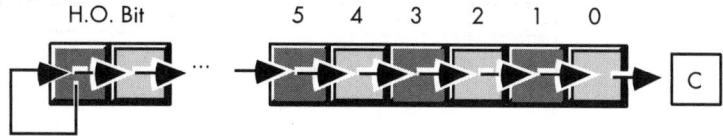

Figure 2-13: SAR(1, dest) Operation.

Once again, Intel's documents suggest that shifts of more than one bit leave the carry in an undefined state.

Another pair of useful operations are *rotate left* and *rotate right*. These operations behave like the shift left and shift right operations with one major difference: The bit shifted out from one end is shifted back in at the other end. Figures 2-14 and 2-15 diagram these operations.

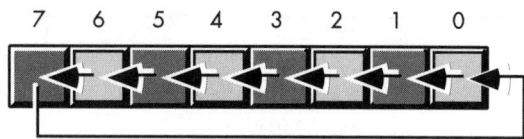

Figure 2-14: Rotate Left Operation.

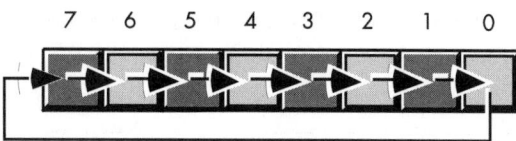

Figure 2-15: Rotate Right Operation.

The 80x86 provides rol (rotate left) and ror (rotate right) instructions that do these basic operations on their operands. The syntax for these two instructions is similar to the shift instructions:

```
rol( count, dest );
ror( count, dest );
```

Once again, these instructions provide a special behavior if the shift count is one. Under this condition these two instructions also copy the bit shifted out of the destination operand into the carry flag, as Figures 2-16 and 2-17 show.

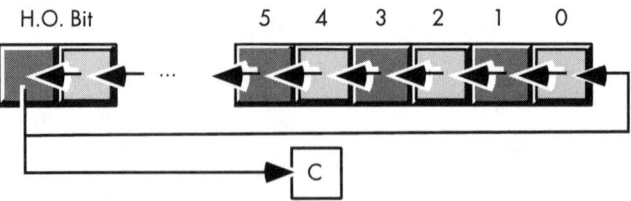

Figure 2-16: ROL(1, Dest) Operation.

Note that, Intel's documents suggest that rotates of more than one bit leave the carry in an undefined state.

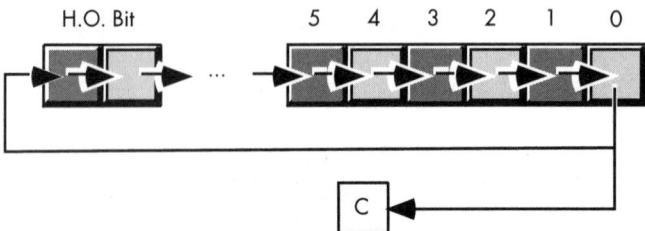

Figure 2-17: ROR(1, Dest) Operation.

It will turn out that it is often more convenient for the rotate operation to shift the output bit through the carry and shift the previous carry value back into the input bit of the shift operation. The 80x86 rcl (rotate through, carry left) and rcr (rotate through, carry right) instructions achieve this for you. These instructions use the following syntax:

```
rcl( count, dest );
rcr( count, dest );
```

As is true for the other shift and rotate instructions, the count operand is either a constant or the CL register and the destination operand is a memory location or register. The count operand must be a value that is less than the number of bits in the destination operand. For a count value of one, these two instructions do the rotation shown in Figures 2-18 and 2-19.

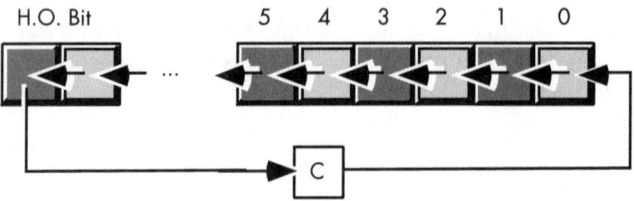

Figure 2-18: RCL(1, Dest) Operation.

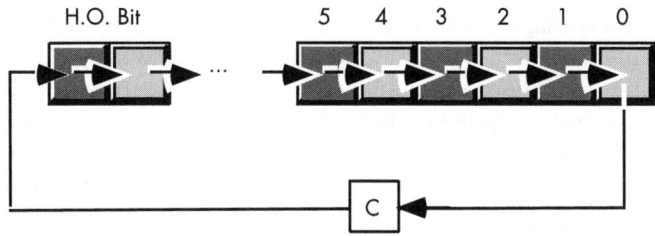

H.O. Bit   5 4 3 2 1 0

C

Figure 2-19: RCR(1, Dest) Operation.

Again, Intel's documents suggest that rotates of more than one bit leave the carry in an undefined state.

2.12   Bit Fields and Packed Data

Although the 80x86 operates most efficiently on byte, word, and double word data types, occasionally you'll need to work with a data type that uses some number of bits other than 8, 16, or 32. For example, consider a date of the form "04/02/01." It takes three numeric values to represent this date: a month, day, and year value. Months, of course, take on the values 1..12. It will require at least 4 bits (maximum of 16 different values) to represent the month. Days range between 1..31. So it will take 5 bits (maximum of 32 different values) to represent the day entry. The year value, assuming that we're working with values in the range 0..99, requires 7 bits (that can be used to represent up to 128 different values). Four plus five plus seven is 16 bits, or two bytes. In other words, we can pack our date data into two bytes rather than the three that would be required if we used a separate byte for each of the month, day, and year values. This saves one byte of memory for each date stored, which could be a substantial saving if you need to store a lot of dates. The bits could be arranged as shown in Figure 2-20.

15 14 13 12 11 10 9 8 7 6 5 4 3 2 1 0

| M | M | M | M | D | D | D | D | D | Y | Y | Y | Y | Y | Y | Y |

Figure 2-20: Short Packed Date Format (Two Bytes).

MMMM represents the 4 bits making up the month value; DDDDD represents the 5 bits making up the day, and YYYYYYY is the 7 bits comprising the year. Each collection of bits representing a data item is a *bit field.* April 2, 2001 would be represented as $4101:

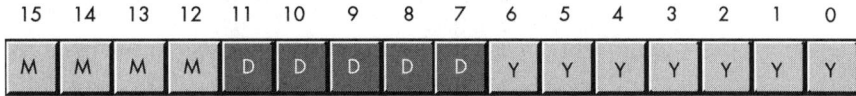

0100	00010	0000001	= %0100_0001_0000_0001 or $4101
4	2	01	

Although packed values are *space efficient* (that is, very efficient in terms of memory usage), they are computationally *inefficient* (slow!). The reason? It takes extra instructions to unpack the data packed into the various bit fields. These extra instructions take additional time to execute (and additional bytes to hold the instructions); hence, you must carefully consider whether packed data fields will save you anything. The sample program in Listing 2-9 demonstrates the effort that must go into packing and unpacking this 16-bit date format.

Listing 2-9: Packing and Unpacking Date Data.

```
program dateDemo;

#include( "stdlib.hhf" )

static
    day:        uns8;
    month:      uns8;
    year:       uns8;

    packedDate: word;

begin dateDemo;

    stdout.put( "Enter the current month, day, and year: " );
    stdin.get( month, day, year );

    // Pack the data into the following bits:
    //
    // 15 14 13 12 11 10  9  8  7  6  5  4  3  2  1  0
    //  m  m  m  m  d  d  d  d  d  y  y  y  y  y  y  y

    mov( 0, ax );
    mov( ax, packedDate );  //Just in case there is an error.
    if( month > 12 ) then

        stdout.put( "Month value is too large", nl );

    elseif( month = 0 ) then

        stdout.put( "Month value must be in the range 1..12", nl );

    elseif( day > 31 ) then

        stdout.put( "Day value is too large", nl );

    elseif( day = 0 ) then

        stdout.put( "Day value must be in the range 1..31", nl );
```

```
        elseif( year > 99 ) then

            stdout.put( "Year value must be in the range 0..99", nl );

        else

            mov( month, al );
            shl( 5, ax );
            or( day, al );
            shl( 7, ax );
            or( year, al );
            mov( ax, packedDate );

        endif;

        // Okay, display the packed value:

        stdout.put( "Packed data = $", packedDate, nl );



        // Unpack the date:

        mov( packedDate, ax );
        and( $7f, al );         // Retrieve the year value.
        mov( al, year );

        mov( packedDate, ax );  // Retrieve the day value.
        shr( 7, ax );
        and( %1_1111, al );
        mov( al, day );

        mov( packedDate, ax );  // Retrive the month value.
        rol( 4, ax );
        and( %1111, al );
        mov( al, month );

        stdout.put( "The date is ", month, "/", day, "/", year, nl );



    end dateDemo;
```

Of course, having gone through the problems with Y2K, using a date format that
limits you to 100 years (or even 127 years) would be quite foolish at this time. If
you're concerned about your software running 100 years from now, perhaps it
would be wise to use a three-byte date format rather than a two-byte format. As
you will see in the chapter on arrays, however, you should always try to create data
objects whose length are an even power of two (one byte, two bytes, four bytes,

eight bytes, and so on) or you will pay a performance penalty. Hence, it is probably wise to go ahead and use four bytes and pack this data into a double word variable. Figure 2-21 shows one possible data organization for a four-byte date.

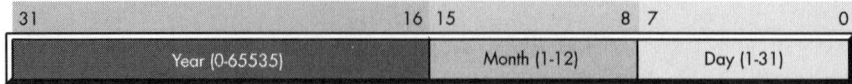

Figure 2-21: Long Packed Date Format (Four Bytes).

In this long packed data format several changes were made beyond simply extending the number of bits associated with the year. First, because there are extra bits in a 32-bit double word variable, this format allocates extra bits to the month and day fields. Because these two fields now consist of 8 bits each, they can be easily extracted as a byte object from the double word. This leaves fewer bits for the year, but 65,536 years is probably sufficient; you can probably assume without too much concern that your software will not still be in use 63,000 years from now when this date format will no longer work.

Of course, you could argue that this is no longer a packed date format. After all, we needed three numeric values, two of which fit just nicely into one byte each and one that should probably have at least two bytes. Because this "packed" date format consumes the same four bytes as the unpacked version, what is so special about this format? Well, another difference you will note between this long packed date format and the short date format appearing in Figure 2-20 is the fact that this long date format rearranges the bits so the Year is in the H.O. bit positions, the Month field is in the middle bit positions, and the Day field is in the L.O. bit positions. This is important because it allows you to very easily compare two dates to see if one date is less than, equal to, or greater than another date. Consider the following code:

```
mov( Date1, eax );          // Assume Date1 and Date2 are dword variables
if( eax > Date2 ) then      //   using the Long Packed Date format.

    << do something if Date1 > Date2 >>

endif;
```

Had you kept the different date fields in separate variables or organized the fields differently, you would not have been able to compare Date1 and Date2 in such a straight-forward fashion. Therefore, this example demonstrates another reason for packing data even if you don't realize any space savings: It can make certain computations more convenient or even more efficient (contrary to what normally happens when you pack data).

Examples of practical packed data types abound. You could pack eight boolean values into a single byte; you could pack two BCD digits into a byte, and so on. Of course, a classic example of packed data is the EFLAGS register (see Figure 2-22). This register packs nine important boolean objects (along with seven important system flags) into a single 16-bit register. You will commonly need to access many of these flags. For this reason, the 80x86 instruction set provides many ways to manipulate the individual bits in the flags register. Of course, you can test many of the condition code flags using the HLA @c, @nc, @z, @nz, and so on pseudo-boolean variables in an if statement or other statement using a boolean expression.

In addition to the condition codes, the 80x86 provides instructions that directly affect certain flags (Table 2-7).

Table 2-7: Instructions That Affect Certain Flags

Instruction	Explanation
cld();	Clears (sets to zero) the direction flag.
std();	Sets (to one) the direction flag.
cli();	Clears the interrupt disable flag.
sti();	Sets the interrupt disable flag.
clc();	Clears the carry flag.
stc();	Sets the carry flag.
cmc();	Complements (inverts) the carry flag.
sahf();	Stores the AH register into the L.O. 8 bits of the flags register.
lahf();	Loads AH from the L.O. 8 bits of the flags register.

There are other instructions that affect the flags register as well; these instructions, however, demonstrate how to access several of the packed boolean values in the flags register. The lahf and sahf instructions, in particular, provide a convenient way to access the L.O. 8 bits of the flags register as an 8-bit byte (rather than as eight separate 1-bit values). See Figure 2-22 for a layout of the flags register.

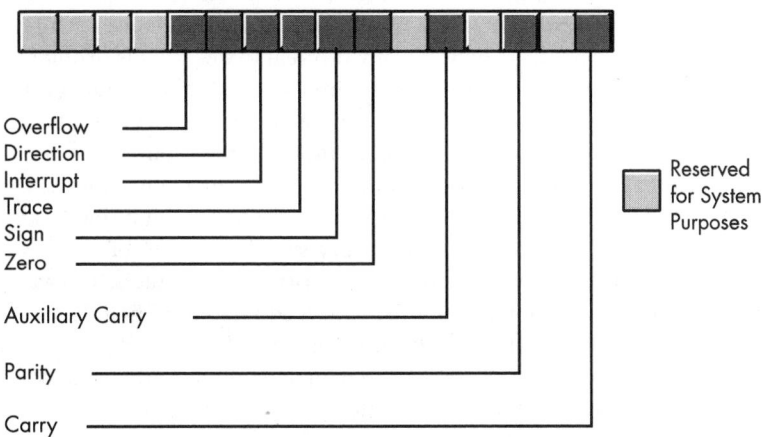

Figure 2-22: Layout of the flags register.

The lahf (load AH with the L.O. 8 bits of the flags register) and the sahf (store AH into the L.O. byte of the flags register) use the following syntax:

```
lahf();
sahf();
```

2.13   An Introduction to Floating Point Arithmetic

Integer arithmetic does not let you represent fractional numeric values. Therefore, modern CPUs support an approximation of real arithmetic: floating point arithmetic. A big problem with floating point arithmetic is that it does not follow the standard rules of algebra. Nevertheless, many programmers apply normal algebraic rules when using floating point arithmetic. This is a source of defects in many programs. One of the primary goals of this section is to describe the limitations of floating point arithmetic so you will understand how to use it properly.

Normal algebraic rules apply only to *infinite precision* arithmetic. Consider the simple statement "x:=x+1," x is an integer. On any modern computer this statement follows the normal rules of algebra *as long as overflow does not occur.* That is, this statement is valid only for certain values of x (*minint <= x < maxint*). Most programmers do not have a problem with this because they are well aware of the fact that integers in a program do not follow the standard algebraic rules (e.g., $5/2 \neq 2.5$).

Integers do not follow the standard rules of algebra because the computer represents them with a finite number of bits. You cannot represent any of the (integer) values above the maximum integer or below the minimum integer. Floating point values suffer from this same problem, only worse. After all, the integers are a subset of the real numbers. Therefore, the floating point values must represent the same infinite set of integers. However, there are an infinite number of values between any two real values, so this problem is infinitely worse. Therefore, as well as having to limit your values between a maximum and minimum range, you cannot represent all the values between those two ranges, either.

To represent real numbers, most floating point formats employ scientific notation and use some number of bits to represent a *mantissa* and a smaller number of bits to represent an *exponent.* The end result is that floating point numbers can only represent numbers with a specific number of *significant* digits. This has a big impact on how floating point arithmetic operates. To easily see the impact of limited precision arithmetic, we will adopt a simplified decimal floating point format for our examples. Our floating point format will provide a mantissa with three significant digits and a decimal exponent with two digits. The mantissa and exponents are both signed values, as shown in Figure 2-23.

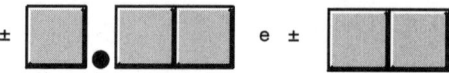

Figure 2-23: Long Packed Date Format (Four Bytes).

When adding and subtracting two numbers in scientific notation, you must adjust the two values so that their exponents are the same. For example, when adding 1.23e1 and 4.56e0, you must adjust the values so they have the same exponent. One way to do this is to convert 4.56e0 to 0.456e1 and then add. This produces 1.686e1. Unfortunately, the result does not fit into three significant digits, so we must either *round* or *truncate* the result to three significant digits. Rounding generally produces the most accurate result, so let's round the result to obtain 1.69e1. As you can see, the lack of *precision* (the number of digits or bits we maintain in a computation) affects the accuracy (the correctness of the computation).

In the previous example, we were able to round the result because we maintained *four* significant digits *during* the calculation. If our floating point calculation is limited to three significant digits *during* computation, we would have had to truncate the last digit of the smaller number, obtaining 1.68e1, a value that is even less correct. To improve the accuracy of floating point calculations, it is necessary to add extra digits for use during the calculation. Extra digits available during a computation are known as *guard digits* (or *guard bits* in the case of a binary format). They greatly enhance accuracy during a long chain of computations.

The accuracy loss during a single computation usually isn't enough to worry about unless you are greatly concerned about the accuracy of your computations. However, if you compute a value that is the result of a sequence of floating point operations, the error can *accumulate* and greatly affect the computation itself. For example, suppose we were to add 1.23e3 with 1.00e0. Adjusting the numbers so their exponents are the same before the addition produces 1.23e3 + 0.001e3. The sum of these two values, even after rounding, is 1.23e3. This might seem perfectly reasonable to you; after all, we can only maintain three significant digits, adding in a small value shouldn't affect the result at all. However, suppose we were to add 1.00e0 to 1.23e3 *ten times*. The first time we add 1.00e0 to 1.23e3 we get 1.23e3. Likewise, we get this same result the second, third, fourth . . . , and tenth time we add 1.00e0 to 1.23e3. On the other hand, had we added 1.00e0 to itself ten times, then added the result (1.00e1) to 1.23e3, we would have gotten a different result, 1.24e3. This is an important thing to know about limited precision arithmetic:

- The order of evaluation can affect the accuracy of the result.

You will get more accurate results if the relative magnitudes (that is, the exponents) are close to one another when adding and subtracting floating point values. If you are performing a chain calculation involving addition and subtraction, you should attempt to group the values appropriately.

Another problem with addition and subtraction is that you can wind up with *false precision*. Consider the computation 1.23e0 - 1.22 e0. This produces 0.01e0. Although this is mathematically equivalent to 1.00e - 2, this latter form suggests that the last two digits are exactly zero. Unfortunately, we've only got a single significant digit at this time. Indeed, some FPUs or floating point software packages might actually insert random digits (or bits) into the L.O. positions. This brings up a second important rule concerning limited precision arithmetic:

- Whenever subtracting two numbers with the same signs or adding two numbers with different signs, the accuracy of the result may be less than the precision available in the floating point format.

Multiplication and division do not suffer from the same problems as addition and subtraction because you do not have to adjust the exponents before the operation; all you need to do is add the exponents and multiply the mantissas (or subtract the exponents and divide the mantissas). By themselves, multiplication and division do not produce particularly poor results. However, they tend to multiply any error that already exists in a value. For example, if you multiply 1.23e0 by two, when you should be multiplying 1.24e0 by two, the result is even less accurate. This brings up a third important rule when working with limited precision arithmetic:

- When performing a chain of calculations involving addition, subtraction, multiplication, and division, try to perform the multiplication and division operations first.

Often, by applying normal algebraic transformations, you can arrange a calculation so the multiply and divide operations occur first. For example, suppose you want to compute x*(y+z). Normally you would add y and z together and multiply their sum by x. However, you will get a little more accuracy if you transform x*(y+z) to get x*y+x*z and compute the result by performing the multiplications first.[7]

Multiplication and division are not without their own problems. When multiplying two very large or very small numbers, it is quite possible for *overflow* or *underflow* to occur. The same situation occurs when dividing a small number by a large number or dividing a large number by a small number. This brings up a fourth rule you should attempt to follow when multiplying or dividing values:

- When multiplying and dividing sets of numbers, try to arrange the multiplications so that they multiply large and small numbers together; likewise, try to divide numbers that have the same relative magnitudes.

Comparing floating point numbers is very dangerous. Given the inaccuracies present in any computation (including converting an input string to a floating point value), you should *never* compare two floating point values to see if they are equal. In a binary floating point format, different computations that produce the same (mathematical) result may differ in their least significant bits. For example, adding 1.31e0+1.69e0 should produce 3.00e0. Likewise, adding 1.50e0+1.50e0 should produce 3.00e0. However, were you to compare (1.31e0+1.69e0) against (1.50e0+1.50e0) you might find out that these sums are *not* equal to one another. The test for equality succeeds if and only if all bits (or digits) in the two operands are exactly the same. Because this is not necessarily true after two different floating point computations that should produce the same result, a straight test for equality may not work.

---

[7] Of course, the drawback is that you must now perform two multiplications rather than one, so the result may be slower.

The standard way to test for equality between floating point numbers is to determine how much error (or tolerance) you will allow in a comparison and check to see if one value is within this error range of the other. The straightforward way to do this is to use a test like the following:

```
if Value1 >= (Value2-error) and Value1 <= (Value2+error) then ...
```

Another common way to handle this same comparison is to use a statement of the form:

```
if abs(Value1-Value2) <= error then ...
```

You must exercise care when choosing the value for error. This should be a value slightly greater than the largest amount of error that will creep into your computations. The exact value will depend upon the particular floating point format you use, but more on that a little later. The final rule we will state in this section is

- When comparing two floating point numbers, always compare one value to see if it is in the range given by the second value plus or minus some small error value.

There are many other little problems that can occur when using floating point values. This text can only point out some of the major problems and make you aware of the fact that you cannot treat floating point arithmetic like real arithmetic: The inaccuracies present in limited precision arithmetic can get you into trouble if you are not careful. A good text on numerical analysis or even scientific computing can help fill in the details that are beyond the scope of this text. If you are going to be working with floating point arithmetic, *in any language*, you should take the time to study the effects of limited precision arithmetic on your computations.

HLA's if statement does not support boolean expressions involving floating point operands. Therefore, you cannot use statements like "if(x < 3.141) then . . ." in your programs. In a later chapter that discusses floating point operations on the 80x86 you'll learn how to do floating point comparisons.

2.13.1   IEEE Floating Point Formats

When Intel planned to introduce a floating point unit (FPU) for its new 8086 microprocessor, it was smart enough to realize that the electrical engineers and solid-state physicists who design chips were, perhaps, not the best people to do the necessary numerical analysis to pick the best possible binary representation for a floating point format. So Intel went out and hired the best numerical analyst it could find to design a floating point format for its 8087 FPU. That person then hired two other experts in the field and the three of them (Kahn, Coonan, and Stone) designed Intel's floating point format. They did such a good job designing the KCS Floating Point Standard that the IEEE organization adopted this format for the IEEE floating point format.[8]

---

[8] There were some minor changes to the way certain degenerate operations were handled, but the bit representation remained essentially unchanged.

To handle a wide range of performance and accuracy requirements, Intel actually introduced *three* floating point formats: single precision, double precision, and extended precision. The single and double precision formats corresponded to C's float and double types or FORTRAN's real and double precision types. Intel intended to use extended precision for long chains of computations. Extended precision contains 16 extra bits that the calculations could use as guard bits before rounding down to a double precision value when storing the result.

The single precision format uses a *one's complement 24-bit mantissa* and an *8-bit excess-127 exponent.* The mantissa usually represents a value between 1.0 to just under 2.0. The H.O. bit of the mantissa is always assumed to be one and represents a value just to the left of the *binary point.*[9] *The remaining 23 mantissa bits appear to the right of the binary point. Therefore, the mantissa represents the value:*

```
1.mmmmmmm mmmmmmmm mmmmmmmm
```

The "mmmm . . ." characters represent the 23 bits of the mantissa. Keep in mind that we are working with binary numbers here. Therefore, each position to the right of the binary point represents a value (zero or one) times a successive negative power of two. The implied one bit is always multiplied by 2^0, which is one. This is why the mantissa is always greater than or equal to one. Even if the other mantissa bits are all zero, the implied one bit always gives us the value one.[10] Of course, even if we had an almost infinite number of one bits after the binary point, they still would not add up to two. This is why the mantissa can represent values in the range one to just under two.

Although there are an infinite number of values between one and two, we can only represent eight million of them because we use a 23-bit mantissa (the 24th bit is always one). This is the reason for inaccuracy in floating point arithmetic—we are limited to 23 bits of precision in computations involving single precision floating point values.

The mantissa uses a one's complement format rather than two's complement. This means that the 24-bit value of the mantissa is simply an unsigned binary number and the sign bit determines whether that value is positive or negative. One's complement numbers have the unusual property that there are two representations for zero (with the sign bit set or clear). Generally, this is important only to the person designing the floating point software or hardware system. We will assume that the value zero always has the sign bit clear.

To represent values outside the range 1.0 to just under 2.0, the exponent portion of the floating point format comes into play. The floating point format raises two to the power specified by the exponent and then multiplies the mantissa by this value. The exponent is 8 bits and is stored in an *excess-127* format. In excess-127 format, the exponent 2^0 is represented by the value 127 ($7F). Therefore, to convert an exponent to excess-127 format simply add 127 to the

---

[9] The binary point is the same thing as the decimal point except it appears in binary numbers rather than decimal numbers.

[10] Actually, this isn't necessarily true. The IEEE floating point format supports *denormalized* values where the H.O. bit is not zero. However, we will ignore denormalized values in our discussion.

exponent value. The use of excess-127 format makes it easier to compare floating point values. The single precision floating point format takes the form shown in Figure 2-24.

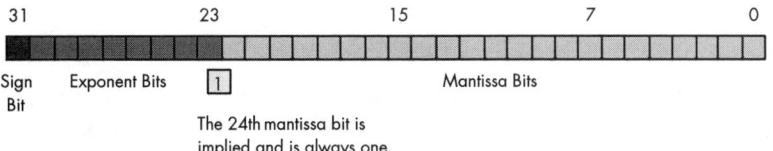

Figure 2-24: Single Precision (32-bit) Floating Point Format

With a 24-bit mantissa, you will get approximately $6 \, 1/2$ digits of precision (one-half digit of precision means that the first six digits can all be in the range 0..9 but the seventh digit can only be in the range 0..x where $x < 9$ and is generally close to five). With an 8-bit excess-127 exponent, the dynamic range of single precision floating point numbers is approximately $2^{\pm 128}$ or about $10^{\pm 38}$.

Although single precision floating point numbers are perfectly suitable for many applications, the dynamic range is somewhat limited and is unsuitable for many financial, scientific, and other applications. Furthermore, during long chains of computations, the limited accuracy of the single precision format may introduce serious error.

The double precision format helps overcome the problems of single precision floating point. Using twice the space, the double precision format has an 11-bit excess-1023 exponent and a 53-bit mantissa (with an implied H.O. bit of one) plus a sign bit. This provides a dynamic range of about $10^{\pm 308}$ and $14 \, 1/2$ digits of precision, sufficient for most applications. Double precision floating point values take the form shown in Figure 2-25.

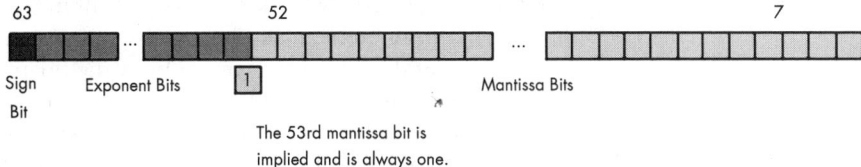

Figure 2-25: 64-Bit Double Precision Floating Point Format.

In order to help ensure accuracy during long chains of computations involving double precision floating point numbers, Intel designed the extended precision format. The extended precision format uses 80 bits. Twelve of the additional 16 bits are appended to the mantissa, four of the additional bits are appended to the end of the exponent. Unlike the single and double precision values, the extended precision format's mantissa does not have an implied H.O. bit, which is always one. Therefore, the extended precision format provides a 64-bit mantissa, a 15-bit excess-16383 exponent, and a 1-bit sign. The format for the extended precision floating point value is shown in Figure 2-26 on the following page.

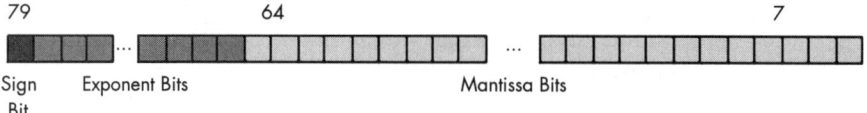

Sign Bit   Exponent Bits   Mantissa Bits

Figure 2-26: 80-Bit Extended Precision Floating Point Format.

On the FPUs all computations are done using the extended precision form. Whenever you load a single or double precision value, the FPU automatically converts it to an extended precision value. Likewise, when you store a single or double precision value to memory, the FPU automatically rounds the value down to the appropriate size before storing it. By always working with the extended precision format, Intel guarantees a large number of guard bits are present to ensure the accuracy of your computations. Some texts erroneously claim that you should never use the extended precision format in your own programs, because Intel only guarantees accurate computations when using the single or double precision formats. This is foolish. By performing all computations using 80 bits, Intel helps ensure (but not guarantee) that you will get full 32- or 64-bit accuracy in your computations. Because the FPUs do not provide a large number of guard bits in 80-bit computations, some error will inevitably creep into the L.O. bits of an extended precision computation. However, if your computation is correct to 64 bits, the 80-bit computation will always provide *at least* 64 accurate bits. Most of the time you will get even more. While you cannot assume that you get an accurate 80-bit computation, you can usually do better than 64 bits when using the extended precision format.

To maintain maximum precision during computation, most computations use *normalized* values. A normalized floating point value is one whose H.O. mantissa bit contains one. Almost any non-normalized value can be normalized; shift the mantissa bits to the left and decrement the exponent until a one appears in the H.O. bit of the mantissa. Remember, the exponent is a binary exponent. Each time you increment the exponent, you multiply the floating point value by two. Likewise, whenever you decrement the exponent, you divide the floating point value by two. By the same token, shifting the mantissa to the left one bit position multiplies the floating point value by two; likewise, shifting the mantissa to the right divides the floating point value by two. Therefore, shifting the mantissa to the left one position *and* decrementing the exponent does not change the value of the floating point number at all.

Keeping floating point numbers normalized is beneficial because it maintains the maximum number of bits of precision for a computation. If the H.O. bits of the mantissa are all zero, the mantissa has that many fewer bits of precision available for computation. Therefore, a floating point computation will be more accurate if it involves only normalized values.

There are two important cases where a floating point number cannot be normalized. Zero is a one of these special cases. Obviously it cannot be normalized because the floating point representation for zero has no one bits in the mantissa. This, however, is not a problem because we can exactly represent the value zero with only a single bit.

The second case is when we have some H.O. bits in the mantissa that are zero but the biased exponent is also zero (and we cannot decrement it to normalize the mantissa). Rather than disallow certain small values, whose H.O. mantissa bits and biased exponent are zero (the most negative exponent possible), the IEEE standard allows special *denormalized* values to represent these smaller values.[11] Although the use of denormalized values allows IEEE floating point computations to produce better results than if underflow occurred, keep in mind that denormalized values offer fewer bits of precision.

2.13.2   HLA Support for Floating Point Values

HLA provides several data types and library routines to support the use of floating point data in your assembly language programs. These include built-in types to declare floating point variables as well as routines that provide floating point input, output, and conversion.

Perhaps the best place to start when discussing HLA's floating point facilities is with a description of floating point literal constants. HLA floating point constants allow the following syntax:

- An optional "+" or "-" symbol, denoting the sign of the mantissa (if this is not present, HLA assumes that the mantissa is positive)

- Followed by one or more decimal digits

- Optionally followed by a decimal point and one or more decimal digits

- Optionally followed by an "e" or "E", optionally followed by a sign ("+" or "-") and one or more decimal digits

Note that the decimal point or the "e"/"E" must be present in order to differentiate this value from an integer or unsigned literal constant. Here are some examples of legal literal floating point constants:

```
1.234  3.75e2  -1.0  1.1e-1  1e+4  0.1  -123.456e+789  +25e0
```

Notice that a floating point literal constant cannot begin with a decimal point; it must begin with a decimal digit so you must use "0.1" to represent ".1" in your programs.

HLA also allows you to place an underscore character ("_") between any two consecutive decimal digits in a floating point literal constant. You may use the underscore character in place of a comma (or other language-specific separator character) to help make your large floating point numbers easier to read. Here are some examples:

```
1_234_837.25  1_000.00  789_934.99  9_999.99
```

To declare a floating point variable you use the real32, real64, or real80 data types. Like their integer and unsigned brethren, the number at the end of these data type declarations specifies the number of bits used for each type's binary representation. Therefore, you use real32 to declare single precision real values,

---

[11] The alternative would be to underflow the values to zero.

real64 to declare double precision floating point values, and real80 to declare extended precision floating point values. Other than the fact that you use these types to declare floating point variables rather than integers, their use is nearly identical to that for int8, int16, int32, and so on. The following examples demonstrate these declarations and their syntax:

```
static

        fltVar1:     real32;
        fltVar1a:    real32 := 2.7;
        pi:          real32 := 3.14159;
        DblVar:      real64;
        DblVar2:     real64 := 1.23456789e+10;
        XPVar:       real80;
        XPVar2:      real80 := -1.0e-104;
```

To output a floating point variable in ASCII form, you would use one of the stdout.putr32, stdout.putr64, or stdout.putr80 routines. These procedures display a number in decimal notation — that is, a string of digits, an optional decimal point and a closing string of digits. Other than their names, these three routines use exactly the same calling sequence. Here are the calls and parameters for each of these routines:

```
stdout.putr80( r:real80; width:uns32; decpts:uns32 );
stdout.putr64( r:real64; width:uns32; decpts:uns32 );
stdout.putr32( r:real32; width:uns32; decpts:uns32 );
```

The first parameter to these procedures is the floating point value you wish to print. The size of this parameter must match the procedure's name (e.g., the r parameter must be an 80-bit extended precision floating point variable when calling the stdout.putr80 routine). The second parameter specifies the field width for the output text; this is the number of print positions the number will require when the procedure displays it. Note that this width must include print positions for the sign of the number and the decimal point. The third parameter specifies the number of print positions after the decimal point. For example,

```
stdout.putr32( pi, 10, 4 );
```

displays the value

```
_ _ _ _ 3.1416
```

(the underscores represent leading spaces in this example).

Of course, if the number is very large or very small, you will want to use scientific notation rather than decimal notation for your floating point numeric output. The HLA Standard Library stdout.pute32, stdout.pute64, and stdout.pute80 routines provide this facility. These routines use the following procedure prototypes:

```
stdout.pute80( r:real80; width:uns32 );
stdout.pute64( r:real64; width:uns32 );
stdout.pute32( r:real32; width:uns32 );
```

Unlike the decimal output routines, these scientific notation output routines do not require a third parameter specifying the number of digits after the decimal point to display. The width parameter, indirectly, specifies this value because all but one of the mantissa digits always appear to the right of the decimal point. These routines output their values in decimal notation, similar to the following:

```
1.23456789e+10  -1.0e-104  1e+2
```

You can also output floating point values using the HLA Standard Library stdout.put routine. If you specify the name of a floating point variable in the stdout.put parameter list, the stdout.put code will output the value using scientific notation. The actual field width varies depending on the size of the floating point variable (the stdout.put routine attempts to output as many significant digits as possible, in this case). Example:

```
stdout.put( "XPVar2 = ", XPVar2 );
```

If you specify a field width specification, by using a colon followed by a signed integer value, then the stdout.put routine will use the appropriate *stdout.puteXX* routine to display the value. That is, the number will still appear in scientific notation, but you get to control the field width of the output value. Like the field width for integer and unsigned values, a positive field width right justifies the number in the specified field, a negative number left justifies the value. Here is an example that prints the XPVar2 variable using ten print positions:

```
stdout.put( "XPVar2 = ", XPVar2:10 );
```

If you wish to use stdout.put to print a floating point value in decimal notation, you need to use the following syntax:

```
Variable_Name : Width : DecPts
```

Note that the DecPts field must be a non-negative integer value.

When `stdout.put` contains a parameter of this form, it calls the corresponding *stdout.putrXX* routine to display the specified floating point value. As an example, consider the following call:

```
stdout.put( "Pi = ", pi:5:3 );
```

The corresponding output is

```
3.141
```

The HLA Standard Library provides several other useful routines you can use when outputting floating point values. Consult the HLA Standard Library Reference Manual for more information on these routines.

The HLA Standard Library provides several routines to let you display floating point values in a wide variety of formats. In contrast, the HLA Standard Library only provides two routines to support floating point input: `stdin.getf()` and `stdin.get()`. The `stdin.getf()` routine requires the use of the 80x86 FPU stack, a hardware component that this chapter is not going to cover. Therefore, we'll defer the discussion of the `stdin.getf()` routine until a later chapter. Because the `stdin.get()` routine provides all the capabilities of the `stdin.getf()` routine, this deference will not prove to be a problem.

You've already seen the syntax for the `stdin.get()` routine; its parameter list simply contains a list of variable names. The `stdin.get()` function reads appropriate values for the user for each of the variables appearing in the parameter list. If you specify the name of a floating point variable, the `stdin.get()` routine automatically reads a floating point value from the user and stores the result into the specified variable. The following example demonstrates the use of this routine:

```
stdout.put( "Input a double precision floating point value: " );
stdin.get( DblVar );
```

CAUTION *This section has discussed how you would declare floating point variables and how you would input and output them. It did not discuss arithmetic. Floating point arithmetic is different than integer arithmetic; you cannot use the 80x86* add *and* sub *instructions to operating on floating point values. Floating point arithmetic will be the subject of a later chapter in this text.*

2.14 Binary Coded Decimal (BCD) Representation

Although the integer and floating point formats cover most of the numeric needs of an average program, there are some special cases where other numeric representations are convenient. In this section we'll discuss the binary coded decimal (BCD) format because the 80x86 CPU provides a small amount of hardware support for this data representation.

BCD values are a sequence of nibbles with each nibble representing a value in the range 0..9. Of course, you can represent values in the range 0..15 using a nibble; the BCD format, however, uses only 10 of the possible 16 different values for each nibble.

Each nibble in a BCD value represents a single decimal digit. Therefore, with a single byte (i.e., two digits) we can represent values containing two decimal digits, or values in the range 0..99 (see Figure 2-27). With a word, we can represent values having four decimal digits, or values in the range 0..9999. Likewise, with a double word we can represent values with up to eight decimal digits (because there are eight nibbles in a double word value).

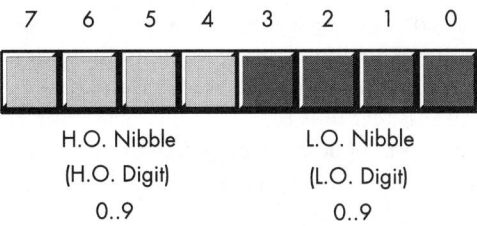

Figure 2-27: BCD Data Representation in Memory.

As you can see, BCD storage isn't particularly memory efficient. For example, an 8-bit BCD variable can represent values in the range 0..99 while that same 8 bits, when holding a binary value, can represent values in the range 0..255. Likewise, a 16-bit binary value can represent values in the range 0..65535 while a 16-bit BCD value can only represent about $1/6$ of those values (0..9999). Inefficient storage isn't the only problem. BCD calculations tend to be slower than binary calculations.

At this point, you're probably wondering why anyone would ever use the BCD format. The BCD format does have two saving graces: It's very easy to convert BCD values between the internal numeric representation and their string representation; also, it's very easy to encode multidigit decimal values in hardware (e.g., using a "thumb wheel" or dial) using BCD than it is using binary. For these two reasons, you're likely to see people using BCD in embedded systems (e.g., toaster ovens and alarm clocks) but rarely in general purpose computer software.

A few decades ago people mistakenly thought that calculations involving BCD (or just "decimal") arithmetic were more accurate than binary calculations. Therefore, they would often perform "important" calculations, like those involving dollars and cents (or other monetary units) using decimal-based arithmetic. While it is true that certain calculations can produce more accurate results in BCD, this statement is not true in general. Indeed, for most calculations (even those involving fixed point decimal arithmetic), the binary representation is more accurate. For this reason, most modern computer programs represent all values in a binary form. For example, the Intel 80x86 floating point unit (FPU) supports a pair of instructions for loading and storing BCD values. Internally, however, the FPU converts these BCD values to binary and performs all calculations in binary. It only uses BCD as an external data format (external to the FPU, that is). This generally produces more accurate results and requires far less silicon than having a separate coprocessor that supports decimal arithmetic.

2.15   Characters

Perhaps the most important data type on a personal computer is the character data type. The term "character" refers to a human or machine readable symbol that is typically a non-numeric entity. In general, the term "character" refers to any symbol that you can normally type on a keyboard (including some symbols that may require multiple key presses to produce) or display on a video display. Many beginners often confuse the terms "character" and "alphabetic character." These terms are not the same. Punctuation symbols, numeric digits, spaces, tabs, carriage returns (ENTER), other control characters, and other special symbols are also characters. When this text uses the term "character" it refers to any of these characters, not just the alphabetic characters. When this text refers to alphabetic characters, it will use phrases like "alphabetic characters," "upper case characters," or "lower case characters."

Another common problem beginners have when they first encounter the character data type is differentiating between numeric characters and numbers. The character '1' is distinct from the value one. The computer (generally) uses two different internal representations for numeric characters ('0,' '1,' . . . , '9') versus the numeric values 0..9. You must take care not to confuse the two.

Most computer systems use a one- or two-byte sequence to encode the various characters in binary form. Windows and Linux certainly fall into this category, using either the ASCII or Unicode encodings for characters. This section will discuss the ASCII character set and the character declaration facilities that HLA provides.

2.15.1   The ASCII Character Encoding

The ASCII (American Standard Code for Information Interchange) character set maps 128 textual characters to the unsigned integer values 0..127 ($0..$7F). Internally, of course, the computer represents everything using binary numbers so it should come as no surprise that the computer also uses binary values to represent non-numeric entities such as characters. Although the exact mapping of characters to numeric values is arbitrary and unimportant, it is important to use a standardized code for this mapping because you will need to communicate with other programs and peripheral devices, and you need to talk the same "language" as these other programs and devices. This is where the ASCII code comes into play; it is a standardized code that nearly everyone has agreed upon. Therefore, if you use the ASCII code 65 to represent the character "A" then you know that some peripheral device (such as a printer) will correctly interpret this value as the character "A" whenever you transmit data to that device.

You should not get the impression that ASCII is the only character set in use on computer systems. IBM uses the EBCDIC character set family on many of its mainframe computer systems. Another common character set in use is the Unicode character set. Unicode is an extension to the ASCII character set that uses

16 bits rather than 7 to represent characters. This allows the use of 65,536 different characters in the character set, allowing the inclusion of most symbols in the world's different languages into a single unified character set.

Because the ASCII character set provides only 128 different characters and a byte can represent 256 different values, an interesting question arises: "What do we do with the values 128..255 that one could store into a byte?" One answer is to ignore those extra values. That will be the primary approach of this text. Another possibility is to extend the ASCII character set and add an additional 128 characters to the character set. Of course, this would tend to defeat the whole purpose of having a standardized character set unless you could get everyone to agree upon the extensions. That is a difficult task.

When IBM first created its IBM-PC, it defined these extra 128 character codes to contain various non-English alphabetic characters, some line drawing graphics characters, some mathematical symbols, and several other special characters. Because IBM's PC was the foundation for what we typically call a PC today, that character set has become a pseudo-standard on all IBM-PC compatible machines. Even on modern machines, which are not IBM-PC compatible and cannot run early PC software, the IBM extended character set still survives. Note, however, that this PC character set (an extension of the ASCII character set) is not universal. Most printers will not print the extended characters when using native fonts and many programs (particularly in non-English countries) do not use those characters for the upper 128 codes in an 8-bit value. For these reasons, this text will generally stick to the standard 128-character ASCII character set.

Despite the fact that it is a "standard," simply encoding your data using standard ASCII characters does not guarantee compatibility across systems. While it's true that an "A" on one machine is most likely an "A" on another machine, there is very little standardization across machines with respect to the use of the control characters. Indeed, of the 32 control codes plus DELETE, there are only four control codes commonly supported — backspace (BS), tab, carriage return (CR), and line feed (LF). Worse still, different machines often use these control codes in different ways. End of line is a particularly troublesome example. Windows, MS-DOS, CP/M, and other systems mark end of line by the two-character sequence CR/LF. Apple Macintosh and many other systems mark the end of line by a single CR character. Linux, BeOS, and other UNIX systems mark the end of a line with a single LF character. Needless to say, attempting to exchange simple text files between such systems can be an experience in frustration. Even if you use standard ASCII characters in all your files on these systems, you will still need to convert the data when exchanging files between them. Fortunately, such conversions are rather simple.

Despite some major shortcomings, ASCII data is *the* standard for data interchange across computer systems and programs. Most programs can accept ASCII data; likewise most programs can produce ASCII data. Because you will be dealing with ASCII characters in assembly language, it would be wise to study the layout of the character set and memorize a few key ASCII codes (e.g., "0," "A," "a," and so on).

The ASCII character set is divided into four groups of 32 characters. The first 32 characters, ASCII codes 0..$1F (31), form a special set of non-printing characters, the *control characters*. We call them control characters because they perform various printer/display control operations rather than displaying symbols. Examples include *carriage return*, which positions the cursor to the left side of the current line of characters,[12] line feed (that moves the cursor down one line on the output device), and backspace (that moves the cursor back one position to the left). Unfortunately, different control characters perform different operations on different output devices. There is very little standardization among output devices. To find out exactly how a control character affects a particular device, you will need to consult its manual.

The second group of 32 ASCII character codes contains various punctuation symbols, special characters, and the numeric digits. The most notable characters in this group include the space character (ASCII code $20) and the numeric digits (ASCII codes $30..$39).

The third group of 32 ASCII characters contains the upper case alphabetic characters. The ASCII codes for the characters "A".."Z" lie in the range $41..$5A (65..90). Because there are only 26 different alphabetic characters, the remaining six codes hold various special symbols.

The fourth, and final, group of 32 ASCII character codes represents the lower case alphabetic symbols, five additional special symbols, and another control character (DELETE). Note that the lower case character symbols use the ASCII codes $61..$7A. If you convert the codes for the upper and lower case characters to binary, you will notice that the upper case symbols differ from their lower case equivalents in exactly one bit position. For example, consider the character code for "E" and "e" appearing in Figure 2-28.

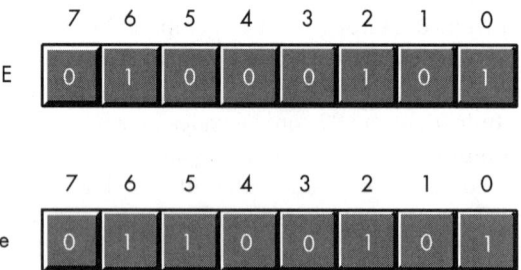

Figure 2-28: ASCII Codes for "E" and "e."

The only place these two codes differ is in bit 5. Upper case characters always contain a 0 in bit 5; lower case alphabetic characters always contain a 1 in bit 5. You can use this fact to quickly convert between upper and lower case. If you have an upper case character you can force it to lower case by setting bit 5 to 1. If you have a lower case character and you wish to force it to upper case, you can do so by setting bit 5 to 0. You can toggle an alphabetic character between upper and lower case by simply inverting bit 5.

---

[12] Historically, carriage return refers to the *paper carriage* used on typewriters. A carriage return consisted of physically moving the carriage all the way to the right so that the next character typed would appear at the left-hand side of the paper.

Indeed, bits 5 and 6 determine which of the four groups in the ASCII character set you're in, as Table 2-8 shows.

Table 2-8: ASCII Groups

Bit 6	Bit 5	Group
0	0	Control characters
0	1	Digits & punctuation
1	0	Upper case & special
1	1	Lower case & special

So you could, for instance, convert any upper or lower case (or corresponding special) character to its equivalent control character by setting bits 5 and 6 to 0.

Consider, for a moment, the ASCII codes of the numeric digit characters appearing in Table 2-9.

Table 2-9: ASCII Codes for Numeric Digits

Character	Decimal	Hexadecimal
"0"	48	$30
"1"	49	$31
"2"	50	$32
"3"	51	$33
"4"	52	$34
"5"	53	$35
"6"	54	$36
"7"	55	$37
"8"	56	$38
"9"	57	$39

The decimal representations of these ASCII codes are not very enlightening. However, the hexadecimal representation of these ASCII codes reveals something very important: The L.O. nibble of the ASCII code is the binary equivalent of the represented number. By stripping away (i.e., setting to zero) the H.O. nibble of a numeric character, you can convert that character code to the corresponding binary representation. Conversely, you can convert a binary value in the range 0..9 to its ASCII character representation by simply setting the H.O. nibble to three. Note that you can use the logical-AND operation to force the H.O. bits to zero; likewise, you can use the logical-OR operation to force the H.O. bits to %0011 (three).

Note that you *cannot* convert a string of numeric characters to their equivalent binary representation by simply stripping the H.O. nibble from each digit in the string. Converting 123 ($31 $32 $33) in this fashion yields three bytes: $010203; the correct value for 123 is $7B. Converting a string of digits to an integer requires more sophistication than this; the conversion above works only for single digits.

2.15.2   HLA Support for ASCII Characters

Although you could easily store character values in byte variables and use the corresponding numeric equivalent ASCII code when using a character literal in your program, such agony is unnecessary: HLA provides good support for character variables and literals in your assembly language programs.

Character literal constants in HLA take one of two forms: a single character surrounded by apostrophes or a pound symbol ("#") followed by a numeric constant in the range 0..127 specifying the ASCII code of the character. Here are some examples:

```
'A'   #65    #$41    #%0100_0001
```

Note that these examples all represent the same character ('A') because the ASCII code of 'A' is 65.

With one exception, only a single character may appear between the apostrophes in a literal character constant. That single exception is the apostrophe character itself. If you wish to create an apostrophe literal constant, place four apostrophes in a row (i.e., double up the apostrophe inside the surrounding apostrophes):

```
''''
```

The pound sign operator ("#") must precede a legal HLA numeric constant (either decimal, hexadecimal, or binary as the examples above indicate). In particular, the pound sign is not a generic character conversion function; it cannot precede registers or variable names, only constants.

As a general rule, you should always use the apostrophe form of the character literal constant for graphic characters (that is, those that are printable or displayable). Use the pound sign form for control characters (that are invisible or do funny things when you print them) or for extended ASCII characters that may not display or print properly within your source code.

Notice the difference between a character literal constant and a string literal constant in your programs. Strings are sequences of zero or more characters surrounded by quotation marks; characters are surrounded by apostrophes. It is especially important to realize that

```
'A' ≠ "A"
```

The character constant 'A' and the string containing the single character "A" have two completely different internal representations. If you attempt to use a string containing a single character where HLA expects a character constant, HLA will report an error. Strings and string constants will be the subject of a later chapter.

To declare a character variable in an HLA program, you use the char data type. The following declaration, for example, demonstrates how to declare a variable named UserInput:

```
static
    UserInput:          char;
```

This declaration reserves one byte of storage that you could use to store any character value (including 8-bit extended ASCII characters). You can also initialize character variables as the following example demonstrates:

```
static

    TheCharA:           char := 'A';
    ExtendedChar:       char := #128;
```

Because character variables are 8-bit objects, you can manipulate them using 8-bit registers. You can move character variables into 8-bit registers and you can store the value of an 8-bit register into a character variable.

The HLA Standard Library provides a handful of routines that you can use for character I/O and manipulation; these include stdout.putc, stdout.putcSize, stdout.put, stdin.getc, and stdin.get.

The stdout.putc routine uses the following calling sequence:

```
                    stdout.putc( chvar );
```

This procedure outputs the single character parameter passed to it as a character to the standard output device. The parameter may be any char constant or variable, or a byte variable or register.[13]

The stdout.putcSize routine provides output width control when displaying character variables. The calling sequence for this procedure is

```
                stdout.putcSize( charvar, widthInt32, fillchar );
```

This routine prints the specified character (parameter c) using at least width print positions.[14] If the absolute value of width is greater than one, then stdout.putcSize prints the fill character as padding. If the value of width is positive, then stdout.putcSize prints the character right justified in the print field; if width is negative, then stdout.putcSize prints the character left justified in the print field. Because character output is usually left justified in a field, the width value will normally be negative for this call. The space character is the most common fill value.

You can also print character values using the generic stdout.put routine. If a character variable appears in the stdout.put parameter list, then stdout.put will automatically print it as a character value, e.g.,

```
        stdout.put( "Character c = '", c, "'", nl );
```

---

[13] If you specify a byte variable or a byte-sized register as the parameter, the *stdout.putc* routine will output the character whose ASCII code appears in the variable or register.

[14] The only time *stdout.putcSize* uses more print positions than you specify is when you specify zero as the width; then this routine uses exactly one print position.

You can read characters from the standard input using the stdin.getc and stdin.get routines. The stdin.getc routine does not have any parameters. It reads a single character from the standard input buffer and returns this character in the AL register. You may then store the character value away or otherwise manipulate the character in the AL register. The program in Listing 2-10 reads a single character from the user, converts it to upper case if it is a lower case character, and then displays the character.

Listing 2-10: Character Input Sample.

```
program charInputDemo;
#include( "stdlib.hhf" )
static
    c:char;

begin charInputDemo;

    stdout.put( "Enter a character: " );
    stdin.getc();
    if( al >= 'a' ) then

        if( al <= 'z' ) then

            and( $5f, al );

        endif;

    endif;
    stdout.put
    (
        "The character you entered, possibly ", nl,
        "converted to upper case, was '"
    );
    stdout.putc( al );
    stdout.put( "'", nl );

end charInputDemo;
```

You can also use the generic stdin.get routine to read character variables from the user. If a stdin.get parameter is a character variable, then the stdin.get routine will read a character from the user and store the character value into the specified variable. Listing 2-11 is a rewrite of Listing 2-10 using the stdin.get routine.

Listing 2-11: stdin.get Character Input Sample.

```
program charInputDemo2;
#include( "stdlib.hhf" )
static
    c:char;

begin charInputDemo2;

    stdout.put( "Enter a character: " );
    stdin.get(c);
    if( c >= 'a' ) then

        if( c <= 'z' ) then

            and( $5f, c );

        endif;

    endif;
    stdout.put
    (
        "The character you entered, possibly ", nl,
        "converted to upper case, was '",
        c,
        "'", nl
    );

end charInputDemo2;
```

As you may recall from the last chapter, the HLA Standard Library buffers its input. Whenever you read a character from the standard input using stdin.getc or stdin.get, the library routines read the next available character from the buffer; if the buffer is empty, then the program reads a new line of text from the user and returns the first character from that line. If you want to guarantee that the program reads a new line of text from the user when you read a character variable, you should call the stdin.flushInput routine before attempting to read the character. This will flush the current input buffer and force the input of a new line of text on the next input (probably a stdin.getc or stdin.get call).

The end of line is problematic. Different operating systems handle the end of line differently on output versus input. From the console device, pressing the ENTER key signals the end of a line; however, when reading data from a file, you get an end-of-line sequence that is a line feed or a carriage return/line feed pair (under Windows) or just a line feed (under Linux). To help solve this problem, HLA's Standard Library provides an "end of line" function. This procedure returns true (one) in the AL register if all the current input characters have been exhausted; it returns false (zero) otherwise. The sample program in Listing 2-12 is a rewrite of the above code using the stdin.eoln function.

Listing 2-12: Testing for End of Line Using Stdin.eoln.

```
program eolnDemo2;
#include( "stdlib.hhf" )
begin eolnDemo2;

    stdout.put( "Enter a short line of text: " );
    stdin.flushInput();
    repeat

        stdin.getc();
        stdout.putc( al );
        stdout.put( "=$", al, nl );

    until( stdin.eoln() );

end eolnDemo2;
```

The HLA language and the HLA Standard Library provide many other procedures and additional support for character objects. Later chapters in this textbook, as well as the HLA reference documentation, describe how to use these features.

2.16 The Unicode Character Set

Although the ASCII character set is, unquestionably, the most popular character representation on computers, it is certainly not the only format around. For example, IBM uses the EBCDIC code on many of its mainframe and mini-computer lines. Because EBCDIC appears mainly on IBM's big iron and you'll rarely encounter it on personal computer systems, we will not consider that character set in this text. Another character representation that is becoming popular on small computer systems (and large ones, for that matter) is the Unicode character set. Unicode overcomes two of ASCII's greatest limitations: the limited character space (i.e., a maximum of 128/256 characters in an 8-bit byte) and the lack of international (beyond the USA) characters.

Unicode uses a 16-bit word to represent a single character. Therefore, Unicode supports up to 65,536 different character codes. This is obviously a huge advance over the 256 possible codes we can represent with an 8-bit byte. Unicode is upward compatible from ASCII. Specifically, if the H.O. 9 bits of a Unicode character contain zero, then the L.O. 7 bits represent the same character as the ASCII character with the same character code. If the H.O. 9 bits contain some non-zero value, then the character represents some other value. If you're wondering why so many different character codes are necessary, simply note that certain Asian character sets contain 4096 characters (at least, their Unicode subset).

This text will stick to the ASCII character set except for a few brief mentions of Unicode here and there. Eventually, this text may have to eliminate the discussion of ASCII in favor of Unicode because many new operating systems are using Unicode internally (and convert to ASCII as necessary). Unfortunately, many string algorithms are not as conveniently written for Unicode as for ASCII (especially character set functions) so we'll stick with ASCII in this text as long as possible.

2.17 For More Information

The unabridged electronic edition of this book (on the accompanying CD-ROM) contains some additional information on data representation you may find useful. For general information about data representation, you should consider reading a textbook on data structures and algorithms (available at any bookstore).

3

MEMORY ACCESS AND ORGANIZATION

3.1 Chapter Overview

Earlier chapters in this text show you how to declare and access simple variables in an assembly language program. In this chapter you get the full picture on 80x86 memory access. You also learn how to efficiently organize your variable declarations to speed up access to their data. This chapter will also teach you about the 80x86 stack and how to manipulate data on the stack. Finally, this chapter will teach you about dynamic memory allocation and the *heap*.

3.2 The 80x86 Addressing Modes

The 80x86 processors let you access memory in many different ways. Until now, you've only seen a single way to access a variable, the so-called *displacement-only* addressing mode. In this section you'll see some additional ways your programs can access memory using 80x86 *memory addressing modes*. The 80x86 memory addressing modes provide flexible access to memory, allowing you to easily access variables, arrays, records, pointers, and other complex data types. Mastery of the 80x86 addressing modes is the first step toward mastering 80x86 assembly language.

When Intel designed the original 8086 processor, it provided it with a flexible, though limited, set of memory addressing modes. Intel added several new addressing modes when it introduced the 80386 microprocessor while retaining all the modes of the previous processors. However, in 32-bit environments like Windows, BeOS, and Linux, these earlier addressing modes are not very useful; indeed, HLA doesn't even support the use of these older, 16-bit-only addressing modes. Fortunately, anything you can do with the older addressing modes can be done with the new addressing modes as well (even better, as a matter of fact). Therefore, you won't need to bother learning the old 16-bit addressing modes when writing code for today's high-performance operating systems. Do keep in mind, however, that if you intend to work under MS-DOS or some other 16-bit operating system, you will need to study up on those old addressing modes (see the 16-bit edition of this book on the accompanying CD-ROM for details).

3.2.1 80x86 Register Addressing Modes

Most 80x86 instructions can operate on the 80x86's general purpose register set. By specifying the name of the register as an operand to the instruction, you can access the contents of that register. Consider the 80x86 mov (move) instruction:

```
mov( source, destination );
```

This instruction copies the data from the *source* operand to the *destination* operand. The 8-bit, 16-bit, and 32-bit registers are certainly valid operands for this instruction. The only restriction is that both operands must be the same size. Now let's look at some actual 80x86 mov instructions:

```
mov( bx, ax );        // Copies the value from BX into AX
mov( al, dl );        // Copies the value from AL into DL
mov( edx, esi );      // Copies the value from EDX into ESI
mov( bp, sp );        // Copies the value from BP into SP
mov( cl, dh );        // Copies the value from CL into DH
mov( ax, ax );        // Yes, this is legal!
```

The registers are the best place to keep variables. Instructions using the registers are shorter and faster than those that access memory. Of course, most computations require at least one register operand, so the register addressing mode is very popular in 80x86 assembly code. Throughout this chapter you'll see the abbreviated operands *reg* and *r/m* (register/memory) used wherever you may use one of the 80x86's general purpose registers.

3.2.2 80x86 32-Bit Memory Addressing Modes

The 80x86 provides hundreds of different ways to access memory. This may seem like quite a bit at first, but fortunately most of the addressing modes are simple variants of one another so they're very easy to learn. And learn them you should! The key to good assembly language programming is the proper use of memory addressing modes.

The addressing modes provided by the 80x86 family include displacement-only, base, displacement plus base, base plus indexed, and displacement plus base plus indexed. Variations on these five forms provide all the different addressing modes on the 80x86. See, from hundreds down to five. It's not so bad after all!

3.2.2.1 The Displacement-Only Addressing Mode

The most common addressing mode, and the one that's easiest to understand, is the *displacement-only* (or *direct*) addressing mode. The displacement-only addressing mode consists of a 32-bit constant that specifies the address of the target location. Assuming that variable J is an int8 variable appearing at address $8088, the instruction "mov(J, al);" loads the AL register with a copy of the byte at memory location $8088. Likewise, if int8 variable K is at address $1234 in memory, then the instruction "mov(dl, K);" stores the value in the DL register to memory location $1234 (see Figure 3-1).

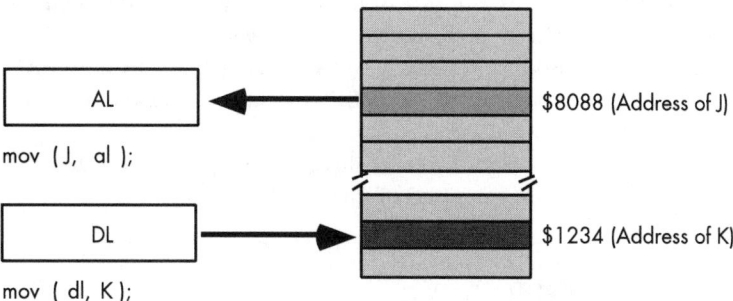

Figure 3-1: Displacement-Only (Direct) Addressing Mode.

The displacement-only addressing mode is perfect for accessing simple scalar variables.

Intel named this the displacement-only addressing mode because a 32-bit constant (displacement) follows the mov opcode in memory. On the 80x86 processors, this displacement is an offset from the beginning of memory (that is, address zero). The examples in this chapter will often access bytes in memory. Don't forget, however, that you can also access words and double words on the 80x86 processors by specifying the address of their first byte (see Figure 3-2).

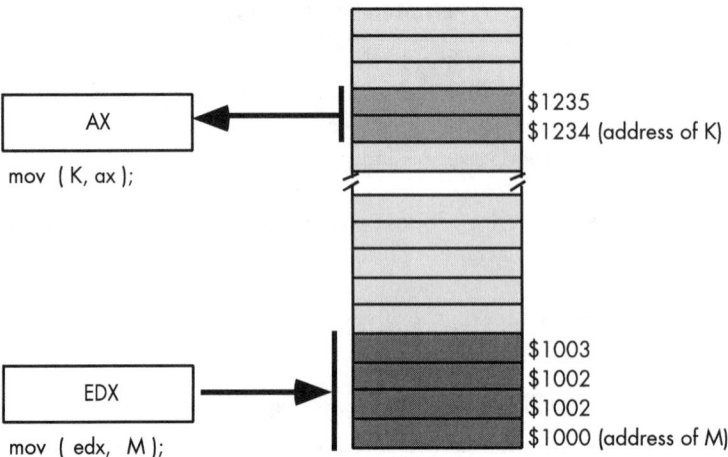

Figure 3-2: Accessing a Word or DWord Using the Displacement Only Addressing Mode.

3.2.2.2 The Register Indirect Addressing Modes

The 80x86 CPUs let you access memory indirectly through a register using the register indirect addressing modes. The term "indirect" means that the operand is not the actual address, but rather, the operand's value specifies the memory address to use. In the case of the register indirect addressing modes, the value the register holds is the address of the memory location to access. For example, the instruction "mov(eax, [ebx]);" tells the CPU to store EAX's value at the location whose address is in EBX (the square brackets around EBX tell HLA to use the register indirect addressing mode).

There are eight forms of this addressing mode on the 80x86; the following instructions are examples of these eight forms:

```
mov( [eax], al );
mov( [ebx], al );
mov( [ecx], al );
mov( [edx], al );
mov( [edi], al );
mov( [esi], al );
mov( [ebp], al );
mov( [esp], al );
```

These eight addressing modes reference the memory location at the offset found in the register enclosed by brackets (EAX, EBX, ECX, EDX, EDI, ESI, EBP, or ESP, respectively).

Note that the register indirect addressing modes require a 32-bit register. You cannot specify a 16-bit or 8-bit register when using an indirect addressing mode.[1] Technically, you could load a 32-bit register with an arbitrary numeric value and access that location indirectly using the register indirect addressing mode:

```
mov( $1234_5678, ebx );
mov( [ebx], al );        // Attempts to access location $1234_5678.
```

Unfortunately (or fortunately, depending on how you look at it), this will probably cause the operating system to generate a protection fault because it's not always legal to access arbitrary memory locations. As it turns out, there are better ways to load the address of some object into a register; you'll see how to do this shortly.

The register indirect addressing mode has many uses. You can use it to access data referenced by a pointer, you can use it to step through array data, and, in general, you can use it whenever you need to modify the address of a variable while your program is running.

The register indirect addressing mode provides an example of an *anonymous* variable. When using the register indirect addressing mode you refer to the value of a variable by its numeric memory address (e.g., the value you load into a register) rather than by the name of the variable. Hence the phrase "anonymous variable."

HLA provides a simple operator that you can use to take the address of a static variable and put this address into a 32-bit register. This is the "&" (address of) operator (note that this is the same symbol that C/C++ uses for the address-of operator). The following example loads the address of variable J into EBX and then stores EAX's current value into J using the register indirect addressing mode:

```
mov( &J, ebx );          // Load address of J into EBX.
mov( eax, [ebx] );       // Store EAX into J.
```

Of course, it would have been easier to store EAX's value directly into J rather than using two instructions to do this indirectly. However, you can easily imagine a code sequence where the program loads one of several different addresses into EBX prior to the execution of the "mov(eax, [ebx]);" statement, thus storing EAX into one of several different locations depending on the execution path of the program.

CAUTION *The "&" (address-of) operator is not a general address-of operator like the "&" operator in C/C++. You may only apply this operator to static variables.[2] You cannot apply it to generic address expressions or other types of variables. Later, you will learn about the "load effective address" instruction that provides a general solution for obtaining the address of some variable in memory.*

---

[1] Actually, the 80x86 does support addressing modes involving certain 16-bit registers, as mentioned earlier. However, HLA does not support these modes and they are not useful under 32-bit operating systems.

[2] Note: The term "static" here indicates a static, read only, or storage object.

3.2.2.3 Indexed Addressing Modes

The indexed addressing modes use the following syntax:

```
mov( VarName[ eax ], al );
mov( VarName[ ebx ], al );
mov( VarName[ ecx ], al );
mov( VarName[ edx ], al );
mov( VarName[ edi ], al );
mov( VarName[ esi ], al );
mov( VarName[ ebp ], al );
mov( VarName[ esp ], al );
```

VarName is the name of some variable in your program.

The indexed addressing mode computes an effective address[3] by adding the address of the variable to the value of the 32-bit register appearing inside the square brackets. Their sum is the actual address in memory the instruction accesses. So if VarName is at address $1100 in memory and EBX contains an eight, then "mov(VarName[ebx], al);" loads the byte at address $1108 into the AL register (see Figure 3-3).

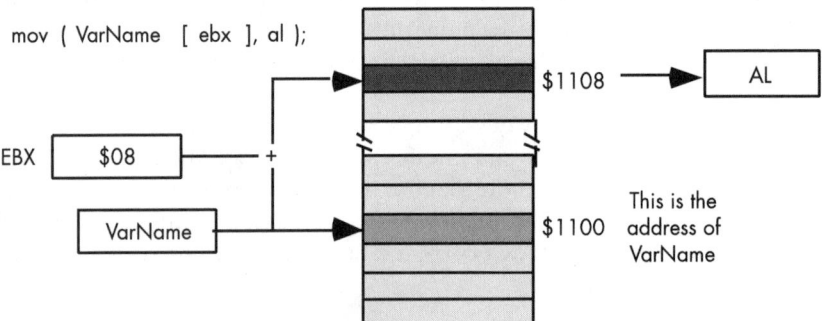

Figure 3-3: Indexed Addressing Mode.

The indexed addressing mode is really handy for accessing elements of arrays. You will see how to use this addressing mode for that purpose a little later in this book.

3.2.2.4 Variations on the Indexed Addressing Mode

There are two important syntactical variations of the indexed addressing mode. Both forms generate the same basic machine instructions, but their syntax suggests other uses for these variants.

The first variant uses the following syntax:

```
mov( [ ebx + constant ], al );
mov( [ ebx - constant ], al );
```

---

[3] The effective address is the ultimate address in memory that an instruction will access, once all the address calculations are complete.

These examples use only the EBX register. However, you can use any of the other 32-bit general purpose registers in place of EBX. This addressing mode computes its effective address by adding the value in EBX to the specified constant, or subtracting the specified constant from EBX (see Figures 3-4 and 3-5).

mov ([ebx + constant],   al);

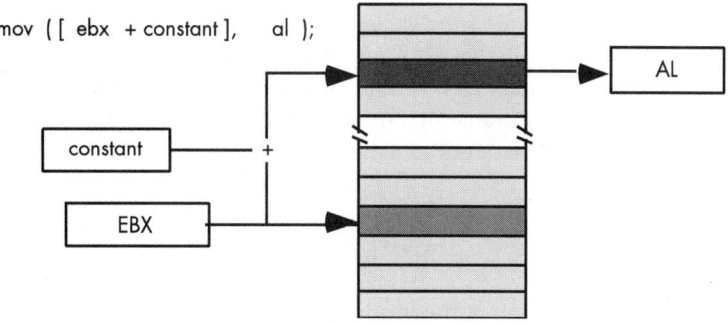

Figure 3-4: Indexed Addressing Mode Using a Register Plus a Constant.

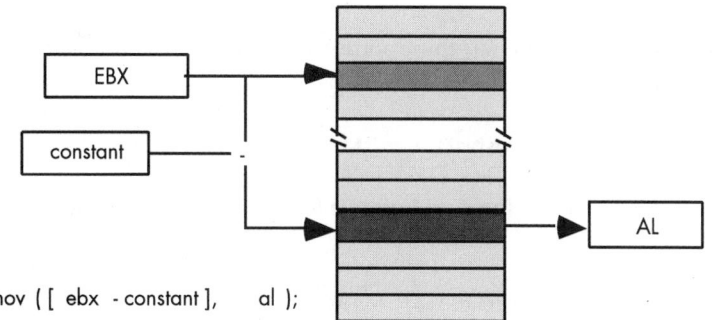

mov ([ebx - constant],   al);

Figure 3-5: Indexed Addressing Mode Using a Register Minus a Constant.

This particular variant of the addressing mode is useful if a 32-bit register contains the base address of a multibyte object and you wish to access a memory location some number of bytes before or after that location. One important use of this addressing mode is accessing fields of a record (or structure) when you have a pointer to the record data. This addressing mode is also invaluable for accessing automatic (local) variables in procedures (see the chapter on procedures for more details).

The second variant of the indexed addressing mode is actually a combination of the previous two forms. The syntax for this version is the following:

```
mov( VarName[ ebx + constant ], al );
mov( VarName[ ebx - constant ], al );
```

Once again, this example uses only the EBX register. You may, however, substitute any of the 32-bit general purpose registers in lieu of EBX in these two examples. This particular form is quite useful when accessing elements of an array of records (structures) in an assembly language program (more on that in the next chapter).

These instructions compute their effective address by adding or subtracting the constant value from VarName's address and then adding the value in EBX to this result. Note that HLA, not the CPU, computes the sum or difference of VarName's address and constant. The actual machine instructions above contain a single constant value that the instructions add to the value in EBX at runtime. Because HLA substitutes a constant for VarName, it can reduce an instruction of the form

```
mov( VarName[ ebx + constant], al );
```

to an instruction of the form

```
mov( constant1[ ebx + constant2], al );
```

Because of the way these addressing modes work, this is semantically equivalent to

```
mov( [ebx + (constant1 + constant2)], al );
```

HLA will add the two constants together at compile time, effectively producing the following instruction:

```
mov( [ebx + constant_sum], al );
```

Of course, there is nothing special about subtraction. You can easily convert the addressing mode involving subtraction to addition by simply taking the two's complement of the 32-bit constant and then adding this complemented value (rather than subtracting the uncomplemented value).

3.2.2.5 Scaled Indexed Addressing Modes

The scaled indexed addressing modes are similar to the indexed addressing modes with two differences: (1) the scaled indexed addressing modes allow you to combine two registers plus a displacement, and (2) the scaled indexed addressing modes let you multiply the index register by a (scaling) factor of 1, 2, 4, or 8. The syntax for these addressing modes is

```
VarName[ IndexReg₃₂*scale ]
VarName[ IndexReg₃₂*scale + displacement ]
VarName[ IndexReg₃₂*scale - displacement ]


[ BaseReg₃₂ + IndexReg₃₂*scale ]
[ BaseReg₃₂ + IndexReg₃₂*scale + displacement ]
[ BaseReg₃₂ + IndexReg₃₂*scale - displacement ]
```

```
VarName[ BaseReg_32 + IndexReg_32*scale ]
VarName[ BaseReg_32 + IndexReg_32*scale + displacement ]
VarName[ BaseReg_32 + IndexReg_32*scale - displacement ]
```

In these examples, $BaseReg_{32}$ represents any general purpose 32-bit register; $IndexReg_{32}$ represents any general purpose 32-bit register except ESP, and scale must be one of the constants: 1, 2, 4, or 8.

The primary difference between the scaled indexed addressing mode and the indexed addressing mode is the inclusion of the $IndexReg_{32}$*scale component. These modes compute the effective address by adding in the value of this new register multiplied by the specified scaling factor (see Figure 3-6 for an example involving EBX as the base register and ESI as the index register).

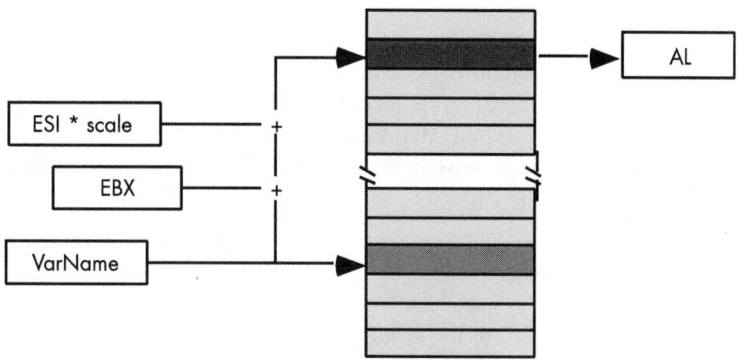

```
mov ( VarName   [ ebx  + esi *scale ],   al );
```

Figure 3-6: The Scaled Indexed Addressing Mode.

In Figure 3-6, suppose that EBX contains $100, ESI contains $20, and VarName is at base address $2000 in memory. Then the following instruction:

```
mov( VarName[ ebx + esi*4 + 4 ], al );
```

will move the byte at address $2184 ($2000 + $100 + $20*4 + 4) into the AL register.

The scaled indexed addressing mode is useful for accessing elements of arrays whose elements are 2, 4, or 8 bytes each. This addressing mode is also useful for access elements of an array when you have a pointer to the beginning of the array.

CAUTION   *Although this addressing mode contains two variable components (the base and index registers), don't get the impression that you use this addressing mode to access elements of a two-dimensional array by loading the two array indices into the two registers. Two-dimensional array access is quite a bit more complicated than this. The next chapter will consider multi-dimensional array access and discuss how to do this.*

3.2.2.6 Addressing Mode Wrap-Up

Well, believe it or not, you've just learned several hundred addressing modes! That wasn't hard now, was it? If you're wondering where all these modes came from, just consider the fact that the register indirect addressing mode isn't a single addressing mode, but eight different addressing modes (involving the eight different registers). Combinations of registers, constant sizes, and other factors multiply the number of possible addressing modes on the system. In fact, you need only memorize about two dozen forms and you've got it made. In practice, you'll use less than half the available addressing modes in any given program (and many addressing modes you may never use at all). So learning all these addressing modes is actually much easier than it sounds.

3.3 Run-Time Memory Organization

An operating system like Linux or Windows tends to put different types of data into different sections (or segments) of memory. Although it is possible to reconfigure memory to your choice by running the linker and specify various parameters, by default Windows loads an HLA program into memory using the organization appearing in Figure 3-7 (Linux is similar, though it rearranges some of the sections).

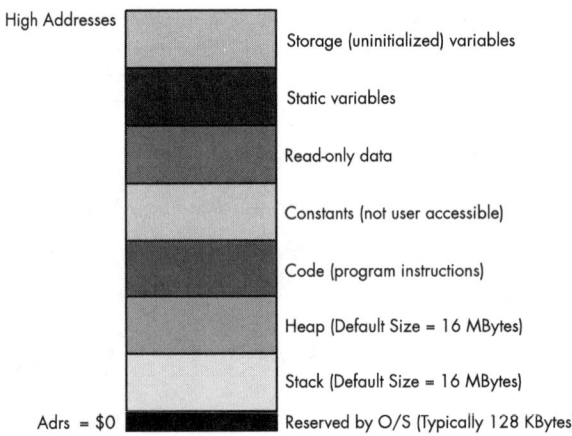

Figure 3-7: HLA Typical Run-Time Memory Organization.

The operating system reserves the lowest memory addresses. Generally, your application cannot access data (or execute instructions) at these low addresses. One reason the OS reserves this space is to help trap NULL pointer references. If you attempt to access memory location zero, the operating system will generate a "general protection fault" meaning you've accessed a memory location that doesn't contain valid data. Because programmers often initialize pointers to NULL (zero) to indicate that the pointer is not pointing anywhere, an access of location zero typically means that the programmer has made a mistake and has not properly initialized a pointer to a legal (non-NULL) value. Also note that if you attempt to use one of the 80x86 16-bit addressing modes (HLA doesn't allow this, but were you to encode the instruction yourself and execute it . . .) the address will always be in the range 0..$1FFFE.[4] This will also access a location in the reserved area, generating a fault.

The remaining six areas in the memory map hold different types of data associated with your program. These sections of memory include the stack section, the heap section, the code section, the readonly section, the static section, and the storage section. Each of these memory sections correspond to some type of data you can create in your HLA programs. The following sections discuss each of these sections in detail.

3.3.1   The Code Section

The code section contains the machine instructions that appear in an HLA program. HLA translates each machine instruction you write into a sequence of one or more byte values. The CPU interprets these byte values as machine instructions during program execution.

By default, when HLA links your program it tells the system that your program can execute instructions in the code segment and you can read data from the code segment. Note, specifically, that you cannot write data to the code segment. The operating system will generate a general protection fault if you attempt to store any data into the code segment.

Machine instructions are nothing more than data bytes. In theory, you could write a program that stores data values into memory and then transfers control to the data it just wrote, thereby producing a program that writes itself as it executes. This possibility produces romantic visions of *artificially intelligent* programs that modify themselves to produce some desired result. In real life, the effect is somewhat less glamorous.

Prior to the popularity of *protected mode operating systems*, like Windows and Linux, a program could overwrite the machine instructions during execution. Most of the time this was due to defects in a program, not because the program was artificially intelligent. A program would begin writing data to some array and fail to stop once it reached the end of the array, eventually overwriting the executing instructions that make up the program. Far from improving the quality of the code, such a defect usually causes the program to fail spectacularly.

Of course, if a feature is available, someone is bound to take advantage of it. Some programmers have discovered that in some special cases, using *self-modifying code* — that is, a program that modifies its machine instructions during execution — can produce slightly faster or slightly smaller programs. Unfortunately, self-modifying code is very difficult to test and debug. Given the speed of modern processors combined with their instruction set and wide variety of addressing modes, there is almost no reason to use self-modifying code in a modern program. Indeed, protected mode operating systems like Linux and Windows make it difficult for you to write self-modifying code.

---

[4] It's $1FFFE, not $FFFF, because you could use the indexed addressing mode with a displacement of $FFFF along with the value $FFFF in a 16-bit register.

HLA automatically stores the data associated with your machine code into the code section. In addition to machine instructions, you can also store data into the code section by using the following pseudo-opcodes:[5]

- byte
- word
- dword
- uns8
- uns16
- uns32
- int8
- int16
- in32
- boolean
- char

The following byte statement exemplifies the syntax for each of these pseudo-opcodes:

```
byte comma_separated_list_of_byte_constants ;
```

Here are some examples:

```
boolean    true;
char        'A';
byte        0, 1, 2;
byte        "Hello", 0
word        0, 2;
int8        -5;
uns32        356789, 0;
```

If more than one value appears in the list of values after the pseudo-opcode, HLA emits each successive value to the code stream. So the first byte statement above emits three bytes to the code stream, the values zero, one, and two. If a string appears within a byte statement, HLA emits one byte of data for each character in the string. Therefore, the second byte statement above emits six bytes: the characters 'H', 'e', 'l', 'l', and 'o', followed by a zero byte.

Keep in mind that the CPU will attempt to treat data you emit to the code stream as machine instructions unless you take special care not to allow the execution of the data. For example, if you write something like the following:

```
mov( 0, ax );
byte 0,1,2,3;
add( bx, cx );
```

[5] This isn't a complete list. HLA generally allows you to use any scalar data type name as a statement to reserve storage in the code section. You'll learn more about the available data types later in this text.

Your program will attempt to execute the 0, 1, 2, and 3 byte values as a machine instruction after executing the mov. Unless you know the machine code for a particular instruction sequence, sticking such data values into the middle of your code will almost always produce unexpected results. More often than not, this will crash your program. Therefore, you should never insert arbitrary data bytes into the middle of an instruction stream unless you understand exactly what you are doing. Typically when you place such data in your programs, you'll execute some code that transfers control around the data.

3.3.2 The Static Sections

The static section is where you will typically declare your variables. Although the static section syntactically appears as part of a program or procedure, keep in mind that HLA moves all static variables to the static section in memory. Therefore, HLA does not sandwich the variables you declare in the static section between procedures in the code section.

In addition to declaring static variables, you can also embed lists of data into the static declaration section. You use the same technique to embed data into your static section that you use to embed data into the code section: You use the byte, word, dword, uns32, and so on, pseudo-opcodes. Consider the following example:

```
static
    b:      byte := 0;
            byte 1,2,3;

    u:      uns32 := 1;
            uns32 5,2,10;

    c:      char;
            char 'a', 'b', 'c', 'd', 'e', 'f';

    bn: boolean;
            boolean true;
```

Data that HLA writes to the static memory segment using these pseudo-opcodes is written to the segment after the preceding variables. For example, the byte values 1, 2, and 3 are emitted to the static section after b's 0 byte. Because there aren't any labels associated with these values, you do not have direct access to these values in your program. You can use the indexed addressing modes to access these extra values (examples will appear a little later in this chapter).

In the examples above, note that the c and bn variables do not have an (explicit) initial value. However, if you don't provide an initial value, HLA will initialize the variables in the static section to all zero bits, so HLA assigns the NULL character (ASCII code zero) to c as its initial value. Likewise, HLA assigns false as the initial value for bn. In particular, you should note that your variable declarations in the static section always consume memory, even if you haven't assigned them an initial value. Any data you declare in a pseudo-opcode like byte will always follow the actual data associated with the variable declaration.

3.3.3   The Read-Only Data Section

The readonly data section holds constants, tables, and other data that your program cannot change during execution. You create read-only objects by declaring them in the readonly declaration section. The readonly section is very similar to the static section with three primary differences:

- The readonly section begins with the reserved word readonly rather than static.
- All declarations in the readonly section generally have an initializer.
- The system does not allow you to store data into a readonly object while the program is running.

Example:

```
readonly
    pi:             real32 := 3.14159;
    e:              real32 := 2.71;
    MaxU16:         uns16 := 65_535;
    MaxI16:         int16 := 32_767;
```

All readonly object declarations must have an initializer because you cannot initialize the value under program control.[6] For all intents and purposes, you can think of readonly objects as constants. However, these constants consume memory and other than you cannot write data to readonly objects, they behave like, and you can use them like, static variables. Because they behave like static objects, you cannot use a readonly object everywhere a constant is allowed; in particular, readonly objects are memory objects, so you cannot supply a readonly object and some other memory object as the operands to an instruction.[7]

Like the static section, you may embed data values in the readonly section using the byte, word, dword, and so on, data declarations, e.g.,

```
readonly
    roArray: byte := 0;
                    byte 1, 2, 3, 4, 5;
    qwVal: qword := 1;
            qword 0;
```

---

[6] There is one exception you'll see a little later in this chapter.

[7] mov is an exception to this rule because HLA emits special code for memory-to-memory move operations.

3.3.4 The Storage Section

The readonly section requires that you initialize all objects you declare. The static section lets you optionally initialize objects (or leave them uninitialized, in which case they have the default initial value of zero). The storage section completes the initialization coverage: You use it to declare variables that are always uninitialized when the program begins running. The storage section begins with the storage reserved word and contains variable declarations without initializers. Here is an example:

```
storage
    UninitUns32:     uns32;
    i:               int32;
    character:       char;
    b:               byte;
```

Linux and Windows will initialize all storage objects to zero when they load your program into memory. However, it's probably not a good idea to depend upon this implicit initialization. If you need an object initialized with zero, declare it in a static section and explicitly set it to zero.

Variables you declare in the storage section may consume less disk space in the executable file for the program. This is because HLA writes out initial values for readonly and static objects to the executable file, but uses a compact representation for uninitialized variables you declare in the storage section; note, however, that this behavior is OS and object-module format dependent. Because the storage section does not allow initialized values, you *cannot* put unlabeled values in the storage section using the byte, word, dword, and so on, pseudo-opcodes.

3.3.5 The @NOSTORAGE Attribute

The @nostorage attribute lets you declare variables in the static data declaration sections (i.e., static, readonly, and storage) without actually allocating memory for the variable. The @nostorage option tells HLA to assign the current address in a declaration section to a variable but do not allocate any storage for the object. That variable will share the same memory address as the next object appearing in the variable declaration section. Here is the syntax for the @nostorage option:

```
    variableName: varType; @nostorage;
```

Note that you follow the type name with "@nostorage;" rather than some initial value or just a semicolon. The following code sequence provides an example of using the @nostorage option in the readonly section:

```
readonly
    abcd: dword; nostorage;
            byte 'a', 'b', 'c', 'd';
```

In this example, *abcd* is a double word whose L.O. byte contains 97 ('a'), byte #1 contains 98 ('b'), byte #2 contains 99 ('c'), and the H.O. byte contains 100 ('d'). HLA does not reserve storage for the abcd variable, so HLA associates the following four bytes in memory (allocated by the byte directive) with abcd.

Note that the @nostorage attribute is only legal in the static, storage, and readonly sections (the so-called *static* declarations sections). HLA does not allow its use in the var section that you'll read about next.

3.3.6   *The Var Section*

HLA provides another variable declaration section, the var section, that you can use to create *automatic* variables. Your program will allocate storage for automatic variables whenever a program unit (i.e., main program or procedure) begins execution, and it will deallocate storage for automatic variables when that program unit returns to its caller. Of course, any automatic variables you declare in your main program have the same *lifetime*[8] as all the static, readonly, and storage objects, so the automatic allocation feature of the var section is wasted in the main program. In general, you should only use automatic objects in procedures (see the chapter on procedures for details). HLA allows them in your main program's declaration section as a generalization.

Because variables you declare in the var section are created at runtime, HLA does not allow initializers on variables you declare in this section. So the syntax for the var section is nearly identical to that for the storage section; the only real difference in the syntax between the two is the use of the var reserved word rather than the storage reserved word.[9] The following example illustrates this:

```
var
    vInt:       int32;
    vChar:      char;
```

HLA allocates variables you declare in the var section in the stack memory section. HLA does not allocate var objects at fixed locations within the stack segment; instead, it allocates these variables in an activation record associated with the current program unit. The chapter on procedures, later in this book, will discuss activation records in greater detail; for now it is important only to realize that HLA programs use the EBP register as a pointer to the current activation record. Therefore, any time you access a var object, HLA automatically replaces the variable name with "[EBP±displacement]". Displacement is the offset of the object in the activation record. This means that you cannot use the full scaled indexed addressing mode (a base register plus a scaled index register) with var objects because var objects already use the EBP register as their base register. Although you will not directly use the two register addressing modes often, the fact that the var section has this limitation is a good reason to avoid using the var section in your main program.

---

[8] The lifetime of a variable is the point from which memory is first allocated to the point the memory is deallocated for that variable.

[9] Actually, there are a few other, minor differences, but we won't deal with those differences in this text. See the HLA Reference Manual for more details.

3.3.7 Organization of Declaration Sections Within Your Programs

The static, readonly, storage, and var sections may appear zero or more times between the program header and the associated begin for the main program. Between these two points in your program, the declaration sections may appear in any order, as the following example demonstrates:

```
program demoDeclarations;

static
    i_static:     int32;

var
    i_auto:     int32;

storage
    i_uninit:     int32;

readonly
    i_readonly: int32 := 5;

static
    j:      uns32;

var
    k:      char;

readonly
    i2:     uns8 := 9;

storage
    c:      char;

storage
    d:      dword;

begin demoDeclarations;

    << code goes here >>

end demoDeclarations;
```

In addition to demonstrating that the sections may appear in an arbitrary order, this section also demonstrates that a given declaration section may appear more than once in your program. When multiple declaration sections of the same type (e.g., the three storage sections above) appear in a declaration section of your program, HLA combines them into a single group.

3.4 How HLA Allocates Memory for Variables

As you've seen, the 80x86 CPU doesn't deal with variables that have names like I, Profits, and LineCnt. The CPU deals strictly with numeric addresses it can place on the address bus like $1234_5678, $0400_1000, and $8000_CC00. HLA, on the other hand, does not force you refer to variable objects by their addresses (which is nice, because names are so much easier to remember). This abstraction (allowing the use of names rather than numeric addresses in your programs) is nice, but it does obscure what is really going on. In this section, we'll take a look at how HLA associates numeric addresses with your variables so you'll understand (and appreciate) the process that is taking place behind your back.

Take another look at Figure 3-7. As you can see, the various memory sections tend to be adjacent to one another. Therefore, if the size of one memory section changes, then this affects the starting address of all the following sections in memory. For example, if you add a few additional machine instructions to your program and increase the size of the code section, this may affect the starting address of the static section in memory, thus changing the addresses of all your static variables.[10] Keeping track of variables by their numeric address (rather than by their names) is difficult enough; imagine how much worse it would be if the addresses were constantly shifting around as you add and remove machine instructions in your program! Fortunately, you don't have to keep track of all of this, HLA does that bookkeeping for you.

HLA associates a current *location counter* with each of the three static declaration sections (static, readonly, and storage). These location counters initially contain zero and whenever you declare a variable in one of the static sections, HLA associates the current value of that section's location counter with the variable; HLA also bumps up the value of that location counter by the size of the object you're declaring. As an example, assume that the following is the only static declaration section in a program:

```
static
    b    :byte;                  // Location counter = 0, size = 1
    w    :word;                  // Location counter = 1, size = 2
    d    :dword;                 // Location counter = 3, size = 4
    q    :qword;                 // Location counter = 7, size = 8
    l    :lword;                 // Location counter = 15, size = 16
    // Location counter is now 31.
```

Of course, the run-time address of each of these variables is not the value of the location counter. First of all, HLA adds in the base address of the static memory section to each of these location counter values (that we call *displacements* or *offsets*). Secondly, there may be other static objects in modules that you link with your program (e.g., from the HLA Standard Library), or even additional static sections in the same source file, and the linker has to merge the static sections together. Hence, these offsets may have very little bearing on the final address of

---

[10] Note that the operating system typically aligns the static section on a 4,096-byte boundary, so you many need to add a sufficient number of new instructions to cause the code section to grow in size across a 4K boundary before the static addresses actually change. This isn't necessarily true for all memory sections, however.

these variables in memory. Nevertheless, one important fact remains: HLA allocates variables you declare in a single static declaration section in contiguous memory locations. That is, given the declaration above, w will immediately follow b in memory, d will immediately follow w in memory, q will immediately follow d, and so on. Generally, it's not good coding style to assume that the system allocates variables this way, but sometimes it's convenient to do so.

Note that HLA allocates memory objects you declare in readonly, static, and storage sections in completely different regions of memory. Therefore, you cannot assume that the following three memory objects appear in adjacent memory locations (indeed, they probably will not):

```
static
    b       :byte;
readonly
    w       :word := $1234;
storage
    d       :dword;
```

In fact, HLA will not even guarantee that variables you declare in separate static (or whatever) sections are adjacent in memory, even if there is nothing between the declarations in your code (e.g., you cannot assume that b, w, and d are in adjacent memory locations in the following declarations, nor can you assume that they *won't* be adjacent in memory):

```
static
    b       :byte;
static
    w       :word := $1234;
static
    d       :dword;
```

If your code requires these variables to consume adjacent memory locations, you must declare them in the same static section.

Note that HLA handles variables you declare in the var section a little differently than the variables you declare in one of the static sections. We'll discuss the allocation of offsets to var objects in the chapter on procedures.

3.5 HLA Support for Data Alignment

In order to write fast programs, you need to ensure that you properly align data objects in memory. Proper alignment means that the starting address for an object is a multiple of some size, usually the size of object if the object's size is a power of two for values up to 16 bytes in length. For objects greater than 16 bytes, aligning the object on an 8-byte or 16-byte address boundary is probably sufficient. For objects less than 16 bytes, aligning the object at an address that is the next power of two greater than the object's size is usually fine.[11] Accessing

---

[11] An exception are the real80 and tbyte (80-bit) types. These only need to be aligned on an address that is a multiple of eight bytes in memory.

data that is not aligned on at an appropriate address may require extra time; so if you want to ensure that your program runs as rapidly as possible, you should try to align data objects according to their size.

Data becomes misaligned whenever you allocate storage for different-sized objects in adjacent memory locations. For example, if you declare a byte variable, it will consume one byte of storage, and the next variable you declare in that declaration section will have the address of that byte object plus one. If the byte variable's address happens to be an address that is an even address, then the variable following that byte will start at an odd address. If that following variable is a word or double word object, then its starting address will not be optimal. In this section, we'll explore ways to ensure that a variable is aligned at an appropriate starting address based on that object's size.

Consider the following HLA variable declarations:

```
static
      dw:     dword;
      b:      byte;
      w:      word;
      dw2:    dword;
      w2:     word;
      b2:     byte;
      dw3:    dword;
```

The first static declaration in a program (running under Windows, Linux, and most 32-bit operating systems) places its variables at an address that is an even multiple of 4096 bytes. Whatever variable first appears in the static declaration is guaranteed to be aligned on a reasonable address. Each successive variable is allocated at an address that is the sum of the sizes of all the preceding variables plus the starting address of that static section. Therefore, assuming HLA allocates the variables in the previous example at a starting address of 4096, HLA will allocate them at the following addresses:

```
                      // Start Adrs        Length
      dw:     dword;  //     4096          4
      b:      byte;   //     4100          1
      w:      word;   //     4101          2
      dw2:    dword;  //     4103          4
      w2:     word;   //     4107          2
      b2:     byte;   //     4109          1
      dw3:    dword;  //     4110          4
```

With the exception of the first variable (that is aligned on a 4K boundary) and the byte variables (whose alignment doesn't matter), all of these variables are misaligned. The w, w2, and dw2 variables start at odd addresses, and the dw3 variable is aligned on an even address that is not a multiple of four.

An easy way to guarantee that your variables are aligned properly is to put all the double word variables first, the word variables second, and the byte variables last in the declaration:

```
static
    dw:     dword;
    dw2:    dword;
    dw3:    dword;
    w:      word;
    w2:     word;
    b:      byte;
    b2:     byte;
```

This organization produces the following addresses in memory:

		// Start Adrs	Length
dw:	dword;	// 4096	4
dw2:	dword;	// 4100	4
dw3:	dword;	// 4104	4
w:	word;	// 4108	2
w2:	word;	// 4110	2
b:	byte;	// 4112	1
b2:	byte;	// 4113	1

As you can see, these variables are all aligned at reasonable addresses.

Unfortunately, it is rarely possible for you to arrange your variables in this manner. While there are many technical reasons that make this alignment impossible, a good practical reason for not doing this is because it doesn't let you organize your variable declarations by logical function (that is, you probably want to keep related variables next to one another regardless of their size).

To resolve this problem, HLA provides the align directive. The align directive uses the following syntax:

```
align( integer_constant );
```

The integer constant must be one of the following small unsigned integer values: 1, 2, 4, 8, or 16. If HLA encounters the align directive in a static section, it will align the very next variable on an address that is an even multiple of the specified alignment constant. The previous example could be rewritten, using the align directive, as follows:

```
static
    align( 4 );
    dw:     dword;
    b:      byte;
    align( 2 );
    w:      word;
    align( 4 );
    dw2:    dword;
    w2:     word;
    b2:     byte;
```

```
align( 4 );
dw3:    dword;
```

If you're wondering how the align directive works, it's really quite simple. If HLA determines that the current address (location counter value) is not an even multiple of the specified value, HLA will quietly emit extra bytes of padding after the previous variable declaration until the current address in the static section is an even multiple of the specified value. This has the effect of making your program slightly larger (by a few bytes) in exchange for faster access to your data; given that your program will only grow by a few bytes when you use this feature, this is probably a good trade-off.

As a general rule, if you want the fastest possible access you should choose an alignment value that is equal to the size of the object you want to align. That is, you should align words to even boundaries using an "align(2);" statement, double words to four-byte boundaries using "align(4);", quad words to eight-byte boundaries using "align(8);", and so on. If the object's size is not a power of two, align it to the next higher power of two (up to a maximum of 16 bytes). Note, however, that you need only align real80 (and tbyte) objects on an eight-byte boundary.

Note that data alignment isn't always necessary. The cache architecture of modern 80x86 CPUs actually handles most misaligned data. Therefore, you should only use the alignment directives with variables for whom speedy access is absolutely critical. This is a reasonable space/speed trade-off.

3.6   Address Expressions

Earlier, this chapter points out that addressing modes take a couple generic forms, including:

```
VarName[ Reg32 ]
VarName[ Reg32 + offset ]
VarName[ RegNotESP32*Scale ]
VarName[ Reg32 + RegNotESP32*Scale ]
VarName[ RegNotESP32*Scale + offset ]
and
VarName[ Reg32 + RegNotESP32*Scale + offset ]
```

Another legal form, which isn't actually a new addressing mode but simply an extension of the displacement-only addressing mode, is

```
VarName[ offset ]
```

This latter example computes its effective address by adding the constant offset within the brackets to the variable's address. For example, the instruction "mov(Address[3], AL);" loads the AL register with the byte in memory that is three bytes beyond the Address object (see Figure 3-8).

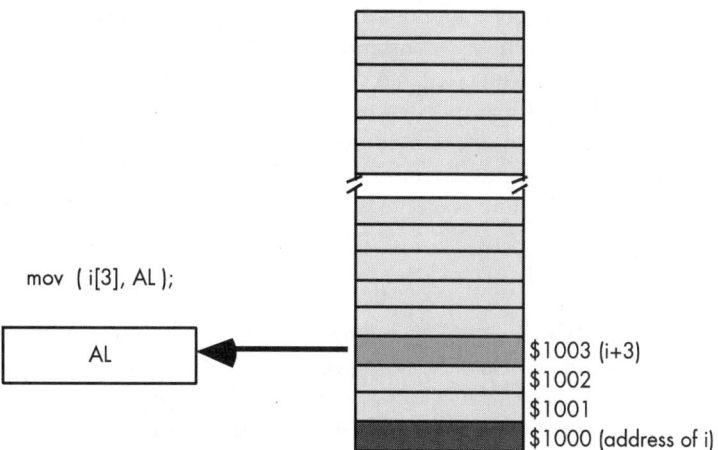

mov (i[3], AL);

AL

$1003 (i+3)
$1002
$1001
$1000 (address of i)

Figure 3-8: Using an Address Expression to Access Data Beyond a Variable.

Always remember that the offset value in these examples must be a constant. If Index is an int32 variable, then Variable[Index] is not a legal address expression. If you wish to specify an index that varies at runtime, then you must use one of the indexed or scaled indexed addressing modes.

Another important thing to remember is that the offset in Address[offset] is a byte address. Despite the fact that this syntax is reminiscent of array indexing in a high level language like C/C++ or Pascal, this does not properly index into an array of objects unless Address is an array of bytes.

This text will consider an *address expression* to be any legal 80x86 addressing mode that includes a displacement (i.e., variable name) or an offset. In addition to the above forms, the following are also address expressions:

$$[\ Reg_{32} + offset \ ]$$
$$[\ Reg_{32} + RegNotESP_{32}*Scale + offset \ ]$$

This book will *not* consider the following to be address expressions because they do not involve a displacement or offset component:

$$[\ Reg_{32} \ ]$$
$$[\ Reg_{32} + RegNotESP_{32}*Scale \ ]$$

Address expressions are special because those instructions containing an address expression always encode a displacement constant as part of the machine instruction. That is, the machine instruction contains some number of bits (usually 8 or 32) that hold a numeric constant. That constant is the sum of the displacement (i.e., the address or offset of the variable) plus the offset. Note that HLA automatically adds these two values together for you (or subtracts the offset if you use the "-" rather than "+" operator in the addressing mode).

Until this point, the offset in all the addressing mode examples has always been a single numeric constant. However, HLA also allows a *constant expression* anywhere an offset is legal. A constant expression consists of one or more constant terms manipulated by operators such as addition, subtraction, multiplication, division, modulo, and a wide variety of other operators. Most address expressions, however, will only involve addition, subtraction, multiplication, and sometimes, division. Consider the following example:

```
mov( X[ 2*4+1 ], al );
```

This instruction will move the byte at address X+9 into the AL register.

The value of an address expression is always computed at compiletime, never while the program is running. When HLA encounters the instruction above, it calculates 2*4+1 on the spot and adds this result to the base address of X in memory. HLA encodes this single sum (base address of X plus nine) as part of the instruction; HLA does not emit extra instructions to compute this sum for you at runtime (which is good, because doing so would be less efficient). Because HLA computes the value of address expressions at compiletime, all components of the expression must be constants because HLA cannot know the run-time value of a variable while it is compiling the program.

Address expressions are useful for accessing the data in memory beyond a variable, particularly when you've used the byte, word, dword, and so on, statements in a static or readonly section to tack on additional bytes after a data declaration. For example, consider the program in Listing 3-1.

Listing 3-1: Demonstration of Address Expressions.

```
program adrsExpressions;
#include( "stdlib.hhf" )
static
  i: int8; @nostorage;
    byte 0, 1, 2, 3;

begin adrsExpressions;

  stdout.put
  (
    "i[0]=", i[0], nl,
    "i[1]=", i[1], nl,
    "i[2]=", i[2], nl,
    "i[3]=", i[3], nl
  );

end adrsExpressions;
```

The program in Listing 3-1 will display the four values 0, 1, 2, and 3 as though they were array elements. This is because the value at the address of i is 0 (this program declares i using the @nostorage option, so i is the address of the next object in the static section, which just happens to be the value 0 appearing as part of the byte statement). The address expression "i[1]" tells HLA to fetch the byte appearing at i's address plus one. This is the value one, because the byte statement in this program emits the value one to the static segment immediately after the value 0. Likewise for i[2] and i[3], this program displays the values 2 and 3.

3.7 Type Coercion

Although HLA is fairly loose when it comes to type checking, HLA does ensure that you specify appropriate operand sizes to an instruction. For example, consider the following (incorrect) program:

```
program hasErrors;
static
      i8:      int8;
      i16:     int16;
      i32:     int32;
begin hasErrors;

      mov( i8, eax );
      mov( i16, al );
      mov( i32, ax );

end hasErrors;
```

HLA will generate errors for these three mov instructions. This is because the operand sizes are incompatible. The first instruction attempts to move a byte into EAX, the second instruction attempts to move a word into AL and the third instruction attempts to move a double word into AX. The mov instruction, of course, requires both operands to be the same size.

While this is a good feature in HLA,[12] there are times when it gets in the way. Consider the following code fragments:

```
static
      byte_values: byte; @nostorage;
                        byte  0, 1;

      ...

            mov( byte_values, ax );
```

In this example let's assume that the programmer really wants to load the word starting at the address of byte_values into the AX register because they want to load AL with 0 and AH with 1 using a single instruction. HLA will refuse, claiming there is a type mismatch error (because byte_values is a byte object and AX is a word object). The programmer could break this into two instructions, one to load AL with the byte at address byte_values and the other to load AH with

---

[12] After all, if the two operand sizes are different this usually indicates an error in the program.

the byte at address byte_values[1]. Unfortunately, this decomposition makes the program slightly less efficient (which was probably the reason for using the single mov instruction in the first place). Somehow, it would be nice if we could tell HLA that we know what we're doing and we want to treat the byte_values variable as a word object. HLA's *type coercion* facilities provide this capability.

Type coercion[13] is the process of telling HLA that you want to treat an object as an explicit type, regardless of its actual type. To coerce the type of a variable, you use the following syntax:

```
(type newTypeName addressExpression)
```

The newTypeName item is the new type you wish to associate with the memory location specified by addressExpression. You may use this coercion operator anywhere a memory address is legal. To correct the previous example, so HLA doesn't complain about type mismatches, you would use the following statement:

```
mov( (type word byte_values), ax );
```

This instruction tells HLA to load the AX register with the word starting at address byte_values in memory. Assuming byte_values still contains its initial values, this instruction will load zero into AL and one into AH.

Type coercion is necessary when you specify an anonymous variable as the operand to an instruction that directly modifies memory (e.g., neg, shl, not, and so on). Consider the following statement:

```
not( [ebx] );
```

HLA will generate an error on this instruction because it cannot determine the size of the memory operand. The instruction does not supply sufficient information to determine whether the program should invert the bits in the byte pointed at by EBX, the word pointed at by EBX, or the double word pointed at by EBX. You must use type coercion to explicitly specify size of anonymous references with these types of instructions:

```
not( (type byte [ebx]) );
not( (type dword [ebx]) );
```

CAUTION *Do not use the type coercion operator unless you know exactly what you are doing and fully understand the effect it has on your program. Beginning assembly language programmers often use type coercion as a tool to quiet the compiler when it complains about type mismatches without solving the underlying problem. Consider the following statement (where byteVar is an 8-bit variable):*

```
mov( eax, (type dword byteVar) );
```

Without the type coercion operator, HLA complains about this instruction because it attempts to store a 32-bit register into an 8-bit memory location. A beginning programmer, wanting their program to compile, may take a shortcut

[13] Also called *type casting* in some languages.

and use the type coercion operator as shown in this instruction; this certainly quiets the compiler — it will no longer complain about a type mismatch. So the beginning programmer is happy. But the program is still incorrect; the only difference is that HLA no longer warns you about your error. The type coercion operator does not fix the problem of attempting to store a 32-bit value into an 8-bit memory location — it simply allows the instruction to store a 32-bit value *starting at the address specified by the 8-bit variable.* The program still stores four bytes, overwriting the three bytes following byteVar in memory. This often produces unexpected results including the phantom modification of variables in your program.[14] Another, rarer, possibility is for the program to abort with a general protection fault. This can occur if the three bytes following byteVar are not allocated in real memory or if those bytes just happen to fall in a read-only segment in memory. The important thing to remember about the type coercion operator is this: "If you cannot exactly state the affect this operator has, don't use it."

Also keep in mind that the type coercion operator does not perform any translation of the data in memory. It simply tells the compiler to treat the bits in memory as a different type. It will not automatically sign extend an 8-bit value to 32 bits nor will it convert an integer to a floating point value. It simply tells the compiler to treat the bit pattern of the memory operand as a different type.

3.8   Register Type Coercion

You can also cast a register to a specific type using the type coercion operator. By default, the 8-bit registers are of type byte, the 16-bit registers are of type word, and the 32-bit registers are of type dword. With type coercion, you can cast a register as a different type *as long as the size of the new type agrees with the size of the register.* This is an important restriction that does not exist when applying type coercion to a memory variable.

Most of the time you do not need to coerce a register to a different type. As byte, word, and dword objects, registers are already compatible with all one, two, and four byte objects. However, there are a few instances where register type coercion is handy, if not downright necessary. Two examples include boolean expressions in HLA high level language statements (e.g., if and while) and register I/O in the stdout.put and stdin.get (and related) statements.

In boolean expressions, HLA always treats byte, word, and dword objects as unsigned values. Therefore, without type coercion, the following if statement always evaluates false (because there is no unsigned value less than zero):

```
if( eax < 0 ) then

    stdout.put( "EAX is negative!", nl );

endif;
```

---

[14] If you have a variable immediately following byteVar in this example, the mov instruction will surely overwrite the value of that variable, whether or not you intend for this to happen.

You can overcome this limitation by casting EAX as an int32 value:

```
if( (type int32 eax) < 0 ) then

    stdout.put( "EAX is negative!", nl );

endif;
```

In a similar vein, the HLA Standard Library stdout.put routine always outputs byte, word, and dword values as hexadecimal numbers. Therefore, if you attempt to print a register, the stdout.put routine will print it as a hex value. If you would like to print the value as some other type, you can use register type coercion to achieve this:

```
stdout.put( "AL printed as a char = '", (type char al), "'", nl );
```

The same is true for the stdin.get routine. It will always read a hexadecimal value for a register unless you coerce its type to something other than byte, word, or dword.

3.9 The Stack Segment and the PUSH and POP Instructions

This chapter mentions that all variables you declare in the var section wind up in the stack memory segment. However, var objects are not the only things in the stack memory section; your programs manipulate data in the stack segment in many different ways. This section introduces the push and pop instructions that also manipulate data in stack memory.

The stack segment in memory is where the 80x86 maintains the stack. The *stack* is a dynamic data structure that grows and shrinks according to certain needs of the program. The stack also stores important information about program including local variables, subroutine information, and temporary data.

The 80x86 controls its stack via the ESP (stack pointer) register. When your program begins execution, the operating system initializes ESP with the address of the last memory location in the stack memory segment. Data is written to the stack segment by "pushing" data onto the stack and "popping" or "pulling" data off of the stack. Whenever you push data onto the stack, the 80x86 decrements the stack pointer by the size of the data you are pushing, and then it copies the data to memory where ESP is then pointing. Therefore, the stack grows and shrinks as you push data onto the stack and pop data from the stack.

3.9.1 The Basic PUSH Instruction

Consider the syntax for the 80x86 push instruction:

```
push( reg16 );
push( reg32 );
push( memory16 );
```

```
push( memory_{32} );
pushw( constant );
pushd( constant );
```

The pushw and pushd operands are always two- or four-byte constants, respectively.

These six forms allow you to push word or dword registers, memory locations, and constants. You should specifically note that you cannot push byte values onto the stack.

The push instruction does the following:

```
ESP := ESP - Size_of_Register_or_Memory_Operand (2 or 4)
[ESP] := Operand's_Value
```

Assuming that ESP contains $00FF_FFE8, then the instruction "push(eax);" will set ESP to $00FF_FFE4, and store the current value of EAX into memory location $00FF_FFE4 as Figures 3-9 and 3-10 show.

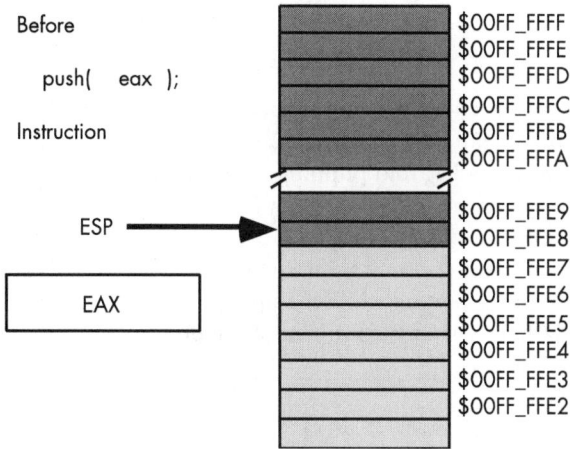

Figure 3-9: Before "PUSH(EAX);" Operation.

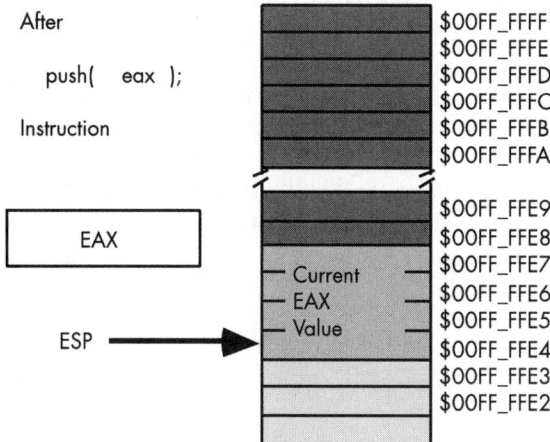

Figure 3-10: Stack Segment After "PUSH(EAX);" Operation.

Note that the "push(eax);" instruction does not affect the value of the EAX register.

Although the 80x86 supports 16-bit push operations, their primary use in is 16-bit environments such as DÔS. For maximum performance, the stack pointer's value should always be an even multiple of four; indeed, your program may malfunction under Windows or Linux if ESP contains a value that is not a multiple of four and you make an operating system API call. The only practical reason for pushing less than four bytes at a time on the stack is because you're building up a double word via two successive word pushes.

3.9.2 The Basic POP Instruction

To retrieve data you've pushed onto the stack, you use the pop instruction. The basic pop instruction allows the following different forms:

```
pop( reg16 );
pop( reg32 );
pop( memory16 );
pop( memory32 );
```

Like the push instruction, the pop instruction only supports 16-bit and 32-bit operands; you cannot pop an 8-bit value from the stack. Also like the push instruction, you should avoid popping 16-bit values (unless you do two 16-bit pops in a row) because 16-bit pops may leave the ESP register containing a value that is not an even multiple of four. One major difference between push and pop is that you cannot pop a constant value (which makes sense, because the operand for push is a source operand while the operand for pop is a destination operand).

Formally, here's what the pop instruction does:

```
Operand := [ESP]
ESP := ESP + Size_of_Operand (2 or 4)
```

As you can see, the pop operation is the converse of the push operation. Note that the pop instruction copies the data from memory location [ESP] before adjusting the value in ESP. See Figures 3-11 and 3-12 for details on this operation.

Note that the value popped from the stack is still present in memory. Popping a value does not erase the value in memory; it just adjusts the stack pointer so that it points at the next value above the popped value. However, you should never attempt to access a value you've popped off the stack. The next time something is pushed onto the stack, the popped value will be obliterated. Because your code isn't the only thing that uses the stack (i.e., the operating system uses the stack as do subroutines), you cannot rely on data remaining in stack memory once you've popped it off the stack.

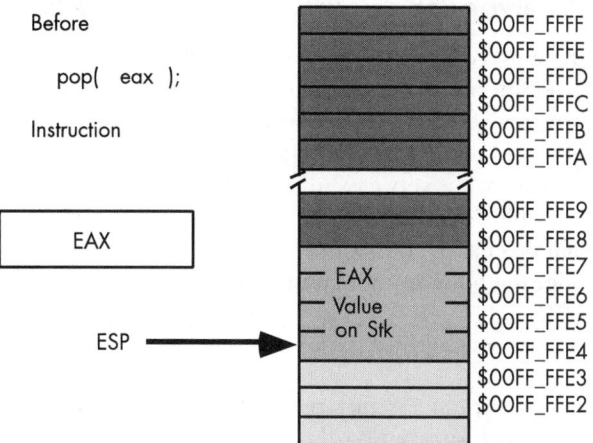

Figure 3-11: Memory Before a "POP(EAX);" Operation.

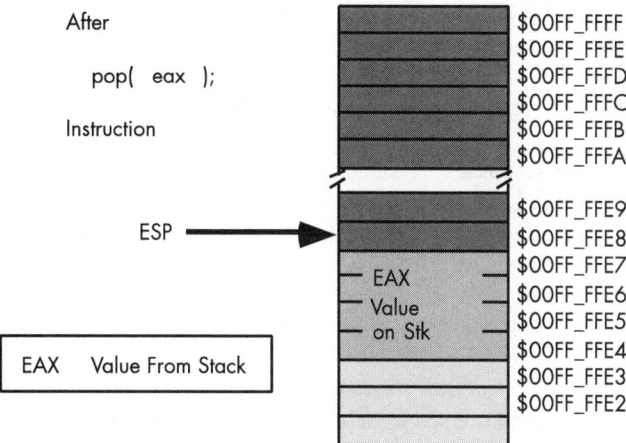

Figure 3-12: Memory After the "POP(EAX);" Instruction.

As Chapter One notes, HLA provides an extended syntax for the mov instruction that allows two memory operands (that is, the instruction provides a memory-to-memory move). HLA actually generates the following two instructions in place of such a mov:

```
// mov( src, dest );

        push( src );
        pop( dest );
```

This is the reason that the memory-to-memory form of the mov instruction only allows 16-bit and 32-bit operands — because push and pop only allow 16-bit and 32-bit operands.

3.9.3 Preserving Registers with the PUSH and POP Instructions

Perhaps the most common use of the push and pop instructions is to save register values during intermediate calculations. A problem with the 80x86 architecture is that it provides very few general purpose registers. Because registers are the best place to hold temporary values, and registers are also needed for the various addressing modes, it is very easy to run out of registers when writing code that performs complex calculations. The push and pop instructions can come to your rescue when this happens.

Consider the following program outline:

```
<< Some sequence of instructions that use the EAX register >>

<< Some sequence of instructions that need to use EAX, for a
      different purpose than the above instructions >>

<< Some sequence of instructions that need the original value in EAX >>
```

The push and pop instructions are perfect for this situation. By inserting a push instruction before the middle sequence and a pop instruction after the middle sequence above, you can preserve the value in EAX across those calculations:

```
<< Some sequence of instructions that use the EAX register >>
push( eax );
<< Some sequence of instructions that need to use EAX, for a
    different purpose than the above instructions >>
pop( eax );
<< Some sequence of instructions that need the original value in EAX >>
```

The push instruction above copies the data computed in the first sequence of instructions onto the stack. Now the middle sequence of instructions can use EAX for any purpose it chooses. After the middle sequence of instructions finishes, the pop instruction restores the value in EAX so the last sequence of instructions can use the original value in EAX.

3.9.4 The Stack Is a LIFO Data Structure

You can push more than one value onto the stack without first popping previous values off the stack. However, the stack is a *last-in, first-out* (LIFO) data structure, so you must be careful how you push and pop multiple values. For example, suppose you want to preserve EAX and EBX across some block of instructions. The following code demonstrates the obvious way to handle this:

```
push( eax );
push( ebx );
<< Code that uses EAX and EBX goes here >>
pop( eax );
pop( ebx );
```

Unfortunately, this code will not work properly! Figures 3-13 through 3-16 show the problem. Because this code pushes EAX first and EBX second, the stack pointer is left pointing at EBX's value on the stack. When the "pop(eax);" instruction comes along, it removes the value that was originally in EBX from the stack and places it in EAX! Likewise, the "pop(EBX);" instruction pops the value that was originally in EAX into the EBX register. The end result is that this code manages to swap the values in the registers by popping them in the same order that it pushes them.

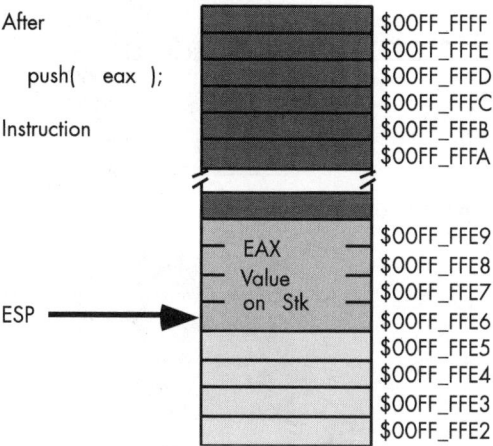

Figure 3-13: Stack After Pushing EAX.

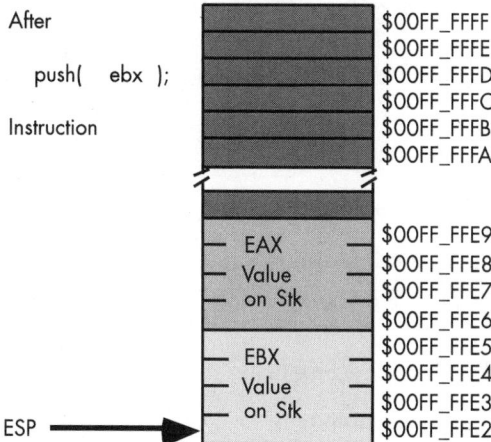

Figure 3-14: Stack After Pushing EBX.

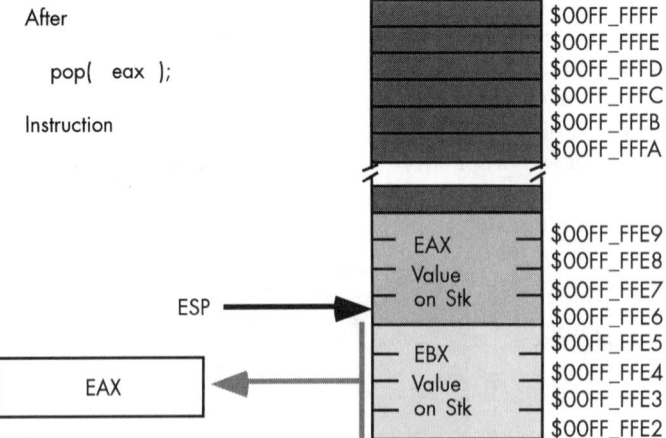

Figure 3-15: Stack After Popping EAX.

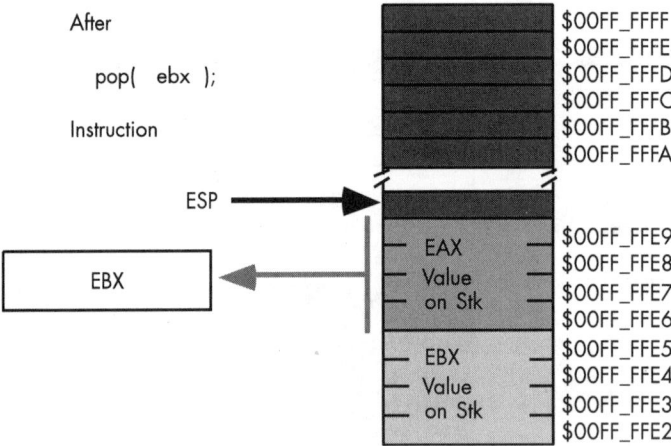

Figure 3-16: Stack After Popping EBX.

To rectify this problem, you must note that the stack is a LIFO data structure, so the first thing you must pop is the last thing you push onto the stack. Therefore, you must always observe the following maxim:

• Always pop values in the reverse order that you push them.

The correction to the previous code is

```
push( eax );
push( ebx );
<< Code that uses EAX and EBX goes here >>
pop( ebx );
pop( eax );
```

Another important maxim to remember is

• Always pop exactly the same number of bytes that you push.

This generally means that the number of pushes and pops must exactly agree. If you have too few pops, you will leave data on the stack, which may confuse the running program: If you have too many pops, you will accidentally remove previously pushed data, often with disastrous results.

A corollary to the maxim above is, "Be careful when pushing and popping data within a loop." Often it is quite easy to put the pushes in a loop and leave the pops outside the loop (or vice versa), creating an inconsistent stack. Remember, it is the execution of the push and pop instructions that matters, not the number of push and pop instructions that appear in your program. At runtime, the number (and order) of the push instructions the program executes must match the number (and reverse order) of the pop instructions.

3.9.5   Other PUSH and POP Instructions

The 80x86 provides several additional push and pop instructions in addition to the basic push/pop instructions. These instructions include the following:

- pusha
- pushad
- pushf
- pushfd
- popa
- popad
- popf
- popfd

The pusha instruction pushes all the general purpose 16-bit registers onto the stack. This instruction exists primarily for older 16-bit operating systems like DOS. In general, you will have very little need for this instruction. The pusha instruction pushes the registers onto the stack in the following order:

ax
cx
dx
bx
sp
bp
si
di

The pushad instruction pushes all the 32-bit (double word) registers onto the stack. It pushes the registers onto the stack in the following order:

eax
ecx
edx
ebx

```
esp
ebp
esi
edi
```

Because the pusha and pushad instructions inherently modify the SP/ESP register, you may wonder why Intel bothered to push this register at all. It was probably easier in the hardware to go ahead and push SP/ESP rather than make a special case out of it. In any case, these instructions do push SP or ESP, so don't worry about it too much — there is nothing you can do about it.

The popa and popad instructions provide the corresponding "pop all" operation to the pusha and pushad instructions. This will pop the registers pushed by pusha or pushad in the appropriate order (that is, popa and popad will properly restore the register values by popping them in the reverse order that pusha or pushad pushed them).

Although the pusha/popa and pushad/popad sequences are short and convenient, they are actually slower than the corresponding sequence of push/pop instructions, this is especially true when you consider that you rarely need to push a majority, much less all the registers.[15] So if you're looking for maximum speed, you should carefully consider whether to use the pusha(d)/popa(d) instructions.

The pushf, pushfd, popf, and popfd instructions push and pop the (E)FLAGs register. These instructions allow you to preserve condition code and other flag settings across the execution of some sequence of instructions. Unfortunately, unless you go to a lot of trouble, it is difficult to preserve individual flags. When using the pushf(d) and popf(d) instructions it's an all-or-nothing proposition: You preserve all the flags when you push them; you restore all the flags when you pop them.

Like the pushad and popad instructions, you should really use the pushfd and popfd instructions to push the full 32-bit version of the EFLAGs register. Although the extra 16 bits you push and pop are essentially ignored when writing applications, you still want to keep the stack aligned by pushing and popping only double words.

3.9.6   Removing Data from the Stack Without Popping It

Once in a while you may discover that you've pushed data onto the stack that you no longer need. Although you could pop the data into an unused register or memory location, there is an easier way to remove unwanted data from the stack: Simply adjust the value in the ESP register to skip over the unwanted data on the stack.

Consider the following dilemma:

```
    push( eax );
    push( ebx );
```

---

[15] For example, it is extremely rare for you to need to push and pop the ESP register with the PUSHAD/POPAD instruction sequence.

```
        << Some code that winds up computing some values we want to keep
            into EAX and EBX >>

    if( Calculation_was_performed ) then

            // Whoops, we don't want to pop EAX and EBX!
            // What to do here?

    else

            // No calculation, so restore EAX, EBX.

            pop( ebx );
            pop( eax );

    endif;
```

Within the then section of the if statement, this code wants to remove the old
values of EAX and EBX without otherwise affecting any registers or memory
locations. How to do this?

Because the ESP register simply contains the memory address of the item on
the top of the stack, we can remove the item from the top of stack by adding the
size of that item to the ESP register. In the preceding example, we wanted to
remove two double word items from the top of stack. We can easily accomplish
this by adding eight to the stack pointer (see Figures 3-17 and 3-18 for the
details):

```
    push( eax );
    push( ebx );

        << Some code that winds up computing some values we want to keep
            into EAX and EBX >>

    if( Calculation_was_performed ) then

            add( 8, ESP );       // Remove unneeded EAX and EBX values

    else

            // No calculation, so restore EAX, EBX.

            pop( ebx );
            pop( eax );

    endif;
```

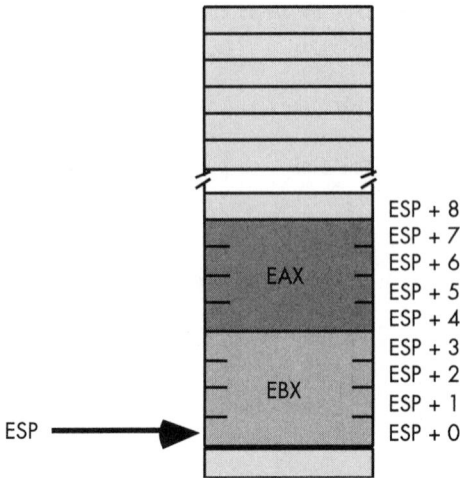

Figure 3-17: Removing Data from the Stack, Before ADD(8, ESP).

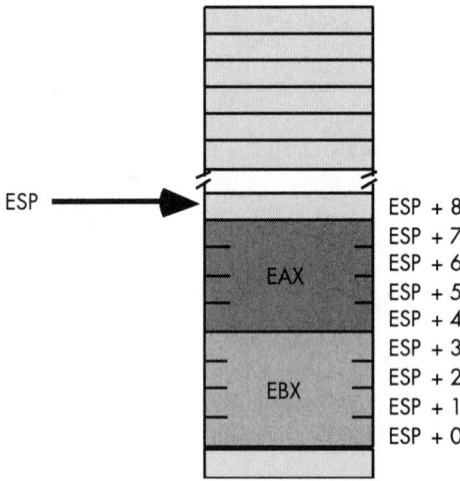

Figure 3-18: Removing Data from the Stack, After ADD(8, ESP).

Effectively, this code pops the data off the stack without moving it anywhere. Also note that this code is faster than two dummy pop instructions because it can remove any number of bytes from the stack with a single add instruction.

CAUTION   *Remember to keep the stack aligned on a double word boundary. Therefore, you should always add a constant that is an even multiple of four to ESP when removing data from the stack.*

3.9.7 Accessing Data You've Pushed on the Stack Without Popping It

Once in a while you will push data onto the stack and you will want to get a copy of that data's value, or perhaps you will want to change that data's value, without actually popping the data off the stack (that is, you wish to pop the data off the stack at a later time). The 80x86 "[reg$_{32}$ + offset]" addressing mode provides the mechanism for this.

Consider the stack after the execution of the following two instructions (see Figure 3-19):

```
        push( eax );
        push( ebx );
```

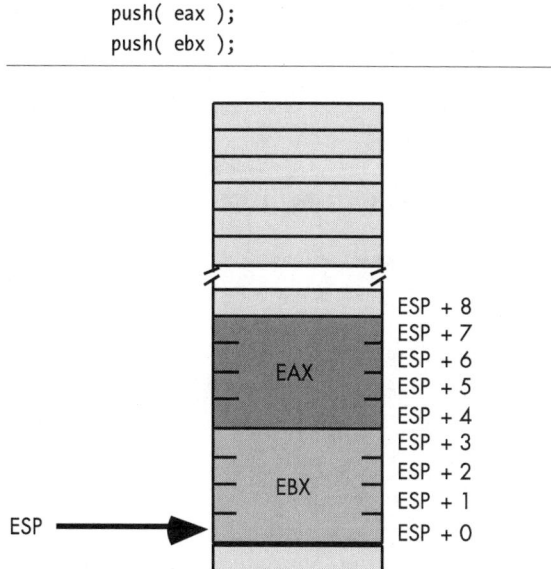

Figure 3-19: Stack After Pushing EAX and EBX.

If you wanted to access the original EBX value without removing it from the stack, you could cheat and pop the value and then immediately push it again. Suppose, however, that you wish to access EAX's old value, or some other value even farther up on the stack. Popping all the intermediate values and then pushing them back onto the stack is problematic at best and impossible at worst. However, as you will notice from Figure 3-19, each of the values pushed on the stack is at some offset from the ESP register in memory. Therefore, we can use the "[ESP + offset]" addressing mode to gain direct access to the value we are interested in. In the example above, you can reload EAX with its original value by using the single instruction

```
        mov( [esp+4], eax );
```

This code copies the four bytes starting at memory address ESP + 4 into the EAX register. This value just happens to be the previous value of EAX that was pushed onto the stack. You can use this same technique to access other data values you've pushed onto the stack.

Don't forget that the offsets of values from ESP into the stack change every time you push or pop data. Abusing this feature can create code that is hard to modify; if you use this feature throughout your code, it will make it difficult to push and pop other data items between the point you first push data onto the stack and the point you decide to access that data again using the "[ESP + offset]" memory addressing mode.

The previous section pointed out how to remove data from the stack by adding a constant to the ESP register. That code example could probably be written more safely as:

```
        push( eax );
        push( ebx );

        << Some code that winds up computing some values we want to keep
            into EAX and EBX >>

        if( Calculation_was_performed ) then

            << Overwrite saved values on stack with new EAX/EBX values.
              (so the pops that follow won't change the values in EAX/EBX.) >>

            mov( eax, [esp+4] );
            mov( ebx, [esp] );

        endif;
        pop( ebx );
        pop( eax );
```

In this code sequence, the calculated result was stored over the top of the values saved on the stack. Later on, when the program pops the values, it loads these calculated values into EAX and EBX.

3.10 Dynamic Memory Allocation and the Heap Segment

Although static and automatic variables are all simple programs may need, more sophisticated programs need the ability to allocate and deallocate storage dynamically (at runtime) under program control. In the C language, you would use the *malloc* and *free* functions for this purpose. C++ provides the *new* and *delete* operators. Pascal uses *new* and *dispose*. Other languages provide comparable facilities. These memory allocation routines share a couple of things in common: They let the programmer request how many bytes of storage to allocate, they return a *pointer* to the newly allocated storage, and they provide a facility for returning the storage to the system so the system can reuse it in a future allocation call. As you've probably guessed, HLA also provides a set of routines in the HLA Standard Library that handle memory allocation and deallocation.

The HLA Standard Library malloc and free routines handle the memory allocation and deallocation chores (respectively). The malloc routine uses the following calling sequence:

```
malloc( Number_of_Bytes_Requested );
```

The single parameter is a double word value specifying the number of bytes of storage you need. This procedure allocates storage in the *heap* segment in memory. The HLA malloc function locates an unused block of memory of the size you specify in the heap segment and marks the block as "in use" so that future calls to malloc will not allocate this same storage. After marking the block as "in use" the malloc routine returns a pointer to the first byte of this storage in the EAX register.

For many objects, you will know the number of bytes that you need in order to represent that object in memory. For example, if you wish to allocate storage for an uns32 variable, you could use the following call to the malloc routine:

```
malloc( 4 );
```

Although you can specify a literal constant as this example suggests, it's generally a poor idea to do so when allocating storage for a specific data type. Instead, use the HLA built-in *compile time function*[16] @size to compute the size of some data type. The @size function uses the following syntax:

```
@size( variable_or_type_name )
```

The @size function returns an unsigned integer constant that is the size of its parameter in bytes. So you should rewrite the previous call to malloc as follows:

```
malloc( @size( uns32 ));
```

This call will properly allocate a sufficient amount of storage for the specified object, regardless of its type. While it is unlikely that the number of bytes required by an uns32 object will ever change, this is not necessarily true for other data types, so you should always use @size rather than a literal constant in these calls.

Upon return from the malloc routine, the EAX register contains the address of the storage you have requested (see Figure 3-20 on the following page).

---

[16] A compile time function is one that HLA evaluates during the compilation of your program rather than at runtime.

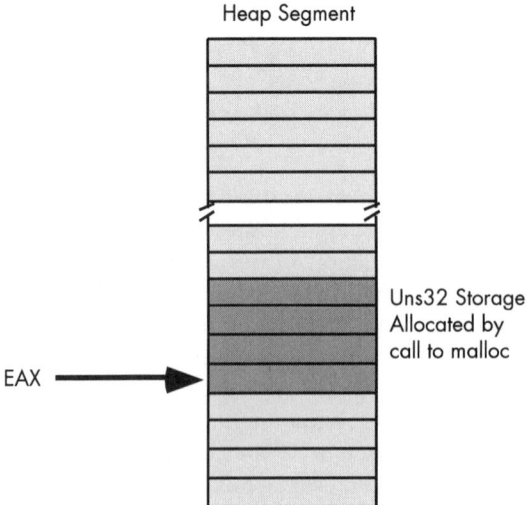

Heap Segment

Uns32 Storage
Allocated by
call to malloc

EAX

Figure 3-20: Call to malloc Returns a Pointer in the EAX Register.

To access the storage malloc allocates you must use a register indirect addressing mode. The following code sequence demonstrates how to assign the value 1234 to the uns32 variable malloc creates:

```
malloc( @size( uns32 ));
mov( 1234, (type uns32 [eax]));
```

Note the use of the type coercion operator. This is necessary in this example because anonymous variables don't have a type associated with them, and the constant 1234 could be a word or dword value. The type coercion operator eliminates the ambiguity.

The malloc routine may not always succeed. If there isn't a single contiguous block of free memory in the heap segment that is large enough to satisfy the request, then the malloc routine will raise an ex.MemoryAllocationFailure exception. If you do not provide a try..exception..endtry handler to deal with this situation, a memory allocation failure will cause your program to stop. Because most programs do not allocate massive amounts of dynamic storage using malloc, this exception rarely occurs. However, you should never assume that the memory allocation will always occur without error.

When you are done using a value that malloc allocates on the heap, you can release the storage (that is, mark it as "no longer in use") by calling the free procedure. The free routine requires a single parameter that must be an address returned by a previous call to malloc (that you have not already freed). The following code fragment demonstrates the nature of the malloc/free pairing:

```
        malloc( @size( uns32));

            << use the storage pointed at by EAX >>
            << Note: this code must not modify EAX >>

    free( eax );
```

This code demonstrates a very important point: In order to properly free the storage that malloc allocates, you must preserve the value that malloc returns. There are several ways to do this if you need to use EAX for some other purpose; you could save the pointer value on the stack using push and pop instructions, or you could save EAX's value in a variable until you need to free it.

Storage you release is available for reuse by future calls to the malloc routine. The ability to allocate storage when you need it and then free the storage for other use when you are done with it improves the memory efficiency of your program. By deallocating storage once you are finished with it, your program can reuse that storage for other purposes, allowing your program to operate with less memory than it would if you statically allocated storage for the individual objects.

Several problems can occur when you use pointers. You should be aware of a few common errors that beginning programmers make when using dynamic storage allocation routines like malloc and free:

- Mistake #1: Continuing to refer to storage after you free it. Once you return storage to the system via the call to free, you should no longer access that storage. Doing so may cause a protection fault or, worse yet, corrupt other data in your program without indicating an error.

- Mistake #2: Calling free twice to release a single block of storage. Doing so may accidentally free some other storage that you did not intend to release or, worse yet, it may corrupt the system memory management tables.

The next chapter will discuss some additional problems you will typically encounter when dealing with dynamically allocated storage.

The examples thus far in this section have all allocated storage for a single unsigned 32-bit object. Obviously you can allocate storage for any data type using a call to malloc by simply specifying the size of that object as malloc's parameter. It is also possible to allocate storage for a sequence of contiguous objects in memory when calling malloc. For example, the following code will allocate storage for a sequence of eight characters:

```
malloc( @size( char ) * 8 );
```

Note the use of the constant expression to compute the number of bytes required by an eight-character sequence. Because "@size(char)" always returns a constant value (one in this case), the compiler can compute the value of the expression "@size(char) * 8" without generating any extra machine instructions.

Calls to malloc always allocate multiple bytes of storage in contiguous memory locations. Hence the former call to malloc produces the sequence appearing in Figure 3-21.

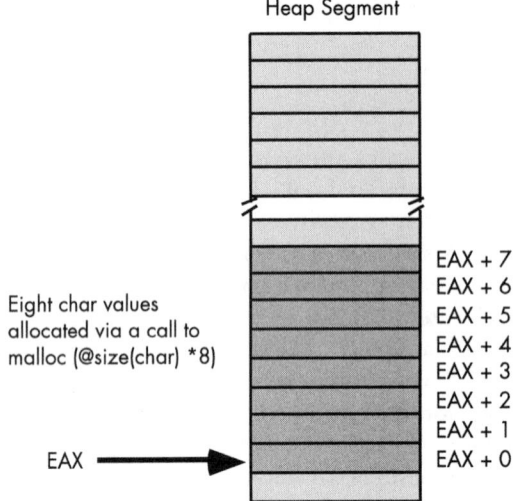

Figure 3-21: Allocating a Sequence of Eight-Character Objects Using Malloc.

To access these extra character values you use an offset from the base address (contained in EAX upon return from malloc). For example, "mov(ch, [eax + 2]);" stores the character found in CH into the third byte that malloc allocates. You can also use an addressing mode like "[EAX + EBX]" to step through each of the allocated objects under program control. For example, the following code will set all the characters in a block of 128 bytes to the NULL character (#0):

```
malloc( 128 );
for( mov( 0, ebx ); ebx < 128; add( 1, ebx ) ) do

    mov( 0, (type byte [eax+ebx]) );

endfor;
```

The next chapter discusses composite data structures (including arrays) and describes additional ways to deal with blocks of memory.

You should note that a call to malloc will actually allocate slightly more memory than you request. For one thing, memory allocation requests are generally of some minimum size (often a power of 2 between 4 and 16, though this is OS dependent). Furthermore, malloc requests also require a few bytes of overhead for each request (generally around 8 to 16 bytes) to keep track of allocated and free blocks. Therefore, it is not efficient to allocate a large number of small objects with individual calls to malloc. The overhead for each allocation may be greater than the storage you actually use. Typically, you'll use malloc to allocate storage for arrays or large records (structures) rather than small objects.

3.11   The INC and DEC Instructions

As the example in the last section indicates, indeed, as several examples up to this point have indicated, adding or subtracting one from a register or memory location is a very common operation. In fact, this operation is so common that Intel's engineers included a pair of instructions to perform these specific operations: the inc (increment) and dec (decrement) instructions.

The inc and dec instructions use the following syntax:

```
inc( mem/reg );
dec( mem/reg );
```

The single operand can be any legal 8-bit, 16-bit, or 32-bit register or memory operand. The inc instruction will add one to the specified operand; the dec instruction will subtract one from the specified operand.

These two instructions are slightly more efficient (they are smaller) than the corresponding add or sub instructions. There is also one slight difference between these two instructions and the corresponding add or sub instructions: they do not affect the carry flag.

As an example of the inc instruction, consider the example from the previous section, recoded to use inc rather than add:

```
        malloc( 128 );
        for( mov( 0, ebx ); ebx < 128; inc( ebx ) ) do

            mov( 0, (type byte [eax+ebx]) );

        endfor;
```

3.12   Obtaining the Address of a Memory Object

An earlier section of this chapter discusses how to use the address-of operator, "&", to take the address of a static variable.[17] Unfortunately, you cannot use the address-of operator to take the address of an automatic variable (one you declare in the var section); you cannot use it to compute the address of an anonymous variable, nor can you use this operator to take the address of a memory reference that uses an indexed or scaled indexed addressing mode (even if a static variable is part of the address expression). You may only use the address-of operator to take the address of a simple static object. Often, you will need to take the address of other memory objects as well; fortunately, the 80x86 provides the *load effective address* instruction, lea, to give you this capability.

The lea instruction uses the following syntax:

```
lea( reg32, Memory_operand );
```

---

[17] A static variable is one that you declare in the static, readonly, *or* storage of your program.

The first operand must be a 32-bit register; the second operand can be any legal memory reference using any valid memory addressing mode. This instruction will load the address of the specified memory location into the register. This instruction does not access or modify the value of the memory operand in any way.

Once you load the effective address of a memory location into a 32-bit general purpose register, you can use the register indirect, indexed, or scaled indexed addressing modes to access the data at the specified memory address. Consider the following code fragment:

```
static
    b:byte; @nostorage;
        byte 7, 0, 6, 1, 5, 2, 4, 3;
            .
            .
            .
    lea( ebx, b );
    for( mov( 0, ecx ); ecx < 8; inc( ecx )) do

        stdout.put( "[ebx+ecx]=", (type byte [ebx+ecx]), nl );

    endwhile;
```

This code steps through each of the eight bytes following the b label in the static section and prints their values. Note the use of the "[ebx+ecx]" addressing mode. The EBX register holds the base address of the list (that is, the address of the first item in the list), and ECX contains the byte index into the list.

3.13   For More Information

The CD-ROM that accompanies this book contains an older, 16-bit version of *The Art of Assembly Language Programming*. In that text you will find information about the 80x86's 16-bit addressing modes and segmentation. Please consult that documentation for more details.

4

CONSTANTS, VARIABLES, AND DATA TYPES

4.1 Chapter Overview

Chapter 2 discussed the basic format for data in memory. Chapter 3 covered how a computer system physically organizes that data in memory. This chapter finishes the discussion by connecting the concept of *data representation* to its actual physical representation. As the title implies, this chapter concerns itself with three main topics: constants, variables, and data structures. This chapter does not assume that you've had a formal course in data structures, though such experience would be useful.

This chapter discusses how to declare and use constants, scalar variables, integers, reals, data types, pointers, arrays, records/structures, unions, and namespaces. You must master these subjects before going on to the next chapter. Declaring and accessing arrays, in particular, seems to present a multitude of problems to beginning assembly language programmers. However, the rest of this text depends on your understanding of these data structures and their memory representation. Do not try to skim over this material with the expectation that you will pick it up as you need it later. You will need it right away, and trying to learn this material along with later material will only confuse you more.

4.2   Some Additional Instructions: INTMUL, BOUND, INTO

This chapter introduces arrays and other concepts that will require the expansion of your 80x86 instruction set knowledge. In particular, you will need to learn how to multiply two values; hence the first instruction we will look at is the intmul *(integer multiply)* instruction. Another common task when accessing arrays is to check to see if an array index is within bounds. The 80x86 bounds instruction provides a convenient way to check a register's value to see if it is within some range. Finally, the into *(interrupt on overflow)* instruction provides a quick check for signed arithmetic overflow. Although into isn't really necessary for array (or other data type access), its function is very similar to bound, hence the presentation at this point.

The intmul instruction takes one of the following forms:

```
// The following compute destreg = destreg * constant

intmul( constant, destreg16 );
intmul( constant, destreg32 );

// The following compute dest = src * constant

intmul( constant, srcreg16, destreg16 );
intmul( constant, srcmem16, destreg16 );

intmul( constant, srcreg32, destreg32 );
intmul( constant, srcmem32, destreg32 );

// The following compute dest = dest * src

intmul( srcreg16, destreg16 );
intmul( srcmem16, destreg16 );
intmul( srcreg32, destreg32 );
intmul( srcmem32, destreg32 );
```

Note that the syntax of the intmul instruction is different than the add and sub instructions. In particular, note that the destination operand must be a register (add and sub both allow a memory operand as a destination). Also note that intmul allows three operands when the first operand is a constant. Another important difference is that the intmul instruction only allows 16-bit and 32-bit operands; it does not multiply 8-bit operands.

intmul computes the product of its specified operands and stores the result into the destination register. If an overflow occurs (which is always a signed overflow, because intmul only multiplies signed integer values), then this instruction sets both the carry and overflow flags. intmul leaves the other condition code flags undefined (so, for example, you cannot check the sign flag or the zero flag after intmul and expect them to tell you anything about the intmul operation).

The bound instruction checks a 16-bit or 32-bit register to see if it is between one of two values. If the value is outside this range, the program raises an exception and aborts. This instruction is particularly useful for checking to see if an array index is within a given range. The bound instruction takes one of the following forms:

```
bound( reg16, LBconstant, UBconstant );
bound( reg32, LBconstant, UBconstant );

bound( reg16, Mem16[2] );[1]
bound( reg32, Mem32[2] );[2]
```

The bound instruction compares its register operand against an unsigned lower bound value and an unsigned upper bound value to ensure that the register is in the range:

```
lower_bound <= register <= upper_bound
```

The form of the bound instruction with three operands compares the register against the second and third parameters (the lower bound and upper bound, respectively).[3] The bound instruction with two operands checks the register against one of the following ranges:

$$Mem_{16}[0] <= register_{16} <= Mem_{16}[2]$$
$$Mem_{32}[0] <= register_{32} <= Mem_{32}[4]$$

If the specified register is not within the given range, then the 80x86 raises an exception. You can trap this exception using the HLA try..endtry exception handling statement. The *excepts.hhf* header file defines an exception, ex.BoundInstr, specifically for this purpose. The program in Listing 4-1 demonstrates how to use the bound instruction to check some user input.

Listing 4-1: Demonstration of the BOUND Instruction.

```
program BoundDemo;
#include( "stdlib.hhf" );

static
    InputValue:int32;
    GoodInput:boolean;

begin BoundDemo;
```

[1] The "[2]" suggests that this variable must be an array of two consecutive word values in memory.

[2] Likewise, this memory operand must be two consecutive dwords in memory.

[3] This form isn't a true 80x86 instruction. HLA converts this form of the bound instruction to the two-operand form by creating two readonly memory variables initialized with the specified constants.

```
// Repeat until the user enters a good value:

repeat

    // Assume the user enters a bad value.

    mov( false, GoodInput );

    // Catch bad numeric input via the try..endtry statement.

    try

        stdout.put( "Enter an integer between 1 and 10: " );
        stdin.flushInput();
        stdin.geti32();

        mov( eax, InputValue );

        // Use the BOUND instruction to verify that the
        // value is in the range 1..10.

        bound( eax, 1, 10 );

        // If we get to this point, the value was in the
        // range 1..10, so set the boolean "GoodInput"
        // flag to true so we can exit the loop.

        mov( true, GoodInput );


        // Handle inputs that are not legal integers.

    exception( ex.ConversionError )

      stdout.put( "Illegal numeric format, reenter", nl );


        // Handle integer inputs that don't fit into an int32.

    exception( ex.ValueOutOfRange )

      stdout.put( "Value is *way* too big, reenter", nl );


        // Handle values outside the range 1..10 (BOUND instruction)

      /*
    exception( ex.BoundInstr )
```

```
            stdout.put
            (
                "Value was ",
                InputValue,
                ", it must be between 1 and 10, reenter",
                nl
            );
          */

        endtry;

    until( GoodInput );
    stdout.put( "The value you entered, ", InputValue, " is valid.", nl );

end BoundDemo;
```

The into instruction, like bound, also generates an exception under certain conditions. Specifically, into generates an exception if the overflow flag is set. Normally, you would use into immediately after a signed arithmetic operation (e.g., intmul) to see if an overflow occurs. If the overflow flag is not set, the system ignores the into instruction; however, if the overflow flag is set, then the into instruction raises the HLA ex.IntoInstr exception. The program in Listing 4-2 demonstrates the use of the into instruction.

Listing 4-2: Demonstration of the INTO Instruction.

```
program INTOdemo;
#include( "stdlib.hhf" );

static
    LOperand:int8;
    ResultOp:int8;

begin INTOdemo;

    // The following try..endtry checks for bad numeric
    // input and handles the integer overflow check:

    try

        // Get the first of two operands:

        stdout.put( "Enter a small integer value (-128..+127):" );
        stdin.geti8();
        mov( al, LOperand );

        // Get the second operand:
```

```
        stdout.put( "Enter a second small integer value (-128..+127):" );
        stdin.geti8();

        // Produce their sum and check for overflow:

        add( LOperand, al );
        into();

        // Display the sum:

        stdout.put( "The eight-bit sum is ", (type int8 al), nl );


        // Handle bad input here:

    exception( ex.ConversionError )

        stdout.put( "You entered illegal characters in the number", nl );


        // Handle values that don't fit in a byte here:

    exception( ex.ValueOutOfRange )

        stdout.put( "The value must be in the range -128..+127", nl );


        // Handle integer overflow here:

    /*
    exception( ex.IntoInstr )

        stdout.put
        (
            "The sum of the two values is outside the range -128..+127",
            nl
        );
    */

    endtry;

end INTOdemo;
```

4.3   The TBYTE Data Types

HLA lets you declare ten-byte variables using the *tbyte* data type. Because HLA
does not allow the use of 80-bit non–floating point constants, you may not
associate an initializer with this data type. However, if you wish to reserve storage
for an 80-bit variable, you may use this data type to do so.

The tbyte directive allocates ten bytes of storage. There are two data types indigenous to the 80x87 (math coprocessor) family that use a ten-byte data type: ten-byte BCD values and extended precision (80-bit) floating point values. Because you would normally use the real80 data type for floating point values, about the only purpose of tbyte in HLA is to reserve storage for a ten-byte BCD value (or other data type that needs 80 bits). The chapter on arithmetic will provide some insight into the use of this data type. However, except for very advanced applications, you could probably ignore this data type and not suffer.

4.4   HLA Constant and Value Declarations

HLA's const and val sections let you declare symbolic constants. The const section lets you declare identifiers whose value is constant throughout compilation and runtime; the val section lets you declare symbolic constants whose values can change at compile time, but whose values are constant at runtime (that is, the same name can have a different value at several points in the source code, but the value of a val symbol at a given point in the program cannot change while the program is running).

The const section appears in the same declaration section of your program that contains the static, readonly, storage, and var sections. It begins with the const reserved word and has a syntax that is nearly identical to the readonly section; that is, the const section contains a list of identifiers followed by a type and a constant expression. The following example will give you an idea of what the const section looks like:

```
const
    pi:                real32 := 3.14159;
    MaxIndex:          uns32  := 15;
    Delimiter:         char   := '/';
    BitMask:           byte   := $F0;
    DebugActive:       boolean:= true;
```

Once you declare these constants in this manner, you may use the symbolic identifiers anywhere the corresponding literal constant is legal. These constants are known as *manifest constants*. A manifest constant is a symbolic representation of a constant that allows you to substitute the literal value for the symbol anywhere in the program. Contrast this with readonly variables; a readonly variable is certainly a constant value because you cannot change such a variable at runtime. However, a memory location associated with readonly variables and the operating system, not the HLA compiler, enforces the read-only attribute at runtime. Although it will certainly crash your program when it runs, it is perfectly legal to write an instruction like "mov(eax, ReadOnlyVar);". On the other hand, it is no more legal to write "mov(eax, MaxIndex);" (using the declaration above) than it is to write "mov(eax, 15);". In fact, both of these statements are equivalent because the compiler substitutes "15" for MaxIndex whenever it encounters this manifest constant.

If there is absolutely no ambiguity about a constant's type, then you may declare a constant by specifying only the name and the constant's value, omitting the type specification. In the example earlier, the pi, Delimiter, MaxIndex, and DebugActive constants could use the following declarations:

```
const
    pi              := 3.14159;     // Default type is real80.
    MaxIndex        := 15;          // Default type is uns32.
    Delimiter       := '/';         // Default type is char.
    DebugActive     := true;        // Default type is boolean.
```

Symbolic constants that have an integer literal constant are always given the smallest possible unsigned type if the constant is zero or positive, or the smallest possible integer type (int8, int16, and so on) if the value is negative.

Constant declarations are great for defining "magic" numbers that might possibly change during program modification. The program in Listing 4-3 provides an example of using constants to parameterize "magic" values in the program.

Listing 4-3: Data Alignment Program Rewritten Using CONST Definitions.

```
program ConstDemo;
#include( "stdlib.hhf" );

const
    MemToAllocate   := 4_000_000;
    NumDWords       := MemToAllocate div 4;
    MisalignBy      := 62;

    MainRepetitions := 1000;
    DataRepetitions := 999_900;

    CacheLineSize   := 16;

begin ConstDemo;

    //console.cls();
    stdout.put
    (
        "Memory Alignment Exercise",nl,
        nl,
        "Using a watch (preferably a stopwatch), time the execution of", nl
        "the following code to determine how many seconds it takes to", nl
        "execute.", nl
        nl
        "Press Enter to begin timing the code:"
    );
```

```
// Allocate enough dynamic memory to ensure that it does not
// all fit inside the cache.  Note: the machine had better have
// at least four megabytes free or virtual memory will kick in
// and invalidate the timing.

malloc( MemToAllocate );

// Zero out the memory (this loop really exists just to
// ensure that all memory is mapped in by the OS).

mov( NumDWords, ecx );
repeat

    dec( ecx );
    mov( 0, (type dword [eax+ecx*4]));

until( !ecx );  // Repeat until ECX = 0.


// Okay, wait for the user to press the Enter key.

stdin.readLn();

// Note: as processors get faster and faster, you may
// want to increase the size of the following constant.
// Execution time for this loop should be approximately
// 10-30 seconds.

mov( MainRepetitions, edx );
add( MisalignBy, eax );      // Force misalignment of data.

repeat

    mov( DataRepetitions, ecx );
    align( CacheLineSize );
    repeat

        sub( 4, ecx );
        mov( [eax+ecx*4], ebx );
        mov( [eax+ecx*4], ebx );
        mov( [eax+ecx*4], ebx );
        mov( [eax+ecx*4], ebx );

    until( !ecx );
    dec( edx );

until( !edx ); // Repeat until EAX is zero.

stdout.put( stdio.bell, "Stop timing and record time spent", nl, nl );
```

```
        // Okay, time the aligned access.

        stdout.put
        (
            "Press Enter again to begin timing access to aligned variable:"
        );
        stdin.readLn();

        // Note: if you change the constant above, be sure to change
        // this one, too!

        mov( MainRepetitions, edx );
        sub( MisalignBy, eax );      // Realign the data.
        repeat

            mov( DataRepetitions, ecx );
            align( CacheLineSize );
            repeat

                sub( 4, ecx );
                mov( [eax+ecx*4], ebx );
                mov( [eax+ecx*4], ebx );
                mov( [eax+ecx*4], ebx );
                mov( [eax+ecx*4], ebx );

            until( !ecx );
            dec( edx );

        until( !edx ); // Repeat until EAX is zero.

        stdout.put( stdio.bell, "Stop timing and record time spent", nl, nl );
        free( eax );


end ConstDemo;
```

4.4.1 Constant Types

Manifest constants can be any of the HLA primitive types plus a few of the composite types this chapter discusses. Chapters 1, 2, and 3 discussed most of the primitive types; the primitive types include the following:[4]

- Boolean constants (true or false).
- Uns8 constants (0..255).
- Uns16 constants (0..65535).
- Uns32 constants (0..4,294,967,295).

---

[4] This is not a complete list. HLA also supports 64-bit and 128-bit data types. We'll discuss those later.

- Int8 constants (-128..+127).

- Int16 constants (-32768..+32767).

- Int32 constants (-2,147,483,648..+2,147,483,647).

- Char constants (any ASCII character with a character code in the range 0..255).

- Byte constants (any eight-bit value including integers, booleans, and characters).

- Word constants (any 16-bit value).

- Dword constants (any 32-bit value).

- Real32 constants (floating point values).

- Real64 constants (floating point values).

- Real80 constants (floating point values).

In addition to the constant types appearing above, the const section supports six additional constant types:

- String constants

- Text constants

- Enumerated constant values

- Array constants

- Record/Union constants

- Character set constants

These data types are the subject of this chapter, and the discussion of most of them appears a little later. However, the string and text constants are sufficiently important to warrant an early discussion of these constant types.

4.4.2 *String and Character Literal Constants*

HLA, like most programming languages, draws a distinction between a sequence of characters, a *string*, and a single character. This distinction is present both in the type declarations and in the syntax for literal character and string constants. Until now, this text has not drawn a fine distinction between character and string literal constants; now is time to do so.

String literal constants consist of a sequence of zero or more characters surrounded by the ASCII quote characters. The following are all examples of legal literal string constants:

```
"This is a string"      // String with 16 characters.
""                      // Zero length string.
"a"                     // String with a single character.
"123"                   // String of length three.
```

A string of length one is not the same thing as a character constant. HLA uses two completely different internal representations for character and string values. Hence, "a" is not a character value; it is a string value that just happens to contain a single character.

Character literal constants take a couple forms, but the most common form consists of a single character surrounded by ASCII apostrophe characters:

'2'	// Character constant equivalent to ASCII code $32.
'a'	// Character constant for lower case 'A'.

As noted above, "a" and 'a' are not equivalent.

Those who are familiar with C, C++, or Java probably recognize these literal constant forms, because they are similar to the character and string constants in C/C++/Java. In fact, this text has made a tacit assumption to this point that you are somewhat familiar with C/C++ insofar as examples appearing up to this point use character and string constants without an explicit definition of them.[5]

Another similarity between C/C++ strings and HLAs is the automatic concatenation of adjacent literal string constants within your program. For example, HLA concatenates the two string constants

```
"First part of string, " "second part of string"
```

to form the single string constant

```
"First part of string, second part of string"
```

Beyond these few similarities, however, HLA strings and C/C++ strings differ. For example, C/C++ strings let you specify special character values using the escape character sequence consisting of a backslash character followed by one or more special characters; HLA does not use this escape character mechanism. HLA does provide, however, several other ways to insert special characters into a string or character constant.

Because HLA does not allow escape character sequences in literal string and character constants, the first question you might ask is "How does one embed quote characters in string constants and apostrophe characters in character constants?" To solve this problem, HLA uses the same technique as Pascal and many other languages: You insert two quotes in a string constant to represent a single quote or you place two apostrophes in a character constant to represent a single apostrophe character, e.g.,

```
"He wrote a ""Hello World"" program as an example."
```

---

[5] Apologies are due to those of you who do not know C/C++/Java or a language that shares these string and constant definitions.

The previous is equivalent to:

```
He wrote a "Hello World" program as an example.

''''
```

The following is equivalent to a single apostrophe character.

HLA provides a couple of other features that eliminate the need for escape characters. In addition to concatenating two adjacent string constants to form a longer string constant, HLA will also concatenate any combination of adjacent character and string constants to form a single string constant:

```
'1' '2' '3' // Equivalent to "123"
"He wrote a " '"' "Hello World" '"' " program as an example."
```

Note that the two "He wrote . . ." strings in the these examples are identical to HLA.

HLA provides a second way to specify character constants that handles all the other C/C++ escape character sequences: the ASCII code literal character constant. This literal character constant form uses the syntax:

```
#integer_constant
```

This form creates a character constant whose value is the ASCII code specified by integer_constant. The numeric constant can be a decimal, hexadecimal, or binary value, e.g.,

```
#13        #$d        #%1101      // All three are the same character,
                                  // a carriage return.
```

Because you may concatenate character literals with strings, and the *#constant* form is a character literal; the following are all legal strings:

```
"Hello World" #13 #10      // #13 #10 is the Windows newline sequence
                           // (carriage return followed by line feed).

"Error: Bad Value" #7      // #7 is the bell character.
"He wrote a " #$22 "Hello World" #$22 " program as an example."
```

Because $22 is the ASCII code for the quote character, this last example is yet a third form of the *"He wrote . . ."* string literal.

4.4.3 String and Text Constants in the CONST Section

String and text constants in the const section use the following declaration syntax:

```
const
    AStringConst:    string := "123";
    ATextConst:      text   := "123";
```

Other than the data type of these two constants, their declarations are identical. However, their behavior in an HLA program is quite different.

Whenever HLA encounters a symbolic string constant within your program, it substitutes the string literal constant in place of the string name. So a statement like "stdout.put(AStringConst);" prints the string "123" (without quotes, of course) to the display. No real surprise here.

Whenever HLA encounters a symbolic text constant within your program, it substitutes the text of that string (rather than the string literal constant) for the identifier. That is, HLA substitutes the characters between the delimiting quotes in place of the symbolic text constant. Therefore, the following statement is perfectly legal given the previous declarations:

```
        mov( ATextConst, al );        // equivalent to mov( 123, al );
```

Note that substituting AStringConst for ATextConst in this example is illegal:

```
        mov( AStringConst, al );      // equivalent to mov( "123", al );
```

This latter example is illegal because you cannot move a string literal constant into the AL register.

Whenever HLA encounters a symbolic text constant in your program, it immediately substitutes the value of the text constant's string for that text constant and continues the compilation as though you had written the text constant's value rather than the symbolic identifier in your program. This can save some typing and help make your programs a little more readable if you often enter some sequence of text in your program. For example, consider the nl (newline) text constant declaration found in the HLA *stdio.hhf* library header file:

```
const
    nl: text := "#$d #$a";  // Windows version.  Linux is just a line feed.
```

Whenever HLA encounters the symbol nl, it immediately substitutes the value of the string "#$d #$a" for the nl identifier. When HLA sees the #$d (carriage return) character constant followed by the #$a (line feed) character constants, it concatenates the two to form the string containing the Windows newline sequence (a carriage return followed by a line feed). Consider the following two statements:

```
stdout.put( "Hello World", nl );
stdout.put( "Hello World" nl );
```

(Notice that the second statement above does not separate the string literal and
the nl symbol with a comma.) In the first example, HLA emits code that prints
the string "Hello World" and then emits some additional code that prints a
newline sequence. In the second example, HLA expands the nl symbol as follows:

```
stdout.put( "Hello World" #$d #$a );
```

Now HLA sees a string literal constant ("Hello World") followed by two character
constants. It concatenates the three of them together to form a single string and
then prints this string with a single call. Therefore, leaving off the comma
between the string literal and the nl symbol produces slightly more efficient
code. Keep in mind that this only works with string literal constants. You cannot
concatenate string variables, or a string variable with a string literal, by using this
technique.

Linux users should note that the Linux end-of-line sequence is just a single
line feed character. Therefore, the declaration for nl is slightly different in Linux
(to always guarantee that nl expands to a string constant rather than a character
constant).

In the constant section, if you specify only a constant identifier and a string
constant (i.e., you do not supply a type), HLA defaults to type string. If you want
to declare a text constant you must explicitly supply the type.

```
const
    AStrConst := "String Constant";
    ATextConst: text := "mov( 0, eax );";
```

4.4.4 Constant Expressions

Thus far, this chapter has given the impression that a symbolic constant definition consists of an identifier, an optional type, and a literal constant. Actually,
HLA constant declarations can be a lot more sophisticated than this because
HLA allows the assignment of a constant expression, not just a literal constant, to
a symbolic constant. The generic constant declaration takes one of the following
two forms:

```
Identifier : typeName := constant_expression ;
Identifier := constant_expression ;
```

Constant expressions take the familiar form you're used to in high level languages like C/C++ and Pascal. They may contain literal constant values, previously declared symbolic constants, and various arithmetic operators. The
following lists some of the operations possible in a constant expression:

Arithmetic Operators

-	(unary negation) Negates the expression immediately following the "-".
*	Multiplies the integer or real values around the asterisk.
div	Divides the left integer operand by the right integer operand producing an integer (truncated) result.
mod	Divides the left integer operand by the right integer operand producing an integer remainder.
/	Divides the left numeric operand by the second numeric operand producing a floating point result.
+	Adds the left and right numeric operands.
-	Subtracts the right numeric operand from the left numeric operand.

Comparison Operators

=, ==	Compares left operand with right operand. Returns TRUE if equal.
<>, !=	Compares left operand with right operand. Returns TRUE if not equal.
<	Returns true if left operand is less than right operand.
<=	Returns true if left operand is <= right operand.
>	Returns true if left operand is greater than right operand.
>=	Returns true if left operand is >= right operand.

Logical Operators:[6]

&	For boolean operands, returns the logical AND of the two operands.
|	For boolean operands, returns the logical OR of the two operands.
^	For boolean operands, returns the logical exclusive-OR.
!	Returns the logical NOT of the single operand following "!".

Bitwise Logical Operators:

&	For integer numeric operands, returns bitwise AND of the operands.
|	For integer numeric operands, returns bitwise OR of the operands.
^	For integer numeric operands, returns bitwise XOR of the operands.
!	For an integer numeric operand, returns bitwise NOT of the operand.

String Operators:

'+'	Returns the concatenation of the left and right string operands.

The constant expression operators follow standard precedence rules; you may use the parentheses to override the precedence if necessary. See the HLA Reference Manual on the CD-ROM for the exact precedence relationships between the operators. In general, if the precedence isn't obvious, use parentheses to

---

[6] Note to C/C++ and Java users. HLA's constant expressions use complete boolean evaluation rather than short-circuit boolean evaluation. Hence, HLA constant expressions do not behave identically to C/C++/Java expressions.

exactly state the order of evaluation. HLA actually provides a few more operators than these, though the ones above are the ones you will most commonly use; the HLA documentation provides a complete list of constant expression operators.

If an identifier appears in a constant expression, that identifier must be a constant identifier that you have previously defined in your program. You may not use variable identifiers in a constant expression; their values are not defined at compile time when HLA evaluates the constant expression. Also, don't confuse compile time and run-time operations:

```
// Constant expression, computed while HLA is compiling your program:

const
        x           := 5;
        y           := 6;
        Sum         := x + y;



// Run-time calculation, computed while your program is running, long after
// HLA has compiled it:

    mov( x, al );
    add( y, al );
```

HLA directly interprets the value of a constant expression during compilation. It does not emit any machine instructions to compute "x+y" in the constant expression above. Instead, it directly computes the sum of these two constant values. From that point forward in the program, HLA associates the value 11 with the constant Sum just as if the program had contained the statement "Sum := 11;" rather than "Sum := x+y;" On the other hand, HLA does not precompute the value 11 in AL for the mov and add instructions above;[7] it faithfully emits the object code for these two instructions and the 80x86 computes their sum when the program is run (sometime after the compilation is complete).

In general, constant expressions don't get very sophisticated in assembly language programs. Usually, you're adding, subtracting, or multiplying two integer values. For example, the following const section defines a set of constants that have consecutive values:

```
const
        TapeDAT             :=      1;
        Tape8mm             :=      TapeDAT + 1;
        TapeQIC80           :=      Tape8mm + 1;
        TapeTravan          :=      TapeQIC80 + 1;
        TapeDLT             :=      TapeTravan + 1;
```

[7] Technically, if HLA had an optimizer it could replace these two instructions with a single "mov(11, al);" instruction. HLA 1.x, however, does not do this.

The constants above have the following values: TapeDAT = 1, Tape8mm = 2, TapeQIC80 = 3, TapeTravan = 4, and TapeDLT = 5.

4.4.5 Multiple CONST Sections and Their Order in an HLA Program

Although const sections must appear in the declaration section of an HLA program (e.g., between the "program *pgmname,*" header and the corresponding "begin *pgmname,*" statement), they do not have to appear before or after any other items in the declaration section. In fact, like the variable declaration sections, you can place multiple const sections in a declaration section. The only restriction on HLA constant declarations is that you must declare any constant symbol before you use it in your program.

Some C/C++ programmers, for example, are more comfortable writing their constant declarations as follows (because this is closer to C/C++'s syntax for declaring constants):

```
const        TapeDAT        :=    1;
const        Tape8mm        :=    TapeDAT + 1;
const        TapeQIC80      :=    Tape8mm + 1;
const        TapeTravan     :=    TapeQIC80 + 1;
const        TapeDLT        :=    TapeTravan + 1;
```

The placement of the const section in a program seems to be a personal issue among programmers. Other than the requirements of defining all constants before you use them, you may feel free to insert the constant declaration section anywhere in the declaration section. Some programmers prefer to put all their const declarations at the beginning of their declaration section, some programmers prefer to spread them throughout declaration section, defining the constants just before they need them for some other purpose. Putting all your constants at the beginning of an HLA declaration section is probably the wisest choice right now. Later in this text you'll see reasons why you might want to define your constants later in a declaration section.

4.4.6 The HLA VAL Section

You cannot change the value of a constant you define in the const section. While this seems perfectly reasonable (constants after all, are supposed to be, well, constant), there are different ways we can define the term "constant" and const objects only follow the rules of one specific definition. HLA's val section lets you define constant objects that follow slightly different rules. This section will discuss the val section and the difference between val constants and const constants.

The concept of "const-ness" can exist at two different times: while HLA is compiling your program and later when your program executes (and HLA is no longer running). All reasonable definitions of a constant require that a value not change while the program is running. Whether or not the value of a "constant" can change during compilation is a separate issue. The difference between HLA const objects and HLA val objects is whether the value of the constant can change during compilation.

Once you define a constant in the const section, the value of that constant is immutable from that point forward *both at runtime and while HLA is compiling your program.* Therefore, an instruction like "mov(SymbolicCONST, EAX);" always moves the same value into EAX, regardless of where this instruction appears in the HLA main program. Once you define the symbol *SymbolicCONST* in the const section, this symbol has the same value from that point forward.

The HLA val section lets you declare symbolic constants, just like the const section. However, HLA val constants can change their value throughout the source code in your program. The following HLA declarations are perfectly legal:

```
val      InitialValue      := 0;
const    SomeVal           := InitialValue + 1;      // = 1
const    AnotherVal        := InitialValue + 2;      // = 2

val      InitialValue      := 100;
const    ALargerVal        := InitialValue;          // = 100
const    LargeValTwo       := InitialValue*2;        // = 200
```

All of the symbols appearing in the const sections use the symbolic value InitialValue as part of the definition. Note, however, that InitialValue has different values at various points in this code sequence; at the beginning of the code sequence InitialValue has the value zero, while later it has the value 100.

Remember, at runtime a val object is not a variable; it is still a manifest constant and HLA will substitute the current value of a val identifier for that identifier.[8] Statements like "mov(25, InitialValue);" are no more legal than "mov(25, 0);" or "mov(25, 100);".

4.4.7 *Modifying VAL Objects at Arbitrary Points in Your Programs*

If you declare all your val objects in the declaration section, it would seem that you would not be able to change the value of a val object between the begin and end statements of your program. After all, the val section must appear in the declaration section of the program, and the declaration section ends before the begin statement. Later, you will learn that most val object modifications occur between the begin and end statements; hence, HLA must provide some way to change the value of a val object outside the declaration section. The mechanism to do this is the "?" operator.

Not only does HLA allow you to change the value of a val object outside the declaration section, it allows you to change the value of a val object almost *anywhere* in the program. Anywhere a space is allowed inside an HLA program, you can insert a statement of the form:

```
? ValIdentifier := constant_expression ;
```

---

[8] In this context, *current* means the value last assigned to a val object looking backward in the source code.

This means that you could write a short program like the one appearing in Listing 4-4.

Listing 4-4: Demonstration of VAL Redefinition Using "?" Operator.

```
program VALdemo;
#include( "stdlib.hhf" )

val
    NotSoConstant := 0;

begin VALdemo;

    mov( NotSoConstant, eax );
    stdout.put( "EAX = ", (type uns32 eax ), nl );

    ?NotSoConstant := 10;
    mov( NotSoConstant, eax );
    stdout.put( "EAX = ", (type uns32 eax ), nl );

    ?NotSoConstant := 20;
    mov( NotSoConstant, eax );
    stdout.put( "EAX = ", (type uns32 eax ), nl );

    ?NotSoConstant := 30;
    mov( NotSoConstant, eax );
    stdout.put( "EAX = ", (type uns32 eax ), nl );

end VALdemo;
```

You probably won't have much use for val objects at this time. When this text discusses HLA's macros and compile time language, you'll see how useful val objects can be to you.

4.5   The HLA TYPE Section

Let's say that you simply do not like the names that HLA uses for declaring byte, word, double word, real, and other variables. Let's say that you prefer Pascal's naming convention or, perhaps, C's naming convention. You want to use terms like *integer, float, double,* or whatever. If HLA were Pascal you could redefine the names in the type section of the program. With C you could use a #define or a typedef statement to accomplish the task. Well, HLA, like Pascal, has its own type statement that also lets you create aliases of these names. The following example demonstrates how to set up some C-/C++-/Pascal-compatible names in your HLA programs:

```
type
    integer:            int32;
    float:              real32;
```

```
        double:                 real64;
        colors:                 byte;
```

Now you can declare your variables with more meaningful statements like:

```
static
        i:                      integer;
        x:                      float;
        HouseColor:             colors;
```

If you are an Ada, C/C++, or FORTRAN programmer (or any other language, for that matter), you can pick type names you're more comfortable with. Of course, this doesn't change how the 80x86 or HLA reacts to these variables one iota, but it does let you create programs that are easier to read and understand because the type names are more indicative of the actual underlying types. One warning for C/C++ programmers: Don't get too excited and go off and define an int data type. Unfortunately, int is an 80x86 machine instruction (interrupt) and therefore, this is a reserved word in HLA.

The type section is useful for much more than creating type isomorphisms (that is, giving a new name to an existing type). The following sections will demonstrate many of the possible things you can do in the type section.

4.6 ENUM and HLA Enumerated Data Types

In a previous section discussing constants and constant expressions, you saw the following example:

```
const        TapeDAT         :=      1;
const        Tape8mm         :=      TapeDAT + 1;
const        TapeQIC80       :=      Tape8mm + 1;
const        TapeTravan      :=      TapeQIC80 + 1;
const        TapeDLT         :=      TapeTravan + 1;
```

This example demonstrates how to use constant expressions to develop a set of constants that contain unique, consecutive values. There are, however, a couple of problems with this approach. First, it involves a lot of typing (and extra reading when reviewing this program). Second, it's very easy make a mistake when creating long lists of unique constants and reuse or skip some values. The HLA enum type provides a better way to create a list of constants with unique values.

enum is an HLA type declaration that lets you associate a list of names with a new type. HLA associates a unique value with each name (that is, it *enumerates* the list). The enum keyword typically appears in the type section, and you use it as follows:

```
type
        enumTypeID:             enum { comma_separated_list_of_names };
```

The symbol enumTypeID becomes a new type whose values are specified by the specified list of names. As a concrete example, consider the data type TapeDrives and a corresponding variable declaration of type TypeDrives:

```
type
    TapeDrives: enum{ TapeDAT, Tape8mm, TapeQIC80, TapeTravan, TapeDLT};

static
    BackupUnit:    TapeDrives := TapeDAT;



    .
    .
    .


    mov( BackupUnit, al );
    if( al = Tape8mm ) then

        ...

    endif;

    // etc.
```

By default, HLA reserves one byte of storage for enumerated data types. So the backupunit variable will consume one byte of memory, and you would typically use an 8-bit register to access it.[9] As for the constants, HLA associates consecutive uns8 constant values starting at zero with each of the enumerated identifiers. In the TapeDrives example, the tape drive identifiers would have the values TapeDAT=0, Tape8mm=1, TapeQIC80=2, TapeTravan=3, and TapeDLT=4. You may use these constants exactly as though you had defined them with these values in a const section.

4.7   Pointer Data Types

Some people refer to pointers as scalar data types; others refer to them as composite data types. This text will treat them as scalar data types even though they exhibit some tendencies of both scalar and composite data types.

Of course, the place to start is with the question "What is a pointer?" Now you've probably experienced pointers firsthand in the Pascal, C, or Ada programming languages, and you're probably getting worried right now. Almost everyone has a real bad experience when they first encounter pointers in a high level language. Well, fear not! Pointers are actually *easier* to deal with in assembly language. Besides, most of the problems you had with pointers probably had nothing to do with pointers, but rather with the linked list and tree data structures you were trying to implement with them. Pointers, on the other hand, have many uses in assembly language that have nothing to do with linked lists, trees,

---

[9] HLA provides a mechanism by which you can specify that enumerated data types consume two or four bytes of memory. See the HLA documentation for more details.

and other scary data structures. Indeed, simple data structures like arrays and records often involve the use of pointers. So if you've got some deep-rooted fear about pointers, well forget everything you know about them. You're going to learn how *great* pointers really are.

Probably the best place to start is with the definition of a pointer. Just exactly what is a pointer, anyway? Unfortunately, high level languages like Pascal tend to hide the simplicity of pointers behind a wall of abstraction. This added complexity (which exists for good reason, by the way) tends to frighten programmers because *they don't understand what's going on.*

Now if you're afraid of pointers, well, let's just ignore them for the time being and work with an array. Consider the following array declaration in Pascal:

```
M: array [0..1023] of integer;
```

Even if you don't know Pascal, the concept here is pretty easy to understand. M is an array with 1024 integers in it, indexed from *M[0]* to *M[1023]*. Each one of these array elements can hold an integer value that is independent of all the others. In other words, this array gives you 1024 different integer variables, each of which you refer to by number (the array index) rather than by name.

If you encounter a program that has the statement "M[0]:=100;" you probably wouldn't have to think at all about what is happening with this statement. It is storing the value 100 into the first element of the array M. Now consider the following two statements:

```
i := 0; (* Assume "i" is an integer variable *)
M [i] := 100;
```

You should agree, without too much hesitation, that these two statements perform the same operation as "M[0]:=100;". Indeed, you're probably willing to agree that you can use any integer expression in the range 0...1023 as an index into this array. The following statements *still* perform the same operation as our single assignment to index zero:

```
i := 5;                (* assume all variables are integers*)
j := 10;
k := 50;
m [i*j-k] := 100;
```

"Okay, so what's the point?" you're probably thinking. "Anything that produces an integer in the range 0...1023 is legal. So what?" Okay, how about this:

```
M [1] := 0;
M [ M [1] ] := 100;
```

Whoa! Now that takes a few moments to digest. However, if you take it slowly, it makes sense, and you'll discover that these two instructions perform the exact same operation you've been doing all along. The first statement stores zero into array element M[1]. The second statement fetches the value of M[1], which is an integer so you can use it as an array index into M, and uses that value (zero) to control where it stores the value 100.

If you're willing to accept the above as reasonable, perhaps bizarre, but usable nonetheless, then you'll have no problems with pointers. *Because m[1] is a pointer!* Well, not really, but if you were to change "M" to "memory" and treat this array as all of memory, this is the exact definition of a pointer.

4.7.1   Using Pointers in Assembly Language

A *pointer* is simply a memory location whose value is the address (or index, if you prefer) of some other memory location. Pointers are very easy to declare and use in an assembly language program. You don't even have to worry about array indices or anything like that.

An HLA pointer is a 32-bit value that may contain the address of some other variable. If you have a dword variable p that contains $1000_0000, then p "points" at memory location $1000_0000. To access the dword that p points at, you could use code like the following:

```
mov( p, ebx );           // Load EBX with the value of pointer p.
mov( [ebx], eax );       // Fetch the data that p points at.
```

By loading the value of p into EBX this code loads the value $1000_0000 into EBX (assuming p contains $1000_0000 and, therefore, points at memory location $1000_0000). The second instruction above loads the EAX register with the word starting at the location whose offset appears in EBX. Because EBX now contains $1000_0000, this will load EAX from locations $1000_0000 through $1000_0003.

Why not just load EAX directly from location $1000_0000 using an instruction like "mov(mem, EAX);" (assuming mem is at address $1000_0000)? Well, there are a lot of reasons. But the primary reason is that this single instruction always loads EAX from location mem. You cannot change the address from which it loads EAX. The former instructions, however, always load EAX from the location where p is pointing. This is very easy to change under program control. In fact, the simple instruction "mov(&mem2, p);" will cause those same two instructions above to load EAX from mem2 the next time they execute. Consider the following instruction sequence:

```
mov( &i, p );              // Assume all variables are STATIC variables.
        .
        .
        .
if( some_expression ) then


    mov( &j, p );              // Assume the code above skips this
                               // instruction and
                               // you get to the next instruction by jumping
                               // to this point from somewhere else.
        .
        .
        .
```

```
        endif;
        mov( p, ebx );              // Assume both of the above code paths
        mov( [ebx], eax );          // wind up down here.
```

This short example demonstrates two execution paths through the program. The first path loads the variable p with the address of the variable i. The second path through the code loads p with the address of the variable j. Both execution paths converge on the last two mov instructions that load EAX with i or j depending upon which execution path was taken. In many respects, this is like a *parameter* to a procedure in a high level language like Pascal. Executing the same instructions accesses different variables depending on whose address (i or j) winds up in p.

4.7.2 Declaring Pointers in HLA

Because pointers are 32 bits long, you could simply use the dword type to allocate storage for your pointers. However, there is a much better way to do this: HLA provides the "pointer to" phrase specifically for declaring pointer variables. Consider the following example:

```
static
    b:          byte;
    d:          dword;
    pByteVar:   pointer to byte := &b;
    pDWordVar:  pointer to dword := &d;
```

This example demonstrates that it is possible to initialize as well as declare pointer variables in HLA. Note that you may only take addresses of static variables (static, readonly, and storage objects) with the address-of operator, so you can only initialize pointer variables with the addresses of static objects.

You can also define your own pointer types in the type section of an HLA program. For example, if you often use pointers to characters, you'll probably want to use a type declaration like the one in the following example:

```
type
    ptrChar:    pointer to char;

static
    cString:    ptrChar;
```

4.7.3 Pointer Constants and Pointer Constant Expressions

HLA allows two literal pointer constant forms: the address-of operator followed by the name of a static variable or the constant NULL. In addition to these two literal pointer constants, HLA also supports simple pointer constant expressions.

The constant zero represents the NULL pointer — that is, an illegal address that does not exist.[10] Programs typically initialize pointers with NULL to indicate that a pointer has explicitly *not* been initialized.

In addition to simple address literals and the value zero, HLA allows very simple constant expressions wherever a pointer constant is legal. Pointer constant expressions take one of the three following forms:

```
&StaticVarName [ PureConstantExpression ]
&StaticVarName + PureConstantExpression
&StaticVarName - PureConstantExpression
```

The *PureConstantExpression* term is a numeric constant expression that does not involve any pointer constants. This type of expression produces a memory address that is the specified number of bytes before or after ("-" or "+", respectively) the StaticVarName variable in memory. Note that the first two forms above are semantically equivalent; they both return a pointer constant whose address is the sum of the static variable and the constant expression.

Because you can create pointer constant expressions, it should come as no surprise to discover that HLA lets you define manifest pointer constants in the const section. The program in Listing 4-5 demonstrates how you can do this.

Listing 4-5: Pointer Constant Expressions in an HLA Program.

```
program PtrConstDemo;
#include( "stdlib.hhf" );

static
    b:  byte := 0;
        byte    1, 2, 3, 4, 5, 6, 7;

const
    pb:= &b + 1;

begin PtrConstDemo;

    mov( pb, ebx );
    mov( [ebx], al );
    stdout.put( "Value at address pb = $", al, nl );

end PtrConstDemo;
```

Upon execution, this program prints the value of the byte just beyond b in memory (which contains the value $01).

---

[10]Actually, address zero does exist, but if you try to access it under Windows or Linux you will get a general protection fault.

4.7.4 Pointer Variables and Dynamic Memory Allocation

Pointer variables are the perfect place to store the return result from the HLA Standard Library malloc function. The malloc function returns the address of the storage it allocates in the EAX register; therefore, you can store the address directly into a pointer variable with a single mov instruction immediately after a call to malloc:

```
type
     bytePtr:      pointer to byte;

var
     bPtr: bytePtr;
          .
          .
          .
     malloc( 1024 );                    // Allocate a block of 1,024 bytes.
     mov( eax, bPtr );                  // Store address of block in bPtr.
          .
          .
          .
     free( bPtr );                      // Free the allocated block when done
                                        // using it.
          .
          .
          .
```

In addition to malloc and free, the HLA Standard Library provides a realloc procedure. The realloc routine takes two parameters: a pointer to a block of storage that malloc (or realloc) previously created and a new size. If the new size is less than the old size, realloc releases the storage at the end of the allocated block back to the system. If the new size is larger than the current block, then realloc will allocate a new block and move the old data to the start of the new block, then free the old block.

Typically, you would use realloc to correct a bad guess about a memory size you'd made earlier. For example, suppose you want to read a set of values from the user but you won't know how many memory locations you'll need to hold the values until after the user has entered the last value. You could make a wild guess and then allocate some storage using malloc based on your estimate. If, during the input, you discover that your estimate was too low, simply call realloc with a larger value. Repeat this as often as required until all the input is read. Once input is complete, you can make a call to realloc to release any unused storage at the end of the memory block.

The *realloc* procedure uses the following calling sequence:

```
realloc( ExistingPointer, NewSize );
```

Realloc returns a pointer to the newly allocated block in the EAX register.

One danger exists when using realloc. If you've made multiple copies of pointers into a block of storage on the heap and then call realloc to resize that block, all the existing pointers are now invalid. Effectively realloc frees the existing storage and then allocates a new block. That new block may not be in the same memory location at the old block, so any existing pointers (into the block) that you have will be invalid after the realloc call.

4.7.5 Common Pointer Problems

There are five common problems programmers encounter when using pointers. Some of these errors will cause your programs to immediately stop with a diagnostic message; other problems are more subtle, yielding incorrect results without otherwise reporting an error or simply affecting the performance of your program without displaying an error. These five problems are

- Using an uninitialized pointer
- Using a pointer that contains an illegal value (e.g., NULL)
- Continuing to use malloc'd storage after that storage has been freed
- Failing to free storage once the program is done using it
- Accessing indirect data using the wrong data type

The first problem above is using a pointer variable before you have assigned a valid memory address to the pointer. Beginning programmers often don't realize that declaring a pointer variable only reserves storage for the pointer itself, it does not reserve storage for the data that the pointer references. The short program in Listing 4-6 demonstrates this problem.

Listing 4-6: Uninitialized Pointer Demonstration.

```
// Program to demonstrate use of
// an uninitialized pointer.  Note
// that this program should terminate
// with a Memory Access Violation exception.

program UninitPtrDemo;
#include( "stdlib.hhf" );

static

    // Note: by default, varibles in the
    // static section are initialized with
    // zero (NULL) hence the following
    // is actually initialized with NULL,
    // but that will still cause our program
    // to fail because we haven't initialized
    // the pointer with a valid memory address.

    Uninitialized: pointer to byte;
```

```
begin UninitPtrDemo;

    mov( Uninitialized, ebx );
    mov( [ebx], al );
    stdout.put( "Value at address Uninitialized: = $", al, nl );

end UninitPtrDemo;
```

Although variables you declare in the static section are, technically, initialized, static initialization still doesn't initialize the pointer in this program with a valid address (it initializes them with zero, which is NULL).

Of course, there is no such thing as a truly uninitialized variable on the 80x86. What you really have are variables that you've explicitly given an initial value and variables that just happen to inherit whatever bit pattern was in memory when storage for the variable was allocated. Much of the time, these garbage bit patterns laying around in memory don't correspond to a valid memory address. Attempting to *dereference* such a pointer (that is, access the data in memory at which it points) typically raises a *Memory Access Violation* exception.

Sometimes, however, those random bits in memory just happen to correspond to a valid memory location you can access. In this situation, the CPU will access the specified memory location without aborting the program. Although to a naive programmer this situation may seem preferable to stopping the program, in reality this is far worse because your defective program continues to run without alerting you to the problem. If you store data through an uninitialized pointer, you may very well overwrite the values of other important variables in memory. This defect can produce some very difficul- to-locate problems in your program.

The second problem programmers have with pointers is storing invalid address values into a pointer. The first problem, described previously, is actually a special case of this second problem (with garbage bits in memory supplying the invalid address rather than you producing via a miscalculation). The effects are the same; if you attempt to dereference a pointer containing an invalid address you will either get a Memory Access Violation exception or you will access an unexpected memory location.

The third problem listed previously is also known as the *dangling pointer problem*. To understand this problem, consider the following code fragment:

```
    malloc( 256 );          // Allocate some storage.
    mov( eax, ptr );        // Save address away in a pointer variable.
        .
        .                   // Code that use the pointer variable "ptr".
        .
    free( ptr );            // Free the storage associated with "ptr".
        .
        .                   // Code that does not change the value in
        .                   // "ptr".
        .
```

```
mov( ptr, ebx );
mov( al, [ebx] );
```

In this example you will note that the program allocates 256 bytes of storage and saves the address of that storage in the ptr variable. Then the code uses this block of 256 bytes for a while and frees the storage, returning it to the system for other uses. Note that calling free does not change the value of ptr in any way; ptr still points at the block of memory allocated by malloc earlier. Indeed, free does not change any data in this block, so upon return from free, ptr still points at the data stored into the block by this code. However, note that the call to free tells the system that this 256-byte block of memory is no longer needed by the program, and the system can use this region of memory for other purposes. The free function cannot enforce the fact that you will never access this data again; you are simply promising that you won't. Of course, the code fragment above breaks this promise; as you can see in the last two instructions above the program fetches the value in ptr and accesses the data it points at in memory.

The biggest problem with dangling pointers is that you can get away with using them a good part of the time. As long as the system doesn't reuse the storage you've freed, using a dangling pointer produces no ill effects in your program. However, with each new call to malloc, the system may decide to reuse the memory released by that previous call to free. When this happens, any attempt to dereference the dangling pointer may produce some unintended consequences. The problems range from reading data that has been overwritten (by the new, legal use of the data storage) to overwriting the new data and to (the worst case) overwriting system heap management pointers (doing so will probably cause your program to crash). The solution is clear: *Never use a pointer value once you free the storage associated with that pointer.*

Of all the problems, the fourth (failing to free allocated storage) will probably have the least impact on the proper operation of your program. The following code fragment demonstrates this problem:

```
malloc( 256 );
mov( eax, ptr );
        .                   // Code that uses the data where ptr is pointing.
        .                   // This code does not free up the storage
        .                   // associated with ptr.
malloc( 512 );
mov( eax, ptr );

// At this point, there is no way to reference the original
// block of 256 bytes pointed at by ptr.
```

In this example the program allocates 256 bytes of storage and references this storage using the *ptr* variable. At some later time the program allocates another block of bytes and overwrites the value in ptr with the address of this new block. Note that the former value in ptr is lost. Because the program no longer has this address value, there is no way to call free to return the storage for later use. As a result, this memory is no longer available to your program. While making 256 bytes of memory inaccessible to your program may not seem like a big deal, imagine that this code is in a loop that repeats over and over again. With each execution of the loop the program loses another 256 bytes of memory. After a sufficient number of loop iterations, the program will exhaust the memory available on the heap. This problem is often called a *memory leak* because the effect is the same as though the memory bits were leaking out of your computer (yielding less and less available storage) during program execution.[11]

Memory leaks are far less damaging than using dangling pointers. Indeed, there are only two problems with memory leaks: the danger of running out of heap space (which, ultimately, may cause the program to abort, though this is rare) and performance problems due to virtual memory page swapping. Nevertheless, you should get in the habit of always freeing all storage once you are done using it. When your program quits, the operating system reclaims all storage including the data lost via memory leaks. Therefore, memory lost via a leak is only lost to your program, not the whole system.

The last problem with pointers is the lack of type-safe access. This can occur because HLA cannot and does not enforce pointer type checking. For example, consider the program in Listing 4-7.

Listing 4-7: Type-Unsafe Pointer Access Example.

```
// Program to demonstrate use of
// lack of type checking in pointer
// accesses.

program BadTypePtrDemo;
#include( "stdlib.hhf" );

static
    ptr:    pointer to char;
    cnt:    uns32;

begin BadTypePtrDemo;

    // Allocate sufficient characters
    // to hold a line of text input
    // by the user:

    malloc( 256 );
    mov( eax, ptr );


    // Okay, read the text a character
    // at a time by the user:
```

---

[11]Note that the storage isn't lost from you computer; once your program quits, it returns all memory (including unfreed storage) to the O/S. The next time the program runs it will start with a clean slate.

```
        stdout.put( "Enter a line of text: ");
        stdin.flushInput();
        mov( 0, cnt );
        mov( ptr, ebx );
        repeat

            stdin.getc();          // Read a character from the user.
            mov( al, [ebx] );      // Store the character away.
            inc( cnt );            // Bump up count of characters.
            inc( ebx );            // Point at next position in memory.


        until( stdin.eoln());


        // Okay, we've read a line of text from the user,
        // now display the data:

        mov( ptr, ebx );
        for( mov( cnt, ecx ); ecx > 0; dec( ecx )) do

            mov( [ebx], eax );
            stdout.put( "Current value is $", eax, nl );
            inc( ebx );

        endfor;
        free( ptr );


end BadTypePtrDemo;
```

This program reads in data from the user as character values and then displays the data as double word hexadecimal values. While a powerful feature of assembly language is that it lets you ignore data types at will and automatically coerce the data without any effort, this power is a two-edged sword. If you make a mistake and access indirect data using the wrong data type, HLA and the 80x86 may not catch the mistake, and your program may produce inaccurate results. Therefore, you need to take care when using pointers and indirection in your programs that you use the data consistently with respect to data type.

4.8   The HLA Standard Library CHARS.HHF Module

The HLA Standard Library *chars.hhf* module provides a couple of routines that convert characters from one form to another and several routines that classify characters according to their graphic representation. These functions are especially useful for processing user input to verify that it is correct.

The first two routines we will consider are the translation/conversion functions. These functions are chars.toUpper and chars.toLower. These functions use the following syntax:

```
        chars.toLower( characterValue ); // Returns converted character in AL.
        chars.toUpper( characterValue ); // Returns converted character in AL.
```

These two functions require a byte-sized parameter (typically an 8-bit register or a char variable). They check the character to see if it is an alphabetic character; if it is not, then these functions return the unmodified parameter value in the AL register. If the character is an alphabetic character, then these functions may translate the value depending on the particular function. The chars.toUpper function translates lower case alphabetic characters to upper case; it returns other characters unmodified. The chars.toLower function does the converse: It translates upper case characters to lower case characters and leaves other characters alone.

These two functions are especially useful when processing user input containing alphabetic characters. For example, suppose you expect a "Y" or "N" answer from the user at some point in your program. You code might look like the following:

```
forever

        stdout.put( "Answer 'Y' or 'N':" );
        stdin.FlushInput();   // Force input of new line of text.
        stdin.getc();  // Read user input in AL.
        breakif( al = 'Y' ||  al = 'N' );
        stdout.put( "Illegal input, please reenter", nl );

endfor;
```

The problem with this program is that the user must answer exactly "Y" or "N" (using upper case) or the program will reject the user's input. This means that the program will reject "y" and "n" because the ASCII codes for these characters are different than "Y" and "N."

One way to solve this problem is to include an additional breakif statement in the code above that test for "y" and "n" as well as "Y" and "N." The problem with this approach is that AL will still contain one of four different characters, complicating tests of AL once the program exits the loop. A better solution is to use either chars.toUpper or chars.toLower to translate all alphabetic characters to a single case. Then you can test AL for a single pair of characters, both in the loop and outside the loop. The resulting code would look like the following:

```
forever

        stdout.put( "Answer 'Y' or 'N':" );
        stdin.FlushInput();   // Force input of new line of text.
        stdin.getc();         // Read user input in AL.
        chars.toUpper( al );  // Convert "y" and "n" to "Y" and "N".
        breakif( al = 'Y' ||  al = 'N' );
        stdout.put( "Illegal input, please reenter", nl );
```

```
        endfor;
    << test for "Y" or "N" down here to determine user input >>
```

As you can see from this example, the case conversion functions can be quite
useful when processing user input. As a final example, consider a program that
presents a menu of options to the user, and the user selects an option using an
alphabetic character. Once again, you can use chars.toUpper or chars.toLower to
map the input character to a single case so that it is easier to process the user's
input:

```
stdout.put( "Enter selection (A-G):" );
stdin.FlushInput();
stdin.getc();
chars.toLower( al );
if( al = 'a' ) then

    << Handle Menu Option A >>

elseif( al = 'b' ) then

    << Handle Menu Option B >>

elseif( al = 'c' ) then

    << Handle Menu Option C >>

elseif( al = 'd' ) then

    << Handle Menu Option D >>

elseif( al = 'e' ) then

    << Handle Menu Option E >>

elseif( al = 'f' ) then

    << Handle Menu Option F >>

elseif( al = 'g' ) then

    << Handle Menu Option G >>

else

    stdout.put( "Illegal input!" nl );

endif;
```

The remaining functions in the *chars.hhf* module all return a boolean result depending on the type of the character you pass them as a parameter. These classification functions let you quickly and easily test a character to determine whether its type is valid for the some intended use. These functions expect a single-byte (char) parameter and they return true (1) or false (0) in the EAX register. These functions use the following calling syntax:

```
chars.isAlpha( c );       // Returns true if c is alphabetic
chars.isUpper( c );       // Returns true if c is upper case alphabetic.
chars.isLower( c );       // Returns true if c is lower case alphabetic.
chars.isAlphaNum( c );    // Returns true if c is alphabetic or numeric.
chars.isDigit( c );       // Returns true if c is a decimal digit.
chars.isXDigit( c );      // Returns true if c is a hexadecimal digit.
chars.isGraphic( c );     // See notes below.
chars.isSpace( c );       // Returns true if c is a whitespace character.
chars.isASCII( c );       // Returns true if c is in the range #$00..#$7f.
chars.isCtrl( c );        // Returns true if c is a control character.
```

Notes: Graphic characters are the printable characters whose ASCII codes fall in the range $21..$7E. Note that a space is not considered a graphic character (nor are the control characters). Whitespace characters are the space, the tab, the carriage return, and the line feed. Control characters are those characters whose ASCII code is in the range $00..$1F and $7F.

Although the *chars.hhf* module's classification functions handle many common situations, you may find that you need to test a character to see whether it belongs in a class that the *chars.hhf* module does not handle. Fear not, checking for such characters is very easy. The section on character sets later in this chapter will explain how to do this.

4.9   Composite Data Types

Composite data types, also known as *aggregate* data types, are those that are built up from other (generally scalar) data types. This chapter will cover several of the more important composite data types — character strings, character sets, arrays, records, and unions. A string is a good example of a composite data type: It is a data structure built up from a sequence of individual characters and some other data.

4.10   Character Strings

After integer values, character strings are probably the most common data type that modern programs use. The 80x86 does support a handful of string instructions, but these instructions are really intended for block memory operations, not a specific implementation of a character string. Therefore, this section will concentrate mainly on the HLA definition of character strings and also discuss the string handling routines available in the HLA Standard Library.

In general, a *character string* is a sequence of ASCII characters that possesses two main attributes: a *length* and the *character data*. Different languages use different data structures to represent strings. To better understand the reasoning behind the design of HLA strings, it is probably instructive to look at two different string representations popularized by various high level languages.

Without question, *zero terminated strings* are probably the most common string representation in use today because this is the native string format for C, C++, C#, Java, and other languages. A zero terminated string consists of a sequence of zero or more ASCII characters ending with a byte containing zero. For example, in C/C++, the string "abc" requires four bytes: the three characters 'a', 'b', and 'c' followed by a byte containing zero. As you'll soon see, HLA character strings are upward compatible with zero terminated strings, but in the meantime you should note that it is very easy to create zero terminated strings in HLA. The easiest place to do this is in the static section using code like the following:

```
static
    zeroTerminatedString:    char; @nostorage;
                    byte "This is the zero terminated string", 0;
```

Remember, when using the @nostorage option, HLA doesn't reserve any space for the variable, so the zeroTerminatedString variable's address in memory corresponds to the first character in the following byte directive. Whenever a character string appears in the byte directive as it does here, HLA emits each character in the string to successive memory locations. The zero value at the end of the string properly terminates this string.

Zero terminated strings have two principle attributes: They are very simple to implement and the strings can be any length. On the other hand, zero terminated strings have a few drawbacks. First, though not usually important, zero terminated strings cannot contain the NUL character (whose ASCII code is zero). Generally, this isn't a problem, but it does create havoc once in a great while. The second problem with zero terminated strings is that many operations on them are somewhat inefficient. For example, to compute the length of a zero terminated string you must scan the entire string looking for that zero byte (counting characters up to the zero). The following program fragment demonstrates how to compute the length of the string above:

```
        mov( &zeroTerminatedString, ebx );
        mov( 0, eax );
        while( (type byte [ebx+eax]) <> 0 ) do

            inc( eax );

        endwhile;

        // String length is now in EAX.
```

As you can see from this code, the time it takes to compute the length of the string is proportional to the length of the string; as the string gets longer it will take longer to compute its length.

A second string format, *length prefixed strings*, overcomes some of the problems with zero terminated strings. length prefixed strings are common in languages like Pascal; they generally consist of a length byte followed by zero or more character values. The first byte specifies the length of the string, the remaining bytes (up to the specified length) are the character data itself. In a length prefixed scheme, the string "abc" would consist of the four bytes — $03 (the string length) followed by 'a', 'b', and 'c'. You can create length prefixed strings in HLA using code like the following:

```
static
    lengthPrefixedString:char; @nostorage;
            byte 3, "abc";
```

Counting the characters ahead of time and inserting them into the byte statement, as was done here, may seem like a major pain. Fortunately, there are ways to have HLA automatically compute the string length for you.

Length prefixed strings solve the two major problems associated with zero terminated strings. It is possible to include the NUL character in length prefixed strings and those operations on zero terminated strings that are relatively inefficient (e.g., string length) are more efficient when using length prefixed strings. However, length prefixed strings have their own drawbacks. The principal drawback to length prefixed strings, as described, is that they are limited to a maximum of 255 characters in length (assuming a one-byte length prefix).

HLA uses an expanded scheme for strings that is upwards compatible with both zero terminated and length prefixed strings. HLA strings enjoy the advantages of both zero terminated and length prefixed strings without the disadvantages. In fact, the only drawback to HLA strings over these other formats is that HLA strings consume a few additional bytes (the overhead for an HLA string is 9 to 12 bytes, compared to 1 byte for zero terminated or length prefixed strings; the overhead being the number of bytes needed above and beyond the actual characters in the string).

An HLA string value consists of four components. The first element is a double word value that specifies the maximum number of characters that the string can hold. The second element is a double word value specifying the current length of the string. The third component is the sequence of characters in the string. The final component is a zero terminating byte. You could create an HLA-compatible string in the static section using code like the following:[12]

```
static
        align(4);
        dword 11;
        dword 11;
```

---

[12] Actually, there are some restrictions on the placement of HLA strings in memory. This text will not cover those issues. See the HLA documentation for more details.

```
TheString: char; @nostorage;
    byte "Hello there";
    byte 0;
```

Note that the address associated with the HLA string is the address of the first character, not the maximum or current length values.

"So what is the difference between the current and maximum string lengths?" you're probably wondering. Well, in a fixed string like the preceding one they are usually the same. However, when you allocate storage for a string variable at runtime, you will normally specify the maximum number of characters that can go into the string. When you store actual string data into the string, the number of characters you store must be less than or equal to this maximum value. The HLA Standard Library string routines will raise an exception if you attempt to exceed this maximum length (something the C/C++ and Pascal formats can't do).

The zero terminating byte at the end of the HLA string lets you treat an HLA string as a zero terminated string if it is more efficient or more convenient to do so. For example, most calls to Windows and Linux require zero terminated strings for their string parameters. Placing a zero at the end of an HLA string ensures compatibility with Windows, Linux, and other library modules that use zero terminated strings.

4.11   HLA Strings

As the previous section notes, HLA strings consist of four components: a maximum length, a current string length, character data, and a zero terminating byte. However, HLA never requires you to create string data by manually emitting these components yourself. HLA is smart enough to automatically construct this data for you whenever it sees a string literal constant. So if you use a string constant like the following, understand that somewhere HLA is creating the four-component string in memory for you:

```
stdout.put( "This gets converted to a four-component string by HLA" );
```

HLA doesn't actually work directly with the string data described in the previous section. Instead, when HLA sees a string object it always works with a *pointer* to that object rather than working directly with the object. Without question, this is the most important fact to know about HLA strings and is the biggest source of problems beginning HLA programmers have with strings in HLA: *strings are pointers!* A string variable consumes exactly four bytes, the same as a pointer (because it *is* a pointer!). Having said all that, let's take a look at a simple string variable declaration in HLA:

```
static
    StrVariable:                string;
```

Because a string variable is a pointer, you must initialize it before you can use it. There are three general ways you may initialize a string variable with a legal string address: using static initializers, using the stralloc routine, or calling some other HLA Standard Library that initializes a string or returns a pointer to a string.

In one of the static declaration sections that allow initialized variables (static, and readonly) you can initialize a string variable using the standard initialization syntax, e.g.,

```
static
    InitializedString: string := "This is my string";
```

Note that this does not initialize the string variable with the string data. Instead, HLA creates the string data structure (see the previous section) in a special, hidden memory segment and initializes the InitializedString variable with the address of the first character in this string (the "T" in "This"). *Remember, strings are pointers!* The HLA compiler places the actual string data in a read-only memory segment. Therefore, you cannot modify the characters of this string literal at runtime. However, because the string variable (a pointer, remember) is in the static section, you can change the string variable so that it points at different string data.

Because string variables are pointers, you can load the value of a string variable into a 32-bit register. The pointer itself points at the first character position of the string. You can find the current string length in the double word four bytes prior to this address, you can find the maximum string length in the double word eight bytes prior to this address. The program in Listing 4-8 demonstrates one way to access this data.[13]

Listing 4-8: Accessing the Length and Maximum Length Fields of a String.

```
// Program to demonstrate accessing Length and Maxlength fields of a string.

program StrDemo;
#include( "stdlib.hhf" );

static
    theString:string := "String of length 19";

begin StrDemo;

    mov( theString, ebx );  // Get pointer to the string.

    mov( [ebx-4], eax );    // Get current length
    mov( [ebx-8], ecx );    // Get maximum length

    stdout.put
```

---

[13] Note that this scheme is not recommended. If you need to extract the length information from a string, use the routines provided in the HLA String Library for this purpose.

```
        (
            "theString = '", theString, "'", nl,
            "length( theString )= ", (type uns32 eax ), nl,
            "maxLength( theString )= ", (type uns32 ecx ), nl
        );

end StrDemo;
```

When accessing the various fields of a string variable it is not wise to access them using fixed numeric offsets as done in Listing 4-8. In the future, the definition of an HLA string may change slightly. In particular, the offsets to the maximum length and length fields are subject to change. A safer way to access string data is to coerce your string pointer using the str.strRec data type. The str.strRec data type is a record data type (see the section on records a little later in this chapter) that defines symbolic names for the offsets of the length and maximum length fields in the string data type. Were the offsets to the length and maximum length fields to change in a future version of HLA, then the definitions in str.strRec would also change, so if you use str.strRec then recompiling your program would automatically make any necessary changes to your program.

To use the str.strRec data type properly, you must first load the string pointer into a 32-bit register, e.g., "mov(SomeString, EBX);". Once the pointer to the string data is in a register, you can coerce that register to the str.strRec data type using the HLA construct "(type str.strRec [EBX])". Finally, to access the length or maximum length fields, you would use either "(type str.strRec [EBX]).length" or "(type str.strRec [EBX]).MaxStrLen", (respectively). Although there is a little more typing involved (versus using simple offsets like "-4" or "-8"), these forms are far more descriptive and much safer than straight numeric offsets. The program in Listing 4-9 corrects the example in Listing 4-8 by using the str.strRec data type.

Listing 4-9: Correct Way to Access Length and MaxStrLen Fields of a String.

```
// Program to demonstrate accessing Length and Maxlength fields of a string.

program LenMaxlenDemo;
#include( "stdlib.hhf" );

static
    theString:string := "String of length 19";

begin LenMaxlenDemo;

    mov( theString, ebx );  // Get pointer to the string.

    mov( (type str.strRec [ebx]).length, eax );    // Get current length
    mov( (type str.strRec [ebx]).MaxStrLen, ecx ); // Get maximum length

    stdout.put
```

```
    (
        "theString = '", theString, "'", nl,
        "length( theString )= ", (type uns32 eax ), nl,
        "maxLength( theString )= ", (type uns32 ecx ), nl
    );

end LenMaxlenDemo;
```

A second way to manipulate strings in HLA is to allocate storage on the heap to hold string data. Because strings can't directly use pointers returned by malloc (because strings will access the eight bytes prior to the address), you shouldn't use malloc to allocate storage for string data. Fortunately, the HLA Standard Library memory module provides a memory allocation routine specifically designed to allocate storage for strings: stralloc. Like malloc, stralloc expects a single double word parameter. This value specifies the (maximum) number of characters needed for the string. The stralloc routine will allocate the specified number of bytes of memory, plus between 9 and 13 additional bytes to hold the extra string information.[14]

The stralloc routine will allocate storage for a string, initialize the maximum length to the value passed as the stralloc parameter, initialize the current length to zero, and store a zero (terminating byte) in the first character position of the string. After all this, stralloc returns the address of the zero terminating byte (that is, the address of the first character element) in the EAX register.

Once you've allocated storage for a string, you can call various string manipulation routines in the HLA Standard Library to manipulate the string. The next section will discuss the HLA string routines in detail; this section will introduce a couple of string related routines for the sake of example. The first such routine is the "stdin.gets(strvar);". This routine reads a string from the user and stores the string data into the string storage pointed at by the string parameter (strvar in this case). If the user attempts to enter more characters than the maximum the string allows, then stdin.gets raises the ex.StringOverflow exception. The program in Listing 4-10 demonstrates the use of stralloc.

Listing 4-10: Reading a String from the User.

```
// Program to demonstrate stralloc and stdin.gets.

program strallocDemo;
#include( "stdlib.hhf" );

static
    theString:string;

begin strallocDemo;
```

---

[14] *Stralloc* may allocate more than nine bytes for the overhead data because the memory allocated to an HLA string must always be double word aligned, and the total length of the data structure must be an even multiple of four.

```
    stralloc( 16 );          // Allocate storage for the string and store
    mov( eax, theString );   //  the pointer into the string variable.

    // Prompt the user and read the string from the user:

    stdout.put( "Enter a line of text (16 chars, max): " );
    stdin.flushInput();
    stdin.gets( theString );

    // Echo the string back to the user:

    stdout.put( "The string you entered was: ", theString, nl );

end strallocDemo;
```

If you look closely, you see a slight defect in the program above. It allocates storage for the string by calling stralloc, but it never frees the storage allocated. Even though the program immediately exits after the last use of the string variable, and the operating system will deallocate the storage anyway, it's always a good idea to explicitly free up any storage you allocate. Doing so keeps you in the habit of freeing allocated storage (so you don't forget to do it when it's important) and, also, programs have a way of growing such that an innocent defect that doesn't affect anything in today's program becomes a showstopping defect in tomorrow's version.

To free storage you allocate via stralloc, you must call the strfree routine, passing the string pointer as the single parameter. The program in Listing 4-11 is a correction of the program Listing 4-10 with this defect corrected.

Listing 4-11: Corrected Program That Reads a String from the User.

```
// Program to demonstrate stralloc, strfree, and stdin.gets.

program strfreeDemo;
#include( "stdlib.hhf" );

static
    theString:string;

begin strfreeDemo;

    stralloc( 16 );          // Allocate storage for the string and store
    mov( eax, theString );   //  the pointer into the string variable.

    // Prompt the user and read the string from the user:

    stdout.put( "Enter a line of text (16 chars, max): " );
    stdin.flushInput();
    stdin.gets( theString );
```

```
    // Echo the string back to the user:

    stdout.put( "The string you entered was: ", theString, nl );

    // Free up the storage allocated by stralloc:

    strfree( theString );

end strfreeDemo;
```

When looking at this corrected program, please take note that the stdin.gets
routine expects you to pass it a string parameter that points at an allocated string
object. Without question, one of the most common mistakes beginning HLA
programmers make is to call stdin.gets and pass it a string variable that they have
not initialized. This may be getting old now, but keep in mind that *strings are
pointers!* Like pointers, if you do not initialize a string with a valid address, your
program will probably crash when you attempt to manipulate that string object.
The call to stralloc plus moving the returned result into theString is how the
programs above initialize the string pointer. If you are going to use string
variables in your programs, you must ensure that you allocate storage for the
string data prior to writing data to the string object.

Allocating storage for a string option is such a common operation that many
HLA Standard Library routines will automatically do the allocation to save you
the effort. Generally, such routines have an "a_" prefix as part of their name. For
example, the stdin.a_gets combines a call to stralloc and stdin.gets into the same
routine. This routine, which doesn't have any parameters, reads a line of text
from the user, allocates a string object to hold the input data, and then returns a
pointer to the string in the EAX register. Listing 4-12 presents an adaptation of
the two programs in Listings 4-10 and 4-11 that uses stdin.a_gets.

Listing 4-12: Reading a String from the User with stdin.a_gets.

```
// Program to demonstrate strfree and stdin.a_gets.

program strfreeDemo2;
#include( "stdlib.hhf" );

static
    theString:string;

begin strfreeDemo2;


    // Prompt the user and read the string from the user:

    stdout.put( "Enter a line of text: " );
    stdin.flushInput();
    stdin.a_gets();
    mov( eax, theString );
```

```
    // Echo the string back to the user:

    stdout.put( "The string you entered was: ", theString, nl );

    // Free up the storage allocated by stralloc:

    strfree( theString );

end strfreeDemo2;
```

Note that, as before, you must still free up the storage stdin.a_gets allocates by calling the strfree routine. One big difference between this routine and the previous two is the fact that HLA will automatically allocate exactly enough space for the string read from the user. In the previous programs, the call to stralloc only allocates 16 bytes. If the user types more than 16 characters, then the program raises an exception and quits. If the user types less than 16 characters, then some space at the end of the string is wasted. The stdin.a_gets routine, on the other hand, always allocates the minimum necessary space for the string read from the user. Because it allocates the storage, there is little chance of overflow.[15]

4.12   Accessing the Characters Within a String

Extracting individual characters from a string is a very common and easy task. In fact, it is so easy that HLA doesn't provide any specific procedure or language syntax to accomplish this: You simply use machine instructions to accomplish this. Once you have a pointer to the string data, a simple indexed addressing mode will do the rest of the work for you.

Of course, the most important thing to keep in mind is that *strings are pointers*. Therefore, you cannot apply an indexed addressing mode directly to a string variable and expect to extract characters from the string. That is, if s is a string variable, then "mov(s[ebx], al);" does not fetch the character at position EBX in string s and place it in the AL register. Remember, s is just a pointer variable; an addressing mode like s[ebx] will simply fetch the byte at offset EBX in memory starting at the address of s (see Figure 4-1).

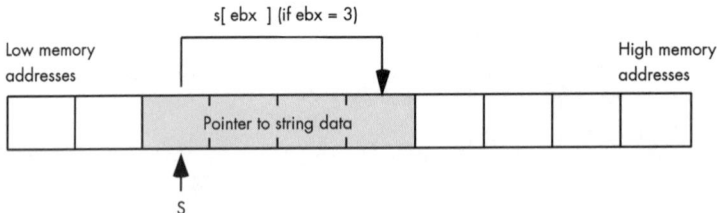

Figure 4-1: Incorrectly Indexing off a String Variable.

---

[15] Actually, there are limits on the maximum number of characters that stdin.a_gets will allocate. This is typically between 1,024 bytes and 4,096 bytes; see the HLA Standard Library source listings and your operating system documentation for the exact value.

In Figure 4-1, assuming EBX contains three, s[ebx] does not access the fourth character in the string s; instead it fetches the fourth byte of the pointer to the string data. It is very unlikely that this is what you would want. Figure 4-2 shows the operation that is necessary to fetch a character from the string, assuming EBX contains the value of s.

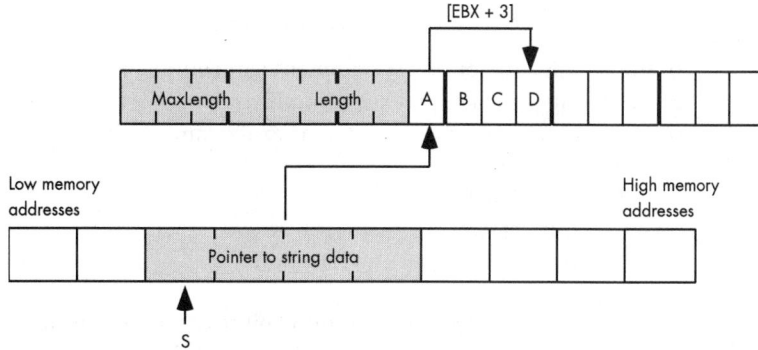

Figure 4-2: Correctly Indexing off the Value of a String Variable.

In Figure 4-2 EBX contains the value of string s. The value of s is a pointer to the actual string data in memory. Therefore, EBX will point at the first character of the string when you load the value of s into EBX. The following code demonstrates how to access the fourth character of string s in this fashion:

```
mov( s, ebx );          // Get pointer to string data into EBX.
mov( [ebx+3], al );     // Fetch the fourth character of the string.
```

If you want to load the character at a variable, rather than fixed, offset into the string, then you can use one of the 80x86's scaled indexed addressing modes to fetch the character. For example, if an uns32 variable index contains the desired offset into the string, you could use the following code to access the character at s[index]:

```
mov( s, ebx );          // Get address of string data into EBX.
mov( index, ecx );      // Get desired offset into string.
mov( [ebx+ecx], al );   // Get the desired character into AL.
```

There is only one problem with the code above: Iit does not check to ensure that the character at offset index actually exists. If index is greater than the current length of the string, then this code will fetch a garbage byte from memory. Unless you can apriori determine that index is always less than the length of the string, code like this is dangerous to use. A better solution is to check the index against the string's current length before attempting to access the character. The following code provides one way to do this.

```
mov( s, ebx );
mov( index, ecx );
if( ecx < (type str.strRec [ebx]).Length ) then
```

```
        mov( [ebx+ecx], al );

    else

        << error, string index is of bounds >>

    endif;
```

In the else portion of this if statement you could take corrective action, print an error message, or raise an exception. If you want to explicitly raise an exception, you can use the HLA raise statement to accomplish this. The syntax for the raise statement is

```
raise( integer_constant );
raise( reg32 );
```

The value of the integer_constant or 32-bit register must be an exception number. Usually, this is one of the predefined constants in the *excepts.hhf* header file. An appropriate exception to raise when a string index is greater than the length of the string is ex.StringIndexError. The following code demonstrates raising this exception if the string index is out of bounds:

```
        mov( s, ebx );
        mov( index, ecx );
        if( ecx < (type str.strRec [ebx]).Length ) then

            mov( [ebx+ecx], al );

        else

            raise( ex.StringIndexError );

        endif;
```

Another way to check to see if the string index is within bounds is to use the 80x86 bound instruction.

4.13   The HLA String Module and Other String-Related Routines

Although HLA provides a powerful definition for string data, the real power behind HLA's string capabilities lies in the HLA Standard Library, not in the definition of HLA string data. HLA provides several dozen string manipulation routines that far exceed the capabilities found in standard high level languages like C/C++, Java, or Pascal; indeed, HLA's string handling capabilities rival those in string processing languages like Icon or SNOBOL4. While it is premature to introduce all of HLA's character string handling routines, this chapter will discuss many of the string facilities that HLA provides.

Perhaps the most basic string operation you will need is to assign one string to another. There are three different ways to assign strings in HLA: by reference, by copying a string, and by duplicating a string. Of these, assignment by reference is the fastest and easiest. If you have two strings and you wish to assign one string to the other, a simple and fast way to do this is to copy the string pointer. The following code fragment demonstrates this:

```
static
        string1:                string              := "Some String Data";
        string2:                string;
            .
            .
            .
        mov( string1, eax );
        mov( eax, string2 );
            .
            .
            .
```

String assignment by reference is very efficient because it only involves two simple mov instructions regardless of the string length. Assignment by reference works great if you never modify the string data after the assignment operation. Do keep in mind, though, that both string variables (string1 and string2 in the example above) *wind up pointing at the same data.* So if you make a change to the data pointed at by one string variable, you will change the string data pointed at by the second string object because both objects point at the same data. Listing 4-13 provides a program that demonstrates this problem.

Listing 4-13: Problem with String Assignment by Copying Pointers.

```
// Program to demonstrate the problem
// with string assignment by reference.

program strRefAssignDemo;
#include( "stdlib.hhf" );

static
    string1:    string;
    string2:    string;

begin strRefAssignDemo;

    // Get a value into string1

    forever

        stdout.put( "Enter a string with at least three characters: " );
        stdin.a_gets();
        mov( eax, string1 );
```

```
        breakif( (type str.strRec [eax]).length >= 3 );

        stdout.put( "Please enter a string with at least three chars." nl );

    endfor;

    stdout.put( "You entered: '", string1, "'" nl );

    // Do the string assignment by copying the pointer

    mov( string1, ebx );
    mov( ebx, string2 );

    stdout.put( "String1= '", string1, "'" nl );
    stdout.put( "String2= '", string2, "'" nl );

    // Okay, modify the data in string1 by overwriting
    // the first three characters of the string (note that
    // a string pointer always points at the first character
    // position in the string and we know we've got at least
    // three characters here).

    mov( 'a', (type char [ebx]) );
    mov( 'b', (type char [ebx+1]) );
    mov( 'c', (type char [ebx+2]) );

    // Okay, demonstrate the problem with assignment via
    // pointer copy.

    stdout.put
    (
        "After assigning 'abc' to the first three characters in string1:"
        nl
        nl
    );
    stdout.put( "String1= '", string1, "'"nl );
    stdout.put( "String2= '", string2, "'"nl );

    strfree( string1 );      // Don't free string2 as well!


end strRefAssignDemo;
```

Because both string1 and string2 point at the same string data in this example, any change you make to one string is reflected in the other. While this is sometimes acceptable, most programmers expect assignment to produce a different copy of a string; that is, they expect the semantics of string assignment to produce two unique copies of the string data.

An important point to remember when using *copy by reference* (this term means copying a pointer) is that you have created an *alias* to the string data. The term "alias" means that you have two names for the same object in memory (e.g., in the program above, string1 and string2 are two different names for the same string data). When you read a program it is reasonable to expect that different variables refer to different memory objects. Aliases violate this rule, thus making your program harder to read and understand because you've got to remember that aliases do not refer to different objects in memory. Failing to keep this in mind can lead to subtle bugs in your program. For instance, in the example above you have to remember that string1 and string2 are aliases so as not to free both objects at the end of the program. Worse still, you have to remember that string1 and string2 are aliases so that you don't continue to use string2 after freeing string1 in this code because string2 would be a dangling reference at that point.

Because using copy by reference makes your programs harder to read and increases the possibility that you might introduce subtle defects in your programs, you might wonder why someone would use copy by reference at all. There are two reasons for this: First, copy by reference is very efficient; it only involves the execution of two mov instructions. Second, some algorithms actually depend on copy by reference semantics. Nevertheless, you should carefully consider whether copying string pointers is the appropriate way to do a string assignment in your program before using this technique.

The second way to assign one string to another is to copy the string data. The HLA Standard Library str.cpy routine provides this capability. A call to the str.cpy procedure using the following call syntax:[16]

```
str.cpy( source_string, destination_string );
```

The source and destination strings must be string variables (pointers) or 32-bit registers containing the addresses of the string data in memory.

The str.cpy routine first checks the maximum length field of the destination string to ensure that it is at least as big as the current length of the source string. If it is not, then str.cpy raises the ex.StringOverflow exception. If the destination string's maximum length is large enough, then str.cpy copies the string length, the characters, and the zero terminating byte from the source string to the destination string's data area. When this process is complete, the two strings point at identical data, but they do not point at the same data in memory.[17] The program in Listing 4-14 is a rework of the example in Listing 4-13 using str.cpy rather than copy by reference.

---

[16] Warning to C/C++ users: Note that the order of the operands is opposite the C Standard Library strcpy function.

[17] Unless, of course, both string pointers contained the same address to begin with, in which case str.cpy copies the string data over the top of itself.

Listing 4-14: Copying Strings Using str.cpy.

```
// Program to demonstrate string assignment using str.cpy.

program strcpyDemo;
#include( "stdlib.hhf" );

static
    string1:    string;
    string2:    string;

begin strcpyDemo;

    // Allocate storage for string2:

    stralloc( 64 );
    mov( eax, string2 );

    // Get a value into string1

    forever

        stdout.put( "Enter a string with at least three characters: ");
        stdin.a_gets();
        mov( eax, string1 );

        breakif( (type str.strRec [eax]).length >= 3 );

        stdout.put( "Please enter a string with at least three chars." nl );

    endfor;


    // Do the string assignment via str.cpy

    str.cpy( string1, string2 );

    stdout.put( "String1= '", string1, "'" nl );
    stdout.put( "String2= '", string2, "'" nl );

    // Okay, modify the data in string1 by overwriting
    // the first three characters of the string (note that
    // a string pointer always points at the first character
    // position in the string and we know we've got at least
    // three characters here).

    mov( string1, ebx );
    mov( 'a', (type char [ebx]) );
    mov( 'b', (type char [ebx+1]) );
```

```
    mov( 'c', (type char [ebx+2]) );

    // Okay, demonstrate that we have two different strings
    // because we used str.cpy to copy the data:

    stdout.put
    (
        "After assigning 'abc' to the first three characters in string1:"
        nl
        nl
    );
    stdout.put( "String1= '", string1, "'" nl );
    stdout.put( "String2= '", string2, "'" nl );


    // Note that we have to free the data associated with both
    // strings because they are not aliases of one another.

    strfree( string1 );
    strfree( string2 );


end strcpyDemo;
```

There are two really important things to note about the program in Listing 4-14.
First, note that this program begins by allocating storage for string2. Remember,
the str.cpy routine does not allocate storage for the destination string; it assumes
that the destination string already has storage allocated. Keep in mind that
str.cpy does not initialize string2; it only copies data to the location where string2
is pointing. It is the program's responsibility to initialize the string by allocating
sufficient memory before calling str.cpy. The second thing to notice here is that
the program calls strfree to free up the storage for both string1 and string2
before the program quits.

Allocating storage for a string variable prior to calling str.cpy is so common
that the HLA Standard Library provides a routine that allocates and copies the
string: str.a_cpy. This routine uses the following call syntax:

```
str.a_cpy( source_string );
```

Note that there is no destination string. This routine looks at the length of the
source string, allocates sufficient storage, makes a copy of the string, and then
returns a pointer to the new string in the EAX register. The program in Listing
4-15 demonstrates how to do the same thing as the program in Listing 4-14 using
the str.a_cpy procedure.

Listing 4-15: Copying Strings Using str.a_cpy.

```
// Program to demonstrate string assignment using str.a_cpy.

program stra_cpyDemo;
#include( "stdlib.hhf" );

static
    string1:    string;
    string2:    string;

begin stra_cpyDemo;


    // Get a value into string1

    forever

        stdout.put( "Enter a string with at least three characters: " );
        stdin.a_gets();
        mov( eax, string1 );

        breakif( (type str.strRec [eax]).length >= 3 );

        stdout.put( "Please enter a string with at least three chars." nl );

    endfor;


    // Do the string assignment via str.a_cpy

    str.a_cpy( string1 );
    mov( eax, string2 );

    stdout.put( "String1= '", string1, "'" nl );
    stdout.put( "String2= '", string2, "'" nl );

    // Okay, modify the data in string1 by overwriting
    // the first three characters of the string (note that
    // a string pointer always points at the first character
    // position in the string and we know we've got at least
    // three characters here).

    mov( string1, ebx );
    mov( 'a', (type char [ebx]) );
    mov( 'b', (type char [ebx+1]) );
    mov( 'c', (type char [ebx+2]) );
```

```
    // Okay, demonstrate that we have two different strings
    // because we used str.cpy to copy the data:

    stdout.put
    (
        "After assigning 'abc' to the first three characters in string1:"
        nl
        nl
    );
    stdout.put( "String1= '", string1, "'" nl );
    stdout.put( "String2= '", string2, "'" nl );


    // Note that we have to free the data associated with both
    // strings because they are not aliases of one another.

    strfree( string1 );
    strfree( string2 );


end stra_cpyDemo;
```

Whenever using copy by reference or str.a_cpy *to assign a string, don't forget to free the storage associated with the string when you are (completely) done with that string's data. Failure to do so may produce a memory leak if you do not have another pointer to the previous string data laying around.*

Obtaining the length of a character string is so common that the HLA Standard Library provides a str.length routine specifically for this purpose. Of course, you can fetch the length by using the str.strRec data type to access the length field directly, but constant use of this mechanism can be tiring because it involves a lot of typing. The str.length routine provides a more compact and convenient way to fetch the length information. You call str.length using one of the following two formats:

```
str.length( Reg32 );
str.length( string_variable );
```

This routine returns the current string length in the EAX register.

Another pair of useful string routines are the str.cat and str.a_cat procedures. They use the following syntax:

```
str.cat( srcRStr, destLStr );
str.a_cat( srcLStr, srcRStr );
```

These two routines concatenate two strings (that is, they create a new string by joining the two strings together). The str.cat procedure concatenates the source string to the end of the destination string. Before the concatenation actually takes place, str.cat checks to make sure that the destination string is large enough to hold the concatenated result; it raises the ex.StringOverflow exception if the destination string's maximum length is too small.

The str.a_cat routine, as its name suggests, allocates storage for the resulting string before doing the concatenation. This routine will allocate sufficient storage to hold the concatenated result; then it will copy the src1Str to the allocated storage. Finally it will append the string data pointed at by src2Str to the end of this new string and return a pointer to the new string in the EAX register.

CAUTION *Note a potential source of confusion. The* str.cat *procedure concatenates its first operand to the end of the second operand. Therefore,* str.cat *follows the standard (src, dest) operand format present in many HLA statements. The* str.a_cat *routine, on the other hand, has two source operands rather than a source and destination operand. The* str.a_cat *routine concatenates its two operands in an intuitive left-to-right fashion. This is the opposite of* str.cat. *Keep this in mind when using these two routines.*

Listing 4-16 demonstrates the use of the str.cat and str.a_cat routines:

Listing 4-16: Demonstration of str.cat and str.a_cat Routines.

```
// Program to demonstrate str.cat and str.a_cat.

program strcatDemo;
#include( "stdlib.hhf" );

static
    UserName:   string;
    Hello:      string;
    a_Hello:    string;

begin strcatDemo;

    // Allocate storage for the concatenated result:

    stralloc( 1024 );
    mov( eax, Hello );

    // Get some user input to use in this example:

    stdout.put( "Enter your name: ");
    stdin.flushInput();
    stdin.a_gets();
    mov( eax, UserName );

    // Use str.cat to combine the two strings:

    str.cpy( "Hello ", Hello );
    str.cat( UserName, Hello );
```

```
    // Use str.a_cat to combine the string strings:

    str.a_cat( "Hello ", UserName );
    mov( eax, a_Hello );

    stdout.put( "Concatenated string #1 is '", Hello, "'" nl );
    stdout.put( "Concatenated string #2 is '", a_Hello, "'" nl );

    strfree( UserName );
    strfree( a_Hello );
    strfree( Hello );

end strcatDemo;
```

The str.insert and str.a_insert routines are similar to the string concatenation procedures. However, the str.insert and str.a_insert routines let you insert one string anywhere into another string, not just at the end of the string. The calling sequences for these two routines are

```
str.insert( src, dest, index );
str.a_insert( StrToInsert, StrToInsertInto, index );
```

These two routines insert the source string (src or StrToInsert) into the destination string (dest or StrToInsertInto) starting at character position index. The str.insert routine inserts the source string directly into the destination string; if the destination string is not large enough to hold both strings, str.insert raises an ex.StringOverflow exception. The str.a_insert routine first allocates a new string on the heap, copies the destination string (StrToInsertInto) to the new string, and then inserts the source string (StrToInsert) into this new string at the specified offset; str.a_insert returns a pointer to the new string in the EAX register.

Indexes into a string are zero based. This means that if you supply the value zero as the index in str.insert or str.a_insert, then these routines will insert the source string before the first character of the destination string. Likewise, if the index is equal to the length of the string, then these routines will simply concatenate the source string to the end of the destination string.

NOTE   *If the* index *is greater than the length of the string, the* str.insert *and* str.a_insert *procedures will not raise an exception; instead, they will simply append the source string to the end of the destination string.*

The str.delete and str.a_delete routines let you remove characters from a string. They use the following calling sequence:

```
str.delete( strng, StartIndex, Length );
str.a_delete( strng, StartIndex, Length );
```

Both routines delete Length characters starting at character position StartIndex in string strng. The difference between the two is that str.delete deletes the characters directly from strng, whereas str.a_delete first allocates storage and copies strng, then deletes the characters from the new string (leaving *strng* untouched). The str.a_delete routine returns a pointer to the new string in the EAX register.

The str.delete and str.a_delete routines are very forgiving with respect to the values you pass in StartIndex and Length. If StartIndex is greater than the current length of the string, these routines do not delete any characters from the string. If StartIndex is less than the current length of the string, but StartIndex+Length is greater than the length of the string, then these routines will delete all characters from StartIndex to the end of the string.

Another very common string operation is the need to copy a portion of a string to another string without otherwise affecting the source string. The str.substr and str.a_substr routines provide this capability. These routines use the following syntax:

```
str.substr( src, dest, StartIndex, Length );
str.a_substr( src, StartIndex, Length );
```

The str.substr routine copies length characters, starting at position StartIndex, from the src string to the dest string. The dest string must have sufficient storage to hold the new string or str.substr will raise an ex.StringOverflow exception. If the StartIndex value is greater than the length of the string, then str.substr will raise an ex.StringIndexError exception. If StartIndex+Length is greater than the length of the source string, but StartIndex is less than the length of the string, then str.substr will extract only those characters from StartIndex to the end of the string.

The str.a_substr procedure behaves in a fashion nearly identical to str.substr except it allocates storage on the heap for the destination string. Other than overflow never occurs, str.a_substr handles exceptions the identically to str.substr.[18] As you can probably guess by now, str.a_substr returns a pointer to the newly allocated string in the EAX register.

After you begin working with string data for a little while, the need will invariably arise to compare two strings. A first attempt at string comparison, using the standard HLA relational operators, will compile but not necessarily produce the desired result:

```
    mov( s1, eax );
    if( eax = s2 ) then

        << code to execute if the strings are equal >>

    else
```

---

[18] Technically, *str.a_substr*, like all routines that call *malloc* to allocate storage, can raise an *ex.MemoryAllocationFailure* exception, but this is very unlikely to occur.

```
        << code to execute if the strings are not equal >>

    endif;
```

As just stated, this code will compile and execute just fine. However, it's probably not doing what you expect it to do. Remember, *strings are pointers*. This code compares the two pointers to see if they are equal. If they are equal, clearly the two strings are equal (because both s1 and s2 point at the exact same string data). However, the fact that the two pointers are different doesn't necessarily mean that the strings are not equivalent. Both s1 and s2 could contain different values (that is, they point at different addresses in memory), yet the string data at those two different addresses could be identical. Most programmers expect a string comparison for equality to be true if the data for the two strings is the same. Clearly a pointer comparison does not provide this type of comparison. To overcome this problem, the HLA Standard Library provides a set of string comparison routines that will compare the string data, not just their pointers. These routines use the following calling sequences:

```
str.eq( src1, src2 );
str.ne( src1, src2 );
str.lt( src1, src2 );
str.le( src1, src2 );
str.gt( src1, src2 );
str.ge( src1, src2 );
```

Each of these routines compares the src1 string to the src2 string and return true (1) or false (0) in the EAX register depending on the comparison. For example, "str.eq(s1, s2);" returns true in EAX if s1 is equal to s2. HLA provides a small extension that allows you to use the string comparison routines within an if statement.[19] The following code demonstrates the use of some of these comparison routines within an if statement:

```
        stdout.put( "Enter a single word: " );
        stdin.a_gets();
        if( str.eq( eax, "Hello" )) then

            stdout.put( "You entered 'Hello'", nl );

        endif;
        strfree( eax );
```

Note that the string the user enters in this example must exactly match "Hello", including the use of an upper case "H" at the beginning of the string. When processing user input, it is best to ignore alphabetic case in string comparisons because different users have different ideas about when they should be pressing the shift key on the keyboard. An easy solution is to use the HLA case-insensitive

---

[19] This extension is actually a little more general than this section describes. A later chapter will explain it fully.

string comparison functions. These routines compare two strings ignoring any differences in alphabetic case. These routines use the following calling sequences:

```
str.ieq( src1, src2 );
str.ine( src1, src2 );
str.ilt( src1, src2 );
str.ile( src1, src2 );
str.igt( src1, src2 );
str.ige( src1, src2 );
```

Other than they treat upper case characters the same as their lower case equivalents, these routines behave exactly like the former routines, returning true or false in EAX depending on the result of the comparison.

Like most high level languages, HLA compares strings using *lexicographical ordering*. This means that two strings are equal if and only if their lengths are the same and the corresponding characters in the two strings are exactly the same. For less than or greater than comparisons, lexicographical ordering corresponds to the way words appear in a dictionary. That is, "a" is less than "b" is less than "c," and so on. Actually, HLA compares the strings using the ASCII numeric codes for the characters, so if you are unsure whether "a" is less than a period, simply consult the ASCII character chart (incidentally, "a" is greater than a period in the ASCII character set, just in case you were wondering).

If two strings have different lengths, lexicographical ordering only worries about the length if the two strings exactly match up through the length of the shorter string. If this is the case, then the longer string is greater than the shorter string (and, conversely, the shorter string is less than the longer string). Note, however, that if the characters in the two strings do not match at all, then HLA's string comparison routines ignore the length of the string; e.g., "z" is always greater than "aaaaa" even though it is shorter.

The str.eq routine checks to see if two strings are equal. Sometimes, however, you might want to know whether one string *contains* another string. For example, you may want to know if some string contains the substring "north" or "south" to determine some action to take in a game. The HLA str.index routine lets you check to see if one string is contained as a substring of another. The str.index routine uses the following calling sequence:

```
str.index( StrToSearch, SubstrToSearchFor );
```

This function returns, in EAX, the offset into StrToSearch where SubstrToSearchFor appears. This routine returns -1 in EAX if SubstrToSearchFor is not present in StrToSearch. Note that str.index will do a case-sensitive search. Therefore the strings must exactly match. There is no case-insensitive variant of str.index you can use.[20]

---

[20] However, HLA does provide routines that will convert all the characters in a string to one case or another. So you can make copies of the strings, convert all the characters in both copies to lower case, and then search using these converted strings. This will achieve the same result.

The HLA string module contains many additional routines besides those this section presents. Space limitations and prerequisite knowledge prevent the presentation of all the string functions here; however, this does not mean that the remaining string functions are unimportant. You should definitely take a look at the HLA Standard Library documentation to learn everything you can about the powerful HLA string library routines.

4.14   In-Memory Conversions

The HLA Standard Library's string module contains dozens of routines for converting between strings and other data formats. Although it's a little premature in this text to present a complete description of those functions, it would be rather criminal not to discuss at least one of the available functions: the str.put routine. This one routine (which is actually a macro) encapsulates the capabilities of all the other string conversion functions, so if you learn how to use this one, you'll have most of the capabilities of those other routines at your disposal. For more information on the other string conversions, check out the HLA Standard Library documentation.

You use the str.put routine in a manner very similar to the stdout.put routine. The only difference is that the str.put routine "writes" its data to a string instead of the standard output device. A call to str.put has the following syntax:

```
str.put( destString, values_to_convert );
```

Example of a call to *str.put*:

```
str.put( destString, "I =", i:4, " J= ", j, " s=", s );
```

NOTE   *Generally, you would not put a newline character sequence at the end of the string as you would if you were printing the string to the standard output device.*

The destString parameter at the beginning of the *str.put* parameter list must be a string variable, and it must already have storage associated with it. If str.put attempts to store more characters than allowed into the destString parameter, then this function raises the *ex.StringOverflow* exception.

Most of the time you won't know the length of the string that *str.put* will produce. In those instances, you should simply allocate sufficient storage for a really large string, one that is way larger than you expect, and use this string data as the first parameter of the str.put call. This will prevent an exception from crashing your program. Generally, if you expect to produce about one screen line of text, you should probably allocate at least 256 characters for the destination string. If you're creating longer strings, you should probably use a default of 1024 characters (or more, if you're going to produce *really* large strings).

Example:

```
static
    s: string;
        .

        .

        .

    stralloc( 256 );
    mov( eax, s );
        .

        .

        .

    str.put( s, "R: ", r:16:4, "strval: '", strval:-10, "'");
```

You can use the str.put routine to convert any data to a string that you can print using stdout.put. You will probably find this routine invaluable for common value-to-string conversions.

At the time of this writing, there is no corresponding str.get routine that will read values from an input string (this routine will probably appear in a future version of the HLA Standard Library, so watch out for it). In the meantime, the HLA strings and conversions modules in the Standard Library do provide several stand-alone conversion functions you can use to convert string data to some other format. See the HLA Standard Library documentation for more details about these routines.

4.15 Character Sets

Character sets are another composite data type, like strings, built upon the character data type. A *character set* is a mathematical set of characters with the most important attribute being membership. That is, a character is either a member of a set or it is not a member of a set. The concept of sequence (e.g., whether one character comes before another, as in a string) is completely foreign to a character set. If two characters are members of a set, their order in the set is irrelevant. Also, membership is a binary relation; a character is either in the set or it is not in the set; you cannot have multiple copies of the same character in a character set. Finally, there are various operations that are possible on character sets including the mathematical set operations of union, intersection, difference, and membership test.

HLA implements a restricted form of character sets that allows set members to be any of the 128 standard ASCII characters (i.e., HLA's character set facilities do not support extended character codes in the range #128..#255). Despite this restriction, however, HLA's character set facilities are very powerful and are very handy when writing programs that work with string data. The following sections describe the implementation and use of HLA's character set facilities so you may take advantage of character sets in your own programs.

4.16 Character Set Implementation in HLA

There are many different ways to represent character sets in an assembly language program. HLA implements character sets by using an array of 128 boolean values. Each boolean value determines whether the corresponding character is or is not a member of the character set — i.e., a true boolean value indicates that the specified character is a member of the set; a false value indicates that the corresponding character is not a member of the set. To conserve memory, HLA allocates only a single bit for each character in the set; therefore, HLA character sets consume 16 bytes of memory because there are 128 bits in 16 bytes. This array of 128 bits is organized in memory, as shown in Figure 4-3.

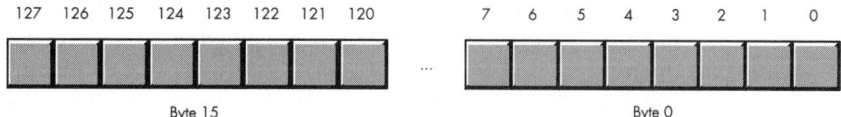

Figure 4-3: Bit Layout of a Character Set Object.

Bit zero of byte zero corresponds to ASCII code zero (the NUL character). If this bit is one, then the character set contains the NUL character; if this bit contains false, then the character set does not contain the NUL character. Likewise, bit zero of byte one (the eighth bit in the 128-bit array) corresponds to the backspace character (ASCII code is eight). Bit one of byte eight corresponds to ASCII code 65, an upper case 'A.' Bit 65 will contain a one if 'A' is a current member of the character set, it will contain zero if 'A' is not a member of the set.

While there are other possible ways to implement character sets, this bit vector implementation has the advantage that it is very easy to implement set operations like union, intersection, difference comparison, and membership tests.

HLA supports character set variables using the cset data type. To declare a character set variable, you would use a declaration like the following:

```
static
      CharSetVar: cset;
```

This declaration will reserve 16 bytes of storage to hold the 128 bits needed to represent a set of ASCII characters.

Although it is possible to manipulate the bits in a character set using instructions like and, or, xor, and so on, the 80x86 instruction set includes several bit test, set, reset, and complement instructions that are nearly perfect for manipulating character sets. The bt (bit test) instruction, for example, will copy a single bit in memory to the carry flag. The bt instruction allows the following syntactical forms:

```
        bt( BitNumber, BitsToTest );


        bt( reg16, reg16 );
        bt( reg32, reg32 );
        bt( constant, reg16 );
        bt( constant, reg32 );


        bt( reg16, mem16 );
        bt( reg32, mem32 );        //HLA treats cset objects as dwords within bt.
        bt( constant, mem16 );
        bt( constant, mem32 );     //HLA treats cset objects as dwords within bt.
```

The first operand holds a bit number; the second operand specifies a register or memory location whose bit should be copied into the carry flag. If the second operand is a register, the first operand must contain a value in the range $0..n\text{-}1$, where n is the number of bits in the second operand. If the first operand is a constant and the second operand is a memory location, the constant must be in the range 0..255. Here are some examples of these instructions:

```
    bt( 7, ax );              // Copies bit #7 of AX into the carry flag (CF).
    mov( 20, eax );
    bt( eax, ebx );           // Copies bit #20 of EBX into CF.

    // Copies bit #0 of the byte at CharSetVar+3 into CF.

    bt( 24, CharSetVar );

    // Copies bit #4 of the byte at DWmem+2 into CF.

    bt( eax, DWmem );
```

The bt instruction turns out to be quite useful for testing set membership. For example, to see if the character 'A' is a member of a character set, you could use a code sequence like the following:

```
        bt( 'A', CharSetVar );
        if( @c ) then

            << Do something if 'A' is a member of the set >>

        endif;
```

The bts (bit test and set), btr (bit test and reset), and btc (bit test and complement) instructions are also quite useful for manipulating character set variables. Like the bt instruction, these instructions copy the specified bit into the carry flag; after copying the specified bit, these instructions will set (bts), clear (btr), or invert (btc) the specified bit. Therefore, you can use the bts instruction to add a character to a character set via set union (that is, it adds a character to the set if the character was not already a member of the set; otherwise the set is unaffected). You can use the btr instruction to remove a character from a character set via set intersection (that is, it removes a character from the set if and only if it was previously in the set; otherwise it has no effect on the set). The btc instruction lets you add a character to the set if it wasn't previously in the set; it removes the character from the set if it was previously a member (that is, it toggles the membership of that character in the set).

4.17 HLA Character Set Constants and Character Set Expressions

HLA supports literal character set constants. These cset constants make it easy to initialize cset variables at compile time and they make it very easy to pass character set constants as procedure parameters. An HLA character set constant takes the following form:

```
{ Comma_separated_list_of_characters_and_character_ranges }
```

The following is an example of a simple character set holding the numeric digit characters:

```
{ '0', '1', '2', '3', '4', '5', '6', '7', '8', '9' }
```

When specifying a character set literal that has several contiguous values, HLA lets you concisely specify the values using only the starting and ending values of the range thusly:

```
{ '0'..'9' }
```

You may combine characters and various ranges within the same character set constant. For example, the following character set constant is all the alphanumeric characters:

```
{ '0'..'9', 'a'..'z', 'A'..'Z' }
```

You can use these cset literal constants in the const and val sections. The following example demonstrates how to create the symbolic constant AlphaNumeric using the character set above:

```
const
    AlphaNumeric: cset := {'0'..'9', 'a'..'z', 'A'..'Z' };
```

After the above declaration, you can use the identifier AlphaNumeric anywhere the character set literal is legal.

You can also use character set literals (and, of course, character set symbolic constants) as the initializer field for a static or readonly variable. The following code fragment demonstrates this:

```
static
    Alphabetic: cset := { 'a'..'z', 'A'..'Z' };
```

Anywhere you can use a character set literal constant, a character set constant expression is also legal. HLA supports the following operators in character set constant expressions:

CSetConst + CSetConst	Computes the union of the two sets.[21]
CSetConst * CSetConst	Computes the intersection of the two sets.[22]
CSetConst - CSetConst	Computes the set difference of the two sets.[23]
-CSetConst	Computes the set complement.[24]

Note that these operators only produce compile time results. That is, the expressions above are computed by the compiler during compilation; they do not emit any machine code. If you want to perform these operations on two different sets while your program is running, the HLA Standard Library provides routines you can call to achieve the results you desire.

4.18 The IN Operator in HLA HLL Boolean Expressions

The HLA IN operator combined with character sets can dramatically reduce the logic in your HLA programs. This text has waited until now to discuss this operator because certain forms require a knowledge of character sets and character set constants. Now that you've seen character set constants, there is no need to delay the introduction of this important language feature.

In addition to the standard boolean expressions in if, while, repeat..until, and other statements, HLA also supports boolean expressions that take the following forms:

```
reg₈ in CSetConstant
reg₈ not in CSetConstant
reg₈ in CSetVariable
reg₈ not in CSetVariable
```

These four forms of the in and not in operators check to see if a character in an 8-bit register is a member of a character set (either a character set constant or a character set variable). The following code fragment demonstrates these operators:

---

[21] The set union is the set of all characters that are in either set.

[22] The set intersection is the set of all characters that appear in both operand sets.

[23] The set difference is the set of characters that appear in the first set but do not appear in the second set.

[24] The set complement is the set of all characters not in the set.

```
const

    Alphabetic: cset := {'a'..'z', 'A'..'Z'};

        .
        .
        .

    stdin.getc();
    if( al in Alphabetic ) then

        stdout.put( "You entered an alphabetic character" nl );

    elseif( al in {'0'..'9'} ) then

        stdout.put( "You entered a numeric character" nl );

    endif;
```

4.19   Character Set Support in the HLA Standard Library

The HLA Standard Library provides several character set routines you may find useful. The character set support routines fall into four categories: standard character set functions, character set tests, character set conversions, and character set I/O. This section describes these routines in the HLA Standard Library.

To begin with, let's consider the Standard Library routines that help you construct character sets. These routines include: cs.empty, cs.cpy, cs.charToCset, cs.unionChar, cs.removeChar, cs.rangeChar, cs.strToCset, and cs.unionStr. These procedures let you build up character sets at run-time using character and string objects.

The cs.empty procedure initializes a character set variable to the empty set by setting all the bits in the character set to zero. This procedure call uses the following syntax (CSvar is a character set variable):

```
cs.empty( CSvar );
```

The cs.cpy procedure copies one character set to another, replacing any data previously held by the destination character set. The syntax for cs.cpy is

```
cs.cpy( srcCsetValue, destCsetVar );
```

The cs.cpy source character set can be either a character set constant or a character set variable. The destination character set must be a character set variable.

The cs.unionChar procedure adds a character to a character set. It uses the following calling sequence:

```
cs.unionChar( CharVar, CSvar );
```

This call will add the first parameter, a character, to the set via set union. Note that you could use the bts instruction to achieve this same result, although the cs.unionChar call is often more convenient (though slower).

The cs.charToCset function creates a singleton set (a set containing a single character). The calling format for this function is

```
cs.charToCset( CharValue, CSvar );
```

The first operand, the character value CharValue, can be an 8-bit register, a constant, or a character variable. The second operand (CSvar) must be a character set variable. This function clears the destination character set to all zeros and then unions the specified character into the character set.

The cs.removeChar procedure lets you remove a single character from a character set without affecting the other characters in the set. This function uses the same syntax as cs.charToCset and the parameters have the same attributes. The calling sequence is

```
cs.removeChar( CharValue, CSVar );
```

Note that if the character was not in the CSVar set to begin with, cs.removeChar will not affect the set.

The cs.rangeChar constructs a character set containing all the characters between two characters you pass as parameters. This function sets all bits outside the range of these two characters to zero. The calling sequence is

```
cs.rangeChar( LowerBoundChar, UpperBoundChar, CSVar );
```

The LowerBoundChar and UpperBoundChar parameters can be constants, registers, or character variables. CSVar, the destination character set, must be a cset variable.

The cs.strToCset procedure creates a new character set containing the union of all the characters in a character string. This procedure begins by setting the destination character set to the empty set and then it unions in the characters in the string one by one until it exhausts all characters in the string. The calling sequence is

```
cs.strToCset( StringValue, CSVar );
```

Technically, the StringValue parameter can be a string constant as well as a string variable; however, it doesn't make any sense to call cs.strToCset like this because cs.cpy is a much more efficient way to initialize a character set with a constant set of characters. As usual, the destination character set must be a cset variable. Typically, you'd use this function to create a character set based on a string input by the user.

The cs.unionStr procedure will add the characters in a string to an existing character set. Like cs.strToCset, you'd normally use this function to union characters into a set based on a string input by the user. The calling sequence for this is

```
cs.unionStr( StringValue, CSVar );
```

Standard set operations include union, intersection, and set difference. The HLA Standard Library routines cs.setunion, cs.intersection, and cs.difference provide these operations, respectively.[25] These routines all use the same calling sequence:

```
cs.setunion( srcCset, destCset );
cs.intersection( srcCset, destCset );
cs.difference( srcCset, destCset );
```

The first parameter can be a character set constant or a character set variable. The second parameter must be a character set variable. These procedures compute "destCset := destCset op srcCset" where *op* represents set union, intersection, or difference, depending on the function call.

The third category of character set routines test character sets in various ways. They typically return a boolean value indicating the result of the test. The HLA character set routines in this category include cs.IsEmpty, cs.member, cs.subset, cs.psubset, cs.superset, cs.psuperset, cs.eq, and cs.ne.

The cs.IsEmpty function tests a character set to see if it is the empty set. The function returns true or false in the EAX register. This function uses the following calling sequence:

```
cs.IsEmpty( CSetValue );
```

The single parameter may be a constant or a character set variable, although it doesn't make much sense to pass a character set constant to this procedure (because you would know at compile time whether this set is empty).

The cs.member function tests to see if a character value is a member of a set. This function returns true in the EAX register if the supplied character is a member of the specified set. Note that you can use the bt instruction to (more efficiently) test this same condition. However, the cs.member function is probably a little more convenient to use. The calling sequence for cs.member is

```
cs.member( CharValue, CsetValue );
```

The first parameter is a register, a character variable, or a constant. The second parameter is either a character set constant or a character set variable. It would be unusual for both parameters to be constants.

---

[25] cs.setunion was used rather than cs.union because "union" is an HLA reserved word.

The cs.subset, cs.psubset (proper subset), cs.superset, and cs.psuperset (proper superset) functions let you check to see if one character set is a subset or superset of another. The calling sequence for these four routines is nearly identical; it is one of the following:

```
cs.subset( CsetValue1, CsetValue2 );
cs.psubset( CsetValue1, CsetValue2 );
cs.superset( CsetValue1, CsetValue2 );
cs.psuperset( CsetValue1, CsetValue2 );
```

These routines compare the first parameter against the second parameter and return true or false in the EAX register depending upon the result of the comparison. One set is a subset of another if all the members of the first character set are present in the second character set. It is a proper subset if the second character set also contains characters not found in the first (left) character set. Likewise, one character set is a superset of another if it contains all the characters in the second (right) set (and, possibly, more). A proper superset contains additional characters above and beyond those found in the second set. The parameters can be either character set variables or character set constants; however, it would be unusual for both parameters to be character set constants (because you can determine this at compile time, there would be no need to call a run-time function to compute this).

The cs.eq and cs.ne check to see if two sets are equal or not equal. These functions return true or false in EAX depending upon the set comparison. The calling sequence is identical to the subset/superset functions above:

```
cs.eq( CsetValue1, CsetValue2 );
cs.ne( CsetValue1, CsetValue2 );
```

The cs.extract routine removes an arbitrary character from a character set and returns that character in the EAX register.[26] The calling sequence is the following:

```
cs.extract( CsetVar );
```

The single parameter must be a character set variable. Note that this function will modify the character set variable by removing some character from the character set. This function returns $FFFF_FFFF (-1) in EAX if the character set was empty prior to the call.

In addition to the routines found in the *cset.hhf* (character set) library module, the string and standard output modules also provide functions that allow or expect character set parameters. For example, if you supply a character set value as a parameter to stdout.put, the stdout.put routine will print the characters currently in the set. See the HLA Standard Library documentation for more details on character set–handling procedures.

---

[26] This routine returns the character in AL and zeros out the H.O. three bytes of EAX.

4.20   Using Character Sets in Your HLA Programs

Character sets are valuable for many different purposes in your programs. For example, one common use of character sets is to validate user input. This section will also present a couple of other applications for character sets to help you start thinking about how you could use them in your program.

Consider the following short code segment that gets a yes/no-type answer from the user:

```
static
    answer: char;
        .
        .
        .
    repeat
            .
            .
            .
        stdout.put( "Would you like to play again? " );
        stdin.FlushInput();
        stdin.get( answer );

    until( answer = 'n' );
```

A major problem with this code sequence is that it will only stop if the user presses a lower case 'n' character. If they type anything other than 'n' (including upper case 'N') the program will treat this as an affirmative answer and transfer back to the beginning of the repeat..until loop. A better solution would be to validate the user input before the until clause above to ensure that the user has only typed "n," "N," "y," or "Y." The following code sequence will accomplish this:

```
    repeat
            .
            .
            .
        repeat

            stdout.put( "Would you like to play again? " );
            stdin.FlushInput();
            stdin.get( answer );

        until( cs.member( answer, { 'n', 'N', 'Y', 'y' } );
        if( answer = 'N' ) then

            mov( 'n', answer );
```

```
            endif;

    until( answer = 'n' );
```

While an excellent use for character sets is to validate user input, especially when you must restrict the user to a small set of noncontiguous input characters, you should not use the cs.member function to test to see if a character value is within literal set. For example, you should never do something like the following:

```
    repeat

        stdout.put( "Enter a character between 0..9: " );
        stdin.getc();

    until( cs.member( al, {'0'..'9' } ) );
```

While there is nothing logically wrong with this code, keep in mind that HLA run-time boolean expressions allow simple membership tests using the in operator. You could write the code above far more efficiently using the following sequence:

```
    repeat

        stdout.put( "Enter a character between 0..9: ");
        stdin.getc();

    until( al in '0'..'9' );
```

The place where the cs.member function becomes useful is when you need to see if an input character is within a set of characters that you build at runtime.

4.21   Arrays

Along with strings, arrays are probably the most commonly used composite data. Yet most beginning programmers have a weak understanding of how arrays operate and their associated efficiency trade-offs. It's surprising how many novice (and even advanced!) programmers view arrays from a completely different perspective once they learn how to deal with arrays at the machine level.

Abstractly, an array is an aggregate data type whose members (elements) are all the same type. Selection of a member from the array is by an integer index.[27] Different indices select unique elements of the array. This text assumes that the integer indices are contiguous (though this is by no means required). That is, if the number x is a valid index into the array and y is also a valid index, with x < y, then all i such that x < i < y are valid indices into the array.

---

[27] Or some value whose underlying representation is integer, such as character, enumerated, and boolean types.

Whenever you apply the indexing operator to an array, the result is the specific array element chosen by that index. For example, A[i] chooses the ith element from array A. Note that there is no formal requirement that element i be anywhere near element i+1 in memory. As long as A[i] always refers to the same memory location and A[i+1] always refers to its corresponding location (and the two are different), the definition of an array is satisfied.

In this text, we will assume that array elements occupy contiguous locations in memory. An array with five elements will appear in memory, as shown in Figure 4-4.

The *base address* of an array is the address of the first element on the array and always appears in the lowest memory location. The second array element directly follows the first in memory, the third element follows the second, and so on. Note that there is no requirement that the indices start at zero. They may start with any number as long as they are contiguous. However, for the purposes of discussion, it's easier to discuss accessing array elements if the first index is zero. This text generally begins most arrays at index zero unless there is a good reason to do otherwise. However, this is for consistency only. There is no efficiency benefit one way or another to starting the array index at zero.

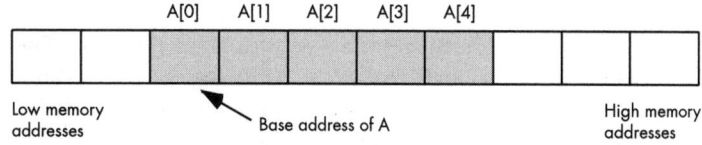

Figure 4-4: Array Layout in Memory.

To access an element of an array, you need a function that translates an array index to the address of the indexed element. For a single dimension array, this function is very simple. It is

---

Element_Address = Base_Address + ((Index - Initial_Index) * Element_Size)

---

where Initial_Index is the value of the first index in the array (which you can ignore if zero) and the value Element_Size is the size, in bytes, of an individual element of the array.

4.22   Declaring Arrays in Your HLA Programs

Before you access elements of an array, you need to set aside storage for that array. Fortunately, array declarations build on the declarations you've seen thus far. To allocate n elements in an array, you would use a declaration like the following in one of the variable declaration sections:

ArrayName: basetype[n];

ArrayName is the name of the array variable and basetype is the type of an element of that array. This sets aside storage for the array. To obtain the base address of the array, just use ArrayName.

The "[n]" suffix tells HLA to duplicate the object n times. Now let's look at some specific examples:

```
static

    CharArray: char[128];        // Character array with elements 0..127.
    IntArray: integer[ 8 ];      // "integer" array with elements 0..7.
    ByteArray: byte[10];         // Array of bytes with elements 0..9.
    PtrArray: dword[4];          // Array of double words with elements 0..3.
```

The second example, of course, assumes that you have defined the integer data type in the type section of the program.

These examples all allocate storage for uninitialized arrays. You may also specify that the elements of the arrays be initialized to a single value using declarations like the following in the static and readonly sections:

```
RealArray: real32[8] := [ 1.0, 1.0, 1.0, 1.0, 1.0, 1.0, 1.0, 1.0 ];
IntegerAry: integer[8] := [ 1, 1, 1, 1, 1, 1, 1, 1 ];
```

These definitions both create arrays with eight elements. The first definition initializes each four-byte real value to 1.0; the second declaration initializes each integer element to one. Note that the number of constants within the square brackets must exactly match the size of the array.

This initialization mechanism is fine if you want each element of the array to have the same value. What if you want to initialize each element of the array with a (possibly) different value? No sweat; just specify a different set of values in the list surrounded by the square brackets in the preceding example:

```
RealArray: real32[8] := [ 1.0, 2.0, 3.0, 4.0, 5.0, 6.0, 7.0, 8.0 ];
IntegerAry: integer[8] := [ 1, 2, 3, 4, 5, 6, 7, 8 ];
```

4.23   HLA Array Constants

The last few examples in the previous section demonstrate the use of HLA array constants. An HLA array constant is nothing more than a list of values surrounded by a pair of brackets. The following are all legal array constants:

```
[ 1, 2, 3, 4 ]
[ 2.0, 3.14159, 1.0, 0.5 ]
[ 'a', 'b', 'c', 'd' ]
[ "Hello", "world", "of", "assembly" ]
```

(Note that this last array constant contains four double word pointers to the four HLA strings appearing elsewhere in memory.)

As you saw in the previous section you can use array constants in the static and readonly sections to provide initial values for array variables. Of course, the number of comma-separated items in an array constant must exactly match the number of array elements in the variable declaration. Likewise, the type of the array constant's elements must match the array variable's element type.

Using array constants to initialize small arrays is very convenient. Of course, if your array has several thousand elements, typing them all will not be very much fun. Most arrays initialized this way have no more than a couple hundred entries, and generally far less than a hundred. It is reasonable to use an array constant to initialize such variables. However, at some point it will become far too tedious and error-prone to initialize arrays in this fashion. You probably would not want to manually initialize an array with 1,000 different elements using an array constant. However, if you want to initialize all the elements of an array with the same value, HLA does provide a special array constant syntax for doing so. Consider the following declaration:

```
BigArray: uns32[ 1000 ] := 1000 dup [ 1 ];
```

This declaration creates a 1,000-element integer array initializing each element of the array with the value one. The "1000 dup [1]" expression tells HLA to create an array constant by duplicating the single value "[1]" 1,000 times. You can even use the dup operator to duplicate a series of values (rather than a single value), as the following example indicates:

```
SixteenInts: int32[16] := 4 dup [1,2,3,4];
```

This example initializes SixteenInts with four copies of the sequence "1, 2, 3, 4" yielding a total of sixteen different integers (i.e., 1, 2, 3, 4, 1, 2, 3, 4, 1, 2, 3, 4, 1, 2, 3, 4).

You will see some more possibilities with the dup operator when looking at multidimensional arrays a little later.

4.24 Accessing Elements of a Single Dimension Array

To access an element of a zero-based array, you can use the simplified formula:

```
Element_Address = Base_Address + index * Element_Size
```

For the Base_Address entry you can use the name of the array (because HLA associates the address of the first element of an array with the name of that array). The Element_Size entry is the number of bytes for each array element. If the object is an array of bytes, the Element_Size field is one (resulting in a very simple computation). If each element of the array is a word (or other two-byte type) then Element_Size is two. And so on. To access an element of the SixteenInts array in the previous section, you'd use the formula:

```
Element_Address = SixteenInts + index*4
```

The 80x86 code equivalent to the statement "EAX:=SixteenInts[index]" is

```
mov( index, ebx );
shl( 2, ebx );           //Sneaky way to compute 4*ebx
mov( SixteenInts[ ebx ], eax );
```

There are two important things to notice here. First of all, this code uses the shl instruction rather than the intmul instruction to compute 4*index. The main reason for choosing shl is that it was more efficient. It turns out that shl is a *lot* faster than intmul on many processors.

The second thing to note about this instruction sequence is that it does not explicitly compute the sum of the base address plus the index times two. Instead, it relies on the indexed addressing mode to implicitly compute this sum. The instruction "mov(SixteenInts[ebx], eax);" loads EAX from location Sixteen-Ints+EBX, which is the base address plus index*4 (because EBX contains index*4). Sure, you could have used

```
lea( eax, SixteenInts );
mov( index, ebx );
shl( 2, ebx );           //Sneaky way to compute 4*ebx
add( eax, ebx );         //Compute base address plus index*4
mov( [ebx], eax );
```

in place of the previous sequence, but why use five instructions where three will do the same job? This is a good example of why you should know your addressing modes inside and out. Choosing the proper addressing mode can reduce the size of your program, thereby speeding it up.

Of course, as long as we're discussing efficiency improvements, it's worth pointing out that the 80x86 scaled indexed addressing modes let you automatically multiply an index by one, two, four, or eight. Because this current example multiplies the index by four, we can simplify the code even further by using the scaled indexed addressing mode:

```
mov( index, ebx );
mov( SixteenInts[ ebx*4 ], eax );
```

Note, however, that if you need to multiply by some constant other than one, two, four, or eight, then you cannot use the scaled indexed addressing modes. Similarly, if you need to multiply by some element size that is not a power of two, you will not be able to use the shl instruction to multiply the index by the element size; instead, you will have to use intmul or some other instruction sequence to do the multiplication.

The indexed addressing mode on the 80x86 is a natural for accessing elements of a single dimension array. Indeed, its syntax even suggests an array access. The only thing to keep in mind is that you must remember to multiply the index by the size of an element. Failure to do so will produce incorrect results.

Before moving on to multidimensional arrays, a couple of additional points about addressing modes and arrays are in order. The above sequences work great if you only access a single element from the SixteenInts array. However, if you access several different elements from the array within a short section of code, and you can afford to dedicate another register to the operation, you can certainly shorten your code and, perhaps, speed it up as well. Consider the following code sequence:

```
lea( ebx, SixteenInts );
mov( index, esi );
mov( [ebx+esi*4], eax );
```

Now EBX contains the base address, and ESI contains the index value. Of course, this hardly appears to be a good trade-off. However, when accessing additional elements in SixteenInts you do not have to reload EBX with the base address of SixteenInts for the next access. The following sequence is a little shorter than the comparable sequence that doesn't load the base address into EBX:

```
lea( ebx, SixteenInts );
mov( index, esi );
mov( [ebx+esi*4], eax );
     .
     .                          //Assumption: EBX is left alone
     .                          //    through this code.
mov( index2, esi );
mov( [ebx+esi*4], eax );
```

This code is slightly shorter because the "mov([ebx+esi*4], eax);" instruction is slightly shorter than the "mov(SixteenInts[ebx*4], eax);" instruction. Of course the more accesses to SixteenInts you make without reloading EBX, the greater your savings will be. Tricky little code sequences such as this one sometimes pay off handsomely. However, the savings depend entirely on which processor you're using. Code sequences that run faster on one 80x86 CPU might actually run *slower* on a different CPU. Unfortunately, if speed is what you're after there are no hard and fast rules. In fact, it is very difficult to predict the speed of most instructions on the 80x86 CPUs.

4.24.1 *Sorting an Array of Values*

Almost every textbook on this planet gives an example of a sort when introducing arrays. Because you've probably seen how to do a sort in high level languages already, it's probably instructive to take a quick look at a sort in HLA. The example code in this section will use a variant of the bubble sort, which is great for short lists of data and lists that are nearly sorted, but horrible for just about everything else.[28]

---

[28] Fear not; you'll see some better sorting algorithms in the chapter on procedures and recursion.

```
const
    NumElements:= 16;

static
    DataToSort: uns32[ NumElements ] :=
                    [
                        1, 2, 16, 14,
                        3, 9, 4,  10,
                        5, 7, 15, 12,
                        8, 6, 11, 13
                    ];


    NoSwap: boolean;

        .
        .
        .


// Bubble sort for the DataToSort array:

repeat

    mov( true, NoSwap );
    for( mov( 0, ebx ); ebx <= NumElements-2; inc( ebx )) do

        mov( DataToSort[ ebx*4], eax );
        if( eax > DataToSort[ ebx*4 + 4] ) then

            mov( DataToSort[ ebx*4 + 4 ], ecx );
            mov( ecx, DataToSort[ ebx*4 ] );
            mov( eax, DataToSort[ ebx*4 + 4 ] ); // Note: EAX contains
            mov( false, NoSwap );                //  DataToSort[ ebx*4 ]

        endif;

    endfor;

until( NoSwap );
```

The bubble sort works by comparing adjacent elements in an array. The
interesting thing to note in this code fragment is how it compares adjacent
elements. You will note that the if statement compares EAX (which contains
"DataToSort[ebx*4]") against "DataToSort[EBX*4 + 4]". Because each element
of this array is four bytes (uns32), the index "[EBX*4 + 4]" references the next
element beyond "[EBX*4]".

As is typical for a bubble sort, this algorithm terminates if the innermost loop
completes without swapping any data. If the data is already presorted, then the
bubble sort is very efficient, making only one pass over the data. Unfortunately, if

the data is not sorted (worst case, if the data is sorted in reverse order), then this algorithm is extremely inefficient. Indeed, although it is possible to modify the code above so that, on the average, it runs about twice as fast, such optimizations are wasted on such a poor algorithm. However, the bubble sort is very easy to implement and understand (which is why introductory texts continue to use it in examples).

4.25   Multidimensional Arrays

The 80x86 hardware can easily handle single dimension arrays. Unfortunately, there is no magic addressing mode that lets you easily access elements of multidimensional arrays. That's going to take some work and several instructions.

Before discussing how to declare or access multidimensional arrays, it would be a good idea to figure out how to implement them in memory. The first problem is to figure out how to store a multidimensional object into a one-dimensional memory space.

Consider for a moment a Pascal array of the form "A:array[0..3,0..3] of char;". This array contains 16 bytes organized as four rows of four characters. Somehow you've got to draw a correspondence with each of the 16 bytes in this array and 16 contiguous bytes in main memory. Figure 4-5 shows one way to do this:

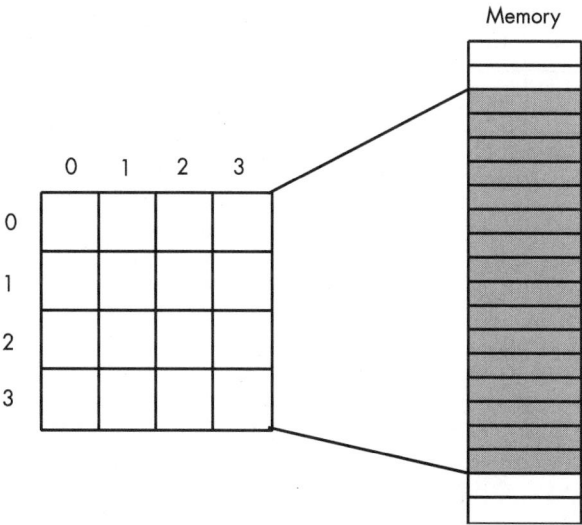

Figure 4-5: Mapping a 4x4 Array to Sequential Memory Locations.

The actual mapping is not important as long as two things occur: (1) each element maps to a unique memory location, (that is, no two entries in the array occupy the same memory locations) and (2) the mapping is consistent. That is, a given element in the array always maps to the same memory location. So what you really need is a function with two input parameters (row and column) that produce an offset into a linear array of 16 memory locations.

Now any function that satisfies the above constraints will work fine. Indeed, you could randomly choose a mapping as long as it was unique. However, what you really want is a mapping that is efficient to compute at runtime and works for any-sized array (not just 4x4 or even limited to two dimensions). While there are a large number of possible functions that fit this bill, there are two functions in particular that most programmers and most high level languages use: *row major ordering* and *column major ordering*.

4.25.1 Row Major Ordering

Row major ordering assigns successive elements, moving across the rows and then down the columns, to successive memory locations. This mapping is demonstrated in Figure 4-6.

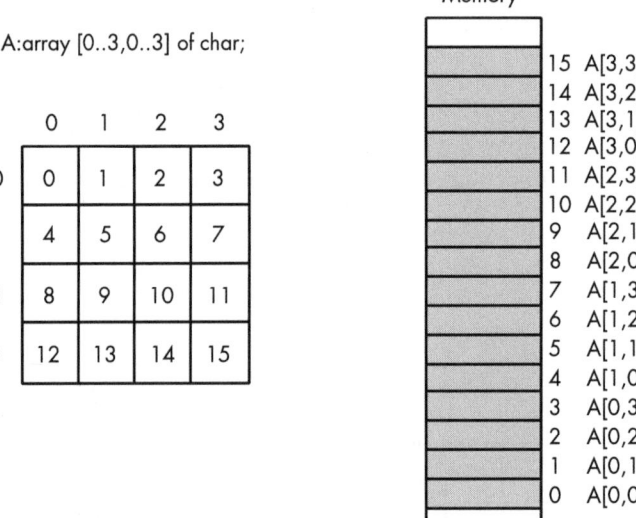

Figure 4-6: Row Major Array Element Ordering.

Row major ordering is the method employed by most high level programming languages including Pascal, C/C++, Java, Ada, and Modula-2. It is very easy to implement and easy to use in machine language. The conversion from a two-dimensional structure to a linear array is very intuitive. You start with the first row (row number zero) and then concatenate the second row to its end. You then concatenate the third row to the end of the list, then the fourth row, and so on (see Figure 4-7).

The actual function that converts a list of index values into an offset is a slight modification of the formula for computing the address of an element of a single dimension array. The formula to compute the offset for a 4x4 two-dimensional row major ordered array is

---

```
Element_Address = Base_Address + (colindex * row_size + rowindex) * Element_Size
```

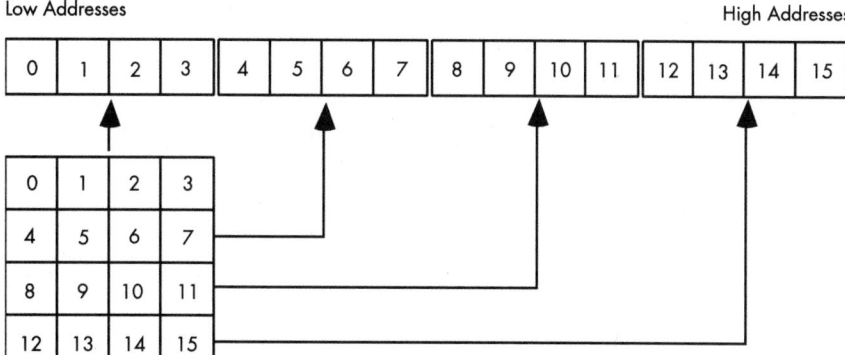

Figure 4-7: Another View of Row Major Ordering for a 4x4 Array.

As usual, Base_Address is the address of the first element of the array (A[0][0] in this case), and Element_Size is the size of an individual element of the array in bytes. colindex is the leftmost index, and rowindex is the rightmost index into the array. Row_size is the number of elements in one row of the array (four, in this case, because each row has four elements). Assuming Element_Size is one, this formula computes the following offsets from the base address:

Column Index	Row Index	Offset into Array
0	0	0
0	1	1
0	2	2
0	3	3
1	0	4
1	1	5
1	2	6
1	3	7
2	0	8
2	1	9
2	2	10
2	3	11
3	0	12
3	1	13
3	2	14
3	3	15

For a three-dimensional array, the formula to compute the offset into memory is the following:

```
Address = Base + ((depthindex*col_size+colindex) * row_size + rowindex) *
            Element_Size
```

col_size is the number of items in a column; row_size is the number of items in a row. In C/C++, if you've declared the array as "*type* A[i] [j] [k];" then row_size is equal to k and col_size is equal to j.

For a four-dimensional array, declared in C/C++ as "*type* A[i] [j] [k] [m];" the formula for computing the address of an array element is

---

```
Address =
Base + (((LeftIndex * depth_size + depthindex)*col_size+colindex) * row_size +
rowindex) * Element_Size
```

---

depth_size is equal to j, col_size is equal to k, and row_size is equal to m. leftIndex represents the value of the leftmost index.

By now you're probably beginning to see a pattern. There is a generic formula that will compute the offset into memory for an array with *any* number of dimensions; however, you'll rarely use more than four.

Another convenient way to think of row major arrays is as arrays of arrays. Consider the following single dimension Pascal array definition:

```
A: array [0..3] of  sometype;
```

Assume that sometype is the type "sometype = array [0..3] of char;".

A is a single dimension array. Its individual elements happen to be arrays, but you can safely ignore that for the time being. The formula to compute the address of an element of a single dimension array is

---

```
Element_Address = Base + Index * Element_Size
```

In this case Element_Size happens to be four because each element of A is an array of four characters. So what does this formula compute? It computes the base address of each row in this 4x4 array of characters (see Figure 4-8):

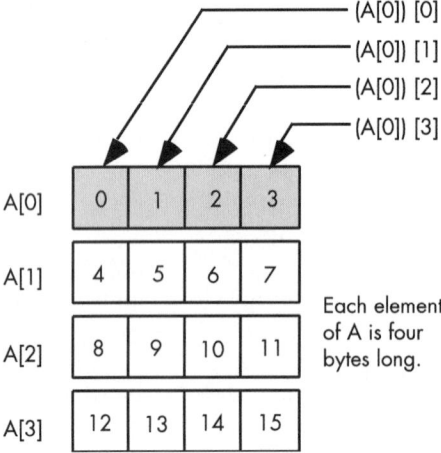

Figure 4-8: Viewing a 4x4 Array as an Array of Arrays.

Of course, once you compute the base address of a row, you can reapply the single dimension formula to get the address of a particular element. While this doesn't affect the computation at all, conceptually it's probably a little easier to deal with several single dimension computations rather than a complex multidimensional array element address computation.

Consider a Pascal array defined as "A:array [0..3] [0..3] [0..3] [0..3] [0..3] of char;". You can view this five-dimension array as a single dimension array of arrays. The following Pascal code provides such a definition:

```
type
        OneD = array [0..3] of char;
        TwoD = array [0..3] of OneD;
        ThreeD = array [0..3] of TwoD;
        FourD = array [0..3] of ThreeD;
var
        A : array [0..3] of FourD;
```

The size of OneD is four bytes. Because TwoD contains four OneD arrays, its size is 16 bytes. Likewise, ThreeD is four TwoDs, so it is 64 bytes long. Finally, FourD is four ThreeDs, so it is 256 bytes long. To compute the address of "A [b, c, d, e, f]" you could use the following steps:

- Compute the address of A [b] as "Base + b * size". Here size is 256 bytes. Use this result as the new base address in the next computation.

- Compute the address of A [b, c] by the formula "Base + c*size", where Base is the value obtained immediately above, and size is 64. Use the result as the new base in the next computation.

- Compute the base address of A [b, c, d] by "Base + d*size" with Base coming from the previous computation and size being 16. Use the result as the new base in the next computation.

- Compute the address of A [b, c, d, e] with the formula "Base + e*size" with Base from the preceding computation and size being four. Use this value as the base for the next computation.

- Finally, compute the address of A [b, c, d, e, f] using the formula "Base + f*size" where Base comes from the above computation and size is one (obviously you can simply ignore this final multiplication). The result you obtain at this point is the address of the desired element.

One of the main reasons you won't find higher-dimension arrays in assembly language is that assembly language emphasizes the inefficiencies associated with such access. It's easy to enter something like "A [b,c,d,e,f]" into a Pascal program, not realizing what the compiler is doing with the code. Assembly language programmers are not so cavalier: They see the mess you wind up with when you use higher-dimension arrays. Indeed, good assembly language programmers try to avoid two-dimension arrays and often resort to tricks in order to access data in such an array when its use becomes absolutely mandatory. But more on that a little later.

4.25.2 Column Major Ordering

Column major ordering is the other function frequently used to compute the address of an array element. FORTRAN and various dialects of BASIC (e.g., older versions of Microsoft BASIC) use this method to index arrays.

In row major ordering the rightmost index increases the fastest as you moved through consecutive memory locations. In column major ordering the leftmost index increases the fastest. Pictorially, a column major ordered array is organized as shown in Figure 4-9.

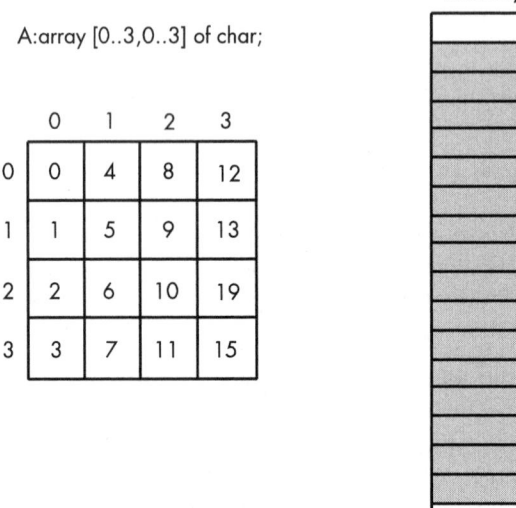

Figure 4-9: Column Major Array Element Ordering.

The formulae for computing the address of an array element when using column major ordering is very similar to that for row major ordering. You simply reverse the indexes and sizes in the computation:

```
For a two-dimension column major array:
Element_Address = Base_Address + (rowindex * col_size + colindex) * Element_Size


For a three-dimension column major array:
Address = Base + ((rowindex*col_size+colindex) * depth_size + depthindex) *
Element_Size


For a four-dimension column major array:
Address =
    Base + (((rowindex * col_size + colindex)*depth_size + depthindex) *
        Left_size + Leftindex) * Element_Size
```

4.26 Allocating Storage for Multidimensional Arrays

If you have an m x n array, it will have m * n elements and require m*n*Element_Size bytes of storage. To allocate storage for an array you must reserve this memory. As usual, there are several different ways of accomplishing this task. Fortunately, HLA's array declaration syntax is very similar to high level language array declaration syntax, so C/C++, BASIC, and Pascal programmers will feel right at home. To declare a multidimensional array in HLA, you use a declaration like the following:

```
ArrayName: elementType [ comma_separated_list_of_dimension_bounds ];
```

For example, here is a declaration for a 4x4 array of characters:

```
GameGrid: char[ 4, 4 ];
```

Here is another example that shows how to declare a three-dimensional array of strings:

```
NameItems: string[ 2, 3, 3 ];
```

Remember, string objects are really pointers, so this array declaration reserves storage for 18 double word pointers (2*3*3=18).

As was the case with single dimension arrays, you may initialize every element of the array to a specific value by following the declaration with the assignment operator and an array constant. Array constants ignore dimension information; all that matters is that the number of elements in the array constant correspond to the number of elements in the actual array. The following example shows the GameGrid declaration with an initializer:

```
GameGrid: char[ 4, 4 ] :=
    [
        'a', 'b', 'c', 'd',
        'e', 'f', 'g', 'h',
        'i', 'j', 'k', 'l',
        'm', 'n', 'o', 'p'
    ];
```

Note that HLA ignores the indentation and extra whitespace characters (e.g., newlines) appearing in this declaration. It was laid out to enhance readability (which is always a good idea). HLA does not interpret the four separate lines as representing rows of data in the array. Humans do, which is why it's good to lay out the initial data in this manner, but HLA completely ignores the physical layout of the declaration. All that matters is that there are 16 (4*4) characters in the array constant. You'll probably agree that this is much easier to read than

```
GameGrid: char[ 4,4 ] :=
    [ 'a', 'b', 'c', 'd', 'e', 'f', 'g', 'h', 'i', 'j', 'k', 'l', 'm',
      'n', 'o', 'p' ];
```

Of course, if you have a large array, an array with really large rows, or an array with many dimensions, there is little hope for winding up with something readable. That's when comments that carefully explain everything come in handy.

As with single dimension arrays, you can use the dup operator to initialize each element of a really large array with the same value. The following example initializes a 256x64 array of bytes so that each byte contains the value $FF:

```
StateValue: byte[ 256, 64 ] := 256*64 dup [$ff];
```

Note the use of a constant expression to compute the number of array elements rather than simply using the constant 16,384 (256*64). The use of the constant expression more clearly suggests that this code is initializing each element of a 256x64 element array than does the simple literal constant 16,384.

Another HLA trick you can use to improve the readability of your programs is to use *nested array constants*. The following is an example of an HLA nested array constant:

```
[ [0, 1, 2], [3, 4], [10, 11, 12, 13] ]
```

Whenever HLA encounters an array constant nested inside another array constant, it simply removes the brackets surrounding the nested array constant and treats the whole constant as a single array constant. For example, HLA converts the preceding nested array constant to the following:

```
[ 0, 1, 2, 3, 4, 10, 11, 12, 13 ]
```

You can take advantage of this fact to help make your programs a little more readable. For multidimensional array constants you can enclose each row of the constant in square brackets to denote that the data in each row is grouped and separate from the other rows. As an example, consider the following declaration for the GameGrid array that is identical (as far as HLA is concerned) to the previous declaration:

```
GameGrid: char[ 4, 4 ] :=
    [
        [ 'a', 'b', 'c', 'd' ],
        [ 'e', 'f', 'g', 'h' ],
        [ 'i', 'j', 'k', 'l' ],
        [ 'm', 'n', 'o', 'p' ]
    ];
```

This declaration makes it clearer that the array constant is a 4x4 array rather than just a 16-element one-dimensional array whose elements wouldn't fit all on one line of source code. Little aesthetic improvements like this are what separate mediocre programmers from good programmers.

4.27 Accessing Multidimensional Array Elements in Assembly Language

Well, you've seen the formulae for computing the address of an array element. Now it's time to see how to access elements of those arrays using assembly language.

The mov, shl, and intmul instructions make short work of the various equations that compute offsets into multidimensional arrays. Let's consider a two-dimensional array first:

```
static
    i:          int32;
    j:          int32;
    TwoD:         int32[ 4, 8 ];


            .
            .
            .


// To peform the operation TwoD[i,j] := 5; you'd use code like the following.
// Note that the array index computation is (i*8 + j)*4.

        mov( i, ebx );
        shl( 3, ebx );          // Multiply by eight (shl by 3 is a multiply by 8).
        add( j, ebx );
        mov( 5, TwoD[ ebx*4 ] );
```

Note that this code does *not* require the use of a two-register addressing mode on the 80x86. Although an addressing mode like TwoD[ebx][esi] looks like it should be a natural for accessing two-dimensional arrays, that isn't the purpose of this addressing mode.

Now consider a second example that uses a three-dimensional array:

```
static
    i:              int32;
    j:              int32;
    k:              int32;
    ThreeD:           int32[ 3, 4, 5 ];
            .
            .
            .
```

```
// To peform the operation ThreeD[i,j,k] := ESI; you'd use the following code
// that computes ((i*4 + j)*5 + k )*4 as the address of ThreeD[i,j,k].

        mov( i, ebx );
        shl( 2, ebx );                          // Four elements per column.
        add( j, ebx );
        intmul( 5, ebx );                       // Five elements per row.
        add( k, ebx );
        mov( esi, ThreeD[ ebx*4 ] );
```

Note that this code uses the intmul instruction to multiply the value in EBX by
five. Remember, the shl instruction can only multiply a register by a power of two.
While there are ways to multiply the value in a register by a constant other than a
power of two, the intmul instruction is more convenient.[29]

4.28 Large Arrays and MASM (Windows Programmers Only)

There is a defect in later versions of MASM 6.*x* that creates some problems when
you declare large static arrays in your programs. Now you may be wondering what
this has to do with you because we're using HLA, but don't forget that HLA 1.*x*
under Windows compiles to MASM assembly code and then runs MASM to
assemble this output. Therefore, any defect in MASM is going to be a problem
for HLA users writing Windows code (obviously, this doesn't affect Linux users
where HLA generates Gas code).

The problem occurs when the total number of array elements you declare in
a static section (static, readonly, or storage) starts to get large. Large in this case is
CPU dependent, but it falls somewhere between 128,000 and one million
elements for most systems. MASM, for whatever reason, uses a very slow
algorithm to emit array code to the object file; by the time you declare 64K array
elements, MASM starts to produce a noticeable delay while assembling your
code. After that point, the delay grows linearly with the number of array elements
(i.e., as you double the number of array elements you double the assembly time)
until the data saturates MASM's internal buffers and the cache. Then there is a
big jump in execution time. For example, on a 300 MHz Pentium II processor,
compiling a program with an array with 256,000 elements takes about
30 seconds; compiling a program with an array having 512,000 element takes
several minutes. Compiling a program with a one-megabyte array seems to take
forever.

There are a couple of ways to solve this problem. First, of course, you can
limit the size of your arrays in your program. Unfortunately, this isn't always an
option available to you. The second possibility is to use MASM 6.11; the defect
was introduced in MASM after this version. The problem with MASM 6.11 is that
it doesn't support the MMX instruction set, so if you're going to compile MMX
instructions (or other instructions that MASM 6.11 doesn't support) with HLA

---

[29] A full discussion of multiplication by constants other than a power of two appears in the
chapter on arithmetic.

you will not be able to use this option. A third option is to put your arrays in a var section rather than a static declaration section; HLA processes arrays you declare in the var section so MASM never sees them. Hence, arrays you declare in the var section don't suffer from this problem.

4.29   Records

Another major composite data structure is the Pascal record or C/C++ structure.[30] The Pascal terminology is probably better, because it tends to avoid confusion with the more general term data structure. Because HLA uses the term "record" we'll adopt that term here.

Whereas an array is homogeneous, whose elements are all the same, the elements in a record can have different types. Arrays let you select a particular element via an integer index. With records, you must select an element (known as a *field*) by name.

The whole purpose of a record is to let you encapsulate different, but logically related, data into a single package. The Pascal record declaration for a student is a typical example:

```
student =
    record
        Name: string [64];
        Major: integer;
        SSN:    string[11];
        Midterm1: integer;
        Midterm2: integer;
        Final: integer;
        Homework: integer;
        Projects: integer;
    end;
```

Most Pascal compilers allocate each field in a record to contiguous memory locations. This means that Pascal will reserve the first 65 bytes for the name[31]; the next two bytes hold the major code, the next 12 the Social Security Number, and so on.

In HLA, you can also create structure types using the record/endrecord declaration. You would encode the above record in HLA as follows:

```
type
    student:    record
        Name: char[65];
        Major: int16;
        SSN:    char[12];
        Midterm1: int16;
        Midterm2: int16;
```

---

[30] It also goes by some other names in other languages, but most people recognize at least one of these names.

[31] Strings require an extra byte, in addition to all the characters in the string, to encode the length.

```
        Final: int16;
        Homework: int16;
        Projects: int16;
    endrecord;
```

As you can see, the HLA declaration is very similar to the Pascal declaration. Note that, to be true to the Pascal declaration, this example uses character arrays rather than strings for the Name and SSN (U.S. Social Security Number) fields. In a real HLA record declaration you'd probably use a string type for at least the name (keeping in mind that a string variable is only a four-byte pointer).

The field names within the record must be unique. That is, the same name may not appear two or more times in the same record. However, all field names are local to that record. Therefore, you may reuse those field names elsewhere in the program or in different records.

The record/endrecord declaration may appear in a variable declaration section (e.g., static or var) or in a type declaration section. In the previous example the Student declaration appears in the type section, so this does not actually allocate any storage for a Student variable. Instead, you have to explicitly declare a variable of type Student. The following example demonstrates how to do this:

```
var
    John: Student;
```

This allocates 81 bytes of storage laid out in memory as shown in Figure 4-10.

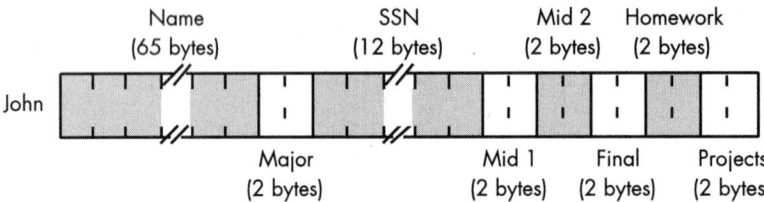

Figure 4-10: Student Data Structure Storage in Memory.

If the label John corresponds to the *base address* of this record, then the Name field is at offset John+0, the Major field is at offset John+65, the SSN field is at offset John+67, and so on.

To access an element of a structure you need to know the offset from the beginning of the structure to the desired field. For example, the Major field in the variable John is at offset 65 from the base address of John. Therefore, you could store the value in AX into this field using the instruction

```
mov( ax, (type word John[65]) );
```

Unfortunately, memorizing all the offsets to fields in a record defeats the whole purpose of using them in the first place. After all, if you've got to deal with these numeric offsets why not just use an array of bytes instead of a record?

Well, as it turns out, HLA lets you refer to field names in a record using the same mechanism C/C++/C# and Pascal use: the dot operator. To store AX into the Major field, you could use "mov(ax, John.Major);" instead of the previous instruction. This is much more readable and certainly easier to use.

Note that the use of the dot operator does *not* introduce a new addressing mode. The instruction "mov(ax, John.Major);" still uses the displacement only addressing mode. HLA simply adds the base address of John with the offset to the Major field (65) to get the actual displacement to encode into the instruction.

Like any type declaration, HLA requires all record type declarations to appear in the program before you use them. However, you don't have to define all records in the type section to create record variables. You can use the record/endrecord declaration directly in a variable declaration section. This is convenient if you have only one instance of a given record object in your program. The following example demonstrates this:

```
storage
    OriginPoint:    record
        x: uns8;
        y: uns8;
        z: uns8;
    endrecord;
```

4.30   Record Constants

HLA lets you define record constants. In fact, HLA supports both symbolic record constants and literal record constants. Record constants are useful as initializers for static record variables. They are also quite useful as compile time data structures when using the HLA compile time language (see the HLA Reference Manual for more details on the HLA compile time language). This section discusses how to create record constants.

A literal record constant takes the following form:

```
RecordTypeName:[ List_of_comma_separated_constants ]
```

The RecordTypeName is the name of a record data type you've defined in an HLA type section prior to this point.

The constant list appearing between the brackets are the data items for each of the fields in the specified record. The first item in the list corresponds to the first field of the record, the second item in the list corresponds to the second field, and so on. The data types of each of the constants appearing in this list must match their respective field types. The following example demonstrates how to use a literal record constant to initialize a record variable:

```
type
    point:    record
        x:int32;
        y:int32;
        z:int32;
```

```
            endrecord;

    static
            Vector: point := point:[ 1, -2, 3 ];
```

This declaration initializes Vector.x with 1, Vector.y with -2, and Vector.z with 3.

You can also create symbolic record constants by declaring record objects in the const or val sections of your program. You access fields of these symbolic record constants just as you would access the field of a record variable, using the dot operator. Because the object is a constant, you can specify the field of a record constant anywhere a constant of that field's type is legal. You can also employ symbolic record constants as record variable initializers. The following example demonstrates this:

```
type
    point:       record
            x:int32;
            y:int32;
            z:int32;
        endrecord;

const
    PointInSpace: point := point:[ 1, 2, 3 ];

static
    Vector: point := PointInSpace;
    XCoord: int32 := PointInSpace.x;
            .

            .

            .

    stdout.put( "Y Coordinate is ", PointInSpace.y, nl );
            .

            .

            .
```

4.31   Arrays of Records

It is a perfectly reasonable operation to create an array of records. To do so, you simply create a record type and then use the standard array declaration syntax. The following example demonstrates how you could do this:

```
type
    recElement:
        record
            << fields for this record >>
        endrecord;
            .

            .
```

```
static
    recArray: recElement[4];
```

To access an element of this array you use the standard array indexing techniques. Because recArray is a single dimension array, you'd compute the address of an element of this array using the formula "baseAddress + index*@size(recElement)". For example, to access an element of recArray you'd use code like the following:

```
// Access element i of recArray:

    intmul( @size( recElement ), i, ebx );  // ebx := i*@size( recElement )
    mov( recArray.someField[ebx], eax );
```

Note that the index specification follows the entire variable name; remember, this is assembly, not a high level language (in a high level language you'd probably use "recArray[i].someField").

Naturally, you can create multidimensional arrays of records as well. You would use the row major or column major order functions to compute the address of an element within such records. The only thing that really changes (from the discussion of arrays) is that the size of each element is the size of the record object.

```
static
    rec2D: recElement[ 4, 6 ];
        .
        .
        .
    // Access element [i,j] of rec2D and load "someField" into EAX:

    intmul( 6, i, ebx );
    add( j, ebx );
    intmul( @size( recElement ), ebx );
    mov( rec2D.someField[ ebx ], eax );
```

4.32   Arrays/Records as Record Fields

Records may contain other records or arrays as fields. Consider the following definition:

```
type
    Pixel:
        record
            Pt:      point;
            color:   dword;
        endrecord;
```

The definition above defines a single point with a 32-bit color component. When initializing an object of type Pixel, the first initializer corresponds to the Pt field, *not the x-coordinate field*. **The following definition is incorrect:**

```
static
    ThisPt: Pixel := Pixel:[ 5, 10 ];    // Syntactically incorrect!
```

The value of the first field ("5") is not an object of type point. Therefore, the assembler generates an error when encountering this statement. HLA will allow you to initialize the fields of Pixel using declarations like the following:

```
static
    ThisPt: Pixel := Pixel:[ point:[ 1, 2, 3 ], 10 ];
    ThatPt: Pixel := Pixel:[ point:[ 0, 0, 0 ], 5 ];
```

Accessing Pixel fields is very easy. Like a high level language you use a single period to reference the Pt field and a second period to access the x, y, and z fields of point:

```
    stdout.put( "ThisPt.Pt.x = ", ThisPt.Pt.x, nl );
    stdout.put( "ThisPt.Pt.y = ", ThisPt.Pt.y, nl );
    stdout.put( "ThisPt.Pt.z = ", ThisPt.Pt.z, nl );
        .
        .
        .

    mov( eax, ThisPt.Color );
```

You can also declare arrays as record fields. The following record creates a data type capable of representing an object with eight points (e.g., a cube):

```
type
    Object8:
        record
            Pts:        point[8];
            Color:      dword;
        endrecord;
```

This record allocates storage for eight different points. Accessing an element of the Pts array requires that you know the size of an object of type point (remember, you must multiply the index into the array by the size of one element, 12 in this particular case). Suppose, for example, that you have a variable CUBE of type Object8. You could access elements of the Pts array as follows:

```
// CUBE.Pts[i].x := 0;

        mov( i, ebx );
        intmul( 12, ebx );
        mov( 0, CUBE.Pts.x[ebx] );
```

The one unfortunate aspect of all this is that you must know the size of each element of the Pts array. Fortunately, you can rewrite the code above using @size as follows:

```
// CUBE.Pts[i].x := 0;

        mov( i, ebx );
        intmul( @size( point ), ebx );
        mov( 0, CUBE.Pts.x[ebx] );
```

Note in this example that the index specification ("[ebx]") follows the whole object name even though the array is Pts, not x. Remember, the "[ebx]" specification is an indexed addressing mode, not an array index. Indexes always follow the entire name; you do not attach them to the array component as you would in a high level language like C/C++ or Pascal. This produces the correct result because addition is commutative, and the dot operator (as well as the index operator) corresponds to addition. In particular, the expression "CUBE.Pts.x[ebx]" tells HLA to compute the sum of CUBE (the base address of the object) plus the offset to the Pts field, plus the offset to the x field plus the value of EBX. Technically, we're really computing offset(CUBE)+offset(Pts)+EBX+offset(x) but we can rearrange this because addition is commutative.

You can also define two-dimensional arrays within a record. Accessing elements of such arrays is no different than any other two-dimensional array other than the fact that you must specify the array's field name as the base address for the array. For example:

```
type
    RecW2DArray:
        record
            intField: int32;
            aField: int32[4,5];

                    .

                    .

                    .

        endrecord;

static
    recVar: RecW2DArray;

        .

        .

        .

    // Access element [i,j] of the aField field using Row-major ordering:

    mov( i, ebx );
    intmul( 5, ebx );
```

```
        add( j, ebx );
        mov( recVar.aField[ ebx*4 ], eax );
                .
                .
                .
```

The preceding code uses the standard row major calculation to index into a 4x5 array of double words. The only difference between this example and a stand-alone array access is the fact that the base address is recVar.aField.

There are two common ways to nest record definitions. As noted earlier in this section, you can create a record type in a type section and then use that type name as the data type of some field within a record (e.g., the Pt:point field in the Pixel data type above). It is also possible to declare a record directly within another record without creating a separate data type for that record; the following example demonstrates this:

```
type
      NestedRecs:
            record
                  iField: int32;
                  sField: string;
                  rField:
                        record
                              i:int32;
                              u:uns32;
                        endrecord;
                  cField:char;
            endrecord;
```

Generally, it's a better idea to create a separate type rather than embed records directly in other records, but nesting them is perfectly legal and a reasonable thing to do on occasion.

If you have an array of records and one of the fields of that record type is an array, you must compute the indexes into the arrays independently of one another and then use the sum of these indexes as the ultimate index. The following example demonstrates how to do this:

```
type
      recType:
            record
                  arrayField: dword[4,5];
                  << Other Fields >>
            endrecord;

static
      aryOfRecs: recType[3,3];
                .
                .
                .
```

```
            // Access aryOfRecs[i,j].arrayField[k,l]:

            intmul( 5, i, ebx );                // Computes index into aryOfRecs
            add( j, ebx );                      // as (i*5 +j)*@size( recType ).
            intmul( @size( recType ), ebx );

            intmul( 3, k, eax );                // Computes index into arrayField
            add( l, eax );                      // as (k*3 + j) (*4 handled later).

            mov( aryOfRecs.arrayField[ ebx + eax*4 ], eax );
```

Note the use of the base plus scaled indexed addressing mode to simplify this operation.

4.33   Controlling Field Offsets Within a Record

By default, whenever you create a record, HLA automatically assigns the offset zero to the first field of that record. This corresponds to record offsets in a high level language and is the intuitive default. In some instances, however, you may want to assign a different starting offset to the first field of the record. HLA provides a mechanism that lets you set the starting offset of the first field in the record.

The syntax to set the first offset is

```
name:
    record := startingOffset;
        << Record Field Declarations >>
    endrecord;
```

Using the syntax above, the first field will have the starting offset specified by the startingOffset int32 constant expression. Because this is an int32 value, the starting offset value can be positive, zero, or negative.

One circumstance where this feature is invaluable is when you have a record whose base address is actually somewhere within the data structure. The classic example is an HLA string. An HLA string uses a record declaration similar to the following:

```
record
    MaxStrLen: dword;
    length: dword;
    charData: char[xxxx];
endrecord;
```

As you're well aware by now, HLA string pointers do not contain the address of the MaxStrLen field; they point at the charData field. The str.strRec record type found in the HLA Standard Library string module uses a record declaration similar to the following:

```
type
    strRec:
        record := -8;
            MaxStrLen: dword;
            length: dword;
            charData: char;
        endrecord;
```

The starting offset for the MaxStrLen field is -8. Therefore, the offset for the length field is -4 (four bytes later), and the offset for the charData field is zero. Therefore, if EBX points at some string data, then "(type str.strRec [ebx]).length" is equivalent to "[ebx-4]" because the length field has an offset of -4.

Generally, you will not use HLA's ability to specify the starting field offset when creating your own record types. Instead, this feature is most useful when you are mapping an HLA data type over the top of some other predefined data type in memory (strings are a good example, but there are many other examples as well).

4.34   Aligning Fields Within a Record

To achieve maximum performance in your programs, or to ensure that HLA's records properly map to records or structures in some high level language, you will often need to be able to control the alignment of fields within a record. For example, you might want to ensure that a double word field's offset is an even multiple of four. You use the align directive to do this, the same way you would use align in the static declaration section of your program. The following example shows how to align some fields on important boundaries:

```
type
    PaddedRecord:
        record
            c:char;
            align(4);
            d:dword;
            b:boolean;
            align(2);
            w:word;
        endrecord;
```

Whenever HLA encounters the align directive within a record declaration, it automatically adjusts the following field's offset so that it is an even multiple of the value the align directive specifies. It accomplishes this by increasing the offset of that field, if necessary. In the example above, the fields would have the following offsets: c:0, d:4, b:8, w:10. Note that HLA inserts three bytes of padding between c and d and it inserts one byte of padding between b and w. It goes without saying that you should never assume that this padding is present. If you want to use those extra bytes, then declare fields for them.

Note that specifying alignment within a record declaration does not guarantee that the field will be aligned on that boundary in memory; it only ensures that the field's offset is a multiple of the value you specify. If a variable of type PaddedRecord starts at an odd address in memory, then the d field will also start at an odd address (because any odd address plus four is an odd address). If you want to ensure that the fields are aligned on appropriate boundaries in memory, you must also use the align directive before variable declarations of that record type, e.g.,

```
static
        .
        .
        .
    align(4);
    PRvar: PaddedRecord;
```

The value of the align operand should be an even value that is evenly divisible by the largest align expression within the record type (four is the largest value in this case, and it's already evenly divisible by two).

If you want to ensure that the record's size is a multiple of some value, then simply stick an align directive as the last item in the record declaration. HLA will emit an appropriate number of bytes of padding at the end of the record to fill it in to the appropriate size. The following example demonstrates how to ensure that the record's size is a multiple of four bytes:

```
type
    PaddedRec:
        record
            << some field declarations >>

            align(4);
        endrecord;
```

HLA provides some additional alignment directives for records that let you easily control the alignment of all fields within a record. We'll consider those directives in a later chapter when discussing the interface between HLA and high level languages. In the meantime, if you're interested in more information about record field alignment, please consult the HLA Reference Manual.

4.35   Pointers to Records

During execution, your program may refer to structure objects directly or indirectly using a pointer. When you use a pointer to access fields of a structure, you must load one of the 80x86's 32-bit registers with the address of the desired record. Suppose you have the following variable declarations (assuming the Object8 structure from an earlier section):

```
static
    Cube:          Object8;
    CubePtr:       pointer to Object8 := &Cube;
```

CubePtr contains the address of (i.e., it is a pointer to) the Cube object. To access the *Color* field of the Cube object, you could use an instruction like "mov(Cube.Color, eax);". When accessing a field via a pointer you need to load the address of the object into a 32-bit register such as EBX. The instruction "mov(CubePtr EBX);" will do the trick. After doing so, you can access fields of the Cube object using the "[EBX+offset]" addressing mode. The only problem is "How do you specify which field to access?" Consider briefly, the following *incorrect* code:

```
    mov( CubePtr, ebx );
    mov( [ebx].Color, eax );        // This does not work!
```

There is one major problem with the code above. Because field names are local to a structure and it's possible to reuse a field name in two or more structures, how does HLA determine which offset Color represents? When accessing structure members directly (e.g., "mov(Cube.Color, EAX);") there is no ambiguity because Cube has a specific type that the assembler can check. "[EBX]", on the other hand, can point at *anything*. In particular, it can point at any structure that contains a Color field. So the assembler cannot, on its own, decide which offset to use for the Color symbol.

HLA resolves this ambiguity by requiring that you explicitly supply a type. To do this, you must coerce "[EBX]" to type Cube. Once you do this, you can use the normal dot operator notation to access the Color field:

```
    mov( CubePtr, ebx );
    mov( (type Cube [ebx]).Color, eax );
```

By specifying the record name, HLA knows which offset value to use for the Color symbol.

If you have a pointer to a record and one of that record's fields is an array, the easiest way to access elements of that field is by using the base plus indexed addressing mode. To do so, you just load the pointer's value into one register and compute the index into the array in a second register. Then you combine these two registers in the address expression. In the example above, the Pts field is an array of eight point objects. To access field x of the ith element of the Cube.Pts field, you'd use code like the following:

```
    mov( CubePtr, ebx );
    intmul( @size( point ), i, esi );   // Compute index into point array.
    mov( (type Object8 [ebx]).Pts.x[ esi*4 ], eax );
```

If you use a pointer to a particular record type frequently in your program, typing a coercion operator, like "(type Object8 [ebx])" can get old pretty quick. One way to reduce the typing needed to coerce EBX is to use a text constant. For example, consider the following statement in a program:

```
const
    O8ptr: text := "(type Object8 [ebx])";
```

With this statement at the beginning of your program you can use o8ptr in place of the type coercion operator and HLA will automatically substitute the appropriate text. With a text constant like the above, the former example becomes a little more readable and writable:

```
        mov( CubePtr, ebx );
        intmul( @size( point ), i, esi );   // Compute index into point array.
        mov( O8Ptr.Pts.x[ esi*4 ], eax );
```

4.36   Unions

A record definition assigns different offsets to each field in the record according to the size of those fields. This behavior is quite similar to the allocation of memory offsets in a var or static section. HLA provides a second type of structure declaration, the union, that does not assign different addresses to each object; instead, each field in a union declaration has the same offset — zero. The following example demonstrates the syntax for a union declaration:

```
type
    unionType:
        union
            << fields (syntactically identical to record declarations) >>
        endunion;
```

You access the fields of a union exactly the same way you access the fields of a record: using dot notation and field names. The following is a concrete example of a union type declaration and a variable of the union type:

```
type
    numeric:
        union
            i: int32;
            u: uns32;
            r: real64;
        endunion;

        .
        .
        .
```

```
static
    number: numeric;
            .
            .
            .

    mov( 55, number.u );
            .
            .
            .

    mov( -5, number.i );
            .
            .
            .

    stdout.put( "Real value = ", number.r, nl );
```

The important thing to note about union objects is that all the fields of a union have the same offset in the structure. In the example above, the number.u, number.i, and number.r fields all have the same offset: zero. Therefore, the fields of a union overlap in memory; this is very similar to the way the 80x86 8-, 16-, and 32-bit registers overlap one another. Usually, access to the fields of a union are mutually exclusive; that is, you do not manipulate separate fields of a particular union variable concurrently because writing to one field overwrites the other fields. In the example above, any modification of number.u would also change number.i and number.r.

Programmers typically use unions for two different reasons: to conserve memory or to create aliases. Memory conservation is the intended use of this data structure facility. To see how this works, let's compare the *numeric* union above with a corresponding record type:

```
type
    numericRec:
        record
            i: int32;
            u: uns32;
            r: real64;
        endrecord;
```

If you declare a variable, say n, of type numericRec, you access the fields as n.i, n.u, and n.r exactly as though you had declared the variable to be type numeric. The difference between the two is that numericRec variables allocate separate storage for each field of the record, while numeric objects allocate the same storage for all fields. Therefore, @size(numericRec) is 16 because the record contains two double word fields and a quad word (real64) field. @size(numeric), however, is eight. This is because all the fields of a union occupy the same memory locations, and the size of a union object is the size of the largest field of that object (see Figure 4-11).

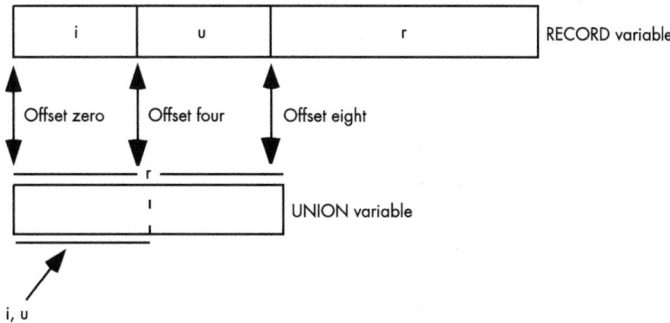

Figure 4-11: Layout of a UNION vs. a RECORD Variable.

In addition to conserving memory, programmers often use unions to create aliases in their code. As you may recall, an alias is a different name for the same memory object. Aliases are often a source of confusion in a program so you should use them sparingly; sometimes, however, using an alias can be quite convenient. For example, in some section of your program you might need to constantly use type coercion to refer to an object using a different type. Although you can use an HLA text constant to simplify this process, another way to do this is to use a union variable with the fields representing the different types you want to use for the object. As an example, consider the following code:

```
type
     CharOrUns:
          union
                  c:char;
                  u:uns32;
          endrecord;

static
     v:CharOrUns;
```

With a declaration like the above, you can manipulate an uns32 object by accessing v.u. If, at some point, you need to treat the L.O. byte of this uns32 variable as a character, you can do so by simply accessing the v.c variable, e.g.,

```
     mov( eax, v.u );
     stdout.put( "v, as a character, is '", v.c, "'" nl );
```

You can use unions exactly the same way you use records in an HLA program. In particular, union declarations may appear as fields in records, record declarations may appear as fields in unions, array declarations may appear within unions, you can create arrays of unions, and so on.

4.37 Anonymous Unions

Within a record declaration you can place a union declaration without specifying a field name for the union object. The following example demonstrates the syntax for this:

```
type
    HasAnonUnion:
        record
            r:real64;
            union
                    u:uns32;
                    i:int32;
            endunion;
            s:string;
        endrecord;

static
    v: HasAnonUnion;
```

Whenever an anonymous union appears within an record you can access the fields of the union as though they were direct fields of the record. In the example above, for example, you would access v's u and i fields using the syntax "v.u" and "v.i," respectively. The u and i fields have the same offset in the record (eight, because they follow a real64 object). The fields of v have the following offsets from v's base address:

v.r	0
v.u	8
v.i	8
v.s	12

@size(v) is 16 because the u and i fields only consume four bytes.

HLA also allows anonymous records within unions. Please see the HLA documentation for more details, though the syntax and usage is identical to anonymous unions within records.

4.38 Variant Types

One big use of unions in programs is to create *variant* types. A variant variable can change its type dynamically while the program is running. A variant object can be an integer at one point in the program, switch to a string at a different part of the program, and then change to a real value at a later time. Many very high level language systems use a dynamic type system (i.e., variant objects) to reduce the overall complexity of the program; indeed, proponents of many very high level languages insist that the use of a dynamic typing system is one of the reasons you can write complex programs in so few lines using very high level languages. Of course, if you can create variant objects in a very high level language, you can certainly do it in assembly language. In this section we'll look at how we can use the union structure to create variant types.

At any one given instant during program execution a variant object has a specific type, but under program control the variable can switch to a different type. Therefore, when the program processes a variant object it must use an if statement or switch statement to execute a different sequence of instructions based on the object's current type. Very high level languages do this transparently. In assembly language you will have to provide the code to test the type yourself. To achieve this, the variant type needs some additional information beyond the object's value. Specifically, the variant object needs a field that specifies the current type of the object. This field (often known as the *tag* field) is a small enumerated type or integer that specifies the type of the object at any given instant. The following code demonstrates how to create a variant type:

```
type
    VariantType:
        record
            tag:uns32;   // 0-uns32, 1-int32, 2-real64
            union
                u:uns32;
                i:int32;
                r:real64;
            endunion;
        endrecord;

static
    v:VariantType;
```

The program would test the v.tag field to determine the current type of the v object. Based on this test, the program would manipulate the v.i, v.u, or v.r field.

Of course, when operating on variant objects, the program's code must constantly be testing the tag field and executing a separate sequence of instructions for uns32, int32, or real64 values. If you use the variant fields often, it makes a lot of sense to write procedures to handle these operations for you (e.g., vadd, vsub, vmul, and vdiv).

4.39   Union Constants

Like records, HLA allows you to create union constants within your HLA source files. However, because all the fields of a union occupy the same storage at runtime, union constants only let you specify a single value. The question is, "which value?" Well, when you create a union constant, you have to explicitly specify the field whose value you want provide. You do this using the following syntax:

```
typename.fieldname:[ field_value ]
```

The typename item must be a union type you've previously defined in a type section. The fieldname item must be a valid field from that union type. The field_value item must be an appropriate constant whose type matches the typename.fieldname field. Here is a quick example:

```
type
    utype:
        union
            b:byte;
            c:char;
            w:word;
        endunion;

const
    u :utype := utype.c[ 'c' ];
```

You can also create union constants for anonymous unions. Obviously, such constants may only appear inside a record constant (because anonymous unions always appear within a record). The union, however, doesn't have a name associated with it, so you cannot use the previous syntax for such a constant. Instead, substitute union for the typename item in the union constant. Here's an example of an anonymous union constant (using the VariantType record type from the previous section):

```
const
    vt      :VariantType := VariantType:[ 0, union.u:[0]];
```

Please consult the HLA Reference Manual for more details about union constants.

4.40   Namespaces

One really nice feature of records and unions is that the field names are local to a given record or union declaration. That is, you can reuse field names in different records or unions. This is an important feature of HLA because it helps avoid *namespace pollution*. Namespace pollution occurs when you use up all the "good" names within the current scope and you have to start creating nondescriptive names for some object because you've already used the most appropriate name for something else. Because you can reuse names in different record/union definitions (and you can even reuse those names outside of the record/union definitions) you don't have to dream up new names for the objects that have less meaning. We use the term "namespace" to describe how HLA associates names with a particular object. The field names of a record have a namespace that is limited to objects of that record type. HLA provides a generalization of this namespace mechanism that lets you create arbitrary namespaces. These namespace objects let you shield the names of constants, types, variables, and other objects so their names do not interfere with other declarations in your program.

An HLA `namespace` section encapsulates a set of generic declarations in much the same way that a `record` encapsulates a set of variable declarations. A `namespace` declaration takes the following form:

```
namespace name;

    << declarations >>

end name;
```

The `name` identifier provides the name for the `namespace`. The identifier after the `end` clause must exactly match the identifier after `namespace`. Note that a `namespace` declaration section is a section unto itself. It does not have to appear in a type or var section. A `namespace` may appear anywhere one of the HLA declaration sections is legal. A program may contain any number of `namespace` declarations; in fact, the namespace identifiers don't even have to be unique, as you will soon see.

The declarations that appear between the `namespace` and `end` clauses are all the standard HLA declaration sections, except that you cannot nest namespace declarations. You may, however, put `const`, `val`, `type`, `static`, `readonly`, `storage`, and `var` sections within a `namespace`.[32] The following code provides an example of a typical `namespace` declaration in an HLA program:

```
namespace myNames;

    type
        integer: int32;

    static
        i:integer;
        j:uns32;

    const
        pi:real64 := 3.14159;

end myNames;
```

To access the fields of a namespace you use the same dot notation that records and unions use. For example, to access the fields of `myNames` outside of the name space you'd use the following identifiers:

myNames.integer	- A type declaration equivalent to int32.
myNames.i	- An integer variable (int32).
myNames.j	- An uns32 variable.
myNames.pi	- A real64 constant.

---

[32] Procedure and macro declarations, the subjects of later chapters, are also legal within a name space declaration section.

This example also demonstrates an important point about namespace declarations: within a namespace you may reference other identifiers in that same namespace declaration without using the dot notation. For example, the i field uses type integer from the myNames namespace without the "myNames." prefix.

What is not obvious from the example is that namespace declarations create a clean symbol table whenever you open up a namespace. The only external symbols that HLA recognizes in a namespace declaration are the predefined type identifiers (e.g., int32, uns32, and char). HLA does not recognize any symbols you've declared outside the namespace while it is processing your namespace declaration. This creates a problem if you want to use symbols from outside the namespace when declaring other symbols inside the namespace. For example, suppose the type integer had been defined outside myNames as follows:

```
type
    integer: int32;

namespace myNames;


    static
        i:integer;
        j:uns32;

    const
        pi:real64 := 3.14159;

end myNames;
```

If you were to attempt to compile this code, HLA would complain that the symbol integer is undefined. Clearly integer is defined in this program, but HLA hides all external symbols when creating a namespace so that you can reuse (and redefine) those symbols within the namespace. Of course, this doesn't help much if you actually want to use a name that you've defined outside myNames within that namespace. HLA provides a solution to this problem: the @global: operator. If, within a namespace declaration section, you prefix a name with "@global:", then HLA will use the global definition of that name rather than the local definition (if a local definition even exists). To correct the problem in the previous example, you'd use the following code:

```
type
    integer: int32;

namespace myNames;


    static
        i:@global:integer;
        j:uns32;
```

```
    const
        pi:real64 := 3.14159;

end myNames;
```

With the @global: prefix, the i variable will be type int32 even if a different declaration of integer appears within the myNames namespace.

You cannot nest namespace declarations. Logically, there doesn't seem to be any need for this; hence its omission from the HLA language.

You can have multiple namespace declarations in the same program that use the same name space identifier, e.g.,

```
namespace ns;

    << declaration group #1 >>

end ns;
        .
        .
        .
namespace ns;

    << declaration group #2 >>

end ns;
```

When HLA encounters a second namespace declaration for a given identifier, it simply appends the declarations in the second group to the end of the symbol list it created for the first group. Therefore, after processing the two namespace declarations, the ns namespace would contain the set of all symbols you've declared in both namespace blocks.

Perhaps the most common use of namespaces is in library modules. If you create a set of library routines to use in various projects or distribute to others, you have to be careful about the names you choose for your functions and other objects. If you use common names like get and put, the users of your module will complain when your names collide with theirs. An easy solution is to put all your code in a namespace block. Then the only name you have to worry about is the namespace identifier itself. This is the only name that will collide with other users' identifiers. This can happen, but it's much less likely to happen than if you don't use a namespace and your library module introduces dozens, if not hundreds, of new names into the global namespace.[33] The HLA Standard Library provides many good examples of namespaces in use. The HLA Standard Library defines several namespaces like stdout, stdin, str, cs, and chars. You refer to functions in these namespaces using names like stdout.put, stdin.get, cs.intersection, str.eq, and chars.toUpper. The use of namespaces in the HLA Standard Library prevents conflicts with similar names in your own programs.

---

[33] The global namespace is the global section of your program.

4.41 Dynamic Arrays in Assembly Language

One problem with arrays as this chapter describes them is that their size is static. That is, the number of elements in all of the examples was chosen when writing the program; it was not selected while the program runs (i.e., dynamically). Alas, sometimes you simply don't know how big an array needs to be when you're writing the program; you can only determine the size of the array while the program is running. This section describes how to allocate storage for arrays dynamically so you can set their size at runtime.

Allocating storage for a single dimension array, and accessing elements of that array, is a nearly trivial task at runtime. All you need to do is call the HLA Standard Library malloc routine specifying the size of the array, in bytes. malloc will return a pointer to the base address of the new array in the EAX register. Typically, you would save this address in a pointer variable and use that value as the base address of the array in all future array accesses.

To access an element of a single -dimensional dynamic array, you would generally load the base address into a register and compute the index in a second register. Then you could use the based indexed addressing mode to access elements of that array. This is not a whole lot more work than accessing elements of a statically allocated array. The following code fragment demonstrates how to allocate and access elements of a single dimension dynamic array:

```
static
      ArySize:      uns32;
      BaseAdrs:     pointer to uns32;
          .
          .
          .

      stdout.put( "How many elements do you want in your array? " );
      stdin.getu32();
      mov( eax, ArySize;       // Save away the upper bounds on this array.
      shl( 2, eax );           // Multiply eax by four to compute the number of bytes.
      malloc( eax );           // Allocate storage for the array.
      mov( eax, BaseAdrs );    // Save away the base address of the new array.
          .
          .
          .


      // Zero out each element of the array:

      mov( BaseAdrs, ebx );
      mov( 0, eax );
      for( mov(0, esi); esi < ArySize; inc( esi )) do

          mov( eax, [ebx + esi*4 ]);

      endfor;
```

Dynamically allocating storage for a multidimensional array is fairly straightforward. The number of elements in a multidimensional array is the product of all the dimension values; e.g., a 4x5 array has 20 elements. So if you get the bounds for each dimension from the user, all you need do is compute the product of all of these bound values and multiply the final result by the size of a single element. This computes the total number of bytes in the array, the value that malloc expects.

Accessing elements of multidimensional arrays is a little more problematic. The problem is that you need to keep the dimension information (that is, the bounds on each dimension) around because these values are needed when computing the row major (or column major) index into the array.[34] The conventional solution is to store these bounds into a static array (generally you know the *arity*, or number of dimensions, at compile time, so it is possible to statically allocate storage for this array of dimension bounds). This array of dynamic array bounds is known as a *dope vector*. The following code fragment shows how to allocate storage for a two-dimensional dynamic array using a simple dope vector.

```
var
    ArrayPtr:    pointer to uns32;
    ArrayDims:   uns32[2];

        .
        .
        .

    // Get the array bounds from the user:

    stdout.put( "Enter the bounds for dimension #1: ");
    stdin.get( ArrayDims[0] );

    stdout.put( "Enter the bounds for dimension #2: ");
    stdin.get( ArrayDims[1*4] );

    // Allocate storage for the array:

    mov( ArrayDims[0], eax );
    intmul( ArrayDims[1*4], eax );
    shl( 2, eax );            // Multiply by four because each element is 4 bytes.
    malloc( eax );            // Allocate storage for the array and
    mov( eax, ArrayPtr );     //   save away the pointer to the array.


    // Initialize the array:

    mov( 0, edx );
    mov( ArrayPtr, edi );
    for( mov( 0, ebx ); ebx < ArrayDims[0]; inc( ebx )) do
```

---

[34] Technically, you don't need the value of the leftmost dimension bound to compute an index into the array. However, if you want to check the index bounds using the bound instruction (or some other technique), you will need this value around at runtime as well.

```
        for( mov( 0, ecx ); ecx < ArrayDims[1*4]; inc( ecx )) do

            // Compute the index into the array
            // as esi := ( ebx * ArrayDims[1*4] + ecx ) * 4
            // (Note that the final multiplication by four is
            //  handled by the scaled indexed addressing mode below.)

            mov( ebx, esi );
            intmul( ArrayDims[1*4], esi );
            add( ecx, esi );

            // Initialize the current array element with edx.

            mov( edx, [edi+esi*4] );
            inc( edx );

        endfor;

    endfor;
```

4.42   HLA Standard Library Array Support

The HLA Standard Library provides an array module that helps reduce the effort
needed to support static and dynamic arrays in your program. The *arrays.hhf*
library module provides code to declare and allocate dynamic arrays, compute
the index into an array, copy arrays, perform row reductions, transpose arrays,
and more. This section will explore some of the more useful features the arrays
module provides.

One of the more interesting features of the HLA Standard Library arrays
module is that most of the array manipulation procedures support both statically
allocated and dynamically allocated arrays. In fact, the HLA array procedures can
automatically figure out if an array is static or dynamic and generate the appropriate code for that array. There is one catch, however. In order for HLA to be
able to differentiate statically and dynamically allocated arrays, you must use the
dynamic array declarations found in the arrays package. This won't be a problem
because HLA's dynamic array facilities are powerful and very easy to use.

To declare a dynamic array with the HLA arrays package, you use a variable
declaration like the following:

```
variableName: array.dArray( elementType, Arity );
```

The elementType parameter is a regular HLA data type identifier (e.g., int32 or
some type identifier you've defined in the type section). The Arity parameter is a
constant that specifies the number of dimensions for the array ("arity" is the
formal name for "number of dimensions"). Note that you do not specify the
bounds of each dimension in this declaration. Storage allocation occurs later, at
runtime. The following is an example of a declaration for a dynamically allocated
two-dimensional matrix:

```
ScreenBuffer: array.dArray( char, 2 );
```

The array.dArray data type is actually an HLA macro that expands the above to the following:

```
ScreenBuffer:
    record
                dataPtr:        dword;
                dopeVector:     uns32[ 2 ];
                elementType:    char;
    endrecord;
```

The dataPtr field will hold the base address of the array once the program allocates storage for it. The dopeVector array has one element for each array dimension (the macro uses the second parameter of the array.dArray type as the number of elements for the dopeVector array). The elementType field is a single object that has the same type as an element of the dynamic array.

After you declare a dynamic array, you must initialize the dynamic array object before attempting to use the array. The HLA Standard Library array.daAlloc routine handles this task for you. This routine uses the following syntax:

```
array.daAlloc( arrayName, comma_separated_list_of_array_bounds );
```

To allocate storage for the ScreenBuffer variable in the previous example you could use a call like the following:

```
array.daAlloc( ScreenBuffer, 20, 40 );
```

This call will allocate storage for a 20x40 array of characters. It will store the base address of the array into the ScreenBuffer.dataPtr field. It will also initialize Screen-Buffer.dopeVector[0] with 20 and ScreenBuffer.dopeVector[1*4] with 40. To access elements of the ScreenBuffer array you can use the techniques of the previous section, or you could use the array.index function.

The array.index function automatically computes the address of an array element for you. This function uses the following call syntax:

```
array.index( reg_32, arrayName, comma_separated_list_of_index_values );
```

The first parameter must be a 32-bit register. The array.index function will store the address of the specified array element in this register. The second array.index parameter must be the name of an array; this can be either a statically allocated array or an array you've declared with array.dArray and allocated dynamically with array.daAlloc. Following the array name parameter is a list of one or more array indices. The number of array indices must match the arity of the array. These array indices can be constants, double word memory variables, or registers (however, you must not specify the same register that appears in the first parameter as one of the array indices). Upon return from this function, you may access the specified array element using the register indirect addressing mode and the register appearing as the first parameter.

One last routine you'll want to know about when manipulating HLA dynamic arrays is the array.daFree routine. This procedure expects a single parameter that is the name of an HLA dynamic array. Calling array.daFree will free the storage associated with the dynamic array. The following code fragment is a rewrite of the example from the previous section using HLA dynamic arrays:

```
var
    da:     array.dArray( uns32, 2 );
    Bnd1:   uns32;
    Bnd2:   uns32;
            .
            .
            .

    // Get the array bounds from the user:

    stdout.put( "Enter the bounds for dimension #1: " );
    stdin.get( Bnd1 );

    stdout.put( "Enter the bounds for dimension #2: " );
    stdin.get( Bnd2 );

    // Allocate storage for the array:

    array.daAlloc( da, Bnd1, Bnd2 );


    // Initialize the array:

    mov( 0, edx );
    for( mov( 0, ebx ); ebx < Bnd1; inc( ebx )) do

        for( mov( 0, ecx ); ecx < Bnd2; inc( ecx )) do

            // Initialize the current array element with edx.
            // Use array.index to compute the address of the array element.

            array.index( edi, da, ebx, ecx );
            mov( edx, [edi] );
            inc( edx );

        endfor;

    endfor;
```

Another extremely useful library module is the `array.cpy` routine. This procedure will copy the data from one array to another. The calling syntax is:

```
array.cpy( sourceArrayName, destArrayName );
```

The source and destination arrays can be static or dynamic arrays. The `array.cpy` automatically adjusts and emits the proper code for each combination of parameters. With most of the array manipulation procedures in the HLA Standard Library, you pay a small performance penalty for the convenience of these library modules. Not so with `array.cpy`. This procedure is very, very fast — much faster than writing a loop to copy the data element by element.

4.43   For More Information

In the electronic edition of this book, which you'll find on the accompanying CD-ROM, you will find additional information about data types. For an in-depth discussion of data types, you should read a textbook on data structures and algorithms.

5

PROCEDURES AND UNITS

5.1 Chapter Overview

In a procedural programming language the basic unit of code is the
procedure. A *procedure* is a set of instructions that compute some
value or take some action (such as printing or reading a character
value). The definition of a procedure is very similar to the definition of
an *algorithm*. A procedure is a set of rules to follow which, if they conclude,
produce some result. An algorithm is also such a sequence, but an algorithm is guaranteed to terminate whereas a procedure offers no such guarantee.

This chapter discusses how HLA implements procedures. It begins by discussing
HLA's high level syntax for procedure declarations and invocations, but it also
describes the low level implementation of procedures at the machine level. At this
point, you should be getting comfortable with assembly language programming, so
it's time to start presenting "pure" assembly language rather than continuing to rely
on HLA's high level syntax as a crutch.

5.2   Procedures

Most procedural programming languages implement procedures using the call/ return mechanism. That is, some code calls a procedure, the procedure does its thing, and then the procedure returns to the caller. The call and return instructions provide the 80x86's *procedure invocation mechanism.* The calling code calls a procedure with the call instruction; the procedure returns to the caller with the ret instruction. For example, the following 80x86 instruction calls the HLA Standard Library stdout.newln routine:[1]

```
call stdout.newln;
```

The stdout.newln procedure prints a newline sequence to the console device and returns control to the instruction immediately following the "call stdout.newln;" instruction.

Alas, the HLA Standard Library does not supply all the routines you will need. Most of the time you'll have to write your own procedures. To do this, you will use HLA's procedure declaration facilities. A basic HLA procedure declaration takes the following form:

```
procedure ProcName;
    << Local declarations >>
begin ProcName;
    << procedure statements >>
end ProcName;
```

Procedure declarations appear in the declaration section of your program. That is, anywhere you can put a static, const, type, or other declaration section, you may place a procedure declaration. In the preceding syntax example, ProcName represents the name of the procedure you wish to define. This can be any valid (and unique) HLA identifier. Whatever identifier follows the procedure reserved word must also follow the begin and end reserved words in the procedure. As you've probably noticed, a procedure declaration looks a whole lot like an HLA program. In fact, the only difference (so far) is the use of the procedure reserved word rather than the program reserved word.

Here is a concrete example of an HLA procedure declaration. This procedure stores zeros into the 256 double words that EBX points at upon entry into the procedure:

```
procedure zeroBytes;
begin zeroBytes;

    mov( 0, eax );
    mov( 256, ecx );
    repeat
```

---

[1] Normally you would call newln using the high level "newln();" syntax, but the call instruction works as well.

```
        mov( eax, [ebx] );
        add( 4, ebx );
        dec( ecx );

    until( @z );   // That is, until ECX=0.

end zeroBytes;
```

You can use the 80x86 call instruction to call this procedure. When, during program execution, the code falls into the "end zeroBytes;" statement, the procedure returns to whoever called it and begins executing the first instruction beyond the call instruction. The program in Listing 5-1 provides an example of a call to the zeroBytes routine.

Listing 5-1: Example of a Simple Procedure.

```
program zeroBytesDemo;
#include( "stdlib.hhf" )


    procedure zeroBytes;
    begin zeroBytes;

        mov( 0, eax );
        mov( 256, ecx );
        repeat

            mov( eax, [ebx] );   // Zero out current dword.
            add( 4, ebx );       // Point ebx at next dword.
            dec( ecx );          // Count off 256 dwords.

        until( ecx = 0 );        // Repeat for 256 dwords.

    end zeroBytes;

static
    dwArray: dword[256];

begin zeroBytesDemo;

    lea( ebx, dwArray );
    call zeroBytes;

end zeroBytesDemo;
```

As you may have noticed when calling HLA Standard Library procedures, you don't have to use the call instruction to call HLA procedures. There is nothing special about the HLA Standard Library procedures versus your own procedures. Although the formal 80x86 mechanism for calling procedures is to use the call instruction, HLA provides a high level extension that lets you call a procedure by simply specifying the procedure's name followed by an empty set of parentheses.[2] For example, either of the following statements will call the HLA Standard Library stdout.newln procedure:

```
call stdout.newln;
stdout.newln();
```

Likewise, either of the following statements will call the zeroBytes procedure in Listing 5-1:

```
call zeroBytes;
zeroBytes();
```

The choice of calling mechanism is strictly up to you. Most people, however, find the high level syntax easier to read.

5.3   Saving the State of the Machine

Take a look at the program in Listing 5-2. This section of code attempts to print 20 lines of 40 spaces and an asterisk. Unfortunately, there is a subtle bug that creates an infinite loop. The main program uses the repeat..until loop to call PrintSpaces 20 times. PrintSpaces uses ECX to count off the 40 spaces it prints. PrintSpaces returns with ECX containing zero. The main program then prints an asterisk, calls a newline, decrements ECX, and then repeats because ECX isn't zero (it will always contain $FFFF_FFFF at this point).

The problem here is that the PrintSpaces subroutine doesn't preserve the ECX register. Preserving a register means you save it upon entry into the subroutine and restore it before leaving. Had the PrintSpaces subroutine preserved the contents of the ECX register, the program in Listing 5-2 would have functioned properly.

Listing 5-2: Program with an Unintended Infinite Loop.

```
program nonWorkingProgram;
#include( "stdlib.hhf" );


    procedure PrintSpaces;
    begin PrintSpaces;

        mov( 40, ecx );
        repeat

            stdout.put( ' ' );  // Print 1 of 40 spaces.
            dec( ecx );         // Count off 40 spaces.
```

---

[2] This assumes that the procedure does not have any parameters.

```
        until( ecx = 0 );

    end PrintSpaces;

begin nonWorkingProgram;

    mov( 20, ecx );
    repeat

        PrintSpaces();
        stdout.put( '*', nl );
        dec( ecx );

    until( ecx = 0 );

end nonWorkingProgram;
```

You can use the 80x86's push and pop instructions to preserve register values while you need to use them for something else. Consider the following code for PrintSpaces:

```
    procedure PrintSpaces;
    begin PrintSpaces;

        push( eax );
        push( ecx );
        mov( 40, ecx );
        repeat

            stdout.put( ' ' );     // Print 1 of 40 spaces.
            dec( ecx );            // Count off 40 spaces.

        until( ecx = 0 );
        pop( ecx );
        pop( eax );

    end PrintSpaces;
```

Note that PrintSpaces saves and restores EAX and ECX (because this procedure modifies these registers). Also, note that this code pops the registers off the stack in the reverse order that it pushed them. The last-in, first-out operation of the stack imposes this ordering.

Either the caller (the code containing the call instruction) or the callee (the subroutine) can take responsibility for preserving the registers. In the example above, the callee preserved the registers. The example in Listing 5-3 shows what this code might look like if the caller preserves the registers:

Listing 5-3: Demonstration of Caller Register Preservation.

```
program callerPreservation;
#include( "stdlib.hhf" );


    procedure PrintSpaces;
    begin PrintSpaces;

        mov( 40, ecx );
        repeat

            stdout.put( ' ' );  // Print 1 of 40 spaces.
            dec( ecx );         // Count off 40 spaces.

        until( ecx = 0 );

    end PrintSpaces;

begin callerPreservation;

    mov( 20, ecx );
    repeat

        push( eax );
        push( ecx );
        PrintSpaces();
        pop( ecx );
        pop( eax );
        stdout.put( '*', nl );
        dec( ecx );

    until( ecx = 0 );

end callerPreservation;
```

There are two advantages to callee preservation: space and maintainability. If the callee (the procedure) preserves all affected registers, then there is only one copy of the push and pop instructions, those the procedure contains. If the caller saves the values in the registers, the program needs a set of push and pop instructions around every call. Not only does this make your programs longer, it also makes them harder to maintain. Remembering which registers to push and pop on each procedure call is not something easily done.

On the other hand, a subroutine may unnecessarily preserve some registers if it preserves all the registers it modifies. In the examples above, the code needn't save EAX. Although PrintSpaces changes AL, this won't affect the program's operation. If the caller is preserving the registers, it doesn't have to save registers it doesn't care about (see the program in Listing 5-4).

Listing 5-4: Demonstrating That Caller Preservation Need Not Save All Registers.

```
program callerPreservation2;
#include( "stdlib.hhf" );


    procedure PrintSpaces;
    begin PrintSpaces;

        mov( 40, ecx );
        repeat

            stdout.put( ' ' );  // Print 1 of 40 spaces.
            dec( ecx );         // Count off 40 spaces.

        until( ecx = 0 );

    end PrintSpaces;

begin callerPreservation2;

    mov( 10, ecx );
    repeat

        push( ecx );
        PrintSpaces();
        pop( ecx );
        stdout.put( '*', nl );
        dec( ecx );

    until( ecx = 0 );


    mov( 5, ebx );
    while( ebx > 0 ) do

        PrintSpaces();

        stdout.put( ebx, nl );
        dec( ebx );

    endwhile;


    mov( 110, ecx );
    for( mov( 0, eax );  eax < 7; inc( eax )) do

        push ( eax );
        push ( ecx );
```

```
        PrintSpaces();

        pop( ecx );
        pop( eax );
        stdout.put( eax, " ", ecx, nl );
        dec( ecx );

    endfor;

end callerPreservation2;
```

This example in Listing 5-4 provides three different cases. The first loop
(repeat..until) only preserves the ECX register. Modifying the AL register won't
affect the operation of this loop. Immediately after the first loop, this code calls
PrintSpaces again in the while loop. However, this code doesn't save EAX or ECX
because it doesn't care whether PrintSpaces changes them. Because the final loop
(for) uses EAX and ECX, it saves them both.

One big problem with having the caller preserve registers is that your
program may change. You may modify the calling code or the procedure so that
they use additional registers. Such changes, of course, may change the set of
registers that you must preserve. Worse still, if the modification is in the
subroutine itself, you will need to locate *every* call to the routine and verify that
the subroutine does not change any registers the calling code uses.

Preserving registers isn't all there is to preserving the environment. You can
also push and pop variables and other values that a subroutine might change.
Because the 80x86 allows you to push and pop memory locations, you can easily
preserve these values as well.

5.4   Prematurely Returning from a Procedure

The HLA exit and exitif statements let you return from a procedure without
having to fall into the corresponding end statement in the procedure. These
statements behave a whole lot like the break and breakif statements for loops,
except they transfer control to the bottom of the procedure rather than out of
the current loop. These statements are quite useful in many cases.

The syntax for these two statements is the following:

```
exit procedurename;
exitif( boolean_expression ) procedurename;
```

The procedurename operand is the name of the procedure you wish to exit. If you
specify the name of your main program, the exit and exitif statements will
terminate program execution (even if you're currently inside a procedure rather
than the body of the main program).

The exit statement immediately transfers control out of the specified
procedure or program. The conditional exitif statement first tests the boolean
expression and exits if the result is true. It is semantically equivalent to the
following:

```
    if( boolean_expression ) then

        exit procedurename;

    endif;
```

Although the exit and exitif statements are invaluable in many cases, you should try to avoid using them without careful consideration. If a simple if statement will let you skip the rest of the code in your procedure, by all means use the if statement. Procedures that contain a lot of exit and exitif statements will be harder to read, understand, and maintain than procedures without these statements (after all, the exit and exitif statements are really nothing more than GOTO statements, and you've probably heard already about the problems with GOTOs). exit and exitif are convenient when you got to return from a procedure inside a sequence of nested control structures and slapping an if..endif around the remaining code in the procedure is not possible.

5.5   Local Variables

HLA procedures, like procedures and functions in most high level languages, let you declare *local variables*. Local variables are generally accessible only within the procedure, they are not accessible by the code that calls the procedure. Local variable declarations are identical to variable declarations in your main program except, of course, you declare the variables in the procedure's declaration section rather than the main program's declaration section. Actually, you may declare anything in the procedure's declaration section that is legal in the main program's declaration section, including constants, types, and even other procedures.[3] In this section, however, we'll concentrate on local variables.

Local variables have two important attributes that differentiate them from the variables in your main program (i.e., *global* variables): *lexical scope* and *lifetime*. Lexical scope, or just *scope*, determines where an identifier is usable in your program. Lifetime determines when a variable has memory associated with it and is capable of storing data. Because these two concepts differentiate local and global variables, it is wise to spend some time discussing these two attributes.

Perhaps the best place to start when discussing the scope and lifetimes of local variables is with the scope and lifetimes of global variables — those variables you declare in your main program. Until now, the only rule you've had to follow concerning the declaration of your variables has been "you must declare all variables that you use in your programs." The position of the HLA declaration section with respect to the program statements automatically enforces the other major rule which is "you must declare all variables before their first use." With the introduction of procedures, it is now possible to violate this rule because (1) procedures may access global variables, and (2) procedure declarations may appear anywhere in a declaration section, even before some variable declarations. The program in Listing 5-5 demonstrates this source code organization.

---

[3] Strictly speaking, this is not true. You may not declare external objects within a procedure. External objects are the subject of a later section in this chapter.

Listing 5-5: Demonstration of Global Scope.

```
program demoGlobalScope;
#include( "stdlib.hhf" );

static
    AccessibleInProc: char;


    procedure aProc;
    begin aProc;

        mov( 'a', AccessibleInProc );

    end aProc;



static
    InaccessibleInProc: char;


begin demoGlobalScope;


    mov( 'b', InaccessibleInProc );
    aProc();
    stdout.put
    (
        "AccessibleInProc   = '", AccessibleInProc,   "'" nl
        "InaccessibleInProc = '", InaccessibleInProc, "'" nl
    );



end demoGlobalScope;
```

This example demonstrates that a procedure can access global variables in the main program as long as you declare those global variables before the procedure. In this example, the aProc procedure cannot access the InaccessibleInProc variable because its declaration appears after the procedure declaration. However, aProc may reference AccessibleInProc because its declaration appears before the aProc procedure.

A procedure can access any static, storage, or readonly object exactly the same way the main program accesses such variables — by simply referencing the name. Although a procedure may access global var objects, a different syntax is necessary, and you need to learn a little more before you will understand the purpose of the additional syntax (for more details, please consult the HLA Reference Manual).

Accessing global objects is convenient and easy. Unfortunately, as you've probably learned when studying high level language programming, accessing global objects makes your programs harder to read, understand, and maintain. Like most introductory programming texts, this book discourages the use of global variables within procedures. Accessing global variables within a procedure is sometimes the best solution to a given problem. However, such (legitimate) access typically occurs only in advanced programs involving multiple threads of execution or in other complex systems. Because it is unlikely you would be writing such code at this point, it is equally unlikely that you will absolutely need to access global variables in your procedures so you should carefully consider your options before accessing global variables within your procedures.[4]

Declaring local variables in your procedures is very easy; you use the same declaration sections as the main program: static, readonly, storage, and var. The same rules and syntax for the declaration sections and the access of variables you declare in these sections applies in your procedure. The example code in Listing 5-6 demonstrates the declaration of a local variable.

Listing 5-6: Example of a Local Variable in a Procedure.

```
program demoLocalVars;
#include( "stdlib.hhf" );

    // Simple procedure that displays 0..9 using
    // a local variable as a loop control variable.

    procedure CntTo10;
    var
        i: int32;

    begin CntTo10;

        for( mov( 0, i ); i < 10; inc( i )) do

            stdout.put( "i=", i, nl );

        endfor;

    end CntTo10;


begin demoLocalVars;

    CntTo10();

end demoLocalVars;
```

[4] Note that this argument against accessing global variables does not apply to other global symbols. It is perfectly reasonable to access global constants, types, procedures, and other objects in your programs.

Local variables you declare in a procedure are accessible only within that procedure.[5] Therefore, the variable i in procedure CntTo10 in Listing 5-6 is not accessible in the main program.

HLA relaxes, somewhat, the rule that identifiers must be unique in a program for local variables. In an HLA program, all identifiers must be unique within a given *scope.* Therefore, all global names must be unique with respect to one another. Similarly, all local variables within a given procedure must have unique names *but only with respect to other local symbols in that same procedure.* In particular, a local name may be the same as a global name. When this occurs, HLA creates two separate variables. Within the scope of the procedure any reference to the common name accesses the local variable; outside that procedure, any reference to the common name references the global identifier. Although the quality of the resultant code is questionable, it is perfectly legal to have a global identifier named MyVar with the same local name in two or more different procedures. The procedures each have their own local variant of the object which is independent of MyVar in the main program. Listing 5-7 provides an example of an HLA program that demonstrates this feature.

Listing 5-7: Local Variables Need Not Have Globally Unique Names.

```
program demoLocalVars2;
#include( "stdlib.hhf" );

static
    i:  uns32 := 10;
    j:  uns32 := 20;



    // The following procedure declares "i" and "j"
    // as local variables, so it does not have access
    // to the global variables by the same name.

    procedure First;
    var
        i: int32;
        j:uns32;

    begin First;

        mov( 10, j );
        for( mov( 0, i ); i < 10; inc( i )) do

            stdout.put( "i=", i," j=", j, nl );
            dec( j );

        endfor;
```

```
        end First;


        // This procedure declares only an "i" variable.
        // It cannot access the value of the global "i"
        // variable but it can access the value of the
        // global "j" object because it does not provide
        // a local variant of "j".

        procedure Second;
        var
             i:uns32;

        begin Second;

             mov( 10, j );
             for( mov( 0, i ); i < 10; inc( i )) do

                  stdout.put( "i=", i," j=", j, nl );
                  dec( j );

             endfor;

        end Second;



begin demoLocalVars2;

     First();
     Second();

     // Because the calls to First and Second have not
     // modified variable "i", the following statement
     // should print "i=10".  However, because the Second
     // procedure manipulated global variable "j", this
     // code will print "j=0" rather than "j=20".

     stdout.put(  "i=", i, " j=", j, nl );

end demoLocalVars2;
```

There are good and bad points to be made about reusing global names within a procedure. On the one hand, there is the potential for confusion. If you use a name like ProfitsThisYear as a global symbol and you reuse that name within a procedure, someone reading the procedure might think that the procedure refers to the global symbol rather than the local symbol. On the other hand, simple names like i, j, and k are nearly meaningless (almost everyone expects the program to use them as loop control variables or for other local uses), so reusing these names as local objects is probably a good idea. From a software engineering perspective, it is probably a good idea to keep all variables names that have a very specific meaning (like ProfitsThisYear) unique throughout your program. General names that have a nebulous meaning (like index, counter, and names like i, j, or k) will probably be okay to reuse as global variables

There is one last point to make about the scope of identifiers in an HLA program: Variables in separate procedures are separate, even if they have the same name. The First and Second procedures in Listing 5-7, for example, share the same name (i) for a local variable. However, the i in First is a completely different variable than the i in Second.

The second major attribute that differentiates (certain) local variables from global variables is *lifetime*. The lifetime of a variable spans from the point the program first allocates storage for a variable to the point the program deallocates the storage for that variable. Note that lifetime is a dynamic attribute (controlled at runtime), whereas scope is a static attribute (controlled at compile time). In particular, a variable can actually have several lifetimes if the program repeatedly allocates and then deallocates the storage for that variable.

Global variables always have a single lifetime that spans from the moment the main program first begins execution to the point the main program terminates. Likewise, all static objects have a single lifetime that spans the execution of the program (remember, static objects are those you declare in the static, readonly, or storage sections). This is true even within procedures. So there is no difference between the lifetime of a local static object and the lifetime of a global static object. Variables you declare in the var section, however, are a different matter. var objects use automatic storage allocation. *Automatic storage allocation* means that the procedure automatically allocates storage for a local variable upon entry into a procedure. Similarly, the program deallocates storage for automatic objects when the procedure returns to its caller. Therefore, the lifetime of an automatic object is from the point of the execution of the first statement in a procedure to the point it returns to its caller.

Perhaps the most important thing to note about automatic variables is that you cannot expect them to maintain their values between calls to the procedure. Once the procedure returns to its caller, the storage for the automatic variable is lost and, therefore, the value is lost as well. Thus, *you must always assume that a local* var *object is uninitialized upon entry into a procedure*, even if you know you've called the procedure before and the previous procedure invocation initialized that variable. Whatever value the last call stored into the variable was lost when the procedure returned to its caller. If you need to maintain the value of a variable between calls to a procedure, you should use one of the static variable declaration types.

Given that automatic variables cannot maintain their values across procedure calls, you might wonder why you would want to use them at all. However, there are several benefits to automatic variables that static variables do not have. The biggest disadvantage to static variables is that they consume memory even when the (only) procedure that references them is not running. Automatic variables, on the other hand, only consume storage while their associated procedure is executing. Upon return, the procedure returns any automatic storage it allocated back to the system for reuse by other procedures. You'll see some additional advantages to automatic variables later in this chapter.

5.6   Other Local and Global Symbol Types

As the previous section notes, HLA procedures let you declare constants, values, types, and almost everything else legal in the main program's declaration section. The same rules for scope apply to these identifiers. Therefore, you can reuse constant names, procedure names, type names, and so on, in local declarations.

Referencing global constants, values, and types does not present the same software engineering problems that occur when you reference global variables. The problem with referencing global variables is that a procedure can change the value of a global variable in a non-obvious way. This makes programs more difficult to read, understand, and maintain because you can't often tell that a procedure is modifying memory by looking only at the call to that procedure. Constants, values, types, and other non-variable objects don't suffer from this problem because you cannot change them at runtime. Therefore, the pressure to avoid global objects at nearly all costs doesn't apply to non-variable objects.

Having said that it's okay to access global constants, types, and so on, it's also worth pointing out that you should declare these objects locally within a procedure if the only place your program references such objects is within that procedure. Doing so will make your programs a little easier to read because the person reading your code won't have to search all over the place for the symbol's definition.

5.7   Parameters

Although there is a large class of procedures that are totally self-contained, most procedures require some input data and return some data to the caller. Parameters are values that you pass to and from a procedure. In straight assembly language, passing parameters can be a real chore. Fortunately, HLA provides a high level language–like syntax for procedure declarations and for procedure calls involving parameters. This section will present HLA's high level parameter syntax. Later sections in this chapter will deal with the low level mechanisms for passing parameters in pure assembly code.

The first thing to consider when discussing parameters is *how* we pass them to a procedure. If you are familiar with Pascal or C/C++, you've probably seen two ways to pass parameters: pass by value and pass by reference. HLA certainly supports these two parameter passing mechanisms. However, HLA also supports pass by value/result, pass by result, pass by name, and pass by lazy evaluation. Of course, HLA is assembly language, so it is possible to pass parameters in HLA using any scheme you can dream up (at least, any scheme that is possible at all on the CPU). However, HLA provides special high level syntax for pass by value, reference, value/result, result, name, and lazy evaluation.

Because pass by value/result, result, name, and lazy evaluation are somewhat advanced, this chapter will not deal with those parameter passing mechanisms. If you're interested in learning more about these parameter passing schemes, see the HLA Reference Manual or check out the electronic versions of this text on the accompanying CD-ROM.

Another concern you will face when dealing with parameters is *where* you pass them. There are a lot of different places to pass parameters; in this section, because we're using HLA's high level syntax for declaring and calling procedures, we'll wind up passing procedure parameters on the stack. You don't really need to concern yourself with the details because HLA abstracts them away for you; however, do keep in mind that procedure calls and procedure parameters make use of the stack. Therefore, whatever you push on the stack immediately before a procedure call is not going to be on the top of the stack upon entry into the procedure.

5.7.1 Pass by Value

A parameter passed by value is just that: The caller passes a value to the procedure. Pass by value parameters are input-only parameters. That is, you can pass them to a procedure but the procedure cannot return values through them. In HLA the idea of a pass by value parameter being an input only parameter makes a lot of sense. Given the HLA procedure call:

```
CallProc(I);
```

If you pass I by value, then CallProc does not change the value of I, regardless of what happens to the parameter inside CallProc.

Because you must pass a copy of the data to the procedure, you should only use this method for passing small objects like bytes, words, and double words. Passing large arrays and records by value is very inefficient (because you must create and pass a copy of the object to the procedure).

HLA, like Pascal and C/C++, passes parameters by value unless you specify otherwise. Here's what a typical function looks like with a single pass by value parameter:

```
procedure PrintNSpaces( N:uns32 );
begin PrintNSpaces;

    push( ecx );
    mov( N, ecx );
    repeat

        stdout.put( ' ' );  // Print 1 of N spaces.
        dec( ecx );         // Count off N spaces.

    until( ecx = 0 );
    pop( ecx );

end PrintNSpaces;
```

The parameter N in PrintNSpaces is known as a *formal parameter*. Anywhere the name N appears in the body of the procedure the program references the value passed through N by the caller.

The calling sequence for PrintNSpaces can be any of the following:

```
PrintNSpaces( constant );
PrintNSpaces( reg32 );
PrintNSpaces( uns32_variable );
```

Here are some concrete examples of calls to PrintNSpaces:

```
PrintNSpaces( 40 );
PrintNSpaces( EAX );
PrintNSpaces( SpacesToPrint );
```

The parameter in the calls to PrintNSpaces is known as an *actual parameter*. In the examples above, 40, EAX, and SpacesToPrint are the actual parameters.

Note that pass by value parameters behave exactly like local variables you declare in the var section with the single exception that the procedure's caller initializes these local variables before it passes control to the procedure.

HLA uses positional parameter notation just like most high level languages. Therefore, if you need to pass more than one parameter, HLA will associate the actual parameters with the formal parameters by their position in the parameter list. The following PrintNChars procedure demonstrates a simple procedure that has two parameters.

```
procedure PrintNChars( N:uns32; c:char );
begin PrintNChars;

    push( ecx );
    mov( N, ecx );
    repeat

        stdout.put( c );      // Print 1 of N characters.
        dec( ecx );           // Count off N characters.

    until( ecx = 0 );
    pop( ecx );

end PrintNChars;
```

The following is an invocation of the PrintNChars procedure that will print 20 asterisk characters:

```
PrintNChars( 20, '*' );
```

Note that HLA uses semicolons to separate the formal parameters in the procedure declaration, and it uses commas to separate the actual parameters in the procedure invocation (Pascal programmers should be comfortable with this notation). Also note that each HLA formal parameter declaration takes the following form:

---

parameter_identifier : type_identifier

In particular, note that the parameter type has to be an identifier. None of the following are legal parameter declarations because the data type is not a single identifier:

```
PtrVar: pointer to uns32
ArrayVar: uns32[10]
recordVar: record i:int32; u:uns32; endrecord
DynArray: array.dArray( uns32, 2 )
```

However, don't get the impression that you cannot pass pointer, array, record, or dynamic array variables as parameters. The trick is to declare a data type for each of these types in the type section. Then you can use a single identifier as the type in the parameter declaration. The following code fragment demonstrates how to do this with the four data types in the preceding list:

```
type
     uPtr:       pointer to uns32;
     uArray10:   uns32[10];
     recType:    record i:int32; u:uns32; endrecord
     dType:      array.dArray( uns32, 2 );

     procedure FancyParms
     (
          PtrVar: uPtr;
          ArrayVar:uArray10;
          recordVar:recType;
          DynArray: dtype
     );
     begin FancyParms;
          .
          .
          .
     end FancyParms;
```

By default, HLA assumes that you intend to pass a parameter by value. HLA also lets you explicitly state that a parameter is a value parameter by prefacing the formal parameter declaration with the val keyword. The following is a version of the PrintNSpaces procedure that explicitly states that N is a pass by value parameter:

```
procedure PrintNSpaces( val N:uns32 );
begin PrintNSpaces;

    push( ecx );
    mov( N, ecx );
    repeat

        stdout.put( ' ' );  // Print 1 of N spaces.
        dec( ecx );         // Count off N spaces.

    until( ecx = 0 );
    pop( ecx );

end PrintNSpaces;
```

Explicitly stating that a parameter is a pass by value parameter is a good idea if you have multiple parameters in the same procedure declaration that use different passing mechanisms.

When you pass a parameter by value and call the procedure using the HLA high level language syntax, HLA will automatically generate code that will make a copy of the actual parameter's value and copy this data into the local storage for that parameter (i.e., the formal parameter). For small objects pass by value is probably the most efficient way to pass a parameter. For large objects, however, HLA must generate code that copies each and every byte of the actual parameter into the formal parameter. For large arrays and records this can be a very expensive operation.[6] Unless you have specific semantic concerns that require you to pass a large array or record by value, you should use pass by reference or some other parameter passing mechanism for arrays and records.

When passing parameters to a procedure, HLA checks the type of each actual parameter and compares this type to the corresponding formal parameter. If the types do not agree, HLA then checks to see if either the actual or formal parameter is a byte, word, or double word object and the other parameter is one, two, or four bytes in length (respectively). If the actual parameter does not satisfy either of these conditions, HLA reports a parameter type mismatch error. If, for some reason, you need to pass a parameter to a procedure using a different type than the procedure calls for, you can always use the HLA type coercion operator to override the type of the actual parameter.

5.7.2 Pass by Reference

To pass a parameter by reference, you must pass the address of a variable rather than its value. In other words, you must pass a pointer to the data. The procedure must dereference this pointer to access the data. Passing parameters by reference is useful when you must modify the actual parameter or when you pass large data structures between procedures.

---

[6] Note to C/C++ programmers: HLA does not automatically pass arrays by reference. If you specify an array type as a formal parameter, HLA will emit code that makes a copy of each and every byte of that array when you call the associated procedure.

To declare a pass by reference parameter you must preface the formal parameter declaration with the var keyword. The following code fragment demonstrates this:

```
procedure UsePassByReference( var PBRvar: int32 );
begin UsePassByReference;

    .

    .

    .

end UsePassByReference;
```

Calling a procedure with a pass by reference parameter uses the same syntax as pass by value except that the parameter has to be a memory location; it cannot be a constant or a register. Furthermore, the type of the memory location must exactly match the type of the formal parameter. The following are legal calls to the procedure above (assuming i32 is an int32 variable):

```
UsePassByReference( i32 );
UsePassByReference( (type int32 [ebx] ) );
```

The following are all illegal UsePassbyReference invocations (assumption: charVar is of type char):

```
UsePassByReference( 40 );          // Constants are illegal.
UsePassByReference( EAX );         // Bare registers are illegal.
UsePassByReference( charVar );     // Actual parameter type must match
                                   //  the formal parameter type.
```

Unlike the high level languages Pascal and C++, HLA does not completely hide the fact that you are passing a pointer rather than a value. In a procedure invocation, HLA will automatically compute the address of a variable and pass that address to the procedure. Within the procedure itself, however, you cannot treat the variable like a value parameter (as you could in most high level languages). Instead, you treat the parameter as a double word variable containing a pointer to the specified data. You must explicitly dereference this pointer when accessing the parameter's value. The example appearing in Listing 5-8 provides a simple demonstration of this.

Listing 5-8: Accessing Pass by Reference Parameters.

```
program PassByRefDemo;
#include( "stdlib.hhf" );

var
    i:  int32;
    j:  int32;
```

```
            procedure pbr( var a:int32; var b:int32 );
            const
                aa: text := "(type int32 [ebx])";
                bb: text := "(type int32 [ebx])";

            begin pbr;

                push( eax );
                push( ebx );          // Need to use EBX to dereference a and b.

                // a = -1;

                mov( a, ebx );        // Get ptr to the "a" variable.
                mov( -1, aa );        // Store -1 into the "a" parameter.

                // b = -2;

                mov( b, ebx );        // Get ptr to the "b" variable.
                mov( -2, bb );        // Store -2 into the "b" parameter.

                // Print the sum of a+b.
                // Note that ebx currently contains a pointer to "b".

                mov( bb, eax );
                mov( a, ebx );        // Get ptr to "a" variable.
                add( aa, eax );
                stdout.put( "a+b=", (type int32 eax), nl );

            end pbr;

        begin PassByRefDemo;

            // Give i and j some initial values so
            // we can see that pass by reference will
            // overwrite these values.

            mov( 50, i );
            mov( 25, j );

            // Call pbr passing i and j by reference

            pbr( i, j );

            // Display the results returned by pbr.
```

```
    stdout.put
    (
        "i= ", i, nl,
        "j= ", j, nl
    );


end PassByRefDemo;
```

Passing parameters by reference can produce some peculiar results in some rare circumstances. Consider the pbr procedure in Listing 5-8. Were you to modify the call in the main program to be "pbr(i,i)" rather than "pbr(i,j);", the program would produce the following non-intuitive output:

```
a+b=-4
i=  -2;
j=  25;
```

The reason this code displays "a+b=-4" rather than the expected "a+b=-3" is because the "pbr(i,i);" call passes the same actual parameter for a and b. As a result, the a and b reference parameters both contain a pointer to the same memory location — that of the variable i. In this case, a and b are *aliases* of one another. Therefore, when the code stores -2 at the location pointed at by b, it overwrites the -1 stored earlier at the location pointed at by a. When the program fetches the value pointed at by a and b to compute their sum, both a and b point at the same value, which is -2. Summing -2 + -2 produces the -4 result that the program displays. This non-intuitive behavior is possible any time you encounter aliases in a program. Passing the same variable as two different reference parameters probably isn't very common. But you could also create an alias if a procedure references a global variable and you pass that same global variable by reference to the procedure (this is a good example of yet one more reason why you should avoid referencing global variables in a procedure).

Pass by reference is usually less efficient than pass by value. You must dereference all pass by reference parameters on each access; this is slower than simply using a value because it typically requires at least two instructions. However, when passing a large data structure, pass by reference is faster because you do not have to copy the large data structure before calling the procedure. Of course, you'd probably need to access elements of that large data structure (e.g., an array) using a pointer, so very little efficiency is lost when you pass large arrays by reference.

5.8   Functions and Function Results

Functions are procedures that return a result. In assembly language, there are very few syntactical differences between a procedure and a function, which is why HLA doesn't provide a specific declaration for a function. Nevertheless, although there is very little *syntactical* difference between assembly procedures and functions, there are considerable *semantic* differences. That is, although you can declare them the same way in HLA, you use them differently.

Procedures are a sequence of machine instructions that fulfill some task. The end result of the execution of a procedure is the accomplishment of that activity. Functions, on the other hand, execute a sequence of machine instructions specifically to compute some value to return to the caller. Of course, a function can perform some activity as well and procedures can undoubtedly compute some values, but the main difference is that the purpose of a function is to return some computed result; procedures don't have this requirement.

A good example of a procedure is the stdout.puti32 procedure. This procedure requires a single int32 parameter. The purpose of this procedure is to print the decimal conversion of this integer value to the standard output device. Note that stdout.puti32 doesn't return any kind of value that is usable by the calling program.

A good example of a function is the cs.member function. This function expects two parameters: The first is a character value, and the second is a character set value. This function returns true (1) in EAX if the character is a member of the specified character set. It returns false if the character parameter is not a member of the character set.

Logically, the fact that cs.member returns a usable value to the calling code (in EAX) while stdout.puti32 does not is a good example of the main difference between a function and a procedure. So, in general, a procedure becomes a function by virtue of the fact that you explicitly decide to return a value somewhere upon procedure return. No special syntax is needed to declare and use a function. You still write the code as a procedure.

5.8.1   Returning Function Results

The 80x86's registers are the most common place to return function results. The cs.member routine in the HLA Standard Library is a good example of a function that returns a value in one of the CPU's registers. It returns true (1) or false (0) in the EAX register. By convention, programmers try to return 8-, 16-, and 32-bit (non-real) results in the AL, AX, and EAX registers, respectively.[7] For example, this is where most high level languages return these types of results.

Of course, there is nothing particularly sacred about the AL/AX/EAX register. You can return function results in any register if it is more convenient to do so. However, if you don't have a good reason for not using AL/AX/EAX, then you should follow the convention. Doing so will help others understand your code better because they will generally assume that your functions return small results in the AL/AX/EAX register set.

If you need to return a function result that is larger than 32 bits, you obviously must return it somewhere other than in EAX (which can hold values 32 bits or less). For values slightly larger than 32 bits (e.g., 64 bits or maybe even as many as 128 bits) you can split the result into pieces and return those parts in two or more registers. It is very common to see programs returning 64-bit values in the EDX:EAX register pair (e.g., the HLA Standard Library stdin.geti64 function returns a 64-bit integer in the EDX:EAX register pair).

---

[7] In the next chapter, you'll see where most programmers return real results.

If you need to return a really large object as a function result — say, an array of 1,000 elements — you obviously are not going to be able to return the function result in the registers. There are two common ways to deal with really large function return results: Either pass the return value as a reference parameter or allocate storage on the heap (using malloc) for the object and return a pointer to it in a 32-bit register. Of course, if you return a pointer to storage you've allocated on the heap, the calling program must free this storage when it is done with it.

5.8.2 Instruction Composition in HLA

Several HLA Standard Library functions allow you to call them as operands of other instructions. For example, consider the following code fragment:

```
if( cs.member( al, {'a'..'z'}) ) then

  .

  .
  .

endif;
```

As your high level language experience (and HLA experience) should suggest, this code calls the cs.member function to check to see if the character in AL is a lower case alphabetic character. If the cs.member function returns true then this code fragment executes the then section of the if statement; however, if cs.member returns false, this code fragment skips the if..then body. There is nothing spectacular here except for the fact that HLA doesn't support function calls as boolean expressions in the if statement (look back at Chapter 1 to see the complete set of allowable expressions). How then, does this program compile and run producing the intuitive results?

The very next section will describe how you can tell HLA that you want to use a function call in a boolean expression. However, to understand how this works, you need to first learn about *instruction composition* in HLA.

Instruction composition lets you use one instruction as the operand of another. For example, consider the mov instruction. It has two operands, a source operand and a destination operand. Instruction composition lets you substitute a valid 80x86 machine instruction for either (or both) operands. The following is a simple example:

```
mov( mov( 0, eax ), ebx );
```

Of course the immediate question is, "What does this mean?" To understand what is going on, you must first realize that most instructions "return" a value to the compiler while they are being compiled. For most instructions, the value they "return" is their destination operand. Therefore, "mov(0, eax);" returns the string "eax" to the compiler during compilation because EAX is the destination operand. Most of the time, specifically when an instruction appears on a line by itself, the compiler ignores the string result the instruction returns. However, HLA uses this string result whenever you supply an instruction in place of some operand; specifically, HLA uses that string in place of the instruction as the operand. Therefore, the mov instruction above is equivalent to the following two instruction sequences:

```
mov( 0, eax );      // HLA compiles interior instructions first.
mov( eax, ebx );
```

When processing composed instructions (that is, instruction sequences that have other instructions as operands), HLA always works in a "left-to-right then depth-first (inside-out)" manner. To make sense of this, consider the following instructions:

```
add( sub( mov( i, eax ), mov( j, ebx )), mov( k, ecx ));
```

To interpret what is happening here, begin with the source operand. It consists of the following:

```
sub( mov( i, eax ), mov( j, ebx ))
```

The source operand for this instruction is "mov(i, eax)" and this instruction does not have any composition, so HLA emits this instruction and returns its destination operand (EAX) for use as the source to the sub instruction. This effectively gives us the following:

```
sub( eax, mov( j, ebx ))
```

Now HLA compiles the instruction that appears as the destination operand ("mov(j, ebx)") and returns its destination operand (EBX) to substitute for this mov in the sub instruction. This yields the following:

```
sub( eax, ebx )
```

This is a complete instruction, without composition, that HLA can compile. So it compiles this instruction and returns its destination operand (EBX) as the string result to substitute for the sub in the original add instruction. So the original add instruction now becomes:

```
add( ebx, mov(i, ecx ));
```

HLA next compiles the mov instruction appearing in the destination operand. It returns its destination operand as a string that HLA substitutes for the mov, finally yielding the simple instruction:

```
add( ebx, ecx );
```

The compilation of the original add instruction, therefore, yields the following instruction sequence:

```
mov( i, eax );
mov( j, ebx );
sub( eax, ebx );
mov( k, ecx );
add( ebx, ecx );
```

Whew! It's rather difficult to look at the original instruction and easily see that this sequence is the result. As you can easily see in this example, *overzealous use of instruction composition can produce nearly unreadable programs*. You should be very careful about using instruction composition in your programs. With only a few exceptions, writing a composed instruction sequence makes your program harder to read.

Note that the excessive use of instruction composition may make errors in your program difficult to decipher. Consider the following HLA statement:

```
add( mov( eax, i ), mov( ebx, j ) );
```

This instruction composition yields the 80x86 instruction sequence:

```
mov( eax, i );
mov( ebx, j );
add( i, j );
```

Of course, the compiler will complain that you're attempting to add one memory location to another. However, the instruction composition effectively masks this fact and makes it difficult to comprehend the cause of the error message. Moral of the story: Avoid using instruction composition unless it really makes your program easier to read. The few examples in this section demonstrate how *not* to use instruction composition.

There are two main areas where using instruction composition can help make your programs more readable. The first is in HLA's high level language control structures. The other is in procedure parameters. Although instruction composition is useful in these two cases (and probably a few others as well), this doesn't give you a license to use extremely convoluted instructions like the add instruction in the previous example. Instead, most of the time you will use a single instruction or a function call in place of a single operand in a high level language boolean expression or in a procedure/function parameter.

While we're on the subject, exactly what does a procedure call return as the string that HLA substitutes for the call in an instruction composition? For that matter, what do statements like if..endif return? How about instructions that don't have a destination operand? Well, function return results are the subject of the very next section so you'll read about that in a few moments. As for all the other statements and instructions, you should check out the HLA Reference Manual. It lists each instruction and its "returns" value. The "returns" value is the string that HLA will substitute for the instruction when it appears as the operand to another instruction. Note that many HLA statements and instructions return the empty string as their "returns" value (by default, so do procedure calls). If an instruction returns the empty string as its composition value, then HLA will report an error if you attempt to use it as the operand of another instruction. For example, the if..endif statement returns the empty string as its "returns" value, so you may not bury an if..endif inside another instruction.

5.8.3   The HLA @RETURNS Option in Procedures

HLA procedure declarations allow a special option that specifies the string to use when a procedure invocation appears as the operand of another instruction: the @returns option. The syntax for a procedure declaration with the @returns option is as follows:

```
procedure ProcName ( optional parameters );  @returns( string_constant );
    << Local declarations >>
begin ProcName;
    << procedure statements >>
end ProcName;
```

If the @returns option is not present, HLA associates the empty string with the @returns value for the procedure. This effectively makes it illegal to use that procedure invocation as the operand to another instruction.

The @returns option requires a single string expression surrounded by parentheses. HLA will substitute this string constant for the procedure call if it ever appears as the operand of another instruction. Typically this string constant is a register name; however, any text that would be legal as an instruction operand is okay here. For example, you could specify memory address or constants. For purposes of clarity, you should always specify the location of a function's return value in the @returns parameter.

As an example, consider the following boolean function that returns true or false in the EAX register if the single character parameter is an alphabetic character:[8]

```
procedure IsAlphabeticChar( c:char ); @returns( "EAX" );
begin IsAlphabeticChar;

    // Note that cs.member returns true/false in EAX

    cs.member( c, {'a'..'z', 'A'..'Z'} );

end IsAlphabeticChar;
```

---

[8] Before you run off and actually use this function in your own programs, note that the HLA Standard Library provides the *char.isAlpha* function that provides this test. See the HLA documentation for more details.

Once you tack the @returns option on the end of this procedure declaration you can legally use a call to IsAlphabeticChar as an operand to other HLA statements and instructions:

```
mov( IsAlphabeticChar( al ), EBX );
      .
      .
      .
if( IsAlphabeticChar( ch ) ) then
      .
      .
      .
endif;
```

The last example above demonstrates that, via the @returns option, you can embed calls to your own functions in the boolean expression field of various HLA statements. Note that the code above is equivalent to

```
IsAlphabeticChar( ch );
if( EAX ) then
      .
      .
endif;
```

Not all HLA high level language statements expand composed instructions before the statement. For example, consider the following while statement:

```
while( IsAlphabeticChar( ch ) ) do
      .
      .
      .
endwhile;
```

This code does not expand to the following:

```
IsAlphabeticChar( ch );
while( EAX ) do
      .
      .
      .
endwhile;
```

Instead, the call to IsAlphabeticChar expands inside the while's boolean expression so that the program calls this function on each iteration of the loop.

You should exercise caution when entering the @returns parameter. HLA does not check the syntax of the string parameter when it is compiling the procedure declaration (other than to verify that it is a string constant). Instead, HLA checks the syntax when it replaces the function call with the @returns string.

So if you had specified "EAZ" instead of "EAX" as the @returns parameter for IsAlphabeticChar in the previous examples, HLA would not have reported an error until you actually used IsAlphabeticChar as an operand. Then of course, HLA complains about the illegal operand and it's not at all clear what the problem is by looking at the IsAlphabeticChar invocation. So take special care not to introduce typographical errors in the @returns string; figuring out such errors later can be very difficult.

5.9   Recursion

Recursion occurs when a procedure calls itself. The following, for example, is a recursive procedure:

```
procedure Recursive;
begin Recursive;

    Recursive();

end Recursive;
```

Of course, the CPU will never return from this procedure. Upon entry into Recursive, this procedure will immediately call itself again and control will never pass to the end of the procedure. In this particular case, runaway recursion results in an infinite loop.[9]

Like a looping structure, recursion requires a termination condition in order to stop infinite recursion. Recursive could be rewritten with a termination condition as follows:

```
procedure Recursive;
begin Recursive;

    dec( eax );
    if( @nz ) then

            Recursive();

    endif;

end Recursive;
```

This modification to the routine causes Recursive to call itself the number of times appearing in the EAX register. On each call, Recursive decrements the EAX register by one and calls itself again. Eventually, Recursive decrements EAX to zero and returns. Once this happens, each successive call returns back to Recursive until control returns to the original call to Recursive.

---

[9] Well, not really infinite. The stack will overflow and Windows or Linux will raise an exception at that point.

So far, however, there hasn't been a real need for recursion. After all, you could efficiently code this procedure as follows:

```
procedure Recursive;
begin Recursive;

    repeat
        dec( eax );
    until( @z );

end Recursive;
```

Both examples would repeat the body of the procedure the number of times passed in the EAX register.[10] As it turns out, there are only a few recursive algorithms that you cannot implement in an iterative fashion. However, many recursively implemented algorithms are more efficient than their iterative counterparts, and most of the time the recursive form of the algorithm is much easier to understand.

The quicksort algorithm is probably the most famous algorithm that usually appears in recursive form (see a textbook on data structures and algorithms for a discussion of this algorithm). An HLA implementation of this algorithm appears in Listing 5-9.

Listing 5-9: Recursive Quicksort Program.

```
program QSDemo;
#include( "stdlib.hhf" );

type
    ArrayType:  uns32[ 10 ];

static
    theArray:   ArrayType := [1,10,2,9,3,8,4,7,5,6];


    procedure quicksort( var a:ArrayType; Low:int32; High: int32 );
    const
        i:      text := "(type int32 edi)";
        j:      text := "(type int32 esi)";
        Middle: text := "(type uns32 edx)";
        ary:    text := "[ebx]";

    begin quicksort;

        push( eax );
        push( ebx );
        push( ecx );
```

___

[10] Although the latter version will do it considerably faster because it doesn't have the overhead of the CALL/RET instructions.

```
        push( edx );
        push( esi );
        push( edi );

        mov( a, ebx );        // Load BASE address of "a" into EBX

        mov( Low, edi);       // i := Low;
        mov( High, esi );     // j := High;

        // Compute a pivotal element by selecting the
        // physical middle element of the array.

        mov( i, eax );
        add( j, eax );
        shr( 1, eax );
        mov( ary[eax*4], Middle );  // Put middle value in EDX

        // Repeat until the EDI and ESI indicies cross one
        // another (EDI works from the start toward the end
        // of the array, ESI works from the end toward the
        // start of the array).

    repeat

            // Scan from the start of the array forward
            // looking for the first element greater or equal
            // to the middle element).

            while( Middle > ary[i*4] ) do

                inc( i );

            endwhile;

            // Scan from the end of the array backward looking
            // for the first element that is less than or equal
            // to the middle element.

            while( Middle < ary[j*4] ) do

                dec( j );

            endwhile;

            // If we've stopped before the two pointers have
            // passed over one another, then we've got two
            // elements that are out of order with respect
            // to the middle element.  So swap these two elements.
```

```
            if( i <= j ) then

                mov( ary[i*4], eax );
                mov( ary[j*4], ecx );
                mov( eax, ary[j*4] );
                mov( ecx, ary[i*4] );
                inc( i );
                dec( j );

            endif;

        until( i > j );

        // We have just placed all elements in the array in
        // their correct positions with respect to the middle
        // element of the array.  So all elements at indicies
        // greater than the middle element are also numerically
        // greater than this element.  Likewise, elements at
        // indicies less than the middle (pivotal) element are
        // now less than that element.  Unfortunately, the
        // two halves of the array on either side of the pivotal
        // element are not yet sorted.  Call quicksort recursively
        // to sort these two halves if they have more than one
        // element in them (if they have zero or one elements, then
        // they are already sorted).

        if( Low < j ) then

            quicksort( a, Low, j );

        endif;
        if( i < High ) then

quicksort( a, i, High );

        endif;

        pop( edi );
        pop( esi );
        pop( edx );
        pop( ecx );
        pop( ebx );
        pop( eax );

    end quicksort;

begin QSDemo;

    stdout.put( "Data before sorting: " nl );
```

```
    for( mov( 0, ebx ); ebx < 10; inc( ebx )) do

        stdout.put( theArray[ebx*4]:5 );

    endfor;
    stdout.newln();

    quicksort( theArray, 0, 9 );

    stdout.put( "Data after sorting: " nl );
    for( mov( 0, ebx ); ebx < 10; inc( ebx )) do

        stdout.put( theArray[ebx*4]:5 );

    endfor;
    stdout.newln();

end QSDemo;
```

Note that this quicksort procedure uses registers for all non-parameter local variables. Also note how quicksort uses text constant definitions to provide more readable names for the registers. This technique can often make an algorithm easier to read; however, one must take care when using this trick not to forget that those registers are being used.

5.10 Forward Procedures

As a general rule HLA requires that you declare all symbols before their first use in a program.[11] Therefore, you must define all procedures before their first call. There are two reasons this isn't always practical: *mutual recursion* (two procedures call each other) and *source code organization* (you prefer to place a procedure in your code after the point you've first called it). Fortunately, HLA lets you use a forward procedure definition to declare a procedure prototype. Forward declarations let you define a procedure before you actually supply the code for that procedure.

A *forward procedure declaration* is a familiar procedure declaration that uses the reserved word @forward in place of the procedure's declaration section and body. The following is a forward declaration for the quicksort procedure appearing in the last section:

```
procedure quicksort( var a:ArrayType; Low:int32; High: int32 ); @forward;
```

A forward declaration in an HLA program is a promise to the compiler that the actual procedure declaration will appear, exactly as stated in the forward declaration, at a later point in the source code. "Exactly as stated" means exactly

---

[11] There are a few minor exceptions to this rule, but it is certainly true for procedure calls.

that. The forward declaration must have the same parameters, they must be passed the same way, and they must all have the same types as the formal parameters in the procedure.[12]

Routines that are mutually recursive (that is, procedure A calls procedure B, and procedure B calls procedure A) require at least one forward declaration because you may only declare one of procedure A or B before the other. In practice, however, mutual recursion (direct or indirect) doesn't occur very frequently, so the need for forward declarations is not that great.

In the absence of mutual recursion, it is always possible to organize your source code so that each procedure declaration appears before its first invocation. What's possible and what's desired are two different things, however. You might want to group a related set of procedures at the beginning of your source code and a different set of procedures toward the end of your source code. This logical grouping, by function rather than by invocation, may make your programs much easier to read and understand. However, this organization may also yield code that attempts to call a procedure before its declaration. No sweat. Just use a forward procedure definition to resolve the problem.

One major difference between the forward definition and the actual procedure declaration has to do with the procedure options. Some options, like @returns may appear only in the forward declaration (if a @forward declaration is present). Other options may only appear in the actual procedure declaration (we haven't covered any of the other procedure options yet, so don't worry about them just yet). If your procedure requires a @returns option, the @returns option must appear before the @forward reserved word. For example:

```
procedure IsItReady( valueToTest: dword ); @returns( "EAX" ); @forward;
```

The @returns option must not also appear in the actual procedure declaration later in your source file.

5.11   Low Level Procedures and the CALL Instruction

The 80x86 call instruction does two things. First, it pushes the address of the instruction immediately following the call onto the stack; then it transfers control to the address of the specified procedure. The value that call pushes onto the stack is known as the *return address*. When the procedure wants to return to the caller and continue execution with the first statement following the call instruction, the procedure simply pops the return address off the stack and jumps (indirectly) to that address. Most procedures return to their caller by executing a ret (return) instruction. The ret instruction pops a return address off the stack and transfers control indirectly to the address it pops off the stack.

---

[12] Actually, "exactly" is too strong a word. You will see some exceptions in a moment.

By default, the HLA compiler automatically places a ret instruction (along with a few other instructions) at the end of each HLA procedure you write. This is why you haven't had to explicitly use the ret instruction up to this point. To disable the default code generation in an HLA procedure, specify the following options when declaring your procedures:

```
procedure ProcName; @noframe; @nodisplay;
begin ProcName;

    .
    .
    .

end ProcName;
```

The @noframe and @nodisplay clauses are examples of procedure *options*. HLA procedures support several such options, including @returns, @noframe, @nodisplay, and @noalignstack. You'll see the purpose of @noalignstack and a couple of other procedure options a little later in this chapter. These procedure options may appear in any order following the procedure name (and parameters, if any). Note that @noframe and @nodisplay (as well as @noalignstack) may only appear in an actual procedure declaration. You cannot specify these options in a forward declaration.

The @noframe option tells HLA that you don't want the compiler to automatically generate entry and exit code for the procedure. This tells HLA not to automatically generate the ret instruction (along with several other instructions).

The @nodisplay option tells HLA that it should not allocate storage in procedure's local variable area for a *display*. The display is a mechanism you use to access nonlocal var objects in a procedure. Therefore, a display is only necessary if you nest procedures in your programs. This book will not consider the display or nested procedures; for more details on the display and nested procedures see the appropriate chapter in the electronic edition appearing on the CD-ROM or check out the HLA Reference Manual. Until then, you can safely specify the @nodisplay option on all your procedures. Indeed, for all of the procedures appearing in this chapter up to this point specifying the @nodisplay option makes a lot of sense because none of those procedures actually use the display. Procedures that have the @nodisplay option are a tiny bit faster and a tiny bit shorter than those procedures that do not specify this option.

The following is an example of the minimal procedure:

```
procedure minimal; @nodisplay; @noframe; @noalignstack;
begin minimal;

    ret();

end minimal;
```

If you call this procedure with the `call` instruction, `minimal` will simply pop the return address off the stack and return back to the caller. You should note that a `ret` instruction is absolutely necessary when you specify the `@noframe` procedure option.[13] If you fail to put the `ret` instruction in the procedure, the program will not return to the caller upon encountering the "end minimal;" statement. Instead, the program will fall through to whatever code happens to follow the procedure in memory. The example program in Listing 5-10 demonstrates this problem.

Listing 5-10: Effect of Missing RET Instruction in a Procedure.

```
program missingRET;
#include( "stdlib.hhf" );

    // This first procedure has the NOFRAME
    // option but does not have a RET instruction.

    procedure firstProc; @noframe; @nodisplay;
    begin firstProc;

        stdout.put( "Inside firstProc" nl );

    end firstProc;



    // Because the procedure above does not have a
    // RET instruction, it will "fall through" to
    // the following instruction.  Note that there
    // is no call to this procedure anywhere in
    // this program.

    procedure secondProc; @noframe; @nodisplay;
    begin secondProc;

        stdout.put( "Inside secondProc" nl );
        ret();

end secondProc;


begin missingRET;

    // Call the procedure that doesn't have
    // a RET instruction.
```

---

[13] Strictly speaking, this isn't true. But some mechanism that pops the return address off the stack and jumps to the return address is necessary in the procedure's body.

```
        call firstProc;

end missingRET;
```

Although this behavior might be desirable in certain rare circumstances, it usually represents a defect in most programs. Therefore, if you specify the @noframe option, always remember to explicitly return from the procedure using the ret instruction.

5.12   Procedures and the Stack

Because procedures use the stack to hold the return address, you must exercise caution when pushing and popping data within a procedure. Consider the following simple (and defective) procedure:

```
procedure MessedUp; noframe; nodisplay;
begin MessedUp;

    push( eax );
    ret();

end MessedUp;
```

At the point the program encounters the ret instruction, the 80x86 stack takes the form shown in Figure 5-1.

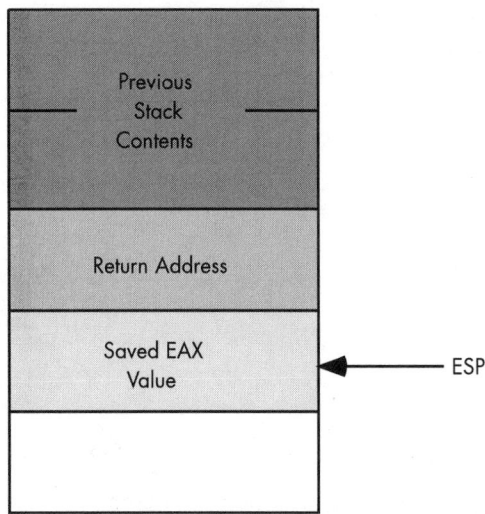

Figure 5-1: Stack Contents Before RET in "MessedUp" Procedure.

The ret instruction isn't aware that the value on the top of stack is not a valid address. It simply pops whatever value is on the top of the stack and jumps to that location. In this example, the top of stack contains the saved EAX value. Because it is very unlikely that EAX contains the proper return address (indeed, there is about a one in four billion chance it is correct), this program will probably crash or exhibit some other undefined behavior. Therefore, you must take care when pushing data onto the stack within a procedure that you properly pop that data prior to returning from the procedure.

NOTE *If you do not specify the @noframe option when writing a procedure, HLA automatically generates code at the beginning of the procedure that pushes some data onto the stack. Therefore, unless you understand exactly what is going on and you've taken care of this data HLA pushes on the stack, you should never execute the bare ret instruction inside a procedure that does not have the @noframe option. Doing so will attempt to return to the location specified by this data (which is not a return address) rather than properly returning to the caller. In procedures that do not have the @noframe option, use the exit or exitif statements to return from the procedure.*

Popping extra data off the stack prior to executing the ret statement can also create havoc in your programs. Consider the following defective procedure:

```
procedure MessedUpToo; @noframe; @nodisplay;
begin MessedUpToo;

    pop( eax );
    ret();

end MessedUpToo;
```

Upon reaching the ret instruction in this procedure, the 80x86 stack looks something like that shown in Figure 5-2.

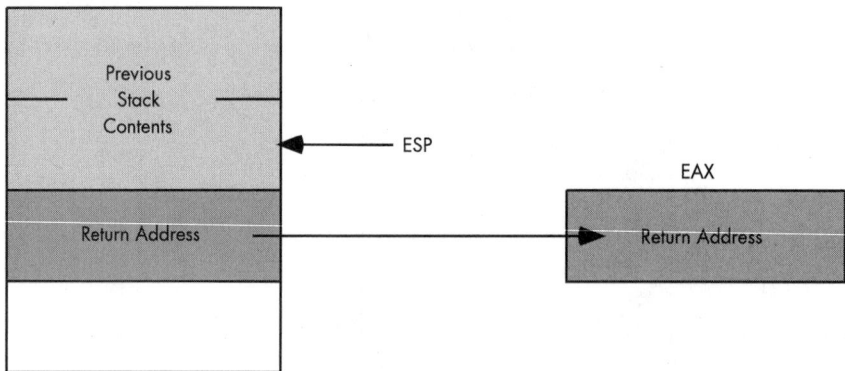

Figure 5-2: Stack Contents Before RET in MessedUpToo.

Once again, the ret instruction blindly pops whatever data happens to be on the top of the stack and attempts to return to that address. Unlike the previous example, where it was very unlikely that the top of stack contained a valid return address (because it contained the value in EAX), there is a small possibility that the top of stack in this example actually *does* contain a return address. However, this will not be the proper return address for the MessedUpToo procedure; instead, it will be the return address for the procedure that called MessUpToo. To understand the effect of this code, consider the program in Listing 5-11.

Listing 5-11: Effect of Popping Too Much Data off the Stack.

```
program extraPop;
#include( "stdlib.hhf" );



    // Note that the following procedure pops
    // excess data off the stack (in this case,
    // it pops messedUpToo's return address).

    procedure messedUpToo; @noframe; @nodisplay;
    begin messedUpToo;

        stdout.put( "Entered messedUpToo" nl );
        pop( eax );
        ret();

    end messedUpToo;



    procedure callsMU2; @noframe; @nodisplay;
    begin callsMU2;

        stdout.put( "calling messedUpToo" nl );
        messedUpToo();

        // Because messedUpToo pops extra data
        // off the stack, the following code
        // never executes (because the data popped
        // off the stack is the return address that
        // points at the following code.

        stdout.put( "Returned from messedUpToo" nl );
        ret();

    end callsMU2;



begin extraPop;
```

```
stdout.put( "Calling callsMU2" nl );
callsMU2();
stdout.put( "Returned from callsMU2" nl );
```

end extraPop;

Because a valid return address is sitting on the top of the stack, you might think that this program will actually work (properly). However, note that when returning from the MessedUpToo procedure, this code returns directly to the main program rather than to the proper return address in the EndSkipped procedure. Therefore, all code in the callsMU2 procedure that follows the call to MessedUpToo does not execute. When reading the source code, it may be very difficult to figure out why those statements are not executing because they immediately follow the call to the MessUpToo procedure. It isn't clear, unless you look very closely, that the program is popping an extra return address off the stack and, therefore, doesn't return back to callsMU2 but, rather, returns directly to whomever calls callsMU2. Of course, in this example it's fairly easy to see what is going on (because this example is a demonstration of this problem). In real programs, however, determining that a procedure has accidentally popped too much data off the stack can be much more difficult. Therefore, you should always be careful about pushing and popping data in a procedure. You should always verify that there is a one-to-one relationship between the pushes in your procedures and the corresponding pops.

5.13   Activation Records

Whenever you call a procedure there is certain information the program associates with that procedure call. The return address is a good example of some information the program maintains for a specific procedure call. Parameters and automatic local variables (i.e., those you declare in the var section) are additional examples of information the program maintains for each procedure call. *Activation record* is the term we'll use to describe the information the program associates with a specific call to a procedure.[14]

Activation record is an appropriate name for this data structure. The program creates an activation record when calling (activating) a procedure and the data in the structure is organized in a manner identical to records. Perhaps the only thing unusual about an activation record (when comparing it to a standard record) is that the base address of the record is in the middle of the data structure, so you must access fields of the record at positive and negative offsets.

Construction of an activation record begins in the code that calls a procedure. The caller pushes the parameter data (if any) onto the stack. Then the execution of the call instruction pushes the return address onto the stack. At this point, construction of the activation record continues within the procedure itself. The procedure pushes registers and other important state information and

---

[14] *Stack frame* is another term many people use to describe the activation record.

then makes room in the activation record for local variables. The procedure must also update the EBP register so that it points at the base address of the activation record.

To see what a typical activation record looks like, consider the following HLA procedure declaration:

```
procedure ARDemo( i:uns32; j:int32; k:dword ); @nodisplay;
var
    a:int32;
    r:real32;
    c:char;
    b:boolean;
    w:word;
begin ARDemo;

    .
    .
    .

end ARDemo;
```

Whenever an HLA program calls this ARDemo procedure, it begins by pushing the data for the parameters onto the stack. The calling code will push the parameters onto the stack in the order they appear in the parameter list, from left to right. Therefore, the calling code first pushes the value for the i parameter, then it pushes the value for the j parameter, and it finally pushes the data for the k parameter. After pushing the parameters, the program calls the ARDemo procedure. Immediately upon entry into the ARDemo procedure, the stack contains these four items arranged as shown in Figure 5-3.

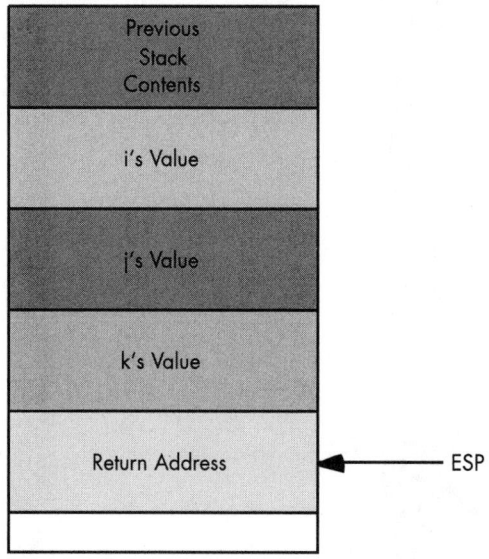

Figure 5-3: Stack Organization Immediately Upon Entry into ARDemo.

The first few instructions in ARDemo (note that it does not have the @noframe option) will push the current value of EBP onto the stack and then copy the value of ESP into EBP. Next, the code drops the stack pointer down in memory to make room for the local variables. This produces the stack organization shown in Figure 5-4.

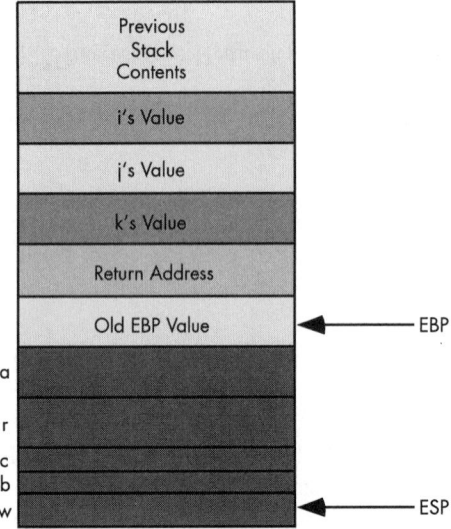

Figure 5-4: Activation Record for ARDemo.

To access objects in the activation record you must use offsets from the EBP register to the desired object. The two items of immediate interest to you are the parameters and the local variables. You can access the parameters at positive offsets from the EBP register, you can access the local variables at negative offsets from the EBP register, as Figure 5-5 shows.

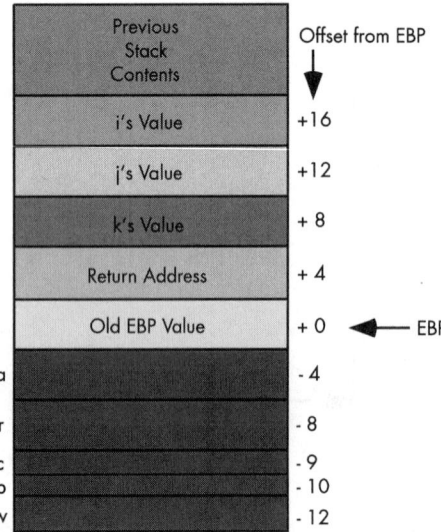

Figure 5-5: Offsets of Objects in the ARDemo Activation Record.

Intel specifically reserves the EBP (Extended Base Pointer) register for use as a pointer to the base of the activation record. This is why you should never use the EBP register for general calculations. If you arbitrarily change the value in the EBP register you will lose access to the current procedure's parameters and local variables.

5.14   The Standard Entry Sequence

The caller of a procedure is responsible for pushing the parameters onto the stack. Of course, the call instruction pushes the return address onto the stack. It is the procedure's responsibility to construct the rest of the activation record. You can accomplish this by using the following *standard entry sequence* code:

```
push( ebp );         // Save a copy of the old EBP value
mov( esp, ebp );     // Get ptr to base of activation record into EBP
sub( NumVars, esp ); // Allocate storage for local variables.
```

If the procedure doesn't have any local variables, the third instruction above, "sub(NumVars, esp);" isn't necessary. NumVars represents the number of *bytes* of local variables needed by the procedure. This is a constant that should be an even multiple of four (so the ESP register remains aligned on a double word boundary). If the number of bytes of local variables in the procedure is not an even multiple of four, you should round the value up to the next higher multiple of four before subtracting this constant from ESP. Doing so will slightly increase the amount of storage the procedure uses for local variables but will not otherwise affect the operation of the procedure.

CAUTION   *If the NumVars constant is not an even multiple of four, subtracting this value from ESP (which, presumably, contains a double word–aligned pointer) will virtually guarantee that all future stack accesses are misaligned because the program almost always pushes and pops double word values. This will have a very negative performance impact on the program. Worse still, many OS API calls will fail if the stack is not double word–aligned upon entry into the operating system. Therefore, you must always ensure that your local variable allocation value is an even multiple of four.*

Because of the problems with a misaligned stack, by default HLA will also emit a fourth instruction as part of the standard entry sequence. The HLA compiler actually emits the following standard entry sequence for the ARDemo procedure defined earlier:

```
push( ebp );
mov( esp, ebp );
sub( 12, esp );          // Make room for ARDemo's local variables.
and( $FFFF_FFFC, esp );  // Force dword stack alignment.
```

The and instruction at the end of this sequence forces the stack to be aligned on a four-byte boundary (it reduces the value in the stack pointer by one, two, or three if the value in ESP is not an even multiple of four). Although the ARDemo entry code correctly subtracts 12 from ESP for the local variables (12 is both an even multiple of four and the number of bytes of local variables), this only leaves ESP double word aligned if it was double word aligned immediately upon entry into the procedure. Had the caller messed with the stack and left ESP containing a value that was not an even multiple of four, subtracting 12 from ESP would leave ESP containing an unaligned value. The and instruction in the sequence above, however, guarantees that ESP is dword aligned regardless of ESP's value upon entry into the procedure. The few bytes and CPU cycles needed to execute this instruction pay off handsomely if ESP was not double word aligned.

Although it is always safe to execute the and instruction in the standard entry sequence, it might not be necessary. If you always ensure that ESP contains a double word aligned value, the and instruction in the standard entry sequence above is unnecessary. Therefore, if you've specified the @noframe procedure option, you don't have to include that instruction as part of the entry sequence.

If you haven't specified the @noframe option (i.e., you're letting HLA emit the instructions to construct the standard entry sequence for you), you can still tell HLA not to emit the extra and instruction if you're sure the stack will be double word aligned whenever someone calls the procedure. To do this, use the @noalignstack procedure option, e.g.,

```
procedure NASDemo( i:uns32; j:int32; k:dword ); @noalignstack;
var
      LocalVar:int32;
begin NASDemo;
      .
      .
      .
end NASDemo;
```

HLA emits the following entry sequence for the procedure above:

```
        push( ebp );
        mov( esp, ebp );
        sub( 4, esp );
```

5.15 The Standard Exit Sequence

Before a procedure returns to its caller, it needs to clean up the activation record. Although it is possible to share the cleanup duties between the procedure and the procedure's caller, Intel has included some features in the instruction set that allows the procedure to efficiently handle all the cleanup chores itself. Standard HLA procedures and procedure calls, therefore, assume that it is the procedure's responsibility to clean up the activation record (including the parameters) when the procedure returns to its caller.

If a procedure does not have any parameters, the calling sequence is very simple. It requires only three instructions:

```
mov( ebp, esp );      // Deallocate locals and clean up stack.
pop( ebp );           // Restore pointer to caller's activation record.
ret();                // Return to the caller.
```

If the procedure has some parameters, then a slight modification to the standard exit sequence is necessary in order to remove the parameter data from the stack. Procedures with parameters use the following standard exit sequence:

```
mov( ebp, esp );      // Deallocate locals and clean up stack.
pop( ebp );           // Restore pointer to caller's activation record.
ret( ParmBytes );     // Return to the caller and pop the parameters.
```

The ParmBytes operand of the ret instruction is a constant that specifies the number of *bytes* of parameter data to remove from the stack after the return instruction pops the return address. For example, the ARDemo example code in the previous sections has three double word parameters. Therefore, the standard exit sequence would take the following form:

```
mov( ebp, esp );
pop( ebp );
ret( 12 );
```

If you've declared your parameters using HLA syntax (i.e., a parameter list follows the procedure declaration), then HLA automatically creates a local constant in the procedure, _parms_, that is equal to the number of bytes of parameters in that procedure. Therefore, rather than counting the number of parameter bytes yourself, you can use the following standard exit sequence for any procedure that has parameters:

```
mov( ebp, esp );
pop( ebp );
ret( _parms_ );
```

Note that if you do not specify a byte constant operand to the ret instruction, the 80x86 will not pop the parameters off the stack upon return. Those parameters will still be sitting on the stack when you execute the first instruction following the call to the procedure. Similarly, if you specify a value that is too small, some of the parameters will be left on the stack upon return from the procedure. If the ret operand you specify is too large, the ret instruction will actually pop some of the caller's data off the stack, usually with disastrous consequences.

If you wish to return early from a procedure that doesn't have the @noframe option, and you don't particularly want to use the exit or exitif statement, you must execute the standard exit sequence to return to the caller. A simple ret instruction is insufficient because local variables and the old EBP value are probably sitting on the top of the stack.

5.16 Low Level Implementation of Automatic (Local) Variables

Your program accesses local variables in a procedure using negative offsets from the activation record base address (EBP). Consider the following HLA procedure (which, admittedly, doesn't do much other than demonstrate the use of local variables):

```
procedure LocalVars; @nodisplay;
var
     a:int32;
     b:int32;
begin LocalVars;

    mov( 0, a );
    mov( a, eax );
    mov( eax, b );

end LocalVars;
```

The activation record for LocalVars appears in Figure 5-6.

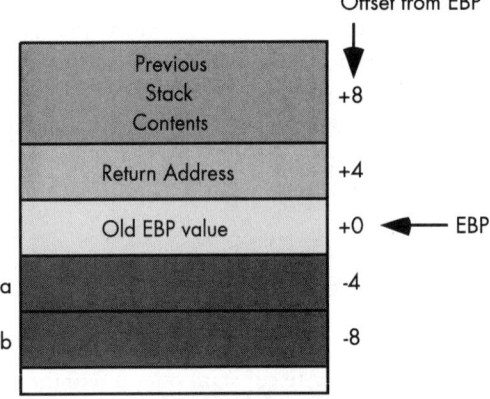

Figure 5-6: Activation Record for LocalVars Procedure.

The HLA compiler emits code that is roughly equivalent to the following for the body of this procedure:[15]

```
        mov( 0, (type dword [ebp-4]));
        mov( [ebp-4], eax );
        mov( eax, [ebp-8] );
```

---

[15] Ignoring the code associated with the standard entry and exit sequences.

You could actually type these statements into the procedure yourself and they would work. Of course, using memory references like "[ebp-4]" and "[ebp-8]" rather than a or b makes your programs very difficult to read and understand. Therefore, you should always declare and use HLA symbolic names rather than offsets from EBP.

The standard entry sequence for this LocalVars procedure will be:[16]

```
push( ebp );
mov( esp, ebp );
sub( 8, esp );
```

This code subtracts eight from the stack pointer because there are eight bytes of local variables (two double word objects) in this procedure. Unfortunately, as the number of local variables increases, especially if those variables have different types, computing the number of bytes of local variables becomes rather tedious. Fortunately, for those who wish to write the standard entry sequence themselves, HLA automatically computes this value for you and creates a constant, _vars_, that specifies the number of bytes of local variables.[17] Therefore, if you intend to write the standard entry sequence yourself, you should use the _vars_ constant in the sub instruction when allocating storage for the local variables:

```
push( ebp );
mov( esp, ebp );
sub( _vars_, esp );
```

Now that you've seen how assembly language allocates and deallocates storage for local variables, it's easy to understand why automatic (var) variables do not maintain their values between two calls to the same procedure. Because the memory associated with these automatic variables is on the stack, when a procedure returns to its caller the caller can push other data onto the stack obliterating the values of the local variable values previously held on the stack. Furthermore, intervening calls to other procedures (with their own local variables) may wipe out the values on the stack. Also, upon reentry into a procedure, the procedure's local variables may correspond to different physical memory locations; hence the values of the local variables would not be in their proper locations.

One big advantage to automatic storage is that it efficiently shares a fixed pool of memory among several procedures. For example, if you call three procedures in a row,

```
ProcA();
ProcB();
ProcC();
```

---

[16] This code assumes that ESP is dword aligned upon entry so the "AND($FFFF_FFFC, ESP);" instruction is unnecessary.

[17] HLA even rounds this constant up to the next even multiple of four so you don't have to worry about stack alignment.

the first procedure (ProcA in the code above) allocates its local variables on the stack. Upon return, ProcA deallocates that stack storage. Upon entry into ProcB, the program allocates storage for ProcB's local variables *using the same memory locations just freed by* ProcA. Likewise, when ProcB returns and the program calls ProcC, ProcC uses the same stack space for its local variables that ProcB recently freed up. This memory reuse makes efficient use of the system resources and is probably the greatest advantage to using automatic (var) variables.

5.17 Low Level Parameter Implementation

Earlier, when discussing HLA's high level parameter passing mechanism, there were several questions concerning parameters. Some important questions are:

- Where is the data coming from?
- What mechanism do you use to pass and return data?
- How much data are you passing?

In this section we will take another look at the two most common parameter passing mechanisms: pass by value and pass by reference. We will discuss three popular places to pass parameters by reference or by value: in the registers, on the stack, and in the code stream. The amount of parameter data has a direct bearing on where and how to pass it. The following sections take up these issues.

5.17.1 *Passing Parameters in Registers*

Having touched on *how* to pass parameters to a procedure earlier in this chapter, the next thing to discuss is *where* to pass parameters. Where you pass parameters depends on the size and number of those parameters. If you are passing a small number of bytes to a procedure, then the registers are an excellent place to pass parameters to a procedure. If you are passing a single parameter to a procedure you should use the following registers for the accompanying data types:

Data Size	Pass in this Register
Byte:	al
Word:	ax
Double Word:	eax
Quad Word:	edx:eax

This is not a hard and fast rule. If you find it more convenient to pass 16-bit values in the SI or BX register, do so. However, most programmers use the registers above to pass parameters.

If you are passing several parameters to a procedure in the 80x86's registers, you should probably use up the registers in the following order:

First		Last
	eax, edx, ecx, esi, edi, ebx	

In general, you should avoid using the EBP register. If you need more than six double words, perhaps you should pass your values elsewhere. This choice of priorities is not completely arbitrary. Many high level languages will attempt to pass parameters in the EAX, EDX, and ECX register (generally, in that order). Furthermore, the Intel ABI (application binary interface) allows high level language procedures to use EAX, EDX, and ECX without preserving their values. Hence, these three registers are a great place to pass parameters because a lot of code assumes their values are modified across procedure calls.

As an example, consider the following "strfill(str,c);" procedure that copies the character c (passed by value in AL) to each character position in s (passed by reference in EDI) up to a zero terminating byte:

```
// strfill-  Overwrites the data in a string with a character.
//
//    EDI-   pointer to zero terminated string (e.g., an HLA string)
//    AL-    character to store into the string.

procedure strfill; @nodisplay;
begin strfill;

    push( edi );  // Preserve this because it will be modified.
    while( (type char [edi] <> #0 ) do

        mov( al, [edi] );
        inc( edi );

    endwhile;
    pop( edi );

end strfill;
```

To call the strfill procedure you would load the address of the string data into EDI and the character value into AL prior to the call. The following code fragment demonstrates a typical call to strfill:

```
mov( s, edi );  // Get ptr to string data into edi (assumes s:string).
mov( ' ', al );
strfill();
```

Don't forget that HLA string variables are pointers. This example assumes that s is an HLA string variable and, therefore, contains a pointer to a zero terminated string. Therefore, the "mov(s, edi);" instruction loads the address of the zero terminated string into the EDI register (hence this code passes the address of the string data to strfill — that is, it passes the string by reference).

One way to pass parameters in the registers is to simply load them with the appropriate values prior to a call and then reference those registers within the procedure. This is the traditional mechanism for passing parameters in registers in an assembly language program. HLA, being somewhat more high level than traditional assembly language, provides a formal parameter declaration syntax that lets you tell HLA you're passing certain parameters in the general purpose registers. This declaration syntax is the following:

```
parmName: parmType in reg
```

Where parmName is the parameter's name, parmType is the type of the object, and reg is one of the 80x86's general purpose 8-, 16-, or 32-bit registers. The size of the parameter's type must be equal to the size of the register or HLA will report an error. Here is a concrete example:

```
procedure HasRegParms( count: uns32 in ecx; charVal:char in al );
```

One nice feature to this syntax is that you can call a procedure that has register parameters exactly like any other procedure in HLA using the high level syntax, e.g.,

```
HasRegParms( ecx, bl );
```

If you specify the same register as an actual parameter that you've declared for the formal parameter, HLA does not emit any extra code; it assumes that the parameter's value is already in the appropriate register. For example, in the call above the first actual parameter is the value in ECX; because the procedure's declaration specifies that first parameter is in ECX, HLA will not emit any code. On the other hand, the second actual parameter is in BL while the procedure will expect this parameter value in AL. Therefore, HLA will emit a "mov(bl, al);" instruction prior to calling the procedure so that the value is in the proper register upon entry to the procedure.

You can also pass parameters by reference in a register. Consider the following declaration:

```
procedure HasRefRegParm( var myPtr:uns32 in edi );
```

A call to this procedure always requires some memory operand as the actual parameter. HLA will emit the code to load the address of that memory object into the parameter's register (EDI in this case). Note that when passing reference parameters, the register must be a 32-bit general purpose register because addresses are 32 bits long. Here's an example of a call to HasRefRegParm:

```
        HasRefRegParm( x );
```

HLA will emit either a "mov(&x, edi);" or "lea(edi, x);" instruction to load the address of x into the EDI registers prior to the call instruction.[18]

If you pass an anonymous memory object (e.g., "[edi]" or "[ecx]") as a parameter to HasRefRegParm, HLA will not emit any code if the memory reference uses the same register that you declare for the parameter (i.e., "[edi]"). It will use

---

[18] The choice of instructions is dictated by whether x is a static variable (mov for static objects, lea for other objects).

a simple mov instruction to copy the actual address into EDI if you specify an indirect addressing mode using a register other than EDI (e.g., "[ecx]"). It will use an lea instruction to compute the effective address of the anonymous memory operand if you use a more complex addressing mode like "[edi+ecx*4+2]".

Within the procedure's code, HLA creates text equates for these register parameters that map their names to the appropriate register. In the HasRegParms example, any time you reference the count parameter, HLA substitutes "ecx" for count. Likewise, HLA substitutes "al" for charVal throughout the procedure's body. Because these names are aliases for the registers, you should take care to always remember that you cannot use ECX and AL independently of these parameters. It would be a good idea to place a comment next to each use of these parameters to remind the reader that count is equivalent to ECX and charVal is equivalent to AL.

5.17.2   Passing Parameters in the Code Stream

Another place where you can pass parameters is in the code stream immediately after the call instruction. Consider the following print routine that prints a literal string constant to the standard output device:

```
call print;
byte "This parameter is in the code stream.",0;
```

Normally, a subroutine returns control to the first instruction immediately following the call instruction. Were that to happen here, the 80x86 would attempt to interpret the ASCII codes for "This..." as an instruction. This would produce undesirable results. Fortunately, you can skip over this string when returning from the subroutine.

So how do you gain access to these parameters? Easy. The return address on the stack points at them. Consider the implementation of print appearing in Listing 5-12.

Listing 5-12: Print Procedure Implementation (Using Code Stream Parameters).

```
program printDemo;
#include( "stdlib.hhf" );

    // print-
    //
    //  This procedure writes the literal string
    //  immediately following the call to the
    //  standard output device. The literal string
    //  must be a sequence of characters ending with
    //  a zero byte (i.e., a C string, not an HLA
    //  string).

    procedure print; @noframe; @nodisplay;
    const
```

```
            // RtnAdrs is the offset of this procedure's
            // return address in the activation record.

            RtnAdrs:text := "(type dword [ebp+4])";

begin print;

            // Build the activation record (note the
            // "@noframe" option above).

            push( ebp );
            mov( esp, ebp );

            // Preserve the registers this function uses.

            push( eax );
            push( ebx );

            // Copy the return address into the EBX
            // register. Because the return address points
            // at the start of the string to print, this
            // instruction loads EBX with the address of
            // the string to print.

            mov( RtnAdrs, ebx );

            // Until we encounter a zero byte, print the
            // characters in the string.

            forever

                mov( [ebx], al );    // Get the next character.
                breakif( !al );      // Quit if it's zero.
                stdout.putc( al );   // Print it.
                inc( ebx );          // Move on to the next char.

            endfor;

            // Skip past the zero byte and store the resulting
            // address over the top of the return address so
            // we'll return to the location that is one byte
            // beyond the zero terminating byte of the string.

            inc( ebx );
            mov( ebx, RtnAdrs );

            // Restore EAX and EBX.

            pop( ebx );
```

```
        pop( eax );

        // Clean up the activation record and return.

        pop( ebp );
        ret();

    end print;


begin printDemo;

    // Simple test of the print procedure.

    call print;
    byte "Hello World!", 13, 10, 0 ;

end printDemo;
```

Besides showing how to pass parameters in the code stream, the print routine also exhibits another concept: *variable length parameters*. The string following the call can be any practical length. The zero terminating byte marks the end of the parameter list. There are two easy ways to handle variable length parameters. Either use some special terminating value (like zero) or you can pass a special length value that tells the subroutine how many parameters you are passing. Both methods have their advantages and disadvantages. Using a special value to terminate a parameter list requires that you choose a value that never appears in the list. For example, print uses zero as the terminating value, so it cannot print the NUL character (whose ASCII code is zero). Sometimes this isn't a limitation. Specifying a special length parameter is another mechanism you can use to pass a variable length parameter list. While this doesn't require any special codes or limit the range of possible values that can be passed to a subroutine, setting up the length parameter and maintaining the resulting code can be a real nightmare.[19]

Despite the convenience afforded by passing parameters in the code stream, there are some disadvantages to passing parameters there. First, if you fail to provide the exact number of parameters the procedure requires, the subroutine will get confused. Consider the print example. It prints a string of characters up to a zero terminating byte and then returns control to the first instruction following the zero terminating byte. If you leave off the zero terminating byte, the print routine happily prints the following opcode bytes as ASCII characters until it finds a zero byte. Because zero bytes often appear in the middle of an instruction, the print routine might return control into the middle of some other instruction. This will probably crash the machine. Inserting an extra zero, which occurs more often than you might think, is another problem programmers have with the print routine. In such a case, the print routine would return upon encountering the first zero byte and attempt to execute the following ASCII

---

[19] Especially if the parameter list changes frequently.

characters as machine code. Once again, this usually crashes the machine. These are the some of the reasons why the HLA stdout.put code does *not* pass its parameters in the code stream. Problems notwithstanding, however, the code stream is an efficient place to pass parameters whose values do not change.

5.17.3 Passing Parameters on the Stack

Most high level languages use the stack to pass parameters because this method is fairly efficient. By default, HLA also passes parameters on the stack. Although passing parameters on the stack is slightly less efficient than passing those parameters in registers, the register set is very limited and you can only pass a few value or reference parameters through registers. The stack, on the other hand, allows you to pass a large amount of parameter data without any difficulty. This is the principal reason that most programs pass their parameters on the stack.

HLA typically passes parameters you specify using the high level procedure call syntax on the stack. For example, suppose you define strfill from earlier as follows:

```
procedure strfill( s:string; chr:char );
```

Calls of the form "strfill(s, ' ');" will pass the value of s (which is an address) and a space character on the 80x86 stack. When you specify a call to strfill in this manner, HLA automatically pushes the parameters for you, so you don't have to push them onto the stack yourself. Of course, if you choose to do so, HLA will let you manually push the parameters onto the stack prior to the call.

To manually pass parameters on the stack, push them immediately before calling the subroutine. The subroutine then reads this data from the stack memory and operates on it appropriately. Consider the following HLA procedure call:

```
CallProc(i,j,k);
```

HLA pushes parameters onto the stack in the order that they appear in the parameter list.[20] Therefore, the 80x86 code HLA emits for this subroutine call (assuming you're passing the parameters by value) is

```
        push( i );
        push( j );
        push( k );
        call CallProc;
```

Upon entry into CallProc, the 80x86's stack looks like that shown in Figure 5-7.

---

[20]Assuming, of course, that you don't instruct HLA otherwise. It is possible to tell HLA to reverse the order of the parameters on the stack. See the chapter on mixed language programming for more details.

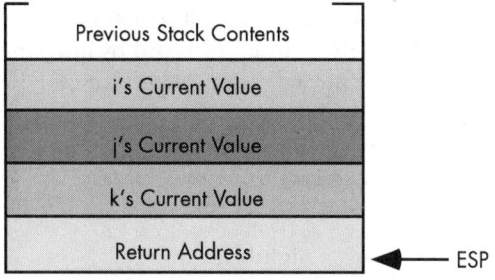

Figure 5-7: Stack Layout upon Entry into CallProc.

You could gain access to the parameters passed on the stack by removing the data from the stack as the following code fragment demonstrates:

```
// Note: To extract parameters off the stack by popping it is very important
// to specify both the @nodisplay and @noframe procedure options.

static
    RtnAdrs: dword;
    p1Parm: dword;
    p2Parm: dword;
    p3Parm: dword;

procedure CallProc( p1:dword; p2:dword; p3:dword ); @nodisplay; @noframe;
begin CallProc;

    pop( RtnAdrs );
    pop( p3Parm );
    pop( p2Parm );
    pop( p1Parm );
    push( RtnAdrs );
        .
        .
        .
    ret();

end CallProc;
```

As you can see from this code, it first pops the return address off the stack and into the RtnAdrs variable; then it pops (in reverse order) the values of the p1, p2, and p3 parameters; finally, it pushes the return address back onto the stack (so the ret instruction will operate properly). Within the CallProc procedure, you may access the p1Parm, p2Parm, and p3Parm variables to use the p1, p2, and p3 parameter values.

There is, however, a better way to access procedure parameters. If your procedure includes the standard entry and exit sequences, then you may directly access the parameter values in the activation record by indexing off the EBP register. Consider the layout of the activation record for CallProc that uses the following declaration:

```
procedure CallProc( p1:dword; p2:dword; p3:dword ); @nodisplay; @noframe;
begin CallProc;

    push( ebp );      // This is the standard entry sequence.
    mov( esp, ebp );  // Get base address of A.R. into EBP.
        .
        .
        .
```

Take a look at the stack immediately after the execution of "mov(esp, ebp);" in CallProc. Assuming you've pushed three double word parameters onto the stack, it should look something like that shown in Figure 5-8.

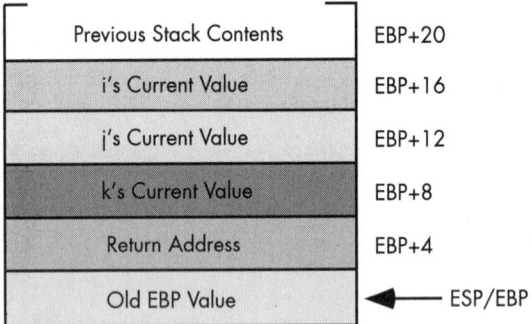

Figure 5-8: Activation Record for CallProc After Standard Entry Sequence Execution.

Now you can access the parameters by indexing off the EBP register:

```
    mov( [ebp+16], eax );   // Accesses the first parameter.
    mov( [ebp+12], ebx );   // Accesses the second parameter.
    mov( [ebp+8], ecx );    // Accesses the third parameter.
```

Of course, like local variables, you'd never really access the parameters in this way. You can use the formal parameter names (p1, p2, and p3), and HLA will substitute a suitable "[ebp+*displacement*]" memory address. Even though you shouldn't actually access parameters using address expressions like "[ebp+12]" it's important to understand their relationship to the parameters in your procedures.

Other items that often appear in the activation record are register values your procedure preserves. The most rational place to preserve registers in a procedure is in the code immediately following the standard entry sequence. In a standard HLA procedure (one where you do not specify the @noframe option), this simply means that the code that preserves the registers should appear first in the procedure's body. Likewise, the code to restore those register values should appear immediately before the end clause for the procedure.[21]

5.17.3.1 Accessing Value Parameters on the Stack

Accessing a parameter's passed by value is no different than accessing a local var object. As long as you've declared the parameter in a formal parameter list and the procedure executes the standard entry sequence upon entry into the program, all you need do is specify the parameter's name to reference the value of that parameter. Listing 5-13 provides an example program whose procedure accesses a parameter the main program passes to it by value.

Listing 5-13: Demonstration of Value Parameters.

```
program AccessingValueParameters;
#include( "stdlib.hhf" )

    procedure ValueParm( theParameter: uns32 ); @nodisplay;
    begin ValueParm;

        mov( theParameter, eax );
        add( 2, eax );
        stdout.put
        (
            "theParameter + 2 = ",
            (type uns32 eax),
            nl
        );

    end ValueParm;


begin AccessingValueParameters;

    ValueParm( 10 );
    ValueParm( 135 );

end AccessingValueParameters;
```

Although you could access the value of theParameter using the anonymous address "[EBP+8]" within your code, there is absolutely no good reason for doing so. If you declare the parameter list using the HLA high level language syntax, you can access the value parameter by specifying its name within the procedure.

---

[21]Note that if you use the exit statement to exit a procedure, you must duplicate the code to pop the register values and place this code immediately before the exit clause. This is a good example of a maintenance nightmare, and is also a good reason why you should only have one exit point in your program.

5.17.3.2 Passing Value Parameters on the Stack

As Listing 5-13 demonstrates, passing a value parameter to a procedure is very easy. Just specify the value in the actual parameter list as you would for a high level language call. Actually, the situation is a little more complicated than this. Passing value parameters is easy if you're passing constant, register, or variable values. It gets a little more complex if you need to pass the result of some expression. This section deals with the different ways you can pass a parameter by value to a procedure.

Of course, you do not have to use the HLA high level syntax to pass value parameters to a procedure. You can push these values on the stack yourself. Because there are many times it is more convenient or more efficient to manually pass the parameters, describing how to do this is a good place to start.

As noted earlier in this chapter, when passing parameters on the stack you push the objects in the order they appear in the formal parameter list (from left to right). When passing parameters by value, you should push the values of the actual parameters onto the stack. The program in Listing 5-14 demonstrates how to do this.

Listing 5-14: Manually Passing Parameters on the Stack.

```
program ManuallyPassingValueParameters;
#include( "stdlib.hhf" )

    procedure ThreeValueParms( p1:uns32; p2:uns32; p3:uns32 ); @nodisplay;
    begin ThreeValueParms;

        mov( p1, eax );
        add( p2, eax );
        add( p3, eax );
        stdout.put
        (
            "p1 + p2 + p3 = ",
            (type uns32 eax),
            nl
        );

    end ThreeValueParms;


static
    SecondParmValue:uns32 := 25;

begin ManuallyPassingValueParameters;
```

```
    pushd( 10 );                // Value associated with p1.
    pushd( SecondParmValue);    // Value associated with p2.
    pushd( 15 );                // Value associated with p3.

    call ThreeValueParms;

end ManuallyPassingValueParameters;
```

Note that if you manually push the parameters onto the stack as this example does, you must use the call instruction to call the procedure. If you attempt to use a procedure invocation of the form "ThreeValueParms();" then HLA will complain about a mismatched parameter list. HLA won't realize that you've manually pushed the parameters (as far as HLA is concerned, those pushes appear to preserve some other data).

Generally, there is little reason to manually push a parameter onto the stack if the actual parameter is a constant, a register value, or a variable. HLA's high level syntax handles most such parameters for you. There are several instances, however, where HLA's high level syntax won't work. The first such example is passing the result of an arithmetic expression as a value parameter. Because arithmetic expressions don't exist in HLA, you will have to manually compute the result of the expression and pass that value yourself. There are two possible ways to do this: Calculate the result of the expression and manually push that result onto the stack, or compute the result of the expression into a register and pass the register as a parameter to the procedure. The program in Listing 5-15 demonstrates these two mechanisms.

Listing 5-15: Passing the Result of Some Arithmetic Expression as a Parameter.

```
program PassingExpressions;
#include( "stdlib.hhf" )

    procedure ExprParm( exprValue:uns32 ); @nodisplay;
    begin ExprParm;

        stdout.put( "exprValue = ", exprValue, nl );

    end ExprParm;


static
    Operand1: uns32 := 5;
    Operand2: uns32 := 20;

begin PassingExpressions;

    // ExprParm( Operand1 + Operand2 );
    //
    // Method one: Compute the sum and manually
    //   push the sum onto the stack.
```

```
    mov( Operand1, eax );
    add( Operand2, eax );
    push( eax );
    call ExprParm;

    // Method two: Compute the sum in a register and
    // pass the register using the HLA high level
    // language syntax.

    mov( Operand1, eax );
    add( Operand2, eax );
    ExprParm( eax );
```

end PassingExpressions;

The examples up to this point in this section have made an important assumption: that the parameter you are passing is a double word value. The calling sequence changes somewhat if you're passing parameters that are not four-byte objects. Because HLA can generate relatively inefficient code when passing objects that are not four bytes long, manually passing such objects is a good idea if you want to have the fastest possible code.

HLA requires that all value parameters be an even multiple of four bytes long.[22] If you pass an object that is less than four bytes long, HLA requires that you pad the parameter data with extra bytes so that you always pass an object that is at least four bytes in length. For parameters that are larger than four bytes, you must ensure that you pass an even multiple of four bytes as the parameter value, adding extra bytes at the high order end of the object to pad it, as necessary.

Consider the following procedure prototype:

procedure OneByteParm(b:byte);

The activation record for this procedure appears in Figure 5-9.

As you can see, there are four bytes on the stack associated with the b parameter, but only one of the four bytes contains valid data (the L.O. byte). The remaining three bytes are just padding, and the procedure should ignore these bytes. In particular, you should never assume that these extra bytes contain zeros or some other consistent value. Depending on the type of parameter you pass, HLA's automatic code generation may or may not push zero bytes as the extra data on the stack.

---

[22] This only applies if you use the HLA high level language syntax to declare and access parameters in your procedures. Of course, if you manually push the parameters yourself and you access the parameters inside the procedure using an addressing mode like "[ebp+8]" then you can pass any sized object you choose. Of course, keep in mind that most operating systems expect the stack to be dword aligned, so parameters you push should be a multiple of four bytes long.

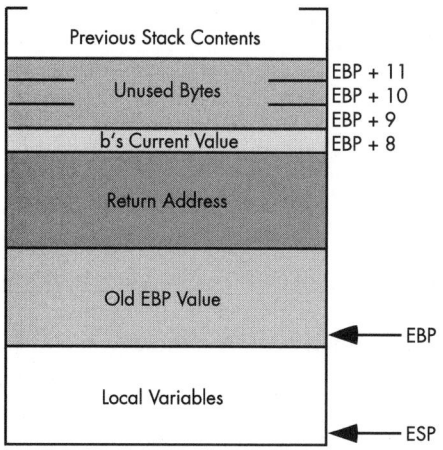

Figure 5-9: OneByteParm Activation Record.

When passing a byte parameter to a procedure, HLA will automatically emit code that pushes four bytes on the stack. Because HLA's parameter passing mechanism guarantees not to disturb any register or other values, HLA often generates more code than is actually needed to pass a byte parameter. For example, if you decide to pass the AL register as the byte parameter, HLA will emit code that pushes the EAX register onto the stack. This single push instruction is a very efficient way to pass AL as a four-byte parameter object. On the other hand, if you decide to pass the AH register as the byte parameter, pushing EAX won't work because this would leave the value in AH at offset EBP+9 in the activation record shown in Figure 5-9. Unfortunately, the procedure expects this value at offset EBP+8 so simply pushing EAX won't do the job. If you pass AH, BH, CH, or DH as a byte parameter, HLA emits code like the following:

```
sub( 4, esp );    // Make room for the parameter on the stack.
mov( ah, [esp] ); // Store AH into the L.O. byte of the parameter.
```

As you can clearly see, passing one of the "H" registers as a byte parameter is less efficient (two instructions) than passing one of the "L" registers. So you should attempt to use the "L" registers whenever possible if passing an eight-bit register as a parameter.[23] Note, by the way, that there is very little you can do about the difference in efficiency, even if you manually pass the parameters yourself.

If the byte parameter you decide to pass is a variable rather than a register, HLA generates decidedly worse code. For example, suppose you call OneByteParm as follows:

```
OneByteParm( uns8Var );
```

---

[23] Or better yet, pass the parameter directly in the register if you are writing the procedure yourself.

For this call, HLA will emit code similar to the following to push this single byte parameter:

```
push( eax );
push( eax );
mov( uns8Var, al );
mov( al, [esp+4] );
pop( eax );
```

As you can plainly see, this is a lot of code to pass a single byte on the stack! HLA emits this much code because (1) it guarantees not to disturb any registers, and (2) it doesn't know whether uns8Var is the last variable in allocated memory. You can generate much better code if you don't have to enforce either of these two constraints.

If you've got a spare 32-bit register laying around (especially one of EAX, EBX, ECX, or EDX) then you can pass a byte parameter on the stack using only two instructions. Move (or move with zero/sign extension) the byte value into the register and then push the register onto the stack. For the current call to OneByteParm, the calling sequence would look like the following in EAX is available:

```
mov( uns8Var, al );
push( eax );
call OneByteParm;
```

If only ESI or EDI were available, you could use code like this:

```
movzx( uns8Var, esi );
push( esi );
call OneByteParm;
```

Another trick you can use to pass the parameter with only a single push instruction is to coerce the byte variable to a double word object, e.g.,

```
push( (type dword uns8Var));
call OneByteParm;
```

This last example is very efficient. Note that it pushes the first three bytes of whatever value happens to follow uns8Var in memory as the padding bytes. HLA doesn't use this technique because there is a (very tiny) chance that using this scheme will cause the program to fail. If it turns out that the uns8Var object is the last byte of a given page in memory and the next page of memory is unreadable, the push instruction will cause a memory access exception. To be on the safe side, the HLA compiler does not use this scheme. However, if you always ensure that the actual parameter you pass in this fashion is not the last variable you declare in a static section, then you can get away with code that uses this technique. Because it is nearly impossible for the byte object to appear at the last accessible address on the stack, it is probably safe to use this technique with var objects.

When passing word parameters on the stack you must also ensure that you include padding bytes so that each parameter consumes an even multiple of four bytes. You can use the same techniques we use to pass bytes except, of course, there are two valid bytes of data to pass instead of one. For example, you could use either of the following two schemes to pass a word object w to a OneWordParm procedure:

```
mov( w, ax );
push( eax );
call OneWordParm;
```

```
push( (type dword w) );
call OneWordParm;
```

When passing large objects by value on the stack (e.g., records and arrays), you do not have to ensure that each element or field of the object consumes an even multiple of four bytes; all you need to do is ensure that the entire data structure consumes an even multiple of four bytes on the stack. For example, if you have an array of ten three-byte elements, the entire array will need two bytes of padding (10*3 is 30 bytes, which is not evenly divisible by four, but 10*3 + 2 is 32, which is divisible by four). HLA does a fairly good job of passing large data objects by value to a procedure. For larger objects, you should use the HLA high level language procedure invocation syntax unless you have some special requirements. Of course, if you want efficient operation, you should try to avoid passing large data structures by value.

By default, HLA guarantees that it won't disturb the values of any registers when it emits code to pass parameters to a procedure. Sometimes this guarantee isn't necessary. For example, if you are returning a function result in EAX and you are not passing a parameter to a procedure in EAX, there really is no reason to preserve EAX upon entry into the procedure. Rather than generating some crazy code like the following to pass a byte parameter:

```
push( eax );
push( eax );
mov( uns8Var, al );
mov( al, [esp+4] );
pop( eax );
```

HLA could generate much better code if it knows that it can use EAX (or some other register):

```
mov( uns8Var, al );
push( eax );
```

You can use the @use procedure option to tell HLA that it can modify a register's value if doing so would improve the code it generates when passing parameters. The syntax for this option is

@use genReg$_{32}$;

The *genReg$_{32}$* operand can be EAX, EBX, ECX, EDX, ESI, or EDI. You'll obtain the best results if this register is one of EAX, EBX, ECX, or EDX. Particularly, you should note that you cannot specify EBP or ESP here (because the procedure already uses those registers).

The @use procedure option tells HLA that it's okay to modify the value of the register you specify as an operand. Therefore, if HLA can generate better code by not preserving that register's value, it will do so. For example, when the "@use eax;" option is provided for the OneByteParm procedure given earlier, HLA will only emit the two instructions immediately above rather than the five-instruction sequence that preserves EAX.

You must exercise care when specifying the @use procedure option. In particular, you should not be passing any parameters in the same register you specify in the @use option (because HLA may inadvertently scramble the parameter's value if you do this). Likewise, you must ensure that it's really okay for the procedure to change the register's value. As noted above, the best choice for an @use register is EAX when the procedure is returning a function result in EAX (because, clearly, the caller will not expect the procedure to preserve EAX).

If your procedure has a @forward or @external declaration (see the section on external declarations later in this chapter), the @use option must only appear in the @forward or @external definition, not in the actual procedure declaration. If no such procedure prototype appears, then you must attach the @use option to the procedure declaration.

Example:

```
procedure OneByteParm( b:byte ); @nodisplay; @use EAX;
begin OneByteParm;

    << Do something with b >>

end OneByteParm;
    .
    .
    .
static
    byteVar:byte;
        .
        .
        .
    OneByteParm( byteVar );
```

This call to OneByteParm emits the following instructions:

```
mov( uns8Var, al );
push( eax );
call OneByteParm;
```

5.17.3.3   Accessing Reference Parameters on the Stack

Because HLA passes the address for reference parameters, accessing the reference parameters within a procedure is slightly more difficult than accessing value parameters because you have to dereference the pointers to the reference parameters. Unfortunately, HLA's high level syntax for procedure declarations and invocations does not (and cannot) abstract this detail away for you. You will have to manually dereference these pointers yourself. This section reviews how you do this.

In Listing 5-16 the RefParm procedure has a single pass by reference parameter. Pass by reference parameters are always a pointer to an object of the type specified by the parameter's declaration. Therefore, theParameter is actually an object of type "pointer to uns32" rather than an uns32 value. In order to access the value associated with theParameter, this code has to load that double word address into a 32-bit register and access the data indirectly. The "mov(theParameter, eax);" instruction in Listing 5-16 fetches this pointer into the EAX register and then procedure RefParm uses the "[eax]" addressing mode to access the actual value of theParameter.

Listing 5-16: Accessing a Reference Parameter

```
program AccessingReferenceParameters;
#include( "stdlib.hhf" )

    procedure RefParm( var theParameter: uns32 ); @nodisplay;
    begin RefParm;

        // Add two directly to the parameter passed by
        // reference to this procedure.

        mov( theParameter, eax );
        add( 2, (type uns32 [eax]) );

        // Fetch the value of the reference parameter
        // and print its value.

        mov( [eax], eax );
        stdout.put
        (
            "theParameter now equals ",
            (type uns32 eax),
            nl
        );
```

```
        end RefParm;


static
     p1: uns32 := 10;
     p2: uns32 := 15;

begin AccessingReferenceParameters;

     RefParm( p1 );
     RefParm( p2 );

     stdout.put( "On return, p1=", p1, " and p2=", p2, nl );

end AccessingReferenceParameters;
```

Because this procedure accesses the data of the actual parameter, adding two to this data affects the values of the variables passed to the RefParm procedure from the main program. Of course, this should come as no surprise because these are the standard semantics for pass by reference parameters.

As you can see, accessing (small) pass by reference parameters is a little less efficient than accessing value parameters because you need an extra instruction to load the address into a 32-bit pointer register (not to mention, you have to reserve a 32-bit register for this purpose). If you access reference parameters frequently, these extra instructions can really begin to add up, reducing the efficiency of your program. Furthermore, it's easy to forget to dereference a reference parameter and use the address of the value in your calculations (this is especially true when passing double word parameters, like the uns32 parameter in the example above, to your procedures). Therefore, unless you really need to affect the value of the actual parameter, you should use pass by value to pass small objects to a procedure.

Passing large objects, like arrays and records, is where using reference parameters becomes efficient. When passing these objects by value, the calling code has to make a copy of the actual parameter; if the actual parameter is a large object, the copy process can be very inefficient. Because computing the address of a large object is just as efficient as computing the address of a small scalar object, there is no efficiency loss when passing large objects by reference. Within the procedure you must still dereference the pointer to access the object but the efficiency loss due to indirection is minimal when you contrast this with the cost of copying that large object. The program in Listing 5-17 demonstrates how to use pass by reference to initialize an array of records.

Listing 5-17: Passing an Array of Records by Referencing.

```
program accessingRefArrayParameters;
#include( "stdlib.hhf" )


const
     NumElements := 64;
```

```
type
    Pt: record

            x:uns8;
            y:uns8;

        endrecord;

    Pts: Pt[NumElements];


    procedure RefArrayParm( var ptArray: Pts ); @nodisplay;
    begin RefArrayParm;

        push( eax );
        push( ecx );
        push( edx );

        mov( ptArray, edx );      // Get address of parameter into EDX.

        for( mov( 0, ecx ); ecx < NumElements; inc( ecx )) do

            // For each element of the array, set the "x" field
            // to (ecx div 8) and set the "y" field to (ecx mod 8).

            mov( cl, al );
            shr( 3, al );    // ECX div 8.
            mov( al, (type Pt [edx+ecx*2]).x );

            mov( cl, al );
            and( %111, al );  // ECX mod 8.
            mov( al, (type Pt [edx+ecx*2]).y );

        endfor;
        pop( edx );
        pop( ecx );
        pop( eax );

    end RefArrayParm;


static
    MyPts: Pts;

begin accessingRefArrayParameters;

    // Initialize the elements of the array.
```

```
    RefArrayParm( MyPts );


    // Display the elements of the array.

    for( mov( 0, ebx ); ebx < NumElements; inc( ebx )) do

        stdout.put
        (
            "RefArrayParm[",
            (type uns32 ebx):2,
            "].x=",
            MyPts.x[ ebx*2 ],

            " RefArrayParm[",
            (type uns32 ebx):2,
            "].y=",
            MyPts.y[ ebx*2 ],
            nl
        );

    endfor;

end accessingRefArrayParameters;
```

As you can see from this example, passing large objects by reference is relatively efficient. Other than tying up the EDX register throughout the RefArrayParm procedure plus a single instruction to load EDX with the address of the reference parameter, the RefArrayParm procedure doesn't require many more instructions than the same procedure where you would pass the parameter by value.

5.17.3.4 Passing Reference Parameters on the Stack

HLA's high level syntax often makes passing reference parameters a breeze. All you need to do is specify the name of the actual parameter you wish to pass in the procedure's parameter list. HLA will automatically emit some code that will compute the address of the specified actual parameter and push this address onto the stack. However, like the code HLA emits for value parameters, the code HLA generates to pass the address of the actual parameter on the stack may not be the most efficient that is possible. Therefore, if you want to write fast code, you may want to manually write the code to pass reference parameters to a procedure. This section discusses how to do exactly that.

Whenever you pass a static object as a reference parameter, HLA generates very efficient code to pass the address of that parameter to the procedure. As an example, consider the following code fragment:

```
    procedure HasRefParm( var d:dword );
        .
        .
        .
```

```
static
    FourBytes:dword;

var
    v: dword;
    .
    .
    .

HasRefParm( FourBytes );
    .
    .
    .
```

For the call to the HasRefParm procedure, HLA emits the following instruction sequence:

```
pushd( &FourBytes );
call HasRefParm;
```

You really aren't going to be able to do substantially better than this if you are passing your reference parameters on the stack. So if you're passing static objects as reference parameters, HLA generates fairly good code and you should stick with the high level syntax for the procedure call.

Unfortunately, when passing automatic (var) objects or indexed variables as reference parameters, HLA needs to compute the address of the object at run-time. This generally requires the use of the lea instruction. Unfortunately, the lea instruction requires the use of a 32-bit register and HLA promises not to disturb the values in any registers when it automatically generates code for you.[24] Therefore, HLA needs to preserve the value in whatever register it uses when it computes an address via lea to pass a parameter by reference. The following example shows you the code that HLA actually emits:

```
// Call to the HasRefParm procedure:

    HasRefParm( v );

// HLA actually emits the following code for the above call:

    push( eax );
    push( eax );
    lea( eax, v );
    mov( eax, [esp+4] );
    pop( eax );
    call HasRefParm;
```

---

[24] This isn't entirely true. You'll see the exception in the chapter on classes and objects. Also, using the @USE procedure option tells HLA that it's okay to modify the value in one of the registers.

As you can see, this is quite a bit of code, especially if you have a 32-bit register available and you don't need to preserve that register's value. Here's a better code sequence given the availability of EAX:

```
        lea( eax, v );
        push( eax );
        call HasRefParm;
```

Remember, when passing an actual parameter by reference, you must compute the address of that object and push the address onto the stack. For simple static objects you can use the address-of operator ("&") to easily compute the address of the object and push it onto the stack; however, for indexed and automatic objects, you will probably need to use the lea instruction to compute the address of the object. Here are some examples that demonstrate this using the HasRefParm procedure from the previous examples:

```
static
        i:      int32;
        Ary:    int32[16];
        iptr: pointer to int32 := &i;

var
        v:      int32;
        AV:     int32[10];
        vptr: pointer to int32;
        .
        .
        .
        lea( eax, v );
        mov( eax, vptr );
        .
        .
        .

// HasRefParm( i );

        push( &i );                 // Simple static object, so just use "&".
        call HasRefParm;

// HasRefParm( Ary[ebx] );          // Pass element of Ary by reference.

        lea( eax, Ary[ ebx*4 ]);    // Must use LEA for indexed addresses.
        push( eax );
        call HasRefParm;

// HasRefParm( *iptr );    -- Pass object pointed at by iptr

        push( iptr );               // Pass address (iptr's value) on stack.
        call HasRefParm;
```

```
// HasRefParm( v );

    lea( eax, v );              // Must use LEA to compute the address
    push( eax );                //  of automatic vars passed on stack.
    call HasRefParm;

// HasRefParm( AV[ esi ] );   -- Pass element of AV by reference.

    lea( eax, AV[ esi*4] );     // Must use LEA to compute address of the
    push( eax );                //  desired element.
    call HasRefParm;

// HasRefParm( *vptr );   -- Pass address held by vptr...

    push( vptr );               // Just pass vptr's value as the specified
    call HasRefParm;            //  address.
```

If you have an extra register to spare, you can tell HLA to use that register when computing the address of reference parameters (without emitting the code to preserve that register's value). The @use option will tell HLA that it's okay to use the specified register without preserving its value. As noted in the section on value parameters, the syntax for this procedure option is

$$\text{@use } reg_{32};$$

where reg_{32} may be any of EAX, EBX, ECX, EDX, ESI, or EDI. Because reference parameters always pass a 32-bit value, all of these registers are equivalent as far as HLA is concerned (unlike value parameters, that may prefer the EAX, EBX, ECX, or EDX register). Your best choice would be EAX if the procedure is not passing a parameter in the EAX register and the procedure is returning a function result in EAX; otherwise, any currently unused register will work fine.

With the "@USE EAX;" option, HLA emits the shorter code given in the previous examples. It does not emit all the extra instructions needed to preserve EAX's value. This makes your code much more efficient, especially when passing several parameters by reference or when calling procedures with reference parameters several times.

5.17.3.5 Passing Formal Parameters as Actual Parameters

The examples in the previous two sections show how to pass static and automatic variables as parameters to a procedure, either by value or by reference. There is one situation that these examples don't handle properly: the case when you are passing a formal parameter in one procedure as an actual parameter to another procedure. The following simple example demonstrates the different cases that can occur for pass by value and pass by reference parameters:

```
procedure p1( val v:dword;  var r:dword );
begin p1;
        .
```

```
            .
            .

    end p1;

    procedure p2( val v2:dword; var r2:dword );
    begin p2;

        p1( v2, r2 );    // (1) First call to p1.
        p1( r2, v2 );    // (2) Second call to p1.

    end p2;
```

In the statement labeled (1), procedure p2 calls procedure p1 and passes its two formal parameters as parameters to p1. Note that this code passes the first parameter of both procedures by value, and it passes the second parameter of both procedures by reference. Therefore, in statement (1), the program passes the v2 parameter into p2 by value and passes it on to p1 by value; likewise, the program passes r2 in by reference and it passes the value onto p2 by reference.

Because p2's caller passes v2 in by value and p2 passes this parameter to p1 by value, all the code needs to do is make a copy of v2's value and pass this on to p1. The code to do this is nothing more than a single push instruction, e.g.,

```
    push( v2 );
    << code to handle r2 >>
    call p1;
```

As you can see, this code is identical to passing an automatic variable by value. Indeed, it turns out that the code you need to write to pass a value parameter to another procedure is identical to the code you would write to pass a local, automatic variable to that other procedure.

Passing r2 in statement (1) preceding requires a little more thought. You do not take the address of r2 using the lea instruction as you would a value parameter or an automatic variable. When passing r2 on through to p1, the author of this code probably expects the *r* formal parameter to contain the address of the variable whose address p2's caller passed into p2. In plain English, this means that p2 must pass the address of *r2*'s actual parameter on through to p1. Because the r2 parameter is a double word value containing the address of the corresponding actual parameter, this means that the code must pass the double word value of r2 on to p1. The complete code for statement (1) above looks like the following:

```
    push( v2 );    // Pass the value passed in through v2 to p1.
    push( r2 );    // Pass the address passed in through r2 to p1.
    call p1;
```

The important thing to note in this example is that passing a formal reference parameter (r2) as an actual reference parameter (r) does not involve taking the address of the formal parameter (r2). p2's caller has already done this; p2 simply passes this address on through to p1.

In the second call to p1 in the example above (2), the code swaps the actual parameters so that the call to p1 passes r2 by value and v2 by reference. Specifically, p1 expects p2 to pass it the value of the double word object associated with r2; likewise, it expects p2 to pass it the address of the value associated with v2.

To pass the value of the object associated with r2, your code must dereference the pointer associated with r2 and directly pass the value. Here is the code HLA automatically generates to pass r2 as the first parameter to p1 in statement (2):

```
sub( 4, esp );      // Make room on stack for parameter.
push( eax );        // Preserve EAX's value.
mov( r2, eax );     // Get address of object passed in to p2.
mov( [eax], eax );  // Dereference to get the value of this object.
mov( eax, [esp+4]); // Put value of parameter into its location on stack.
pop( eax );         // Restore original EAX value.
```

As usual, HLA generates a little more code than may be necessary because it won't destroy the value in the EAX register (you may use the @use procedure option to tell HLA that it's okay to use EAX's value, thereby reducing the code it generates). You can write more efficient code if a register is available to use in this sequence. If EAX is unused, you could trim this down to the following:

```
mov( r2, eax );     // Get the pointer to the actual object.
pushd( [eax] );     // Push the value of the object onto the stack.
```

Because you can treat value parameters exactly like local (automatic) variables, you use the same code to pass v2 by reference to p1 as you would to pass a local variable in p2 to p1. Specifically, you use the lea instruction to compute the address of the value in the v2. The code HLA automatically emits for statement (2) above preserves all registers and takes the following form (same as passing an automatic variable by reference):

```
push( eax );        // Make room for the parameter.
push( eax );        // Preserve EAX's value.
lea( eax, v2 );     // Compute address of v2's value.
mov( eax, [esp+4]); // Store away address as parameter value.
pop( eax );         // Restore EAX's value.
```

Of course, if you have a register available, you can improve on this code. Here's the complete code that corresponds to statement (2) above:

```
mov( r2, eax );     // Get the pointer to the actual object.
pushd( [eax] );     // Push the value of the object onto the stack.
lea( eax, v2 );     // Push the address of V2 onto the stack.
```

```
    push( eax );
    call p1;
```

5.17.3.6   HLA Hybrid Parameter Passing Facilities

Like control structures, HLA provides a high level language syntax for procedure
calls that is convenient to use and easy to read. However, this high level language
syntax is sometimes inefficient and may not provide the capabilities you need
(for example, you cannot specify an arithmetic expression as a value parameter
as you can in high level languages). HLA lets you overcome these limitations by
writing low level ("pure") assembly language code. Unfortunately, the low level
code is harder to read and maintain than procedure calls that use the high level
syntax. Furthermore, it's quite possible that HLA generates perfectly fine code
for certain parameters while only one or two parameters present a problem.
Fortunately, HLA provides a hybrid syntax for procedure calls that allows you to
use both high level and low level syntax as appropriate for a given actual
parameter. This lets you use the high level syntax where appropriate and then
drop down into pure assembly language to pass those special parameters that
HLA's high level language syntax cannot handle efficiently (if at all).

   Within an actual parameter list (using the high level language syntax), if
HLA encounters "#{" followed by a sequence of statements and a closing "}#",
HLA will substitute the instructions between the braces in place of the code it
would normally generate for that parameter. For example, consider the following
code fragment:

```
procedure HybridCall( i:uns32; j:uns32 );
begin HybridCall;
    .
    .
    .
end HybridCall;
    .
    .
    .

    // Equivalent to HybridCall( 5, i+j );

    HybridCall
    (
        5,
        #{
            mov( i, eax );
            add( j, eax );
            push( eax );
        }#
    );
```

The call to HybridCall immediately above is equivalent to the following "pure"
assembly language code:

```
    pushd( 5 );
    mov( i, eax );
    add( j, eax );
    push( eax );
    call HybridCall;
```

As a second example, consider the example from the previous section:

```
procedure p2( val v2:dword; var r2:dword );
begin p2;

    p1( v2, r2 );    // (1) First call to p1.
    p1( r2, v2 );    // (2) Second call to p1.

end p2;
```

HLA generates exceedingly mediocre code for the second call to p1 in this example. If efficiency is important in the context of this procedure call, and you have a free register available, you might want to rewrite this code as follows:[25]

```
procedure p2( val v2:dword; var r2:dword );
begin p2;

    p1( v2, r2 );    // (1) First call to p1.
    p1              // (2) Second call to p1.
    (               //      This code assumes EAX is free.
        #{
            mov( r2, eax );
            pushd( [eax] );
        }#,

        #{
            lea( eax, v2 );
            push( eax );
        }#
    );

end p2;
```

Note that specifying the "@use reg;" option tells HLA that the register is always available for use wherever you call a procedure. If there is one case where the procedure's invocation must preserve the specified register, then you cannot use the @use option to generate better code. However, you may use the hybrid parameter passing mechanism on a case-by-base basis to improve the performance of those particular calls.

---

[25] Of course, you could also use the "@use eax;" procedure option to achieve the same effect in this example.

5.17.3.7   Mixing Register and Stack Based Parameters

You can mix register parameters and standard (stack based) parameters in the same high level procedure declaration, e.g.,

```
procedure HasBothRegAndStack( var dest:dword in edi; count:un32 );
```

When constructing the activation record, HLA ignores the parameters you pass in registers and only processes those parameters you pass on the stack. Therefore, a call to the HasBothRegAndStack procedure will push only a single parameter onto the stack (count). It will pass the dest parameter in the EDI register. When this procedure returns to its caller, it will only remove four bytes of parameter data from the stack.

Note that when you pass a parameter in a register, you should avoid specifying that same register in the @use procedure option. In the example above, HLA might not generate any code whatsoever at all for the dest parameter (because the value is already in EDI). Had you specified "@use edi;" and HLA decided it was okay to disturb EDI's value, this would destroy the parameter value in EDI; that won't actually happen in this particular example (because HLA never uses a register to pass a double word value parameter like count), but keep this problem in mind.

5.18   Procedure Pointers

The 80x86 call instruction allows three basic forms: direct calls (via a procedure name), indirect calls through a 32-bit general purpose register, and indirect calls through a double word pointer variable. The call instruction supports the following (low level) syntax:

```
call Procname;     // Direct call to procedure "Procname" (or stmt label).
call( Reg32 );     // Indirect call to procedure whose address appears
                   //    in the Reg32 general purpose 32-bit register.
call( dwordVar );  // Indirect call to the procedure whose address appears
                   //    in the dwordVar double word variable.
```

The first form we've been using throughout this chapter, so there is little need to discuss it further here. The second form, the register indirect call, calls the procedure whose address is held in the specified 32-bit register. The address of a procedure is the byte address of the first instruction to execute within that procedure. Remember, on a Von Neumann architecture machine (like the 80x86), the system stores machine instructions in memory along with other data. The CPU fetches the instruction opcode values from memory prior to executing them. When you execute the register indirect call instruction, the 80x86 first pushes the return address onto the stack and then begins fetching the next opcode byte (instruction) from the address specified by the register's value.

The third form of the call instruction above fetches the address of some procedure's first instruction from a double word variable in memory. Although this instruction suggests that the call uses the displacement only addressing mode, you should realize that any legal memory addressing mode is legal here;

e.g., "call(procPtrTable[ebx*4]);" is perfectly legitimate, this statement fetches the double word from the array of double words (procPtrTable) and calls the procedure whose address is the value contained within that double word.

HLA treats procedure names like static objects. Therefore, you can compute the address of a procedure by using the address-of ("&") operator along with the procedure's name or by using the lea instruction. For example, "&Procname" is the address of the very first instruction of the Procname procedure. So all three of the following code sequences wind up calling the Procname procedure:

```
call Procname;
    .
    .
    .
mov( &Procname, eax );
call( eax );
    .
    .
    .
lea( eax, Procname );
call( eax );
```

Because the address of a procedure fits in a 32-bit object, you can store such an address into a double word variable; in fact, you can initialize a double word variable with the address of a procedure using code like the following:

```
procedure p;
begin p;
end p;
    .
    .
    .
static
    ptrToP: dword := &p;
    .
    .
    .
call( ptrToP );  // Calls the "p" procedure if ptrToP has not changed.
```

Because the use of procedure pointers occurs frequently in assembly language programs, HLA provides a special syntax for declaring procedure pointer variables and for calling procedures indirectly through such pointer variables. To declare a procedure pointer in an HLA program, you can use a variable declaration like the following:

```
static
    procPtr: procedure;
```

Note that this syntax uses the keyword procedure as a data type. It follows the variable name and a colon in one of the variable declaration sections (static, readonly, storage, or var). This sets aside exactly four bytes of storage for the procPtr variable. To call the procedure whose address is held by procPtr, you can use either of the following two forms:

```
call( procPtr );    // Low level syntax.
procPtr();          // High level language syntax.
```

Note that the high level syntax for an indirect procedure call is identical to the high level syntax for a direct procedure call. HLA can figure out whether to use a direct call or an indirect call by the type of the identifier. If you've specified a variable name, HLA assumes it needs to use an indirect call; if you specify a procedure name, HLA uses a direct call.

Like all pointer objects, you should not attempt to indirectly call a procedure through a pointer variable unless you've initialized that variable with an appropriate address. There are two ways to initialize a procedure pointer variable: static and readonly objects allow an initializer, or you can compute the address of a routine (as a 32-bit value) and store that 32-bit address directly into the procedure pointer at runtime. The following code fragment demonstrates both ways you can initialize a procedure pointer:

```
static
    ProcPtr: procedure := &p;    // Initialize ProcPtr with the address of p.
    .
    .
    .
    ProcPtr();                    // First invocation calls p.

    mov( &q, ProcPtr );          // Reload ProcPtr with the address of q.
    .
    .
    .
    ProcPtr();                    // This invocation calls the "q" procedure.
```

Procedure pointer variable declarations also allow the declaration of parameters. To declare a procedure pointer with parameters, you must use a declaration like the following:

```
static
    p:procedure( i:int32; c:char );
```

This declaration states that p is a 32-bit pointer that contains the address of a procedure requiring two parameters. If desired, you could also initialize this variable p with the address of some procedure by using a static initializer, e.g.,

```
static
    p:procedure( i:int32; c:char ) := &SomeProcedure;
```

Note that SomeProcedure must be a procedure whose parameter list exactly matches p's parameter list (i.e., two value parameters, the first is an int32 parameter and the second is a char parameter). To indirectly call this procedure, you could use either of the following sequences:

```
    push( << Value for i >> );
    push( << Value for c >> );
    call( p );
-or-
    p( <<Value for i>>, <<Value for c>> );
```

The high level language syntax has the same features and restrictions as the high level syntax for a direct procedure call. The only difference is the actual call instruction HLA emits at the end of the calling sequence.

Although all of the examples in this section use static variable declarations, don't get the idea that you can only declare simple procedure pointers in the static or other variable declaration sections. You can also declare procedure pointer types in the type section, and you can declare procedure pointers as fields of a record or a union. Assuming you create a type name for a procedure pointer in the type section, you can even create arrays of procedure pointers. The following code fragments demonstrate some of the possibilities:

```
type
        pptr:           procedure;
        prec:           record
                        p:pptr;
                        // other fields...
                endrecord;
static
        p1:pptr;
        p2:pptr[2]
        p3:prec;
        .

        .

        .
        p1();
        p2[ebx*4]();
        p3.p();
```

One very important thing to keep in mind when using procedure pointers is that HLA does not (and cannot) enforce strict type checking on the pointer values you assign to a procedure pointer variable. In particular, if the parameter lists do not agree between the declarations of the pointer variable and the procedure whose address you assign to the pointer variable, the program will probably crash if you attempt to call the mismatched procedure indirectly through the pointer using the high level syntax. Like the low level "pure" procedure calls, it is your responsibility to ensure that the proper number and types of parameters are on the stack prior to the call.

5.19   Procedure Parameters

One place where procedure pointers are quite invaluable is in parameter lists. Selecting one of several procedures to call by passing the address of some procedure is not an uncommon operation. Therefore, HLA lets you declare procedure pointers as parameters.

There is nothing special about a procedure parameter declaration. It looks exactly like a procedure variable declaration except it appears within a parameter list rather than within a variable declaration section. The following are some typical procedure prototypes that demonstrate how to declare such parameters:

```
procedure p1( procparm: procedure ); @forward;
procedure p2( procparm: procedure( i:int32 ) ); @forward;
procedure p3( val procparm: procedure ); forward;
```

The last in the preceding list is identical to the first. It does point out, though, that you generally pass procedural parameters by value. This may seem counterintuitive because procedure pointers are addresses and you will need to pass an address as the actual parameter; however, a pass by reference procedure parameter means something else entirely. Consider the following (legal!) declaration:

```
procedure p4( var procPtr:procedure ); @forward;
```

This declaration tells HLA that you are passing a procedure *variable* by reference to p4. The address HLA expects must be the address of a procedure pointer variable, not a procedure.

When passing a procedure pointer by value, you may specify either a procedure variable (whose value HLA passes to the actual procedure) or a procedure pointer constant. A procedure pointer constant consists of the address-of operator ("&") immediately followed by a procedure name. Passing procedure constants is probably the most convenient way to pass procedure parameters. For example, the following calls to the Plot routine might plot out the function passed as a parameter from -2 to +2.

```
Plot( &sineFunc );
Plot( &cosFunc  );
Plot( &tanFunc  );
```

Note that you cannot pass a procedure as a parameter by simply specifying the procedure's name — i.e., "Plot(sineFunc);" will not work. Simply specifying the procedure name doesn't work because HLA will attempt to directly call the procedure whose name you specify (remember, a procedure name inside a parameter list invokes instruction composition). If you did not specify a parameter list, or at least an empty pair of parentheses, after the parameter/

procedure's name, HLA generates a syntax error message. Moral of the story: Don't forget to preface procedure parameter constant names with the address-of operator ('&').

5.20 Untyped Reference Parameters

Sometimes you will want to write a procedure to which you pass a generic memory object by reference without regard to the type of that memory object. A classic example is a procedure that zeros out some data structure. Such a procedure might have the following prototype:

```
procedure ZeroMem( var mem:byte; count:uns32 );
```

This procedure would zero out count bytes starting at the address the first parameter specifies. The problem with this procedure prototype is that HLA will complain if you attempt to pass anything other than a byte object as the first parameter. Of course, you can overcome this problem using type coercion like the following, but if you call this procedure several times with a lot of different data types, then the following coercion operator is rather tedious to use:

```
ZeroMem( (type byte MyDataObject), @size( MyDataObject ));
```

Of course, you can always use hybrid parameter passing or manually push the parameters yourself, but these solutions are even more work than using the type coercion operation. Fortunately, HLA provides a far more convenient solution: untyped reference parameters.

Untyped reference parameters are exactly that — pass by reference parameters on which HLA doesn't bother to compare the type of the actual parameter against the type of the formal parameter. With an untyped reference parameter, the call to ZeroMem above would take the following form:

```
ZeroMem( MyDataObject, @size( MyDataObject ));
```

MyDataObject could be any type and multiple calls to ZeroMem could pass different typed objects without any objections from HLA.

To declare an untyped reference parameter, you specify the parameter using the normal syntax except that you use the reserved word var in place of the parameter's type. This var keyword tells HLA that any variable object is legal for that parameter. Note that you must pass untyped reference parameters by reference, so the var keyword must precede the parameter's declaration as well. Here's the correct declaration for the ZeroMem procedure using an untyped reference parameter:

```
procedure ZeroMem( var mem:var; count:uns32 );
```

With this declaration, HLA will compute the address of whatever memory object you pass as an actual parameter to ZeroMem and pass this on the stack.

5.21   Managing Large Programs

Most assembly language source files are not stand-alone programs. In general, you will call various Standard Library or other routines that are not defined in your main program. For example, you've probably noticed by now that the 80x86 doesn't provide any machine instructions like "read," "write," or "put" for doing I/O operations. Of course, you can write your own procedures to accomplish this. Unfortunately, writing such routines is a complex task, and beginning assembly language programmers are not ready for such tasks. That's where the HLA Standard Library comes in. This is a package of procedures you can call to perform simple I/O operations like stdout.put.

The HLA Standard Library contains tens of thousands of lines of source code. Imagine how difficult programming would be if you had to merge these thousands of lines of code into your simple programs! Imagine how slow compiling your programs would be if you had to compile those tens of thousands of lines with each program you write. Fortunately, you don't have to do this.

For small programs, working with a single source file is fine. For large programs this gets very cumbersome (consider the example above of having to include the entire HLA Standard Library into each of your programs). Furthermore, once you've debugged and tested a large section of your code, continuing to assemble that same code when you make a small change to some other part of your program is a waste of time. The HLA Standard Library, for example, takes several minutes to assemble, even on a fast machine. Imagine having to wait five or ten minutes on a fast Pentium machine to assemble a program to which you've made a one line change!

As with high level languages, the solution is *separate compilation*. First, you break up your large source files into manageable chunks. Then you compile the separate files into object code modules. Finally, you link the object modules together to form a complete program. If you need to make a small change to one of the modules, you only need to reassemble that one module; you do not need to reassemble the entire program.

The HLA Standard Library works in precisely this way. The Standard Library is already compiled and ready to use. You simply call routines in the Standard Library and link your code with the Standard Library using a *linker* program. This saves a tremendous amount of time when developing a program that uses the Standard Library code. Of course, you can easily create your own object modules and link them together with your code. You could even add new routines to the Standard Library so they will be available for use in future programs you write.

"Programming in the large" is a phrase software engineers have coined to describe the processes, methodologies, and tools for handling the development of large software projects. While everyone has their own idea of what "large" is, separate compilation and some conventions for using separate compilation are among the more popular techniques that support "programming in the large." The following sections describe the tools HLA provides for separate compilation and how to effectively employ these tools in your programs.

5.22   The #INCLUDE Directive

The #include directive, when encountered in a source file, switches program input from the current file to the file specified in the parameter list of the include directive. This allows you to construct text files containing common constants, types, source code, and other HLA items, and include such files into the assembly of several separate programs. The syntax for the #include directive is

```
#include( "filename" )
```

Filename must be a valid filename. HLA merges the specified file into the compilation at the point of the #include directive. Note that you can nest #include statements inside files you include. That is, a file being included into another file during assembly may itself include a third file. In fact, the *stdlib.hhf* header file you see in most example programs is really nothing more than a bunch of includes (see Listing 5-18).

Listing 5-18: The stdlib.hhf Header File, as of 01/01/2000.

```
#include( "hla.hhf" )
#include( "x86.hhf" )
#include( "misctypes.hhf" )
#include( "hll.hhf" )

#include( "excepts.hhf" )
#include( "memory.hhf" )

#include( "args.hhf" )
#include( "conv.hhf" )
#include( "strings.hhf" )
#include( "cset.hhf" )
#include( "patterns.hhf" )
#include( "tables.hhf" )
#include( "arrays.hhf" )
#include( "chars.hhf" )

#include( "math.hhf" )
#include( "rand.hhf" )

#include( "stdio.hhf" )
#include( "stdin.hhf" )
#include( "stdout.hhf" )
```

By including *stdlib.hhf* in your source code, you automatically include all the HLA library modules. It's often more efficient (in terms of compile time and size of code generated) to provide only those #include statements for the modules you actually need in your program. However, including *stdlib.hhf* is extremely convenient and takes up less space in this text, which is why most programs appearing in this text use *stdlib.hhf.*

Note that the #include directive does not need to end with a semicolon. If you put a semicolon after the #include, that semicolon becomes part of the source file and is the first character following the included source during compilation. HLA generally allows spare semicolons in various parts of the program, so you will often see a #include statement ending with a semicolon. In general, though, you should not get in the habit of putting semicolons after #include statements because there is the slight possibility this could create a syntax error in certain circumstances.

Using the #include directive by itself does not provide separate compilation. You *could* use the #include directive to break up a large source file into separate modules and join these modules together when you compile your file. The following example would include the *printf.hla* and *putc.hla* files during the compilation of your program:

```
#include( "printf.hla" )
#include( "putc.hla" )
```

Now your program *will* benefit from the modularity gained by this approach. Alas, you will not save any development time. The #include directive inserts the source file at the point of the #include during compilation, exactly as though you had typed that code yourself. HLA still has to compile the code and that takes time. Were you to include all the files for the Standard Library routines in this manner, your compilations would take *forever.*

In general, you should *not* use the #include directive to include source code as shown above.[26] Instead, you should use the #include directive to insert a common set of constants, types, external procedure declarations, and other such items into a program. Typically an assembly language include file does not contain any machine code (outside of a macro; see the chapter on macros for details). The purpose of using #include files in this manner will become clearer after you see how the external declarations work.

5.23   Ignoring Duplicate #INCLUDE Operations

As you begin to develop sophisticated modules and libraries, you eventually discover a big problem: Some header files will need to include other header files (e.g., the *stdlib.hhf* header file includes all the other HLA Standard Library header files). Well, this isn't actually a big problem, but a problem will occur when one header file includes another, and that second header file includes another, and that third header file includes another, and . . . that last header file includes the first header file. Now *this* is a big problem.

There are two problems with a header file indirectly including itself. First, this creates an infinite loop in the compiler. The compiler will happily go on about its business including all these files over and over again until it runs out of memory or some other error occurs. Clearly this is not a good thing. The second problem that occurs (usually before the problem above) is that the second time HLA includes a header file, it starts complaining bitterly about duplicate symbol

---

[26] There is nothing wrong with this, other than the fact that it does not take advantage of separate compilation.

definitions. After all, the first time it reads the header file it processes all the declarations in that file, the second time around it views all those symbols as duplicate symbols.

HLA provides a special include directive that eliminates this problem: #includeonce. You use this directive exactly like you use the #include directive, e.g.,

---

```
#includeonce( "myHeaderFile.hhf" )
```

If *myHeaderFile.hhf* directly or indirectly includes itself (with a #includeonce directive), then HLA will ignore the new request to include the file. Note, however, that if you use the #include directive, rather than #includeonce, HLA will include the file a second time. This was done in case you really do need to include a header file twice, for some.

The bottom line is this: You should always use the #includeonce directive to include header files you've created. In fact, you should get in the habit of always using #includeonce, even for header files created by others (the HLA Standard Library already has provisions to prevent recursive includes, so you don't have to worry about using #includeonce with the Standard Library header files).

There is another technique you can use to prevent recursive includes — using conditional compilation. A later chapter will discuss this option.

5.24   UNITs and the EXTERNAL Directive

Technically, the #include directive provides you with all the facilities you need to create modular programs. You can create several modules, each containing some specific routine, and include those modules, as necessary, in your assembly language programs using #include. However, HLA provides a better way: external and public symbols.

One major problem with the #include mechanism is that once you've debugged a routine, including it into a compilation still wastes time because HLA must recompile bug-free code every time you assemble the main program. A much better solution would be to preassemble the debugged modules and link the object code modules together. This is what the @external directive allows you to do.

To use the @external facilities, you must create at least two source files. One file contains a set of variables and procedures used by the second. The second file uses those variables and procedures without knowing how they're implemented. The only problem is that if you create two separate HLA programs, the linker will get confused when you try to combine them. This is because both HLA programs have their own main program. Which main program does the OS run when it loads the program into memory? To resolve this problem, HLA uses a different type of compilation module, the unit, to compile programs without a main program. The syntax for an HLA unit is actually simpler than that for an HLA program; it takes the following form:

```
unit unitname;

    << declarations >>

end unitname;
```

With one exception (the var section), anything that can go in the declaration section of an HLA program can go into the declaration section of an HLA unit. Notice that a unit does not have a begin clause and there are no program statements in the unit;[27] a unit only contains declarations.

In addition to the fact that a unit does not contain a main program section, there is one other difference between units and programs. Units cannot have a var section. This is because the var section declares variables that are local to the main program's source code. Because there is no "main program" associated with a unit, var sections are illegal.[28]

To demonstrate, consider the two modules in Listings 5.19 and 5.20.

Listing 5-19: Example of a Simple HLA Unit.

```
unit Number1;

static
    Var1:   uns32;
    Var2:   uns32;

    procedure Add1and2;
    begin Add1and2;

        push( eax );
        mov( Var2, eax );
        add( eax, Var1 );

    end Add1and2;

end Number1;
```

Listing 5-20: Main Program That References External Objects.

```
program main;
#include( "stdlib.hhf" );

begin main;

    mov( 2, Var2 );
    mov( 3, Var1 );
```

[27] Of course, units may contain procedures and those procedures may have statements, but the unit itself does not have any executable instructions associated with it.

[28] Of course, procedures in the unit may have their own var sections, but the procedure's declaration section is separate from the unit's declaration section.

```
        Add1and2();
        stdout.put( "Var1=", Var1, nl );


end main;
```

The main program references Var1, Var2, and Add1and2, yet these symbols are external to this program (they appear in unit Number1). If you attempt to compile the main program as it stands, HLA will complain that these three symbols are undefined.

Therefore, you must declare them external with the @external option. An external procedure declaration looks just like a forward declaration except you use the reserved word @external rather than @forward. To declare external static variables, simply follow those variables' declarations with the reserved word @external. The program in Listing 5-21 is a modification to the program in Listing 5-20 that includes the external declarations.

Listing 5-21: Modified Main Program with Extrenal Declarations.

```
program main;
#include( "stdlib.hhf" );

    procedure Add1and2; external;

static
    Var1: uns32; @external;
    Var2: uns32; @external;

begin main;

    mov( 2, Var2 );
    mov( 3, Var1 );
    Add1and2();
    stdout.put( "Var1=", Var1, nl );

end main;
```

If you attempt to compile this second version of main, using the typical HLA compilation command "HLA main2.hla" you will be somewhat disappointed. This program will actually compile without error. However, when HLA attempts to link this code it will report that the symbols Var1, Var2, and Add1and2 are undefined. This happens because you haven't compiled and linked in the associated unit with this main program. Before you try that, and discover that it still doesn't work, you should know that all symbols in a unit, by default, are *private* to that unit. This means that those symbols are inaccessible in code outside that unit unless you explicitly declare those symbols as *public* symbols. To declare symbols as public, you simply put external declarations for those symbols in the unit before the actual symbol declarations. If an external declaration appears in the same source file as the actual declaration of a symbol, HLA assumes that the name is needed externally and makes that symbol a public (rather than private) symbol. The unit in Listing 5-22 is a correction to the Number1 unit that properly declares the external objects.

Listing 5-22: Correct Number1 Unit with External Declarations.

```
unit Number1;

static
    Var1:   uns32; @external;
    Var2:   uns32; @external;

    procedure Add1and2; @external;

static
    Var1:   uns32;
    Var2:   uns32;


    procedure Add1and2;
    begin Add1and2;

        push( eax );
        mov( Var2, eax );
        add( eax, Var1 );

    end Add1and2;

end Number1;
```

It may seem redundant declaring these symbols twice as occurs in Listings 5.21 and 5.22, but you'll soon seen that you don't normally write the code this way.

If you attempt to compile the main program or the Number1 unit using the typical HLA statement, i.e.,

```
HLA main2.hla
HLA unit2.hla
```

you'll quickly discover that the linker still returns errors. It returns an error on the compilation of *main2.hla* because you still haven't told HLA to link in the object code associated with *unit2.hla*. Likewise, the linker complains if you attempt to compile *unit2.hla* by itself because it can't find a main program. The simple solution is to compile both of these modules together with the following single command:

```
HLA main2.hla unit2.hla
```

This command will properly compile both modules and link together their object code.

Unfortunately, the command above defeats one of the major benefits of separate compilation. When you issue this command it will compile both main2 and unit2 prior to linking them together. Remember, a major reason for separate compilation is to reduce compilation time on large projects. While the above command is convenient, it doesn't achieve this goal.

To separately compile the two modules you must run HLA separately on them. Of course, we saw earlier that attempting to compile these modules separately produced linker errors. To get around this problem, you need to compile the modules without linking them. The "-c" (compile-only) HLA command line option achieves this. To compile the two source files without running the linker, you would use the following commands:

```
HLA -c main2.hla
HLA -c unit2.hla
```

This produces two object code files, *main2.obj* and *unit2.obj*, that you can link together to produce a single executable. You could run the linker program directly, but an easier way is to use the HLA compiler to link the object modules together for you:

```
HLA main2.obj unit2.obj
```

Under Windows, this command produces an executable file named *main2.exe*;[29] under Linux, this command produces a file named *main2*. You could also type the following command to compile the main program and link it with a previously compiled *unit2* object module:

```
HLA main2.hla unit2.obj
```

In general, HLA looks at the suffixes of the filenames following the HLA commands. If the filename doesn't have a suffix, HLA assumes it to be ".HLA." If the filename has a suffix, then HLA will do the following with the file:

- If the suffix is ".HLA," HLA will compile the file with the HLA compiler.
- If the suffix is ".ASM," HLA will assemble the file with MASM (Windows) or Gas (Linux).
- If the suffix is ".OBJ" or ".LIB" (Windows), or ".o" or ".a" (Linux), then HLA will link that module with the rest of the compilation.

---

[29] If you want to explicitly specify the name of the output file, HLA provides a command line option to achieve this. You can get a menu of all legal command line options by entering the command "HLA -?".

5.24.1 Behavior of the EXTERNAL Directive

Whenever you declare a symbol using the @external directive, keep in mind several limitations of @external objects:

- Only one @external declaration of an object may appear in a given source file. That is, you cannot define the same symbol twice as an @external object.
- Only procedure, static, readonly, and storage variable objects can be external. var, type, const and parameter objects cannot be external.
- External objects must appear at the global declaration level. You cannot declare @external objects within a procedure or other nested structure.[30]
- @external objects publish their name globally. Therefore, you must carefully choose the names of your @external objects so they do not conflict with other symbols.

This last point is especially important to keep in mind. As this text is being written, the HLA compiler translates your HLA source code into assembly code. HLA assembles the output by using MASM (the Microsoft Macro Assembler), Gas (Gnu's as), or some other assembler. Finally, HLA links your modules using a linker. At each step in this process, your choice of external names could create problems for you.

Consider the following HLA external/public declaration:

```
static
        extObj:        uns32; @external;
        extObj:        uns32;
        localObject:   uns32;
```

When you compile a program containing these declarations, HLA automatically generates a "munged" name for the localObject variable that probably isn't ever going to have any conflicts with system-global external symbols.[31] Whenever you declare an external symbol, however, HLA uses the object's name as the default external name. This can create some problems if you inadvertently use some global name as your variable name. Worse still, the assembler will not be able to properly process HLA's output if you happen to choose an identifier that is legal in HLA but is one of the assembler's reserved words. For example, if you attempt to compile the following code fragment as part of an HLA program (producing MASM output), it will compile properly, but MASM will not be able to assemble the code:

```
static
    c: char; @external;
    c: char;
```

---

[30] There are a few exceptions, but you cannot declare external procedures or variables except at the global level.

[31] Typically, HLA creates a name like *?001A_localObject* out of *localObject*. This is a legal MASM identifier, but it is not likely it will conflict with any other global symbols when HLA compiles the program with MASM.

The reason MASM will have trouble with this is because HLA will write the identifier "c" to the assembly language output file, and it turns out that "c" is a MASM reserved word (MASM uses it to denote C-language linkage).

To get around the problem of conflicting external names, HLA supports an additional syntax for the @external option that lets you explicitly specify the external name. The following example demonstrates this extended syntax:

```
static
    c: char; @external( "var_c" );
    c: char;
```

If you follow the @external keyword with a string constant enclosed by parentheses, HLA will continue to use the declared name (c in this example) as the identifier within your HLA source code. Externally (i.e., in the assembly code) HLA will substitute the name var_c whenever you reference c. This feature helps you avoid problems with the misuse of assembler reserved words, or other global symbols, in your HLA programs.

You should also note that this feature of the @external option lets you create aliases. For example, you may want to refer to an object by the name StudentCount in one module while refer to the object as PersonCount in another module (you might do this because you have a general library module that deals with counting people and you want to use the object in a program that deals only with students). Using a declaration like the following lets you do this:

```
static
    StudentCount: uns32; @external( "PersonCount" );
```

Of course, you've already seen some of the problems you might encounter when you start creating aliases. So you should use this capability sparingly in your programs. Perhaps a more reasonable use of this feature is to simplify certain OS APIs. For example, the Win32 API uses some really long names for certain procedure calls. You can use the @external directive to provide a more meaningful name than the standard one the operating system specifies.

5.24.2   Header Files in HLA

HLA's technique of using the same @external declaration to define public as well as external symbols may seem somewhat counter-intuitive. Why not use a @public reserved word for public symbols and the @external keyword for external definitions? Well, as counterintuitive as HLA's external declarations may seem, they are founded on decades of solid experience with the C/C++ programming language that uses a similar approach to public and external symbols.[32] Combined with a *header file,* HLA's external declarations make large program maintenance a breeze.

---

[32] Actually, C/C++ is a little different. All global symbols in a module are assumed to be public unless explicitly declared private. HLA's approach (forcing the declaration of public items via external) is a little safer.

An important benefit of the @external directive (versus separate @public and @external directives) is that it lets you minimize duplication of effort in your source files. Suppose, for example, you want to create a module with a bunch of support routines and variables for use in several different programs (e.g., the HLA Standard Library). In addition to sharing some routines and some variables, suppose you want to share constants, types, and other items as well.

The #include file mechanism provides a perfect way to handle this. You simply create a #include file containing the constants, macros, and @external definitions and include this file in the module that implements your routines and in the modules that use those routines (see Figure 5-10).

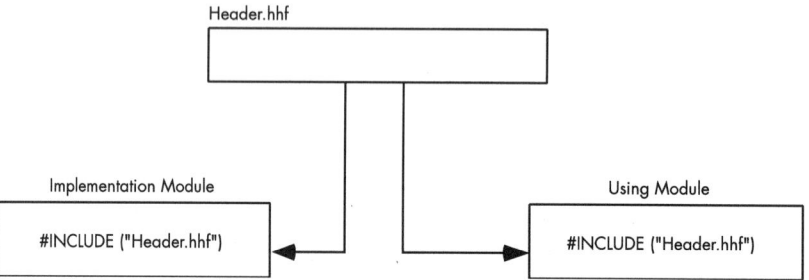

Figure 5-10: Using Header Files in HLA Programs.

A typical header file contains only const, val, type, static, readonly, storage, and procedure prototypes (plus a few others we haven't looked at yet, like macros). Objects in the static, readonly, and storage sections, as well as all procedure declarations, are always @external objects. In particular, you should not put any var objects in a header file, nor should you put any non-external variables or procedure bodies in a header file. If you do, HLA will make duplicate copies of these objects in the different source files that include the header file. Not only will this make your programs larger, but it will cause them to fail under certain circumstances. For example, you generally put a variable in a header file so you can share the value of that variable among several different modules. However, if you fail to declare that symbol as external in the header file and just put a standard variable declaration there, each module that includes the source file will get its own separate variable: The modules will not share a common variable.

If you create a standard header file, containing const, val, and type declarations, and external objects, you should always be sure to include that file in the declaration section of all modules that need the definitions in the header file. Generally, HLA programs include all their header files in the first few statements after the program or unit header.

This text adopts the HLA Standard Library convention of using an ".hhf" suffix for HLA header files ("HHF" stands for HLA header file).

5.25 Namespace Pollution

One problem with creating libraries with a lot of different modules is namespace pollution. A typical library module will have a #include file associated with it that provides external definitions for all the routines, constants, variables, and other symbols provided in the library. Whenever you want to use some routines or other objects from the library, you would typically #include the library's header file in your project. As your libraries get larger and you add declarations in the header file, it becomes likely that the names you've chosen for your library's identifiers will conflict with names you want to use in your current project. This is known as *namespace pollution*: Library header files pollute the namespace with names you typically don't need in order to gain easy access to the few routines in the library you actually use. Most of the time those names don't harm anything — unless you want to use those names for your own purposes.

HLA requires that you declare all external symbols at the global (program/unit) level. You cannot, therefore, include a header file with external declarations within a procedure. As such, there will be no naming conflicts between external library symbols and symbols you declare locally within a procedure; the conflicts will only occur between the external symbols and your global symbols. While this is a good argument for avoiding global symbols as much as possible in your program, the fact remains that most symbols in an assembly language program will have global scope. So another solution is necessary.

HLA's solution, is to put most of the library names in a namespace declaration section. A namespace declaration encapsulates all declarations and exposes only a single name (the namespace identifier) at the global level. You access the names within the namespace by using the familiar dot notation (see the discussion of namespaces in the previous chapter). This reduces the effect of namespace pollution from many dozens or hundreds of names down to a single name.

Of course, one disadvantage of using a namespace declaration is that you have to type a longer name in order to reference a particular identifier in that name space (i.e., you have to type the namespace identifier, a period, and then the specific identifier you wish to use). For a few identifiers you use frequently, you might elect to leave those identifiers outside of any namespace declaration. For example, the HLA Standard Library does not define the symbols malloc, free, or nl (among others) within a namespace. However, you want to minimize such declarations in your libraries to avoid conflicts with names in your own programs. Often, you can choose a namespace identifier to complement your routine names. For example, the HLA Standard Library's string copy routine was named after the equivalent C Standard Library function, *strcpy*. HLA's version is str.cpy. The actual function name is cpy; it happens to be a member of the str namespace, hence the full name str.cpy, which is very similar to the comparable C function. The HLA Standard Library contains several examples of this convention. The arg.c and arg.v functions are another pair of such identifiers (corresponding to the C identifiers *argc* and *argv*).

Using a namespace in a header file is no different than using a namespace in a program or unit, though you do not normally put actual procedure bodies in a namespace. Here's an example of a typical header file containing a namespace declaration:

```
// myHeader.hhf -
//
// Routines supported in the myLibrary.lib file.
```

```
namespace myLib;

    procedure func1; @external;
    procedure func2; @external;
    procedure func3; @external;

end myLib;
```

Typically, you would compile each of the functions (func1..func3) as separate units (so each has its own object file and linking in one function doesn't link them all). Here's what a sample unit declaration for one of these functions:

```
unit func1Unit;
#includeonce( "myHeader.hhf" )

procedure myLib.func1;
begin func1;

    << code for func1 >>

end func1;

end func1Unit;
```

You should notice two important things about this unit. First, you do not put the actual func1 procedure code within a namespace declaration block. By using the identifier myLib.func1 as the procedure's name, HLA automatically realizes that this procedure declaration belongs in a namespace. The second thing to note is that you do not preface func1 with "myLib." after the begin and end clauses in the procedure. HLA automatically associates the begin and end identifiers with the procedure declaration, so it knows that these identifiers are part of the myLib namespace and it doesn't make you type the whole name again.

Important note: When you declare external names within a namespace, as was done in func1Unit previously, HLA uses only the function name (func1 in this example) as the external name. This creates a namespace pollution problem in the external namespace. For example, if you have two different namespaces, myLib and yourLib and they both define a func1 procedure, the linker will complain about a duplicate definition for func1 if you attempt to use functions from both these library modules. There is an easy work-around to this problem: Use the extended form of the @external directive to explicitly supply an external name for all external identifiers appearing in a namespace declaration. For example, you could solve this problem with the following simple modification to the *myHeader.hhf* file above:

```
// myHeader.hhf -
//
// Routines supported in the myLibrary.lib file.

namespace myLib;

    procedure func1; @external( "myLib_func1" );
    procedure func2; @external( "myLib_func2" );
    procedure func3; @external( "myLib_func3" );

end myLib;
```

This example demonstrates an excellent convention you should adopt: When exporting names from a namespace, always supply an explicit external name and construct that name by concatenating the namespace identifier with an underscore and the object's internal name.

The use of namespace declarations does not completely eliminate the problems of namespace pollution (after all, the namespace identifier is still a global object, as anyone who has included *stdlib.hhf* and attempted to define a "cs" variable can attest), but namespace declarations come pretty close to eliminating this problem. Therefore, you should use namespace everywhere practical when creating your own libraries.

5.26 For More Information

The electronic edition of this book on the accompanying CD-ROM contains a whole "volume" on advanced and intermediate procedures. The information on this chapter was taken from the introductory and intermediate chapters in the electronic edition. While the information appearing in this chapter covers 99 percent of the material assembly programmers typically use, there is additional information on procedures and parameters that you may find interesting. In particular, the electronic edition covers additional parameter passing mechanisms (pass by value/result, pass by result, pass by name, and pass by lazy evaluation) and goes into greater detail about the places you can pass parameters. The electronic version of this text also covers iterators, thunks, and other advanced procedure types. You should also check out the HLA documentation for more details on HLA's procedure facilities. Finally, a good compiler construction textbook will cover additional details about run-time support for procedures.

This chapter discussed only 32-bit near procedures (appropriate for operating systems like Windows and Linux). For information about procedures in 16-bit code (including near and far procedures), check out the 16-bit edition of this book, also found on the accompanying CD-ROM.

HLA supports the ability to nest procedures; that is, you can declare a procedure in the declaration section of some other procedure and use *displays* and *static links* to access automatic variables in the enclosing procedures. HLA also supports advanced parameter pointer facilities. This text does not discuss these features because they're somewhat advanced, and very few assembly language programmers take advantage of these facilities in their programs. However, these features are very handy in certain situations. Once you're comfortable with procedures and assembly language programming in general, you should read about HLA's facilities for nested procedures in the HLA documentation and in the chapters on intermediate and advanced procedures in the electronic version of this book appearing on the CD-ROM.

6

ARITHMETIC

6.1 Chapter Overview

This chapter discusses arithmetic computation in assembly language. By the conclusion of this chapter you should be able to translate arithmetic expressions and assignment statements from high level languages like Pascal and C/C++ into 80x86 assembly language.

6.2 80x86 Integer Arithmetic Instructions

Before describing how to encode arithmetic expressions in assembly language, it would be a good idea to first discuss the remaining arithmetic instructions in the 80x86 instruction set. Previous chapters have covered most of the arithmetic and logical instructions, so this section will cover the few remaining instructions you'll need.

6.2.1 The MUL and IMUL Instructions

The multiplication instructions provide you with another taste of irregularity in the 80x86's instruction set. Instructions like add, sub, and many others in the 80x86 instruction set support two operands, just like the mov instruction. Unfortunately, there weren't enough bits in the 80x86's opcode byte to support all instructions, so the 80x86 treats the mul (unsigned multiply) and imul (signed integer multiply) instructions as single operand instructions, just like the inc, dec, and neg instructions.

Of course, multiplication *is* a two operand function. To work around this fact, the 80x86 always assumes the accumulator (AL, AX, or EAX) is the destination operand. This irregularity makes using multiplication on the 80x86 a little more difficult than other instructions because one operand has to be in the accumulator. Intel adopted this unorthogonal approach because they felt that programmers would use multiplication far less often than instructions like add and sub.

Another problem with the mul and imul instructions is that you cannot multiply the accumulator by a constant using these instructions. Intel quickly discovered the need to support multiplication by a constant and added the intmul instruction to overcome this problem. Nevertheless, you must be aware that the basic mul and imul instructions do not support the full range of operands that intmul does.

There are two forms of the multiply instruction: unsigned multiplication (mul) and signed multiplication (imul). Unlike addition and subtraction, you need separate instructions for signed and unsigned operations.

The multiply instructions take the following forms:

Unsigned Multiplication:

mul(reg_8);	// returns "ax"
mul(reg_{16});	// returns "dx:ax"
mul(reg_{32});	// returns "edx:eax"
mul(mem_8);	// returns "ax"
mul(mem_{16});	// returns "dx:ax"
mul(mem_{32});	// returns "edx:eax"

Signed (Integer) Multiplication:

imul(reg_8);	// returns "ax"
imul(reg_{16});	// returns "dx:ax"
imul(reg_{32});	// returns "edx:eax"
imul(mem_8);	// returns "ax"
imul(mem_{16});	// returns "dx:ax"
imul(mem_{32});	// returns "edx:eax"

The "returns" values above are the strings these instructions return for use with instruction composition in HLA. (i)mul, available on all 80x86 processors, multiplies 8-, 16-, or 32-bit operands.

When multiplying two n-bit values, the result may require as many as 2*n bits. Therefore, if the operand is an 8-bit quantity, the result could require 16 bits. Likewise, a 16-bit operand produces a 32-bit result and a 32-bit operand requires 64 bits to hold the result.

The (i)mul instruction, with an 8-bit operand, multiplies AL by the operand and leaves the 16-bit product in AX. So

---

or
```
        mul( operand8 );
        imul( operand8 );
```

---

computes

$$AX := AL * operand_8$$

"*" represents an unsigned multiplication for mul and a signed multiplication for imul.

If you specify a 16-bit operand, then mul and imul compute

$$DX:AX := AX * operand_{16}$$

"*" has the same meanings as the preceding computation and DX:AX means that DX contains the H.O. word of the 32-bit result and AX contains the L.O. word of the 32-bit result. If you're wondering why Intel didn't put the 32-bit result in EAX, just note that Intel introduced the mul and imul instructions in the earliest 80x86 processors, before the advent of 32-bit registers in the 80386 CPU.

If you specify a 32-bit operand, then mul and imul compute the following:

$$EDX:EAX := EAX * operand_{32}$$

"*" has the same meanings as again, and EDX:EAX means that EDX contains the H.O. double word of the 64-bit result and EAX contains the L.O. double word of the 64-bit result.

If an 8x8, 16x16, or 32x32-bit product requires more than 8, 16, or 32 bits (respectively), the mul and imul instructions set the carry and overflow flags. mul and imul scramble the sign and zero flags.

NOTE   *Especially note that the sign and zero flags do not contain meaningful values after the execution of these two instructions.*

To help reduce some of the syntax irregularities with the use of the mul and imul instructions, HLA provides an extended syntax that allows the following two-operand forms:

Unsigned Multiplication:

```
        mul( reg8, al );
        mul( reg16, ax );
        mul( reg32, eax );

        mul( mem8, al );
        mul( mem16, ax );
        mul( mem32, eax );
```

```
        mul( constant_8, al );
        mul( constant_16, ax );
        mul( constant_32, eax );
```

Signed (Integer) Multiplication:

```
        imul( reg_8, al );
        imul( reg_16, ax );
        imul( reg_32, eax );

        imul( mem_8, al );
        imul( mem_16, ax );
        imul( mem_32, eax );

        imul( constant_8, al );
        imul( constant_16, ax );
        imul( constant_32, eax );
```

The two operand forms let you specify the (L.O.) destination register as the second operand. By specifying the destination register you can make your programs easier to read. Note that just because HLA allows two operands here, you can't specify an arbitrary register. The destination operand must always be AL, AX, or EAX, depending on the source operand.

HLA provides a form that lets you specify a constant. The 80x86 doesn't actually support a mul or imul instruction that has a constant operand. HLA will take the constant you specify and create a "variable" in a read-only segment in memory and initialize that variable with this value. Then HLA converts the instruction to the "(i)mul(memory);" instruction. Note that when you specify a constant as the source operand, the instruction requires two operands (because HLA uses the second operand to determine whether the multiplication is 8, 16, or 32 bits).

You'll use the mul and imul instructions quite a bit when you learn about extended precision arithmetic in the chapter on Advanced Arithmetic. Unless you're doing multiprecision work, however, you'll probably just want to use the intmul instruction in place of the mul or imul because it is more general. However, intmul is not a complete replacement for these two instructions. Besides the number of operands, there are several differences between the intmul and the mul/imul instructions. Specifically for the intmul instruction:

- There isn't an 8x8-bit intmul instruction available.

- The intmul instruction does not produce a 2*n bit result. That is, a 16x16 multiply produces a 16-bit result. Likewise, a 32x32-bit multiply produces a 32-bit result. These instructions set the carry and overflow flags if the result does not fit into the destination register.

6.2.2　The DIV and IDIV Instructions

The 80x86 divide instructions perform a 64/32 division, a 32/16 division, or a 16/8 division. These instructions take the following form:

```
div( reg8 );                    // returns "al"
div( reg16 );                   // returns "ax"
div( reg32 );                   // returns "eax"

div( reg8, AX );                // returns "al"
div( reg16, DX:AX );
div( reg32, EDX:EAX );

div( mem8 );                    // returns "al"
div( mem16 );                   // returns "ax"
div( mem32 );                   // returns "eax"

div( mem8, AX );                // returns "al"
div( mem16, DX:AX );            // returns "ax"
div( mem32, EDX:EAX );          // returns "eax"

div( constant8, AX );           // returns "al"
div( constant16, DX:AX );       // returns "ax"
div( constant32, EDX:EAX );     // returns "eax"

idiv( reg8 );                   // returns "al"
idiv( reg16 );                  // returns "ax"
idiv( reg32 );                  // returns "eax"

idiv( reg8, AX );               // returns "al"
idiv( reg16, DX:AX );           // returns "ax"
idiv( reg32, EDX:EAX );         // returns "eax"

idiv( mem8 );                   // returns "al"
idiv( mem16 );                  // returns "ax"
idiv( mem32 );                  // returns "eax"

idiv( mem8, AX );               // returns "al"
idiv( mem16, DX:AX );           // returns "ax"
idiv( mem32, EDX:EAX );         // returns "eax"

idiv( constant8, AX );          // returns "al"
idiv( constant16, DX:AX );      // returns "ax"
idiv( constant32, EDX:EAX );    // returns "eax"
```

The div instruction computes an unsigned division. If the operand is an 8-bit operand, div divides the AX register by the operand leaving the quotient in AL and the remainder (modulo) in AH. If the operand is a 16-bit quantity, then the div instruction divides the 32-bit quantity in DX:AX by the operand leaving the quotient in AX and the remainder in DX. With 32-bit operands div divides the 64-bit value in EDX:EAX by the operand leaving the quotient in EAX and the remainder in EDX. Like mul and imul, HLA provides special syntax to allow the use of constant operands even though these instructions don't really support them.

You cannot, on the 80x86, simply divide one 8-bit value by another. If the denominator is an 8-bit value, the numerator must be a 16-bit value. If you need to divide one unsigned 8-bit value by another, you must zero extend the numerator to 16 bits. You can accomplish this by loading the numerator into the AL register and then moving zero into the AH register. Then you can divide AX by the denominator operand to produce the correct result. *Failing to zero extend AL before executing* div *may cause the 80x86 to produce incorrect results!* When you need to divide two 16-bit unsigned values, you must zero extend the AX register (which contains the numerator) into the DX register. To do this, just load zero into the DX register. If you need to divide one 32-bit value by another, you must zero extend the EAX register into EDX (by loading a zero into EDX) before the division.

When dealing with signed integer values, you will need to sign extend AL into AX, AX into DX, or EAX into EDX before executing idiv. To do so, use the cbw, cwd, cdq, or movsx instructions. If the H.O. byte, word, or double word does not already contain significant bits, then you must sign extend the value in the accumulator (AL/AX/EAX) before doing the idiv operation. Failure to do so may produce incorrect results.

There is one other issue with the 80x86's divide instructions: You can get a fatal error when using this instruction. First, of course, you can attempt to divide a value by zero. The second problem is that the quotient may be too large to fit into the EAX, AX, or AL register. For example, the 16/8 division "$8000 / 2" produces the quotient $4000 with a remainder of zero. $4000 will not fit into 8-bits. If this happens, or you attempt to divide by zero, the 80x86 will generate an ex.DivisionError exception or integer overflow error (ex.IntoInstr). This usually means your program will display the appropriate dialog box and abort your program. If this happens to you, chances are you didn't sign or zero extend your numerator before executing the division operation. Because this error may cause your program to crash, you should be very careful about the values you select when using division. Of course, you can use the try..endtry block with the ex.DivisionError and ex.IntoInstr to trap this problem in your program.

The 80x86 leaves the carry, overflow, sign, and zero flags undefined after a division operation. Therefore, you cannot test for problems after a division operation by checking the flag bits.

The 80x86 does not provide a separate instruction to compute the remainder of one number divided by another. The div and idiv instructions automatically compute the remainder at the same time they compute the quotient. HLA, however, provides mnemonics (instructions) for the mod and imod instructions. These special HLA instructions compile into the exact same code as their div and idiv counterparts. The only difference is the "returns" value for the instruction (because these instructions return the remainder in a different location than the quotient). The mod and imod instructions that HLA supports are

```
        mod( reg8 );                   // returns "ah"
        mod( reg16 );                  // returns "dx"
        mod( reg32 );                  // returns "edx"


        mod( reg8, AX );               // returns "ah"
        mod( reg16, DX:AX );           // returns "dx"
        mod( reg32, EDX:EAX );         // returns "edx"


        mod( mem8 );                   // returns "ah"
        mod( mem16 );                  // returns "dx"
        mod( mem32 );                  // returns "edx"


        mod( mem8, AX );               // returns "ah"
        mod( mem16, DX:AX );           // returns "dx"
        mod( mem32, EDX:EAX );         // returns "edx"


        mod( constant8, AX );          // returns "ah"
        mod( constant16, DX:AX );      // returns "dx"
        mod( constant32, EDX:EAX );    // returns "edx"


        imod( reg8 );                  // returns "ah"
        imod( reg16 );                 // returns "dx"
        imod( reg32 );                 // returns "edx"


        imod( reg8, AX );              // returns "ah"
        imod( reg16, DX:AX );          // returns "dx"
        imod( reg32, EDX:EAX );        // returns "edx"


        imod( mem8 );                  // returns "ah"
        imod( mem16 );                 // returns "dx"
        imod( mem32 );                 // returns "edx"


        imod( mem8, AX );              // returns "ah"
        imod( mem16, DX:AX );          // returns "dx"
        imod( mem32, EDX:EAX );        // returns "edx"


        imod( constant8, AX );         // returns "ah"
        imod( constant16, DX:AX );     // returns "dx"
        imod( constant32, EDX:EAX );   // returns "edx"
```

6.2.3   The CMP Instruction

The cmp (compare) instruction is identical to the sub instruction with one crucial semantic difference: It does not retain the difference it computes; it only sets the condition code bits in the flags register. The syntax for the cmp instruction is similar to sub (though the operands are reversed so it reads better), the generic form is

```
cmp( LeftOperand, RightOperand );
```

This instruction computes "LeftOperand - RightOperand" (note the reversal from sub). The specific forms are

```
cmp( reg, reg );            // Registers must be the same size (8, 16,
                            // or 32 bits)
cmp( reg, mem );            // Sizes must match.
cmp( reg, constant );
cmp( mem, constant );
```

Note that both operands are "source" operands, so the fact that a constant appears as the second operand is okay.

The cmp instruction updates the 80x86's flags according to the result of the subtraction operation (LeftOperand - RightOperand). The 80x86 sets the flags in an appropriate fashion so that we can read this instruction as "compare LeftOperand to RightOperand." You can test the result of the comparison by checking the appropriate flags in the flags register using the conditional set instructions (see the next section) or the conditional jump instructions (see the chapter on low level control structures).

Probably the first place to start when exploring the cmp instruction is to take a look at exactly how the cmp instruction affects the flags. Consider the following cmp instruction:

```
cmp( ax, bx );
```

This instruction performs the computation AX - BX and sets the flags depending upon the result of the computation. The flags are set as follows (also see Table 6-1):

- **Z:** The zero flag is set if and only if AX = BX. This is the only time AX - BX produces a zero result. Hence, you can use the zero flag to test for equality or inequality.

- **S:** The sign flag is set to one if the result is negative. At first glance, you might think that this flag would be set if AX is less than BX but this isn't always the case. If AX=$7FFF and BX= -1 ($FFFF), subtracting AX from BX produces $8000, which is negative (and so the sign flag will be set). So, for signed comparisons, anyway, the sign flag doesn't contain the proper status. For unsigned operands, consider AX=$FFFF and BX=1. AX is greater than BX, but their difference is $FFFE, which is still negative. As it turns out, the sign flag and the overflow flag, taken together, can be used for comparing two signed values.

- **O:** The overflow flag is set after a cmp operation if the difference of AX and BX produced an overflow or underflow. As mentioned above, the sign flag and the overflow flag are both used when performing signed comparisons.

- **C:** The carry flag is set after a cmp operation if subtracting BX from AX requires a borrow. This occurs only when AX is less than BX where AX and BX are both unsigned values.

Given that the cmp instruction sets the flags in this fashion, you can test the comparison of the two operands with the following flags:

```
cmp( Left, Right );
```

Table 6-1: Condition Code Settings After CMP

Unsigned Operands	Signed Operands
Z: equality/inequality	Z: equality/inequality
C: Left < Right (C=1) Left > Right (C=0)	C: no meaning
S: no meaning	S: see discussion in this section
O: no meaning	O: see discussion in this section

For signed comparisons, the S (sign) and O (overflow) flags, taken together, have the following meaning:

- If ((S=0) and (O=1)) or ((S=1) and (O=0)) then Left < Right when using a signed comparison.

- If ((S=0) and (O=0)) or ((S=1) and (O=1)) then Left >= Right when using a signed comparison.

Note that (S xor O) is one if the left operand is less than the right operand. Conversely, (S xor O) is zero if the left operand is greater or equal to the right operand.

To understand why these flags are set in this manner, consider the following examples:

Left	minus	Right	S	O
------		------	-	-
$FFFF (-1)	-	$FFFE (-2)	0	0
$8000	-	$0001	0	1
$FFFE (-2)	-	$FFFF (-1)	1	0
$7FFF (32767)	-	$FFFF (-1)	1	1

Remember, the cmp operation is really a subtraction; therefore, the first example above computes (-1)-(-2) which is (+1). The result is positive and an overflow did not occur, so both the S and O flags are zero. Because (S xor O) is zero, Left is greater than or equal to Right.

In the second example, the cmp instruction would compute (-32768)-(+1), which is (-32769). Because a 16-bit signed integer cannot represent this value, the value wraps around to $7FFF (+32767) and sets the overflow flag. The result is positive (at least as a 16-bit value), so the CPU clears the sign flag. (S xor O) is one here, so Left is less than Right.

In the third example, cmp computes (-2)-(-1), which produces (-1). No overflow occurred so the O flag is zero, the result is negative so the sign flag is one. Because (S xor O) is one, Left is less than Right.

In the fourth (and final) example, cmp computes (+32767)-(-1). This produces (+32768), setting the overflow flag. Furthermore, the value wraps around to $8000 (-32768) so the sign flag is set as well. Because (S xor O) is zero, Left is greater than or equal to Right.

You may test the flags after a cmp instruction using HLA high level control statements and the boolean flag expressions (e.g., @c, @nc, @z, @nz, @o, @no, @s, @ns, and so on). Table 6-2 lists the boolean expressions HLA supports that let you check various conditions after a compare instruction.

Table 6-2: HLA Condition Code Boolean Expressions

HLA Syntax	Condition	Comment
@c	Carry set	Carry flag is set if the first operand is less than the second operand (unsigned). Same condition as @b and @nae.
@nc	Carry clear (no carry)	Carry flag is clear if the first operand is greater than or equal to the second (using an unsigned comparison). Same condition as @nb and @ae.
@z	Zero flag set	Zero flag is set if the first operand equals the second operand. Same condition as @e.
@nz	Zero flag clear (no zero)	Zero flag is clear if the first operand is not equal to the second. Same condition as @ne.
@o	Overflow flag set	This flag is set if there was a signed arithmetic overflow as a result of the comparison operation.
@no	Overflow flag clear (no overflow)	The overflow flag is clear if there was no signed arithmetic overflow during the compare operation.
@s	Sign flag set	The sign flag is set if the result of the compare (subtraction) produces a negative result.
@ns	Sign flag clear (no sign)	The sign flag is clear if the compare operation produces a non-negative (zero or positive) result.
@a	Above (unsigned greater than)	The @a condition checks the carry and zero flags to see if @c=0 and @z=0. This condition exists if the first (unsigned) operand is greater than the second (unsigned) operand. This is the same condition as @nbe.
@na	Not above	The @na condition checks to see if the carry flag is set (@c) or the zero flag is set (@z). This is equivalent to an unsigned "not greater than" condition. Note that this condition is the same as @be.

Table 6-2: HLA Condition Code Boolean Expressions

HLA Syntax	Condition	Comment
@ae	Above or equal (unsigned greater than or equal)	The @ae condition is true if the first operand is greater than or equal to the second using an unsigned comparison. This is equivalent to the @nb and @nc conditions.
@nae	Not above or equal	The @nae condition is true if the first operand is not greater than or equal to the second using an unsigned comparison. This is equivalent to the @b and @c conditions.
@b	Below (unsigned less than)	The @b condition is true if the first operand is less than the second using an unsigned comparison. This is equivalent to the @nae and @c conditions.
@nb	Not below	This condition is true if the first operand is not less than the second using an unsigned comparison. This condition is equivalent to the @nc and @ae conditions.
@be	Below or equal (unsigned less than or equal)	The @be condition is true when the first operand is less than or equal to the second using an unsigned comparison. This condition is equivalent to @na.
@nbe	Not below or equal	The @be condition is true when the first operand is not less than or equal to the second using an unsigned comparison. This condition is equivalent to @a.
@g	Greater (signed greater than)	The @g condition is true if the first operand is greater than the second using a signed comparison. This is equivalent to the @nle condition.
@ng	Not greater	The @ng condition is true if the first operand is not greater than the second using a signed comparison. This is equivalent to the @le condition.
@ge	Greater or equal (signed greater than or equal)	The @ge condition is true if the first operand is greater than or equal to the second using a signed comparison. This is equivalent to the @nl condition.
@nge	Not greater or equal	The @nge condition is true if the first operand is not greater than or equal to the second using a signed comparison. This is equivalent to the @l condition.
@l	Less than (signed less than)	The @l condition is true if the first operand is less than the second using a signed comparison. This is equivalent to the @nge condition.
@nl	Not less than	The @ng condition is true if the first operand is not less than the second using a signed comparison. This is equivalent to the @ge condition.
@le	Less than or equal (signed)	The @le condition is true if the first operand is less than or equal to the second using a signed comparison. This is equivalent to the @ng condition.
@nle	Not less than or equal	The @nle condition is true if the first operand is not less than or equal to the second using a signed comparison. This is equivalent to the @g condition
@e	Equal (signed or unsigned)	This condition is true if the first operand equals the second. The @e condition is equivalent to the @z condition.
@ne	Not equal (signed or unsigned)	@ne is true if the first operand does not equal the second. This condition is equivalent to @nz.

You may use the boolean conditions appearing in Table 6-2 within an `if` statement, while statement, or any other HLA high level control statement that allows boolean expressions. Immediately after the execution of a `cmp` instruction, you would typically use one of these conditions in an `if` statement, for example:

```
cmp( eax, ebx );
if( @e ) then

    << do something if eax = ebx >>

endif;
```

Note that the example above is equivalent to:

```
if( eax = ebx ) then

    << do something if eax = ebx >>

endif;
```

6.2.4 The SETcc Instructions

The *set on condition* (or setcc) instructions set a single byte operand (register or memory) to zero or one depending on the values in the flags register. The general formats for the setcc instructions are

```
setcc( reg8 );
setcc( mem8 );
```

setcc represents a mnemonic appearing in Tables 6-3, 6-4, and 6-5, respectively. These instructions store a zero into the corresponding operand if the condition is false; they store a one into the 8-bit operand if the condition is true.

Table 6-3: SETCC Instructions That Test Flags.

Instruction	Description	Condition	Comments
SETC	Set if carry	Carry = 1	Same as SETB, SETNAE
SETNC	Set if no carry	Carry = 0	Same as SETNB, SETAE
SETZ	Set if zero	Zero = 1	Same as SETE
SETNZ	Set if not zero	Zero = 0	Same as SETNE
SETS	Set if sign	Sign = 1	
SETNS	Set if no sign	Sign = 0	
SETO	Set if overflow	Ovrflw=1	
SETNO	Set if no overflow	Ovrflw=0	
SETP	Set if parity	Parity = 1	Same as SETPE
SETPE	Set if parity even	Parity = 1	Same as SETP

Table 6-3: SETCC Instructions That Test Flags.

Instruction	Description	Condition	Comments
SETNP	Set if no parity	Parity = 0	Same as SETPO
SETPO	Set if parity odd	Parity = 0	Same as SETNP

The setcc instructions above simply test the flags without any other meaning attached to the operation. You could, for example, use setc to check the carry flag after a shift, rotate, bit test, or arithmetic operation. You might notice the setp, setpe, and setnp instructions above. They check the *parity* flag. These instructions appear here for completeness, but this text will not spend too much time discussing parity flag (its use is somewhat obsolete).

The cmp instruction works synergistically with the setcc instructions. Immediately after a cmp operation the processor flags provide information concerning the relative values of those operands. They allow you to see if one operand is less than, equal to, greater than, or any combination of these.

There are two additional groups of setcc instructions that are very useful after a cmp operation. The first group deals with the result of an *unsigned* comparison; the second group deals with the result of a *signed* comparison.

Table 6-4: SETcc Instructions for Unsigned Comparisons

Instruction	Description	Condition	Comments
SETA	Set if above (>)	Carry=0, Zero=0	Same as SETNBE
SETNBE	Set if not below or equal (not <=)	Carry=0, Zero=0	Same as SETA
SETAE	Set if above or equal (>=)	Carry = 0	Same as SETNC, SETNB
SETNB	Set if not below (not <)	Carry = 0	Same as SETNC, SETAE
SETB	Set if below (<)	Carry = 1	Same as SETC, SETNAE
SETNAE	Set if not above or equal (not >=)	Carry = 1	Same as SETC, SETB
SETBE	Set if below or equal (<=)	Carry = 1 or Zero = 1	Same as SETNA
SETNA	Set if not above (not >)	Carry = 1 or Zero = 1	Same as SETBE
SETE	Set if equal (=)	Zero = 1	Same as SETZ
SETNE	Set if not equal (¦)	Zero = 0	Same as SETNZ

Table 6-5 lists the corresponding signed comparisons.

Table 6-5: SETcc Instructions for Signed Comparisons

Instruction	Description	Condition	Comments
SETG	Set if greater (>)	Sign = Ovrflw and Zero=0	Same as SETNLE
SETNLE	Set if not less than or equal (not <=)	Sign = Ovrflw or Zero=0	Same as SETG
SETGE	Set if greater than or equal (>=)	Sign = Ovrflw	Same as SETNL
SETNL	Set if not less than (not <)	Sign = Ovrflw	Same as SETGE
SETL	Set if less than (<)	Sign ¦ Ovrflw	Same as SETNGE

Table 6-5: SETcc Instructions for Signed Comparisons

Instruction	Description	Condition	Comments
SETNGE	Set if not greater or equal (not >=)	Sign ¦ Ovrflw	Same as SETL
SETLE	Set if less than or equal (<=)	Sign ¦ Ovrflw or Zero = 1	Same as SETNG
SETNG	Set if not greater than (not >)	Sign ¦ Ovrflw or Zero = 1	Same as SETLE
SETE	Set if equal (=)	Zero = 1	Same as SETZ
SETNE	Set if not equal (¦)	Zero = 0	Same as SETNZ

Note the correspondence between the setcc instructions and the HLA flag conditions that may appear in boolean instructions.

The setcc instructions are particularly valuable because they can convert the result of a comparison to a boolean value (false/true or 0/1). This is especially important when translating statements from a high level language like Pascal or C/C++ into assembly language. The following example shows how to use these instructions in this manner:

```
// Bool := A <= B

        mov( A, eax );
        cmp( eax, B );
        setle( bool );                          // bool is a boolean or byte
                                                // variable.
```

Because the setcc instructions always produce zero or one, you can use the results with the and and or instructions to compute complex boolean values:

```
// Bool := ((A <= B) and (D = E))

        mov( A, eax );
        cmp( eax, B );
        setle( bl );
        mov( D, eax );
        cmp( eax, E );
        sete( bh );
        and( bl, bh );
        mov( bh, Bool );
```

6.2.5   The TEST Instruction

The 80x86 test instruction is to the and instruction what the cmp instruction is to sub. That is, the test instruction computes the logical AND of its two operands and sets the condition code flags based on the result; it does not, however, store the result of the logical AND back into the destination operand. The syntax for the test instruction is similar to and; it is

```
test( operand1, operand2 );
```

The test instruction sets the zero flag if the result of the logical AND operation is zero. It sets the sign flag if the H.O. bit of the result contains a one. test always clears the carry and overflow flags.

The primary use of the test instruction is to check to see if an individual bit contains a zero or a one. Consider the instruction "test(1, AL);". This instruction logically ANDs AL with the value one; if bit one of AL contains zero, the result will be zero (setting the zero flag) because all the other bits in the constant one are zero. Conversely, if bit one of AL contains one, then the result is not zero, so test clears the zero flag. Therefore, you can test the zero flag after this test instruction to see if bit zero contains a zero or a one (e.g., using a setz or setnz instruction).

The test instruction can also check to see if all the bits in a specified set of bits contain zero. The instruction "test($F, AL);" sets the zero flag if and only if the L.O. four bits of AL all contain zero.

One very important use of the test instruction is to check to see if a register contains zero. The instruction "test(reg, reg);" where both operands are the same register will logically AND that register with itself. If the register contains zero, then the result is zero and the CPU will set the zero flag. However, if the register contains a non-zero value, logically ANDing that value with itself produces that same non-zero value, so the CPU clears the zero flag. Therefore, you can test the zero flag immediately after the execution of this instruction (e.g., using the setz or setnz instructions or the @z and @nz boolean conditions) to see if the register contains zero. Examples:

```
test( eax, eax );
setz( bl );          // BL is set to one if EAX contains zero.
    .
    .
    .
test( bx, bx );
if( @nz ) then

    << do something if bx <> 0 >>

endif;
```

6.3   Arithmetic Expressions

Probably the biggest shock to beginners facing assembly language for the very first time is the lack of familiar arithmetic expressions. Arithmetic expressions, in most high level languages, look similar to their algebraic equivalents, e.g.,

```
X:=Y*Z;
```

In assembly language, you'll need several statements to accomplish this same task, e.g.,

```
mov( y, eax );
intmul( z, eax );
mov( eax, x );
```

Obviously the HLL version is much easier to type, read, and understand. This point, more than any other, is responsible for scaring people away from assembly language. Although there is a lot of typing involved, converting an arithmetic expression into assembly language isn't difficult at all. By attacking the problem in steps, the same way you would solve the problem by hand, you can easily break down any arithmetic expression into an equivalent sequence of assembly language statements. By learning how to convert such expressions to assembly language in three steps, you'll discover there is little difficulty to this task.

6.3.1 Simple Assignments

The easiest expressions to convert to assembly language are simple assignments. Simple assignments copy a single value into a variable and take one of two forms:

```
variable := constant
```

or

```
variable := variable
```

Converting the first form to assembly language is trivial, just use the assembly language statement:

```
mov( constant, variable );
```

This mov instruction copies the constant into the variable.

The second assignment above is slightly more complicated because the 80x86 doesn't provide a memory-to-memory mov instruction. Therefore, to copy one memory variable into another, you must move the data through a register. By convention (and for slight efficiency reasons), most programmers tend to use AL/AX/EAX for this purpose. If the AL, AX, or EAX register is available, you should use it for this operation. For example,

```
var1 := var2;
```

becomes

```
mov( var2, eax );
mov( eax, var1 );
```

This is assuming, of course, that var1 and var2 are 32-bit variables. Use AL if they are 8-bit variables; use AX if they are 16-bit variables.

Of course, if you're already using AL, AX, or EAX for something else, one of the other registers will suffice. Regardless, you must use a register to transfer one memory location to another.

Although the 80x86 does not support a memory-to-memory move, HLA does provide an extended syntax for the mov instruction that allows two memory operands. However, both operands have to be 16-bit or 32-bit values; 8-bit values won't work. Assuming you want to copy the value of a word or double word object to another variable, you can use the following syntax:

```
mov( var2, var1 );
```

HLA translates this "instruction" into the following two instruction sequences:

```
push( var2 );
pop( var1 );
```

Although this is slightly slower than the two mov instructions, it is convenient and it doesn't require the use of an intermediate register (important if you don't have any free registers available).

6.3.2 Simple Expressions

The next level of complexity is a simple expression. A simple expression takes the form:

$$var_1 := term_1 \text{ op } term_2;$$

var1 is a variable, term1 and term2 are variables or constants, and op is some arithmetic operator (addition, subtraction, multiplication, and so on). Most expressions take this form. It should come as no surprise, then, that the 80x86 architecture was optimized for just this type of expression.

A typical conversion for this type of expression takes the following form:

```
mov( term₁, eax );
op( term₂, eax );
mov( eax, var₁ )
```

op is the mnemonic that corresponds to the specified operation (e.g., "+" = add, "-" = sub, and so on).

There are a few inconsistencies you need to be aware of. Of course, when dealing with the (i)mul, (i)div, and (i)mod instructions on the 80x86, you must use the AL/AX/EAX and DX/EDX registers. You cannot use arbitrary registers as you can with other operations. Also, don't forget the sign extension instructions if you're performing a division operation and you're dividing one

16-/32-bit number by another. Finally, don't forget that some instructions may cause overflow. You may want to check for an overflow (or underflow) condition after an arithmetic operation.

Examples of common simple expressions:

```
x := y + z;

        mov( y, eax );
        add( z, eax );
        mov( eax, x );


x := y - z;

        mov( y, eax );
        sub( z, eax );
        mov( eax, x );


x := y * z; {unsigned}

        mov( y, eax );
        mul( z, eax );      // Don't forget this wipes out EDX.
        mov( eax, x );


x := y * z; {signed}

        mov( y, eax );
        intmul( z, eax );   // Does not affect EDX!
        mov( eax, x );


x := y div z; {unsigned div}

        mov( y, eax );
        mov( 0, edx );      // Zero extend EAX into EDX.
        div( z, edx:eax );
        mov( eax, x );


x := y idiv z; {signed div}

        mov( y, eax );
        cdq();              // Sign extend EAX into EDX.
        idiv( z, edx:eax );
        mov( eax, z );


x := y mod z; {unsigned remainder}

        mov( y, eax );
        mov( 0, edx );      // Zero extend EAX into EDX.
        mod( z, edx:eax );
        mov( edx, x );      // Note that remainder is in EDX.
```

```
x := y imod z; {signed remainder}

        mov( y, eax );
        cdq();                  // Sign extend EAX into EDX.
        imod( z, edx:eax );
        mov( edx, x );          // Remainder is in EDX.
```

Certain unary operations also qualify as simple expressions. A good example of a unary operation is negation. In a high level language negation takes one of two possible forms:

```
        var := -var   or    var_1 := -var_2
```

Note that var := -constant is really a simple assignment, not a simple expression. You can specify a negative constant as an operand to the mov instruction:

```
        mov( -14, var );
```

To handle "var = -var;" use the single assembly language statement:

```
        // var = -var;

        neg( var );
```

If two different variables are involved, then use the following:

```
        // var1 = -var2;

        mov( var_2, eax );
        neg( eax );
        mov( eax, var_1 );
```

6.3.3   Complex Expressions

A complex expression is any arithmetic expression involving more than two terms and one operator. Such expressions are commonly found in programs written in a high level language. Complex expressions may include parentheses to override operator precedence, function calls, array accesses, and so on. While the conversion of many complex expressions to assembly language is fairly straight-forward, others require some effort. This section outlines the rules you use to convert such expressions.

A complex expression that is easy to convert to assembly language is one that involves three terms and two operators, for example:

```
        w := w - y - z;
```

Clearly the straight-forward assembly language conversion of this statement will require two sub instructions. However, even with an expression as simple as this one, the conversion is not trivial. There are actually *two ways* to convert this from the statement above into assembly language:

```
mov( w, eax );
sub( y, eax );
sub( z, eax );
mov( eax, w );
```

and

```
mov( y, eax );
sub( z, eax );
sub( eax, w );
```

The second conversion, because it is shorter, looks better. However, it produces an incorrect result (assuming Pascal-like semantics for the original statement). Associativity is the problem. The second sequence above computes W := W - (Y - Z) which is not the same as W := (W - Y) - Z. How we place the parentheses around the subexpressions can affect the result. Note that if you are interested in a shorter form, you can use the following sequence:

```
mov( y, eax );
add( z, eax );
sub( eax, w );
```

This computes W:=W-(Y+Z). This is equivalent to W := (W - Y) - Z.

Precedence is another issue. Consider the Pascal expression:

```
X := W * Y + Z;
```

Once again there are two ways we can evaluate this expression:

```
X := (W * Y) + Z;
```

or

```
X := W * (Y + Z);
```

By now, you're probably thinking that this text is crazy. Everyone knows the correct way to evaluate these expressions is by the second form. However, you're wrong to think that way. The APL programming language, for example, evaluates expressions solely from right to left and does not give one operator precedence over another. Which way is "correct" depends entirely on how you define precedence in your arithmetic system.

Most high level languages use a fixed set of precedence rules to describe the order of evaluation in an expression involving two or more different operators. Such programming languages usually compute multiplication and division before addition and subtraction. Those that support exponentiation (e.g., FORTRAN and BASIC) usually compute that before multiplication and division. These rules are intuitive because almost everyone learns them before high school. Consider the expression:

$X op_1 Y op_2 Z$

If op_1 takes precedence over op_2 then this evaluates to $(X op_1 Y) op_2 Z$ otherwise if op_2 takes precedence over op_1 then this evaluates to $X op_1 (Y op_2 Z)$. Depending upon the operators and operands involved, these two computations could produce different results. When converting an expression of this form into assembly language, you must be sure to compute the subexpression with the highest precedence first. The following example demonstrates this technique:

```
// w := x + y * z;

        mov( x, ebx );
        mov( y, eax );      // Must compute y*z first because "*"
        intmul( z, eax );   // has higher precedence than "+".
        add( ebx, eax );
        mov( eax, w );
```

If two operators appearing within an expression have the same precedence, then you determine the order of evaluation using *associativity* rules. Most operators are *left associative,* meaning that they evaluate from left to right. Addition, subtraction, multiplication, and division are all left associative. A *right associative* operator evaluates from right to left. The exponentiation operator in FORTRAN and BASIC is a good example of a right associative operator:

2^2^3 is equal to $2^{(2^3)}$ not $(2^2)^3$

The precedence and associativity rules determine the order of evaluation. Indirectly, these rules tell you where to place parentheses in an expression to determine the order of evaluation. Of course, you can always use parentheses to override the default precedence and associativity. However, the ultimate point is that your assembly code must complete certain operations before others to correctly compute the value of a given expression. The following examples demonstrate this principle:

```
// w := x - y - z

        mov( x, eax );      // All the same operator, so we need
        sub( y, eax );      // to evaluate from left to right
        sub( z, eax );      // because they all have the same
        mov( eax, w );      // precedence and are left associative.
```

```
// w := x + y * z

        mov( y, eax );      // Must compute Y * Z first because
        intmul( z, eax );   // multiplication has a higher
        add( x, eax );      // precedence than addition.
        mov( eax, w );


// w := x / y - z

        mov( x, eax );      // Here we need to compute division
        cdq();              // first because it has the highest
        idiv( y, edx:eax ); // precedence.
        sub( z, eax );
        mov( eax, w );

// w := x * y * z

        mov( y, eax );      // Addition and multiplication are
        intmul( z, eax );   // commutative, therefore the order
        intmul( x, eax );   // of evaluation does not matter.
        mov( eax, w );
```

There is one exception to the associativity rule. If an expression involves multiplication and division it is generally better to perform the multiplication first. For example, given an expression of the form:

```
        W := X/Y * Z        // Note: this is (x*z)/y, not x/(y*z)
```

It is usually better to compute X*Z and then divide the result by Y rather than divide X by Y and multiply the quotient by Z. There are two reasons this approach is better. First, remember that the imul instruction always produces a 64-bit result (assuming 32-bit operands). By doing the multiplication first, you automatically *sign extend* the product into the EDX register so you do not have to sign extend EAX prior to the division. This saves the execution of the cdq instruction. A second reason for doing the multiplication first is to increase the accuracy of the computation. Remember, (integer) division often produces an inexact result. For example, if you compute 5/2 you will get the value 2, not 2.5. Computing (5/2)*3 produces 6. However, if you compute (5*3)/2 you get the value 7 which is a little closer to the real quotient (7.5). Therefore, if you encounter an expression of the form

```
        w := x/y*z;
```

you can usually convert it to the following assembly code:

```
        mov( x, eax );
        imul( z, eax );          // Note the use of IMUL, not INTMUL!
        idiv( y, edx:eax );
        mov( eax, w );
```

Of course, if the algorithm you're encoding depends on the truncation effect of the division operation, you cannot use this trick to improve the algorithm. Moral of the story: always make sure you fully understand any expression you are converting to assembly language. Obviously if the semantics dictate that you must perform the division first, do so.

Consider the following Pascal statement:

```
w := x - y * x;
```

This is similar to a previous example, except it uses subtraction rather than addition. Because subtraction is not commutative, you cannot compute $y * z$ and then subtract x from this result. This tends to complicate the conversion a tiny amount. Rather than a straight-forward multiply and addition sequence, you'll have to load x into a register, multiply y and z leaving their product in a different register, and then subtract this product from x, e.g.,

```
        mov( x, ebx );
        mov( y, eax );
        intmul( x, eax );
        sub( eax, ebx );
        mov( ebx, w );
```

This is a trivial example that demonstrates the need for *temporary variables* in an expression. This code uses the EBX register to temporarily hold a copy of x until it computes the product of y and z. As your expressions increase in complexity, the need for temporaries grows. Consider the following Pascal statement:

```
w := (a + b) * (y + z);
```

Following the normal rules of algebraic evaluation, you compute the subexpressions inside the parentheses (i.e., the two subexpressions with the highest precedence) first and set their values aside. When you've computed the values for both subexpressions you can compute their product. One way to deal with complex expressions like this one is to reduce it to a sequence of simple expressions whose results wind up in temporary variables. For example, we can convert the single expression above into the following sequence:

```
        Temp₁ := a + b;
        Temp₂ := y + z;
        w := Temp₁ * Temp₂;
```

Because converting simple expressions to assembly language is quite easy, it's now a snap to compute the former, complex expression in assembly. The code is

```
mov( a, eax );
add( b, eax );
mov( eax, Temp1 );
mov( y, eax );
add( z, eax );
mov( eax, Temp2 );
mov( Temp1, eax );
intmul( Temp2, eax );
mov( eax, w );
```

Of course, this code is grossly inefficient and it requires that you declare a couple of temporary variables in your data segment. However, it is very easy to optimize this code by keeping temporary variables, as much as possible, in 80x86 registers. By using 80x86 registers to hold the temporary results this code becomes:

```
mov( a, eax );
add( b, eax );
mov( y, ebx );
add( z, ebx );
intmul( ebx, eax );
mov( eax, w );
```

Yet another example:

```
x := (y+z) * (a-b) / 10;
```

This can be converted to a set of four simple expressions:

```
Temp1 := (y+z)
Temp2 := (a-b)
Temp1 := Temp1 * Temp2
X := Temp1 / 10
```

You can convert these four simple expressions into the assembly language statements:

```
mov( y, eax );        // Compute eax = y+z
add( z, eax );
mov( a, ebx );        // Compute ebx = a-b
sub( b, ebx );
imul( ebx, eax );     // This also sign extends eax into edx.
idiv( 10, edx:eax );
mov( eax, x );
```

The most important thing to keep in mind is that you should attempt to keep temporary values, in registers. Remember, accessing an 80x86 register is much more efficient than accessing a memory location. Use memory locations to hold temporaries only if you've run out of registers to use.

Ultimately, converting a complex expression to assembly language is little different than solving the expression by hand. Instead of actually computing the result at each stage of the computation, you simply write the assembly code that computes the result. Because you were probably taught to compute only one operation at a time, this means that manual computation works on "simple expressions" that exist in a complex expression. Of course, converting those simple expressions to assembly is fairly trivial. Therefore, anyone who can solve a complex expression by hand can convert it to assembly language following the rules for simple expressions.

6.3.4 Commutative Operators

If "@" represents some operator, that operator is *commutative* if the following relationship is always true:

(A @ B) = (B @ A)

As you saw in the previous section, commutative operators are nice because the order of their operands is immaterial and this lets you rearrange a computation, often making that computation easier or more efficient. Often, rearranging a computation allows you to use fewer temporary variables. Whenever you encounter a commutative operator in an expression, you should always check to see if there is a better sequence you can use to improve the size or speed of your code. Tables 6-6 and 6-7, respectively, list the commutative and noncommutative operators you typically find in high level languages.

Table 6-6: Some Common Commutative Dyadic (Binary) Operators

Pascal	C/C++	Description
+	+	Addition
*	*	Multiplication
AND	&& or &	Logical or bitwise AND
OR	|| or |	Logical or bitwise OR
XOR	^	(Logical or) bitwise exclusive OR
=	==	Equality
<>	!=	Inequality

Table 6-7: Some Common Noncommutative Dyadic (Binary) Operators

Pascal	C/C++	Description
-	-	Subtraction
/ or DIV	/	Division
MOD	%	Modulo or remainder
<	<	Less than
<=	<=	Less than or equal

Table 6-7: Some Common Noncommutative Dyadic (Binary) Operators

Pascal	C/C++	Description
>	>	Greater than
>=	>=	Greater than or equal

6.4 Logical (Boolean) Expressions

Consider the following expression from a Pascal program:

```
B := ((X=Y) and (A <= C)) or ((Z-A) <> 5);
```

B is a boolean variable and the remaining variables are all integers.

How do we represent boolean variables in assembly language? Although it takes only a single bit to represent a boolean value, most assembly language programmers allocate a whole byte or word for this purpose (as such, HLA also allocates a whole byte for a boolean variable). With a byte, there are 256 possible values we can use to represent the two values *true* and *false*. So which two values (or which two sets of values) do we use to represent these boolean values? Because of the machine's architecture, it's much easier to test for conditions like zero or not zero and positive or negative rather than to test for one of two particular boolean values. Most programmers (and, indeed, some programming languages like "C") choose zero to represent false and anything else to represent true. Some people prefer to represent true and false with one and zero (respectively) and not allow any other values. Others select all one bits ($FFFF_FFFF, $FFFF, or $FF) for true and 0 for false. You could also use a positive value for true and a negative value for false. All these mechanisms have their own advantages and drawbacks.

Using only zero and one to represent false and true offers two very big advantages: (1) The setcc instructions produce these results so this scheme is compatible with those instructions; (2) the 80x86 logical instructions (and, or, xor and, to a lesser extent, not) operate on these values exactly as you would expect. That is, if you have two boolean variables A and B, then the following instructions perform the basic logical operations on these two variables:

```
// c = a AND b;

    mov( a, al );
    and( b, al );
    mov( al, c );

// c = a OR b;

        mov( a, al );
        or( b, al );
        mov( al, c );
```

```
// c = a XOR b;

        mov( a, al );
        xor( b, al );
        mov( al, c );

// b = not a;

        mov( a, al );       // Note that the NOT instruction does not
        not( al );          // properly compute al = not al by itself.
        and( 1, al );       // I.e., (not 0) does not equal one.  The AND
        mov( al, b );       // instruction corrects this problem.

        mov( a, al );       // Another way to do b = not a;
        xor( 1, al );       // Inverts bit zero.
        mov( al, b );
```

Note, as pointed out in the preceding code, that the not instruction will not properly compute logical negation. The bitwise NOT of zero is $FF and the bitwise NOT of one is $FE. Neither result is zero or one. However, by ANDing the result with one you get the proper result. Note that you can implement the NOT operation more efficiently using the "xor(1, ax);" instruction because it only affects the L.O. bit.

As it turns out, using zero for false and anything else for true has a lot of subtle advantages. Specifically, the test for true or false is often implicit in the execution of any logical instruction. However, this mechanism suffers from a very big disadvantage: you cannot use the 80x86 and, or, xor, and not instructions to implement the boolean operations of the same name. Consider the two values $55 and $AA. They're both non-zero so they both represent the value true. However, if you logically AND $55 and $AA together using the 80x86 and instruction, the result is zero. True AND true should produce true, not false. Although you can account for situations like this, it usually requires a few extra instructions and is somewhat less efficient when computing boolean operations.

A system that uses non-zero values to represent true and zero to represent false is an *arithmetic logical system*. A system that uses the two distinct values like zero and one to represent false and true is called a *boolean logical system*, or simply a boolean system. You can use either system, as convenient. Consider again the boolean expression

```
    B := ((X=Y) and (A <= D)) or ((Z-A) <> 5);
```

The simple expressions resulting from this expression might be

```
        mov( x, eax );
        cmp( y, eax );
        sete( al );       // AL := x = y;

        mov( a, ebx );
        cmp( ebx, d );
```

```
setle( bl );      // BL := a <= d;
and( al, bl );    // BL := (x=y) and (a <= d);

mov( z, eax );
sub( a, eax );
cmp( eax, 5 );
setne( al );
or( bl, al );     // AL := ((X=Y) and (A <= D)) or ((Z-A) <> 5);
mov( al, b );
```

When working with boolean expressions don't forget the that you might be able to optimize your code by simplifying those boolean expressions. You can use algebraic transformations to help reduce the complexity of an expression. In the chapter on control structures you'll also see how to use control flow to calculate a boolean result. This is generally quite a bit more efficient than using *complete boolean evaluation,* as the examples in this section teach.

6.5   Machine and Arithmetic Idioms

An *idiom* is an idiosyncrasy. Several arithmetic operations and 80x86 instructions have idiosyncrasies that you can take advantage of when writing assembly language code. Some people refer to the use of machine and arithmetic idioms as "tricky programming" that you should always avoid in well-written programs. While it is wise to avoid tricks just for the sake of tricks, many machine and arithmetic idioms are well known and commonly found in assembly language programs. Some of them can be really tricky, but a good number of them are simply "tricks of the trade." This text cannot even begin to present all of the idioms in common use today; they are too numerous and the list is constantly changing. Nevertheless, there are some very important idioms that you will see all the time, so it makes sense to discuss those.

6.5.1   Multiplying Without MUL, IMUL, or INTMUL

If you take a quick look at the timing for the multiply instruction, you'll notice that the execution time for this instruction is often long.[1] When multiplying by a constant, you can sometimes avoid the performance penalty of the mul, imul, and intmul instructions by using shifts, additions, and subtractions to perform the multiplication.

Remember, a shl instruction computes the same result as multiplying the specified operand by two. Shifting to the left two bit positions multiplies the operand by four. Shifting to the left three bit positions multiplies the operand by eight. In general, shifting an operand to the left n bits multiplies it by 2^n. You can multiply any value by some constant using a series of shifts and adds or shifts and subtractions. For example, to multiply the AX register by ten, you need only multiply it by 8 and then add in two times the original value. That is, $10*AX = 8*AX + 2*AX$. The code to accomplish this is

---

[1] Actually, this is specific to a given processor. Some processors execute the intmul instruction fairly fast.

```
shl( 1, ax );          // Multiply AX by two.
mov( ax, bx);          // Save 2*AX for later.
shl( 2, ax );          // Multiply ax by eight (*4 really, but it
                       // contains *2).
add( bx, ax );         // Add in AX*2 to AX*8 to get AX*10.
```

Many x86 processors can multiply the AX register (or just about any register, for that matter) by various constant values much faster using shl than by using the mul instruction. This may seem hard to believe because it only takes one instruction to compute this product:

```
intmul( 10, ax );
```

However, if you look at the timings, the shift and add example above requires fewer clock cycles on many processors in the 80x86 family than the mul instruction. Of course, the code is somewhat larger (by a few bytes), but the performance improvement is usually worth it. Of course, on the later 80x86 processors, the multiply instructions are quite a bit faster than the earlier processors, but the shift and add scheme is often faster on these processors as well.

You can also use subtraction with shifts to perform a multiplication operation. Consider the following multiplication by seven:

```
mov( eax, ebx );       // Save EAX * 1
shl( 3, eax );         // EAX = EAX * 8
sub( ebx, eax );       // EAX*8 - EAX*1 is EAX*7
```

This follows directly from the fact that EAX*7 = (EAX*8)-EAX.
A common error beginning assembly language programmers make is subtracting or adding one or two rather than EAX*1 or EAX*2. The following does not compute EAX*7:

```
shl( 3, eax );
sub( 1, eax );
```

It computes (8*EAX)-1, something entirely different (unless, of course, EAX = 1). Beware of this pitfall when using shifts, additions, and subtractions to perform multiplication operations.

You can also use the lea instruction to compute certain products. The trick is to use the scaled index addressing modes. The following examples demonstrate some simple cases:

```
lea( eax, [ecx][ecx] );       // EAX := ECX * 2
lea( eax, [eax][eax*2] );     // EAX := EAX * 3
lea( eax, [eax*4] );          // EAX := EAX * 4
lea( eax, [ebx][ebx*4] );     // EAX := EBX * 5
lea( eax, [eax*8] );          // EAX := EAX * 8
lea( eax, [edx][edx*8] );     // EAX := EDX * 9
```

6.5.2 Division Without DIV or IDIV

Much as the shl instruction can be used for simulating a multiplication by some power of two, you may use the shr and sar instructions to simulate a division by a power of two. Unfortunately, you cannot use shifts, additions, and subtractions to perform a division by an arbitrary constant as easily as you can use these instructions to perform a multiplication operation. Therefore, keep in mind that this trick is useful only when dividing by powers of two. Also, don't forget that the sar instruction rounds toward negative infinity rather than toward zero; this is not the way the idiv instruction operates (it rounds toward zero).

Another way to perform division is to use the multiply instructions. You can divide by some value by multiplying by its reciprocal. Because the multiply instruction is faster than the divide instruction, multiplying by a reciprocal is usually faster than division.

Now you're probably wondering, "How does one multiply by a reciprocal when the values we're dealing with are all integers?" The answer, of course, is that we must cheat to do this. If you want to multiply by one-tenth, there is no way you can load the value 1/10th into an 80x86 register prior to performing the multiplication. However, we could multiply 1/10th by 10, perform the multiplication, and then divide the result by ten to get the final result. Of course, this wouldn't buy you anything at all; in fact it would make things worse because you're now doing a multiplication by ten as well as a division by ten. However, suppose you multiply 1/10th by 65,536 (6553), perform the multiplication, and then divide by 65,536. This would still perform the correct operation and, as it turns out, if you set up the problem correctly, you can get the division operation for free. Consider the following code that divides AX by ten:

```
mov( 6554, dx );          // 6554 = round( 65,536/10 ).
mul( dx, ax );
```

This code leaves AX/10 in the DX register.

To understand how this works, consider what happens when you multiply AX by 65,536 ($10000). This simply moves AX into DX and sets AX to zero (a multiply by $10000 is equivalent to a shift left by 16 bits). Multiplying by 6,554 (65,536 divided by ten) puts AX divided by ten into the DX register. Because mul is faster than div, this technique runs a little faster than using a straight division.

Multiplying by the reciprocal works well when you need to divide by a constant. You could even use it to divide by a variable, but the overhead to compute the reciprocal only pays off if you perform the division many, many times (by the same value).

6.5.3 Implementing Modulo-N Counters with AND

If you want to implement a counter variable that counts up to 2^n-1 and then resets to zero, simply use the following code:

```
inc( CounterVar );
and( nBits, CounterVar );
```

where nBits is a binary value containing n one bits right justified in the number. For example, to create a counter that cycles between 0 and 15, you could use the following:

```
inc( CounterVar );
and( %00001111, CounterVar );
```

6.5.4 Careless Use of Machine Idioms

One problem with using machine idioms is that the machines change over time. The DOS/16-bit version of this text recommends the use of several machine idioms in addition to those this chapter presents. Unfortunately, as time passed Intel improved the processor and tricks that used to provide a performance benefit are actually slower on the newer processors. Therefore, you should be careful about employing common "tricks" you pick up; they may not actually improve the code. On the wide range of 80x86 processors available today, it is very difficult to find a machine idiom that provides an improvement on all CPUs. An idiom that works great on a Pentium II may be lousy on a Pentium IV. A trick that works great on a Pentium IV may not produce the best results on an Athlon CPU. So be careful; that tricky code you're writing may actually run slower than the straight-forward code on many CPUs.

6.6 Floating Point Arithmetic

When the 8086 CPU first appeared in the late 1970s, semiconductor technology was not to the point where Intel could put floating point instructions directly on the 8086 CPU. Therefore, it devised a scheme whereby it could use a second chip to perform the floating point calculations — the floating point unit (or FPU).[2] It released its original floating point chip, the 8087, in 1980. This particular FPU worked with the 8086, 8088, 80186, and 80188 CPUs. When Intel introduced the 80286 CPU, it released a redesigned 80287 FPU chip to accompany it. Although the 80287 was compatible with the 80386 CPU, Intel designed a better FPU, the 80387, for use in 80386 systems. The 80486 CPU was the first Intel CPU to include an on-chip floating point unit. Shortly after the release of the 80486, Intel introduced the 80486sx CPU that was an 80486 without the built-in FPU. To get floating point capabilities on this chip, you had to add an 80487 chip, although the 80487 was really nothing more than a full-blown 80486 that took over for the "sx" chip in the system. Intel's Pentium chips provide a high-performance floating point unit directly on the CPU. There is no (Intel) floating point coprocessor available for the Pentium chip.

Collectively, we will refer to all these chips as the 80x87 FPU. Given the obsolescence of the 8086, 80286, 8087, 80287, 80387, and 80487 chips, this text will concentrate on the Pentium and later chips. There are some differences between the Pentium floating point units and the earlier FPUs. If you need to write code that will execute on those earlier machines, you should consult the appropriate Intel documentation for those devices.

---

[2] Intel has also referred to this device as the Numeric Data Processor (NDP), Numeric Processor Extension (NPX), and math coprocessor.

6.6.1 FPU Registers

The 80x86 FPUs add 13 registers to the 80x86 and later processors: 8 floating point data registers, a control register, a status register, a tag register, an instruction pointer, and a data pointer. The data registers are similar to the 80x86's general purpose register set insofar as all floating point calculations take place in these registers. The control register contains bits that let you decide how the FPU handles certain degenerate cases like rounding of inaccurate computations, it contains bits that control precision, and so on. The status register is similar to the 80x86's flags register; it contains the condition code bits and several other floating point flags that describe the state of the FPU. The tag register contains several groups of bits that determine the state of the value in each of the eight general purpose registers. The instruction and data pointer registers contain certain state information about the last floating point instruction executed. We will not consider the last three registers in this text; see the Intel documentation for more details.

6.6.1.1 FPU Data Registers

The FPUs provide eight 80-bit data registers organized as a stack. This is a significant departure from the organization of the general purpose registers on the 80x86 CPU that comprise a standard general purpose register set. HLA refers to these registers as ST0, ST1, ..., ST7.

The biggest difference between the FPU register set and the 80x86 register set is the stack organization. On the 80x86 CPU, the AX register is always the AX register, no matter what happens. On the FPU, however, the register set is an eight-element stack of 80-bit floating point values (see Figure 6-1).

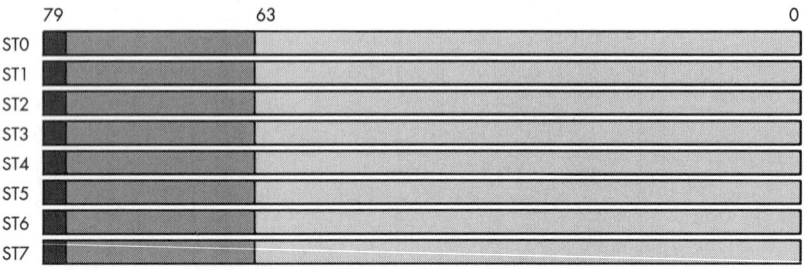

Figure 6-1: FPU Floating Point Register Stack.

ST0 refers to the item on the top of the stack, ST1 refers to the next item on the stack, and so on. Many floating point instructions push and pop items on the stack; therefore, ST1 will refer to the previous contents of ST0 after you push something onto the stack. It will take some thought and practice to get used to the fact that the registers are changing, but this is an easy problem to overcome.

6.6.1.2 The FPU Control Register

When Intel designed the 80x87 (and, essentially, the IEEE floating point standard), there were no standards in floating point hardware. Different (mainframe and mini) computer manufacturers all had different and incompatible floating point formats. Unfortunately, much application software had been written taking into account the idiosyncrasies of these different floating point formats. Intel wanted to design an FPU that could work with the majority of the software out there (keep in mind, the IBM PC was three to four years away when Intel began designing the 8087; it couldn't rely on that "mountain" of software available for the PC to make its chip popular). Unfortunately, many of the features found in these older floating point formats were mutually incompatible. For example, in some floating point systems rounding would occur when there was insufficient precision; in others, truncation would occur. Some applications would work with one floating point system but not with another. Intel wanted as many applications as possible to work with as few changes as possible on its 80x87 FPUs, so it added a special register, the FPU *control register,* that lets the user choose one of several possible operating modes for their FPU.

The 80x87 control register contains 16-bits organized as shown in Figure 6-2.

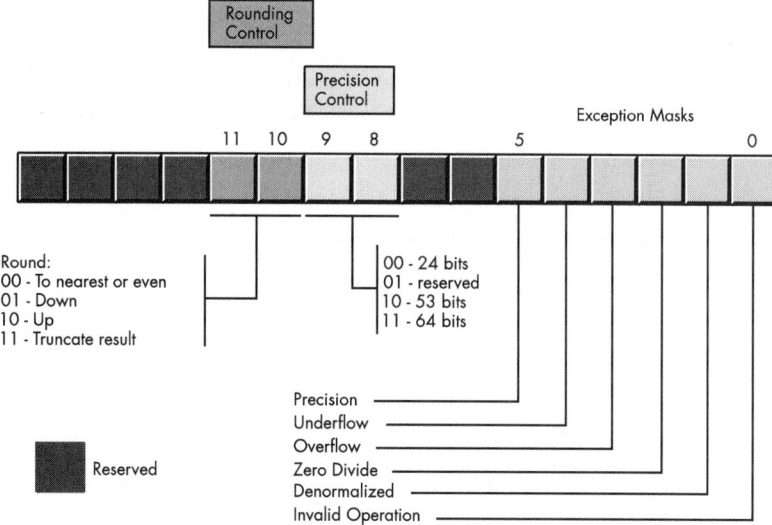

Figure 6-2: FPU Control Register.

Bits 10 and 11 of the FPU control register provide rounding control according to the values appearing in Table 6-8.

Table 6-8: Rounding Control

Bits 10 & 11	Function
00	To nearest or even
01	Round down
10	Round up
11	Truncate

The "00" setting is the default. The FPU rounds values above one-half of the least significant bit up. It rounds values below one-half of the least significant bit down. If the value below the least significant bit is exactly one-half of the least significant bit, the FPU rounds the value toward the value whose least significant bit is zero. For long strings of computations, this provides a reasonable, automatic way to maintain maximum precision.

The round up and round down options are present for those computations where it is important to keep track of the accuracy during a computation. By setting the rounding control to round down and performing the operation, then repeating the operation with the rounding control set to round up, you can determine the minimum and maximum ranges between which the true result will fall.

The truncate option forces all computations to truncate any excess bits during the computation. You will rarely use this option if accuracy is important to you. However, if you are porting older software to the FPU, you might use this option to help when porting the software. One place where this option is extremely useful is when converting a floating point value to an integer. Because most software expects floating point-to-integer conversions to truncate the result, you will need to use the truncation rounding mode to achieve this.

Bits eight and nine of the control register specify the precision during computation. This capability is provided to allow compatibility with older software as required by the IEEE 754 standard. The precision control bits use the values in Table 6-9.

Table 6-9: Mantissa Precision Control Bits

Bits 8 & 9	Precision Control
00	24 bits
01	Reserved
10	53 bits
11	64 bits

Some CPUs may operate faster with floating point values whose precision is 53 bits (i.e., 64-bit floating point format) rather than 64 bits (i.e., 80-bit floating point format). Please see the documentation for your specific processor for details. Generally, the CPU defaults these bits to %11 to select the 64-bit mantissa precision.

Bits zero through five are the *exception masks*. These are similar to the interrupt enable bit in the 80x86's flags register. If these bits contain a one, the corresponding condition is ignored by the FPU. However, if any bit contains zero, and the corresponding condition occurs, then the FPU immediately generates an interrupt so the program can handle the degenerate condition (typically, this would wind up raising in HLA exception; see the *excepts.hhf* header file for the exception values).

Bit zero corresponds to an invalid operation error. This generally occurs as the result of a programming error. Problems that raise the invalid operation exception include pushing more than eight items onto the stack or attempting to pop an item off an empty stack, taking the square root of a negative number, or loading a non-empty register.

Bit one masks the *denormalized* interrupt that occurs whenever you try to manipulate denormalized values. Denormalized exceptions occur when you load arbitrary extended precision values into the FPU or work with very small numbers just beyond the range of the FPU's capabilities. Normally, you would probably *not* enable this exception. If you enable this exception and the FPU generates this interrupt, the HLA run-time system raises the ex.fDenormal exception.

Bit two masks the *zero divide* exception. If this bit contains zero, the FPU will generate an interrupt if you attempt to divide a non-zero value by zero. If you do not enable the zero division exception, the FPU will produce NaN (not a number) whenever you perform a zero division. It's probably a good idea to enable this exception by programming a zero into this bit. Note that if your program generates this interrupt, the HLA run-time system will raise the ex.fDivByZero exception.

Bit three masks the *overflow* exception. The FPU will raise the overflow exception if a calculation overflows or if you attempt to store a value that is too large to fit into the destination operand (e.g., storing a large extended precision value into a single precision variable). If you enable this exception and the FPU generates this interrupt, the HLA run-time system raises the ex.fOverflow exception.

Bit four, if set, masks the *underflow* exception. Underflow occurs when the result is too *small* to fit in the destination operand. Like overflow, this exception can occur whenever you store a small extended precision value into a smaller variable (single or double precision) or when the result of a computation is too small for extended precision. If you enable this exception and the FPU generates this interrupt, the HLA run-time system raises the ex.fUnderflow exception.

Bit five controls whether the *precision* exception can occur. A precision exception occurs whenever the FPU produces an imprecise result, generally the result of an internal rounding operation. Although many operations will produce an exact result, many more will not. For example, dividing one by ten will produce an inexact result. Therefore, this bit is usually one because inexact results are very common. If you enable this exception and the FPU generates this interrupt, the HLA run-time system raises the ex.InexactResult exception.

Bits six and thirteen through fifteen in the control register are currently undefined and reserved for future use. Bit seven is the interrupt enable mask, but it is only active on the 80x87 FPU; a zero in this bit enables 80x87 interrupts and a one disables FPU interrupts.

The FPU provides two instructions, fldcw (load control word) and fstcw (store control word), that let you load and store the contents of the control register. The single operand to these instructions must be a 16-bit memory location. The fldcw instruction loads the control register from the specified memory location, fstcw stores the control register into the specified memory location. The syntax for these instructions is

```
fldcw( mem16 );
fstcw( mem16 );
```

Here's some example code that sets the rounding control to "truncate result" and sets the rounding precision to 24 bits:

```
static
    fcw16: word;
        .
        .
        .
    fstcw( fcw16 );
    mov( fcw16, ax );
    and( $f0ff, ax );      // Clears bits 8-11.
    or( $0c00, ax );       // Rounding control=%11, Precision = %00.
    mov( ax, fcw16 );
    fldcw( fcw16 );
```

6.6.1.3 The FPU Status Register

The FPU status register provides the status of the coprocessor at the instant you read it. The FSTSW instruction stores the 16-bit floating point status register into a word variable. The status register is a 16-bit register; its layout appears in Figure 6-3.

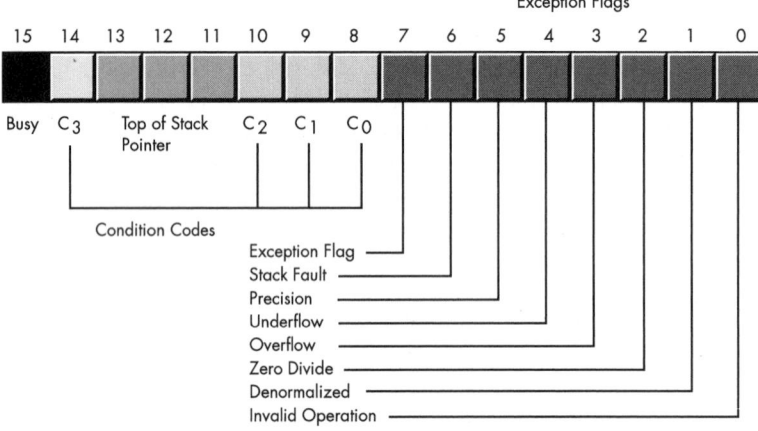

Figure 6-3: The FPU Status Register.

Bits zero through five are the exception flags. These bits are appear in the same order as the exception masks in the control register. If the corresponding condition exists, then the bit is set. These bits are independent of the exception masks in the control register. The FPU sets and clears these bits regardless of the corresponding mask setting.

Bit six indicates a *stack fault*. A stack fault occurs whenever there is a stack overflow or underflow. When this bit is set, the C_1 condition code bit determines whether there was a stack overflow (C_1=1) or stack underflow (C_1=0) condition.

Bit seven of the status register is set if *any* error condition bit is set. It is the logical OR of bits zero through five. A program can test this bit to quickly determine if an error condition exists.

Bits 8, 9, 10, and 14 are the coprocessor condition code bits. Various instructions set the condition code bits, as shown in Tables 6-10 and 6-11, respectively.

Table 6-10: FPU Condition Code Bits

Instruction	Condition Code Bits				Condition
	C3	C2	C1	C0	
fcom,	0	0	X	0	ST>source
fcomp,	0	0	X	1	ST<source
fcompp,	1	0	X	0	ST=source
ficom,	1	1	X	1	ST or source
ficomp					undefined
ftst	0	0	X	0	ST is positive
	0	0	X	1	ST is negative
	1	0	X	0	ST is zero (+ or -)
	1	1	X	1	ST is uncomparable
fxam	0	0	0		+ Unnormalized
	0	0	1	0	-Unnormalized
	0	1	0	0	+Normalized
	0	1	1	0	-Normalized
	1	0	0	0	+0
	1	0	1	0	-0
	1	1	0	0	+Denormalized
	1	1	1	0	-Denormalized
	0	0	0	1	+NaN
	0	0	1	1	-NaN
	0	1	0	1	+Infinity
	0	1	1	1	-Infinity
	1	X	X	1	Empty register
fucom,	0	0	X	0	ST > source
fucomp,	0	0	X	1	ST < source
fucompp	1	0	X	0	ST = source
	1	1	X	1	Unordered
	X = Don't care				

Table 6-11: Condition Code Interpretations

Instructions	Condition Code Bits			
	C0	C3	C2	C1
fcom, fcomp, fcmpp, ftst, fucom, fucomp, fucompp, ficom, ficomp	Result of comparison. See previous table.	Result of comparison. See previous table.	Operands are not comparable.	Result of comparison. See previous table. Also denotes stack overflow/underflow if stack exception bit is set.
fxam	See previous table.	See previous table.	See previous table.	Sign of result, or stack overflow/underflow (if stack exception bit is set).
fprem, fprem1	Bit 2 of remainder	Bit 0 of remainder	0- reduction done. 1- reduction incomplete.	Bit 1 of remainder of stack overflow/underflow (if stack exception bit is set).

Table 6-11: Condition Code Interpretations

Instructions	Condition Code Bits			
fist, fbstp, frndint, fst, fstp, fadd, fmul, fdiv, fdivr, fsub, fsubr, fscale, fsqrt, fpatan, f2xm1, fyl2x, fyl2xp1	Undefined	Undefined	Undefined	Round up occurred or stack overflow/underflow (if stack exception bit is set).
fptan, fsin, fcos, fsincos	Undefined	Undefined	0- reduction done. 1- reduction incomplete.	Round up occurred or stack overflow/underflow (if stack exception bit is set).
fchs, fabs, fxch, fincstp, fdecstp, *constant loads*, fxtract, fld, fild, fbld, fstp (80 bit)	Undefined	Undefined	Undefined	Zero result or stack overflow/underflow (if stack exception bit is set).
fldenv, fstor	Restored from memory operand.	Restored from memory operand.	Restored from memory operand.	Restored from memory operand.
fldcw, fstenv, fstcw, fstsw, fclex	Undefined	Undefined	Undefined	Undefined
finit, fsave	Cleared to zero.	Cleared to zero.	Cleared to zero.	Cleared to zero.

Bits 11-13 of the FPU status register provide the register number of the top of stack. During computations, the FPU adds (modulo 8) the *logical* register numbers supplied by the programmer to these three bits to determine the *physical* register number at runtime.

Bit 15 of the status register is the *busy* bit. It is set whenever the FPU is busy. Most programs will have little reason to access this bit.

6.6.2 FPU Data Types

The FPU supports seven different data types: three integer types, a packed decimal type, and three floating point types. The integer type provides for 64-bit integers, although it is often faster to do the 64-bit arithmetic using the integer unit of the CPU (see the chapter on advanced arithmetic). Certainly it is faster to do 16-bit and 32-bit integer arithmetic using the standard integer registers. The packed decimal type provides a 17-digit signed decimal (BCD) integer. The primary purpose of the BCD format is to convert between strings and floating point values. The remaining three data types are the 32-bit, 64-bit, and 80-bit floating point data types we've looked at so far. The 80x87 data types appear in Figures 6-4, 6-5, and 6-6.

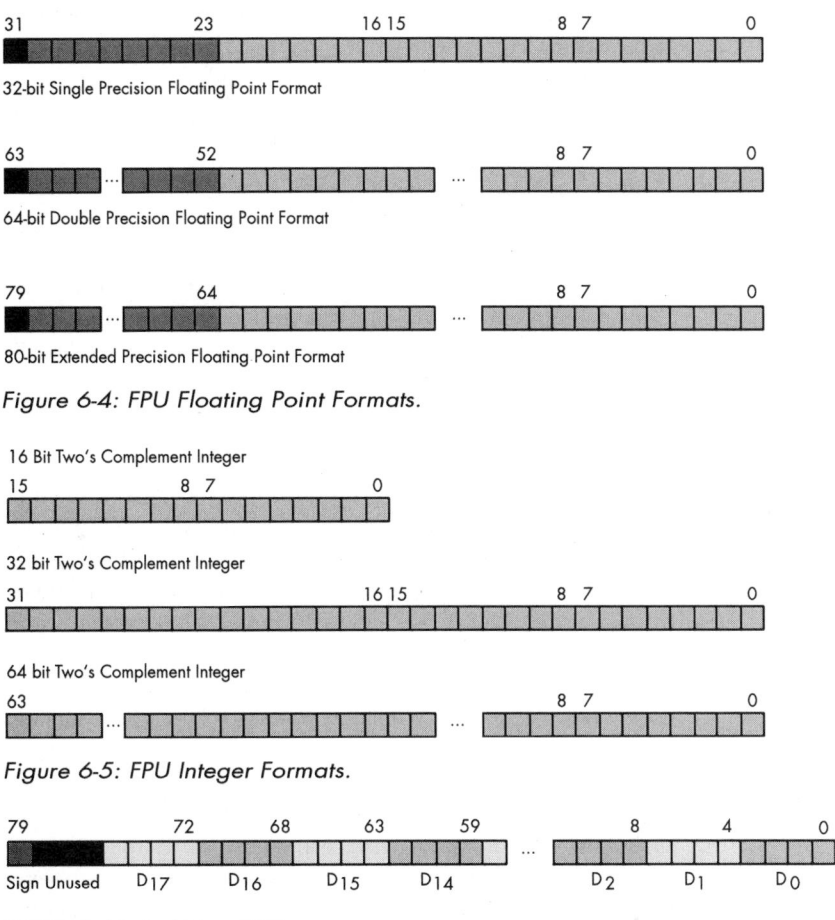

Figure 6-4: FPU Floating Point Formats.

Figure 6-5: FPU Integer Formats.

Figure 6-6: FPU Packed Decimal Format.

The FPU generally stores values in a *normalized* format. When a floating point number is normalized, the H.O. bit of the mantissa is always one. In the 32- and 64-bit floating point formats, the FPU does not actually store this bit, the FPU always assumes that it is one. Therefore, 32- and 64-bit floating point numbers are always normalized. In the extended precision 80-bit floating point format, the FPU does *not* assume that the H.O. bit of the mantissa is one; the H.O. bit of the mantissa appears as part of the string of bits.

Normalized values provide the greatest precision for a given number of bits. However, there is a large number of non-normalized values that we *cannot* represent with the 80-bit format. These values are very close to zero and represent the set of values whose mantissa H.O. bit is not zero. The FPUs support a special 80-bit form known as *denormalized* values. Denormalized values allow the FPU to encode very small values it cannot encode using normalized values, but at a price. Denormalized values offer fewer bits of precision than normalized values. Therefore, using denormalized values in a computation may introduce some slight inaccuracy into a computation. Of course, this is always better than underflowing the denormalized value to zero (which could make the computation even less accurate), but you must keep in mind that if you work with very small values you may lose some accuracy in your computations. Note that the FPU status register contains a bit you can use to detect when the FPU uses a denormalized value in a computation.

6.6.3   The FPU Instruction Set

The FPU adds over 80 new instructions to the 80x86 instruction set. We can classify these instructions as data movement instructions, conversions, arithmetic instructions, comparisons, constant instructions, transcendental instructions, and miscellaneous instructions. The following sections describe each of the instructions in these categories.

6.6.4   FPU Data Movement Instructions

The data movement instructions transfer data between the internal FPU registers and memory. The instructions in this category are fld, fst, fstp, and fxch. The fld instruction always pushes its operand onto the floating point stack. The fstp instruction always pops the top of stack after storing the top of stack. The remaining instructions do not affect the number of items on the stack.

6.6.4.1   The FLD Instruction

The fld instruction loads a 32-bit, 64-bit, or 80-bit floating point value onto the stack. This instruction converts 32- and 64-bit operands to an 80-bit extended precision value before pushing the value onto the floating point stack.

The fld instruction first decrements the top of stack (TOS) pointer (bits 11 through 13 of the status register) and then stores the 80-bit value in the physical register specified by the new TOS pointer. If the source operand of the FLD instruction is a floating point data register, STi, then the actual register the FPU uses for the load operation is the register number *before* decrementing the TOS pointer. Therefore, "fld(st0);" duplicates the value on the top of the stack.

The fld instruction sets the stack fault bit if stack overflow occurs. It sets the denormalized exception bit if you load an 80-bit denormalized value. It sets the invalid operation bit if you attempt to load an empty floating point register onto the top of stack (or perform some other invalid operation). Examples:

```
fld( st1 );
fld( real32_variable );
fld( real64_variable );
fld( real80_variable );
fld( (type real64 [ebx]) );
fld( real_constant );
```

Note that there is no way to directly load a 32-bit integer register onto the floating point stack, even if that register contains a real32 value. To accomplish this, you must first store the integer register into a memory location then you can push that memory location onto the FPU stack using the fld instruction. E.g.,

```
        mov( eax, tempReal32 );      // Save REAL32 value in EAX to memory.
        fld( tempReal32 );           // Push that real value onto the FPU stack.
```

NOTE *Loading a constant via* fld *is actually an HLA extension. The FPU doesn't support this instruction type. HLA creates a* real80 *object in the constants segment and uses the address of this memory object as the true operand for* fld.

6.6.4.2 The FST and FSTP Instructions

The fst and fstp instructions copy the value on the top of the floating point register stack to another floating point register or to a 32-, 64-, or 80-bit memory variable. When copying data to a 32- or 64-bit memory variable, the 80-bit extended precision value on the top of stack is rounded to the smaller format as specified by the rounding control bits in the FPU control register.

The fstp instruction pops the value off the top of stack when moving it to the destination location. It does this by incrementing the top of stack pointer in the status register after accessing the data in ST0. If the destination operand is a floating point register, the FPU stores the value at the specified register number *before* popping the data off the top of the stack.

Executing an "fstp(st0);" instruction effectively pops the data off the top of stack with no data transfer. Examples:

```
        fst( real32_variable );
        fst( real64_variable );
        fst( realArray[ ebx*8 ] );
        fst( real80_variable );
        fst( st2 );
        fstp( st1 );
```

The last example preceding effectively pops ST1 while leaving ST0 on the top of the stack.

The fst and fstp instructions will set the stack exception bit if a stack underflow occurs (attempting to store a value from an empty register stack). They will set the precision bit if there is a loss of precision during the store operation (this will occur, for example, when storing an 80-bit extended precision value into a 32- or 64-bit memory variable and there are some bits lost during conversion). They will set the underflow exception bit when storing an 80-bit value into a 32- or 64-bit memory variable, but the value is too small to fit into the destination operand. Likewise, these instructions will set the overflow exception bit if the value on the top of stack is too big to fit into a 32- or 64-bit memory variable. The fst and fstp instructions set the denormalized flag when you try to store a denormalized value into an 80-bit register or variable.[3] They set the invalid operation flag if an invalid operation (such as storing into an empty register) occurs. Finally, these instructions set the C1 condition bit if rounding occurs during the store operation (this only occurs when storing into a 32- or 64-bit memory variable and you have to round the mantissa to fit into the destination).

---

[3] Storing a denormalized value into a 32- or 64-bit memory variable will always set the underflow exception bit.

Because of an idiosyncrasy in the FPU instruction set related to the encoding of the instructions, you cannot use the fst *instruction to store data into a* real80 *memory variable. You may, however, store 80-bit data using the* fstp *instruction.*

6.6.4.3 The FXCH Instruction

The fxch instruction exchanges the value on the top of stack with one of the other FPU registers. This instruction takes two forms: one with a single FPU register as an operand, the second without any operands. The first form exchanges the top of stack (TOS) with the specified register. The second form of fxch swaps the top of stack with ST1.

Many FPU instructions, e.g., fsqrt, operate only on the top of the register stack. If you want to perform such an operation on a value that is not on the top of stack, you can use the fxch instruction to swap that register with TOS, perform the desired operation, and then use the fxch to swap the TOS with the original register. The following example takes the square root of ST2:

```
fxch( st2 );
fsqrt();
fxch( st2 );
```

The fxch instruction sets the stack exception bit if the stack is empty. It sets the invalid operation bit if you specify an empty register as the operand. This instruction always clears the C_1 condition code bit.

6.6.5 Conversions

The FPU performs all arithmetic operations on 80 bit real quantities. In a sense, the fld and fst/fstp instructions are conversion instructions because they automatically convert between the internal 80-bit real format and the 32- and 64-bit memory formats. Nonetheless, we'll simply classify them as data movement operations, rather than conversions, because they are moving real values to and from memory. The FPU provides five other instructions that convert to or from integer or binary coded decimal (BCD) format when moving data. These instructions are fild, fist, fistp, fbld, and fbstp.

6.6.5.1 The FILD Instruction

The fild (integer load) instruction converts a 16-, 32-, or 64-bit two's complement integer to the 80-bit extended precision format and pushes the result onto the stack. This instruction always expects a single operand. This operand must be the address of a word, double word, or quad word integer variable. You cannot specify one of the 80x86's 16- or 32-bit general purpose registers. If you want to push an 80x86 general purpose register onto the FPU stack, you must first store it into a memory variable and then use fild to push that value of that memory variable.

The fild instruction sets the stack exception bit and C_1 (accordingly) if stack overflow occurs while pushing the converted value. Examples:

```
fild( word_variable );
fild( dword_val[ ecx*4 ] );
fild( qword_variable );
fild( (type int64 [ebx]) );
```

6.6.5.2   The FIST and FISTP Instructions

The fist and fistp instructions convert the 80-bit extended precision variable on
the top of stack to a 16-, 32-, or 64-bit integer and store the result away into the
memory variable specified by the single operand. These instructions convert the
value on TOS to an integer according to the rounding setting in the FPU control
register (bits 10 and 11). As for the fild instruction, the fist and fistp
instructions will not let you specify one of the 80x86's general purpose 16- or
32-bit registers as the destination operand.

The fist instruction converts the value on the top of stack to an integer and
then stores the result; it does not otherwise affect the floating point register
stack. The fistp instruction pops the value off the floating point register stack
after storing the converted value.

These instructions set the stack exception bit if the floating point register
stack is empty (this will also clear C_1). They set the precision (imprecise
operation) and C_1 bits if rounding occurs (that is, if there is any fractional
component to the value in ST0). These instructions set the underflow exception
bit if the result is too small (i.e., less than one but greater than zero or less than
zero but greater than -1). Examples:

```
fist( word_var[ ebx*2 ] );
fist( qword_var );
fistp( dword_var );
```

Don't forget that these instructions use the rounding control settings to
determine how they will convert the floating point data to an integer during the
store operation. Be default, the rounding control is usually set to "round" mode;
yet most programmers expect fist/fistp to truncate the decimal portion during
conversion. If you want fist/fistp to truncate floating point values when converting them to an integer, you will need to set the rounding control bits appropriately in the floating point control register, e.g.,

```
static
    fcw16:              word;
    fcw16_2:            word;
    IntResult:          int32;

        .
        .
        .

    fstcw( fcw16 );
    mov( fcw16, ax );
    or( $0c00, ax );        // Rounding control=%11 (truncate).
    mov( ax, fcw16_2 );     // Store into memory and reload the ctrl word.
```

```
        fldcw( fcw16_2 );

        fistp( IntResult );        // Truncate ST0 and store as int32 object.

        fldcw( fcw16 );            // Restore original rounding control
```

6.6.5.3   The FBLD and FBSTP Instructions

The fbld and fbstp instructions load and store 80-bit BCD values. The fbld
instruction converts a BCD value to its 80-bit extended precision equivalent and
pushes the result onto the stack. The fbstp instruction pops the extended
precision real value on TOS, converts it to an 80 bit BCD value (rounding
according to the bits in the floating point control register), and stores the
converted result at the address specified by the destination memory operand.
Note that there is no fbst instruction.

The fbld instruction sets the stack exception bit and C_1 if stack overflow
occurs. It sets the invalid operation bit if you attempt to load an invalid BCD
value. The fbstp instruction sets the stack exception bit and clears C_1 if stack
underflow occurs (the stack is empty). It sets the underflow flag under the same
conditions as fist and fistp. Examples:

```
// Assuming fewer than 8 items on the stack, the following
// code sequence is equivalent to an fbst instruction:

        fld( st0 );
        fbstp( tbyte_var );

// The following example easily converts an 80-bit BCD value to
// a 64-bit integer:

        fbld( tbyte_var );
        fist( qword_var );
```

These two instructions are especially useful for converting between string and
floating point formats. See the conversion routines in the HLA Standard Library
for more details.

6.6.6   Arithmetic Instructions

The arithmetic instructions make up a small, but important, subset of the FPU's
instruction set. These instructions fall into two general categories — those that
operate on real values and those that operate on a real and an integer value.

6.6.6.1   The FADD and FADDP Instructions

These two instructions take the following forms:

```
        fadd()
        faddp()
        fadd( st0, sti );
```

```
fadd( sti, sto );
faddp( sto, sti );
fadd( mem_32_64 );
fadd( real_constant );
```

The first two forms are equivalent. They pop the two values on the top of stack, add them, and push their sum back onto the stack.

The next two forms of the fadd instruction, those with two FPU register operands, behave like the 80x86's add instruction. They add the value in the source register operand to the value in the destination register operand. Note that one of the register operands must be ST0.

The faddp instruction with two operands adds ST0 (which must always be the source operand) to the destination operand and then pops ST0. The destination operand must be one of the other FPU registers.

The last form above, fadd with a memory operand, adds a 32- or 64-bit floating point variable to the value in ST0. This instruction will convert the 32- or 64-bit operands to an 80-bit extended precision value before performing the addition. Note that this instruction does *not* allow an 80-bit memory operand.

These instructions can raise the stack, precision, underflow, overflow, denormalized, and illegal operation exceptions, as appropriate. If a stack fault exception occurs, C_1 denotes stack overflow or underflow.

Like fld(real_constant), the fadd(real_constant) instruction is an HLA extension. Note that it creates a 64-bit variable holding the constant value and emits the fadd(mem64) instruction, specifying the read-only object it creates in the constants segment.

6.6.6.2 The FSUB, FSUBP, FSUBR, and FSUBRP Instructions

These four instructions take the following forms:

```
fsub()
fsubp()
fsubr()
fsubrp()

fsub( sto, sti )
fsub( sti, sto );
fsubp( sto, sti );
fsub( mem_32_64 );
fsub( real_constant );

fsubr( sto, sti )
fsubr( sti, sto );
fsubrp( sto, sti );
fsubr( mem_32_64 );
fsubr( real_constant );
```

With no operands, the fsub and fsubp instructions operate identically. They pop ST0 and ST1 from the register stack, compute ST1-ST0, and then push the difference back onto the stack. The fsubr and fsubrp instructions (reverse subtraction) operate in an almost identical fashion, except they compute ST0-ST1 and push that difference.

With two register operands (*source, destination*) the fsub instruction computes *destination := destination - source*. One of the two registers must be ST0. With two registers as operands, the fsubp also computes *destination := destination - source* and then it pops ST0 off the stack after computing the difference. For the fsubp instruction, the source operand must be ST0.

With two register operands, the fsubr and fsubrp instruction work in a similar fashion to fsub and fsubp, except they compute *destination := source - destination*.

The fsub(mem) and fsubr(mem) instructions accept a 32- or 64-bit memory operand. They convert the memory operand to an 80-bit extended precision value and subtract this from ST0 (fsub) or subtract ST0 from this value (fsubr) and store the result back into ST0.

These instructions can raise the stack, precision, underflow, overflow, denormalized, and illegal operation exceptions, as appropriate. If a stack fault exception occurs, C_1 denotes stack overflow or underflow.

Note: the instructions that have real constants as operands aren't true FPU instructions. These are extensions provided by HLA. HLA generates a read-only memory object initialized with the constant's value.

6.6.6.3   The FMUL and FMULP Instructions

The fmul and fmulp instructions multiply two floating point values. These instructions allow the following forms:

```
fmul()
fmulp()

fmul( sti, st0 );
fmul( st0, sti );
fmul( mem_32_64 );
fmul( real_constant );

fmulp( st0, sti );
```

With no operands, fmul and fmulp both do the same thing: They pop ST0 and ST1, multiply these values, and push their product back onto the stack. The fmul instructions with two register operands compute *destination := destination * source*. One of the registers (source or destination) must be ST0.

The fmulp(ST0, STi) instruction computes STi := STi * ST0 and then pops ST0. This instruction uses the value for i before popping ST0. The fmul(mem) instruction requires a 32- or 64-bit memory operand. It converts the specified memory variable to an 80-bit extended precision value and then multiplies ST0 by this value.

These instructions can raise the stack, precision, underflow, overflow, denormalized, and illegal operation exceptions, as appropriate. If rounding occurs during the computation, these instructions set the C_1 condition code bit. If a stack fault exception occurs, C_1 denotes stack overflow or underflow.

NOTE *The instruction that has a real constant as its operand isn't a true FPU instruction. It is an extension provided by HLA (see the note at the end of the previous section for details).*

6.6.6.4   The FDIV, FDIVP, FDIVR, and FDIVRP Instructions

These four instructions allow the following forms:

```
fdiv()
fdivp()
fdivr()
fdivrp()

fdiv( sti, st0 );
fdiv( st0, sti );
fdivp( st0, sti );

fdivr( sti, st0 );
fdivr( st0, sti );
fdivrp( st0, sti );

fdiv( mem_32_64 );
fdivr( mem_32_64 );
fdiv( real_constant );
fdivr( real_constant );
```

With no operands, the fdiv and fdivp instructions pop ST0 and ST1, compute ST1/ST0, and push the result back onto the stack. The fdivr and fdivrp instructions also pop ST0 and ST1 but compute ST0/ST1 before pushing the quotient onto the stack.

With two register operands, these instructions compute the following quotients:

```
fdiv( sti, st0 );          // ST0 := ST0/STi
fdiv( st0, sti );          // STi := STi/ST0
fdivp( st0, sti );         // STi := STi/ST0  then pop ST0
fdivr( st0, sti );         // ST0 := ST0/STi
fdivrp( st0, sti );        // STi := ST0/STi then pop ST0
```

The fdivp and fdivrp instructions also pop ST0 after performing the division operation. The value for i in these two instructions is computed before popping ST0.

These instructions can raise the stack, precision, underflow, overflow, denormalized, zero divide, and illegal operation exceptions, as appropriate. If rounding occurs during the computation, these instructions set the C_1 condition code bit. If a stack fault exception occurs, C_1 denotes stack overflow or underflow.

NOTE *The instructions that have real constants as operands aren't true FPU instructions. These are extensions provided by HLA.*

6.6.6.5 The FSQRT Instruction

The fsqrt routine does not allow any operands. It computes the square root of the value on top of stack (TOS) and replaces ST0 with this result. The value on TOS must be zero or positive, otherwise fsqrt will generate an invalid operation exception.

This instruction can raise the stack, precision, denormalized, and invalid operation exceptions, as appropriate. If rounding occurs during the computation, fsqrt sets the C_1 condition code bit. If a stack fault exception occurs, C_1 denotes stack overflow or underflow.

Example:

```
// Compute Z := sqrt(x**2 + y**2);


        fld( x );              // Load X.
        fld( st0 );            // Duplicate X on TOS.
        fmul();                // Compute X**2.

        fld( y );              // Load Y
        fld( st0 );            // Duplicate Y.
        fmul();                // Compute Y**2.

        fadd();                // Compute X**2 + Y**2.
        fsqrt();               // Compute sqrt( X**2 + Y**2 ).
        fstp( z );             // Store result away into Z.
```

6.6.6.6 The FPREM and FPREM1 Instructions

The fprem and fprem1 instructions compute a *partial remainder*. Intel designed the fprem instruction before the IEEE finalized its floating point standard. In the final draft of the IEEE floating point standard, the definition of fprem was a little different than Intel's original design. Unfortunately, Intel needed to maintain compatibility with the existing software that used the fprem instruction, so it designed a new version to handle the IEEE partial remainder operation, fprem1. You should always use fprem1 in new software you write; therefore we will only discuss fprem1 here, although you use fprem in an identical fashion.

fprem1 computes the *partial* remainder of ST0/ST1. If the difference between the exponents of ST0 and ST1 is less than 64, fprem1 can compute the exact remainder in one operation. Otherwise you will have to execute the fprem1 two or more times to get the correct remainder value. The C_2 condition code bit determines when the computation is complete. Note that fprem1 does *not* pop the two operands off the stack; it leaves the partial remainder in ST0 and the original divisor in ST1 in case you need to compute another partial product to complete the result.

The fprem1 instruction sets the stack exception flag if there aren't two values on the top of stack. It sets the underflow and denormal exception bits if the result is too small. It sets the invalid operation bit if the values on TOS are inappropriate for this operation. It sets the C_2 condition code bit if the partial remainder operation is not complete. Finally, it loads C_3, C_1, and C_0 with bits zero, one, and two of the quotient, respectively.

Example:

```
// Compute Z := X mod Y

        fld( y );
        fld( x );
        repeat

            fprem1();
            fstsw( ax );      // Get condition code bits into AX.
            and( 1, ah );     // See if C2 is set.

        until( @z );          // Repeat until C2 is clear.
        fstp( z );            // Store away the remainder.
        fstp( st0 );          // Pop old Y value.
```

6.6.6.7 The FRNDINT Instruction

The frndint instruction rounds the value on the top of stack (TOS) to the nearest integer using the rounding algorithm specified in the control register.

This instruction sets the stack exception flag if there is no value on the TOS (it will also clear C_1 in this case). It sets the precision and denormal exception bits if there was a loss of precision. It sets the invalid operation flag if the value on the TOS is not a valid number. Note that the result on TOS is still a floating point value, it simply does not have a fractional component.

6.6.6.8 The FABS Instruction

fabs computes the absolute value of ST0 by clearing the mantissa sign bit of ST0. It sets the stack exception bit and invalid operation bits if the stack is empty.

Example:

```
// Compute X := sqrt(abs(x));

        fld( x );
        fabs();
        fsqrt();
        fstp( x );
```

6.6.6.9 The FCHS Instruction

fchs changes the sign of ST0's value by inverting the mantissa sign bit (that is, this is the floating point negation instruction). It sets the stack exception bit and invalid operation bits if the stack is empty. Example:

```
// Compute X := -X if X is positive, X := X if X is negative.

        fld( x );
        fabs();
        fchs();
        fstp( x );
```

6.6.7 Comparison Instructions

The FPU provides several instructions for comparing real values. The fcom, fcomp, and fcompp instructions compare the two values on the top of stack and set the condition codes appropriately. The ftst instruction compares the value on the top of stack with zero.

Generally, most programs test the condition code bits immediately after a comparison. Unfortunately, there are no FPU instructions that test the FPU condition codes. Instead, you use the fstsw instruction to copy the floating point status register into the AX register; then you can use the sahf instruction to copy the AH register into the 80x86's condition code bits. After doing this, you can test the standard 80x86 flags to check for some condition. This technique copies C_0 into the carry flag, C_2 into the parity flag, and C_3 into the zero flag. The sahf instruction does not copy C_1 into any of the 80x86's flag bits.

Because the sahf instruction does not copy any FPU status bits into the sign or overflow flags, you cannot use signed comparison instructions. Instead, use unsigned operations (e.g., seta, setb) when testing the results of a floating point comparison. *Yes, these instructions normally test unsigned values, and floating point numbers are signed values.* However, use the unsigned operations anyway; the fstsw and sahf instructions set the 80x86 flags register as though you had compared unsigned values with the cmp instruction.

The Pentium II and (upward) compatible processors provide an extra set of floating point comparison instructions that directly affect the 80x86 condition code flags. These instructions circumvent having to use fstsw and sahf to copy the FPU status into the 80x86 condition codes. These instructions include fcomi and fcomip. You use them just like the fcom and fcomp instructions except, of course, you do not have to manually copy the status bits to the flags register. Do be aware that these instructions are not available on all processors in common use today (as of 10/1/2002). However, as time passes it may be safe to begin assuming that everyone's CPU supports these instructions. Because this text assumes a minimum Pentium CPU, it will not discuss these two instructions any further.

6.6.7.1 The FCOM, FCOMP, and FCOMPP Instructions

The fcom, fcomp, and fcompp instructions compare ST0 to the specified operand and set the corresponding FPU condition code bits based on the result of the comparison. The legal forms for these instructions are

```
fcom()
fcomp()
fcompp()

fcom( sti )
fcomp( sti )

fcom( mem_32_64 )
fcomp( mem_32_64 )
fcom( real_constant )
fcomp( real_constant )
```

With no operands, fcom, fcomp, and fcompp compare ST0 against ST1 and set the
FPU flags accordingly. In addition, fcomp pops ST0 off the stack and fcompp pops
both ST0 and ST1 off the stack.

With a single register operand, fcom and fcomp compare ST0 against the
specified register. fcomp also pops ST0 after the comparison.

With a 32- or 64-bit memory operand, the fcom and fcomp instructions convert
the memory variable to an 80-bit extended precision value and then compare
ST0 against this value, setting the condition code bits accordingly. fcomp also pops
ST0 after the comparison.

These instructions set C_2 (which winds up in the parity flag) if the two
operands are not comparable (e.g., NaN). If it is possible for an illegal floating
point value to wind up in a comparison, you should check the parity flag for an
error before checking the desired condition (e.g., using HLA's @p and @np
conditions, or by using the setp/setnp instructions).

These instructions set the stack fault bit if there aren't two items on the top
of the register stack. They set the denormalized exception bit if either or both
operands are denormalized. They set the invalid operation flag if either or both
operands are quite NaNs. These instructions always clear the C_1 condition code.

Note: The instructions that have real constants as operands aren't true FPU
instructions. These are extensions provided by HLA. When HLA encounters
such an instruction, it creates a real64 read-only variable in the constants segment
and initializes this variable with the specified constant. Then HLA translates the
instruction to one that specifies a real64 memory operand. *Note that because of the
precision differences (64 bits vs. 80 bits), if you use a constant operand in a floating point
instruction you may not get results that are as precise as you would expect.*

Example of a floating point comparison:

```
fcompp();
fstsw( ax );
sahf();
setb( al );    // AL = true if ST1 < ST0.
        .
        .
        .
```

Note that you cannot compare floating point values in an HLA run-time boolean expression (e.g., within an if statement). You may, however, test the conditions in such statements after a floating point comparison like the sequence above, e.g.,

```
fcompp();
fstsw( ax );
sahf();
if( @b ) then

        << Code that executes if ST1 < ST0 >>

endif;
```

6.6.7.2 The FTST Instruction

The ftst instruction compares the value in ST0 against 0.0. It behaves just like the fcom instruction would if ST1 contained 0.0. Note that this instruction does not differentiate -0.0 from +0.0. If the value in ST0 is either of these values, ftst will set C_3 to denote equality. Note that this instruction does *not* pop ST0 off the stack. Example:

```
ftst();
fstsw( ax );
sahf();
sete( al );                        // Set AL to 1 if TOS = 0.0
```

6.6.8 Constant Instructions

The FPU provides several instructions that let you load commonly used constants onto the FPU's register stack. These instructions set the stack fault, invalid operation, and C_1 flags if a stack overflow occurs; they do not otherwise affect the FPU flags. The specific instructions in this category include:

```
fldz()              ;Pushes +0.0.
fld1()              ;Pushes +1.0.
fldpi()             ;Pushes π.
fldl2t()            ;Pushes log2(10).
fldl2e()            ;Pushes log2(e).
fldlg2()            ;Pushes log10(2).
fldln2()            ;Pushes ln(2).
```

6.6.9 Transcendental Instructions

The FPU provides eight transcendental (log and trigonometric) instructions to compute sin, cos, partial tangent, partial arctangent, 2^x-1, y * $\log_2(x)$, and y * $\log_2(x+1)$. Using various algebraic identities, it is easy to compute most of the other common transcendental functions using these instructions.

6.6.9.1　The F2XM1 Instruction

f2xm1 computes $2^{st0}-1$. The value in ST0 must be in the range -1.0<=ST0<=+1.0. If ST0 is out of range f2xm1 generates an undefined result but raises no exceptions. The computed value replaces the value in ST0. Example:

```
; Compute 10ˣ using the identity: 10ˣ = 2ˣ*lg(10) (lg = log₂).

        fld( x );
        fldl2t();
        fmul();
        f2xm1();
        fld1();
        fadd();
```

Note that f2xm1 computes 2^x-1, which is why the code above adds 1.0 to the result at the end of the computation.

6.6.9.2　The FSIN, FCOS, and FSINCOS Instructions

These instructions pop the value off the top of the register stack and compute the sine, cosine, or both, and push the result(s) back onto the stack. The fsincos pushes the sine followed by the cosine of the original operand; hence it leaves cos(ST0) in ST0 and sin(ST0) in ST1.

These instructions assume ST0 specifies an angle in radians, and this angle must be in the range $-2^{63} < ST0 < +2^{63}$. If the original operand is out of range, these instructions set the C_2 flag and leave ST0 unchanged. You can use the fprem1 instruction, with a divisor of 2π, to reduce the operand to a reasonable range.

These instructions set the stack fault/C_1, precision, underflow, denormalized, and invalid operation flags according to the result of the computation.

6.6.9.3　The FPTAN Instruction

fptan computes the tangent of ST0 and pushes this value and then it pushes 1.0 onto the stack. Like the fsin and fcos instructions, the value of ST0 must be in radians and in the range $-2^{63} < ST0 < +2^{63}$. If the value is outside this range, fptan sets C_2 to indicate that the conversion did not take place. As with the fsin, fcos, and fsincos instructions, you can use the fprem1 instruction to reduce this operand to a reasonable range using a divisor of 2π.

If the argument is invalid (i.e., zero or π radians, which causes a division by zero) the result is undefined and this instruction raises no exceptions. fptan will set the stack fault, precision, underflow, denormal, invalid operation, C_2, and C_1 bits as required by the operation.

6.6.9.4　The FPATAN Instruction

This instruction expects two values on the top of stack. It pops them and computes the following:

$$ST0 = \tan^{-1}(ST1 / ST0)$$

The resulting value is the arctangent of the ratio on the stack expressed in radians. If you have a value you wish to compute the arctangent of, use fld1 to create the appropriate ratio and then execute the fpatan instruction.

This instruction affects the stack fault/C_1, precision, underflow, denormal, and invalid operation bits if an problem occurs during the computation. It sets the C_1 condition code bit if it has to round the result.

6.6.9.5   The FYL2X Instruction

This instruction expects two operands on the FPU stack: y is found in ST1, and x is found in ST0. This function computes:

$$ST0 = ST1 * \log_2(ST0)$$

This instruction has no operands (to the instruction itself). The instruction uses the following syntax:

```
fyl2x();
```

Note that this instruction computes the base two logarithm. Of course, it is a trivial matter to compute the log of any other base by multiplying by the appropriate constant.

6.6.9.6   The FYL2XP1 Instruction

This instruction expects two operands on the FPU stack: y is found in ST1, and x is found in ST0. This function computes:

$$ST0 = ST1 * \log_2(ST0 + 1.0)$$

The syntax for this instruction is

```
fyl2xp1();
```

Otherwise, the instruction is identical to fyl2x.

6.6.10   Miscellaneous Instructions

The FPU includes several additional instructions which control the FPU, synchronize operations, and let you test or set various status bits. These instructions include finit/fninit, fldcw, fstcw, fclex/fnclex, and fstsw.

6.6.10.1   The FINIT and FNINIT Instructions

The finit instruction initializes the FPU for proper operation. Your applications should execute this instruction before executing any other FPU instructions. This instruction initializes the control register to $37F, the status register to zero, and the tag word to $FFFF. The other registers are unaffected. Examples:

```
FINIT();
FNINIT();
```

The difference between finit and fninit is that finit first checks for any pending floating point exceptions before initializing the FPU; fninit does not.

6.6.10.2   The FLDCW and FSTCW Instructions

The fldcw and fstcw instructions require a single 16-bit memory operand:

```
fldcw( mem_16 );
fstcw( mem_16 );
```

These two instructions load the control register from a memory location (fldcw) or store the control word to a 16-bit memory location (fstcw).

When using the fldcw instruction to turn on one of the exceptions, if the corresponding exception flag is set when you enable that exception, the FPU will generate an immediate interrupt before the CPU executes the next instruction. Therefore, you should use the fclex instruction to clear any pending interrupts before changing the FPU exception enable bits.

6.6.10.3   The FCLEX and FNCLEX Instructions

The fclex and fnclex instructions clear all exception bits the stack fault bit, and the busy flag in the FPU status register. Examples:

```
fclex();
fnclex();
```

The difference between these instructions is the same as finit and fninit.

6.6.10.4   The FSTSW and FNSTSW Instructions

```
fstsw( ax )
fnstsw( ax )
fstsw( mem_16 )
fnstsw( mem_16 )
```

These instructions store the FPU status register into a 16-bit memory location or the AX register. These instructions are unusual in the sense that they can copy an FPU value into one of the 80x86 general purpose registers (specifically, AX). Of course, the whole purpose behind allowing the transfer of the status register into AX is to allow the CPU to easily test the condition code register with the sahf instruction. The difference between fstsw and fnstsw is the same as for fclex and fnclex.

6.6.11 Integer Operations

The 80x87 FPUs provide special instructions that combine integer to extended precision conversion along with various arithmetic and comparison operations. These instructions are the following:

```
fiadd( int_16_32 )
fisub( int_16_32 )
fisubr( int_16_32 )
fimul( int_16_32 )
fidiv( int_16_32 )
fidivr( int_16_32 )

ficom( int_16_32 )
ficomp( int_16_32 )
```

These instructions convert their 16- or 32-bit integer operands to an 80-bit extended precision floating point value and then use this value as the source operand for the specified operation. These instructions use ST0 as the destination operand.

6.7 Converting Floating Point Expressions to Assembly Language

Because the FPU register organization is different than the 80x86 integer register set, translating arithmetic expressions involving floating point operands is a little different than the techniques for translating integer expressions. Therefore, it makes sense to spend some time discussing how to manually translate floating point expressions into assembly language.

In one respect, it's actually easier to translate floating point expressions into assembly language. The stack architecture of the Intel FPU eases the translation of arithmetic expressions into assembly language. If you've ever used a Hewlett-Packard calculator, you'll be right at home on the FPU because, like the HP calculator, the FPU uses *reverse polish notation*, or *RPN*, for arithmetic calculations. Once you get used to using RPN, it's actually a bit more convenient for translating expressions because you don't have to worry about allocating temporary variables: They always wind up on the FPU stack.

RPN, as opposed to standard *infix notation*, places the operands before the operator. The following examples give some simple examples of infix notation and the corresponding RPN notation:

infix notation	RPN notation
5 + 6	5 6 +
7 - 2	7 2 -
x * y	x y *
a / b	a b /

An RPN expression like "5 6 +" says "push five onto the stack, push six onto the stack, then pop the value off the top of stack (six) and add it to the new top of stack." Sound familiar? This is exactly what the `fld` and `fadd` instructions do. In fact, you can calculate this using the following code:

```
fld( 5.0 );
fld( 6.0 );
fadd();                    // 11.0 is now on the top of the FPU stack.
```

As you can see, RPN is a convenient notation because it's very easy to translate this code into FPU instructions.

One advantage to RPN (or *postfix notation*) is that it doesn't require any parentheses. The following examples demonstrate some slightly more complex infix to postfix conversions:

infix notation	postfix notation
(x + y) * 2	x y + 2 *
x * 2 - (a + b)	x 2 * a b + -
(a + b) * (c + d)	a b + c d + *

The postfix expression "x y + 2 *" says "push x, then push y; next, add those values on the stack (producing x+y on the stack). Next, push 2 and then multiply the two values (two and x+y) on the stack to produce two times the quantity x+y." Once again, we can translate these postfix expressions directly into assembly language. The following code demonstrates the conversion for each of the above expressions:

```
//          x y + 2 *

fld( x );
fld( y );
fadd();
fld( 2.0 );
fmul();


//          x 2 * a b + -

fld( x );
fld( 2.0 );
fmul();
fld( a );
fld( b );
fadd();
fsub();
```

```
//          a b + c d + *

          fld( a );
          fld( b );
          fadd();
          fld( c );
          fld( d );
          fadd();
          fmul();
```

6.7.1 Converting Arithmetic Expressions to Postfix Notation

Because the process of translating arithmetic expressions into assembly language involves postfix (RPN) notation, converting arithmetic expressions into postfix notation seems like a good place to begin our discussion of floating point expression conversion. This section will concentrate on RPN conversion.

For simple expressions, those involving two operands and a single expression, the translation is trivial. Simply move the operator from the infix position to the postfix position (that is, move the operator from in between the operands to after the second operand). For example, "5 + 6" becomes "5 6 +". Other than separating your operands so you don't confuse them (i.e., is it "5" and "6" or "56"?) there isn't much to converting simple infix expressions into postfix notation.

For complex expressions, the idea is to convert the simple subexpressions into postfix notation and then treat each converted subexpression as a single operand in the remaining expression. The following discussion will surround completed conversions in square brackets so it is easy to see which text needs to be treated as a single operand in the conversion.

As for integer expression conversion, the best place to start is in the innermost parenthetical subexpression and then work your way outward considering precedence, associativity, and other parenthetical subexpressions. As a concrete working example, consider the following expression:

x = ((y-z)*a) - (a + b * c)/3.14159

A possible first translation is to convert the subexpression "(y-z)" into postfix notation:

x = ([y z -] * a) - (a + b * c)/3.14159

Square brackets surround the converted postfix code just to separate it from the infix code. These exist only to make the partial translations more readable. Remember, for the purposes of conversion we will treat the text inside the square brackets as a single operand. Therefore, you would treat "[y z -]" as though it were a single variable name or constant.

The next step is to translate the subexpression "([y z -] * a)" into postfix form. This yields the following:

```
x = [y z - a *] - ( a + b * c )/3.14159
```

Next, we work on the parenthetical expression "(a + b * c)." Because multiplication has higher precedence than addition, we convert "b*c" first:

```
x = [y z - a *] - ( a + [b c *])/3.14159
```

After converting "b*c" we finish the parenthetical expression:

```
x = [y z - a *] - [a b c * +]/3.14159
```

This leaves only two infix operators: subtraction and division. Because division has the higher precedence, we'll convert that first:

```
x = [y z - a *] - [a b c * + 3.14159 /]
```

Finally, we convert the entire expression into postfix notation by dealing with the last infix operation, subtraction:

```
x = [y z - a *] [a b c * + 3.14159 /] -
```

Removing the square brackets to give us true postfix notation yields the following RPN expression:

```
x = y z - a * a b c * + 3.14159 / -
```

Here is another example of an infix to postfix conversion:

```
a = (x * y - z + t)/2.0
```

Step 1: Work inside the parentheses. Because multiplication has the highest precedence, convert that first:

```
a = ( [x y *] - z + t)/2.0
```

Step 2: Still working inside the parentheses, we note that addition and subtraction have the same precedence, so we rely upon associativity to determine what to do next. These operators are left associative, so we must translate the expressions in a left to right order. This means translate the subtraction operator first:

```
a = ( [x y * z -] + t)/2.0
```

Step 3: Now translate the addition operator inside the parentheses. Because this finishes the parenthetical operators, we can drop the parentheses:

```
a = [x y * z - t +]/2.0
```

Step 4: Translate the final infix operator (division). This yields the following:

```
a = [x y * z - t + 2.0 / ]
```

Step 5: Drop the square brackets and we're done:

```
a = x y * z - t + 2.0 /
```

6.7.2 Converting Postfix Notation to Assembly Language

Once you've translated an arithmetic expression into postfix notation, finishing the conversion to assembly language is especially easy. All you have to do is issue an fld instruction whenever you encounter an operand and issue an appropriate arithmetic instruction when you encounter an operator. This section will use the completed examples from the previous section to demonstrate how little there is to this process.

```
x = y z - a * a b c * + 3.14159 / -
```

- Step 1: Convert y to fld(y);
- Step 2: Convert z to fld(z);
- Step 3: Convert "-" to fsub();
- Step 4: Convert a to fld(a);
- Step 5: Convert "*" to fmul();
- Steps 6-n: Continuing in a left-to-right fashion, generate the following code for the expression:

```
        fld( y );
        fld( z );
        fsub();
        fld( a );
        fmul();
        fld( a );
        fld( b );
        fld( c );
        fmul();
        fadd();
        fldpi();        // Loads pi (3.14159)
        fdiv();
        fsub();

        fstp( x );      // Store result away into x.
```

Here's the translation for the second example in the previous section:

```
a = x y * z - t + 2.0 /
        fld( x );
        fld( y );
        fmul();
        fld( z );
        fsub();
        fld( t );
        fadd();
        fld( 2.0 );
        fdiv();


        fstp( a );      // Store result away into a.
```

As you can see, the translation is fairly trivial once you've converted the infix notation to postfix notation. Also note that, unlike integer expression conversion, you don't need any explicit temporaries. It turns out that the FPU stack provides the temporaries for you.[4] For these reasons, conversion of floating point expressions into assembly language is actually easier than converting integer expressions.

6.8   HLA Standard Library Support for Floating Point Arithmetic

The HLA Standard Library provides several routines that support the use of real numbers. In Chapters 1 and 2 you saw, with one exception, how the standard input and output routines operate. This section will not repeat that discussion; see those chapters for more details. One input function that Chapter 2 only mentioned briefly was the stdin.getf function. This section will elaborate on that function. The HLA Standard Library also includes the *math.hhf* module that provides several mathematical functions that the FPU doesn't directly support. This section will discuss those functions, as well.

6.8.1   The stdin.getf and fileio.getf Functions

The stdin.getf function reads a floating point value from the standard input device. It leaves the converted value in ST0 (i.e., on the top of the floating point stack). The only reason Chapter 2 did not discuss this function thoroughly was because you hadn't seen the FPU and FPU registers at that point.

The stdin.getf function accepts the same inputs that "stdin.get(fp_variable);" would except. The only difference between the two is where these functions store the floating point value.

---

[4] Assuming, of course, that your calculations aren't so complex that you exceed the eight-element limitation of the FPU stack.

6.8.2 Trigonometric Functions in the HLA Math Library

The FPU provides a small handful of trigonometric functions. It does not, however, support the full range of trig functions. The HLA *math.hhf* module fills in many of the missing functions. The trigonometric functions that HLA provides include

- math.acos(arc cosine)
- math.acot (arc cotangent)
- math.acsc(arc cosecant)
- math.asec (arc secant)
- math.asin (arc sin)
- math.cot (cotangent)
- math.csc (cosecant)
- math.sec (secant)

The HLA Standard Library actually provides five different routines you can call for each of these functions. For example, the prototypes for the first four math.cot (cotangent) routines are:

```
procedure cot32( r32: real32 );
procedure cot64( r64: real64 );
procedure cot80( r80: real80 );
procedure _cot();
```

The first three routines push their parameter onto the FPU stack and compute the cotangent of the result. The fourth routine above (math._cot) computes the cotangent of the value currently held in ST0.

The fifth routine is actually an overloaded procedure that calls one of the four routines above depending on the parameter. This call uses the following syntax:

```
math.cot();          // Calls _cot() to compute cot(ST0).
math.cot( r32 );     // Calls cot32 to compute the cotangent of r32.
math.cot( r64 );     // Calls cot64 to compute the cotangent of r64.
math.cot( r80 );     // Calls cot80 to compute the cotangent of r80.
```

Using this fifth form is probably preferable because it is much more convenient. Note that there is no efficiency loss when you use math.cot rather than one of the other cotangent routines. HLA actually translates this statement directly into one of the other calls.

The HLA trigonometric functions that require an angle expressed in radians, not degrees. Keep in mind that some of these functions produce undefined results for certain input values. If you've enabled exceptions on the FPU, these functions will raise the appropriate FPU exception if an error occurs.

6.8.3 Exponential and Logarithmic Functions in the HLA Math Library

The HLA *math.hhf* module provides several exponential and logarithmic functions in addition to the trigonometric functions. Like the trig functions, the exponential and logarithmic functions provide five different interfaces to each function depending on the size and location of the parameter. Table 6-12 lists the functions that *math.hhf* supports.

Table 6-12: Functions That Support *math.hhf*

Function	Description
math.TwoToX	Raises 2.0 to the specified power.
math.TenToX	Raises 10.0 to the specified power.
math.exp	Raises e [2.718281828...] to the specified power.
math.YtoX	Raises first parameter to the power specified by the second parameter.
math.log	Computes base 10 logarithm.
math.ln	Computes base e logarithm.

Except for the math.YtoX function, all these functions provide the same sort of interface as the math.cot function mentioned in the previous section. For example, the math.exp function provides the following prototypes:

```
procedure math.exp32( r32: real32 );
procedure math.exp64( r64: real64 );
procedure math.exp80( r80: real80 );
procedure math._exp();
```

The math.exp function, by itself, automatically calls one of the above functions depending on the parameter type (and presence of a parameter):

```
math.exp();          // Calls _exp() to compute exp(ST0).
math.exp( r32 );     // Calls exp32 to compute the e**r32.
math.exp( r64 );     // Calls exp64 to compute the e**r64.
math.exp( r80 );     // Calls exp80 to compute the e**r80.
```

The lone exception to the preceding is the math.YtoX function. math.YtoX has its own rules because it has two parameters rather than one (Y and X). math.YtoX provides the following function prototypes:

```
procedure math.YtoX32( y: real32; x: real32 );
procedure math.YtoX64( y: real64; x: real64 );
procedure Ymath.toX80( y: real80; x: real80 );
procedure math._YtoX();
```

The math._YtoX function computes ST1**ST0 (i.e., ST1 raised to the ST0 power).

The math.YtoX function provides the following interface:

```
math.YtoX();                // Calls _YtoX() to compute exp(ST0).
math.YtoX( y32, x32);       // Calls YtoX32 to compute y32**x32.
math.YtoX( y64, x64 );      // Calls YtoX64 to compute y64**x64.
math.YtoX( y80, x80 );      // Calls YtoX80 to compute y80**x80.
```

6.9   Putting It All Together

This chapter finished the presentation of the integer arithmetic instructions on the 80x86. Then it demonstrated how to convert expressions from a high level language syntax into assembly language. This chapter concluded by teaching you a few assembly language tricks you will commonly find in programs. By the conclusion of this chapter you are (hopefully) in a position where you can easily evaluate arithmetic expressions in your assembly language programs.

Between the FPU and the HLA Standard Library, floating point arithmetic is actually quite simple. In this chapter you learned about the floating point instruction set and you learned how to convert arithmetic expressions involving real arithmetic into a sequence of floating point instructions. This chapter also presented several transcendental functions that the HLA Standard Library provides. Armed with the information from this chapter, you should be able to deal with floating point expressions just as easily as integer expressions.

7

LOW LEVEL CONTROL STRUCTURES

7.1 Chapter Overview

This chapter discusses "pure" assembly language control statements. You'll need to master these low level control structures before you can really claim to be an assembly language programmer. By the time you finish this chapter, you should be able to stop using most of HLA's high level control statements and synthesize them using low level 80x86 machine instructions.

The last section of this chapter discusses *hybrid* control structures that combine the features of HLA's high level control statements with the 80x86 control instructions. These combine the power and efficiency of the low level control statements with the readability of high level control statements. Advanced assembly programmers may want to use these hybrid statements to improve their programs' readability without sacrificing efficiency.

7.2 Low Level Control Structures

Until now, most of the control structures you've seen and have used in your programs are similar to the control structures found in high level languages like Pascal, C++, and Ada. While these control structures make learning assembly language easy they are not true assembly language statements. Instead, the HLA compiler translates these control structures into a sequence of "pure" machine instructions that achieve the same result as the high level control structures. This text uses the high level control structures to allow you to learn assembly language without having to learn everything all at once. Now, however, it's time to put aside these high level control structures and learn how to write your programs in *real* assembly language, using low level control structures.

7.3   Statement Labels

HLA low level control structures make extensive use of *labels* within your code. A low level control structure usually transfers control from one point in your program to another point in your program. You typically specify the destination of such a transfer using a *statement label*. A statement label consists of a valid (unique) HLA identifier and a colon, e.g.,

---

aLabel:

Of course, like procedure, variable, and constant identifiers, you should attempt to choose descriptive and meaningful names for your labels. The example identifier above, aLabel, is hardly descriptive or meaningful.

Statement labels have one important attribute that differentiates them from most other identifiers in HLA: you don't have to declare a label before you use it. This is important, because low level control structures must often transfer control to a label at some point later in the code, therefore the label may not be defined at the point you reference it.

You can do three things with labels: transfer control to a label via a jmp (GOTO) instruction, call a label via the call instruction, and take the address of a label. There is very little else you can directly do with a label (of course, there is very little else you would want to do with a label, so this is hardly a restriction). The program in Listing 7-1 demonstrates two ways to take the address of a label in your program and print out the address (using the lea instruction and using the "&" address-of operator):

Listing 7-1: Displaying the Address of Statement Labels in a Program.

```
program labelDemo;
#include( "stdlib.hhf" );

begin labelDemo;

    lbl1:

        lea( ebx, lbl1 );
    mov( &lbl2, eax );
        stdout.put( "&lbl1=$", ebx, "&lbl2=", eax, nl );
```

```
        lbl2:

end labelDemo;
```

HLA also allows you to initialize double word variables with the addresses of statement labels. However, there are some restrictions on labels that appear in the initialization portions of variable declarations. The most important restriction is that you must define the statement label at the same lex level as the variable declaration. That is, if you reference a statement label in the initializer of a variable declaration appearing in the main program, the statement label must also be in the main program. Conversely, if you take the address of a statement label in a local variable declaration, that symbol must appear in the same procedure as the local variable. Listing 7-2 demonstrates the use of statement labels in variable initialization:

Listing 7-2: Initializing DWORD Variables with the Address of Statement Labels.

```
program labelArrays;
#include( "stdlib.hhf" );

static
    labels:dword[2] := [ &lbl1, &lbl2 ];

    procedure hasLabels;
    static
        stmtLbls: dword[2] := [ &label1, &label2 ];

    begin hasLabels;

        label1:

            stdout.put
            (
                "stmtLbls[0]= $", stmtLbls[0], nl,
                "stmtLbls[1]= $", stmtLbls[4], nl
            );

        label2:

    end hasLabels;

begin labelArrays;

    hasLabels();
    lbl1:

        stdout.put( "labels[0]= $", labels[0], " labels[1]=", labels[4], nl );
```

```
lbl2:

end labelArrays;
```

Once in a while, you'll need to refer to a label that is not within the current procedure. The need for this is sufficiently rare that this text will not describe all the details. However, you can look up the details on HLA's label declaration section in the HLA documentation, should the need to do this ever arise.

7.4 Unconditional Transfer of Control (JMP)

The jmp (jump) instruction unconditionally transfers control to another point in the program. There are three forms of this instruction: a direct jump, and two indirect jumps. These instructions take one of the following three forms:

```
jmp label;
jmp( reg32 );
jmp( mem32 );
```

For the first (direct) jump above, you normally specify the target address using a statement label (see the previous section for a discussion of statement labels). The statement label is usually on the same line as an executable machine instruction or appears by itself on a line preceding an executable machine instruction. The direct jump instruction is the most common of these three forms. It is completely equivalent to a GOTO statement in a high level language.[1] Example:

```
        << statements >>
        jmp laterInPgm;

              .

              .

              .

laterInPgm:
        << statements >>
```

The second form of the jmp instruction above, "jmp(reg32);", is a *register indirect* jump instruction. This instruction transfers control to the instruction whose address appears in the specified 32-bit general purpose register. To use this form of the jmp instruction you must load a 32-bit register with the address of some machine instruction prior to the execution of the jmp. You could use this instruction to implement a state machine by loading a register with the address of some label at various points throughout your program; then a single indirect jump at a common point in the program can transfer control to the label whose address you've loaded into the register. The short sample program in Listing 7-3 demonstrates how you could use the jmp in this manner.

---

[1] Unlike high level languages, where your instructors usually forbid you to use GOTO statements, you will find that the use of the jmp instruction in assembly language is absolutely essential.

Listing 7-3: Using Register Indirect JMP Instructions.

```
program regIndJmp;
#include( "stdlib.hhf" );

static
    i:int32;

begin regIndJmp;

    // Read an integer from the user and set EBX to
    // denote the success or failure of the input.

    try

        stdout.put( "Enter an integer value between 1 and 10: " );
        stdin.get( i );
        mov( i, eax );
        if( eax in 1..10 ) then

            mov( &GoodInput, ebx );

        else

            mov( &valRange, ebx );

        endif;

      exception( ex.ConversionError )

        mov( &convError, ebx );

      exception( ex.ValueOutOfRange )

        mov( &valRange, ebx );

    endtry;

    // Okay, transfer control to the appropriate
    // section of the program that deals with
    // the input.

    jmp( ebx );

    valRange:
        stdout.put( "You entered a value outside the range 1..10" nl );
        jmp Done;

    convError:
```

```
            stdout.put( "Your input contained illegal characters" nl );
            jmp Done;

        GoodInput:
            stdout.put( "You entered the value ", i, nl );

        Done:


end regIndJmp;
```

The third form of the jmp instruction is a memory indirect jmp. This form of the jmp instruction fetches a double word value from the specified memory location and transfers control to the instruction at the address specified by the contents of the memory location. This is similar to the register indirect jmp except the address appears in a memory location rather than in a register. Listing 7-4 demonstrates a rather trivial use of this form of the jmp instruction:

Listing 7-4: Using Memory Indirect JMP Instructions.

```
program memIndJmp;
#include( "stdlib.hhf" );

static
    LabelPtr:dword := &stmtLabel;

begin memIndJmp;

    stdout.put( "Before the JMP instruction" nl );
    jmp( LabelPtr );

        stdout.put( "This should not execute" nl );

    stmtLabel:

        stdout.put( "After the LabelPtr label in the program" nl );

end memIndJmp;
```

CAUTION   *Unlike the HLA high level control structures, the low level jmp instructions can get you into a lot of trouble. In particular, if you do not initialize a register with the address of a valid instruction and you jump indirect through that register, the results are undefined (though this will usually cause a general protection fault). Similarly, if you do not initialize a double word variable with the address of a legal instruction, jumping indirect through that memory location will probably crash your program.*

7.5 The Conditional Jump Instructions

Although the jmp instruction provides transfer of control, it does not allow you to make any serious decisions. The 80x86's conditional jump instructions handle this task. The conditional jump instructions are the basic tool for creating loops and other conditionally executable statements like the if..endif statement.

The conditional jumps test one or more flags to see if they match some particular pattern (just like the setcc instructions). If the flag settings match, the instruction transfers to the target location. If the match fails, the CPU ignores the conditional jump and execution continues with the next instruction. Some conditional jump instructions simply test the setting of the sign, carry, overflow, and zero flags. For example, after the execution of an shl instruction, you could test the carry flag to determine if the shl shifted a one out of the H.O. bit of its operand. Likewise, you could test the zero flag after a test instruction to see if any specified bits were one. Most of the time, however, you will probably execute a conditional jump after a cmp instruction. The cmp instruction sets the flags so that you can test for less than, greater than, equality, and so on.

The conditional jmp instructions take the following form:

Jcc label;

The "*cc*" in Jcc indicates that you must substitute some character sequence that specifies the type of condition to test. These are the same characters the setcc instruction uses. For example, "js" stands for jump if the sign flag is set. A typical js instruction looks like this:

---

js ValueIsNegative;

In this example, the js instruction transfers control to the ValueIsNegative statement label if the sign flag is currently set; control falls through to the next instruction following the js instruction if the sign flag is clear.

Unlike the unconditional jmp instruction, the conditional jump instructions do not provide an indirect form. The only form they allow is a branch to a statement label in your program. Conditional jump instructions have a restriction that the target label must be within 32,768 bytes of the jump instruction. However, because this generally corresponds to somewhere between 8,000 and 32,000 machine instructions, it is unlikely you will ever encounter this restriction.

Note: Intel's documentation defines various synonyms or instruction aliases for many conditional jump instructions. Tables 7-1, 7-2, and 7-3 list all the aliases for a particular instruction. These tables also list out the opposite branches. You'll soon see the purpose of the opposite branches.

Table 7-1: JCC Instructions That Test Flags

Instruction	Description	Condition	Aliases	Opposite
JC	Jump if carry	Carry = 1	JB, JNAE	JNC
JNC	Jump if no carry	Carry = 0	JNB, JAE	JC
JZ	Jump if zero	Zero = 1	JE	JNZ
JNZ	Jump if not zero	Zero = 0	JNE	JZ
JS	Jump if sign	Sign = 1		JNS
JNS	Jump if no sign	Sign = 0		JS
JO	Jump if overflow	Ovrflw=1		JNO
JNO	Jump if no overflow	Ovrflw=0	JO	
JP	Jump if parity	Parity = 1	JPE	JNP
JPE	Jump if parity even	Parity = 1	JP	JPO
JNP	Jump if no parity	Parity = 0	JPO	JP
JPO	Jump if parity odd	Parity = 0	JNP	JPE

Table 7-2: JCC Instructions for Unsigned Comparisons

Instruction	Description	Condition	Aliases	Opposites
JA	Jump if above (>)	Carry=0, Zero=0	JNBE	JNA
JNBE	Jump if not below or equal (not <=)	Carry=0, Zero=0	JA	JBE
JAE	Jump if above or equal (>=)	Carry = 0	JNC, JNB	JNAE
JNB	Jump if not below (not <)	Carry = 0	JNC, JAE	JB
JB	Jump if below (<)	Carry = 1	JC, JNAE	JNB
JNAE	Jump if not above or equal (not >=)	Carry = 1	JC, JB	JAE
JBE	Jump if below or equal (<=)	Carry = 1 or Zero = 1	JNA	JNBE
JNA	Jump if not above (not >)	Carry = 1 or Zero = 1	JBE	JA

Table 7-2: JCC Instructions for Unsigned Comparisons

Instruction	Description	Condition	Aliases	Opposites
JE	Jump if equal (=)	Zero = 1	JZ	JNE
JNE	Jump if not equal (¦)	Zero = 0	JNZ	JE

Table 7-3: JCC Instructions for Signed Comparisons

Instruction	Description	Condition	Aliases	Opposite
JG	Jump if greater (>)	Sign = Ovrflw or Zero=0	JNLE	JNG
JNLE	Jump if not less than or equal (not <=)	Sign = Ovrflw or Zero=0	JG	JLE
JGE	Jump if greater than or equal (>=)	Sign = Ovrflw	JNL	JGE
JNL	Jump if not less than (not <)	Sign = Ovrflw	JGE	JL
JL	Jump if less than (<)	Sign <> Ovrflw	JNGE	JNL
JNGE	Jump if not greater or equal (not >=)	Sign <> Ovrflw	JL	JGE
JLE	Jump if less than or equal (<=)	Sign <> Ovrflw or Zero = 1	JNG	JNLE
JNG	Jump if not greater than (not >)	Sign <> Ovrflw or Zero = 1	JLE	JG
JE	Jump if equal (=)	Zero = 1	JZ	JNE
JNE	Jump if not equal (¦)	Zero = 0	JNZ	JE

One brief comment about the "opposites" column is in order. In many instances you will need to be able to generate the opposite of a specific branch instructions (examples appear later in this chapter). With only two exceptions, a very simple rule completely describes how to generate an opposite branch:

- If the second letter of the J*cc* instruction is not an "n", insert an "n" after the "j". E.g., je becomes jne and jl becomes jnl.

- If the second letter of the J*cc* instruction is an "n", then remove that "n" from the instruction. E.g., jng becomes jg and jne becomes je.

The two exceptions to this rule are jpe (jump if parity is even) and jpo (jump if parity is odd). These exceptions cause few problems because (a) you'll hardly ever need to test the parity flag, and (b) you can use the aliases jp and jnp synonyms for jpe and jpo. The "N/No N" rule applies to jp and jnp.

Though you *know* that jge is the opposite of jl, get in the habit of using jnl rather than jge as the opposite jump instruction for jl. It's too easy in an important situation to start thinking "greater is the opposite of less" and substitute jg instead. You can avoid this confusion by always using the "N/No N" rule.

The 80x86 conditional jump instructions give you the ability to split program flow into one of two paths depending upon some condition. Suppose you want to increment the AX register if BX is equal to CX. You can accomplish this with the following code:

```
            cmp( bx, cx );
            jne SkipStmts;
            inc( ax );
SkipStmts:
```

The trick is to use the *opposite* branch to skip over the instructions you want to execute if the condition is true. Always use the "opposite branch (N/no N)" rule given earlier to select the opposite branch.

You can also use the conditional jump instructions to synthesize loops. For example, the following code sequence reads a sequence of characters from the user and stores each character in successive elements of an array until the user presses the ENTER key (carriage return):

```
            mov( 0, edi );
RdLnLoop:
            stdin.getc();              // Read a character into the AL register.
            mov( al, Input[ edi ] );   // Store away the character.
            inc( edi );                // Move on to the next character.
            cmp( al, stdio.cr );       // See if the user pressed Enter.
            jne RdLnLoop;
```

Like the set*cc* instructions, the conditional jump instructions come in two basic categories — those that test specific processor flags (e.g., jz, jc, jno) and those that test some condition (less than, greater than, and so on). When testing a condition, the conditional jump instructions almost always follow a cmp instruction. The cmp instruction sets the flags so you can use a ja, jae, jb, jbe, je, or jne instruction to test for unsigned less than, less than or equal, equality, inequality, greater than, or greater than or equal. Simultaneously, the cmp instruction sets the flags so you can also do a signed comparison using the jl, jle, je, jne, jg, and jge instructions.

The conditional jump instructions only test flags; they do not affect any of the 80x86 flags.

7.6 "Medium Level" Control Structures: JT and JF

HLA provides two special conditional jump instructions: jt (jump if true) and jf (jump if false). These instructions take the following syntax:

```
jt( boolean_expression ) target_label;
jf( boolean_expression ) target_label;
```

The boolean_expression is the standard HLA boolean expression allowed by if..endif and other HLA high level language statements. These instructions evaluate the boolean expression and jump to the specified label if the expression evaluates true (jt) or false (jf).

These are not real 80x86 instructions. HLA compiles them into a sequence of one or more 80x86 machine instructions that achieve the same result. In general, you should not use these two instructions in your main code; they offer few benefits over using an if..endif statement and they are no more readable than the pure assembly language sequences they compile into. HLA provides these "medium-level" instructions so that you may create your own high level control structures using macros (see the chapter on macros and the HLA Reference Manual for more details).

7.7 Implementing Common Control Structures in Assembly Language

Because a primary goal of this chapter is to teach you how to use the low level machine instructions to implement decisions, loops, and other control constructs, it would be wise to show you how to simulate these high level statements using "pure" assembly language. The following sections provide this information.

7.8 Introduction to Decisions

In its most basic form, a decision is some sort of branch within the code that switches between two possible execution paths based on some condition. Normally (though not always), conditional instruction sequences are implemented with the conditional jump instructions. Conditional instructions correspond to the if..then..endif statement in HLA:

```
if( expression ) then
    << statements >>
endif;
```

Assembly language, as usual, offers much more flexibility when dealing with conditional statements. Consider the following C/C++ statement:

```
if( (( x < y ) && ( z > t )) || ( a != b ) )
    stmt1;
```

A "brute force" approach to converting this statement into assembly language might produce:

```
            mov( x, eax );
            cmp( eax, y );
            setl( bl );                 // Store X<Y in bl.
            mov( z, eax );
            cmp( eax, t );
            setg( bh );                 // Store Z > T in bh.
            and( bh, bl );              // Put (X<Y) && (Z>T) into bl.
            mov( a, eax );
            cmp( eax, b );
            setne( bh );                // Store A != B into bh.
            or( bh, bl );               // Put (X<Y) && (Z>T) || (A!=B) into bl
            je SkipStmt1;               // Branch if result is false (OR sets Z-Flag if
                                        // false).


    <Code for stmt1 goes here>

SkipStmt1:
```

As you can see, it takes a considerable number of conditional statements just to process the expression in the example above. This roughly corresponds to the (equivalent) C/C++ statements:

```
        bl = x < y;
        bh = z > t;
        bl = bl && bh;
        bh = a != b;
        bl = bl || bh;
        if( bl )
                stmt1;
```

Now compare this with the following "improved" code:

```
        mov( a, eax );
        cmp( eax, b );
        jne DoStmt;
        mov( x, eax );
        cmp( eax, y );
        jnl SkipStmt;
        mov( z, eax );
        cmp( eax, t );
        jng SkipStmt;
DoStmt:
        << Place code for Stmt1 here >>
SkipStmt:
```

Two things should be apparent from the code sequences above: First, a single conditional statement in C/C++ (or some other HLL) may require several conditional jumps in assembly language; second, organization of complex expressions in a conditional sequence can affect the efficiency of the code. Therefore, care should be exercised when dealing with conditional sequences in assembly language.

Conditional statements may be broken down into three basic categories: if statements, switch/case statements, and indirect jumps. The following sections will describe these program structures, how to use them, and how to write them in assembly language.

7.8.1 IF..THEN..ELSE Sequences

The most common conditional statement is the if..then or if..then..else statement. These two statements take the form shown in Figure 7-1.

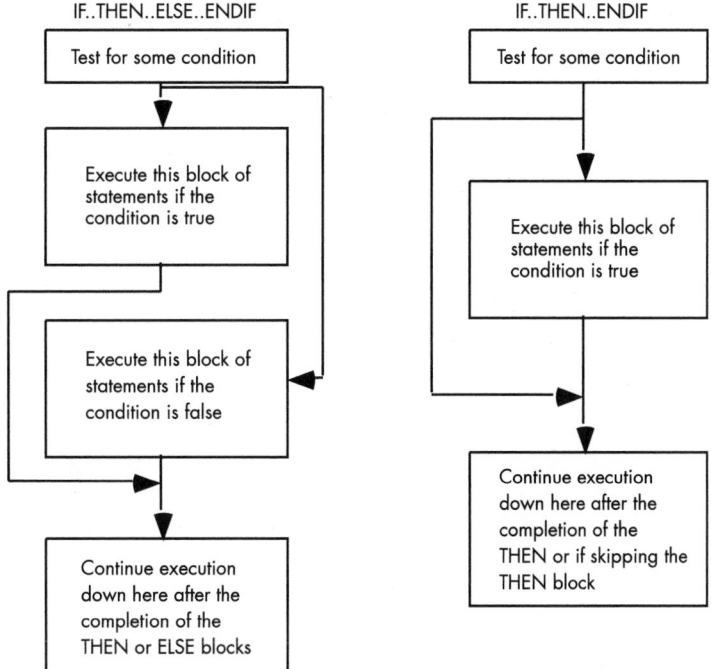

Figure 7-1: IF..THEN..ELSE..ENDIF and IF..ENDIF Statement Flow.

The if..endif statement is just a special case of the if..else..endif statement (with an empty else block). Therefore, we'll only consider the more general if..else..endif form. The basic implementation of an if..then..else statement in 80x86 assembly language looks something like this:

```
{Sequence of statements to test some condition}
      Jcc ElseCode
{Sequence of statements corresponding to the THEN block}

      jmp EndOfIF

ElseCode:
```

```
{Sequence of statements corresponding to the ELSE block}
```

```
EndOfIF:
```

NOTE *Jcc represents some conditional jump instruction.*

For example, to convert the C/C++ statement

```
if( a == b )
        c = d;
else
        b = b + 1;
```

to assembly language, you could use the following 80x86 code:

```
        mov( a, eax );
        cmp( eax, b );
        jne ElsePart;
        mov( d, c );
        jmp EndOfIf;

ElseBlk:
        inc( b );

EndOfIf:
```

For simple expressions like "(a == b)" generating the proper code for an if..else..endif statement is almost trivial. Should the expression become more complex, the associated assembly language code complexity increases as well. Consider the following C/C++ if statement presented earlier:

```
if( (( x > y ) && ( z < t )) || ( a != b ) )
        c = d;
```

When processing complex if statements such as this one, you'll find the conversion task easier if you break this if statement into a sequence of three different if statements as follows:

```
if( a != b ) C = D;
else if( x > y)
        if( z < t )
            C = D;
```

This conversion comes from the following C/C++ equivalences:

```
if( expr1 && expr2 ) stmt;
```

is equivalent to

```
if( expr1 ) if( expr2 ) stmt;
```

and

```
if( expr1 || expr2 ) stmt;
```

is equivalent to

```
if( expr1 ) stmt;
else if( expr2 ) stmt;
```

In assembly language, the former if statement becomes:

```
// if( (( x > y ) && ( z < t )) || ( a != b ) )
//          c = d;

        mov( a, eax );
        cmp( eax, b );
        jne DoIF;
        mov( x, eax );
        cmp( eax, y );
        jng EndOfIF;
        mov( z, eax );
        cmp( eax, t );
        jnl EndOfIf;
DoIf:
        mov( d, c );
EndOfIF:
```

As you can probably tell, the code necessary to test a condition can easily become more complex than the statements appearing in the else and then blocks. Although it seems somewhat paradoxical that it may take more effort to test a condition than to act upon the results of that condition, it happens all the time. Therefore, you should be prepared to accept this.

Probably the biggest problem with complex conditional statements in assembly language is trying to figure out what you've done after you've written the code. A big advantage high level languages offer over assembly language is that expressions are much easier to read and comprehend. This is one of the primary reasons HLA supports high level control structures. The high level version is self-documenting, whereas assembly language tends to hide the true nature of the code. Therefore, well-written comments are an essential ingredient to assembly language implementations of if..then..else statements. An elegant implementation of the example above is:

```
// IF ((X > Y) && (Z < T)) OR (A != B)  C = D;
// Implemented as:
// IF (A != B) THEN GOTO DoIF;
```

```
        mov( a, eax );
        cmp( eax, b );
        jne DoIF;

// if NOT (X > Y) THEN GOTO EndOfIF;

        mov( x, eax );
        cmp( eax, y );
        jng EndOfIF;

// IF NOT (Z < T) THEN GOTO EndOfIF ;

        mov( z, eax );
        cmp( eax, t );
        jnl EndOfIf;

// THEN Block:

DoIf:
        mov( d, c );

// End of IF statement

EndOfIF:
```

Admittedly, this appears to be going overboard for such a simple example. The following would probably suffice:

```
// if( (( x > y ) && ( z < t )) || ( a != b ) )  c = d;
// Test the boolean expression:

        mov( a, eax );
        cmp( eax, b );
        jne DoIF;
        mov( x, eax );
        cmp( eax, y );
        jng EndOfIF;
        mov( z, eax );
        cmp( eax, t );
        jnl EndOfIf;

; THEN Block:

DoIf:
        mov( d, c );

; End of IF statement

EndOfIF:
```

However, as your if statements become complex, the density (and quality) of your comments become more and more important.

7.8.2   Translating HLA IF Statements into Pure Assembly Language

Translating HLA if statements into pure assembly language is very easy. The boolean expressions that the HLA if supports were specifically chosen to expand into a few simple machine instructions. The following paragraphs discuss the conversion of each supported boolean expression into pure machine code.

if(*flag_specification*) then <<*stmts*>> endif;

This form is, perhaps, the easiest HLA if statement to convert. To execute the code immediately following the then keyword if a particular flag is set (or clear), all you need do is skip over the code if the flag is clear (set). This requires only a single conditional jump instruction for implementation as the following examples demonstrate:

```
// if( @c ) then inc( eax );  endif;

        jnc SkipTheInc;

            inc( eax );

        SkipTheInc:

// if( @ns ) then neg( eax ); endif;

        js SkipTheNeg;

            neg( eax );

        SkipTheNeg:
```

if(*register*) then <<*stmts*>> endif;

This form of the if statement uses the test instruction to check the specified register for zero. If the register contains zero (false), then the program jumps around the statements after the then clause with a jz instruction. Converting this statement to assembly language requires a test instruction and a jz instruction as the following examples demonstrate:

```
// if( eax ) then mov( false, eax );  endif;

        test( eax, eax );
        jz DontSetFalse;

            mov( false, eax );

        DontSetFalse:
```

```
// if( al ) then mov( bl, cl );  endif;

        test( al, al );
        jz noMove;

            mov( bl, cl );

        noMove:
```

if(!*register*) then <<*stmts*>> endif;

This form of the if statement uses the test instruction to check the specified register to see if it is zero. If the register is not zero (true), then the program jumps around the statements after the then clause with a jnz instruction. Converting this statement to assembly language requires a test instruction and a jnz instruction in a manner identical to the previous examples.

if(*boolean_variable*) then <<*stmts*>> endif;

This form of the if statement compares the boolean variable against zero (false) and branches around the statements if the variable contains false. HLA implements this statement by using the cmp instruction to compare the boolean variable to zero and then it uses a jz (je) instruction to jump around the statements if the variable is false. The following example demonstrates the conversion:

```
// if( bool ) then mov( 0, al );  endif;

        cmp( bool, false );
        je SkipZeroAL;

            mov( 0, al );

        SkipZeroAL:
```

if(!*boolean_variable*) then <<*stmts*>> endif;

This form of the if statement compares the boolean variable against zero (false) and branches around the statements if the variable contains true (i.e., the opposite condition of the previous example). HLA implements this statement by using the cmp instruction to compare the boolean variable to zero and then it uses a jnz (jne) instruction to jump around the statements if the variable contains true. The following example demonstrates the conversion:

```
// if( !bool ) then mov( 0, al );  endif;

        cmp( bool, false );
        jne SkipZeroAL;

            mov( 0, al );
```

```
SkipZeroAL:
```

if(*mem_reg* *relop* *mem_reg_const*) then <<*stmts*>> endif;

HLA translates this form of the if statement into a cmp instruction and a conditional jump that skips over the statements on the opposite condition specified by the *relop* operator. Table 7-4 lists the correspondence between operators and conditional jump instructions.

Table 7-4: IF Statement Conditional Jump Instructions

Relop	Conditional Jump Instruction If Both Operands Are Unsigned	Conditional Jump Instruction If Either Operand Is Signed
= or ==	JNE	JNE
<> or !=	JE	JE
<	JNB	JNL
<=	JNBE	JNLE
>	JNA	JNG
>=	JNAE	JNGE

Here are a few examples of if statements translated into pure assembly language that use expressions involving relational operators:

```
// if( al == ch ) then inc( cl ); endif;

        cmp( al, ch );
        jne SkipIncCL;

            inc( cl );

        SkipIncCL:

// if( ch >= 'a' ) then and( $5f, ch ); endif;

        cmp( ch, 'a' );
        jnae NotLowerCase

            and( $5f, ch );

        NotLowerCase:

// if( (type int32 eax ) < -5 ) then mov( -5, eax );  endif;

        cmp( eax, -5 );
        jnl DontClipEAX;

            mov( -5, eax );
```

```
            DontClipEAX:

// if( si <> di ) then inc( si );  endif;

            cmp( si, di );
            je DontIncSI;

                inc( si );

            DontIncSI:
```

if(*reg/mem* in *LowConst..HiConst*) then <<*stmts*>> endif;

HLA translates this if statement into a pair of cmp instructions and a pair of conditional jump instructions. It compares the register or memory location against the lower-valued constant and jumps if less than (below) past the statements after the then clause. If the register or memory location's value is greater than or equal to LowConst, the code falls through to the second cmp/conditional jump pair that compares the register or memory location against the higher constant. If the value is greater than (above) this constant, a conditional jump instruction skips the statements in the then clause. Example:

```
// if( eax in 1000..125_000 ) then sub( 1000, eax );  endif;

            cmp( eax, 1000 );
            jb DontSub1000;
            cmp( eax, 125_000 );
            ja DontSub1000;

                sub( 1000, eax );

            DontSub1000:

// if( i32 in -5..5 ) then add( 5, i32 ); endif;

            cmp( i32, -5 );
            jl NoAdd5;
            cmp( i32, 5 );
            jg NoAdd5;

                add(5, i32 );

            NoAdd5:
```

if(*reg/mem* not in *LowConst..HiConst*) then <<*stmts*>> endif;

This form of the HLA if statement tests a register or memory location to see if its value is outside a specified range. The implementation is very similar to the code above exception you branch to the then clause if the value is less than the LowConst value or greater than the HiConst value and you branch over the code in the then clause if the value is within the range specified by the two constants. The following examples demonstrate how to do this conversion:

```
// if( eax not in 1000..125_000 ) then add( 1000, eax );  endif;

        cmp( eax, 1000 );
        jb Add1000;
        cmp( eax, 125_000 );
        jbe SkipAdd1000;

            Add1000:
            add( 1000, eax );

        SkipAdd1000:

// if( i32 not in -5..5 ) theen mov( 0, i32 );  endif;

        cmp( i32, -5 );
        jl Zeroi32;
        cmp( i32, 5 );
        jle SkipZero;

            Zeroi32:
            mov( 0, i32 );

        SkipZero:
```

if(reg₈ in *CSetVar/CSetConst*) then <<*stmts*>> endif;

This statement checks to see if the character in the specified 8-bit register is a member of the specified character set. HLA emits code that is similar to the following for instructions of this form:

```
        movzx( reg₈, eax );
        bt( eax, CsetVar/CsetConst );
        jnc SkipPastStmts;

            << stmts >>

        SkipPastStmts:
```

This example modifies the EAX register (the code HLA generates does not, because it pushes and pops the register it uses). You can easily swap another register for EAX if you've got a value in EAX you need to preserve. In the worst case, if no registers are available, you can push EAX, execute the movzx and bt instructions, and then pop EAX's value from the stack. The following are some actual examples:

```
// if( al in {'a'..'z'} ) then or( $20, al );   endif;

        movzx( al, eax );
        bt( eax, {'a'..'z'} );  // See if we've got a lower case char.
        jnc DontConvertCase;

            or( $20, al );      // Convert to uppercase.

        DontConvertCase:



// if( ch in {'0'..'9'} ) then and( $f, ch );   endif;

        push( eax );
        movzx( ch, eax );
        bt( eax, {'a'..'z'} );  // See if we've got a lower case char.
        pop( eax );
        jnc DontConvertNum;

            and( $f, ch );      // Convert to binary form.

        DontConvertNum:
```

7.8.3   Implementing Complex IF Statements Using Complete Boolean Evaluation

The previous section did not discuss how to translate boolean expressions involving conjunction (AND) or disjunction (OR) into assembly language. This section will begin that discussion. There are two different ways to convert complex boolean expressions involving conjunction and disjunction into assembly language: using complete boolean evaluation or using short-circuit boolean evaluation. This section discusses complete boolean evaluation. The next section discusses short-circuit boolean evaluation, which is the scheme that HLA uses when converting complex boolean expressions to assembly language.

   Using complete boolean evaluation to evaluate a boolean expression for an if statement is almost identical to converting arithmetic expressions into assembly language. Indeed, the previous chapter on arithmetic covers this conversion process. About the only thing worth noting about that process is that you do not need to store the ultimate boolean result in some variable; once the evaluation of the expression is complete you check to see if you have a false (zero) or true (one, or non-zero) result to determine whether to branch around the then portion of the if statement. As you can see in the examples in the preceding sections, you can often use the fact that the last boolean instruction (AND/OR) sets the zero flag if the result is false and clears the zero flag if the result is true. This lets you avoid explicitly testing the result. Consider the following if statement and its conversion to assembly language using complete boolean evaluation:

```
    if( (( x < y ) && ( z > t )) || ( a != b ) )
        Stmt1;



        mov( x, eax );
        cmp( eax, y );
        setl( bl );                  // Store x<y in bl.
        mov( z, eax );
        cmp( eax, t );
        setg( bh );                  // Store z > t in bh.
        and( bh, bl );               // Put (x<y) && (z>t) into bl.
        mov( a, eax );
        cmp( eax, b );
        setne( bh );                 // Store a != b into bh.
        or( bh, bl );                // Put (x<y) && (z>t) || (a != b) into bl
        je SkipStmt1;                // Branch if result is false (OR sets Z-Flag if
false).

        << Code for Stmt1 goes here >>

SkipStmt1:
```

This code computes a boolean value in the BL register and then, at the end of the computation, tests this resulting value to see if it contains true or false. If the result is false, this sequence skips over the code associated with Stmt1. The important thing to note in this example is that the program will execute each and every instruction that computes this boolean result (up to the je instruction).

7.8.4 Short-Circuit Boolean Evaluation

If you are willing to spend a little more effort studying a complex boolean expression, you can usually convert it to a much shorter and faster sequence of assembly language instructions using *short-circuit boolean evaluation*. Short-circuit boolean evaluation attempts to determine whether an expression is true or false by executing only a portion of the instructions that compute the complete expression. By executing only a portion of the instructions, the evaluation is often much faster. For this reason, plus the fact that short-circuit boolean evaluation doesn't require the use of any temporary registers, HLA uses short-circuit evaluation when translating complex boolean expressions into assembly language.

To understand how short-circuit boolean evaluation works, consider the expression "A && B". Once we determine that A is false, there is no need to evaluate B because there is no way the expression can be true. If A and B represent subexpressions rather than simple variables, you can begin to see the savings that are possible with short-circuit boolean evaluation. As a concrete example, consider the subexpression "((x<y) && (z>t))" from the previous section. Once you determine that x is not less than y, there is no need to check to see if z is greater than t because the expression will be false regardless of z and t's values. The following code fragment shows how you can implement short-circuit boolean evaluation for this expression:

```
// if( (x<y) && (z>t) ) then ...

        mov( x, eax );
        cmp( eax, y );
        jnl TestFails;
        mov( z, eax );
        cmp( eax, t );
        jng TestFails;

            << Code for THEN clause of IF statement >>

        TestFails:
```

Notice how the code skips any further testing once it determines that x is not less than y. Of course, if x is less than y, then the program has to test z to see if it is greater than t; if not, the program skips over the then clause. Only if the program satisfies both conditions does the code fall through to the then clause.

For the logical OR operation the technique is similar. If the first subexpression evaluates to true, then there is no need to test the second operand. Whatever the second operand's value is at that point, the full expression still evaluates to true. The following example demonstrates the use of short-circuit evaluation with disjunction (OR):

```
// if( ch < 'A' || ch > 'Z' ) then stdout.put( "Not an upper case char" ); endif;

        cmp( ch, 'A' );
        jb ItsNotUC
        cmp( ch, 'Z' );
        jna ItWasUC;

            ItsNotUC:
            stdout.put( "Not an upper case char" );

        ItWasUC:
```

Because the conjunction and disjunction operators are commutative, you can evaluate the left or right operand first if it is more convenient to do so.[2] As one last example in this section, consider the full boolean expression from the previous section:

---

[2] However, be aware of the fact that some expressions depend upon the leftmost subexpression evaluating one way in order for the rightmost subexpression to be valid; e.g., a common test in C/C++ is "if(x != NULL && x->y) . . .".

```
// if( (( x < y ) && ( z > t )) || ( a != b ) )   Stmt1;

        mov( a, eax );
        cmp( eax, b );
        jne DoStmt1;
        mov( x, eax );
        cmp( eax, y );
        jnl SkipStmt1;
        mov( z, eax );
        cmp( eax, t );
jng SkipStmt1;

        DoStmt1:
        << Code for Stmt1 goes here >>

    SkipStmt1:
```

Notice how the code in this example chose to evaluate "a != b" first and the remaining subexpression last. This is a common technique assembly language programmers use to write better code.

7.8.5 Short-Circuit vs. Complete Boolean Evaluation

One fact about complete boolean evaluation is that every statement in the sequence will execute when evaluating the expression. Short-circuit boolean evaluation may not require the execution of every statement associated with the boolean expression. As you've seen in the previous two sections, code based on short-circuit evaluation is usually shorter and faster. So it would seem that short-circuit evaluation is the technique of choice when converting complex boolean expressions to assembly language.

Sometimes, unfortunately, short-circuit boolean evaluation may not produce the correct result. In the presence of *side effects* in an expression, short-circuit boolean evaluation will produce a different result than complete boolean evaluation. Consider the following C/C++ example:

```
if( ( x == y ) && ( ++z != 0 )) stmt;
```

Using complete boolean evaluation, you might generate the following code:

```
        mov( x, eax );      // See if x == y
        cmp( eax, y );
        sete( bl );
        inc( z );           // ++z
        cmp( z, 0 );        // See if incremented z is zero.
        setne( bh );
        and( bh, bl );      // Test x == y && ++z != 0
```

```
        jz SkipStmt;

        << code for stmt goes here >>

SkipStmt:
```

Using short-circuit boolean evaluation, you might generate the following code:

```
        mov( x, eax );       // See if x == y
        cmp( eax, y );
        jne SkipStmt;
        inc( z );            // ++z
        cmp( z, 0 );         // See if incremented z is zero.
        je SkipStmt;

        << code for stmt goes here >>

SkipStmt:
```

Notice a very subtle but important difference between these two conversions: If it turns out that x is equal to y, then the first version above *still increments* z and compares it to zero before it executes the code associated with *stmt*; the short-circuit version, on the other hand, skips over the code that increments z if it turns out that x is equal to y. Therefore, the behavior of these two code fragments is different with respect to what happens to z if x is equal to y. Neither implementation is particularly wrong, depending on the circumstances you may or may not want the code to increment z if x is equal to y. However, it is important for you to realize that these two schemes produce different results so you can choose an appropriate implementation if the effect of this code on z matters to your program.

Many programs take advantage of short-circuit boolean evaluation and rely upon the fact that the program may not evaluate certain components of the expression. The following C/C++ code fragment demonstrates what is probably the most common example that requires short-circuit boolean evaluation:

```
        if( Ptr != NULL && *Ptr == 'a' ) stmt;
```

If it turns out that Ptr is NULL in this if statement, then the expression is false, and there is no need to evaluate the remainder of the expression (and, therefore, code that uses short-circuit boolean evaluation will not evaluate the remainder of this expression). This statement relies upon the semantics of short-circuit boolean evaluation for correct operation. Were C/C++ to use complete boolean evaluation, and the variable Ptr contained NULL, then the second half of the expression would attempt to dereference a NULL pointer (which tends to crash most programs). Consider the translation of this statement using complete and short-circuit boolean evaluation:

```
// Complete boolean evaluation:

        mov( Ptr, eax );
        test( eax, eax );      // Check to see if EAX is zero (NULL is zero).
        setne( bl );
        mov( [eax], al );      // Get *Ptr into AL.
        cmp( al, 'a' );
        sete( bh );
        and( bh, bl );
        jz SkipStmt;

        << code for stmt goes here >>

SkipStmt:
```

Notice in this example that if Ptr contains NULL (zero), then this program will attempt to access the data at location zero in memory via the "mov([eax], al);" instruction. Under most operating systems this will cause a memory access fault (general protection fault). Now consider the short-circuit boolean conversion:

```
// Short-circuit boolean evaluation

        mov( Ptr, eax );       // See if Ptr contains NULL (zero) and
        test( eax, eax );      // immediately skip past Stmt if this
        jz SkipStmt;           // is the case

        mov( [eax], al );      // If we get to this point, Ptr contains
        cmp( al, 'a' );        // a non-NULL value, so see if it points
        jne SkipStmt;          // at the character 'a'.

        << code for stmt goes here >>

SkipStmt:
```

As you can see in this example, the problem with dereferencing the NULL pointer doesn't exist. If Ptr contains NULL, this code skips over the statements that attempt to access the memory address Ptr contains.

7.8.6 Efficient Implementation of IF Statements in Assembly Language

Encoding if statements efficiently in assembly language takes a bit more thought than simply choosing short-circuit evaluation over complete boolean evaluation. To write code that executes as quickly as possible in assembly language you must carefully analyze the situation and generate the code appropriately. The following paragraphs provide some suggestions you can apply to your programs to improve their performance.

Know Your Data!

A mistake programmers often make is the assumption that data is random. In reality, data is rarely random and if you know the types of values that your program commonly uses, you can use this knowledge to write better code. To see how, consider the following C/C++ statement:

```
if(( a == b ) && ( c < d )) ++i;
```

Because C/C++ uses short-circuit evaluation, this code will test to see if a is equal to b. If so, then it will test to see if c is less than d. If you expect a to be equal to b most of the time but don't expect c to be less than d most of the time, this statement will execute slower than it should. Consider the following HLA implementation of this code:

```
mov( a, eax );
cmp( eax, b );
jne DontIncI;

mov( c, eax );
cmp( eax, d );
jnl DontIncI;

    inc( i );

DontIncI:
```

As you can see in this code, if a is equal to b most of the time and c is not less than d most of the time, you will have to execute the first three instructions nearly every time in order to determine that the expression is false. Now consider the following implementation of the above C/C++ statement that takes advantage of this knowledge and the fact that the "&&" operator is commutative:

```
mov( c, eax );
cmp( eax, d );
jnl DontIncI;

mov( a, eax );
cmp( eax, b );
jne DontIncI;

    inc( i );

DontIncI:
```

In this example the code first checks to see if c is less than d. If most of the time c is less than d, then this code determines that it has to skip to the label DontIncI after executing only three instructions in the typical case (compared with six instructions in the previous example). This fact is much more obvious in assembly language than in a high level language; this is one of the main reasons that assembly programs are often faster than their high level language counterparts: Optimizations are more obvious in assembly language than in a high level language. Of course, the key here is to understand the behavior of your data so you can make intelligent decisions such as the one above.

Rearranging Expressions

Even if your data is random (or you can't determine how the input values will affect your decisions), there may still be some benefit to rearranging the terms in your expressions. Some calculations take far longer to compute than others. For example, the div instruction is much slower than a simple cmp instruction. Therefore, if you have a statement like the following you may want to rearrange the expression so that the cmp comes first:

```
if( (x % 10 = 0 ) && (x != y ) ++x;
```

Converted to assembly code, this if statement becomes:

```
        mov( x, eax );          // Compute X % 10
        cdq();                  // Must sign extend EAX -> EDX:EAX
        imod( 10, edx:eax );    // Remember, remainder goes into EDX
        test( edx, edx );       // See if EDX is zero.
        jnz SkipIF

        mov( x, eax );
        cmp( eax, y );
        je SkipIF

            inc( x );

    SkipIF:
```

The imod instruction is very expensive (often 50 to 100 times slower than most of the other instructions in this example). Unless it is 50 to 100 times more likely that the remainder is zero rather than x is equal to y, it would be better to do the comparison first and the remainder calculation afterward:

```
        mov( x, eax );
        cmp( eax, y );
        je SkipIF

        mov( x, eax );          // Compute X % 10
        cdq();                  // Must sign extend EAX -> EDX:EAX
        imod( 10, edx:eax );    // Remember, remainder goes into EDX
        test( edx, edx );       // See if EDX is zero.
        jnz SkipIF
```

```
        inc( x );


    SkipIF:
```

Of course, in order to rearrange the expression in this manner, the code must
not assume the use of short-circuit evaluation semantics (because the && and ||
operators are not commutative if the code must compute one subexpression
before another).

Destructuring Your Code

Although there is a lot of good things to be said about structured programming
techniques, there are some drawbacks to writing structured code. Specifically,
structured code is sometimes less efficient than unstructured code. Most of the
time this is tolerable because unstructured code is difficult to read and maintain;
it is often acceptable to sacrifice some performance in exchange for
maintainable code. In certain instances, however, you may need all the
performance you can get. In those rare instances you might choose to
compromise the readability of you code in order to gain some additional
performance.

One classic way to do this is to use code movement to move code your
program rarely uses out of the way of code that executes most of the time. For
example, consider the following pseudo C/C++ statement:

```
if( See_If_an_Error_Has_Ocurred )
{
    << Statements to execute if no error >>
}
else
{
    << Error handling statements >>
}
```

In normal code, one does not expect errors to be frequent. Therefore, you would
normally expect the then section of the above if to execute far more often than
the else clause. The code above could translate into the following assembly code:

```
cmp( See_If_an_Error_Has_Ocurred, true );
je HandleTheError

    << Statements to execute if no error >>
    jmp EndOfIF;

HandleTheError:
    << Error handling statements >>
EndOfIf:
```

Notice that if the expression is false this code falls through to the normal statements and then jumps over the error handling statements. Instructions that transfer control from one point in your program to another (e.g., jmp instructions) tend to be slow. It is much faster to execute a sequential set of instructions rather than jump all over the place in your program. Unfortunately, the code above doesn't allow this. One way to rectify this problem is to move the else clause of the code somewhere else in your program. That is, you could rewrite the code as follows:

```
cmp( See_If_an_Error_Has_Ocurred, true );
je HandleTheError

    << Statements to execute if no error >>

EndOfIf:
```

At some other point in your program (typically after a jmp instruction) you would insert the following code:

```
HandleTheError:
    << Error handling statements >>
    jmp EndOfIf;
```

Note that the program isn't any shorter. The jmp you removed from the original sequence winds up at the end of the else clause. However, because the else clause rarely executes, moving the jmp instruction from the then clause (which executes frequently) to the else clause is a big performance win because the then clause executes using only straight-line code. This technique is surprisingly effective in many time-critical code segments.

There is a difference between writing *destructured* code and writing *unstructured* code. Unstructured code is written in an unstructured way to begin with. It is generally hard to read and difficult to maintain, and it often contains defects. Destructured code, on the other hand, starts out as structured code, and you make a conscious decision to eliminate the structure in order to gain a small performance boost. Generally, you've already tested the code in its structured form before destructuring it. Therefore, destructured code is often easier to work with than unstructured code.

Calculation Rather Than Branching

On many processors in the 80x86 family, branches are very expensive compared to many other instructions (perhaps not as bad as imod or idiv, but typically an order of magnitude worse than instructions like add and sub). For this reason it is sometimes better to execute more instructions in a sequence rather than fewer instructions that involve branching. For example, consider the simple assignment "EAX = abs(EAX);". Unfortunately, there is no 80x86 instruction that computes the absolute value of an integer value. The obvious way to handle this is with an instruction sequence like the following:

```
            test( eax, eax );
            jns ItsPositive;

                neg( eax );

        ItsPositive:
```

However, as you can plainly see in this example, it uses a conditional jump to skip over the neg instruction (that creates a positive value in EAX if EAX was negative). Now consider the following sequence that will also do the job:

```
// Set EDX to $FFFF_FFFF if EAX is negative, $0000_0000 if EAX is
// zero or positive:

        cdq();

// If EAX was negative, the following code inverts all the bits in EAX,
// otherwise it has no effect on EAX.

        xor( edx, eax);

// If EAX was negative, the following code adds one to EAX, otherwise
// it doesn't modify EAX's value.

        and( 1, edx );      // EDX = 0 or 1 (1 if EAX was negative).
        add( edx, eax );
```

This code will invert all the bits in EAX and then add one to EAX if EAX was negative prior to the sequence (i.e., it takes the two's complement [negates] the value in EAX). If EAX was zero or positive, then this code does not change the value in EAX.

Note that this sequence takes four instructions rather than the three the previous example requires. However, because there are no transfer of control instructions in this sequence, it may execute faster on many CPUs in the 80x86 family.

7.8.7 SWITCH/CASE Statements

The HLA (Standard Library/ *hll.hhf*) switch statement takes the following form:

```
switch( reg_{32} )
    case( const_1)
        <<stmts_1>>

    case( const_2 )
        <<stmts_2>>
        .
        .
        .
```

```
        case( const_n )
            <<stmts_n >>

        default      // Note that the default section is optional
            <<stmts_default >>

    endswitch;
```

(Note that this statement is not actually built into the HLA language; it is implemented as a macro in the *hll.hhf* header file that *stdlib.hhf* includes.)

When this statement executes, it checks the value of register against the constants $const_1$ ... $const_n$. If a match is found then the corresponding statements execute. HLA places a few restrictions on the switch statement. First, the HLA switch statement only allows a 32-bit register as the switch expression. Second, all the constants appearing as case clauses must be unique. The reason for these restrictions will become clear in a moment.

Most introductory programming texts introduce the switch/case statement by explaining it as a sequence of if..then..elseif statements. They might claim that the following two pieces of HLA code are equivalent:

```
    switch( eax )
        case(0) stdout.put("I=0");
        case(1) stdout.put("I=1");
        case(2) stdout.put("I=2");
    endswitch;

    if( eax = 0 ) then
        stdout.put("I=0")
    elseif( eax = 1 ) then
        stdout.put("I=1")
    elseif( eax = 2 ) then
        stdout.put("I=2");
    endif;
```

While semantically these two code segments may be the same, their implementation is usually different. Whereas the if..then..elseif chain does a comparison for each conditional statement in the sequence, the switch statement normally uses an indirect jump to transfer control to any one of several statements with a single computation. Consider the two examples presented above, they could be written in assembly language with the following code:

```
// IF..THEN..ELSE form:

        mov( i, eax );
        test( eax, eax );   // Check for zero.
        jnz Not0;
            stdout.put( "I=0" );
            jmp EndCase;
```

```
        Not0:
        cmp( eax, 1 );
        jne Not1;
            stdou.put( "I=1" );
            jmp EndCase;

        Not1:
        cmp( eax, 2 );
        jne EndCase;
            stdout.put( "I=2" );
    EndCase:


// Indirect Jump Version

readonly
    JmpTbl:dword[3] := [ &Stmt0, &Stmt1, &Stmt2 ];
            .
            .
            .
    mov( i, eax );
    jmp( JmpTbl[ eax*4 ] );

        Stmt0:
            stdout.put( "I=0" );
            jmp EndCase;

        Stmt1:
            stdout.put( "I=1" );
            jmp EndCase;

        Stmt2:
            stdout.put( "I=2" );

    EndCase:
```

The implementation of the if..then..elseif version is fairly obvious and doesn't need much in the way of explanation. The indirect jump version, however, is probably quite mysterious to you, so let's consider how this particular implementation of the switch statement works.

Remember that there are three common forms of the jmp instruction. The standard unconditional jmp instruction, like the "jmp EndCase;" instruction in the previous examples, transfers control directly to the statement label specified as the jmp operand. The second form of the jmp instruction (i.e., "jmp Reg$_{32}$;") transfers control to the memory location specified by the address found in a 32-bit register. The third form of the jmp instruction, the one the example above uses, transfers control to the instruction specified by the contents of a double word memory location. As this example clearly illustrates, that memory location can use any addressing mode. You are not limited to the displacement only addressing mode. Now let's consider exactly how this second implementation of the switch statement works.

To begin with, a switch statement requires that you create an array of pointers with each element containing the address of a statement label in your code (those labels must be attached to the sequence of instructions to execute for each case in the switch statement). In the example above, the JmpTbl array serves this purpose. Note that this code initializes JmpTbl with the address of the statement labels Stmt0, Stmt1, and Stmt2. The program places this array in the readonly section because the program should never change these values during execution.

CAUTION *Whenever you initialize an array with a set of addresses of statement labels as in this example, the declaration section in which you declare the array (e.g.,* readonly *in this case) must be in the same procedure that contains the statement labels.[3]*

During the execution of this code sequence, the program loads the EAX register with I's value. Then the program uses this value as an index into the JmpTbl array and transfers control to the four-byte address found at the specified location. For example, if EAX contains zero, the "jmp(JmpTbl[eax*4]);" instruction will fetch the double word at address JmpTbl+0 (eax*4=0). Because the first double word in the table contains the address of Stmt0, the jmp instruction will transfer control to the first instruction following the Stmt0 label. Likewise, if I (and therefore, EAX) contains one, then the indirect jmp instruction fetches the double word at offset four from the table and transfers control to the first instruction following the Stmt1 label (because the address of Stmt1 appears at offset four in the table). Finally, if I/EAX contains two, then this code fragment transfers control to the statements following the Stmt2 label because it appears at offset eight in the JmpTbl table.

Two things should become readily apparent: The more (consecutive) cases you have, the more efficient the jump table implementation becomes (both in terms of space and speed) over the if/elseif form. Except for trivial cases, the switch statement is almost always faster and usually by a large margin. As long as the case values are consecutive, the switch statement version is usually smaller as well.

What happens if you need to include nonconsecutive case labels or you cannot be sure that the switch value doesn't go out of range? With the HLA switch statement, such an occurrence will transfer control to the first statement after the endswitch clause. However, this doesn't happen in the example above. If variable I does not contain zero, one, or two, the result of executing the code above is undefined. For example, if I contains five when you execute the code in the previous example, the indirect jmp instruction will fetch the dword at offset 20 (5*4) in JmpTbl and transfer control to that address. Unfortunately, JmpTbl doesn't have six entries; so the program will wind up fetching the value of the third double word following JmpTbl and using that as the target address. This will often

---

[3] If the switch statement appears in your main program, you must declare the array in the declaration section of your main program.

crash your program or transfer control to an unexpected location. Clearly this code does not behave like the HLA switch statement, nor does it have desirable behavior.

The solution is to place a few instructions before the indirect jmp to verify that the switch selection value is within some reasonable range. In the previous example, we'd probably want to verify that I's value is in the range 0..2 before executing the jmp instruction. If I's value is outside this range, the program should simply jump to the endcase label (this corresponds to dropping down to the first statement after the endswitch clause). The following code provides this modification:

```
readonly
    JmpTbl:dword[3] := [ &Stmt0, &Stmt1, &Stmt2 ];
     .
     .
     .
    mov( i, eax );
    cmp( eax, 2 );          // Verify that I is in the range
    ja EndCase;             // 0..2 before the indirect JMP.
    jmp( JmpTbl[ eax*4 ] );


        Stmt0:
            stdout.put( "I=0" );
            jmp EndCase;

        Stmt1:
            stdout.put( "I=1" );
            jmp EndCase;

        Stmt2:
            stdout.put( "I=2" );

    EndCase:
```

Although the example above handles the problem of selection values being outside the range zero through two, it still suffers from a couple of severe restrictions:

- The cases must start with the value zero. That is, the minimum case constant has to be zero in this example.

- The case values must be contiguous; there cannot be any gaps between any two case values.

Solving the first problem is easy, and you deal with it in two steps. First, you must compare the case selection value against a lower and upper bounds before determining if the case value is legal, e.g.,

```
// SWITCH statement specifying cases 5, 6, and 7:
// WARNING: This code does *NOT* work.  Keep reading to find out why.

        mov( i, eax );
        cmp( eax, 5 );
        jb EndCase
        cmp( eax, 7 );                // Verify that I is in the range
        ja EndCase;                   // 5..7 before the indirect JMP.
        jmp( JmpTbl[ eax*4 ] );


            Stmt5:
                stdout.put( "I=5" );
                jmp EndCase;

            Stmt6:
                stdout.put( "I=6" );
                jmp EndCase;

            Stmt7:
                stdout.put( "I=7" );

        EndCase:
```

As you can see, this code adds a pair of extra instructions, cmp and jb, to test the selection value to ensure it is in the range five through seven. If not, control drops down to the EndCase label, otherwise control transfers via the indirect jmp instruction. Unfortunately, as the comments point out, this code is broken. Consider what happens if variable i contains the value five: The code will verify that five is in the range five through seven, and then it will fetch the dword at offset 20 (5*@size(dword)) and jump to that address. As before, however, this loads four bytes outside the bounds of the table and does not transfer control to a defined location. One solution is to subtract the smallest case selection value from EAX before executing the jmp instruction. E.g.,

```
// SWITCH statement specifying cases 5, 6, and 7:
// WARNING: There is a better way to do this.  Keep reading.

readonly
        JmpTbl:dword[3] := [ &Stmt5, &Stmt6, &Stmt7 ];
            .
            .
            .

        mov( i, eax );
        cmp( eax, 5 );
        jb EndCase
        cmp( eax, 7 );                // Verify that I is in the range
        ja EndCase;                   // 5..7 before the indirect JMP.
```

```
        sub( 5, eax );              // 5->0, 6->1, 7->2.
        jmp( JmpTbl[ eax*4 ] );


            Stmt5:
                stdout.put( "I=5" );
                jmp EndCase;

            Stmt6:
                stdout.put( "I=6" );
                jmp EndCase;

            Stmt7:
                stdout.put( "I=7" );

        EndCase:
```

By subtracting five from the value in EAX this code forces EAX to take on the values zero, one, or two prior to the jmp instruction. Therefore, case selection value five jumps to Stmt5, case selection value six transfers control to Stmt6, and case selection value seven jumps to Stmt7.

There is a sneaky way to improve the code above. You can eliminate the sub instruction by merging this subtraction into the jmp instruction's address expression. Consider the following code that does this:

```
// SWITCH statement specifying cases 5, 6, and 7:

readonly
    JmpTbl:dword[3] := [ &Stmt5, &Stmt6, &Stmt7 ];
            .
            .
            .

    mov( i, eax );
    cmp( eax, 5 );
    jb EndCase
    cmp( eax, 7 );              // Verify that I is in the range
    ja EndCase;                 // 5..7 before the indirect JMP.
    jmp( JmpTbl[ eax*4 - 5*@size(dword)] );


            Stmt5:
                stdout.put( "I=5" );
                jmp EndCase;

            Stmt6:
                stdout.put( "I=6" );
                jmp EndCase;

            Stmt7:
```

```
                    stdout.put( "I=7" );

    EndCase:
```

The HLA switch statement provides a default clause that executes if the case selection value doesn't match any of the case values. E.g.,

```
    switch( ebx )

        case( 5 )  stdout.put( "ebx=5" );
        case( 6 )  stdout.put( "ebx=6" );
        case( 7 )  stdout.put( "ebx=7" );
        default
            stdout.put( "ebx does not equal 5, 6, or 7" );

    endswitch;
```

Implementing the equivalent of the default clause in pure assembly language is very easy. Just use a different target label in the jb and ja instructions at the beginning of the code. The following example implements an HLA switch statement similar to the one immediately above:

```
// SWITCH statement specifying cases 5, 6, and 7 with a DEFAULT clause:

readonly
    JmpTbl:dword[3] := [ &Stmt5, &Stmt6, &Stmt7 ];
         .
         .
         .

    mov( i, eax );
    cmp( eax, 5 );
    jb DefaultCase;
    cmp( eax, 7 );                  // Verify that I is in the range
    ja DefaultCase;                 // 5..7 before the indirect JMP.
    jmp( JmpTbl[ eax*4 - 5*@size(dword)] );


        Stmt5:
            stdout.put( "I=5" );
            jmp EndCase;

        Stmt6:
            stdout.put( "I=6" );
            jmp EndCase;

        Stmt7:
            stdout.put( "I=7" );
            jmp EndCase;
```

```
        DefaultCase:
            stdout.put( "I does not equal 5, 6, or 7" );
    EndCase:
```

The second restriction noted earlier, that the case values need to be contiguous, is easy to handle by inserting extra entries into the jump table. Consider the following HLA switch statement:

```
switch( ebx )

    case( 1 ) stdout.put( "ebx = 1" );
    case( 2 ) stdout.put( "ebx = 2" );
    case( 4 ) stdout.put( "ebx = 4" );
    case( 8 ) stdout.put( "ebx = 8" );
    default
        stdout.put( "ebx is not 1, 2, 4, or 8" );

endswitch;
```

The minimum switch value is one, and the maximum value is eight. Therefore, the code before the indirect jmp instruction needs to compare the value in EBX against one and eight. If the value is between one and eight, it's still possible that EBX might not contain a legal case selection value. However, because the jmp instruction indexes into a table of double words using the case selection table, the table must have eight double word entries. To handle the values between one and eight that are not case selection values, simply put the statement label of the default clause (or the label specifying the first instruction after the endswitch if there is no default clause) in each of the jump table entries that don't have a corresponding case clause. The following code demonstrates this technique:

```
readonly
    JmpTbl2: dword :=
                [
                    &Case1, &Case2, &dfltCase, &Case4,
                    &dfltCase, &dfltCase, &dfltCase, &Case8
                ];
        .
        .
        .
    cmp( ebx, 1 );
    jb dfltCase;
    cmp( ebx, 8 );
    ja dfltCase;
    jmp( JmpTbl2[ ebx*4 - 1*@size(dword)] );

        Case1:
            stdout.put( "ebx = 1" );
            jmp EndOfSwitch;
```

```
Case2:
    stdout.put( "ebx = 2" );
    jmp EndOfSwitch;

Case4:
    stdout.put( "ebx = 4" );
    jmp EndOfSwitch;

Case8:
    stdout.put( "ebx = 8" );
    jmp EndOfSwitch;

dfltCase:
    stdout.put( "ebx is not 1, 2, 4, or 8" );


EndOfSwitch:
```

There is a problem with this implementation of the switch statement. If the case values contain nonconsecutive entries that are widely spaced the jump table could become exceedingly large. The following switch statement would generate an extremely large code file:

```
switch( ebx )

    case( 1     ) stmt1;
    case( 100   ) stmt2;
    case( 1_000 ) stmt3;
    case( 10_000 ) stmt4;
    default stmt5;

endswitch;
```

In this situation, your program will be much smaller if you implement the switch statement with a sequence of if statements rather than using an indirect jump statement. However, keep one thing in mind: The size of the jump table does not normally affect the execution speed of the program. If the jump table contains two entries or two thousand, the switch statement will execute the multiway branch in a constant amount of time. The if statement implementation requires a linearly increasing amount of time for each case label appearing in the case statement.

Probably the biggest advantage to using assembly language over a HLL like Pascal or C/C++ is that you get to choose the actual implementation of statements like switch. In some instances you can implement a switch statement as a sequence of if..then..elseif statements, or you can implement it as a jump table, or you can use a hybrid of the two:

```
switch( eax )

    case( 0 ) stmt0;
```

```
        case( 1 ) stmt1;
        case( 2 ) stmt2;
        case( 100 ) stmt3;
        default stmt4;

    endswitch;
```

The preceding code could become:

```
        cmp( eax, 100 );
        je DoStmt3;
        cmp( eax, 2 );
        ja TheDefaultCase;
        jmp( JmpTbl[ eax*4 ]);
        etc.
```

Of course, you could do this in HLA using the following code high level control structures:

```
    if( ebx = 100 ) then
        stmt3;
    else
        switch( eax )
            case(0) stmt0;
            case(1) stmt1;
            case(2) stmt2;
            default stmt4
        endswitch;
    endif;
```

But this tends to destroy the readability of the program. On the other hand, the extra code to test for 100 in the assembly language code doesn't adversely affect the readability of the program (perhaps because it's so hard to read already). Therefore, most people will add the extra code to make their program more efficient.

The C/C++ switch statement is very similar to the HLA switch statement.[4] There is only one major semantic difference: The programmer must explicitly place a break statement in each case clause to transfer control to the first statement beyond the switch. This break corresponds to the jmp instruction at the end of each case sequence in the assembly code above. If the corresponding break is not present, C/C++ transfers control into the code of the following case. This is equivalent to leaving off the jmp at the end of the case's sequence:

```
    switch (i)
    {
        case 0: stmt1;
```

[4] The HLA Standard Library switch statement actually provides an option to support C semantics. See the HLA Standard Library documentation for details.

```
        case 1: stmt2;
        case 2: stmt3;
                break;
        case 3: stmt4;
                break;
        default: stmt5;
    }
```

This translates into the following 80x86 code:

```
readonly
    JmpTbl: dword[4] := [ &case0, &case1, &case2, &case3 ];
        .
        .
        .
    mov( i, ebx );
    cmp( ebx, 3 );
    ja DefaultCase;
    jmp( JmpTbl[ ebx*4 ]);

        case0:
            stmt1;

        case1:
            stmt2;

        case2:
            stmt3;
            jmp EndCase;     // Emitted for the break stmt.

        case3:
            stmt4;
            jmp EndCase;     // Emitted for the break stmt.

        DefaultCase:
            stmt5;

    EndCase:
```

7.9 State Machines and Indirect Jumps

Another control structure commonly found in assembly language programs is
the *state machine*. A state machine uses a *state variable* to control program flow.
The FORTRAN programming language provides this capability with the assigned
GOTO statement. Certain variants of C (e.g., GNU's GCC from the Free Software
Foundation) provide similar features. In assembly language, the indirect jump
provides a mechanism to easily implement state machines.

So what is a state machine? In very basic terms, it is a piece of code[5] that keeps track of its execution history by entering and leaving certain "states." For the purposes of this chapter, we'll not use a very formal definition of a state machine. We'll just assume that a state machine is a piece of code that (somehow) remembers the history of its execution (its *state*) and executes sections of code based upon that history.

In a very real sense, all programs are state machines. The CPU registers and values in memory constitute the "state" of that machine. However, we'll use a much more constrained view. Indeed, for most purposes only a single variable (or the value in the EIP register) will denote the current state.

Now let's consider a concrete example. Suppose you have a procedure that you want to perform one operation the first time you call it, a different operation the second time you call it, yet something else the third time you call it, and then something new again on the fourth call. After the fourth call it repeats these four different operations in order. For example, suppose you want the procedure to add EAX and EBX the first time, subtract them on the second call, multiply them on the third, and divide them on the fourth. You could implement this procedure as follows:

```
procedure StateMachine;
static
    State:byte := 0;
begin StateMachine;

    cmp( State, 0 );
    jne TryState1;

        // State 0: Add EBX to EAX and switch to state 1:

        add( ebx, eax );
        inc( State );
        exit StateMachine;

    TryState1:
    cmp( State, 1 );
    jne TryState2;

        // State 1: subtract ebx from EAX and switch to state 2:

        sub( ebx, eax );
        inc( State );        // State 1 becomes State 2.
        exit StateMachine;

    TryState2:
    cmp( State, 2 );
    jne MustBeState3;
```

---

[5] Note that state machines need not be software based. Many state machines' implementation are hardware based.

```
                // If this is state 2, multiply EAX by EAX and switch to state 3:

        intmul( ebx, eax );
        inc( State );        // State 2 becomes State 3.
        exit StateMachine;

    // If it isn't one of the above states, we must be in state 3
    // So divide eax by ebx and switch back to state zero.

    MustBeState3:
    push( edx );         // Preserve this 'cause it gets whacked by DIV.
    xor( edx, edx );     // Zero extend EAX into EDX.
    div( ebx, edx:eax);
    pop( edx );          // Restore EDX's value preserved above.
    mov( 0, State );     // Reset the state back to zero.

end StateMachine;
```

Technically, this procedure is not the state machine. Instead, it is the variable *State* and the cmp/jne instructions that constitute the state machine.

There is nothing particularly special about this code. It's little more than a switch statement implemented via the if..then..elseif construct. The only thing special about this procedure is that it remembers how many times it has been called[6] and behaves differently depending upon the number of calls. While this is a *correct* implementation of the desired state machine, it is not particularly efficient. The astute reader, of course, would recognize that this code could be made a little faster using an actual switch statement rather than the if..then..elseif implementation. However, there is a better way. . . .

The more common implementation of a state machine in assembly language is to use an *indirect jump*. Rather than having a state variable that contains a value like zero, one, two, or three, we could load the state variable with the *address* of the code to execute upon entry into the procedure. By simply jumping to that address, the state machine could save the tests above needed to execute the proper code fragment. Consider the following implementation using the indirect jump:

```
procedure StateMachine;
static
    State:dword := &State0;
begin StateMachine;

    jmp( State );

        // State 0: Add EBX to EAX and switch to state 1:

    State0:
        add( ebx, eax );
```

---

[6] Actually, it remembers how many times, *MOD 4*, that it has been called.

```
        mov( &State1, State );
        exit StateMachine;

State1:

        // State 1: subtract ebx from EAX and switch to state 2:

        sub( ebx, eax );
        mov( &State2, State );    // State 1 becomes State 2.
        exit StateMachine;

State2:

        // If this is state 2, multiply EAX by EAX and switch to state 3:

        intmul( ebx, eax );
        mov( &State3, State );    // State 2 becomes State 3.
        exit StateMachine;

// State 3: divide eax by ebx and switch back to state zero.

State3:
        push( edx );              // Preserve this 'cause it gets whacked by DIV.
        xor( edx, edx );          // Zero extend EAX into EDX.
        div( ebx, edx:eax);
        pop( edx );               // Restore EDX's value preserved above.
        mov( &State0, State );    // Reset the state back to zero.

end StateMachine;
```

The jmp instruction at the beginning of the StateMachine procedure transfers control to the location pointed at by the State variable. The first time you call StateMachine it points at the State0 label. Thereafter, each subsection of code sets the State variable to point at the appropriate successor code.

7.10   Spaghetti Code

One major problem with assembly language is that it takes several statements to realize a simple idea encapsulated by a single high level language statement. All too often an assembly language programmer will notice that s/he can save a few bytes or cycles by jumping into the middle of some program structure. After a few such observations (and corresponding modifications) the code contains a whole sequence of jumps in and out of portions of the code. If you were to draw a line from each jump to its destination, the resulting listing would end up looking like someone dumped a bowl of spaghetti on your code, hence the term "spaghetti code."

Spaghetti code suffers from one major drawback: It's difficult (at best) to read such a program and figure out what it does. Most programs start out in a "structured" form only to become spaghetti code when sacrificed at the altar of efficiency. Alas, spaghetti code is rarely efficient. Because it's difficult to figure out exactly what's going on, it's very difficult to determine if you can use a better algorithm to improve the system. Hence, spaghetti code may wind up less efficient than structured code.

While it's true that producing some spaghetti code in your programs may improve its efficiency, doing so should always be a last resort after you've tried everything else and you still haven't achieved what you need. Always start out writing your programs with straight-forward if and switch statements. Start combining sections of code (via jmp instructions) once everything is working and well understood. Of course, you should never obliterate the structure of your code unless the gains are worth it.

A famous saying in structured programming circles is "After GOTOs, pointers are the next most dangerous element in a programming language." A similar saying is "Pointers are to data structures what GOTOs are to control structures." In other words, avoid excessive use of pointers. If pointers and GOTOs are bad, then the indirect jump must be the worst construct of all because it involves both GOTOs and pointers! Seriously, though, the indirect jump instructions should be avoided for casual use. They tend to make a program harder to read. After all, an indirect jump can (theoretically) transfer control to any label within a program. Imagine how hard it would be to follow the flow through a program if you have no idea what a pointer contains and you come across an indirect jump using that pointer. Therefore, you should always exercise care when using jump indirect instructions.

7.11   Loops

Loops represent the final basic control structure (sequences, decisions, and loops) that make up a typical program. Like so many other structures in assembly language, you'll find yourself using loops in places you've never dreamed of using loops. Most high level languages have implied loop structures hidden away. For example, consider the BASIC statement "IF A$ = B$ THEN 100". This if statement compares two strings and jumps to statement 100 if they are equal. In assembly language, you would need to write a loop to compare each character in A$ to the corresponding character in B$ and then jump to statement 100 if and only if all the characters matched. In BASIC, there is no loop to be seen in the program. In assembly language, such a simple if statement requires a loop to compare the individual characters in the string.[7] This is but a small example that shows how loops seem to pop up everywhere.

Program loops consist of three components: an optional initialization component, a loop termination test, and the body of the loop. The order with which these components are assembled can dramatically change the way the loop operates. Three permutations of these components appear over and over again. Because of their frequency, these loop structures are given special names in high level languages: while loops, repeat..until loops (do..while in C/C++), and infinite loops (e.g., forever..endfor in HLA).

---

[7] Of course, the HLA Standard Library provides the *str.eq* routine that compares the strings for you, effectively hiding the loop even in an assembly language program.

7.11.1 WHILE Loops

The most general loop is the while loop. In HLA it takes the following form:

```
while( expression ) do <<statements>> endwhile;
```

There are two important points to note about the while loop. First, the test for termination appears at the beginning of the loop. Second as a direct consequence of the position of the termination test, the body of the loop may never execute. If the boolean expression is always false, the loop body will never execute.

Consider the following HLA while loop:

```
mov( 0, I );
while( I < 100 ) do

    inc( I );

endwhile;
```

The "mov(0, I);" instruction is the initialization code for this loop. I is a loop control variable, because it controls the execution of the body of the loop. "I<100" is the loop termination condition. That is, the loop will not terminate as long as I is less than 100. The single instruction "inc(I);" is the loop body. This is the code that executes on each pass of the loop.

Note that an HLA while loop can be easily synthesized using if and jmp statements. For example, you may replace the HLA while loop above by:

```
mov( 0, I );
WhileLp:
if( I < 100 ) then

    inc( i );
    jmp WhileLp;

endif;
```

More generally, any while loop can be built up from the following:

```
<< optional initialization code>>

UniqueLabel:
if( not_termination_condition ) then

    <<loop body>>
    jmp UniqueLabel;

endif;
```

Therefore, you can use the techniques from earlier in this chapter to convert if statements to assembly language along with a single jmp instruction to produce a while loop. The example we've been looking at in this section translates to the following "pure" 80x86 assembly code:[8]

```
mov( 0, i );
WhileLp:
    cmp( i, 100 );
    jnl WhileDone;
    inc( i );
    jmp WhileLp;

WhileDone:
```

7.11.2   REPEAT..UNTIL Loops

The repeat..until (do..while) loop tests for the termination condition at the end of the loop rather than at the beginning. In HLA, the repeat..until loop takes the following form:

```
<< optional initialization code >>
repeat

    <<loop body>>

until( termination_condition );
```

This sequence executes the initialization code and the loop body and then tests some condition to see if the loop should repeat. If the boolean expression evaluates to false, the loop repeats; otherwise the loop terminates. The two things to note about the repeat..until loop are that the termination test appears at the end of the loop and, as a direct consequence of this, the loop body always executes at least once.

Like the while loop, the repeat..until loop can be synthesized with an if statement and a jmp . You could use the following:

```
<< initialization code >>
SomeUniqueLabel:

    << loop body >>

if( not_the_termination_condition ) then jmp SomeUniqueLabel; endif;
```

Based on the material presented in the previous sections, you can easily synthesize repeat..until loops in assembly language. The following is a simple example:

---

[8] Note that HLA will actually convert most while statements to different 80x86 code than this section presents. The reason for the difference appears a little later in this text when we explore how to write more efficient loop code.

```
        repeat

            stdout.put( "Enter a number greater than 100: ");
            stdin.get( i );

        until( i > 100 );

// This translates to the following IF/JMP code:

    RepeatLbl:

            stdout.put( "Enter a number greater than 100: ");
            stdin.get( i );

        if( i <= 100 ) then jmp RepeatLbl; endif;

// It also translates into the following "pure" assembly code:

    RepeatLabel:

            stdout.put( "Enter a number greater than 100: ");
            stdin.get( i );

        cmp( i, 100 );
        jng RepeatLbl;
```

7.11.3   FOREVER..ENDFOR Loops

If while loops test for termination at the beginning of the loop and repeat..until loops check for termination at the end of the loop, the only place left to test for termination is in the middle of the loop. The HLA forever..endfor loop, combined with the break and breakif statements, provide this capability. The forever..endfor loop takes the following form:

```
    forever

        << loop body >>

    endfor;
```

Note that there is no explicit termination condition. Unless otherwise provided for, the forever..endfor construct simply forms an infinite loop. Loop termination is typically handled by a breakif statement. Consider the following HLA code that employs a forever..endfor construct:

```
    forever

        stdin.get( character );
```

```
        breakif( character = '.' );
        stdout.put( character );

    endfor;
```

Converting a forever loop to pure assembly language is trivial. All you need is a label and a jmp instruction. The breakif statement in this example is really nothing more than an if and a jmp instruction. The "pure" assembly language version of the code above looks something like the following:

```
foreverLabel:

        stdin.get( character );
        cmp( character, '.' );
        je ForIsDone;
        stdout.put( character );
        jmp foreverLabel;

ForIsDone:
```

7.11.4   FOR Loops

The for loop is a special form of the while loop that repeats the loop body a specific number of times. In HLA, the for loop takes the following form:

```
for( <<Initialization Stmt>>;   <<Termination Expression>>; <<inc_Stmt>> ) do

    << statements >>

endfor;
```

This is completely equivalent to the following:

```
<< Initialization Stmt>>;
while( <<Termination Expression>> ) do

    << statements >>

    <<inc_Stmt>>

endwhile;
```

Traditionally, the for loop has been used to process arrays and other objects accessed in sequential numeric order. One normally initializes a loop control variable with the initialization statement and then uses the loop control variable as an index into the array (or other data type), e.g.,

```
for( mov(0, esi); esi < 7; inc( esi )) do

    stdout.put( "Array Element = ", SomeArray[ esi*4], nl );

endfor;
```

To convert this to "pure" assembly language, begin by translating the for loop into an equivalent while loop:

```
mov( 0, esi );
while( esi < 7 ) do

    stdout.put( "Array Element = ", SomeArray[ esi*4], nl );

    inc( esi );
endwhile;
```

Now, using the techniques from the section on while loops, translate the code into pure assembly language:

```
mov( 0, esi );
WhileLp:
cmp( esi, 7 );
jnl EndWhileLp;

    stdout.put( "Array Element = ", SomeArray[ esi*4], nl );

    inc( esi );
    jmp WhileLp;

EndWhileLp:
```

7.11.5   The BREAK and CONTINUE Statements

The HLA break and continue statements both translate into a single jmp instruction. The break instruction exits the loop that immediately contains the break statement; the continue statement restarts the loop that immediately contains the continue statement.

Converting a break statement to "pure" assembly language is very easy. Just emit a jmp instruction that transfers control to the first statement following the endxxxx clause of the loop to exit. You can do this by placing a label after the associated endxxxx clause and jumping to that label. The following code fragments demonstrate this technique for the various loops:

```
// Breaking out of a forever loop:

forever
    <<stmts>>
```

```
            //break;
        jmp BreakFromForever;
    <<stmts>>
endfor;
BreakFromForever:

// Breaking out of a FOR loop;
for( <<initStmt>>; <<expr>>; <<incStmt>> ) do
    <<stmts>>
            //break;
        jmp BrkFromFor;
    <<stmts>>
endfor;
BrkFromFor:

// Breaking out of a WHILE loop:

while( <<expr>> ) do
    <<stmts>>
            //break;
        jmp BrkFromWhile;
    <<stmts>>
endwhile;
BrkFromWhile:

// Breaking out of a REPEAT..UNTIL loop:

repeat
    <<stmts>>
            //break;
        jmp BrkFromRpt;
    <<stmts>>
until( <<expr>> );
BrkFromRpt:
```

The continue statement is slightly more difficult to implement that the break statement. The implementation still consists of a single jmp instruction, however the target label doesn't wind up going in the same spot for each of the different loops. Figures 7-2, 7-3, 7-4, and 7-5, respectively, show where the continue statement transfers control for each of the HLA loops.

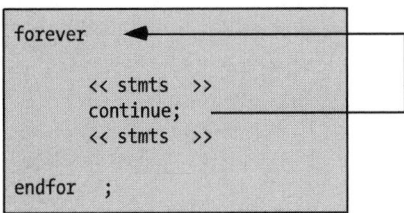

Figure 7-2: CONTINUE Destination for the FOREVER Loop.

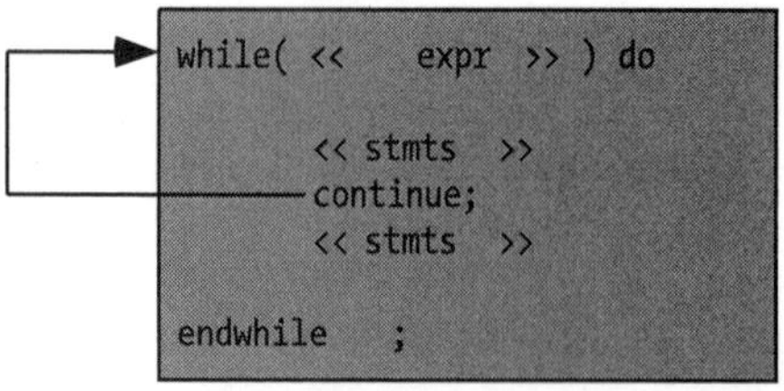

Figure 7-3: CONTINUE Destination and the WHILE Loop.

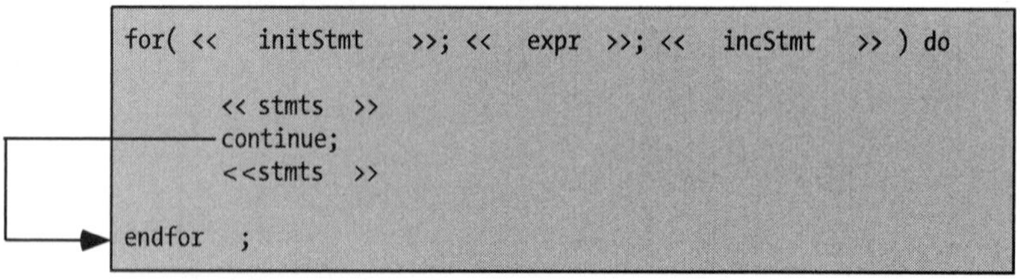

Note: CONTINUE forces the execution of the
<<incStmt>> clause and then transfers control
to the test for loop termination.

Figure 7-4: CONTINUE Destination and the FOR Loop.

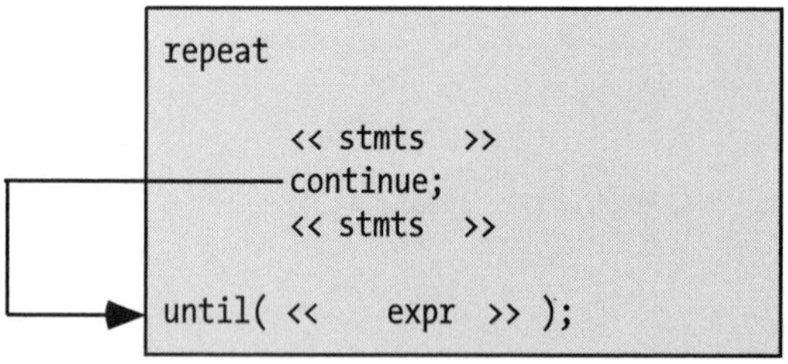

Figure 7-5: CONTINUE Destination and the REPEAT..UNTIL Loop.

The following code fragments demonstrate how to convert the continue statement
into an appropriate jmp instruction for each of these loop types.

forever..continue..endfor

```
// Conversion of forever loop w/continue
// to pure assembly:
forever
    <<stmts>>
    continue;
    <<stmts>>
endfor;

// Converted code:

foreverLbl:
    <<stmts>>
        // continue;
```

```
        jmp foreverLbl;
    <<stmts>>
    jmp foreverLbl;
```

while..continue..endwhile

```
// Conversion of while loop w/continue
// into pure assembly:

while( <<expr>> ) do
    <<stmts>>
    continue;
    <<stmts>>
endwhile;


// Converted code:

whlLabel:
<<Code to evaluate expr>>
Jcc EndOfWhile;  // Skip loop on expr failure.
    <<stmts>
        //continue;
        jmp whlLabel; // Jump to start of loop on continue.
    <<stmts>>
    jmp whlLabel; // Repeat the code.
EndOfwhile:
```

for..continue..endfor

```
// Conversion for a for loop w/continue
// into pure assembly:

for( <<initStmt>>; <<expr>>; <<incStmt>> ) do
    <<stmts>>
    continue;
    <<stmts>>
endfor;


// Converted code

<<initStmt>>
ForLpLbl:
<<Code to evaluate expr>>
Jcc EndOfFor; // Branch if expression fails.
    <<stmts>>
        //continue
        jmp ContFor;  // Branch to <<incStmt>> on continue.
    <<stmts>>
```

```
    ContFor:
    <<incStmt>>
    jmp ForLpLbl;
EndOfFor:
```

repeat..continue..until

```
repeat
    <<stmts>>
    continue;
    <<stmts>>
until( <<expr>> );
```

```
// Converted Code:
```

```
RptLpLbl:
    <<stmts>>
        // continue;
        jmp ContRpt;  // Continue branches to loop termination test.
        <<stmts>>
    ContRpt:
    <<code to test expr>>
    Jcc RptLpLbl;      // Jumps if expression evaluates false.
```

7.11.6   Register Usage and Loops

Given that the 80x86 accesses registers much faster than memory locations, registers are the ideal spot to place loop control variables (especially for small loops). However, there are some problems associated with using registers within a loop. The primary problem with using registers as loop control variables is that registers are a limited resource. The following will not work properly because it attempts to reuse a register (CX) that is already in use:

```
        mov( 8, cx );
    loop1:
        mov( 4, cx );
        loop2:
            <<stmts>>
            dec( cx );
            jnz loop2;
        dec( cx );
        jnz loop1;
```

The intent here, of course, was to create a set of nested loops — that is, one loop inside another. The inner loop (loop2) should repeat four times for each of the eight executions of the outer loop (loop1). Unfortunately, both loops use the same register as a loop control variable. Therefore, this will form an infinite loop because CX will be set to zero at the end of the first loop. Because CX is always zero upon encountering the second dec instruction, control will always transfer to the loop1 label (because decrementing zero produces a non-zero result). The solution here is to save and restore the CX register or to use a different register in place of CX for the outer loop:

```
        mov( 8, cx );
    loop1:
            push( cx );
            mov( 4, cx );
            loop2:
                <<stmts>>
                dec( cx );
                jnz loop2;

            pop( cx );
            dec( cx );
            jnz loop1;
```

or:

```
        mov( 8, dx );
    loop1:
            mov( 4, cx );
            loop2:
                <<stmts>>
                dec( cx );
                jnz loop2;

            dec( dx );
            jnz loop1;
```

Register corruption is one of the primary sources of bugs in loops in assembly language programs; always keep an eye out for this problem.

7.12   Performance Improvements

The 80x86 microprocessors execute sequences of instructions at blinding speeds. Therefore, you'll rarely encounter a program that is slow and that doesn't contain any loops. Because loops are the primary source of performance problems within a program, they are the place to look when attempting to speed up your software. While a treatise on how to write efficient programs is beyond the scope of this chapter, there are some things you should be aware of when designing loops in your programs. They're all aimed at removing unnecessary instructions from your loops in order to reduce the time it takes to execute one iteration of the loop.

7.12.1 Moving the Termination Condition to the End of a Loop

Consider the following flow graphs for the three types of loops presented earlier:

```
repeat..until loop:
    Initialization code
        Loop body
    Test for termination
    Code following the loop


while loop:
    Initialization code
    Loop termination test
        Loop body
        Jump back to test
    Code following the loop


forever..endfor loop:
    Initialization code
        Loop body, part one
        Loop termination test
        Loop body, part two
        Jump back to loop body part 1
    Code following the loop
```

As you can see, the repeat..until loop is the simplest of the bunch. This is reflected in the assembly language code required to implement these loops. Consider the following repeat..until and while loops that are semantically identical:

```
// Example involving a WHILE loop:

    mov( edi, esi );
    sub( 20, esi );
    while( esi <= edi ) do

        <<stmts>>
        inc( esi );

    endwhile;

// Conversion of the code above into pure assembly language:

    mov( edi, esi );
    sub( 20, esi );
    whlLbl:
    cmp( esi, edi );
    jnle EndOfWhile;
```

```
        <<stmts>>
        inc( esi );
        <<stmts>>
        jmp whlLbl;


    EndOfWhile:


//Example involving a REPEAT..UNTIL loop:

    mov( edi, esi );
    sub( 20, esi );
    repeat

        <<stmts>>
        inc( esi );

    until( esi > edi );

// Conversion of the REPEAT..UNTIL loop into pure assembly:

    rptLabel:
        <<stmts>>
        inc( esi );
        cmp( esi, edi );
        jng rptLabel;
```

As you can see by carefully studying the conversion to pure assembly language, testing for the termination condition at the end of the loop allowed us to remove a jmp instruction from the loop. This can be significant if this loop is nested inside other loops. In the preceding example there wasn't a problem with executing the body at least once. Given the definition of the loop, you can easily see that the loop will be executed exactly 20 times. This suggests that the conversion to a repeat..until loop is trivial and always possible. Unfortunately, it's not always quite this easy. Consider the following HLA code:

```
    while( esi <= edi ) do
        <<stmts>>
        inc( esi );
    endwhile;
```

In this particular example, we haven't the slightest idea what ESI contains upon entry into the loop. Therefore, we cannot assume that the loop body will execute at least once. So we must test for loop termination before executing the body of the loop. The test can be placed at the end of the loop with the inclusion of a single jmp instruction:

```
    jmp WhlTest;
    TopOfLoop:
```

```
    <<stmts>>
    inc( esi );
WhlTest:
    cmp( esi, edi );
    jle TopOfLoop;
```

Although the code is as long as the original while loop, the jmp instruction executes only once rather than on each repetition of the loop. Note that this slight gain in efficiency is obtained via a slight loss in readability. The second code sequence above is closer to spaghetti code that the original implementation. Such is often the price of a small performance gain. Therefore, you should carefully analyze your code to ensure that the performance boost is worth the loss of clarity. More often than not, assembly language programmers sacrifice clarity for dubious gains in performance, producing impossible-to-understand programs.

Note, by the way, that HLA translates its while statement into a sequence of instructions that test the loop termination condition at the bottom of the loop using exactly the technique this section describes. Therefore, you do not have to worry about the HLA while statement introducing slower code into your programs.

7.12.2   Executing the Loop Backward

Because of the nature of the flags on the 80x86, loops that repeat from some number down to (or up to) zero are more efficient than any other. Compare the following HLA for loop and the code it generates:

```
for( mov( 1, J); J <= 8; inc(J)) do
    <<stmts>>
endfor;


// Conversion to pure assembly (as well as using a repeat..until form):

mov( 1, J );
ForLp:
    <<stmts>>
    inc( J );
    cmp( J, 8 );
    jnge ForLp;
```

Now consider another loop that also has eight iterations, but runs its loop control variable from eight down to one rather than one up to eight:

```
mov( 8, J );
LoopLbl:
    <<stmts>>
    dec( J );
    jnz LoopLbl;
```

Note that by running the loop from eight down to one we saved a comparison on each repetition of the loop.

Unfortunately, you cannot force all loops to run backward. However, with a little effort and some coercion you should be able to write many for loops so they operate backward. By saving the execution time of the cmp instruction on each iteration of the loop the code may run faster.

The example above worked out well because the loop ran from eight down to one. The loop terminated when the loop control variable became zero. What happens if you need to execute the loop when the loop control variable goes to zero? For example, suppose that the loop above needed to range from seven down to zero. As long as the upper bound is positive, you can substitute the jns instruction in place of the jnz instruction above to repeat the loop some specific number of times:

```
mov( 7, J );
LoopLbl:
    <<stmts>>
    dec( J );
    jns LoopLbl;
```

This loop will repeat eight times with j taking on the values seven down to zero on each execution of the loop. When it decrements zero to minus one, it sets the sign flag and the loop terminates.

Keep in mind that some values may look positive but they are negative. If the loop control variable is a byte, then values in the range 128..255 are negative. Likewise, 16-bit values in the range 32768..65535 are negative. Therefore, initializing the loop control variable with any value in the range 129..255 or 32769..65535 (or, of course, zero) will cause the loop to terminate after a single execution. This can get you into a lot of trouble if you're not careful.

7.12.3 Loop Invariant Computations

A *loop invariant computation* is some calculation that appears within a loop that always yields the same result. You needn't do such computations inside the loop. You can compute them outside the loop and reference the value of the computation inside the loop. The following HLA code demonstrates a loop that contains an invariant computation:

```
for( mov( 0, eax ); eax < n; inc( eax )) do

    mov( eax, edx );
    add( j, edx );
    sub( 2, edx );
    add( edx, k );

endfor;
```

Because j never changes throughout the execution of this loop, the subexpression "j-2" can be computed outside the loop and its value used in the expression inside the loop:

```
mov( j, ecx );
sub( 2, ecx );
for( mov( 0, eax ); eax < n; inc( eax )) do

    mov( eax, edx );
    add( ecx, edx );
    add( edx, k );

endfor;
```

Still, the value in ECX never changes inside this loop, so although we've eliminated a single instruction by computing the subexpression "j-2" outside the loop, there is still an invariant component to this calculation. Because we note that this invariant component executes *n* times in the loop, we can translate the code above to the following:

```
mov( j, ecx );
sub( 2, ecx );
intmul( n, ecx );    // Compute n*(j-2) and add this into k outside
add( ecx, k );       // the loop.
for( mov( 0, eax ); eax < n; inc( eax )) do

    add( eax, k );

endfor;
```

As you can see, we've shrunk the loop body from four instructions down to one. Of course, if you're really interested in improving the efficiency of this particular loop, you can compute it without a loop at all (there is a formula that corresponds to the iterative calculation above). However, simple computations such as this one aren't always possible. Still, this demonstrates that a better algorithm is almost always better than the trickiest code you can come up with.

Removing invariant computations and unnecessary memory accesses from a loop (particularly an inner loop in a set of nested loops) can produce dramatic performance improvements in a program.

7.12.4 Unraveling Loops

For small loops — that is, those whose body is only a few statements — the overhead required to process a loop may constitute a significant percentage of the total processing time. For example, look at the following Pascal code and its associated 80x86 assembly language code:

```
FOR I := 3 DOWNTO 0 DO A [I] := 0;

mov( 3, I );
LoopLbl:
    mov( I, ebx );
    mov( 0, A[ebx*4] );
    dec( I );
    jns LoopLbl;
```

Each iteration of the loop requires four instructions. Only one instruction is performing the desired operation (moving a zero into an element of A). The remaining three instructions control the repetition of the loop. Therefore, it takes 16 instructions to do the operation logically required by 4.

While there are many improvements we could make to this loop based on the information presented thus far, consider carefully exactly what it is that this loop is doing: It's simply storing four zeros into A[0] through A[3]. A more efficient approach is to use four mov instructions to accomplish the same task. For example, if A is an array of double words, then the following code initializes A much faster than the code above:

```
mov( 0, A[0] );
mov( 0, A[4] );
mov( 0, A[8] );
mov( 0, A[12] );
```

Although this is a trivial example, it shows the benefit of *loop unraveling* (also known as *loop unrolling*). If this simple loop appeared buried inside a set of nested loops, the 4:1 instruction reduction could possibly double the performance of that section of your program.

Of course, you cannot unravel all loops. Loops that execute a variable number of times cannot be unraveled because there is rarely a way to determine (at assembly time) the number of times the loop will execute. Therefore, unraveling a loop is a process best applied to loops that execute a known number of times (and the number of times is known at assembly time).

Even if you repeat a loop of some fixed number of iterations, it may not be a good candidate for loop unraveling. Loop unraveling produces impressive performance improvements when the number of instructions required to control the loop (and handle other overhead operations) represent a significant percentage of the total number of instructions in the loop. Had the preceding loop contained 36 instructions in the body of the loop (exclusive of the four overhead instructions), then the performance improvement would be, at best, only 10 percent (compared with the 300 to 400 percent it now enjoys). Therefore, the costs of unraveling a loop — i.e., all the extra code that must be inserted into your program — quickly reaches a point of diminishing returns as the body of the loop grows larger or as the number of iterations increases. Furthermore, entering that code into your program can become quite a chore. Therefore, loop unraveling is a technique best applied to small loops.

Note that the superscalar 80x86 chips (Pentium and later) have *branch prediction hardware* and use other techniques to improve performance. Loop unrolling on such systems may actually *slow down* the code because these processors are optimized to execute short loops.

7.12.5 Induction Variables

Consider the following modification of the loop presented in the previous section:

```
FOR I := 0 TO 255 DO csetVar[I] := {};
```

Here the program is initializing each element of an array of character sets to the empty set. The straight-forward code to achieve this is the following:

```
mov( 0, i );
FLp:

        // Compute the index into the array (note that each element
        // of a CSET array contains 16 bytes).

        mov( i, ebx );
        shl( 4, ebx );

        // Set this element to the empty set (all zero bits).

        mov( 0, csetVar[ ebx ] );
        mov( 0, csetVar[ ebx+4 ] );
        mov( 0, csetVar[ ebx+8 ] );
        mov( 0, csetVar[ ebx+12 ] );

        inc( i );
        cmp( i, 256 );
        jb FLp;
```

Although unraveling this code will still produce a performance improvement, it will take 1024 instructions to accomplish this task, too many for all but the most time-critical applications. However, you can reduce the execution time of the body of the loop using *induction variables*. An induction variable is one whose value depends entirely on the value of some other variable. In the example above, the index into the array csetVar tracks the loop control variable (it's always equal to the value of the loop control variable times 16). Because i doesn't appear anywhere else in the loop, there is no sense in performing all the computations on i. Why not operate directly on the array index value? The following code demonstrates this technique:

```
mov( 0, ebx );
FLp:
        mov( 0, csetVar[ ebx ]);
```

```
mov( 0, csetVar[ ebx+4 ] );
mov( 0, csetVar[ ebx+8 ] );
mov( 0, csetVar[ ebx+12 ] );

add( 16, ebx );
cmp( ebx, 256*16 );
jb FLp;
```

The induction that takes place in this example occurs when the code increments the loop control variable (moved into EBX for efficiency reasons) by 16 on each iteration of the loop rather than by one. Multiplying the loop control variable by 16 allows the code to eliminate multiplying the loop control variable by 16 on each iteration of the loop (i.e., this allows us to remove the shl instruction from the previous code). Further, because this code no longer refers to the original loop control variable (i), the code can maintain the loop control variable strictly in the EBX register.

7.13   Hybrid Control Structures in HLA

The HLA high level language control structures have a few drawbacks: (1) they're not true assembly language instructions; (2) complex boolean expressions only support short-circuit evaluation; and (3) they often introduce inefficient coding practices into a language that most people only use when they need to write high-performance code. On the other hand, while the 80x86 low level control structures let you write efficient code, the resulting code is very difficult to read and maintain. HLA provides a set of hybrid control structures that allow you to use pure assembly language statements to evaluate boolean expressions while using the high level control structures to delineate the statements controlled by the boolean expressions. The result is code that is much more readable than pure assembly language without being a whole lot less efficient.

HLA provides hybrid forms of the if..elseif..else..endif, while..endwhile, repeat..until, breakif, exitif, and continueif statements (i.e., those that involve a boolean expression). For example, a hybrid if statement takes the following form:

```
if( #{  <<instructions>> }# ) then <<statements>> endif;
```

Note the use of #{ and }# operators to surround a sequence of instructions within this statement. This is what differentiates the hybrid control structures from the standard high level language control structures. The remaining hybrid control structures take the following forms:

```
while( #{ <<statements>> }# )  <<statements>> endwhile;
repeat <<statements>> until( #{ <<statements>> }# );
breakif( #{ <<statements>> }# );
exitif( #{ <<statements>> }# );
continueif( #{ <<statements>> }# );
```

The statements within the curly braces replace the normal boolean expression in an HLA high level control structure. These particular statements are special insofar as HLA defines two pseudo-labels, true and false, within their context. HLA associates the label true with the code that would normally execute if a boolean expression were present and that expression's result was true. Similarly, HLA associates the label false with the code that would execute if a boolean expression in one of these statements evaluated false. As a simple example, consider the following two (equivalent) if statements:

```
if( eax < ebx ) then inc( eax ); endif;


if
( #{
    cmp( eax, ebx );
    jnl false;
}# ) then
    inc( eax );

endif;
```

The jnl that transfers control to the false label in this latter example will skip over the inc instruction if EAX is not less than EBX. Note that if EAX is less than EBX, then control falls through to the inc instruction. This is roughly equivalent to the following pure assembly code:

```
cmp( eax, ebx );
jnl falseLabel;
    inc( eax );
falseLabel:
```

As a slightly more complex example, consider the statement

```
if( eax >= J && eax <= K ) then sub( J, eax ); endif;
```

The following hybrid if statement accomplishes the same:

```
if
( #{
    cmp( eax, J );
    jnge false;
    cmp( eax, K );
    jnle false;
}# ) then
    sub( J, eax );

endif;
```

As one final example of the hybrid if statement, consider the following:

```
// if( ((eax > ebx) && (eax < ecx)) || (eax = edx)) then mov( ebx, eax ); endif;

if
( #{
    cmp( eax, edx );
    je true;
    cmp( eax, ebx );
    jng false;
    cmp( eax, ecx );
    jnl false;
}# ) then
    mov( ebx, eax );

endif;
```

Because these examples are rather trivial, they don't really demonstrate how much more readable the code can be when using hybrid statements rather than pure assembly code. However, one thing you notice is that the use of hybrid statements eliminate the need to insert labels throughout your code. This is what makes your programs easier to read and understand.

For the if statement, the true label corresponds to the then clause of the statement; the false label corresponds to the elseif, else, or endif clause (whichever follows the then clause). For the while loop, the true label corresponds to the body of the loop while the false label is attached to the first statement following the corresponding endwhile. For the repeat..until statement, the true label is attached to the code following the until clause while the false label is attached to the first statement of the body of the loop. The breakif, exitif, and continueif statements associate the false label with the statement immediately following one of these statements; they associate the true label with the code normally associated with a break, exit, or continue statement.

7.14   For More Information

HLA contains a few additional high level control structures beyond those this chapter describes. Examples include the try..endtry block and the foreach statement. A discussion of these statements does not appear in this chapter because these are highly advanced control structures, and their implementation is probably a bit too complex to describe this early in the text. For more information on their implementation, see the electronic edition on the accompanying CD-ROM or the HLA Reference Manual.

8

FILES

8.1 Chapter Overview

In this chapter you will learn about the *file* persistent data type. In most assembly languages, file I/O is a major headache. Not so in HLA with the HLA Standard Library. File I/O is no more difficult than writing data to the standard output device or reading data from the standard input device. In this chapter you will learn how to create and manipulate sequential and random access files.

8.2 File Organization

A *file* is a collection of data that the system maintains in persistent storage. *Persistent* means that the storage is non-volatile, which means the system maintains the data even after the program terminates; indeed, even if you shut off the system power. For this reason, plus the fact that different programs can access the data in a file, applications typically use files to maintain data across executions of the application and to share data with other applications.

The operating system typically saves file data on a disk drive or some other form of secondary storage device. Because secondary storage tends to be much slower than main memory, you generally do not store data that a program commonly accesses in files during program execution unless that data is far too large to fit into main memory (e.g., a large database).

Under Linux and Windows, a standard file is simply a stream of bytes that the operating system does not interpret in any way. It is the responsibility of the application to interpret this information, just as it is your application's responsibility to interpret data in memory. The stream of bytes in a file could be a sequence of ASCII characters (e.g., a text file) or they could be pixel values that form a 24-bit color photograph.

Files generally take one of two different forms: *sequential files* or *random access files*. Sequential files are great for data you read or write all at once; random access files work best for data you read and write in pieces (or rewrite, as the case may be). For example, a typical text file (like an HLA source file) is usually a sequential file. Usually your text editor will read or write the entire file at once. Similarly, the HLA compiler will read the data from the file in a sequential fashion without skipping around in the file. A database file, on the other hand, requires random access because the application can read data from anywhere in the file in response to a query.

8.2.1   Files as Lists of Records

A good view of a file is as a list of records. That is, the file is broken down into a sequential string of records that share a common structure. A list is simply an open-ended single dimension array of items, so we can view a file as an array of records. As such, we can index into the file and select record number zero, record number one, record number two, and so on. Using common file access operations, it is quite possible to skip around to different records in a file. Under Windows and Linux, the principle difference between a sequential file and a random access file is the organization of the records and how easy it is to locate a specific record within the file. In this section we'll take a look at the issues that differentiate these two types of files.

The easiest file organization to understand is the random access file. A random access file is a list of records whose lengths are all identical (i.e., random access files require fixed length records). If the record length is n bytes, then the first record appears at byte offset zero in the file, the second record appears at byte offset n in the file, the third record appears at byte offset $n*2$ in the file, and so on. This organization is virtually identical to that of an array of records in main memory; you use the same computation to locate an "element" of this list in the file as you would use to locate an element of an array in memory: The only difference is that a file doesn't have a "base address" in memory; you simply compute the zero-based offset of the record in the file. This calculation is quite simple, and using some file I/O functions you will learn about a little later, you can quickly locate and manipulate any record in a random access file.

Sequential files also consist of a list of records. However, these records do not all have to be the same length.[1] If a sequential file does not use fixed length records then we say that the file uses variable length records. If a sequential file uses variable length records, then the file must contain some kind of marker or other mechanism to separate the records in the file. Typical sequential files use one of two mechanisms: a length prefix or some special terminating value. These two schemes should sound quite familiar to those who have read the chapter on strings. Character strings use a similar scheme to determine the bounds of a string in memory.

A text file is the best example of a sequential file that uses variable length records. Text files use a special marker at the end of each record to delineate the records. In a text file, a record corresponds to a single line of text. Under Linux, the line feed character marks the end of each record. Other operating systems may use a different sequence; e.g., Windows uses a carriage return/line feed sequence, while the Mac OS uses a single carriage return. For the sake of example, this chapter will use the Windows end-of-line sequence because most readers are probably learning assembly under Windows; Linux users should keep in mind that the end-of-line marker is a simple line feed character.

Accessing records in a file containing variable length records is problematic. Unless you have an array of offsets to each record in a variable length file, the only practical way to locate record *n* in a file is to read the first *n-1* records. This is why variable length files are sequential access: You have to read the file sequentially from the start in order to locate a specific record in the file. This will be much slower than accessing the file in a random access fashion. Generally, you would not use a variable length record organization for files you need to access in a random fashion.

At first blush it would seem that fixed length random access files offer all the advantages here. After all, you can access records in a file with fixed length records much more rapidly than files using the variable length record organization. However, there is a cost to this: Your fixed length records have to be large enough to hold the largest possible data object you want to store in a record. To store a sequence of lines in a text file, for example, your record sizes would have to be large enough to hold the longest possible input line. This could be quite large (for example, HLA's stdin.gets procedure allows lines up to 256 characters long). Each record in the file will consume this many bytes even if the record uses substantially less data. For example, an empty line only requires one or two bytes (for the line feed [Linux] or carriage return/line feed [Windows] sequence). If your record size is 256 bytes, then you're wasting 255 or 254 bytes for that blank line in your file. If the average line length is around 60 characters, then each line wastes an average of about 200 characters. This problem, known as *internal fragmentation,* can waste a tremendous amount of space on your disk, especially as your files get larger or you create lots of files. File organizations that use variable length records generally don't suffer from this problem.

---

[1] There is nothing preventing a sequential file from using fixed length records. However, they don't require fixed length records.

8.2.2 Binary vs. Text Files

Another important thing to realize about files is that they don't all contain human-readable text. Object code and executable files are good examples of files that contain binary information rather than text. A text file is a very special kind of variable length sequential file that uses special end-of-line markers (carriage returns/line feeds) at the end of each record (line) in the file. Binary files are everything else.

Binary files are often more compact than text files, and they are usually more efficient to access. Consider a text file that contains the following set of two-byte integer values:

```
1234
543
3645
32000
1
87
0
```

As a text file, this file consumes at least 34 bytes (under Windows) or 27 bytes (under Linux). However, were we to store the data in a fixed–record length binary file, with two bytes per integer value, this file would only consume 14 bytes — less than half the space. Furthermore, because the file now uses fixed length records (two bytes per record) we can efficiently access it in a random fashion. Finally, there is one additional, though hidden, efficiency aspect to the binary format: When a program reads and writes binary data it doesn't have to convert between the binary and string formats. This is an expensive process (with respect to computer time). If a human being isn't going to read this file with a separate program like a text editor, then converting to and from text format on every I/O operation is a wasted effort.

Consider the following HLA record type:

```
type
     person:
          record
               name:string;
               age:int16;
               ssn:char[11];
               salary:real64;
          endrecord;
```

If we were to write this record as text to a text file, a typical record would take the following form (<nl> indicates the end-of-line marker, a line feed or carriage return/line feed pair):

```
Hyde, Randall<nl>
45<nl>
555-55-5555<nl>
123456.78<nl>
```

Presumably, the next *person* record in the file would begin with the next line of text in the text file.

The binary version of this file (using a fixed length record, reserving 64 bytes for the *name* string) appears in Figure 8-1.

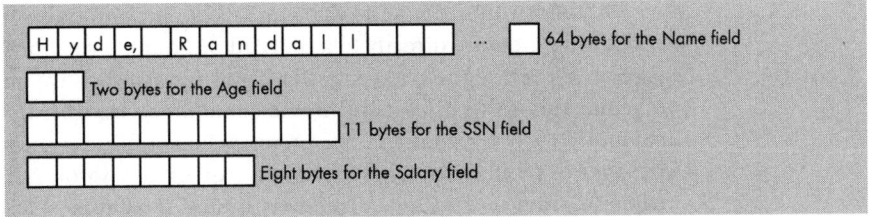

Figure 8-1: Fixed Length Format for Person Record.

Don't get the impression that binary files must use fixed length record sizes. We could create a variable length version of this record by using a zero byte to terminate the string, as Figure 8-2 shows.

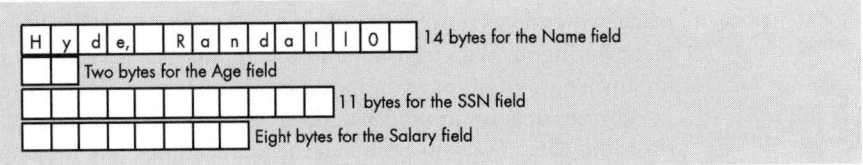

Figure 8-2: Variable Length Format for Person Record.

In this particular record format the age field starts at offset 14 in the record (because the name field and the "end of field" marker [the zero byte] consume 14 bytes). If a different name were chosen, then the age field would begin at a different offset in the record. In order to locate the age, ssn, and salary fields of this record, the program would have to scan past the name and find the zero terminating byte. The remaining fields would follow at fixed offsets from the zero terminating byte. As you can see, it's a bit more work to process this variable length record than the fixed length record. Once again, this demonstrates the performance difference between random access (fixed length) and sequential access (variable length, in this case) files.

Although binary files are often more compact and more efficient to access, they do have their drawbacks. In particular, only applications that are aware of the binary file's record format can easily access the file. If you're handed an arbitrary binary file and asked to decipher its contents, this could be very difficult. Text files, on the other hand, can be read by just about any text editor or filter program out there. Hence, your data files will be more interchangeable with other programs if you use text files. Furthermore, it is easier to debug the output of your programs if they produce text files because you can load a text file into the same editor you use to edit your source files.

8.3   Sequential Files

Sequential files are perfect for three types of persistent data: ASCII text files, "memory dumps," and stream data. Because you're probably familiar with ASCII text files, we'll skip their discussion. The other two methods of writing sequential files deserve more explanation.

A "memory dump" is a file that consists of data you transfer from data structures in memory directly to a file. Although the term "memory dump" suggests that you sequentially transfer data from consecutive memory locations to the file, this isn't necessarily the case. Memory access can, an often does, occur in a random access fashion. However, once the application constructs a record to write to the file, it writes that record in a sequential fashion (i.e., each record is written in order to the file). A "memory dump" is what most applications do when you request that they save the program's current data to a file or read data from a file into application memory. When writing, they gather all the important data from memory and write it to the file in a sequential fashion; when reading (loading) data from a file, they read the data from the file in a sequential fashion and store the data into appropriate memory-based data structures. Generally, when loading or saving file data in this manner, the program opens a file, reads/writes data from/to the file, and closes the file. Very little processing takes place during the data transfer, and the application does not leave the file open for any length of time beyond what is necessary to read or write the file's data.

Stream data on input is like data coming from a keyboard. The program reads the data at various points in the application when it needs new input to continue. Similarly, stream data on output is like a write to the console device. The application writes data to the file at various points in the program after important computations have taken place and the program wishes to report the results of the calculation. When reading data from a sequential file, once the program reads a particular piece of data, that data is no longer available (unless, of course, the program closes and reopens the file). When writing data to a sequential file, once data is written, it becomes a permanent part of the output file.

When doing stream processing the program typically opens a file and then continues execution. As program execution continues, the application can read or write data in the file. At some point, typically toward the end of the application's execution, the program closes the file and commits the data to disk.

Working with sequential files in HLA is very easy. In fact, you already know most of the functions you need in order to read or write sequential files. All that's left to learn is how to open and close files and perform some simple tests (like "Have we reached the end of a file when reading data from the file?").

The file I/O functions are nearly identical to the stdin and stdout functions. Indeed, stdin and stdout are really nothing more than special file I/O functions that read data from the standard input device (a file) or write data to the standard output device (which is also a file). You use the file I/O functions in a manner analogous to stdin and stdout, except you use the fileio prefix rather than stdin or stdout. For example, to write a string to an output file, you could use the fileio.puts function almost the same way you use the stdout.puts routine. Similarly, if you wanted to read a string from a file, you would use fileio.gets. The only real difference between these function calls and their stdin and stdout counterparts is that you must supply an extra parameter to tell the function what file to use for the transfer. This is a double word value known as the *file handle*. You'll see how to initialize this file handle in a moment, but assuming you have a couple of double word variables that hold file handle values, you can use calls like the following to read and write data in sequential files:

```
// Reads i, j, k, from file inputHandle.
fileio.get( inputHandle, i, j, k );
// Writes output to file outputHandle
fileio.put( outputHandle, "I = ", i, "J = ", j, " K = ", k, nl );
```

Although this example only demonstrates the use of get and put, be aware that almost all of the stdin and stdout functions are available as fileio functions, as well (in fact, most of the stdin and stdout functions simply call the appropriate fileio function to do the real work).

There is, of course, the issue of this file handle variable. You're probably wondering what a file handle is and how you tell the fileio routines to work with data in a specific file on your disk. Well, the definition of the file handle object is the easiest to explain: It's just a double word variable that the operating system initializes and uses to keep track of your file. To declare a file handle, you'd just create a dword variable, e.g.,

```
static
    myFileHandle:dword;
```

You should never explicitly manipulate the value of a file handle variable. The operating system will initialize this variable for you (via some calls you'll see in a moment) and the OS expects you to leave this value alone as long as you're working with the file the OS associates with that handle. If you're curious, both Linux and Windows store small integer values into the handle variable. Internally, the OS uses this value as an index into an array that contains pertinent information about open files. If you mess with the file handle's value, you will confuse the OS greatly the next time you attempt to access the file. The moral of the story is leave this value alone while the file is open.

Before you can read or write a file you must open that file and associate a filename with it. The HLA Standard Library provides a couple of functions that provide this service: fileio.open and fileio.openNew. The fileio.open function opens an existing file for reading, writing, or both. Generally, you open sequential files for reading or writing, but not both (though there are some special cases where you can open a sequential file for reading and writing). The syntax for the call to this function is:

```
fileio.open( "filename", access );
```

The first parameter is a string value that specifies the filename of the file to open. This can be a string constant, a register that contains the address of a string value, or a string variable. The second parameter is a constant that specifies how you want to open the file. You may use any of the three predefined constants for the second parameter:

```
        fileio.r
        fileio.w
        fileio.rw
```

fileio.r obviously specifies that you want to open an existing file in order to read the data from that file; likewise, fileio.w says that you want to open an existing file and overwrite the data in that file. The fileio.rw option lets you open a file for both reading and writing.

The fileio.open routine, if successful, returns a *file handle* in the EAX register. Generally, you will want to save the return value into a double word variable for use by the other HLA fileio routines (i.e., the MyFileHandle variable in the earlier example).

If the OS cannot open the file, fileio.open will raise an ex.FileOpenFailure exception. This usually means that it could not find the specified file on the disk.

The fileio.open routine requires that the file exist on the disk or it will raise an exception. If you want to create a new file that might not already exist, the fileio.openNew function will do the job for you. This function uses the following syntax:

```
fileio.openNew( "filename" );
```

Note that this call has only a single parameter, a string specifying the filename. When you open a file with fileio.openNew, the file is always opened for writing. If a file by the specified filename already exists, then this function will delete the existing file and the new data will be written over the top of the old file (*so be careful*).

Like fileio.open, fileio.openNew returns a file handle in the EAX register if it successfully opens the file. You should save this value in a file handle variable. This function raises the ex.FileOpenFailure exception if it cannot open the file.

Once you open a sequential file with fileio.open or fileio.openNew and you save the file handle value away, you can begin reading data from an input file (fileio.r) or writing data to an output file (fileio.w). To do this, you would use functions like fileio.put as just noted.

When the file I/O is complete, you must close the file to commit the file data to the disk. You should always close all files you open as soon as you are through with them so that the program doesn't consume excess system resources. The syntax for fileio.close is very simple; it takes a single parameter, the file handle value returned by fileio.open or fileio.openNew:

```
fileio.close( file_handle );
```

If there is an error closing the file, `fileio.close` will raise the `ex.FileCloseError` exception. Note that Linux and Windows automatically close all open files when an application terminates; however, it is very bad programming style to depend on this feature. If the system crashes (or the user turns off the power) before the application terminates, file data may be lost. So you should always close your files as soon as you are done accessing the data in that file.

The last function of interest to us right now is the `fileio.eof` function. This function returns true (1) or false (0) in the EAX register depending on whether the current file pointer is at the end of the file. Generally you would use this function when reading data from an input file to determine if there is more data to read from the file. You would not normally call this function for output files; it always returns false.[2] Because the `fileio` routines will raise an exception if the disk is full, there is no need to waste time checking for end of file (EOF) when writing data to a file. The syntax for `fileio.eof` is

```
fileio.eof( file_handle );
```

Listing 8-1 demonstrates a complete program that opens and writes a simple text file.

Listing 8-1: A Simple File Output Program.

```
program SimpleFileOutput;
#include( "stdlib.hhf" )

static
  outputHandle:dword;

begin SimpleFileOutput;

  fileio.openNew( "myfile.txt" );
  mov( eax, outputHandle );

  for( mov( 0, ebx ); ebx < 10; inc( ebx )) do

    fileio.put( outputHandle, (type uns32 ebx ), nl );

  endfor;
  fileio.close( outputHandle );

end SimpleFileOutput;
```

Listing 8-2 reads the data that Listing 8-1 produces and writes the data to the standard output device.

---

[2] Actually, it will return true under Windows if the disk is full.

Listing 8-2: A Sample File Input Program.

```
program SimpleFileInput;
#include( "stdlib.hhf" )

static
  inputHandle:dword;
  u:uns32;

begin SimpleFileInput;

  fileio.open( "myfile.txt", fileio.r );
  mov( eax, inputHandle );

  for( mov( 0, ebx ); ebx < 10; inc( ebx )) do

    fileio.get( inputHandle, u );
    stdout.put( "ebx=", ebx, " u=", u, nl );

  endfor;
  fileio.close( inputHandle );

end SimpleFileInput;
```

There are a couple of interesting functions that you can use when working with sequential files. They are the following:

```
fileio.rewind( fileHandle );
fileio.append( fileHandle );
```

The fileio.rewind function resets the "file pointer" (the cursor into the file where the next read or write will take place) back to the beginning of the file. This name is a carry-over from the days of files on tape drives when the system would rewind the tape on the tape drive to move the read/write head back to the beginning of the file.

If you've opened a file for reading, then fileio.rewind lets you begin reading the file from the start (i.e., make a second pass over the data). If you've opened the file for writing, then fileio.rewind will cause future writes to overwrite the data you've previously written; you won't normally use this function with files you've opened only for writing. If you've opened the file for reading and writing (using the fileio.rw option) then you can write the data after you've first opened the file and then rewind the file and read the data you've written. Listing 8-3 is a modification to the program in Listing 8-2 that reads the data file twice. This program also demonstrates the use of fileio.eof to test for the end of the file (rather than just counting the records).

Listing 8-3: Another Sample File Input Program.

```
program SimpleFileInput2;
#include( "stdlib.hhf" )

static
  inputHandle:dword;
  u:uns32;

begin SimpleFileInput2;

  fileio.open( "myfile.txt", fileio.r );
  mov( eax, inputHandle );

  for( mov( 0, ebx ); ebx < 10; inc( ebx )) do

    fileio.get( inputHandle, u );
    stdout.put( "ebx=", ebx, " u=", u, nl );

  endfor;
  stdout.newln();

  // Rewind the file and reread the data from the beginning.
  // This time, use fileio.eof() to determine when we've
  // reached the end of the file.

  fileio.rewind( inputHandle );
  while( fileio.eof( inputHandle ) = false ) do

    // Read and display the next item from the file:

    fileio.get( inputHandle, u );
    stdout.put( "u=", u, nl );

    // Note: After we read the last numeric value, there is still
    // a newline sequence left in the file, if we don't read the
    // newline sequence after each number then EOF will be false
    // at the start of the loop and we'll get an EOF exception
    // when we try to read the next value. Calling fileio.ReadLn
    // "eats" the newline after each number and solves this problem.

    fileio.readLn( inputHandle );


  endwhile;
  fileio.close( inputHandle );

end SimpleFileInput2;
```

The fileio.append function moves the file pointer to the end of the file. This function is really only useful for files you've opened for writing (or reading and writing). After executing fileio.append, all data you write to the file will be written after the data that already exists in the file (i.e., you use this call to append data to the end of a file you've opened). The program in Listing 8-4 demonstrates how to use this program to append data to the file created by the program in Listing 8-1.

Listing 8-4: Demonstration of the fileio.Append Routine.

```
program AppendDemo;
#include( "stdlib.hhf" )

static
  fileHandle:dword;
  u:uns32;

begin AppendDemo;

  fileio.open( "myfile.txt", fileio.rw );
  mov( eax, fileHandle );
  fileio.append( eax );

  for( mov( 10, ecx ); ecx < 20; inc( ecx )) do

    fileio.put( fileHandle, (type uns32 ecx), nl );

  endfor;


  // Okay, let's rewind to the beginning of the file and
  // display all the data from the file, including the
  // new data we just wrote to it:

  fileio.rewind( fileHandle );
  while( !fileio.eof( fileHandle )) do

    // Read and display the next item from the file:

    fileio.get( fileHandle, u );
    stdout.put( "u=", u, nl );
    fileio.readLn( fileHandle );

  endwhile;
  fileio.close( fileHandle );

end AppendDemo;
```

Another function, similar to fileio.eof, that will prove useful when reading data from a file is the fileio.eoln function. This function returns true if the next character(s) to be read from the file are the end-of-line sequence (carriage return, line feed, or the sequence of these two characters under Windows, just a line feed under Linux). This function returns true in the EAX register if it detects an end-of-line sequence. The calling sequence for this function is

fileio.eoln(*fileHandle*);

If fileio.eoln detects an end-of-line sequence, it will read those characters from the file (so the next read from the file will not read the end-of-line characters). If fileio.eoln does not detect the end of line sequence, it does not modify the file pointer position. The program in Listing 8-5 demonstrates the use of fileio.eoln in the *AppendDemo* program, replacing the call to fileio.readLn (because fileio.eoln reads the end-of-line sequence, there is no need for the call to fileio.readLn).

Listing 8-5: fileio.eoln Demonstration Program.

```
program EolnDemo;
#include( "stdlib.hhf" )

static
    fileHandle:dword;
    u:uns32;

begin EolnDemo;

    fileio.open( "myfile.txt", fileio.rw );
    mov( eax, fileHandle );
    fileio.append( eax );

    for( mov( 10, ecx ); ecx < 20; inc( ecx )) do

        fileio.put( fileHandle, (type uns32 ecx), nl );

    endfor;


    // Okay, let's rewind to the beginning of the file and
    // display all the data from the file, including the
    // new data we just wrote to it:

    fileio.rewind( fileHandle );
    while( !fileio.eof( fileHandle )) do

        // Read and display the next item from the file:

        fileio.get( fileHandle, u );
```

```
            stdout.put( "u=", u, nl );
            if( !fileio.eoln( fileHandle )) then

                stdout.put( "Hmmm, expected the end of the line", nl );

            endif;

        endwhile;
        fileio.close( fileHandle );

    end EolnDemo;
```

8.4   Random Access Files

The problem with sequential files is that they are, well, sequential. They are great for dumping and retrieving large blocks of data all at once, but they are not suitable for applications that need to read, write, and rewrite the same data in a file multiple times. In those situations random access files provide the only reasonable alternative.

Windows and Linux don't differentiate sequential and random access files anymore than the CPU differentiates byte and character values in memory; it's up to your application to treat the files as sequential or random access. As such, you use many of the same functions to manipulate random access files as you use to manipulate sequential access files; you just use them differently is all.

You still open files with `fileio.open` and `fileio.openNew`. Random access files are generally opened for reading or reading and writing. You rarely open a random access file as write-only because a program typically needs to read data if it's jumping around in the file.

You still close the files with `fileio.close`.

You can read and write the files with `fileio.get` and `fileio.put`, although you would not normally use these functions for random access file I/O because each record you read or write has to be exactly the same length and these functions aren't particularly suited for fixed length record I/O. Most of the time you will use one of the following functions to read and write fixed length data:

```
fileio.write( fileHandle, buffer, count );
fileio.read( fileHandle, buffer, count );
```

The `fileHandle` parameter is the usual file handle value (a dword variable). The count parameter is an `uns32` object that specifies how many bytes to read or write. The `buffer` parameter must be an object with at least count bytes. This parameter supplies the address of the first byte in memory where the I/O transfer will take place. These functions return the number of bytes read or written in the EAX register. For `fileio.read`, if the return value in EAX does not equal count's value, then you've reached the end of the file. For `fileio.write`, if EAX does not equal count then the disk is full.

Here is a typical call to the `fileio.read` function that will read a record from a file:

```
fileio.read( myHandle, myRecord, @size( myRecord ) );
```

If the return value in EAX does not equal @size(myRecord) and it does not equal zero (indicating end of file), then there is something seriously wrong with the file because the file should contain an integral number of records.

Writing data to a file with `fileio.write` uses a similar syntax to `fileio.read`.

You can use `fileio.read` and `fileio.write` to read and write data from/to a sequential file, just as you can use routines like `fileio.get` and `fileio.put` to read/write data from/to a random access file. You'd typically use these routines to read and write data from/to a binary sequential file.

The functions we've discussed to this point don't let you randomly access records in a file. If you call `fileio.read` several times in a row, the program will read those records sequentially from the text file. To do true random access I/O we need the ability to jump around in the file. Fortunately, the HLA Standard Library's file module provides several functions you can use to accomplish this.

The `fileio.position` function returns the current offset into the file in the EAX register. If you call this function immediately before reading or writing a record to a file, then this function will tell you the exact position of that record. You can use this value to quickly locate that record for a future access. The calling sequence for this function is

```
fileio.position( fileHandle ); // Returns current file position in EAX.
```

The `fileio.seek` function repositions the file pointer to the offset you specify as a parameter. The following is the calling sequence for this function:

```
fileio.seek( fileHandle, offset ); // Repositions file to specified offset.
```

The function call above will reposition the file pointer to the byte offset specified by the offset parameter. If you feed this function the value returned by `fileio.position`, then the next read or write operation will access the record written (or read) immediately after the `fileio.position` call.

You can pass any arbitrary offset value as a parameter to the `fileio.seek` routine; this value does not have to be one that the `fileio.position` function returns. For random access file I/O you would normally compute this offset file by specifying the index of the record you wish to access multiplied by the size of the record. For example, the following code computes the byte offset of record index in the file, repositions the file pointer to that record, and then reads the record:

```
intmul( @size( myRecord ), index, ebx );
fileio.seek( fileHandle, ebx );
fileio.read( fileHandle, (type byte myRecord), @size( myRecord ) );
```

You can use essentially this same code sequence to select a specific record in the file for writing.

Note that it is not an error to seek beyond the current end of file and then write data. If you do this, the OS will automatically fill in the intervening records with uninitialized data. Generally, this isn't a great way to create files, but it is perfectly legal. On the other hand, be aware that if you do this by accident, you may wind up with garbage in the file and no error to indicate that this has happened.

The fileio module provides another routine for repositioning the file pointer: fileio.rSeek. This function's calling sequence is very similar to fileio.seek; it is

```
fileio.rSeek( fileHandle, offset );
```

The difference between this function and the regular fileio.seek function is that this function repositions the file pointer offset bytes from the end of the file (rather than offset bytes from the start of the file). The "r" in "rSeek" stands for "reverse" seek.

Repositioning the file pointer, especially if you reposition it a fair distance from its current location, can be a time-consuming process. If you reposition the file pointer and then attempt to read a record from the file, the system may need to reposition a disk arm (a very slow process) and wait for the data to rotate underneath the disk read/write head. This is why random access I/O is much less efficient than sequential I/O.

The program in Listing 8-6 demonstrates random access I/O by writing and reading a file of records.

Listing 8-6: Random Access File I/O Example.

```
program RandomAccessDemo;
#include( "stdlib.hhf" )

type
  fileRec:
    record
      x:int16;
      y:int16;
      magnitude:uns8;
    endrecord;

const

  // Some arbitrary data we can use to initialize the file:

  fileData:=
    [
      fileRec:[ 2000, 1, 1 ],
      fileRec:[ 1000, 10, 2 ],
      fileRec:[ 750, 100, 3 ],
```

```
        fileRec:[ 500, 500, 4 ],
        fileRec:[ 100, 1000, 5 ],
        fileRec:[ 62, 2000, 6 ],
        fileRec:[ 32, 2500, 7 ],
        fileRec:[ 10, 3000, 8 ]
    ];


static
    fileHandle:      dword;
    RecordFromFile:    fileRec;
    InitialFileData:  fileRec[ 8 ] := fileData;



begin RandomAccessDemo;

    fileio.openNew( "fileRec.bin" );
    mov( eax, fileHandle );

// Okay, write the initial data to the file in a sequential fashion:

    for( mov( 0, ebx ); ebx < 8; inc( ebx )) do

        intmul( @size( fileRec ), ebx, ecx );  // Compute index into fileData
        fileio.write
        (
            fileHandle,
            (type byte InitialFileData[ecx]),
            @size( fileRec )
        );

    endfor;

    // Okay, now let's demonstrate a random access of this file
    // by reading the records from the file backward.

    stdout.put( "Reading the records, backwards:" nl );
    for( mov( 7, ebx ); (type int32 ebx) >= 0; dec( ebx )) do

        intmul( @size( fileRec ), ebx, ecx );  // Compute file offset
        fileio.seek( fileHandle, ecx );
        fileio.read
        (
            fileHandle,
            (type byte RecordFromFile),
            @size( fileRec )
        );
        if( eax = @size( fileRec )) then
```

```
                stdout.put
                (
                  "Read record #",
                  (type uns32 ebx),
                  ", values:" nl
                  " x: ", RecordFromFile.x, nl
                  " y: ", RecordFromFile.y, nl
                  " magnitude: ", RecordFromFile.magnitude, nl nl
                );

            else

                stdout.put( "Error reading record number ", (type uns32 ebx), nl );

            endif;

        endfor;
        fileio.close( fileHandle );

    end RandomAccessDemo;
```

8.5   ISAM (Indexed Sequential Access Method) Files

ISAM is a trick that attempts to allow random access to variable length records in a sequential file. This is a technique employed by IBM on its mainframe data bases in the 1960s and 1970s. Back then, disk space was very precious (remember why we wound up with the Y2K problem?), and IBM's engineers did everything they could to save space. At that time disks held about five megabytes or so, were the size of washing machines, and cost tens of thousands of dollars. You can appreciate why they wanted to make every byte count. Today, database designers have disk drives with hundreds of gigabytes per drive and RAID[3] devices with dozens of these drives installed. They don't bother trying to conserve space at all ("Heck, I don't know how big the person's name can get, so I'll allocate 256 bytes for it!"). Nevertheless, even with large disk arrays, saving space is often a wise idea. Not everyone has a terabyte (1,000 gigabytes) at their disposal, and a user of your application may not appreciate your decision to waste their disk space. Therefore, techniques like ISAM that can reduce disk storage requirements are still important today.

ISAM is actually a very simple concept. Somewhere, the program saves the offset to the start of every record in a file. Because offsets are four bytes long, an array of double words will work quite nicely.[4] Generally, as you construct the file you fill in the list (array) of offsets and keep track of the number of records in the file. For example, if you were creating a text file and you wanted to be able to

---

[3] Redundant array of inexpensive disks. RAID is a mechanism for combining lots of cheap disk drives together to form the equivalent of a really large disk drive.

[4] This assumes, of course, that your files have a maximum size of four gigabytes.

quickly locate any line in the file, you would save the offset into the file of each line you wrote to the file. The following code fragment shows how you could do this:

```
static
    outputLine: string;
    ISAMarray: dword[ 128*1024 ]; // allow up to 128K records.
            .
            .
            .
    mov( 0, ecx );      // Keep record count here.
    forever

        << create a line of text in "outputLine" >>

        fileio.position( fileHandle );
        mov( eax, ISAMarray[ecx*4] ); // Save away current record offset.
        fileio.put( fileHandle, outputLine, nl ); // Write the record.
        inc( ecx ); // Advance to next element of ISAMarray.

        << determine if we're done and BREAK if we are >>

    endfor;

    << At this point, ECX contains the number of records and >>
    << ISAMarray[0]..ISAMarray[ecx-1] contain the offsets to >>
    << each of the records in the file.            >>
```

After building the file using the code above, you can quickly jump to an arbitrary line of text by fetching the index for that line from the ISAMarray list. The following code demonstrates how you could read line *recordNumber* from the file:

```
    mov( recordNumber, ebx );
    fileio.seek( fileHandle, ISAMarray[ ebx*4 ] );
    fileio.a_gets( fileHandle, inputString );
```

As long as you've precalculated the ISAMarray list, accessing an arbitrary line in this text file is a trivial matter.

Of course, back in the days when IBM programmers were trying to squeeze every byte from their databases as possible so they would fit on a 5MB disk drive, they didn't have 512 kilobytes of RAM to hold 128K entries in the ISAMarray list. Although a half a megabyte is no big deal today, there are a couple of reasons why keeping the ISAMarray list in a memory-based array might not be such a good idea. First, databases are much larger these days. Some databases have hundreds of millions of entries. While setting aside a half a megabyte for an ISAM table might not be a bad thing, few people are willing to set aside a half a gigabyte for this purpose. Even if your database isn't amazingly big, there is another reason why you might not want to keep your ISAMarray in main memory; it's the same reason you don't keep the file in memory: Memory is volatile, and the data is lost whenever the application quits or the user removes power from the system. The solution is exactly the same as for the file data: You store the ISAMarray data in its own file. A program that builds the ISAM table while writing the file is a simple modification to the previous ISAM generation program. The trick is to open two files concurrently and write the ISAM data to one file while you're writing the text to the other file:

```
static
    fileHandle: dword;    // file handle for the text file.
    outputLine: string;   // file handle for the ISAM file.
    CurrentOffset: dword; // Holds the current offset into the text file.
        .
        .
        .

    forever

        << create a line of text in "outputLine" >>

        // Get the offset of the next record in the text file
        // and write this offset (sequentially) to the ISAM file.

        fileio.position( fileHandle );
        mov( eax, CurrentOffset );
        fileio.write( isamHandle, (type byte CurrentOffset), 4 );

        // Okay, write the actual text data to the text file:

        fileio.put( fileHandle, outputLine, nl ); // Write the record.

        << determine if we're done and BREAK if we are >>

    endfor;
```

If necessary, you can count the number of records as before. You might write this value to the first record of the ISAM file (because you know the first record of the text file is always at offset zero, you can use the first element of the ISAM list to hold the count of ISAM/text file records).

Because the ISAM file is just a sequence of four-byte integers, each record in the file (i.e., an integer) has the same length. Therefore, we can easily access any value in the ISAM file using the random access file I/O mechanism. In order to read a particular line of text from the text file, the first task is to read the offset from the ISAM file and then use that offset to read the desired line from the text file. The code to accomplish this is as follows:

```
// Assume we want to read the line specified by the "lineNumber" variable.

if( lineNumber <> 0 ) then
```

```
            // If not record number zero, then fetch the offset to the desired
            // line from the ISAM file:

            intmul( 4, lineNumber, eax );  // Compute the index into the ISAM file.
            fileio.seek( isamHandle, eax );
            fileio.read( isamHandle, (type byte CurrentOffset), 4 ); // Read offset

        else
            mov( 0, eax ); // Special case for record zero because the file
                           // contains the record count in this position.

        endif;
        fileio.seek( fileHandle, CurrentOffset ); // Set text file position.
        fileio.a_gets( fileHandle, inputLine );   // Read the line of text.
```

This operation runs at about half the speed of having the ISAM array in memory (because it takes four file accesses rather than two to read the line of text from the file), but the data is non-volatile and is not limited by the amount of available RAM.

If you decide to use a memory-based array for your ISAM table, it's still a good idea to keep that data in a file somewhere so you don't have to recompute it (by reading the entire file) every time your application starts. If the data is present in a file, all you've got to do is read that file data into your ISAMarray list. Assuming you've stored the number of records in element number zero of the ISAM array, you could use the following code to read your ISAM data into the ISAMarray variable:

```
static
    isamSize: uns32;
    isamHandle: dword;
    fileHandle: dword;
    ISAMarray: dword[ 128*1024 ];

         .

         .

         .

    // Read the first record of the ISAM file into the isamSize variable:

    fileio.read( isamHandle, (type byte isamSize), 4 );

    // Now read the remaining data from the ISAM file into the ISAMarray
    // variable:

    if( isamSize >= 128*1024 ) then

        raise( ex.ValueOutOfRange );

    endif;
    intmul( 4, isamSize, ecx ); // #records * 4 is number of bytes to read.
    fileio.read( isamHandle, (type byte ISAMarray), ecx );
```

```
    // At this point, ISAMarray[0]..ISAMarray[isamSize-1] contain the indexes
    // into the text file for each line of text.
```

8.6   Truncating a File

If you open an existing file (using fileio.open) for output and write data to that file, it overwrites the existing data from the start of the file. However, if the new data you write to the file is shorter than the data originally appearing in the file, the excess data from the original file, beyond the end of the new data you've written, will still appear at the end of the new data. Sometimes this might be desirable, but most of the time, you'll want to delete the old data after writing the new data.

One way to delete the old data is to use the fileio.opennew function to open the file. The fileio.opennew function automatically deletes any existing file so only the data you write to the file will be present in the file. However, there may be times when you may want to read the old data first, rewind the file, and then overwrite the data. In this situation, you'll need a function that will *truncate* the old data at the end of the file after you've written the new data. The fileio.truncate function accomplishes this task. This function uses the following calling syntax:

fileio.truncate(fileHandle);

Note that this function does not close the file. You still have to call fileio.close to commit the data to the disk.

The program in Listing 8-7 demonstrates the use of the fileio.truncate function.

Listing 8-7: Using fileio.truncate to Eliminate Old Data from a File.

```
program TruncateDemo;
#include( "stdlib.hhf" )

static
  fileHandle:dword;
  u:uns32;

begin TruncateDemo;

  fileio.openNew( "myfile.txt" );
  mov( eax, fileHandle );
  for( mov( 0, ecx ); ecx < 20; inc( ecx )) do

    fileio.put( fileHandle, (type uns32 ecx), nl );

  endfor;
```

```
// Okay, let's rewind to the beginning of the file and
// rewrite the first ten lines and then truncate the
// file at that point.

fileio.rewind( fileHandle );
for( mov( 0, ecx ); ecx < 10; inc( ecx )) do

  fileio.put( fileHandle, (type uns32 ecx), nl );

endfor;
fileio.truncate( fileHandle );


// Rewind and display the file contents to ensure that
// the file truncation has worked.

fileio.rewind( fileHandle );
while( !fileio.eof( fileHandle )) do

  // Read and display the next item from the file:

  fileio.get( fileHandle, u );
  stdout.put( "u=", u, nl );
  fileio.readLn( fileHandle );

endwhile;
fileio.close( fileHandle );

end TruncateDemo;
```

8.7   For More Information

Most of the information appearing in this chapter is generic — that is, it's not assembly language specific. As such, you'll find a wealth of information on file I/O in data structure texts and other introductory programming texts. The HLA Standard Library provides hundreds of functions and procedures related to file I/O. For more information on those, please consult the HLA Standard Library Reference Manual.

If you're interested in implementing a database engine in assembly language, you should definitely consider obtaining a college textbook on database design. Although such texts almost always use a high level language, most of the theoretical information appearing in such texts is language independent, and you'll find it quite useful when working on your assembly database engine.

9

ADVANCED ARITHMETIC

9.1   Chapter Overview

This chapter deals with those arithmetic operations for which assembly language is especially well suited, but for which high level languages are, in general, poorly suited. It covers four main topics: extended precision arithmetic, arithmetic on operands whose sizes are different, decimal arithmetic, and computation via table look-up.

By far, the most extensive subject this chapter covers is multiprecision arithmetic. By the conclusion of this chapter you will know how to apply arithmetic and logical operations to integer operands of any size. If you need to work with integer values outside the range ±2 billion (or with unsigned values beyond 4 billion), no sweat; this chapter will show you how to get the job done.

Operands whose sizes are not the same also present some special problems in arithmetic operations. For example, you may want to add a 128-bit unsigned integer to a 256-bit signed integer value. This chapter discusses how to convert these two operands to a compatible format so the operation may proceed.

This chapter also discusses decimal arithmetic using the binary coded decimal (BCD) features of the 80x86 instruction set and the FPU. This lets you use decimal arithmetic in those few applications that absolutely require base 10 operations (rather than binary).

Finally, this chapter concludes by discussing the use of tables to speed up complex computations.

9.2 Multiprecision Operations

One big advantage of assembly language over high level languages is that assembly language does not limit the size of integer operations. For example, the standard C programming language defines three different integer sizes: short int, int, and long int.[1] On the PC, these are often 16- and 32-bit integers. Although the 80x86 machine instructions limit you to processing 8-, 16-, or 32-bit integers with a single instruction, you can always use more than one instruction to process integers of any size you desire. If you want to add 256-bit integer values together, no problem; it's relatively easy to accomplish this in assembly language. The following sections describe how extended various arithmetic and logical operations from 16 or 32 bits to as many bits as you please.

9.2.1 HLA Standard Library Support for Extended Precision Operations

Although it is important for you to understand how to do extended precision arithmetic yourself, you should note that the HLA Standard Library provides a full set of 64-bit and 128-bit arithmetic and logical functions that you can use. These routines are very general purpose and are very convenient to use. This section will briefly describe the HLA Standard Library support for extended precision arithmetic.

As noted in earlier chapters, the HLA compiler supports several different 64-bit and 128-bit data types. As a review, here are the extended data types that HLA supports:

- uns64: 64-bit unsigned integers

- int64: 64-bit signed integers

- qword: 64-bit untyped values

- uns128: 128-bit unsigned integers

- int128: 128-bit signed integers

- lword: 128-bit untyped values

HLA also provides a tbyte type, but we will not consider that here (see the section on decimal arithmetic later in this chapter).

HLA lets you create constants, types, and variables whose type is one of the above. HLA fully supports 64-bit and 128-bit literal constants and constant arithmetic. This allows you to initialize 64- and 128-bit static objects using standard decimal, hexadecimal, or binary notation. For example:

```
static
    u128    :uns128 := 12345678901234567890123357890;
    i64     :int64  := -12345678901234567890;
    lw      :lword  := $1234_5678_90ab_cdef_0000_ffff;
```

---

[1] Newer C standards also provide for a "long long int," which is usually a 64-bit integer.

Of course, the 80x86 general purpose integer registers don't support 64-bit or 128-bit operands, so you may not directly manipulate these values with single 80x86 machine instructions (though you'll see how to do this with multiple instructions starting in the next section).

In order to easily manipulate 64-bit and 128-bit values, the HLA Standard Library's math.hhf module provides a set of functions that handle most of the standard arithmetic and logical operations you'll need. You use these functions in a manner quite similar to the standard 32-bit arithmetic and logical instructions. For example, consider the math.addq (qword) and math.addl (lword) functions:

```
math.addq( left64, right64, dest64 );
math.addl( left128, right128, dest128 );
```

These functions compute the following:

```
dest64 := left64 + right64;      // dest64, left64, and right64
                                 //    must be 8-byte operands
dest128 := left128 + right128;   // dest128, left128, and right128
                                 //    must be 16-byte operands
```

These functions also leave all the 80x86 flags set the same way you'd expect them after the execution of an add instruction. Specifically, these functions set the zero flag if the (full) result is zero, they set the carry flag if there is a carry out of the H.O. bit, they set the overflow flag if there is a signed overflow, and they set the sign flag if the H.O. bit of the result contains one.

Most of the remaining arithmetic and logical routines use the same calling sequence as math.addq and math.addl. Briefly, here are the functions that use the same syntax:

```
math.andq( left64, right64, dest64 );
math.andl( left128, right128, dest128 );
math.divq( left64, right64, dest64 );
math.divl( left128, right128, dest128 );
math.idivq( left64, right64, dest64 );
math.idivl( left128, right128, dest128 );
math.modq( left64, right64, dest64 );
math.modl( left128, right128, dest128 );
math.imodq( left64, right64, dest64 );
math.imodl( left128, right128, dest128 );
math.mulq( left64, right64, dest64 );
math.mull( left128, right128, dest128 );
math.imulq( left64, right64, dest64 );
math.imull( left128, right128, dest128 );
math.orq( left64, right64, dest64 );
math.orl( left128, right128, dest128 );
math.subq( left64, right64, dest64 );
math.subl( left128, right128, dest128 );
```

```
math.xorq( left64, right64, dest64 );
math.xorl( left128, right128, dest128 );
```

These functions set the flags the same way as the corresponding 32-bit machine instructions and, in the case of the divide and modulo functions, raise the same exceptions. Note that the multiplication functions do not produce an extended precision result. The destination value is the same size as the source operands. These functions set the overflow and carry flags if the result does not fit into the destination operand. All of these functions compute the following:

```
dest64 := left64 op right64;
dest128 := left128 op right128;
```

where *op* represents the specific operation.

In addition to the above functions, the HLA Standard Library's math module also provides a few additional functions whose syntax is slightly different. This list includes math.negq, math.negl, math.notq, math.notl, math.shlq, math.shll, math.shrq, and math.shrl. Note that there are no rotates or arithmetic shift right functions. However, you'll soon see that these operations are easy to synthesize using standard instructions. Here are the prototypes for these additional functions:

```
math.negq( source:qword; var dest:qword );
math.negl( source:lword; var dest:lword );
math.notq( source:qword; var dest:qword );
math.notl( source:lword; var dest:lword );
math.shlq( count:uns32; source:qword; var dest:qword );
math.shll( count:uns32; source:lword; var dest:lword );
math.shrq( count:uns32; source:qword; var dest:qword );
math.shrl( count:uns32; source:lword; var dest:lword );
```

Again, all these functions set the flags exactly the same way the corresponding machine instructions would set the flags were they to support 64-bit or 128-bit operands.

The HLA Standard Library also provides a full complement of I/O and conversion routines for 64-bit and 128-bit values. For example, you can use stdout.put to display 64- and 128-bit values, you may use stdin.get to read these values, and there are a set of routines in the HLA conversions module that convert between these values and their string equivalents. In general, anything you can do with a 32-bit value can be done with a 64-bit or 128-bit value as well. See the HLA Standard Library documentation for more details.

9.2.2 Multiprecision Addition Operations

The 80x86 add instruction adds two 8-, 16-, or 32-bit numbers. After the execution of the add instruction, the 80x86 carry flag is set if there is an overflow out of the H.O. bit of the sum. You can use this information to do multiprecision addition operations. Consider the way you manually perform a multidigit (multiprecision) addition operation:

Step 1: Add the least significant digits together:

```
  289                      289
 +456    produces         +456
 ----                     ----
                          5 with carry 1.
```

Step 2: Add the next significant digits plus the carry:

```
  1 (previous carry)
  289                      289
 +456    produces         +456
 ----                     ----
   5                      45 with carry 1.
```

Step 3: Add the most significant digits plus the carry:

```
                          1 (previous carry)
  289                      289
 +456    produces         +456
 ----                     ----
  45                      745
```

The 80x86 handles extended precision arithmetic in an identical fashion, except instead of adding the numbers a digit at a time, it adds them together a byte, word, or double word at a time. Consider the three double word (96-bit) addition operation in Figure 9-1 on the following page.

   As you can see from this figure, the idea is to break up a larger operation into a sequence of smaller operations. Because the x86 processor family is capable of adding together, at most, 32 bits at a time, the operation must proceed in blocks of 32 bits or less. So the first step is to add the two L.O. double words together just as we would add the two L.O. digits of a decimal number together in the manual algorithm. There is nothing special about this operation; you can use the add instruction to achieve this.

Step 1: Add the least significant words together:

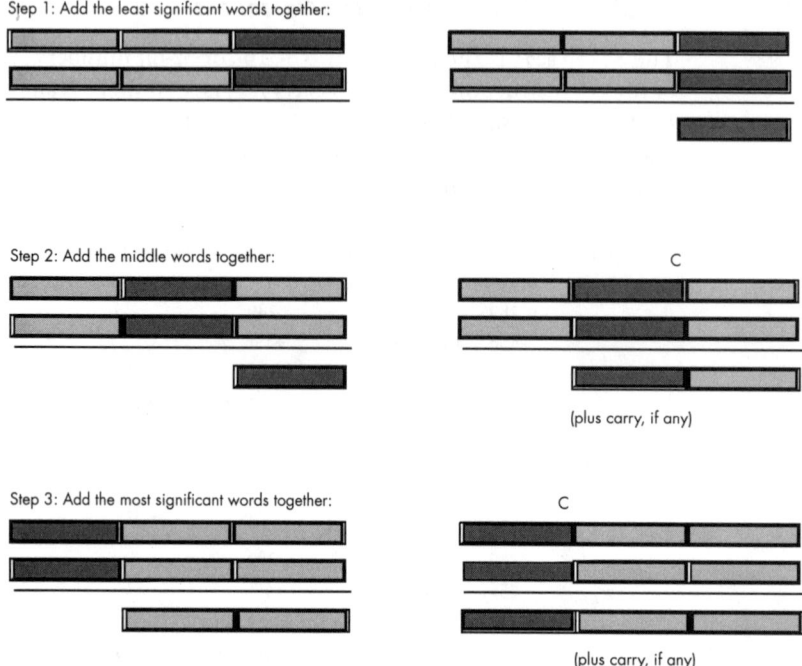

Step 2: Add the middle words together:

C

(plus carry, if any)

Step 3: Add the most significant words together:

C

(plus carry, if any)

Figure 9-1: Adding Two 96-Bit Objects Together.

The second step involves adding together the second pair of double words in the two 96-bit values. Note that in step two, the calculation must also add in the carry out of the previous addition (if any). If there was a carry out of the L.O. addition, the add instruction sets the carry flag to one; conversely, if there was no carry out of the L.O. addition, the earlier add instruction clears the carry flag. Therefore, in this second addition, we really need to compute the sum of the two double words plus the carry out of the first instruction. Fortunately, the x86 CPUs provide an instruction that does exactly this: the adc (add with carry) instruction. The adc instruction uses the same syntax as the add instruction and performs almost the same operation:

```
adc( source, dest );  // dest := dest + source + C
```

As you can see, the only difference between the add and adc instruction is that the adc instruction adds in the value of the carry flag along with the source and destination operands. It also sets the flags the same way the add instruction does (including setting the carry flag if there is an unsigned overflow). This is exactly what we need to add together the middle two double words of our 96-bit sum.

In step three of Figure 9-1, the algorithm adds together the H.O. double words of the 96-bit value. This addition operation must also incorporate the carry out of the sum of the middle two double words; hence the adc instruction is needed here, as well. To sum it up, the add instruction adds the L.O. double words together. The adc (add with carry) instruction adds all other double word pairs together. At the end of the extended precision addition sequence, the carry flag indicates unsigned overflow (if set), a set overflow flag indicates signed overflow, and the sign flag indicates the sign of the result. The zero flag doesn't have any real meaning at the end of the extended precision addition (it simply means that the sum of the H.O. two double words is zero and does not indicate that the whole result is zero); if you want to see how to check for an extended precision zero result, see the source code for the HLA Standard Library math.addq or math.addl function.

For example, suppose that you have two 64-bit values you wish to add together, defined as follows:

```
static
    X: qword;
    Y: qword;
```

Suppose also that you want to store the sum in a third variable, Z, which is also a qword. The following 80x86 code will accomplish this task:

```
mov( (type dword X), eax );         // Add together the L.O. 32 bits
add( (type dword Y), eax );         // of the numbers and store the
mov( eax, (type dword Z) );         // result into the L.O. dword of Z.

mov( (type dword X[4]), eax );       // Add together (with carry) the
adc( (type dword Y[4]), eax );       // H.O. 32 bits and store the result
mov( eax, (type dword Z[4]) );       // into the H.O. dword of Z.
```

Remember, these variables are qword objects. Therefore the compiler will not accept an instruction of the form "mov(X, eax);" because this instruction would attempt to load a 64-bit value into a 32-bit register. This code uses the coercion operator to coerce symbols X, Y, and Z to 32 bits. The first three instructions add the L.O. double words of X and Y together and store the result at the L.O. double word of Z. The last three instructions add the H.O. double words of X and Y together, along with the carry out of the L.O. word, and store the result in the H.O. double word of Z. Remember, address expressions of the form "X[4]" access the H.O. double word of a 64-bit entity. This is due to the fact that the x86 memory space addresses bytes, and it takes four consecutive bytes to form a double word.

You can extend this to any number of bits by using the adc instruction to add in the higher order values. For example, to add together two 128-bit values, you could use code that looks something like the following:

```
type
    tBig: dword[4];   // Storage for four dwords is 128 bits.

static
    BigVal1: tBig;
    BigVal2: tBig;
    BigVal3: tBig;
        .
```

```
        .
        .
        mov( BigVal1[0], eax );      // Note there is no need for (type dword BigValx)
        add( BigVal2[0], eax );      // because the base type of BitValx is dword.
        mov( eax, BigVal3[0] );

        mov( BigVal1[4], eax );
        adc( BigVal2[4], eax );
        mov( eax, BigVal3[4] );

        mov( BigVal1[8], eax );
        adc( BigVal2[8], eax );
        mov( eax, BigVal3[8] );

        mov( BigVal1[12], eax );
        adc( BigVal2[12], eax );
        mov( eax, BigVal3[12] );
```

9.2.3 Multiprecision Subtraction Operations

Like addition, the 80x86 performs multibyte subtraction the same way you would manually, except it subtracts whole bytes, words, or double words at a time rather than decimal digits. The mechanism is similar to that for the add operation. You use the sub instruction on the L.O. byte/word/double word and sbb (subtract with borrow) instruction on the high order values. The following example demonstrates a 64-bit subtraction using the 32-bit registers on the 80x86:

```
static
        Left:       .qword;
        Right:      qword;
        Diff:       qword;

                    .
                    .
                    .

        mov( (type dword Left), eax );
        sub( (type dword Right), eax );
        mov( eax, (type dword Diff) );

        mov( (type dword Left[4]), eax );
        sbb( (type dword Right[4]), eax );
        mov( (type dword Diff[4]), eax );
```

The following example demonstrates a 128-bit subtraction:

```
type
        tBig: dword[4];    // Storage for four dwords is 128 bits.

static
        BigVal1: tBig;
```

```
BigVal2: tBig;
BigVal3: tBig;
     .
     .
     .

// Compute BigVal3 := BigVal1 - BigVal2

mov( BigVal1[0], eax );     // Note there is no need for (type dword BigValx)
sub( BigVal2[0], eax );     // because the base type of BitValx is dword.
mov( eax, BigVal3[0] );

mov( BigVal1[4], eax );
sbb( BigVal2[4], eax );
mov( eax, BigVal3[4] );

mov( BigVal1[8], eax );
sbb( BigVal2[8], eax );
mov( eax, BigVal3[8] );

mov( BigVal1[12], eax );
sbb( BigVal2[12], eax );
mov( eax, BigVal3[12] );
```

9.2.4   Extended Precision Comparisons

Unfortunately, there isn't a "compare with borrow" instruction that you can use to perform extended precision comparisons. Because the cmp and sub instructions perform the same operation, at least as far as the flags are concerned, you'd probably guess that you could use the sbb instruction to synthesize an extended precision comparison; however, you'd only be partly right. There is, however, a better way, so there is no need to explore the use of sbb for extended precision comparison.

Consider the two unsigned values $2157 and $1293. The L.O. bytes of these two values do not affect the outcome of the comparison. Simply comparing the H.O. bytes, $21 with $12, tells us that the first value is greater than the second. In fact, the only time you ever need to look at both bytes of these values is if the H.O. bytes are equal. In all other cases comparing the H.O. bytes tells you everything you need to know about the values. Of course, this is true for any number of bytes, not just two. The following code compares two signed 64-bit integers by comparing their H.O. double words first and comparing their L.O. double words only if the H.O. double words are equal:

```
// This sequence transfers control to location "IsGreater" if
// QwordValue > QwordValue2. It transfers control to "IsLess" if
// QwordValue < QwordValue2. It falls though to the instruction
// following this sequence if QwordValue = QwordValue2. To test for
// inequality, change the "IsGreater" and "IsLess" operands to "NotEqual"
```

```
// in this code.

    mov( (type dword QWordValue[4]), eax );  // Get H.O. dword
    cmp( eax, (type dword QWordValue2[4]));
    jg IsGreater;
    jl IsLess;


    mov( (type dword QWordValue[0]), eax );  // If H.O. dwords were equal,
    cmp( eax, (type dword QWordValue2[0]));  // then we must compare the
    jg IsGreater;                            // L.O. dwords.
    jl IsLess;


// Fall through to this point if the two values were equal.
```

To compare unsigned values, simply use the ja and jb instructions in place of jg and jl.

You can easily synthesize any possible comparison from the preceding sequence. The following examples show how to do this. These examples demonstrate signed comparisons; just substitute ja, jae, jb, and jbe for jg, jge, jl, and jle (respectively) if you want unsigned comparisons.

```
static
    QW1: qword;
    QW2: qword;

const
    QW1d: text := "(type dword QW1)";
    QW2d: text := "(type dword QW2)";

// 64-bit test to see if QW1 < QW2 (signed).
// Control transfers to "IsLess" label if QW1 < QW2. Control falls
// through to the next statement if this is not true.

    mov( QW1d[4], eax );   // Get H.O. dword
    cmp( eax, QW2d[4] );
    jg NotLess;
    jl IsLess;

    mov( QW1d[0], eax );   // Fall through to here if the H.O. dwords are equal.
    cmp( eax, QW2d[0] );
    jl IsLess;
NotLess:

// 64-bit test to see if QW1 <= QW2 (signed).  Jumps to "IsLessEq" if the
// condition is true.

    mov( QW1d[4], eax );   // Get H.O. dword
    cmp( eax, QW2d[4] );
```

```
        jg NotLessEQ;
        jl IsLessEQ;

        mov( QW1d[0], eax );    // Fall through to here if the H.O. dwords are equal.
        cmp( eax, QW2d[0] );
        jle IsLessEQ;
NotLessEQ:


// 64-bit test to see if QW1 > QW2 (signed).  Jumps to "IsGtr" if this condition
// is true.

        mov( QW1d[4], eax );    // Get H.O. dword
        cmp( eax, QW2d[4] );
        jg IsGtr;
        jl NotGtr;

        mov( QW1d[0], eax );    // Fall through to here if the H.O. dwords are equal.
        cmp( eax, QW2d[0] );
        jg IsGtr;
NotGtr:


// 64-bit test to see if QW1 >= QW2 (signed).  Jumps to "IsGtrEQ" if this
// is the case.

        mov( QW1d[4], eax );    // Get H.O. dword
        cmp( eax, QW2d[4] );
        jg IsGtrEQ;
        jl NotGtrEQ;

        mov( QW1d[0], eax );    // Fall through to here if the H.O. dwords are equal.
        cmp( eax, QW2d[0] );
        jge IsGtrEQ;
NotGtrEQ:


// 64-bit test to see if QW1 = QW2 (signed or unsigned). This code branches
// to the label "IsEqual" if QW1 = QW2. It falls through to the next instruction
// if they are not equal.

        mov( QW1d[4], eax );    // Get H.O. dword
        cmp( eax, QW2d[4] );
        jne NotEqual;

        mov( QW1d[0], eax );    // Fall through to here if the H.O. dwords are equal.
        cmp( eax, QW2d[0] );
        je IsEqual;
```

```
NotEqual:


// 64-bit test to see if QW1 <> QW2 (signed or unsigned). This code branches
// to the label "NotEqual" if QW1 <> QW2. It falls through to the next
// instruction if they are equal.

    mov( QW1d[4], eax );    // Get H.O. dword
    cmp( eax, QW2d[4] );
    jne NotEqual;

    mov( QW1d[0], eax );    // Fall through to here if the H.O. dwords are equal.
    cmp( eax, QW2d[0] );
    jne NotEqual;

// Fall through to this point if they are equal.
```

You cannot directly use the HLA high level control structures if you need to
perform an extended precision comparison. However, you may use the HLA
hybrid control structures and bury the appropriate comparison into this
statement. Doing so will probably make your code easier to read. For example,
the following *if..then..else..endif* statement checks to see if QW1 > QW2 using a
64-bit extended precision unsigned comparison:

```
if
( #{
    mov( QW1d[4], eax );
    cmp( eax, QW2d[4] );
    jg true;

    mov( QW1d[0], eax );
    cmp( eax, QW2d[0] );
    jng false;
}# ) then

    << code to execute if QW1 > QW2 >>

else

    << code to execute if QW1 <= QW2 >>

endif;
```

If you need to compare objects that are larger than 64 bits, it is very easy to
generalize the preceding code for 64-bit operands. Always start the comparison
with the H.O. double words of the objects and work you way down toward the

L.O. double words of the objects as long as the corresponding double words are equal. The following example compares two 128-bit values to see if the first is less than or equal (unsigned) to the second:

```
static
    Big1: uns128;
    Big2: uns128;
        .
        .
        .
    if
    ( #{
        mov( Big1[12], eax );
        cmp( eax, Big2[12] );
        jb true;
        jg false;
        mov( Big1[8], eax );
        cmp( eax, Big2[8] );
        jb true;
        jg false;
        mov( Big1[4], eax );
        cmp( eax, Big2[4] );
        jb true;
        jg false;
        mov( Big1[0], eax );
        cmp( eax, Big2[0] );
        jnbe false;
    }# ) then

        << Code to execute if Big1 <= Big2 >>

    else

        << Code to execute if Big1 > Big2 >>

    endif;
```

9.2.5 Extended Precision Multiplication

Although an 8x8, 16x16, or 32x32 multiply is usually sufficient, there are times when you may want to multiply larger values together. You will use the x86 single operand mul and imul instructions for extended precision multiplication.

Not surprisingly (in view of how we achieved extended precision addition using adc and sbb), you use the same techniques to perform extended precision multiplication on the 80x86 that you employ when manually multiplying two values. Consider a simplified form of the way you perform multidigit multiplication by hand:

```
1) Multiply the first two          2) Multiply 5*2:
   digits together (5*3):

     123                                 123
      45                                  45
     ---                                 ---
      15                                  15
                                         10



3) Multiply 5*1:                   4) Multiply 4*3:

     123                                 123
      45                                  45
     ---                                 ---
      15                                  15
      10                                  10
      5                                   5
                                         12



5) Multiply 4*2:                   6) Multiply 4*1:

     123                                 123
      45                                  45
     ---                                 ---
      15                                  15
      10                                  10
      5                                   5
      12                                  12
      8                                   8
                                          4


7) Add all the partial products together:

     123
      45
     ---
      15
      10
      5
      12
      8
      4
     ------
     5535
```

The 80x86 does extended precision multiplication in the same manner except that it works with bytes, words, and double words rather than digits. Figure 9-2 shows how this works.

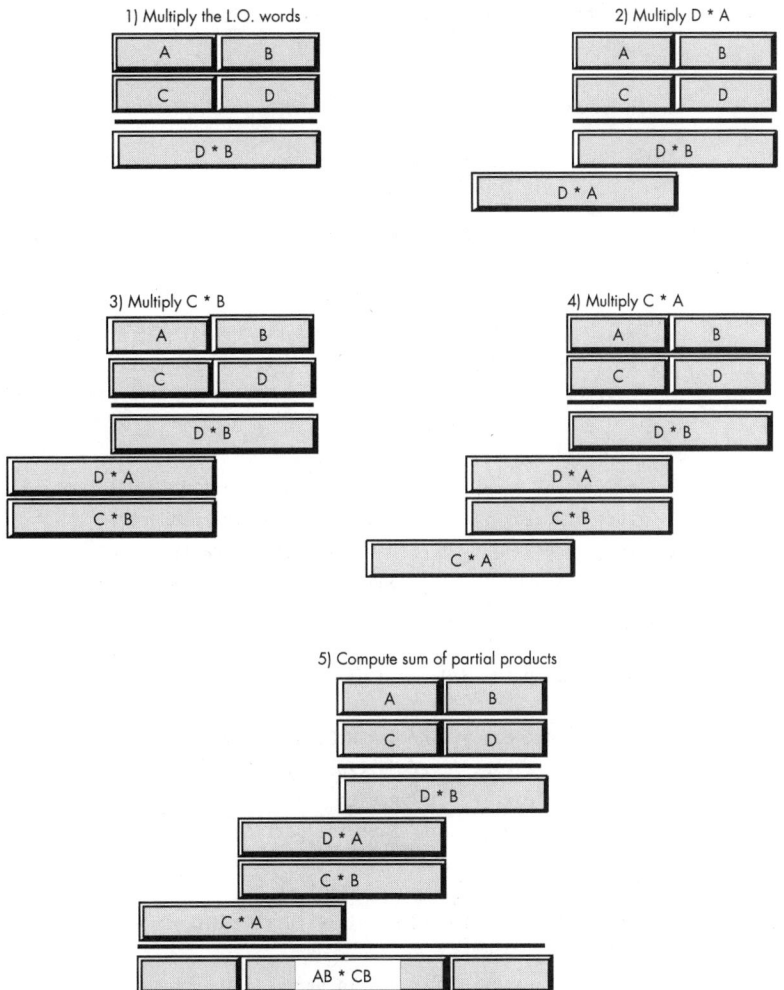

Figure 9-2: Extended Precision Multiplication.

Probably the most important thing to remember when performing an extended precision multiplication is that you must also perform a multiple precision addition at the same time. Adding up all the partial products requires several additions that will produce the result. Listing 9-1 demonstrates the proper way to multiply two 64-bit values on a 32-bit processor:

Listing 9-1: Extended Precision Multiplication.

```
program testMUL64;
#include( "stdlib.hhf" )
```

```
procedure MUL64( Multiplier:qword; Multiplicand:qword; var Product:lword );
const
    mp: text := "(type dword Multiplier)";
    mc: text := "(type dword Multiplicand)";
    prd:text := "(type dword [edi])";

begin MUL64;

    mov( Product, edi );

    // Multiply the L.O. dword of Multiplier times Multiplicand.

    mov( mp, eax );
    mul( mc, eax );       // Multiply L.O. dwords.
    mov( eax, prd );      // Save L.O. dword of product.
    mov( edx, ecx );      // Save H.O. dword of partial product result.

    mov( mp, eax );
    mul( mc[4], eax );    // Multiply mp(L.O.) * mc(H.O.)
    add( ecx, eax );      // Add to the partial product.
    adc( 0, edx );        // Don't forget the carry!
    mov( eax, ebx );      // Save partial product for now.
    mov( edx, ecx );

    // Multiply the H.O. word of Multiplier with Multiplicand.

    mov( mp[4], eax );    // Get H.O. dword of Multiplier.
    mul( mc, eax );       // Multiply by L.O. word of Multiplicand.
    add( ebx, eax );      // Add to the partial product.
    mov( eax, prd[4] );   // Save the partial product.
    adc( edx, ecx );      // Add in the carry!

    mov( mp[4], eax );    // Multiply the two H.O. dwords together.
    mul( mc[4], eax );
    add( ecx, eax );      // Add in partial product.
    adc( 0, edx );        // Don't forget the carry!
    mov( eax, prd[8] );   // Save the partial product.
    mov( edx, prd[12] );

end MUL64;

static
    op1: qword;
    op2: qword;
    rslt: lword;


begin testMUL64;
```

```
// Initialize the qword values (note that static objects
// are initialized with zero bits).

mov( 1234, (type dword op1 ));
mov( 5678, (type dword op2 ));
MUL64( op1, op2, rslt );

// The following only prints the L.O. qword, but
// we know the H.O. qword is zero so this is okay.

stdout.put( "rslt=" );
stdout.putu64( (type qword rslt));
```

```
end testMUL64;
```

One thing you must keep in mind concerning this code is that it only works for unsigned operands. To multiply two signed values you must note the signs of the operands before the multiplication, take the absolute value of the two operands, do an unsigned multiplication, and then adjust the sign of the resulting product based on the signs of the original operands. Multiplication of signed operands is left as an exercise to the reader (or you could just check out the source code in the HLA Standard Library).

The example in Listing 9-1 was fairly straight-forward because it was possible to keep the partial products in various registers. If you need to multiply larger values together, you will need to maintain the partial products in temporary (memory) variables. Other than that, the algorithm that Listing 9-1 uses generalizes to any number of double words.

9.2.6 Extended Precision Division

You cannot synthesize a general n-bit/m-bit division operation using the div and idiv instructions. You must perform such operations using a sequence of shift and subtract instructions, and it is extremely messy. However, a less general operation, dividing an *n*-bit quantity by a 32-bit quantity is easily synthesized using the div instruction. This section presents both methods for extended precision division.

Before describing how to perform a multiprecision division operation, you should note that some operations require an extended precision division even though they may look calculable with a single div or idiv instruction. Dividing a 64-bit quantity by a 32-bit quantity is easy, as long as the resulting quotient fits into 32 bits. The div and idiv instructions will handle this directly. However, if the quotient does not fit into 32 bits then you have to handle this problem as an extended precision division. The trick here is to divide the (zero or sign extended) H.O double word of the dividend by the divisor, and then repeat the process with the remainder and the L.O. dword of the dividend. The following sequence demonstrates this:

```
static
    dividend: dword[2] := [$1234, 4];   // = $4_0000_1234.
    divisor:  dword := 2;               // dividend/divisor = $2_0000_091A
    quotient: dword[2];
    remainder:dword;
    .
    .
    .
    mov( divisor, ebx );
    mov( dividend[4], eax );
    xor( edx, edx );                // Zero extend for unsigned division.
    div( ebx, edx:eax );
    mov( eax, quotient[4] );        // Save H.O. dword of the quotient (2).
    mov( dividend[0], eax );        // Note that this code does *NOT* zero extend
    div( ebx, edx:eax );            //  EAX into EDX before this DIV instr.
    mov( eax, quotient[0] );        // Save L.O. dword of the quotient ($91a).
    mov( edx, remainder );          // Save away the remainder.
```

Because it is perfectly legal to divide a value by one, it is certainly possible that the resulting quotient after a division could require as many bits as the dividend. That is why the quotient variable in this example is the same size (64 bits) as the dividend variable (note the use of an array of two double words rather than a qword type; this spares the code from having to coerce the operands to double words). Regardless of the size of the dividend and divisor operands, the remainder is always no larger than the size of the division operation (32 bits in this case). Hence the remainder variable in this example is just a double word.

Before analyzing this code to see how it works, let's take a brief look at why a single 64/32 division will not work for this particular example even though the div instruction does indeed calculate the result for a 64/32 division. The naive approach, assuming that the x86 were capable of this operation, would look something like the following:

```
// This code does *NOT* work!

    mov( dividend[0], eax );    // Get dividend into edx:eax
    mov( divident[4], edx );
    div( divisor, edx:eax );    // Divide edx:eax by divisor.
```

Although this code is syntactically correct and will compile, if you attempt to run this code it will raise an ex.DivideError[2] exception. The reason, if you'll remember how the div instruction works, is that the quotient must fit into 32 bits; because the quotient turns out to be $2_0000_091A, it will not fit into the EAX register, hence the resulting exception.

Now let's take another look at the former code that correctly computes the 64/32 quotient. This code begins by computing the 32/32 quotient of dividend[4]/divisor. The quotient from this division (2) becomes the H.O. double word of the final quotient. The remainder from this division (0) becomes the

[2] Windows may translate this to an ex.IntoInstr exception.

extension in EDX for the second half of the division operation. The second half of the code divides edx:dividend[0] by divisor to produce the L.O. double word of the quotient and the remainder from the division. Note that the code does not zero extend EAX into EDX prior to the second div instruction. EDX already contains valid bits, and this code must not disturb them.

The 64/32 division operation above is actually just a special case of the more general division operation that lets you divide an arbitrary-sized value by a 32-bit divisor. To achieve this, you begin by moving the H.O. double word of the dividend into EAX and zero extending this into EDX. Next, you divide this value by the divisor. Then, without modifying EDX along the way, you store away the partial quotients, load EAX with the next lower double word in the dividend, and divide it by the divisor. You repeat this operation until you've processed all the double words in the dividend. At that time the EDX register will contain the remainder. The program in Listing 9-2 demonstrates how to divide a 128-bit quantity by a 32-bit divisor, producing a 128-bit quotient and a 32-bit remainder.

Listing 9-2: Unsigned 128/32-Bit Extended Precision Division.

```
program testDiv128;
#include( "stdlib.hhf" )

procedure div128
(
        Dividend:    lword;
        Divisor:     dword;
    var QuotAdrs:    lword;
    var Remainder:   dword
); @nodisplay;

const
    Quotient: text := "(type dword [edi])";

begin div128;

    push( eax );
    push( edx );
    push( edi );

    mov( QuotAdrs, edi );       // Pointer to quotient storage.

    mov( Dividend[12], eax );   // Begin division with the H.O. dword.
    xor( edx, edx );            // Zero extend into EDX.
    div( Divisor, edx:eax );    // Divide H.O. dword.
    mov( eax, Quotient[12] );   // Store away H.O. dword of quotient.

    mov( Dividend[8], eax );    // Get dword #2 from the dividend
    div( Divisor, edx:eax );    // Continue the division.
    mov( eax, Quotient[8] );    // Store away dword #2 of the quotient.
```

```
        mov( Dividend[4], eax );      // Get dword #1 from the dividend.
        div( Divisor, edx:eax );      // Continue the division.
        mov( eax, Quotient[4] );      // Store away dword #1 of the quotient.

        mov( Dividend[0], eax );      // Get the L.O. dword of the dividend.
        div( Divisor, edx:eax );      // Finish the division.
        mov( eax, Quotient[0] );      // Store away the L.O. dword of the quotient.

        mov( Remainder, edi );        // Get the pointer to the remainder's value.
        mov( edx, [edi] );            // Store away the remainder value.

        pop( edi );
        pop( edx );
        pop( eax );

end div128;

static
    op1:    lword   := $8888_8888_6666_6666_4444_4444_2222_2221;
    op2:    dword   := 2;
    quo:    lword;
    rmndr:  dword;


begin testDiv128;

    div128( op1, op2, quo, rmndr );

    stdout.put
    (
        nl
        nl
        "After the division: " nl
        nl
        "Quotient = $",
        quo[12], "_",
        quo[8], "_",
        quo[4], "_",
        quo[0], nl

        "Remainder = ", (type uns32 rmndr )
    );

end testDiv128;
```

You can extend this code to any number of bits by simply adding additional mov/
div/mov instructions to the sequence. Like the extended multiplication the
previous section presents, this extended precision division algorithm works only

for unsigned operands. If you need to divide two signed quantities, you must note their signs, take their absolute values, do the unsigned division, and then set the sign of the result based on the signs of the operands.

If you need to use a divisor larger than 32 bits you're going to have to implement the division using a shift and subtract strategy. Unfortunately, such algorithms are very slow. In this section we'll develop two division algorithms that operate on an arbitrary number of bits. The first is slow but easier to understand; the second is quite a bit faster (in the average case).

As for multiplication, the best way to understand how the computer performs division is to study how you were taught to perform long division by hand. Consider the operation 3456/12 and the steps you would take to manually perform this operation, as shown in Figure 9-3.

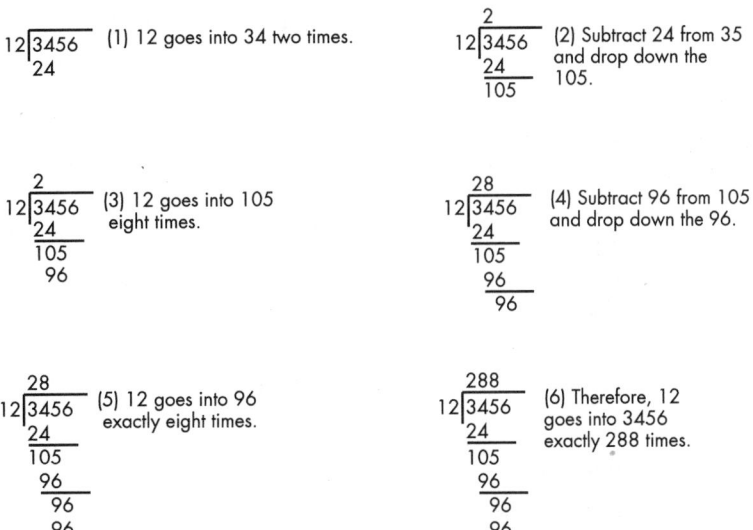

Figure 9-3: Manual Digit-by-digit Division Operation.

This algorithm is actually easier in binary because at each step you do not have to guess how many times 12 goes into the remainder nor do you have to multiply 12 by your guess to obtain the amount to subtract. At each step in the binary algorithm the divisor goes into the remainder exactly zero or one times. As an example, consider the division of 27 (11011) by three (11) that is shown in Figure 9-4.

```
11 | 11011      11 goes into 11 one time.
     11


        1
11 | 11011      Subtract out the 11 and bring down the zero.
     11
     00
```

```
      1
11 ⌐11011          11 goes into 00 zero times.
   11
   ──
   00
   00
```

```
     10
11 ⌐11011          Subtract out the zero and bring down the one.
   11
   ──
   00
   00
   ──
   01
```

```
     10
11 ⌐11011          11 goes into 01 zero times.
   11
   ──
   00
   00
   ──
   01
   00
```

```
    100
11 ⌐11011
   11
   ──
   00
   00               Subtract out the zero and bring down the one.
   ──
   01
   00
   ──
   11
```

```
    100
11 ⌐11011
   11
   ──
   00
   00               11 goes into 11 one time.
   ──
   01
   00
   ──
   11
   11
```

```
   1001
11 ⌐11011
   11
   ──
   00
   00               This produces the final result
   ──               of 1001.
   01
   00
   ──
   11
   11
   ──
   00
```

Figure 9-4: Longhand Division in Binary.

There is a novel way to implement this binary division algorithm that computes the quotient and the remainder at the same time. The algorithm is the following:

```
Quotient := Dividend;
Remainder := 0;
for i:= 1 to NumberBits do

    Remainder:Quotient := Remainder:Quotient SHL 1;
    if Remainder >= Divisor then

        Remainder := Remainder - Divisor;
        Quotient := Quotient + 1;

    endif
endfor
```

NumberBits is the number of bits in the Remainder, Quotient, Divisor, and Dividend variables. Note that the "Quotient := Quotient + 1;" statement sets the L.O. bit of Quotient to one because this algorithm previously shifts Quotient one bit to the left. The program in Listing 9-3 implements this algorithm.

Listing 9-3: Extended Precision Division.

```
program testDiv128b;
#include( "stdlib.hhf" )



// div128-
//
// This procedure does a general 128/128 division operation
// using the following algorithm:
// (all variables are assumed to be 128-bit objects)
//
// Quotient := Dividend;
// Remainder := 0;
// for i:= 1 to NumberBits do
//
//   Remainder:Quotient := Remainder:Quotient SHL 1;
//   if Remainder >= Divisor then
//
//       Remainder := Remainder - Divisor;
//       Quotient := Quotient + 1;
//
//   endif
// endfor
//
```

```
procedure div128
(
        Dividend:    lword;
        Divisor:     lword;
    var QuotAdrs:    lword;
    var RmndrAdrs:   lword
); @nodisplay;

const
    Quotient: text := "Dividend";    // Use the Dividend as the Quotient.

var
    Remainder: lword;

begin div128;

    push( eax );
    push( ecx );
    push( edi );

    mov( 0, eax );                // Set the remainder to zero.
    mov( eax, Remainder[0] );
    mov( eax, Remainder[4] );
    mov( eax, Remainder[8] );
    mov( eax, Remainder[12]);

    mov( 128, ecx );              // Count off 128 bits in ECX.
    repeat

        // Compute Remainder:Quotient := Remainder:Quotient SHL 1:

        shl( 1, Dividend[0] );  // See the section on extended
        rcl( 1, Dividend[4] );  // precision shifts to see how
        rcl( 1, Dividend[8] );  // this code shifts 256 bits to
        rcl( 1, Dividend[12]);  // the left by one bit.
        rcl( 1, Remainder[0] );
        rcl( 1, Remainder[4] );
        rcl( 1, Remainder[8] );
        rcl( 1, Remainder[12]);

        // Do a 128-bit comparison to see if the remainder
        // is greater than or equal to the divisor.

        if
        ( #{
            mov( Remainder[12], eax );
            cmp( eax, Divisor[12] );
            ja true;
            jb false;
```

```
            mov( Remainder[8], eax );
            cmp( eax, Divisor[8] );
            ja true;
            jb false;

            mov( Remainder[4], eax );
            cmp( eax, Divisor[4] );
            ja true;
            jb false;

            mov( Remainder[0], eax );
            cmp( eax, Divisor[0] );
            jb false;
        }# ) then

            // Remainder := Remainder - Divisor

            mov( Divisor[0], eax );
            sub( eax, Remainder[0] );

            mov( Divisor[4], eax );
            sbb( eax, Remainder[4] );

            mov( Divisor[8], eax );
            sbb( eax, Remainder[8] );

            mov( Divisor[12], eax );
            sbb( eax, Remainder[12] );

            // Quotient := Quotient + 1;

            add( 1, Quotient[0] );
            adc( 0, Quotient[4] );
            adc( 0, Quotient[8] );
            adc( 0, Quotient[12] );

        endif;
        dec( ecx );

    until( @z );


    // Okay, copy the quotient (left in the Dividend variable)
    // and the remainder to their return locations.

    mov( QuotAdrs, edi );
    mov( Quotient[0], eax );
    mov( eax, [edi] );
```

```
        mov( Quotient[4], eax );
        mov( eax, [edi+4] );
        mov( Quotient[8], eax );
        mov( eax, [edi+8] );
        mov( Quotient[12], eax );
        mov( eax, [edi+12] );


        mov( RmndrAdrs, edi );
        mov( Remainder[0], eax );
        mov( eax, [edi] );
        mov( Remainder[4], eax );
        mov( eax, [edi+4] );
        mov( Remainder[8], eax );
        mov( eax, [edi+8] );
        mov( Remainder[12], eax );
        mov( eax, [edi+12] );



        pop( edi );
        pop( ecx );
        pop( eax );


end div128;




// Some simple code to test out the division operation:

static
    op1:    lword    := $8888_8888_6666_6666_4444_4444_2222_2221;
    op2:    lword    := 2;
    quo:    lword;
    rmndr:  lword;



begin testDiv128b;

    div128( op1, op2, quo, rmndr );

    stdout.put
    (
        nl
        nl
        "After the division: " nl
        nl
        "Quotient = $",
        quo[12], "_",
        quo[8], "_",
        quo[4], "_",
```

```
        quo[0], nl

    "Remainder = ", (type uns32 rmndr )
);

end testDiv128b;
```

This code looks simple, but there are a few problems with it: It does not check for division by zero (it will produce the value $FFFF_FFFF_FFFF_FFFF if you attempt to divide by zero), it only handles unsigned values, and it is very slow. Handling division by zero is very simple; just check the divisor against zero prior to running this code and return an appropriate error code if the divisor is zero (or raise the ex.DivisionError exception). Dealing with signed values is the same as the earlier division algorithm, note the signs, take the operands' absolute values, do the unsigned division, and then fix the sign afterward. The performance of this algorithm, however, leaves a lot to be desired. It's around an order of magnitude or two worse than the div/idiv instructions on the 80x86, and they are among the slowest instructions on the CPU.

There is a technique you can use to boost the performance of this division by a fair amount: Check to see if the divisor variable uses only 32 bits. Often, even though the divisor is a 128-bit variable, the value itself fits just fine into 32 bits (i.e., the H.O. double words of Divisor are zero). In this special case, which occurs frequently, you can use the div instruction which is much faster. The algorithm is a bit more complex because you have to first compare the H.O. double words for zero, but on the average it runs much faster while remaining capable of dividing any two pair of values.

9.2.7   Extended Precision NEG Operations

Although there are several ways to negate an extended precision value, the shortest way for smaller values (96 bits or less) is to use a combination of neg and sbb instructions. This technique uses the fact that neg subtracts its operand from zero. In particular, it sets the flags the same way the sub instruction would if you subtracted the destination value from zero. This code takes the following form (assuming you want to negate the 64-bit value in EDX:EAX):

```
neg( edx );
neg( eax );
sbb( 0, edx );
```

The sbb instruction decrements EDX if there is a borrow out of the L.O. word of the negation operation (which always occurs unless EAX is zero).

To extend this operation to additional bytes, words, or double words is easy; all you have to do is start with the H.O. memory location of the object you want to negate and work toward the L.O. byte. The following code computes a 128-bit negation:

```
static
    Value: dword[4];

        .
        .
        .

    neg( Value[12] );       // Negate the H.O. double word.
    neg( Value[8] );        // Neg previous dword in memory.
    sbb( 0, Value[12] );    // Adjust H.O. dword.

    neg( Value[4] );        // Negate the second dword in the object.
    sbb( 0, Value[8] );     // Adjust third dword in object.
    sbb( 0, Value[12] );    // Adjust the H.O. dword.

    neg( Value );           // Negate the L.O. dword.
    sbb( 0, Value[4] );     // Adjust second dword in object.
    sbb( 0, Value[8] );     // Adjust third dword in object.
    sbb( 0, Value[12] );    // Adjust the H.O. dword.
```

Unfortunately, this code tends to get really large and slow because you need to propagate the carry through all the H.O. words after each negate operation. A simpler way to negate larger values is to simply subtract that value from zero:

```
static
    Value: dword[5];    // 160-bit value.

        .
        .
        .

    mov( 0, eax );
    sub( Value, eax );
    mov( eax, Value );

    mov( 0, eax );
    sbb( Value[4], eax );
    mov( eax, Value[4] );

    mov( 0, eax );
    sbb( Value[8], eax );
    mov( eax, Value[8] );

    mov( 0, eax );
    sbb( Value[12], eax );
    mov( eax, Value[12] );

    mov( 0, eax );
    sbb( Value[16], eax );
    mov( eax, Value[16] );
```

9.2.8 Extended Precision AND Operations

Performing an n-byte AND operation is very easy : Simply AND the corresponding bytes between the two operands, saving the result. For example, to perform the AND operation where all operands are 64 bits long, you could use the following code:

```
mov( (type dword source1), eax );
and( (type dword source2), eax );
mov( eax, (type dword dest) );

mov( (type dword source1[4]), eax );
and( (type dword source2[4]), eax );
mov( eax, (type dword dest[4]) );
```

This technique easily extends to any number of words; all you need to is logically AND the corresponding bytes, words, or double words together in the operands. Note that this sequence sets the flags according to the value of the last AND operation. If you AND the H.O. double words last, this sets all but the zero flag correctly. If you need to test the zero flag after this sequence, you will need to logically OR the two resulting double words together (or otherwise compare them both against zero).

9.2.9 Extended Precision OR Operations

Multibyte logical OR operations are performed in the same way as multibyte AND operations. You simply OR the corresponding bytes in the two operands together. For example, to logically OR two 96-bit values, use the following code:

```
mov( (type dword source1), eax );
or( (type dword source2), eax );
mov( eax, (type dword dest) );

mov( (type dword source1[4]), eax );
or( (type dword source2[4]), eax );
mov( eax, (type dword dest[4]) );

mov( (type dword source1[8]), eax );
or( (type dword source2[8]), eax );
mov( eax, (type dword dest[8]) );
```

As for the previous example, this does not set the zero flag properly for the entire operation. If you need to test the zero flag after a multiprecision OR, you must logically OR the resulting double words together.

9.2.10 Extended Precision XOR Operations

Extended precision XOR operations are performed in a manner identical to AND/OR: Simply XOR the corresponding bytes in the two operands to obtain the extended precision result. The following code sequence operates on two 64-bit operands, computes their exclusive-or, and stores the result into a 64-bit variable:

```
mov( (type dword source1), eax );
xor( (type dword source2), eax );
mov( eax, (type dword dest) );

mov( (type dword source1[4]), eax );
xor( (type dword source2[4]), eax );
mov( eax, (type dword dest[4]) );
```

The comment about the zero flag in the previous two sections applies here.

9.2.11 Extended Precision NOT Operations

The not instruction inverts all the bits in the specified operand. An extended precision NOT is performed by simply executing the not instruction on all the affected operands. For example, to perform a 64-bit NOT operation on the value in (edx:eax), all you need to do is execute the instructions:

```
not( eax );
not( edx );
```

Keep in mind that if you execute the not instruction twice, you wind up with the original value. Also note that exclusive-ORing a value with all ones ($FF, $FFFF, or $FFFF_FFFF) performs the same operation as the not instruction.

9.2.12 Extended Precision Shift Operations

Extended precision shift operations require a shift and a rotate instruction. Consider what must happen to implement a 64-bit shl using 32-bit operations (see Figure 9-5):

1. A zero must be shifted into bit zero.
2. Bits zero through 30 are shifted into the next higher bit.
3. Bit 31 is shifted into bit 32.
4. Bits 32 through 62 must be shifted into the next higher bit.
5. Bit 63 is shifted into the carry flag.

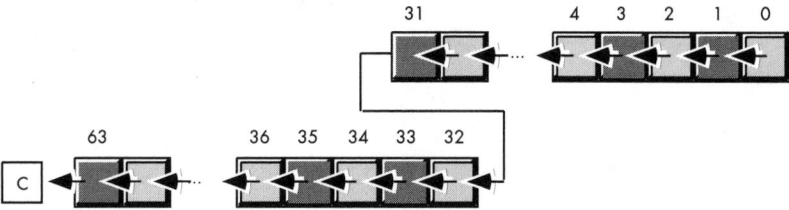

Figure 9-5: 64-Bit Shift Left Operation.

The two instructions you can use to implement this 32-bit shift are shl and rcl. For example, to shift the 64-bit quantity in (EDX:EAX) one position to the left, you'd use the instructions:

```
shl( 1, eax );
rcl( 1, eax );
```

Note that using this technique you can only shift an extended precision value one bit at a time. You cannot shift an extended precision operand several bits using the CL register. Nor can you specify a constant value greater than one using this technique.

To understand how this instruction sequence works, consider the operation of these instructions on an individual basis. The shl instruction shifts a zero into bit zero of the 64-bit operand and shifts bit 31 into the carry flag. The rcl instruction then shifts the carry flag into bit 32 and then shifts bit 63 into the carry flag. The result is exactly what we want.

To perform a shift left on an operand larger than 64 bits, you simply use additional rcl instructions. An extended precision shift left operation always starts with the least significant double word, and each succeeding rcl instruction operates on the next most significant double word. For example, to perform a 96- bit shift left operation on a memory location you could use the following instructions:

```
shl( 1, (type dword Operand[0]) );
rcl( 1, (type dword Operand[4]) );
rcl( 1, (type dword Operand[8]) );
```

If you need to shift your data by two or more bits, you can either repeat the preceding sequence the desired number of times (for a constant number of shifts) or place the instructions in a loop to repeat them some number of times. For example, the following code shifts the 96-bit value Operand to the left the number of bits specified in ECX:

```
ShiftLoop:
    shl( 1, (type dword Operand[0]) );
    rcl( 1, (type dword Operand[4]) );
    rcl( 1, (type dword Operand[8]) );
    dec( ecx );
    jnz ShiftLoop;
```

You implement shr and sar in a similar way, except you must start at the H.O. word of the operand and work your way down to the L.O. word:

```
// Double precision SAR:

    sar( 1, (type dword Operand[8]) );
    rcr( 1, (type dword Operand[4]) );
    rcr( 1, (type dword Operand[0]) );

// Double precision SHR:

    shr( 1, (type dword Operand[8]) );
    rcr( 1, (type dword Operand[4]) );
    rcr( 1, (type dword Operand[0]) );
```

There is one major difference between the extended precision shifts described here and their 8-/16-/32-bit counterparts: The extended precision shifts set the flags differently than the single precision operations. This is because the rotate instructions affect the flags differently than the shift instructions. Fortunately, the carry flag is the one you'll test most often after a shift operation and the extended precision shift operations (i.e., rotate instructions) properly set this flag.

The shld and shrd instructions let you efficiently implement multiprecision shifts of several bits. These instructions have the following syntax:

```
    shld( constant, Operand₁, Operand₂ );
    shld( cl, Operand₁, Operand₂ );
    shrd( constant, Operand₁, Operand₂ );
    shrd( cl, Operand₁, Operand₂ );
```

The shld instruction works as shown in Figure 9-6.

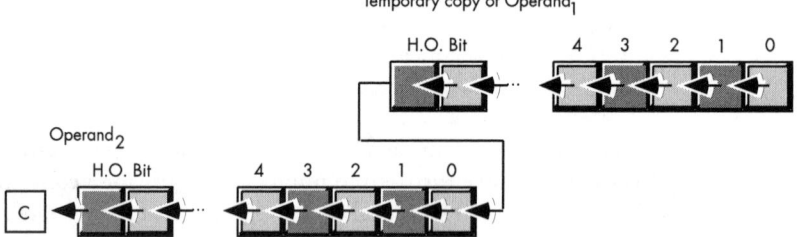

Figure 9-6: SHLD Operation.

Operand₁ must be a 16- or 32-bit register. Operand₂ can be a register or a memory location. Both operands must be the same size. The immediate operand can be a value in the range zero through n-1, where n is the number of bits in the two operands; this operand specifies the number of bits to shift.

The shld instruction shifts bits in Operand$_2$ to the left. The H.O. bits shift into the carry flag and the H.O. bits of Operand1 shift into the L.O. bits of Operand$_2$. Note that this instruction does not modify the value of Operand$_1$; it uses a temporary copy of Operand$_1$ during the shift. The immediate operand specifies the number of bits to shift. If the count is n, then shld shifts bit n-1 into the carry flag. It also shifts the H.O. n bits of Operand$_1$ into the L.O. n bits of Operand$_2$. The shld instruction sets the flag bits as follows:

- If the shift count is zero, the shld instruction doesn't affect any flags.
- The carry flag contains the last bit shifted out of the H.O. bit of the Operand$_2$.
- If the shift count is one, the overflow flag will contain one if the sign bit of Operand$_2$ changes during the shift. If the count is not one, the overflow flag is undefined.
- The zero flag will be one if the shift produces a zero result.
- The sign flag will contain the H.O. bit of the result.

The shrd instruction is similar to shld except, of course; it shifts its bits right rather than left. To get a clear picture of the shrd instruction, consider Figure 9-7.

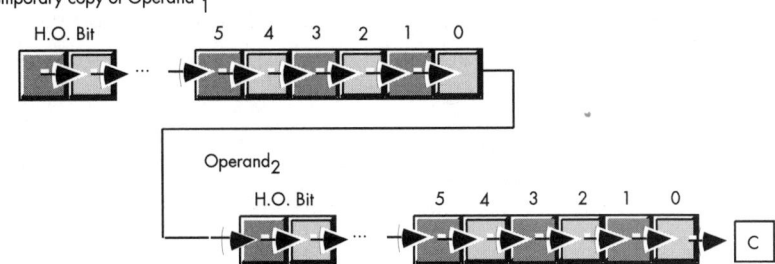

Figure 9-7: SHRD Operation.

The shrd instruction sets the flag bits as follows:

- If the shift count is zero, the shrd instruction doesn't affect any flags.
- The carry flag contains the last bit shifted out of the L.O. bit of the Operand$_2$.
- If the shift count is one, the overflow flag will contain one if the H.O. bit of Operand2 changes. If the count is not one, the overflow flag is undefined.
- The zero flag will be one if the shift produces a zero result.
- The sign flag will contain the H.O. bit of the result.

Consider the following code sequence:

```
static
    ShiftMe: dword[3] := [ $1234, $5678, $9012 ];
    .
    .
    .
    mov( ShiftMe[4], eax )
    shld( 6, eax, ShiftMe[8] );
```

```
mov( ShiftMe[0], eax );
shld( 6, eax, ShiftMe[4] );
shl( 6, ShiftMe[0] );
```

The first shld instruction above shifts the bits from ShiftMe[4] into ShiftMe[8] without affecting the value in ShiftMe[4]. The second shld instruction shifts the bits from ShiftMe into ShiftMe[4]. Finally, the shl instruction shifts the L.O. double word the appropriate amount. There are two important things to note about this code. First, unlike the other extended precision shift left operations, this sequence works from the H.O. double word down to the L.O. double word. Second, the carry flag does not contain the carry out of the H.O. shift operation. If you need to preserve the carry flag at that point, you will need to push the flags after the first shld instruction and pop the flags after the shl instruction.

You can do an extended precision shift right operation using the shrd instruction. It works almost the same way as the preceding code sequence except you work from the L.O. double word to the H.O. double word. The solution is left as an exercise for the reader.

9.2.13   Extended Precision Rotate Operations

The rcl and rcr operations extend in a manner almost identical to shl and shr . For example, to perform 96-bit rcl and rcr operations, use the following instructions:

```
rcl( 1, (type dword Operand[0]) );
rcl( 1, (type dword Operand[4]) );
rcl( 1, (type dword Operand[8]) );


rcr( 1, (type dword Operand[8]) );
rcr( 1, (type dword Operand[4]) );
rcr( 1, (type dword Operand[0]) );
```

The only difference between this code and the code for the extended precision shift operations is that the first instruction is a rcl or rcr rather than a shl or shr instruction.

Performing an extended precision rol or ror instruction isn't quite as simple an operation. You can use the bt, shld, and shrd instructions to implement an extended precision rol or ror instruction. The following code shows how to use the shld instruction to do an extended precision rol:

```
// Compute ROL( 4, EDX:EAX );

        mov( edx, ebx );
        shld, 4, eax, edx );
        shld( 4, ebx, eax );
        bt( 0, eax );          // Set carry flag, if desired.
```

An extended precision ror instruction is similar; just keep in mind that you work on the L.O. end of the object first and the H.O. end last.

9.2.14 Extended Precision I/O

Once you have the ability to compute using extended precision arithmetic, the next problem is how do you get those extended precision values into your program and how do you display those extended precision values to the user? HLA's Standard Library provides routines for unsigned decimal, signed decimal, and hexadecimal I/O for values that are 8, 16, 32, 64, or 128 bits in length. So as long as you're working with values whose size is less than or equal to 128 bits in length, you can use the Standard Library code. If you need to input or output values that are greater than 128 bits in length, you will need to write your own procedures to handle the operation. This section discusses the strategies you will need to write such routines.

The examples in this section work specifically with 128-bit values. The algorithms are perfectly general and extend to any number of bits (indeed, the 128-bit algorithms in this section are really nothing more than the algorithms the HLA Standard Library uses for 128-bit values). Of course, if you need a set of 128-bit unsigned I/O routines, you can use the Standard Library code as-is. If you need to handle larger values, simple modifications to the following code are all that should be necessary.

The sections that follow use a common set of 128-bit data types in order to avoid having to coerce lword/uns128/int128 values in each instruction. Here are these types:

```
type
    h128        :dword[4];
    u128        :dword[4];
    i128        :dword[4];
```

9.2.14.1 Extended Precision Hexadecimal Output

Extended precision hexadecimal output is very easy. All you have to do is output each double word component of the extended precision value from the H.O. double word to the L.O. double word using a call to the stdout.putd routine. The following procedure does exactly this to output an lword value:

```
procedure putb128( b128: h128 ); @nodisplay;
begin putb128;

    stdout.putd( b128[12] );
    stdout.putd( b128[8] );
    stdout.putd( b128[4] );
    stdout.putd( b128[0] );

end putb128;
```

Of course, the HLA Standard Library supplies a stdout.putl procedure that directly writes lword values, so you can call stdout.putl multiple times when outputting larger values (e.g., a 256-bit value). As it turns out, the implementation of the HLA stdlib.putl routine is very similar to putb128, above.

9.2.14.2 Extended Precision Unsigned Decimal Output

Decimal output is a little more complicated than hexadecimal output because the H.O. bits of a binary number affect the L.O. digits of the decimal representation (this was not true for hexadecimal values, which is why hexadecimal output is so easy). Therefore, we will have to create the decimal representation for a binary number by extracting one decimal digit at a time from the number.

The most common solution for unsigned decimal output is to successively divide the value by ten until the result becomes zero. The remainder after the first division is a value in the range 0..9, and this value corresponds to the L.O. digit of the decimal number. Successive divisions by ten (and their corresponding remainder) extract successive digits from the number.

Iterative solutions to this problem generally allocate storage for a string of characters large enough to hold the entire number. Then the code extracts the decimal digits in a loop and places them in the string one by one. At the end of the conversion process, the routine prints the characters in the string in reverse order (remember, the divide algorithm extracts the L.O. digits first and the H.O. digits last, the opposite of the way you need to print them).

In this section, we will employ a recursive solution because it is a little more elegant. The recursive solution begins by dividing the value by ten and saving the remainder in a local variable. If the quotient was not zero, the routine recursively calls itself to print any leading digits first. On return from the recursive call (which prints all the leading digits), the recursive algorithm prints the digit associated with the remainder to complete the operation. Here's how the operation works when printing the decimal value "123":

1. Divide 123 by 10. Quotient is 12; remainder is 3.

2. Save the remainder (3) in a local variable and recursively call the routine with the quotient.

3. [Recursive entry 1.] Divide 12 by 10. Quotient is 1; remainder is 2.

4. Save the remainder (2) in a local variable and recursively call the routine with the quotient.

5. [Recursive entry 2.] Divide 1 by 10. Quotient is 0, remainder is 1.

6. Save the remainder (1) in a local variable. Because the quotient is zero, you don't call the routine recursively.

7. Output the remainder value saved in the local variable (1). Return to the caller (recursive entry 1).

8. [Return to recursive entry 1.] Output the remainder value saved in the local variable in recursive entry 1 (2). Return to the caller (original invocation of the procedure).

9. [Original invocation.] Output the remainder value saved in the local variable in the original call (3). Return to the original caller of the output routine.

The only operation that requires extended precision calculation through this entire algorithm is the "divide by 10" statement. Everything else is simple and straight-forward. We are in luck with this algorithm; because we are dividing an extended precision value by a value that easily fits into a double word, we can use the fast (and easy) extended precision division algorithm that uses the div instruction. The program in Listing 9-4 implements a 128-bit decimal output routine utilizing this technique.

Listing 9-4: 128-Bit Extended Precision Decimal Output Routine.

```
program out128;

#include( "stdlib.hhf" );

// 128-bit unsigned integer data type:

type
    u128: dword[4];




// DivideBy10-
//
// Divides "divisor" by 10 using fast
// extended precision division algorithm
// that employs the DIV instruction.
//
// Returns quotient in "quotient"
// Returns remainder in eax.
// Trashes EBX, EDX, and EDI.

procedure DivideBy10( dividend:u128; var quotient:u128 ); @nodisplay;
begin DivideBy10;

    mov( quotient, edi );
    xor( edx, edx );
    mov( dividend[12], eax );
    mov( 10, ebx );
    div( ebx, edx:eax );
    mov( eax, [edi+12] );

    mov( dividend[8], eax );
    div( ebx, edx:eax );
    mov( eax, [edi+8] );

    mov( dividend[4], eax );
    div( ebx, edx:eax );
    mov( eax, [edi+4] );
```

```
            mov( dividend[0], eax );
            div( ebx, edx:eax );
            mov( eax, [edi+0] );
            mov( edx, eax );

    end DivideBy10;



    // Recursive version of putu128.
    // A separate "shell" procedure calls this so that
    // this code does not have to preserve all the registers
    // it uses (and DivideBy10 uses) on each recursive call.

    procedure recursivePutu128( b128:u128 ); @nodisplay;
    var
        remainder: byte;

    begin recursivePutu128;

        // Divide by ten and get the remainder (the char to print).

        DivideBy10( b128, b128 );
        mov( al, remainder );        // Save away the remainder (0..9).

        // If the quotient (left in b128) is not zero, recursively
        // call this routine to print the H.O. digits.

        mov( b128[0], eax );      // If we logically OR all the dwords
        or( b128[4], eax );       // together, the result is zero if and
        or( b128[8], eax );       // only if the entire number is zero.
        or( b128[12], eax );
        if( @nz ) then

            recursivePutu128( b128 );

        endif;

        // Okay, now print the current digit.

        mov( remainder, al );
        or( '0', al );            // Converts 0..9 -> '0..'9'.
        stdout.putc( al );

    end recursivePutu128;



    // Non-recursive shell to the above routine so we don't bother
    // saving all the registers on each recursive call.
```

```
        procedure putu128( b128:uns128 ); @nodisplay;
        begin putu128;

            push( eax );
            push( ebx );
            push( edx );
            push( edi );

            recursivePutu128( b128 );

            pop( edi );
            pop( edx );
            pop( ebx );
            pop( eax );

        end putu128;



        // Code to test the routines above:

        static
            b0: u128 := [0, 0, 0, 0];          // decimal = 0
            b1: u128 := [1234567890, 0, 0, 0];  // decimal = 1234567890
            b2: u128 := [$8000_0000, 0, 0, 0];  // decimal = 2147483648
            b3: u128 := [0, 1, 0, 0 ];          // decimal = 4294967296

            // Largest uns128 value
            // (decimal=340,282,366,920,938,463,463,374,607,431,768,211,455):

            b4: u128 := [$FFFF_FFFF, $FFFF_FFFF, $FFFF_FFFF, $FFFF_FFFF ];

        begin out128;

            stdout.put( "b0 = " );
            putu128( b0 );
            stdout.newln();

            stdout.put( "b1 = " );
            putu128( b1 );
            stdout.newln();

            stdout.put( "b2 = " );
            putu128( b2 );
            stdout.newln();

            stdout.put( "b3 = " );
            putu128( b3 );
```

```
    stdout.newln();

    stdout.put( "b4 = " );
    putu128( b4 );
    stdout.newln();

end out128;
```

9.2.14.3 Extended Precision Signed Decimal Output

Once you have an extended precision unsigned decimal output routine, writing an extended precision signed decimal output routine is very easy. The basic algorithm takes the following form:

- Check the sign of the number. If it is positive, call the unsigned output routine to print it.
- If the number is negative, print a minus sign. Then negate the number and call the unsigned output routine to print it.

To check the sign of an extended precision integer, of course, you simply test the H.O. bit of the number. To negate a large value, the best solution is to probably subtract that value from zero. Here's a quick version of puti128 that uses the putu128 routine from the previous section.

```
procedure puti128( i128: int128 ); nodisplay;
begin puti128;

    if( (type int32 i128[12]) < 0 ) then

        stdout.put( '-' );

        // Extended Precision Negation:

        push( eax );
        mov( 0, eax );
        sub( i128[0], eax );
        mov( eax, i128[0] );

        mov( 0, eax );
        sbb( i128[4], eax );
        mov( eax, i128[4] );

        mov( 0, eax );
        sbb( i128[8], eax );
        mov( eax, i128[8] );
```

```
            mov( 0, eax );
            sbb( i128[12], eax );
            mov( eax, i128[12] );
            pop( eax );


    endif;
    putu128( (type uns128 i128));


end puti128;
```

9.2.14.4 Extended Precision Formatted Output

The code in the previous two sections prints signed and unsigned integers using the minimum number of necessary print positions. To create nicely formatted tables of values you will need the equivalent of a puti128Size or putu128Size routine. Once you have the "unformatted" versions of these routines, implementing the formatted versions is very easy.

The first step is to write an i128Size and a u128Size routine that compute the minimum number of digits needed to display the value. The algorithm to accomplish this is very similar to the numeric output routines. In fact, the only difference is that you initialize a counter to zero upon entry into the routine (e.g., the non-recursive shell routine), and you increment this counter rather than outputting a digit on each recursive call. (Don't forget to increment the counter inside i128Size if the number is negative; you must allow for the output of the minus sign.) After the calculation is complete, these routines should return the size of the operand in the EAX register.

Once you have the i128Size and u128Size routines, writing the formatted output routines is very easy. Upon initial entry into puti128Size or putu128Size, these routines call the corresponding "size" routine to determine the number of print positions for the number to display. If the value that the "size" routine returns is greater than the absolute value of the minimum size parameter (passed into puti128Size or putu128Size), all you need to do is call the put routine to print the value, no other formatting is necessary. If the absolute value of the parameter size is greater than the value i128Size or u128Size returns, then the program must compute the difference between these two values and print that many spaces (or other filler character) before printing the number (if the parameter size value is positive) or after printing the number (if the parameter size value is negative). The actual implementation of these two routines is left as an exercise (or just check out the source code in the HLA Standard Library for the stdout.putiSize128 and stdout.putuSize128 routines).

The HLA Standard Library implements the i128Size and u128Size by doing a set of successive extended precision comparisons to determine the number of digits in the values. Interested readers may want to take a look at the source code for these routines as well as the source code for the stdout.puti128 and stdout.putu128 procedures (this source code appears on the accompanying CD-ROM).

9.2.14.5 Extended Precision Input Routines

There are a couple of fundamental differences between the extended precision output routines and the extended precision input routines. First of all, numeric output generally occurs without possibility of error;[3] numeric input, on the other hand, must handle the very real possibility of an input error such as illegal characters and numeric overflow. Also, HLA's Standard Library and run-time system encourage a slightly different approach to input conversion. This section discusses those issues that differentiate input conversion from output conversion.

Perhaps the biggest difference between input and output conversion is the fact that output conversion is not bracketed. That is, when converting a numeric value to a string of characters for output, the output routine does not concern itself with characters preceding the output string, nor does it concern itself with the characters following the numeric value in the output stream. Numeric output routines convert their data to a string and print that string without considering the context (i.e., the characters before and after the string representation of the numeric value). Numeric input routines cannot be so cavalier; the contextual information surrounding the numeric string is very important.

A typical numeric input operation consists of reading a string of characters from the user and then translating this string of characters into an internal numeric representation. For example, a statement like "stdin.get(i32);" typically reads a line of text from the user and converts a sequence of digits appearing at the beginning of that line of text into a 32-bit signed integer (assuming i32 is an int32 object). Note, however, that the stdin.get routine skips over certain characters in the string that may appear before the actual numeric characters. For example, stdin.get automatically skips any leading spaces in the string. Likewise, the input string may contain additional data beyond the end of the numeric input (for example, it is possible to read two integer values from the same input line), therefore the input conversion routine must somehow determine where the numeric data ends in the input stream. Fortunately, HLA provides a simple mechanism that lets you easily determine the start and end of the input data: the Delimiters character set.

The Delimiters character set is a variable, internal to the HLA Standard Library, which contains the set of legal characters that may precede or follow a legal numeric value. By default, this character set includes the end of string marker (a zero byte), a tab character, a line feed character, a carriage return character, a space, a comma, a colon, and a semicolon. Therefore, HLA's numeric input routines will automatically ignore any characters in this set that occur on input before a numeric string. Likewise, characters from this set may legally follow a numeric string on input (conversely, if any non-delimiter character follows the numeric string, HLA will raise an ex.ConversionError exception).

The Delimiters character set is a private variable inside the HLA Standard Library. Although you do not have direct access to this object, the HLA Standard Library does provide two accessor functions, conv.setDelimiters and

---

[3] Technically speaking, this isn't entirely true. It is possible for a device error (e.g., disk full) to occur. The likelihood of this is so low that we can effectively ignore this possibility.

conv.getDelimiters that let you access and modify the value of this character set. These two functions have the following prototypes (found in the conv.hhf header file):

```
procedure conv.setDelimiters( Delims:cset );
procedure conv.getDelimiters( var Delims:cset );
```

The conv.setDelimiters procedure will copy the value of the Delims parameter into the internal Delimiters character set. Therefore, you can use this procedure to change the character set if you want to use a different set of delimiters for numeric input. The conv.getDelimiters call returns a copy of the internal Delimiters character set in the variable you pass as a parameter to the conv.getDelimiters procedure. We will use the value returned by conv.getDelimiters to determine the end of numeric input when writing our own extended precision numeric input routines.

When reading a numeric value from the user, the first step will be to get a copy of the Delimiters character set. The second step is to read and discard input characters from the user as long as those characters are members of the Delimiters character set. Once a character is found that is not in the Delimiters set, the input routine must check this character and verify that it is a legal numeric character. If not, the program should raise an ex.IllegalChar exception if the character's value is outside the range $00..$7f or it should raise the ex.ConversionError exception if the character is not a legal numeric character. Once the routine encounters a numeric character, it should continue reading characters as long as they valid numeric characters; while reading the characters the conversion routine should be translating them to the internal representation of the numeric data. If, during conversion, an overflow occurs, the procedure should raise the ex.ValueOutOfRange exception.

Conversion to numeric representation should end when the procedure encounters the first delimiter character at the end of the string of digits. However, it is very important that the procedure does not consume the delimiter character that ends the string. So the following is incorrect:

```
static
    Delimiters: cset;

    .
    .
    .

    conv.getDelimiters( Delimiters );

// Skip over leading delimiters in the string:

    while( stdin.getc() in Delimiters ) do  /* getc did the work */ endwhile;
    while( al in '0'..'9') do

        // Convert character in AL to numeric representation and
        // accumulate result...
```

```
        stdin.getc();

    endwhile;
    if( al not in Delimiters ) then

        raise( ex.ConversionError );

    endif;
```

The first while loop reads a sequence of delimiter characters. When this first while loop ends, the character in AL is not a delimiter character. So far, so good. The second while loop processes a sequence of decimal digits. First, it checks the character read in the previous while loop to see if it is a decimal digit; if so, it processes that digit and reads the next character. This process continues until the call to stdin.getc (at the bottom of the loop) reads a non-digit character. After the second while loop, the program checks the last character read to ensure that it is a legal delimiter character for a numeric input value.

The problem with this algorithm is that it consumes the delimiter character after the numeric string. For example, the colon symbol is a legal delimiter in the default Delimiters character set. If the user types the input "123:456" and executes the code above, this code will properly convert "123" to the numeric value one hundred twenty-three. However, the very next character read from the input stream will be the character "4" not the colon character (":"). While this may be acceptable in certain circumstances, most programmers expect numeric input routines to consume only leading delimiter characters and the numeric digit characters. They do not expect the input routine to consume any trailing delimiter characters (e.g., many programs will read the next character and expect a colon as input if presented with the string "123:456"). Because stdin.getc consumes an input character, and there is no way to "put the character back" onto the input stream, some other way of reading input characters from the user, that doesn't consume those characters, is needed.[4]

The HLA Standard Library comes to the rescue by providing the stdin.peekc function. Like stdin.getc, the stdin.peekc routine reads the next input character from HLA's internal buffer. There are two major differences between stdin.peekc and stdin.getc. First, stdin.peekc will not force the input of a new line of text from the user if the current input line is empty (or you've already read all the text from the input line). Instead, stdin.peekc simply returns zero in the AL register to indicate that there are no more characters on the input line. Because #0 is (by default) a legal delimiter character for numeric values, and the end of line is certainly a legal way to terminate numeric input, this works out rather well. The second difference between stdin.getc and stdin.peekc is that stdin.peekc does not consume the character read from the input buffer. If you call stdin.peekc several times in a row, it will always return the same character; likewise, if you call stdin.getc immediately after stdin.peekc, the call to stdin.getc will generally return the same character as returned by stdin.peekc (the only exception being

---

[4] The HLA Standard Library routines actually buffer up input lines in a string and process characters out of the string. This makes it easy to "peek" ahead one character when looking for a delimiter to end the input value. Your code can also do this; however, the code in this chapter will use a different approach.

the end-of-line condition). So although we cannot put characters back onto the input stream after we've read them with stdin.getc, we can peek ahead at the next character on the input stream and base our logic on that character's value. A corrected version of the previous algorithm might be the following:

```
static
    Delimiters: cset;
        .
        .
        .
    conv.getDelimiters( Delimiters );

    // Skip over leading delimiters in the string:

    while( stdin.peekc() in Delimiters ) do

        // If at the end of the input buffer, we must explicitly read a
        // new line of text from the user. stdin.peekc does not do this
        // for us.

        if( al = #0 ) then

            stdin.ReadLn();

        else

            stdin.getc();   // Remove delimiter from the input stream.

        endif;

    endwhile;
    while( stdin.peekc in '0'..'9') do

        stdin.getc();      // Remove the input character from the input stream.

        // Convert character in AL to numeric representation and
        // accumulate result...

    endwhile;
    if( al not in Delimiters ) then

        raise( ex.ConversionError );

    endif;
```

Note that the call to stdin.peekc in the second while does not consume the delimiter character when the expression evaluates false. Hence, the delimiter character will be the next character read after this algorithm finishes.

The only remaining comment to make about numeric input is to point out that the HLA Standard Library input routines allow arbitrary underscores to appear within a numeric string. The input routines ignore these underscore characters. This allows the user to input strings like "FFFF_F012" and "1_023_596" which are a little more readable than "FFFFF012" or "1023596". To allow underscores (or any other symbol you choose) within a numeric input routine is quite simple; just modify the second while loop above as follows:

```
while( stdin.peekc in {'0'..'9', '_'}) do

    stdin.getc();  // Read the character from the input stream.

    // Ignore underscores while processing numeric input.

    if( al <> '_' ) then

        // Convert character in AL to numeric representation and
        // accumulate result...

    endif;

endwhile;
```

9.2.14.6 Extended Precision Hexadecimal Input

As was the case for numeric output, hexadecimal input is the easiest numeric input routine to write. The basic algorithm for hexadecimal string to numeric conversion is the following:

- Initialize the extended precision value to zero.
- For each input character that is a valid hexadecimal digit, do the following:
- Convert the hexadecimal character to a value in the range 0..15 ($0..$F).
- If the H.O. four bits of the extended precision value are non-zero, raise an exception.
- Multiply the current extended precision value by 16 (i.e., shift left four bits).
- Add the converted hexadecimal digit value to the accumulator.
- Check the last input character to ensure it is a valid delimiter. Raise an exception if it is not.

The program in Listing 9-5 implements this extended precision hexadecimal input routine for 128-bit values.

Listing 9-5: Extended Precision Hexadecimal Input.

```
program Xin128;

#include( "stdlib.hhf" );
```

```
// 128-bit unsigned integer data type:

type
    b128: dword[4];




procedure getb128( var inValue:b128 ); @nodisplay;
const
    HexChars  := {'0'..'9', 'a'..'f', 'A'..'F', '_'};
var
    Delimiters: cset;
    LocalValue: b128;

begin getb128;

    push( eax );
    push( ebx );

    // Get a copy of the HLA standard numeric input delimiters:

    conv.getDelimiters( Delimiters );

    // Initialize the numeric input value to zero:

    xor( eax, eax );
    mov( eax, LocalValue[0] );
    mov( eax, LocalValue[4] );
    mov( eax, LocalValue[8] );
    mov( eax, LocalValue[12] );

    // By default, #0 is a member of the HLA Delimiters
    // character set.  However, someone may have called
    // conv.setDelimiters and removed this character
    // from the internal Delimiters character set. This
    // algorithm depends upon #0 being in the Delimiters
    // character set, so let's add that character in
    // at this point just to be sure.

    cs.unionChar( #0, Delimiters );


    // If we're at the end of the current input
    // line (or the program has yet to read any input),
    // for the input of an actual character.

    if( stdin.peekc() = #0 ) then
```

```
        stdin.readLn();

    endif;



    // Skip the delimiters found on input. This code is
    // somewhat convoluted because stdin.peekc does not
    // force the input of a new line of text if the current
    // input buffer is empty. We have to force that input
    // ourselves in the event the input buffer is empty.

    while( stdin.peekc() in Delimiters ) do

        // If we're at the end of the line, read a new line
        // of text from the user; otherwise, remove the
        // delimiter character from the input stream.

        if( al = #0 ) then

            stdin.readLn(); // Force a new input line.

        else

            stdin.getc();    // Remove the delimiter from the input buffer.

        endif;

    endwhile;

    // Read the hexadecimal input characters and convert
    // them to the internal representation:

    while( stdin.peekc() in HexChars ) do

        // Actually read the character to remove it from the
        // input buffer.

        stdin.getc();

        // Ignore underscores, process everything else.

        if( al <> '_' ) then

            if( al in '0'..'9' ) then

                and( $f, al ); // '0'..'9' -> 0..9

            else
```

```
                    and( $f, al );   // 'a'/'A'..'f'/'F' -> 1..6
                    add( 9, al );    // 1..6 -> 10..15

            endif;


            // Conversion algorithm is the following:
            //
            // (1) LocalValue := LocalValue * 16.
            // (2) LocalValue := LocalValue + al
            //
            // Note that "* 16" is easily accomplished by
            // shifting LocalValue to the left four bits.
            //
            // Overflow occurs if the H.O. four bits of LocalValue
            // contain a non-zero value prior to this operation.

            // First, check for overflow:

            test( $F0, (type byte LocalValue[15]));
            if( @nz ) then

                raise( ex.ValueOutOfRange );

            endif;


            // Now multiply LocalValue by 16 and add in
            // the current hexadecimal digit (in EAX).

            mov( LocalValue[8], ebx );
            shld( 4, ebx, LocalValue[12] );
            mov( LocalValue[4], ebx );
            shld( 4, ebx, LocalValue[8] );
            mov( LocalValue[0], ebx );
            shld( 4, ebx, LocalValue[4] );
            shl( 4, ebx );
            add( eax, ebx );
            mov( ebx, LocalValue[0] );

        endif;

endwhile;

// Okay, we've encountered a non-hexadecimal character.
// Let's make sure it's a valid delimiter character.
// Raise the ex.ConversionError exception if it's invalid.

if( al not in Delimiters ) then
```

```
                raise( ex.ConversionError );

        endif;

        // Okay, this conversion has been a success.  Let's store
        // away the converted value into the output parameter.

        mov( inValue, ebx );
        mov( LocalValue[0], eax );
        mov( eax, [ebx] );

        mov( LocalValue[4], eax );
        mov( eax, [ebx+4] );

        mov( LocalValue[8], eax );
        mov( eax, [ebx+8] );

        mov( LocalValue[12], eax );
        mov( eax, [ebx+12] );

        pop( ebx );
        pop( eax );

end getb128;



// Code to test the routines above:

static
    b1:b128;

begin Xin128;

    stdout.put( "Input a 128-bit hexadecimal value: " );
    getb128( b1 );
    stdout.put
    (
        "The value is: $",
        b1[12], '_',
        b1[8],  '_',
        b1[4],  '_',
        b1[0],
        nl
    );

end Xin128;
```

Extending this code to handle objects that are not 128 bits long is very easy. There are only three changes necessary: You must zero out the whole object at the beginning of the getb128 routine; when checking for overflow (the "test($F, (type byte LocalValue[15]));" instruction) you must test the H.O. 4 bits of the new object you're processing; and you must modify the code that multiplies LocalValue by 16 (via shld) so that it multiplies your object by 16 (i.e., shifts it to the left four bits).

9.2.14.7 Extended Precision Unsigned Decimal Input

The algorithm for extended precision unsigned decimal input is nearly identical to that for hexadecimal input. In fact, the only difference (beyond only accepting decimal digits) is that you multiply the extended precision value by 10 rather than 16 for each input character (in general, the algorithm is the same for any base; just multiply the accumulating value by the input base). The code in Listing 9-6 demonstrates how to write a 128-bit unsigned decimal input routine.

Listing 9-6: Extended Precision Unsigned Decimal Input.

```
program Uin128;

#include( "stdlib.hhf" );

// 128-bit unsigned integer data type:

type
    u128: dword[4];




procedure getu128( var inValue:u128 ); @nodisplay;
var
    Delimiters: cset;
    LocalValue: u128;
    PartialSum: u128;

begin getu128;

    push( eax );
    push( ebx );
    push( ecx );
    push( edx );

    // Get a copy of the HLA standard numeric input delimiters:

    conv.getDelimiters( Delimiters );

    // Initialize the numeric input value to zero:

    xor( eax, eax );
```

```
mov( eax, LocalValue[0] );
mov( eax, LocalValue[4] );
mov( eax, LocalValue[8] );
mov( eax, LocalValue[12] );

    // By default, #0 is a member of the HLA Delimiters
    // character set. However, someone may have called
    // conv.setDelimiters and removed this character
    // from the internal Delimiters character set.  This
    // algorithm depends upon #0 being in the Delimiters
    // character set, so let's add that character in
    // at this point just to be sure.

cs.unionChar( #0, Delimiters );


    // If we're at the end of the current input
    // line (or the program has yet to read any input),
    // for the input of an actual character.

if( stdin.peekc() = #0 ) then

    stdin.readLn();

endif;



    // Skip the delimiters found on input. This code is
    // somewhat convoluted because stdin.peekc does not
    // force the input of a new line of text if the current
    // input buffer is empty. We have to force that input
    // ourselves in the event the input buffer is empty.

while( stdin.peekc() in Delimiters ) do

    // If we're at the end of the line, read a new line
    // of text from the user; otherwise, remove the
    // delimiter character from the input stream.

    if( al = #0 ) then

        stdin.readLn(); // Force a new input line.

    else

        stdin.getc();    // Remove the delimiter from the input buffer.

    endif;
```

```
        endwhile;

        // Read the decimal input characters and convert
        // them to the internal representation:

while( stdin.peekc() in '0'..'9' ) do

        // Actually read the character to remove it from the
        // input buffer.

        stdin.getc();

        // Ignore underscores, process everything else.

        if( al <> '_' ) then

            and( $f, al );                // '0'..'9' -> 0..9
            mov( eax, PartialSum[0] );    // Save to add in later.

            // Conversion algorithm is the following:
            //
            // (1) LocalValue := LocalValue * 10.
            // (2) LocalValue := LocalValue + al
            //
            // First, multiply LocalValue by 10:

            mov( 10, eax );
            mul( LocalValue[0], eax );
            mov( eax, LocalValue[0] );
            mov( edx, PartialSum[4] );

            mov( 10, eax );
            mul( LocalValue[4], eax );
            mov( eax, LocalValue[4] );
            mov( edx, PartialSum[8] );

            mov( 10, eax );
            mul( LocalValue[8], eax );
            mov( eax, LocalValue[8] );
            mov( edx, PartialSum[12] );

            mov( 10, eax );
            mul( LocalValue[12], eax );
            mov( eax, LocalValue[12] );

            // Check for overflow. This occurs if EDX
            // contains a non-zero value.
```

```
            if( edx /* <> 0 */ ) then

                raise( ex.ValueOutOfRange );

            endif;

            // Add in the partial sums (including the
            // most recently converted character).

            mov( PartialSum[0], eax );
            add( eax, LocalValue[0] );

            mov( PartialSum[4], eax );
            adc( eax, LocalValue[4] );

            mov( PartialSum[8], eax );
            adc( eax, LocalValue[8] );

            mov( PartialSum[12], eax );
            adc( eax, LocalValue[12] );

            // Another check for overflow. If there
            // was a carry out of the extended precision
            // addition above, we've got overflow.

            if( @c ) then

                raise( ex.ValueOutOfRange );

            endif;

        endif;

    endwhile;

    // Okay, we've encountered a non-decimal character.
    // Let's make sure it's a valid delimiter character.
    // Raise the ex.ConversionError exception if it's invalid.

    if( al not in Delimiters ) then

        raise( ex.ConversionError );

    endif;

    // Okay, this conversion has been a success. Let's store
    // away the converted value into the output parameter.

    mov( inValue, ebx );
```

```
        mov( LocalValue[0], eax );
        mov( eax, [ebx] );

        mov( LocalValue[4], eax );
        mov( eax, [ebx+4] );

        mov( LocalValue[8], eax );
        mov( eax, [ebx+8] );

        mov( LocalValue[12], eax );
        mov( eax, [ebx+12] );

        pop( edx );
        pop( ecx );
        pop( ebx );
        pop( eax );

end getu128;



// Code to test the routines above:

static
        b1:u128;

begin Uin128;

        stdout.put( "Input a 128-bit decimal value: " );
        getu128( b1 );
        stdout.put
        (
            "The value is: $",
            b1[12], '_',
            b1[8],  '_',
            b1[4],  '_',
            b1[0],
            nl
        );

end Uin128;
```

As for hexadecimal input, extending this decimal input to some number of bits beyond 128 is fairly easy. All you need do is modify the code that zeros out the LocalValue variable and the code that multiplies LocalValue by ten (overflow checking is done in this same code, so there are only two spots in this code that require modification).

9.2.14.8 Extended Precision Signed Decimal Input

Once you have an unsigned decimal input routine, writing a signed decimal input routine is easy. The following algorithm describes how to accomplish this:

- Consume any delimiter characters at the beginning of the input stream.
- If the next input character is a minus sign, consume this character and set a flag noting that the number is negative.
- Call the unsigned decimal input routine to convert the rest of the string to an integer.
- Check the return result to make sure its H.O. bit is clear. Raise the ex.ValueOutOfRange exception if the H.O. bit of the result is set.
- If the code encountered a minus sign in step two above, negate the result.

The actual code is left as a programming exercise (or see the conversion routines in the HLA Standard Library for concrete examples).

9.3 Operating on Different-Sized Operands

Occasionally you may need to do some computation on a pair of operands that are not the same size. For example, you may need to add a word and a double word together or subtract a byte value from a word value. The solution is simple: just extend the smaller operand to the size of the larger operand and then do the operation on two similarly sized operands. For signed operands, you would sign extend the smaller operand to the same size as the larger operand; for unsigned values, you zero extend the smaller operand. This works for any operation, although the following examples demonstrate this for the addition operation.

To extend the smaller operand to the size of the larger operand, use a sign extension or zero extension operation (depending upon whether you're adding signed or unsigned values). Once you've extended the smaller value to the size of the larger, the addition can proceed. Consider the following code that adds a byte value to a word value:

```
static
    var1: byte;
    var2: word;
        .
        .
        .
// Unsigned addition:

    movzx( var1, ax );
    add( var2, ax );

// Signed addition:

movsx( var1, ax );
add( var2, ax );
```

In both cases, the byte variable was loaded into the AL register, extended to 16 bits, and then added to the word operand. This code works out really well if you can choose the order of the operations (e.g., adding the 8-bit value to the 16- bit value). Sometimes, you cannot specify the order of the operations. Perhaps the 16-bit value is already in the AX register and you want to add an 8-bit value to it. For unsigned addition, you could use the following code:

```
mov( var2, ax );   // Load 16-bit value into AX
       .           // Do some other operations leaving
       .           //  a 16-bit quantity in AX.
add( var1, al );   // Add in the eight-bit value
adc( 0, ah );      // Add carry into the H.O. word.
```

The first add instruction in this example adds the byte at var1 to the L.O. byte of the value in the accumulator. The adc instruction above adds the carry out of the L.O. byte into the H.O. byte of the accumulator. Care must be taken to ensure that this adc instruction is present. If you leave it out, you may not get the correct result.

Adding an 8-bit signed operand to a 16-bit signed value is a little more difficult. Unfortunately, you cannot add an immediate value (as above) to the H.O. word of AX. This is because the H.O. extension byte can be either $00 or $FF. If a register is available, the best thing to do is the following:

```
mov( ax, bx );      // BX is the available register.
movsx( var1, ax );
add( bx, ax );
```

If an extra register is not available, you might try the following code:

```
push( ax );         // Save word value.
movsx( var1, ax );  // Sign extend 8-bit operand to 16 bits.
add( [esp], ax );   // Add in previous word value
add( 2, esp );      // Pop junk from stack
```

Another alternative is to store the 16-bit value in the accumulator into a memory location and then proceed as before:

```
mov( ax, temp );
movsx( var1, ax );
add( temp, ax );
```

All the examples above added a byte value to a word value. By zero or sign extending the smaller operand to the size of the larger operand, you can easily add any two different-sized variables together.

As a last example, consider adding an 8-bit signed value to a quadword (64-bit) value:

```
static
    QVal:qword;
    BVal:int8;

    .

    .

    .

    movsx( BVal, eax );
    cdq();
    add( (type dword QVal), eax );
    adc( (type dword QVal[4]), edx );
```

9.4   Decimal Arithmetic

The 80x86 CPUs use the binary numbering system for their native internal representation. The binary numbering system is, by far, the most common numbering system in use in computer systems today. In the old days, however, there were computer systems that were based on the decimal (base 10) numbering system instead of the binary numbering system. Consequently, their arithmetic system was decimal based rather than binary. Such computer systems were very popular in systems targeted for business/commercial systems.[5] Although systems designers have discovered that binary arithmetic is almost always better than decimal arithmetic for general calculations, the myth still persists that decimal arithmetic is better for money calculations than binary arithmetic. Therefore, many software systems still specify the use of decimal arithmetic in their calculations (not to mention that there is lots of legacy code out there whose algorithms are only stable if they use decimal arithmetic). Therefore, despite the fact that decimal arithmetic is generally inferior to binary arithmetic, the need for decimal arithmetic still persists.

Of course, the 80x86 is not a decimal computer; therefore, we have to play tricks in order to represent decimal numbers using the native binary format. The most common technique, even employed by most so-called decimal computers, is to use the binary coded decimal, or BCD, representation. The BCD representation uses 4 bits to represent the 10 possible decimal digits (see Table 9-1). The binary value of those 4 bits is equal to the corresponding decimal value in the range 0..9. Of course, with 4 bits we can actually represent 16 different values, the BCD format ignores the remaining six bit combinations.

Table 9-1: Binary Code Decimal (BCD) Representation

BCD Representation	Decimal Equivalent
0000	0
0001	1
0010	2

---

[5] In fact, until the release of the IBM 360 in the middle 1960s, most scientific computer systems were binary based while most commercial/business systems were decimal based. IBM pushed its system\360 as a single-purpose solution for both business and scientific applications. Indeed, the model designation (360) was derived from the 360 degrees on a compass so as to suggest that the system\360 was suitable for computations "at all points of the compass" (i.e., business and scientific).

Table 9-1: Binary Code Decimal (BCD) Representation

BCD Representation	Decimal Equivalent
0011	3
0100	4
0101	5
0110	6
0111	7
1000	8
1001	9
1010	Illegal
1011	Illegal
1100	Illegal
1101	Illegal
1110	Illegal
1111	Illegal

Because each BCD digit requires 4 bits, we can represent a two-digit BCD value with a single byte. This means that we can represent the decimal values in the range 0..99 using a single byte (versus 0..255 if we treat the value as an unsigned binary number). Clearly it takes more memory to represent the same value in BCD as it does to represent the same value in binary. For example, with a 32-bit value you can represent BCD values in the range 0..99,999,999 (8 significant digits). However, you can represent values in the range 0..4,294,967,295 (more than nine significant digits) by using binary representation.

Not only does the BCD format waste memory on a binary computer (because it uses more bits to represent a given integer value), decimal arithmetic is also slower. For these reasons, you should avoid the use of decimal arithmetic unless it is absolutely mandated for a given application.

Binary coded decimal representation does offer one big advantage over binary representation: it is fairly trivial to convert between the string representation of a decimal number and the BCD representation. This feature is particularly beneficial when working with fractional values because fixed and floating point binary representations cannot exactly represent many commonly used values between zero and one (e.g., $1/10$). Therefore, BCD operations can be efficient when reading from a BCD device, doing a simple arithmetic operation (e.g., a single addition) and then writing the BCD value to some other device.

9.4.1 Literal BCD Constants

HLA does not provide, nor do you need, a special literal BCD constant. Because BCD is just a special form of hexadecimal notation that does not allow the values $A..$F, you can easily create BCD constants using HLA's hexadecimal notation. Of course, you must take care not to include the symbols 'A'..'F' in a BCD constant because they are illegal BCD values. As an example, consider the following mov instruction that copies the BCD value '99' into the AL register:

```
    mov( $99, al );
```

The important thing to keep in mind is that you must not use HLA literal decimal constants for BCD values. That is, "mov(95, al);" does not load the BCD representation for 95 into the AL register. Instead, it loads $5F into AL and that's an illegal BCD value. Any computations you attempt with illegal BCD values will produce garbage results. Always remember that, even though it seems counterintuitive, you use hexadecimal literal constants to represent literal BCD values.

9.4.2 The 80x86 DAA and DAS Instructions

The integer unit on the 80x86 does not directly support BCD arithmetic. Instead, the 80x86 requires that you perform the computation using binary arithmetic and use some auxiliary instructions to convert the binary result to BCD. To support packed BCD addition and subtraction with two digits per byte, the 80x86 provides two instructions: decimal adjust after addition (daa) and decimal adjust after subtraction (das). You would execute these two instructions immediately after an add/adc or sub/sbb instruction to correct the binary result in the AL register.

Two add a pair of two-digit (i.e., single-byte) BCD values together, you would use the following sequence:

```
    mov( bcd_1, al );      // Assume that bcd1 and bcd2 both contain
    add( bcd_2, al );      // value BCD values.
    daa();
```

The first two instructions above add the two-byte values together using standard binary arithmetic. This may not produce a correct BCD result. For example, if bcd_1 contains $9 and bcd_2 contains $1, then the first two instructions above will produce the binary sum $A instead of the correct BCD result $10. The daa instruction corrects this invalid result. It checks to see if there was a carry out of the low order BCD digit and adjusts the value (by adding six to it) if there was an overflow. After adjusting for overflow out of the L.O. digit, the daa instruction repeats this process for the H.O. digit. daa sets the carry flag if the was a (decimal) carry out of the H.O. digit of the operation.

The daa instruction only operates on the AL register. It will not adjust (properly) for a decimal addition if you attempt to add a value to AX, EAX, or any other register. Specifically note that daa limits you to adding two decimal digits (a single byte) at a time. This means that for the purposes of computing decimal sums, you have to treat the 80x86 as though it were an 8-bit processor, capable of adding only 8 bits at a time. If you wish to add more than two digits together, you must treat this as a multiprecision operation. For example, to add four decimal digits together (using daa), you must execute a sequence like the following:

```
// Assume "bcd_1:byte[2];", "bcd_2:byte[2];", and "bcd_3:byte[2];"

mov( bcd_1[0], al );
add( bcd_2[0], al );
daa();
mov( al, bcd_3[0] );
mov( bcd_1[1], al );
adc( bcd_2[1], al );
daa();
mov( al, bcd_3[1], al );
```

// Carry is set at this point if there was unsigned overflow.

Because a binary addition of two words (producing a word result) requires only three instructions, you can see that decimal arithmetic is so expensive.[6]

The das (decimal adjust after subtraction) adjusts the decimal result after a binary sub or sbb instruction. You use it the same way you use the daa instruction. Examples:

```
// Two-digit (one-byte) decimal subtraction:

mov( bcd_1, al );     // Assume that bcd1 and bcd2 both contain
sub( bcd_2, al );     // value BCD values.
das();

// Four-digit (two-byte) decimal subtraction.
// Assume "bcd_1:byte[2];", "bcd_2:byte[2];", and "bcd_3:byte[2];"

mov( bcd_1[0], al );
sub( bcd_2[0], al );
das();
mov( al, bcd_3[0] );
mov( bcd_1[1], al );
sbb( bcd_2[1], al );
das();
mov( al, bcd_3[1], al );
```

// Carry is set at this point if there was unsigned overflow.

Unfortunately, the 80x86 only provides support for addition and subtraction of packed BCD values using the daa and das instructions. It does not support multiplication, division, or any other arithmetic operations. Because decimal arithmetic using these instructions is so limited, you'll rarely see any programs use these instructions.

---

[6] You'll also soon see that it's rare to find decimal arithmetic done this way — so it hardly matters.

9.4.3   The 80x86 AAA, AAS, AAM, and AAD Instructions

In addition to the packed decimal instructions (daa and das), the 80x86 CPUs support four unpacked decimal adjustment instructions. Unpacked decimal numbers store only one digit per 8-bit byte. As you can imagine, this data representation scheme wastes a considerable amount of memory. However, the unpacked decimal adjustment instructions support the multiplication and division operations, so they are marginally more useful.

The instruction mnemonics aaa, aas, aam, and aad stand for "ASCII Adjust for Addition, Subtraction, Multiplication, and Division" (respectively). Despite their name, these instructions do not process ASCII characters. Instead, they support an unpacked decimal value in AL whose L.O. four bits contain the decimal digit and the H.O. four bits contain zero. Note, though, that you can easily convert an ASCII decimal digit character to an unpacked decimal number by simply ANDing AL with the value $0F.

The aaa instruction adjusts the result of a binary addition of two unpacked decimal numbers. If the addition of those two values exceeds ten, then aaa will subtract ten from AL and increment AH by one (as well as set the carry flag). aaa assumes that the two values you add together were legal unpacked decimal values. Other than the fact that aaa works with only one decimal digit at a time (rather than two), you use it the same way you use the daa instruction. Of course, if you need to add together a string of decimal digits, using unpacked decimal arithmetic will require twice as many operations and, therefore, twice the execution time.

You use the aas instruction the same way you use the das instruction except, of course, it operates on unpacked decimal values rather than packed decimal values. As for aaa, aas will require twice the number of operations to add the same number of decimal digits as the das instruction. If you're wondering why anyone would want to use the aaa or aas instructions, keep in mind that the unpacked format supports multiplication and division, while the packed format does not. Because packing and unpacking the data is usually more expensive than working on the data a digit at a time, the aaa and aas instruction are more efficient if you have to work with unpacked data (because of the need for multiplication and division).

The aam instruction modifies the result in the AX register to produce a correct unpacked decimal result after multiplying two unpacked decimal digits using the mul instruction. Because the largest product you may obtain is 81 (9*9 produces the largest possible product of two single-digit values), the result will fit in the AL register. aam unpacks the binary result by dividing it by ten, leaving the quotient (H.O. digit) in AH and the remainder (L.O. digit) in AL. Note that aam leaves the quotient and remainder in different registers than a standard 8-bit div operation.

Technically, you do not have to use the aam instruction for BCD multiplication operations. aam simply divides AL by ten and leaves the quotient and remainder in AH and AL (respectively). If you have need of this particular operation, you may use the aam instruction for this purpose (indeed, that's about the only use for aam in most programs these days).

If you need to multiply more than two unpacked decimal digits together using mul and aam, you will need to devise a multiprecision multiplication that uses the manual algorithm from earlier in this chapter. Because that is a lot of work, this section will not present that algorithm. If you need a multiprecision decimal multiplication, see the next section; it presents a better solution.

The aad instruction, as you might expect, adjusts a value for unpacked decimal division. The unusual thing about this instruction is that you must execute it before a div operation. It assumes that AL contains the least significant digit of a two-digit value and AH contains the most significant digit of a two-digit unpacked decimal value. It converts these two numbers to binary so that a standard div instruction will produce the correct unpacked decimal result. Like aam, this instruction is nearly useless for its intended purpose as extended precision operations (e.g., division of more than one or two digits) are extremely inefficient. However, this instruction is actually quite useful in its own right. It computes AX = AH*10+AL (assuming that AH and AL contain single-digit decimal values). You can use this instruction to convert a two-character string containing the ASCII representation of a value in the range 0..99 to a binary value. For example:

```
mov( '9', al );
mov( '9', ah );     // "99" is in AH:AL.
and( $0F0F, ax );   // Convert from ASCII to unpacked decimal.
aad();              // After this, AX contains 99.
```

The decimal and ASCII adjust instructions provide an extremely poor implementation of decimal arithmetic. To better support decimal arithmetic on 80x86 systems, Intel incorporated decimal operations into the FPU. The next section discusses how to use the FPU for this purpose. However, even with FPU support, decimal arithmetic is inefficient and less precise than binary arithmetic. Therefore, you should consider carefully if you really need to use decimal arithmetic before incorporating it into your programs.

9.4.4 Packed Decimal Arithmetic Using the FPU

To improve the performance of applications that rely on decimal arithmetic, Intel incorporated support for decimal arithmetic directly into the FPU. Unlike the packed and unpacked decimal formats of the previous sections, the FPU easily supports values with up to 18 decimal digits of precision, all at FPU speeds. Furthermore, all the arithmetic capabilities of the FPU (e.g., transcendental operations) are available in addition to addition, subtraction, multiplication, and division. Assuming you can live with only 18 digits of precision and a few other restrictions, decimal arithmetic on the FPU is the right way to go if you must use decimal arithmetic in your programs.

The first fact you must note when using the FPU is that it doesn't really support decimal arithmetic. Instead, the FPU provides two instructions, fbld and fbstp, that convert between packed decimal and binary floating point formats when moving data to and from the FPU. The fbld (float/BCD load) instruction loads an 80-bit packed BCD value unto the top of the FPU stack after converting that BCD value to the IEEE binary floating point format. Likewise, the `fbstp` (float/BCD store and pop) instruction pops the floating point value off the top of stack, converts it to a packed BCD value, and stores the BCD value into the destination memory location.

Once you load a packed BCD value into the FPU, it is no longer BCD. It's just a floating point value. This presents the first restriction on the use of the FPU as a decimal integer processor: Calculations are done using binary arithmetic. If you have an algorithm that absolutely positively depends upon the use of decimal arithmetic, it may fail if you use the FPU to implement it.[7]

The second limitation is that the FPU supports only one BCD data type: a ten-byte, 18-digit packed decimal value. It will not support smaller values nor will it support larger values. Because 18 digits is usually sufficient and memory is cheap, this isn't a big restriction.

A third consideration is that the conversion between packed BCD and the floating point format is not a cheap operation. The `fbld` and `fbstp` instructions can be quite slow (more than two orders of magnitude slower than `fld` and `fstp`, for example). Therefore, these instructions can be costly if you're doing simple additions or subtractions; the cost of conversion far outweighs the time spent adding the values a byte at a time using the `daa` and `das` instructions (multiplication and division, however, are going to be faster on the FPU).

You may be wondering why the FPU's packed decimal format only supports 18 digits. After all, with ten bytes it should be possible to represent 20 BCD digits. As it turns out, the FPU's packed decimal format uses the first nine bytes to hold the packed BCD value in a standard packed decimal format (the first byte contains the two L.O. digits, and the ninth byte holds the H.O. two digits). The H.O. bit of the tenth byte holds the sign bit and the FPU ignores the remaining bits in the tenth byte. If you're wondering why Intel didn't squeeze in one more digit (i.e., use the L.O. four bits of the tenth byte to allow for 19 digits of precision), just keep in mind that doing so would create some possible BCD values that the FPU could not exactly represent in the native floating point format. Hence, you have the limitation of 18 digits.

The FPU uses a one's complement notation for negative BCD values. That is, the sign bit contains a one if the number is negative or zero, and it contains a zero if the number is positive or zero (like the binary one's complement format, there are two distinct representations for zero).

HLA's tbyte type is the standard data type you would use to define packed BCD variables. The `fbld` and `fbstp` instructions require a tbyte operand. Unfortunately, the current version of HLA does not let you (directly) provide an initializer for a tbyte variable. One solution is to use the `@nostorage` option and initialize the data following the variable declaration. For example, consider the following code fragment:

---

[7] An example of such an algorithm might be a multiplication by ten by shifting the number one digit to the left. However, such operations are not possible within the FPU itself, so algorithms that misbehave inside the FPU are actually quite rare.

```
static
    tbyteObject: tbyte; @nostorage
                    qword $123456;
                    word  0;
```

This tbyteObject declaration tells HLA that this is a tbyte object but does not explicitly set aside any space for the variable. The following qword and word directives set aside ten bytes of storage and initializes these ten bytes with the value $123456 (remember that the 80x86 organizes data from the L.O. byte to the H.O. byte in memory, so the word directive's operand provides the H.O. two bytes). While this scheme is inelegant, it will get the job done.

Because the FPU converts packed decimal values to the internal floating point format, you can mix packed decimal, floating point, and (binary) integer formats in the same calculation. The program in Listing 9-7 demonstrates how you might achieve this.

Listing 9-7: Mixed Mode FPU Arithmetic.

```
program MixedArithmetic;
#include( "stdlib.hhf" )

static
    tb: tbyte; @nostorage;
        byte $21,$43,$65,0,0,0,0,0,0,0;

begin MixedArithmetic;

    fbld( tb );
    fmul( 2.0 );
    fiadd( 1 );
    fbstp( tb );
    stdout.put( "bcd value is " );
    stdout.puttb( tb );
    stdout.newln();

end MixedArithmetic;
```

The FPU treats packed decimal values as integer values. Therefore, if your calculations produce fractional results, the fbstp instruction will round the result according to the current FPU rounding mode. If you need to work with fractional values, you need to stick with floating point results.

9.5 Tables

The term "table" has different meanings to different programmers. To most assembly language programmers, a table is nothing more than an array that is initialized with some data. The assembly language programmer often uses tables to compute complex or otherwise slow functions. Many very high level languages (e.g., SNOBOL4 and Icon) directly support a table data type. Tables in these languages are essentially associative arrays whose elements you can access with a non-integer index (e.g., floating point, string, or any other data type). HLA provides a table module that lets you index an array using a string. However, in this chapter we will adopt the assembly language programmer's view of tables.

A table is an array containing preinitialized values that do not change during the execution of the program. A table can be compared to an array in the same way an integer constant can be compared to an integer variable. In assembly language, you can use tables for a variety of purposes: computing functions, controlling program flow, or simply "looking things up." In general, tables provide a fast mechanism for performing some operation at the expense of some space in your program (the extra space holds the tabular data). In the following sections we'll explore some of the many possible uses of tables in an assembly language program.

NOTE *Because tables typically contain preinitialized data that does not change during program execution, the* readonly *section is a good place to put your table objects.*

9.5.1   Function Computation via Table Look-Up

Tables can do all kinds of things in assembly language. In high level languages, like Pascal, it's real easy to create a formula that computes some value. A simple-looking high level language arithmetic expression can be equivalent to a considerable amount of 80x86 assembly language code and, therefore, could be expensive to compute. Assembly language programmers will often precompute many values and use a table look-up of those values to speed up their programs. This has the advantage of being easier, and often more efficient as well. Consider the following Pascal statement:

```
if (character >= 'a') and (character <= 'z') then
 character := chr(ord(character) - 32);
```

This Pascal if statement converts the character variable character from lower case to upper case if character is in the range 'a'..'z'. The HLA code that does the same thing is

```
        mov( character, al );
        if( al in 'a'..'z' ) then

            and( $5f, al );// Same as SUB( 32, al ) in this code.

        endif;
        mov( al, character );
```

Note that HLA's high level if statement translates into four machine instructions in this particular example. Hence, this code requires a total of seven machine instructions.

Had you buried this code in a nested loop, you'd be hard pressed to reduce the size of this code without using a table look-up. Using a table look-up, however, allows you to reduce this sequence of instructions to just four instructions:

```
mov( character, al );
lea( ebx, CnvrtLower );
xlat
mov( al, character );
```

You're probably wondering how this code works and what is this new instruction, xlat? The xlat, or translate, instruction does the following:

```
mov( [ebx+al*1], al );
```

That is, it uses the current value of the AL register as an index into the array whose base address is found in EBX. It fetches the byte at that index in the array and copies that byte into the AL register. Intel calls this instruction *translate* because programmers typically use it to translate characters from one form to another using a look-up table. That's exactly how we are using it here.

In the previous example, CnvrtLower is a 256-byte table that contains the values 0..$60 at indices 0..$60, $41..$5A at indices $61..$7A, and $7B..$FF at indices $7Bh..0FF. Therefore, if AL contains a value in the range $0..$60, the xlat instruction returns the value $0..$60, effectively leaving AL unchanged. However, if AL contains a value in the range $61..$7A (the ASCII codes for 'a'..'z') then the xlat instruction replaces the value in AL with a value in the range $41..$5A. The values $41..$5A just happen to be the ASCII codes for 'A'..'Z.' Therefore, if AL originally contains a lower case character ($61..$7A), the xlat instruction replaces the value in AL with a corresponding value in the range $61..$7A, effectively converting the original lower case character ($61..$7A) to an upper case character ($41..$5A). The remaining entries in the table, like entries $0..$60, simply contain the index into the table of their particular element. Therefore, if AL originally contains a value in the range $7A..$FF, the xlat instruction will return the corresponding table entry that also contains $7A..$FF.

As the complexity of the function increases, the performance benefits of the table look-up method increase dramatically. While you would almost never use a look-up table to convert lower case to upper case, consider what happens if you want to swap cases:

For example, via computation:

```
mov( character, al );
if( al in 'a'..'z' ) then

    and( $5f, al );

elseif( al in 'A'..'Z' ) then
```

```
        or( $20, al );

    endif;
    mov( al, character ):
```

The `if` and `elseif` statements generate 4 and 5 actual machine instructions, respectively, so this code is equivalent to 13 actual machine instructions.

The table look-up code to compute this same function is:

```
    mov( character, al );
    lea( ebx, SwapUL );
    xlat();
    mov( al, character );
```

As you can see, when using a table look-up to compute a function only the table changes, the code remains the same.

Table look-ups suffer from one major problem: Functions computed via table look-up have a limited domain. The domain of a function is the set of possible input values (parameters) it will accept. For example, the upper/lower case conversion functions above have the 256-character ASCII character set as their domain.

A function such as SIN or COS accepts the set of real numbers as possible input values. Clearly the domain for SIN and COS is much larger than for the upper/lower case conversion function. If you are going to do computations via table look-up, you must limit the domain of a function to a small set. This is because each element in the domain of a function requires an entry in the look-up table. You won't find it very practical to implement a function via table look-up whose domain is the set of real numbers.

Most look-up tables are quite small, usually 10 to 128 entries. Rarely do look-up tables grow beyond 1,000 entries. Most programmers don't have the patience to create (and verify the correctness) of a 1,000-entry table.

Another limitation of functions based on look-up tables is that the elements in the domain of the function must be fairly contiguous. Table look-ups take the input value for a function, use this input value as an index into the table, and return the value at that entry in the table. If you do not pass a function any values other than 0, 100, 1,000, and 10,000, it would seem an ideal candidate for implementation via table look-up; its domain consists of only four items. However, the table would actually require 10,001 different elements due to the range of the input values. Therefore, you cannot efficiently create such a function via a table look-up. Throughout this section on tables, we'll assume that the domain of the function is a fairly contiguous set of values.

The best functions you can implement via table look-ups are those whose domain and range is always 0..255 (or some subset of this range). You can efficiently implement such functions on the 80x86 via the xlat instruction. The upper/lower case conversion routines presented earlier are good examples of such a function. Any function in this class (those whose domain and range take on the values 0..255) can be computed using the same two instructions: "lea(table, ebx);" and "xlat();". The only thing that ever changes is the look-up table.

You cannot (conveniently) use the xlat instruction to compute a function value once the range or domain of the function takes on values outside 0..255. There are three situations to consider:

- The domain is outside 0..255, but the range is within 0..255.
- The domain is inside 0..255, but the range is outside 0..255.
- Both the domain and range of the function take on values outside 0..255.

We will consider each of these cases separately.

If the domain of a function is outside 0..255 but the range of the function falls within this set of values, our look-up table will require more than 256 entries, but we can represent each entry with a single byte. Therefore, the look-up table can be an array of bytes. Other than those look-ups that can use the xlat instruction, functions falling into this class are the most efficient. The following Pascal function invocation:

```
B := Func(X);
```

where Func is

```
function Func(X:dword):byte;
```

is easily converted to the following HLA code:

```
mov( X, ebx );
mov( FuncTable[ ebx ], al );
mov( al, B );
```

This code loads the function parameter into EBX, uses this value (in the range 0..??) as an index into the FuncTable table, fetches the byte at that location, and stores the result into B. Obviously, the table must contain a valid entry for each possible value of X. For example, suppose you wanted to map a cursor position on the video screen in the range 0..1999 (there are 2,000 character positions on an 80x25 video display) to its X or Y coordinate on the screen. You could easily compute the X coordinate via the function:

```
X:=Posn mod 80
```

and the Y coordinate with the formula:

```
Y:=Posn div 80
```

(where Posn is the cursor position on the screen). This can be easily computed using the 80x86 code:

```
        mov( Posn, ax );
        div( 80, ax );
```

```
// X is now in AH, Y is now in AL
```

However, the div instruction on the 80x86 is very slow. If you need to do this computation for every character you write to the screen, you will seriously degrade the speed of your video display code. The following code, which realizes these two functions via table look-up, may improve the performance of your code considerably:

```
        movzx( Posn, ebx );// Use a plain MOV instr if Posn is uns32
        mov( YCoord[ebx], al );// rather than an uns16 value.
        mov( XCoord[ebx], ah );
```

If the domain of a function is within 0..255 but the range is outside this set, the look-up table will contain 256 or fewer entries, but each entry will require two or more bytes. If both the range and domains of the function are outside 0..255, each entry will require two or more bytes and the table will contain more than 256 entries.

Recall from the chapter on arrays that the formula for indexing into a single dimension array (of which a table is a special case) is

```
        Address := Base + index * size
```

If elements in the range of the function require two bytes, then you must multiply the index by two before indexing into the table. Likewise, if each entry requires three, four, or more bytes, the index must be multiplied by the size of each table entry before being used as an index into the table. For example, suppose you have a function, F(x), defined by the following (pseudo) Pascal declaration:

```
function F(x:dword):word;
```

You can easily create this function using the following 80x86 code (and, of course, the appropriate table named F):

```
        mov( X, ebx );
        mov( F[ebx*2], ax );
```

Any function whose domain is small and mostly contiguous is a good candidate for computation via table look-up. In some cases, noncontiguous domains are acceptable as well, as long as the domain can be coerced into an appropriate set of values. Such operations are called *conditioning* and are the subject of the next section.

9.5.2 Domain Conditioning

Domain conditioning is taking a set of values in the domain of a function and massaging them so that they are more acceptable as inputs to that function. Consider the following function:

$$\text{sinx} = \text{sinx} | x \lfloor [-2\pi,\ 2\pi]$$

This says that the (computer) function SIN(x) is equivalent to the (mathematical) function *sin x* where:

$$-2\pi\ ..\ x\ ..\ 2\pi$$

As we all know, sine is a circular function, which will accept any real valued input. The formula used to compute sine, however, only accept a small set of these values.

This range limitation doesn't present any real problems; by simply computing "SIN(X mod (2*pi))" we can compute the sine of any input value. Modifying an input value so that we can easily compute a function is called conditioning the input. In the example above we computed "X mod 2*pi" and used the result as the input to the sin function. This truncates X to the domain sin needs without affecting the result. We can apply input conditioning to table look-ups as well. In fact, scaling the index to handle word entries is a form of input conditioning. Consider the following Pascal function:

```
function val(x:word):word; begin
    case x of
        0: val := 1;
        1: val := 1;
        2: val := 4;
        3: val := 27;
        4: val := 256;
        otherwise val := 0;
    end;
end;
```

This function computes some value for x in the range 0..4, and it returns zero if x is outside this range. Because x can take on 65,536 different values (being a 16-bit word), creating a table containing 65,536 words where only the first five entries are non-zero seems to be quite wasteful. However, we can still compute this function using a table look-up if we use input conditioning. The following assembly language code presents this principle:

```
        mov( 0, ax ); // AX = 0, assume X > 4.
        movzx( x, ebx );// Note that H.O. bits of EBX must be zero!
        if( bx <= 4 ) then

            mov( val[ ebx*2 ], ax );

        endif;
```

This code checks to see if x is outside the range 0..4. If so, it manually sets AX to zero; otherwise it looks up the function value through the val table. With input conditioning, you can implement several functions that would otherwise be impractical to do via table look-up.

9.5.3 Generating Tables

One big problem with using table look-ups is creating the table in the first place. This is particularly true if there is a large number of entries in the table. Figuring out the data to place in the table, then laboriously entering the data, and, finally, checking that data to make sure it is valid is a very time-staking and boring process. For many tables, there is no way around this process. For other tables there is a better way - use the computer to generate the table for you. An example is probably the best way to describe this. Consider the following modification to the sine function:

$$(\sin x) \times r = \left\langle \left. \frac{(r \times (1000 \times \sin x))}{1000} \right| x \in [0, 359] \right\rangle$$

This states that x is an integer in the range 0..359 and r must be an integer. The computer can easily compute this with the following code:

```
movzx( x, ebx );
mov( Sines[ ebx*2], eax );// Get SIN(X) * 1000
imul( r, eax );// Note that this extends EAX into EDX.
idiv( 1000, edx:eax );// Compute (R*(SIN(X)*1000)) / 1000
```

Note that integer multiplication and division are not associative. You cannot remove the multiplication by 1000 and the division by 1000 because they appear to cancel one another out. Furthermore, this code must compute this function in exactly this order. All that we need to complete this function is a table containing 360 different values corresponding to the sine of the angle (in degrees) times 1,000. Entering such a table into an assembly language program containing such values is extremely boring, and you'd probably make several mistakes entering and verifying this data. However, you can have the program generate this table for you. Consider the HLA program in Listing 9-8.

Listing 9-8: An HLA Program That Generates a Table of Sines.

```
program GenerateSines;
#include( "stdlib.hhf" );

var
    outFile: dword;
    angle:   int32;
    r:       int32;

readonly
    RoundMode: uns16 := $23f;
```

```
begin GenerateSines;

    // Open the file:

    mov( fileio.openNew( "sines.hla" ), outFile );

    // Emit the initial part of the declaration to the output file:

    fileio.put
    (
        outFile,
        stdio.tab,
        "sines: int32[360] := " nl,
        stdio.tab, stdio.tab, stdio.tab, "[" nl );

    // Enable rounding control (round to the nearest integer).

    fldcw( RoundMode );

    // Emit the sines table:

    for( mov( 0, angle); angle < 359; inc( angle )) do

        // Convert angle in degrees to an angle in radians
        // using "radians := angle * 2.0 * pi / 360.0;"

        fild( angle );
        fld( 2.0 );
        fmul();
        fldpi();
        fmul();
        fld( 360.0 );
        fdiv();

        // Okay, compute the sine of ST0

        fsin();

        // Multiply by 1000 and store the rounded result into
        // the integer variable r.

        fld( 1000.0 );
        fmul();
        fistp( r );
```

```
            // Write out the integers eight per line to the source file:
            // Note: If (angle AND %111) is zero, then angle is evenly
            // divisible by eight and we should output a newline first.

            test( %111, angle );
            if( @z ) then

                fileio.put
                (
                    outFile,
                    nl,
                    stdio.tab,
                    stdio.tab,
                    stdio.tab,
                    stdio.tab,
                    r:5,
                    ','
                );

            else

                fileio.put( outFile, r:5, ',' );

            endif;

        endfor;

        // Output sine(359) as a special case (no comma following it).
        // Note: This value was computed manually with a calculator.

        fileio.put
        (
            outFile,
            "  -17",
            nl,
            stdio.tab,
            stdio.tab,
            stdio.tab,
            "];",
            nl
        );
        fileio.close( outFile );

end GenerateSines;
```

The preceding program produces the following output (truncated for brevity):

```
sines: int32[360] :=
  [

                      0,    17,    35,    52,    70,    87,   105,   122,
                    139,   156,   174,   191,   208,   225,   242,   259,
                    276,   292,   309,   326,   342,   358,   375,   391,
                    407,   423,   438,   454,   469,   485,   500,   515,
                    530,   545,   559,   574,   588,   602,   616,   629,
                    643,   656,   669,   682,   695,   707,   719,   731,

                                        .

                                        .

                                        .

                   -643,  -629,  -616,  -602,  -588,  -574,  -559,  -545,
                   -530,  -515,  -500,  -485,  -469,  -454,  -438,  -423,
                   -407,  -391,  -375,  -358,  -342,  -326,  -309,  -292,
                   -276,  -259,  -242,  -225,  -208,  -191,  -174,  -156,
                   -139,  -122,  -105,   -87,   -70,   -52,   -35,   -17
  ];
```

Obviously it's much easier to write the HLA program that generated this data than to enter (and verify) this data by hand. Of course, you don't even have to write the table generation program in HLA. If you prefer, you might find it easier to write the program in Pascal/Delphi, C/C++, or some other high level language. Because the program will only execute once, the performance of the table generation program is not an issue. If it's easier to write the table generation program in a high level language, by all means do so. Note, also, that HLA has a built-in interpreter that allows you to easily create tables without having to use an external program. For more details, see the chapter on macros and the HLA compile time language.

Once you run your table generation program, all that remains to be done is to cut and paste the table from the file (*sines.hla* in this example) into the program that will actually use the table.

9.5.4 Table Look-Up Performance

In the early days of PCs, table look-ups were a preferred way to do high-performance computations. However, as the speed of new CPUs vastly outpaces the speed of memory, the advantages of look-up tables have been waning. Today, it is not uncommon for a CPU to 10 to 100 times faster than main memory. As a result, using a table look-up may not be faster than doing the same calculation with machine instructions. So it's worthwhile to briefly discuss when table look-ups offer a big advantage.

Although the CPU is much faster than main memory, the on-chip CPU cache memory subsystems operate at near CPU speeds. Therefore, table look-ups can be cost effective if your table resides in cache memory on the CPU. This means that the way to get good performance using table look-ups is to use small tables (because there's only so much room on the cache) and use tables whose entries you reference frequently (so the tables stay in the cache). See the electronic version of *The Art of Assembly Language* on the accompanying CD-ROM for details concerning the operation of cache memory and how you can optimize your use of cache memory.

9.6 For More Information

The HLA Standard Library Reference Manual contains lots of information about the HLA Standard Library's extended precision arithmetic capabilities. You'll also want to check out the source code for several of the HLA Standard Library routines to see how to do various extended precision operations (that properly set the flags once the computation is complete). The HLA Standard Library source code also covers the extended precision I/O operations that do not appear in this chapter.

Donald Knuth's *The Art of Computer Programming, Volume Two: Seminumerical Algorithms* contains a lot of useful information about decimal arithmetic and extended precision arithmetic, though this text is generic and doesn't describe how to do this in x86 assembly language.

10

MACROS AND THE HLA COMPILE TIME LANGUAGE

10.1   Chapter Overview

This chapter discusses the HLA compile time language. This discussion includes what is, perhaps, the most important component of the HLA compile time language, *macros*. Many people judge the power of an assembler by the power of its macro processing capabilities. If you happen to be one of these people, you'll probably agree that HLA is one of the more powerful assemblers on the planet after reading this chapter; HLA has one of the most powerful macro processing facilities of any computer language processing system.

10.2   Introduction to the Compile Time Language (CTL)

HLA is actually two languages rolled into a single program. The *run-time language* is the standard 80x86/HLA assembly language you've been reading about in all the past chapters. This is called the run-time language because the programs you write execute when you run the executable file. HLA contains an interpreter for a second language, the HLA compile time language (or CTL) that executes programs while HLA is compiling a program. The source code for the CTL program is embedded in an HLA assembly language source file; that is, HLA source files contain instructions for both the HLA CTL and the run-time program. HLA executes the CTL program during compilation. Once HLA completes compilation, the CTL program terminates; the CTL application is not a part of the run-time executable that HLA emits, although the CTL application can *write* part of the run-time program for you and, in fact, this is the major purpose of the CTL.

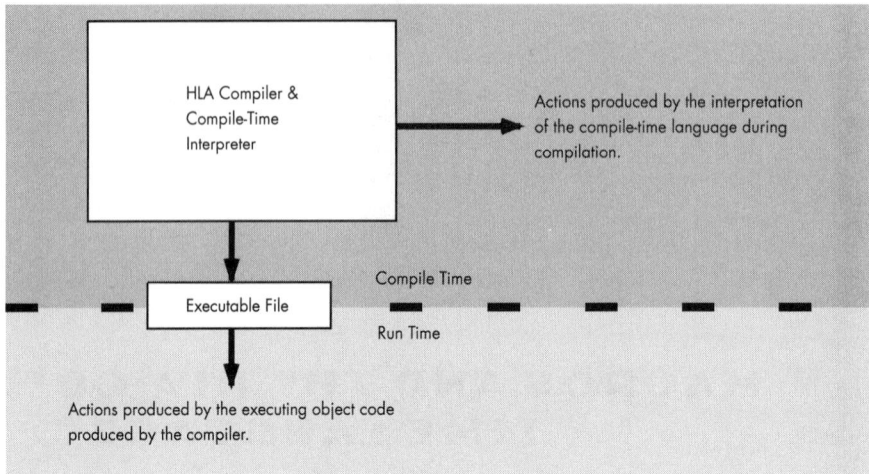

Figure 10-1: Compile Time Versus Run-Time Execution.

It may seem confusing to have two separate languages built into the same compiler. Perhaps you're even questioning why anyone would need a compile time language. To understand the benefits of a compile time language, consider the following statement that you should be very comfortable with at this point:

```
stdout.put( "i32=", i32, " strVar=", strVar, " charVar=", charVar, nl );
```

This statement is neither a statement in the HLA language nor a call to some HLA Standard Library procedure. Instead, stdout.put is actually a statement in a CTL application provided by the HLA Standard Library. The stdout.put "application" processes a list of objects (the parameter list) and makes calls to various other Standard Library procedures; it chooses the procedure to call based on the type of the object it is currently processing. For example, the stdout.put "application" above will emit the following statements to the run-time executable:

```
stdout.puts( "i32=" );
stdout.puti32( i32 );
stdout.puts( " strVar=" );
stdout.puts( strVar );
stdout.puts( " charVar=" );
stdout.putc( charVar );
stdout.newln();
```

Clearly the stdout.put statement is much easier to read and write than the sequence of statements that stdout.put emits in response to its parameter list. This is one of the more powerful capabilities of the HLA programming language: the ability to modify the language to simplify common programming tasks. Printing lots of different data objects in a sequential fashion is a common task; the stdout.put "application" greatly simplifies this process.

The HLA Standard Library is *loaded* with lots of HLA CTL examples. In addition to Standard Library usage, the HLA CTL is quite adept at handling "one-off" or "one-use" applications. A classic example is filling in the data for a look-up table. The previous chapter in this text noted that it is possible to construct look-up tables using the HLA CTL. Not only is this possible, but it is often far less work to use the HLA CTL to construct these look-up tables. This chapter abounds with examples of exactly this application of the CTL.

Although the CTL itself is relatively inefficient and you would not use it to write end-user applications, it does maximize the use of that one precious commodity of which there is so little available: your time. By learning how to use the HLA CTL and applying it properly, you can develop assembly language applications as rapidly as high level language applications (even faster because HLA's CTL lets you create *very* high level language constructs).

10.3   The #PRINT and #ERROR Statements

You may recall that Chapter 1 began with the typical first program most people write when learning a new language, the Hello World program. It is only fitting for this chapter to present that same program when discussing the second language of this text. Listing 10-1 provides the basic Hello World program written in the HLA compile time language.

Listing 10-1: The CTL "Hello World" Program.

```
program ctlHelloWorld;
begin ctlHelloWorld;

    #print( "Hello, World of HLA/CTL" )

end ctlHelloWorld;
```

The only CTL statement in this program is the #print statement. The remaining lines are needed just to keep the compiler happy (though we could have reduced the overhead to two lines by using a unit rather than a program declaration).

The #print statement displays the textual representation of its argument list during the compilation of an HLA program. Therefore, if you compile the program above with the command "hla ctlHW.hla" the HLA compiler will immediately print the text:

```
Hello, World of HLA/CTL
```

Note that there is a big difference between the following two statements in an HLA source file:

```
#print( "Hello World" )
stdout.puts( "Hello World" nl );
```

The first statement prints "Hello World" (and a new line) during the compilation process. This first statement does not have any effect on the executable program. The second line doesn't affect the compilation process (other than the emission of code to the executable file). However, when you run the executable file, the second statement prints the string "Hello World" followed by a newline sequence.

The HLA/CTL #print statement uses the following basic syntax:

```
#print( list_of_comma_separated_constants )
```

Note that a semicolon does not terminate this statement. Semicolons terminate run-time statements; they generally do not terminate compile time statements (there is one big exception, as you will see a little later).

The #print statement must have at least one operand; if multiple operands appear in the parameter list, you must separate each operand with a comma (just like stdout.put). If a particular operand is not a string constant, HLA will translate that constant to its corresponding string representation and print that string. Example:

```
#print( "A string Constant ", 45, ' ', 54.9, ' ', true )
```

You may specify named symbolic constants and constant expressions. However, all #print operands must be constants (either literal constants or constants you define in the const or val sections), and those constants must be defined before you use them in the #print statement. Example:

```
const
    pi := 3.14159;
    charConst := 'c';

#print( "PI = ", pi, "  CharVal=", CharConst )
```

The HLA #print statement is particularly invaluable for debugging CTL programs (because there is no debugger available for CTL code). This statement is also useful for displaying the progress of the compilation and displaying assumptions and default actions that take place during compilation. Other than displaying the text associated with the #print parameter list, the #print statement does not have any affect on the compilation of the program.

The #error statement allows a single string constant operand. Like #print this statement will display the string to the console during compilation. However, the #error statement treats the string as an error message and displays the string as part of an HLA error diagnostic. Further, the #error statement increments the error count, and this will cause HLA to stop the compilation (without assembling or linking) after processing the current source file. You would normally use the #error statement to display an error message during compilation if your CTL code discovers something that prevents it from creating valid code. Example:

```
#error( "Statement must have exactly one operand" )
```

Like the #print statement, the #error statement does not end with a semicolon. Although #error only allows a string operand, it's very easy to print other values by using the compile time string concatenation operator and several of the HLA built-in compile time functions. You'll learn about these a little later in this chapter.

10.4   Compile Time Constants and Variables

Just as the run-time language supports constants and variables, so does the compile time language. You declare compile time constants in the const section, the same as for the run-time language. You declare compile time variables in the val section. Objects you declare in the val section are constants as far as the run-time language is concerned, but remember that you can change the value of an object you declare in the val section throughout the source file. Hence the term "compile time variable." See Chapter 4 in this text for more details.

The CTL assignment statement ("?") computes the value of the constant expression to the right of the assignment operator (":=") and stores the result into the val object name appearing immediately to the left of the assignment operator.[1] This example code may appear anywhere in your HLA source file, not just in the val section of the program.

```
?ConstToPrint := 25;
#print( "ConstToPrint = ", ConstToPrint )
?ConstToPrint := ConstToPrint + 5;
#print( "Now ConstToPrint = ", ConstToPrint )
```

10.5   Compile Time Expressions and Operators

As the previous section states, the HLA CTL supports constant expressions in the CTL assignment statement. Unlike the run-time language (where you have to translate algebraic notation into a sequence of machine instructions), the HLA CTL allows a full set of arithmetic operations using familiar expression syntax. This gives the HLA CTL considerable power, especially when combined with the built-in compile time functions the next section discusses.

---

[1] If the identifier to the left of the assignment operator is undefined, HLA will automatically declare this object at the current scope level.

Tables 10-1 and 10-2 list operators that the HLA CTL supports in compile time expressions.

Table 10-1: Compile Time Operators

Operator(s)	Operand Types[1]	Description
- (unary)	numeric	Negates the specific numeric value (int, uns, real).
	cset	Returns the complement of the specified character set.
! (unary)	integer	Inverts all the bits in the operand (bitwise NOT).
	boolean	Boolean NOT of the operand.
*	numericL * numericR	Multiplies the two operands.
	csetL * csetR	Computes the intersection of the two sets.
div	integerL div integerR	Computes the integer quotient of the two integer (int/uns/dword) operands.
mod	integerL mod integerR	Computes the remainder of the division of the two integer (int/uns/dword) operands.
/	numericL / numericR	Computes the real quotient of the two numeric operands. Returns a real result even if both operands are integers.
<<	integerL << integerR	Shifts integerL operand to the left the number of bits specified by the integerR operand.
>>	integerL >> integerR	Shifts integerL operand to the right the number of bits specified by the integerR operand.
+	numericL + numericR	Adds the two numeric operands.
	csetL + csetR	Computes the union of the two sets.
	strL + strR	Concatenates the two strings.
-	numericL - numericR	Computes the difference between numericL and numericR.
	csetL - csetR	Computes the set difference of csetL-csetR.
= or ==	numericL = numericR	Returns true if the two operands have the same value.
	csetL = csetR	Returns true if the two sets are equal.
	strL = strR	Returns true if the two strings/chars are equal.
	typeL = typeR	Returns true if the two values are equal. They must be the same type.
<> or !=	typeL <> typeR (same as =)	Returns false if the two (compatible) operands are not equal to one another.
<	numericL < numericR	Returns true if numericL is less than numericR.
	csetL < csetR	Returns true if csetL is a proper subset of csetR.
	strL < strR	Returns true if strL is less than strR.
	booleanL < booleanR	Returns true if left operand is less than right operand (note: false < true).
	enumL < enumR	Returns true if enumL appears in the same enum list as enumR and enumL appears first.
<=	Same as <	Returns true if the left operand is less than or equal to the right operand. For character sets, this means that the left operand is a subset of the right operand.

Table 10-1: Compile Time Operators

Operator(s)	Operand Types[1]	Description
>	Same as <	Returns true if the left operand is greater than the right operand. For character sets, this means that the left operand is a proper superset of the right operand.
>=	Same as <=	Returns true if the left operand is greater than or equal to the right operand. For character sets, this means that the left operand is a superset of the right operand.
&	integerL & integerR	Computes the bitwise AND of the two operands.
	booleanL & booleanR	Computes the logical AND of the two operands.
|	integerL | integerR	Computes the bitwise OR of the two operands.
	booleanL | booleanR	Computes the logical OR of the two operands.
^	integerL ^ integerR	Computes the bitwise XOR of the two operands.
	booleanL ^ booleanR	Computes the logical XOR of the two operands. Note that this is equivalent to "booleanL <> booleanR."
in	charL in csetR	Returns true if charL is a member of csetR.

1. Numeric is {intXX, unsXX, byte, word, dword, and realXX} values. cset is a character set operand. Type integer is { intXX, unsXX, byte, word, dword }. Type str is any string or character value. "TYPE" indicates an arbitrary HLA type. Other types specify an explicit HLA data type.

Table 10-2: Operator Precedence and Associativity

Associativity	Precedence (Highest to Lowest)	Operator
Right to left	6	! (unary)
		- (unary)
Left to right	5	*
		div
		mod
		/
		>>
		<<
Left to right	4	+
		-
Left to right	3	= or ==
		<> or !=
		<
		<=
		>
		>=

Table 10-2: Operator Precedence and Associativity

Associativity	Precedence (Highest to Lowest)	Operator
Left to right	2	&
		|
		^
Nonassociative	1	in

Of course, you can always override the default precedence and associativity of an operator by using parentheses in an expression.

10.6 Compile Time Functions

HLA provides a wide range of compile time functions you can use. These functions compute values during compilation the same way a high level language function computes values at runtime. The HLA compile time language includes a wide variety of numeric, string, and symbol table functions that help you write sophisticated compile time programs.

Most of the names of the built-in compile time functions begin with the special symbol "@" and have names like @sin or @length. The use of these special identifiers prevents conflicts with common names you might want to use in your own programs (like length). The remaining compile time functions (those that do not begin with "@") are typically data conversion functions that use type names like int8 and real64. You can even create your own compile time functions using macros (which this chapter discusses a little later).

HLA organizes the compile time functions into various classes depending on the type of operation. For example, there are functions that convert constants from one form to another (e.g., string to integer conversion), there are many useful string functions, and HLA provides a full set of compile time numeric functions.

The complete list of HLA compile time functions is too lengthy to present here. Instead, a complete description of each of the compile time objects and functions appears in the HLA Reference Manual on the accompanying CD-ROM; this section will highlight a few of the functions in order to demonstrate their use. Later sections in this chapter, as well as future chapters, will make extensive use of the various compile time functions.

Perhaps the most important concept to understand about the compile time functions is that they are equivalent to constants in your assembly language code (i.e., the run-time program). For example, the compile time function invocation "@sin(3.1415265358979328)" is roughly equivalent to specifying "0.0" at that point in your program.[2] A function invocation like "@sin(x)" is legal only if x is a constant with a previous declaration at the point of the function call in the source file. In particular, x cannot be a run-time variable or other object whose value exists at runtime rather than compile time. Because HLA replaces compile time function calls with their constant result, you may ask why you should even bother with compile time functions. After all, it's probably more convenient to

---

[2] Actually, because @sin's parameter in this example is not exactly π, you will get a small positive number instead of zero as the function result, but in theory you should get zero.

type "0.0" than it is to type "@sin(3.1415265358979328)" in your program. However, compile time functions are handy for generating look-up tables and other mathematical results that may change whenever you change a const value in your program. Later sections in this chapter will explore these ideas farther.

10.6.1 Type Conversion Compile Time Functions

Probably the most commonly used compile time functions are the type conversion functions. These functions take a single parameter of one type and convert that information to some specified type. These functions use several of the HLA built-in data type names as the function names. Functions in this category are the following:

- boolean
- int8, int16, int32, int64, and int128
- uns8, uns16, uns32, uns64, and uns128
- byte, word, dword, qword, and lword (these are effectively equivalent to uns8, uns16, uns32, uns64, and uns128)
- real32, real64, and real80
- char
- string
- cset
- text

These functions accept a single constant expression parameter and, if at all reasonable, convert that expression's value to the type specified by the type name. For example, the following function call returns the value -128 because it converts the string constant to the corresponding integer value:

```
int8( "-128" )
```

Certain conversions don't make sense or have restrictions associated with them. For example, the boolean function will accept a string parameter, but that string must be "true" or "false" or the function will generate a compile time error. Likewise, the numeric conversion functions (e.g., int8) allow a string operand, but the string operand must represent a legal numeric value. Some conversions (e.g., int8 with a character set parameter) simply don't make sense and are always illegal.

One of the most useful functions in this category is the string function. This function accepts nearly all the constant expression types, and it generates a string that represents the parameter's data. For example, the invocation string(128) produces the string "128" as the return result. This function is real handy when you have a value that you wish to use where HLA requires a string. For example, the #error compile time statement only allows a single string operand. You can use the string function and the string concatenation operator ("+") to easily get around this limitation, e.g.,

```
#error( "theValue (" + string( theValue ) + ") is out of range" )
```

Note that these type functions actually perform a conversion. This means that the bit pattern these functions return may be considerably different than the bit pattern you pass as an argument. For example, consider the following invocation of the real32 function:

```
real32( $3F80_0000 )
```

Now it turns out that $3F80_0000 is the hexadecimal equivalent of the real32 value 1.0. However, the preceding function invocation does not return 1.0; instead it attempts to convert the integer value $3F80_0000 (1,065,353,216) to a real32 value but fails because the value is too large to exactly represent using a real32 object. Contrast this with the following constant function:

```
char( 65 )
```

This CTL function invocation returns the character 'A' (because 65 is the ASCII code for 'A'). Notice how the char function simply uses the bit pattern of the integer argument you pass it as an ASCII code while the real32 function attempts to translate the integer argument to a floating point value. Although the semantics are quite different between these two functions, the bottom line is that they tend to do the intuitive operation, even at the expense of consistency.

Sometimes, however, you might not want these functions to do the "intuitive" thing. For example, you might want the real32 function to simply treat the bit pattern you pass it as a real32 value. To handle this situation, HLA provides a second set of type functions, which are simply the type names with an "@" prefix that simply treat the argument as a bit pattern of the final type. So if you really want to produce 1.0 from $3F80_0000 then you could use the following function invocation:

```
@real32( $3F80_0000 )
```

Generally, type coercion of this form is somewhat advanced in the compile time language, so you'll probably not use it very often. However, when it is needed, it's nice to have around.

10.6.2 Numeric Compile Time Functions

The functions in this category perform standard mathematical operations at compile time. These functions are handy for generating look-up tables and "parameterizing" your source code by recalculating functions on constants defined at the beginning of your program. Functions in this category include the following:

- @abs(n): Absolute value of numeric argument.
- @ceil(r), @floor(r): Extract integer component of floating point value.
- @sin(r), @cos(r),@tan(r): Standard trig functions.

- @exp(r), @log(r), @log10(r): Standard log/exponent functions.
- @min(list),@max(list): Returns min/max value from a list of values.
- @random, @randomize: Returns a pseudo-random int32 value.
- @sqrt(n): Computes the square root of its numeric argument (real result).

See the HLA Reference Manual for more details on these functions.

10.6.3 Character Classification Compile Time Functions

The functions in this group all return a boolean result. They test a character (or all the characters in a string) to see if it belongs to a certain class of characters. The functions in this category include the following:

- @isAlpha(c), @isAlphanum(c)
- @isDigit(c), @isxDigit(c)
- @isLower(c), @isUpper(c)
- @isSpace(c)

In addition to these character classification functions, the HLA language provides a set of pattern matching functions that you can also use to classify character and string data. See the appropriate sections later in this chapter for the discussion of these routines.

10.6.4 Compile Time String Functions

The functions in this category operate on string parameters. Most return a string result, although a few (e.g., @length and @index) return integer results. These functions do not directly affect the values of their parameters; instead, they return an appropriate result that you can assign back to the parameter if you wish to do so.

- @delete, @insert
- @index, @rindex
- @length
- @lowercase, @uppercase
- @strbrk, @strspan
- @strset
- @substr, @tokenize, @trim

For specific details concerning these functions, their parameters, and their types, see the HLA Reference Manual. Note that these are the compile time equivalents of many of the string functions found in the HLA Standard Library.

The @length function deserves a special discussion because it is probably the most popular function in this category. It returns an uns32 constant specifying the number of characters found in its string parameter. The syntax is the following:

```
@length( string_expression )
```

where `string_expression` represents any compile time string expression. As noted, this function returns the length, in characters, of the specified expression.

10.6.5 Compile Time Pattern Matching Functions

HLA provides a very rich set of string/pattern matching functions that let you test a string to see if it begins with certain types of characters or strings. Along with the string processing functions, the pattern matching functions let you extend the HLA language and provide several other benefits as well. There are far too many pattern matching functions to list here (see the HLA Reference Manual for complete details). However, a few examples will demonstrate the power and convenience of these routines.

The pattern matching functions all return a boolean true/false result. If a function returns true, we say that the function *succeeds* in matching its operand. If the function returns false, then we say it *fails* to match its operand. An important feature of the pattern matching functions is that they do not have to match the entire string you supply as a parameter; these patterns will (usually) succeed as long as they match a prefix of the string parameter. The `@matchStr` function is a good example; the following function invocation always returns true:

```
@matchStr( "Hello World", "Hello" )
```

The first parameter of all the pattern matching functions ("Hello World" in this example) is the string to match. The matching functions will attempt to match the characters at the beginning of the string with the other parameters supplied for that particular function. In the `@matchStr` example above, the function succeeds if the first parameter begins with the string specified as the second parameter (which it does). The fact that the "Hello World" string contains additional characters beyond "Hello" is irrelevant; it only needs to begin with the string "Hello" is doesn't require equality with "Hello".

Most of the compile time pattern matching functions support two optional parameters. The functions store additional data into the val objects specified by these two parameters if the function is successful (conversely, if the function fails, it does not modify these objects). The first parameter is where the function stores the remainder. The remainder, after the execution of a pattern matching function, comprises those characters that follow the matched characters in the string. In the example above, the remainder would be " World". If you wanted to capture this remainder data, you would add a third parameter to the `@matchStr` function invocation:

```
@matchStr( "Hello World", "Hello", World )
```

This function invocation would leave " World" sitting in the `World` val object. Note that `World` must be predeclared as a string in the val section (or via the "?" statement) prior to the invocation of this function, e.g., you could use code like the following to define `World`:

```
?World : string;  // No assignment, default is empty string.
```

By using the conjunction operator ("&") you can combine several pattern matching functions into a single expression, e.g.,

```
@matchStr( "Hello There World", "Hello ", tw ) & @matchStr( tw, "There ", World )
```

This full expression returns true and leaves "World" sitting in the World variable. It also leaves "There World" sitting in tw, although tw is probably a temporary object whose value has no meaning beyond this expression. Of course, the preceding could be more efficiently implemented as follows:

```
@matchStr( "Hello There World", "Hello There", World )
```

However, keep in mind that you can combine different pattern matching functions using conjunction; they needn't all be calls to @matchStr.

The second optional parameter to most pattern matching functions holds a copy of the text that the function matched. E.g., the following call to @matchStr returns "Hello" in the Hello val object:[3]

```
@matchStr( "Hello World", "Hello", World, Hello )
```

For more information on these pattern matching functions please consult the HLA Reference Manual. The HLA CTL provides dozens of different compile time pattern matching functions; alas, space restrictions prevent duplicating that information here.

10.6.6   Compile Time Symbol Information

During compilation HLA maintains an internal database known as the *symbol table*. The symbol table contains lots of useful information concerning all the identifiers you've defined up to a given point in the program. In order to generate machine code output, HLA needs to query this database to determine how to treat certain symbols. In your compile time programs, it is often necessary to query the symbol table to determine how to handle an identifier or expression in your code. The HLA compile time symbol information functions handle this task.

Many of the compile time symbol information functions are well beyond the scope of this text. This chapter will present a few of the functions and later chapters will add to this list. For a complete list of the compile time symbol table functions, see the HLA Reference Manual. The functions we will consider in this chapter include the following:

- @size
- @defined
- @typeName
- @elements
- @elementSize

---

[3] Strictly speaking, this example is rather contrived because we generally know the string that @matchStr matches. However, for other pattern matching functions this is not the case.

Without question, the @size function is probably the most important function in this group. Indeed, previous chapters have made use of this function already. The @size function accepts a single HLA identifier or constant expression as a parameter. It returns the size, in bytes, of the data type of that object (or expression). If you supply an identifier, it can be a constant, type, or variable identifier. As you've seen in previous chapters, this function is invaluable for allocating storage via malloc and allocating storage for arrays.

Another very useful function in this group is the @defined function. This function accepts a single HLA identifier as a parameter, e.g.,

---

@defined(MyIdentifier)

This function returns true if the identifier is defined at that point in the program; it returns false otherwise.

The @typeName function returns a string specifying the type name of the identifier or expression you supply as a parameter. For example, if i32 is an int32 object, then "@typeName(i32)" returns the string "int32". This function is useful for testing the types of objects you are processing in your compile time programs.

The @elements function requires an array identifier or expression. It returns the total number of array elements as the function result. Note that for multi-dimensional arrays this function returns the product of all the array dimensions.[4]

The @elementSize function returns the size, in bytes, of an element of an array whose name you pass as a parameter. This function is extremely valuable for computing indices into an array (i.e., this function computes the element_size component of the array index calculation; see Chapter 4 for more details).

10.6.7 Miscellaneous Compile Time Functions

The HLA compile time language contains several additional functions that don't fall into one of the categories above. Some of the more useful miscellaneous functions include

- @odd
- @lineNumber
- @text

The @odd function takes an ordinal value (i.e., non-real numeric or character) as a parameter and returns true if the value is odd, false if it is even. The @lineNumber function requires no parameters; it returns the current line number in the source file. This function is quite useful for debugging compile time (and run-time!) programs.

The @text function is probably the most useful function in this group. It requires a single string parameter. It expands that string as text in place of the @text function call. This function is quite useful in conjunction with the compile time string processing functions. You can build an instruction (or a portion of an

---

[4] There is an @dim function that returns an array specifying the bounds on each dimension of a multidimensional array. See the CD-ROM documentation for more details if you're interested in this function.

instruction) using the string manipulation functions and then convert that string to program source code using the @text function. The following is a trivial example of this function in operation:

```
?id1:string := "eax";
?id2:string := "i32";
@text( "mov( " + id1 + ", " + id2 + ");" )
```

The preceding sequence compiles to

```
mov( eax, i32 );
```

10.6.8   Compile Time Type Conversions of TEXT Objects

Once you create a text constant in your program, it's difficult to manipulate that object. The following example demonstrates a programmer's desire to change the definition of a text symbol within a program:

```
val
    t:text := "stdout.put";
        .
        .
        .
    ?t:text := "fileio.put";
```

The basic idea in this example is that the symbol "t" expands to "stdout.put" in the first half of the code and it expands to "fileio.put" in the second half of the program. Unfortunately, this simple example will not work. The problem is that HLA will expand a text symbol in place almost anywhere it finds that symbol. This includes occurrences of t within this "?" statement. Therefore, the previous code expands to the following (incorrect) text:

```
val
    t:text := "stdout.put";
        .
        .
        .
    ?stdout.put:text := "fileio.put";
```

HLA doesn't know how to deal with this "?" statement, so it generates a syntax error.

At times you may not want HLA to expand a text object. Your code may want to process the string data held by the text object. HLA provides a couple of ways to deal with these two problems:

- @string:*identifier* (also @string(*identifier*))
- @toString:*identifier*

The @string:*identifier* operator consists of @string, immediately followed by a colon and a text identifier (with no interleaving spaces or other characters). HLA returns a string constant corresponding to the text data associated with the text object. In other words, this operator lets you treat a text object as though it were a string constant within an expression. Note that @string(*identifier*) serves the same purpose (this functionality of @string was added to HLA long after @string:*identifier*, so HLA has to support both forms; the @string(identifier) form is preferable, though).

Unfortunately, the @string operator converts a text object to a string constant, not a string identifier. Therefore, you cannot say something like

```
?@string:t := "Hello"
```

This doesn't work because @string:t replaces itself with the string constant associated with the text object t. Given the former assignment to t, this statement expands to

```
?"stdout.put" := "Hello";
```

This statement is still illegal.

The @toString:*identifier* operator comes to the rescue in this case. The @toString operator requires a text object as the associated identifier. It converts this text object to a string object (still maintaining the same string data) and then returns the identifier. Because the identifier is now a string object, you can assign a value to it (and change its type to something else, e.g., text, if that's what you need). To achieve the original goal, therefore, you'd use code like the following:

```
val
    t:text := "stdout.put";
        .
        .
        .
    ?@tostring:t : text := "fileio.put";
```

10.7 Conditional Compilation (Compile Time Decisions)

HLA's compile time language provides an if statement, #if, that lets you make various decisions at compile time. The #if statement has two main purposes: the traditional use of #if is to support *conditional compilation* (or *conditional assembly*) allowing you to include or exclude code during a compilation depending on the status of various symbols or constant values in your program. The second use of this statement is to support the standard if statement decision-making process in the HLA compile time language. This section will discuss these two uses for the HLA #if statement.

The simplest form of the HLA compile time #if statement uses the following syntax:

```
#if( constant_boolean_expression )

    << text >>

#endif
```

Note that you do not place semicolons after the #endif clause. If you place a semicolon after the #endif, it becomes part of the source code, and this would be identical to inserting that semicolon immediately before the next item in the program.

At compile time, HLA evaluates the expression in the parentheses after the #if. This must be a constant expression, and its type must be boolean. If the expression evaluates true, HLA continues to process the text in the source file as though the #if statement was not present. However, if the expression evaluates false, HLA treats all the text between the #if and the corresponding #endif clause as though it were a comment (i.e., it ignores this text), as shown in Figure 10-2.

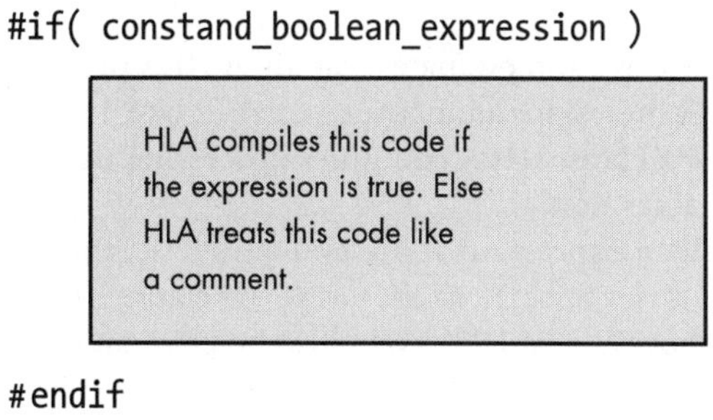

```
#if( constand_boolean_expression )
```

HLA compiles this code if
the expression is true. Else
HLA treats this code like
a comment.

```
#endif
```

Figure 10-2: Operation of HLA Compile Time #IF Statement.

Keep in mind that HLA's constant expressions support a full-expression syntax like you'd find in a high level language like C or Pascal. The #if expression syntax is not limited to the syntax allowed by expressions in the HLA if statement. Therefore, it is perfectly reasonable to write fancy expressions like the following:

```
#if( @length( someStrConst ) < 10*i & ( (MaxItems*2 + 2) < 100 | MinItems-5 < 10 ))

    << text >>

#endif
```

Also keep in mind that the items in a compile time expression must all be const or val identifiers or an HLA compile time function call (with appropriate parameters). In particular, remember that HLA evaluates these expressions at compile time so they cannot contain run-time variables.[5] HLA's compile time language uses complete boolean evaluation, so any side effects that occur in the expression may produce undesired results.

The HLA #if statement supports optional #elseif and #else clauses that behave in the intuitive fashion. The complete syntax for the #if statement looks like the following:

```
#if( constant_boolean_expression1 )

    << text1 >>

#elseif( constant_boolean_expression2 )

    << text2 >>

#else

    << text3 >>

#endif
```

If the first boolean expression evaluates true then HLA processes the text up to the #elseif clause. It then skips all text (i.e., treats it like a comment) until it encounters the #endif clause. HLA continues processing the text after the #endif clause in the normal fashion.

If the first boolean expression above evaluates false, then HLA skips all the text until it encounters a #elseif, #else, or #endif clause. If it encounters a #elseif clause (as above), then HLA evaluates the boolean expression associated with that clause. If it evaluates true, HLA processes the text between the #elseif and the #else clauses (or to the #endif clause if the #else clause is not present). If, during the processing of this text, HLA encounters another #elseif or, as above, a #else clause, then HLA ignores all further text until it finds the corresponding #endif.

If both the first and second boolean expressions in the previous example evaluate false, HLA skips their associated text and begins processing the text in the #else clause. As you can see, the #if statement behaves in a relatively intuitive fashion once you understand how HLA "executes" the body of these statements; the #if statement processes the text or treats it as a comment, depending on the state of the boolean expression. Of course, you can create a nearly infinite variety of different #if statement sequences by including zero or more #elseif clauses and optionally supplying the #else clause. Because the construction is identical to the HLA if..then..elseif..else..endif statement, there is no need to elaborate further here.

A very traditional use of conditional compilation is to develop software that you can easily configure for several different environments. For example, the fcomip instruction makes floating point comparisons very easy, but this instruction is available only on Pentium Pro and later processors. If you want to use this

---

[5] Except, of course, as parameters to certain HLA compile time functions like @size or @typeName.

instruction on the processors that support it and fall back to the standard floating point comparison on the older processors, you would normally have to write two versions of the program — one with the fcomip instruction and one with the traditional floating point comparison sequence. Unfortunately, maintaining two different source files (one for newer processors and one for older processors) is very difficult. Most engineers prefer to use conditional compilation to embed the separate sequences in the same source file. The following example demonstrates how to do this:

```
const
    PentProOrLater: boolean := false;  // Set true to use FCOMIxx instrs.
        .
        .
        .
    #if( PentProOrLater )

        fcomip();        // Compare st1 to st0 and set flags.

    #else

        fcomp();         // Compare st1 to st0.
        fstsw( ax );     // Move the FPU condition code bits
        sahf();          //  into the FLAGS register.

    #endif
```

As currently written, this code fragment will compile the three-instruction sequence in the #else clause and ignore the code between the #if and #else clauses (because the constant PentProOrLater is false). By changing the value of PentProOrLater to true, you can tell HLA to compile the single fcomip instruction rather than the three-instruction sequence. Of course, you can use the PentProOrLater constant in other #if statements throughout your program to control how HLA compiles your code.

Note that conditional compilation does not let you create a single *executable* that runs efficiently on all processors. When using this technique you will still have to create two executable programs (one for Pentium Pro and later processors, one for the earlier processors) by compiling your source file twice: During the first compilation you must set the PentProOrLater constant to false; during the second compilation you must set this constant to true. Although you must create two separate executables, you need only maintain a single source file.

If you are familiar with conditional compilation in other languages, such as the C/C++ language, you may be wondering if HLA supports a statement like C's "#ifdef" statement. The answer is no, it does not. However, you can use the HLA compile time function @defined to easily test to see if a symbol has been defined earlier in the source file. Consider the following modification to the preceding code that uses this technique:

```
const
    // Note: uncomment the following line if you are compiling this
    // code for a Pentium Pro or later CPU.

    // PentProOrLater :=0;   // Value and type are irrelevant
        .
        .
        .
    #if( @defined( PentProOrLater ) )

        fcomip();        // Compare st1 to st0 and set flags.

    #else

        fcomp();         // Compare st1 to st0.
        fstsw( ax );     // Move the FPU condition code bits
        sahf();          //  into the FLAGS register.

    #endif
```

Another common use of conditional compilation is to introduce debugging and testing code into your programs. A typical debugging technique that many HLA programmers use is to insert "print" statements at strategic points throughout their code; this enables them to trace through their code and display important values at various checkpoints. A big problem with this technique, however, is that they must remove the debugging code prior to completing the project. The software's customer (or a student's instructor) probably doesn't want to see debugging output in the middle of a report the program produces. Therefore, programmers who use this technique tend to insert code temporarily and then remove the code once they run the program and determine what is wrong. There are at least two problems with this technique:

- Programmers often forget to remove some debugging statements, and this creates defects in the final program.
- After removing a debugging statement, these programmers often discover that they need that same statement to debug some different problem at a later time. Hence they are constantly inserting, removing, and inserting the same statements over and over again.

Conditional compilation can provide a solution to this problem. By defining a symbol (say, debug) to control debug output in your program, you can easily activate or deactivate *all* debugging output by simply modifying a single line of source code. The following code fragment demonstrates this:

```
const
    debug: boolean := false;   // Set to true to activate debug output.
        .
        .
        .
```

```
#if( debug )

    stdout.put( "At line ", @lineNumber, " i=", i, nl );

#endif
```

As long as you surround all debugging output statements with an #if statement like the preceding, you don't have to worry about debug output accidentally appearing in your final application. By setting the debug symbol to false you can automatically disable all such output. Likewise, you don't have to remove all your debugging statements from your programs once they've served their immediate purpose. By using conditional compilation, you can leave these statements in your code because they are so easy to deactivate. Later, if you decide you need to view this same debugging information during a program run, you won't have to reenter the debugging statement: You simply reactivate it by setting the debug symbol to true.

Although program configuration and debugging control are two of the more common, traditional, uses for conditional compilation, don't forget that the #if statement provides the basic conditional statement in the HLA compile time language. You will use the #if statement in your compile time programs the same way you would use an if statement in HLA or some other language. Later sections in this text will present lots of examples of using the #if statement in this capacity.

10.8   Repetitive Compilation (Compile Time Loops)

HLA's #while..#endwhile and #for..#endfor statements provide compile time loop constructs. The #while statement tells HLA to process the same sequence of statements repetitively during compilation. This is very handy for constructing data tables as well as providing a traditional looping structure for compile time programs. Although you will not employ the #while statement anywhere near as often as the #if statement, this compile time control structure is very important when you write advanced HLA programs.

The #while statement uses the following syntax:

```
#while( constant_boolean_expression )

    << text >>

#endwhile
```

When HLA encounters the #while statement during compilation, it will evaluate the constant boolean expression. If the expression evaluates false, HLA will skip over the text between the #while and the #endwhile clause (the behavior is similar to the #if statement if the expression evaluates false). If the expression evaluates true, then HLA will process the statements between the #while and #endwhile clauses and then "jump back" to the start of the #while statement in the source file and repeat this process, as shown in Figure 10-3.

```
#while(constant_boolean_expression)
```

> HLA repetitively compiles this code
> as long as the expression is true.
> It effectively inserts multiple copies
> of this statement sequence into your
> source file (the exact number of copies
> depends on the value of the loop control
> expression).

```
#endwhile
```

Figure 10-3: HLA Compile Time #WHILE Statement Operation.

To understand how this process works, consider the program in Listing 10-2.

Listing 10-2: #WHILE..#ENDWHILE Demonstration.

```
program ctWhile;
#include( "stdlib.hhf" )

static
ary: uns32[5] := [ 2, 3, 5, 8, 13 ];

begin ctWhile;

    ?i := 0;
    #while( i < 5 )

        stdout.put( "array[ ", i, " ] = ", ary[i*4], nl );
        ?i := i + 1;

    #endwhile

end ctWhile;
```

As you can probably surmise, the output from this program is the following:

```
array[ 0 ] = 2
array[ 1 ] = 3
array[ 2 ] = 4
array[ 3 ] = 5
array[ 4 ] = 13
```

What is not quite obvious is how this program generates this output. Remember, the #while..#endwhile construct is a compile time language feature, not a run-time control construct. Therefore, the previous #while loop repeats five times during *compilation.* On each repetition of the loop, the HLA compiler processes the statements between the #while and #endwhile clauses. Therefore, the preceding program is really equivalent to the code that is shown in Listing 10-3.

Listing 10-3: Program Equivalent to the Code in Listing 10-2.

```
program ctWhile;
#include( "stdlib.hhf" )

static
    ary: uns32[5] := [ 2, 3, 5, 8, 13 ];

begin ctWhile;

    stdout.put( "array[ ", 0, " ] = ", ary[0*4], nl );
    stdout.put( "array[ ", 1, " ] = ", ary[1*4], nl );
    stdout.put( "array[ ", 2, " ] = ", ary[2*4], nl );
    stdout.put( "array[ ", 3, " ] = ", ary[3*4], nl );
    stdout.put( "array[ ", 4, " ] = ", ary[4*4], nl );

end ctWhile;
```

As you can see, the #while statement is very convenient for constructing repetitive-code sequences. This is especially invaluable for unrolling loops. Additional uses of the #while loop appear in later sections of this text.

HLA provides three forms of the #for..#endfor loop. These three loops take the following general form:

```
#for( valObject := startExpr to endExpr )
    .
    .
    .
#endfor

#for( valObject := startExpr downto endExpr )
    .
    .
    .
#endfor

#for( valObject in composite_expr )
    .
    .
    .
#endfor
```

As its name suggests, *valObject* must be an object you've defined in a val declaration (or must be currently undefined; these #for loops will define the symbol locally for you if the loop control variable is undefined).

For the first two forms of the #for loop above, the *startExpr* and *endExpr* components can be any HLA constant expression that yields an integer value. The first of these #for loops is semantically equivalent to the following #while code:

```
?valObject := startExpr;
#while( valObject <= endExpr )

        .

        .

        .
    ?valObject := valObject + 1;
#endwhile
```

The second of these #for loops is semantically equivalent to the #while loop:

```
?valObject := startExpr;
#while( valObject >= endExpr )

        .

        .

        .
    ?valObject := valObject - 1;
#endwhile
```

The third of these #for loops (the one using the in keyword) is especially useful for processing individual items from some composite data type. This loop repeats once for each element, field, character, and so on, of the composite value you specify for *composite_expr*. This can be an array, string, record, or character set expression. For arrays, this #for loop repeats once for each element of the array and on each iteration of the loop; the loop control variable contains the current element's value. For example, the following compile time loop displays the values '1,' '10,' '100,' and '1000':

```
#for( i in [1, 10, 100, 1000])
    #print( i )
#endfor
```

If the *composite_expr* constant is a string constant, the #for loop repeats once for each character in the string and sets the value of the loop control variable to the current character. If the *composite_expr* constant expression is a record constant, then the loop will repeat once for each field of the record and on each iteration the loop control variable will take on the *type and value* of the current field. If the *composite_expr* expression is a character set, the loop will repeat once for each character in the set, and the loop control variable will be assigned that character.

The #for loop actually turns out to be more useful than the #while loop because the larger number of compile time loops you encounter repeat a fixed number of times (e.g., processing a fixed number of array elements, macro parameters, and so on). However, because #for was added relatively late in HLA's design, you'll still see a large number of #while loops in existing source code (most of those are simulating a #for loop).

10.9 Macros (Compile Time Procedures)

Macros are objects that a language processor replaces with other text during compilation. Macros are great devices for replacing long repetitive sequences of text with much shorter sequences of text. In additional to the traditional role that macros play (e.g., "#define" in C/C++), HLA's macros also serve as the equivalent of a compile time language procedure or function. Therefore, macros are very important in HLA's compile time language — just as important as functions and procedures are in other high level languages.

Although macros are nothing new, HLA's implementation of macros far exceeds the macro processing capabilities of most other programming languages (high level or low level). The following sections explore HLA's macro processing facilities and the relationship between macros and other HLA CTL control constructs.

10.9.1 Standard Macros

HLA supports a straight-forward macro facility that lets you define macros in a manner that is similar to declaring a procedure. A typical, simple macro declaration takes the following form:

```
#macro macroname;

   << macro body >>

#endmacro;
```

Although macro and procedure declarations are similar, there are several immediate differences between the two that are obvious from this example. First, of course, macro declarations use the reserved word #macro rather than procedure. Second, you do not begin the body of the macro with a "begin *macroname*;" clause. This is because macros don't have a declaration section like procedures so there is no need for a keyword that separates the macro declarations from the macro body. Finally, you will note that macros end with the #endmacro clause rather than "end *macroname*;". The following code is a concrete example of a macro declaration:

```
#macro neg64;

   neg( edx );
   neg( eax );
   sbb( 0, edx );

#endmacro;
```

Execution of this macro's code will compute the two's complement of the 64-bit value in EDX:EAX (see the description of extended precision neg in the chapter on advanced arithmetic).

To execute the code associated with neg64, you simply specify the macro's name at the point you want to execute these instructions, e.g.,

```
mov( (type dword i64), eax );
mov( (type dword i64+4), edx );
neg64;
```

Note that you do *not* follow the macro's name with a pair of empty parentheses as you would a procedure call (the reason for this will become clear a little later).

Other than the lack of parentheses following neg64's invocation[6] this looks just like a procedure call. You could implement this simple macro as a procedure using the following procedure declaration:

```
procedure neg64p;
begin neg64p;

    neg( edx );
    neg( eax );
    sbb( 0, edx );

end neg64p;
```

Note that the following two statements will both negate the value in EDX:EAX:

```
neg64;              neg64p();
```

The difference between these two (i.e., the macro invocation versus the procedure call) is the fact that macros expand their text in-line, whereas a procedure call emits a call to the associate procedure elsewhere in the text. That is, HLA replaces the invocation "neg64;" directly with the following text:

```
neg( edx );
neg( eax );
sbb( 0, edx );
```

On the other hand, HLA replaces the procedure call "neg64p();" with the single call instruction:

```
call neg64p;
```

Presumably, you've defined the neg64p procedure earlier in the program.

---

[6] To differentiate macros and procedures, this text will use the term "invocation" when describing the use of a macro and "call" when describing the use of a procedure.

You should make the choice of macro versus procedure call on the basis of efficiency. Macros are slightly faster than procedure calls because you don't execute the call and corresponding ret instructions. On the other hand, the use of macros can make your program larger because a macro invocation expands to the text of the macro's body on each invocation. Procedure calls jump to a single instance of the procedure's body. Therefore, if the macro body is large and you invoke the macro several times throughout your program, it will make your final executable much larger. Also, if the body of your macro executes more than a few simple instructions, the overhead of a call/ret sequence has little impact on the overall execution time of the code, so the execution time savings are nearly negligible. On the other hand, if the body of a procedure is very short (like the neg64 example above), you'll discover that the macro implementation is much faster and doesn't expand the size of your program by much. Therefore, a good rule of thumb is:

Use macros for short, time-critical program units. Use procedures for longer blocks of code and when execution time is not as critical.

Macros have many other disadvantages over procedures. Macros cannot have local (automatic) variables, macro parameters work differently than procedure parameters, macros don't support (run-time) recursion, and macros are a little more difficult to debug than procedures (just to name a few disadvantages). Therefore, you shouldn't really use macros as a substitute for procedures except in some rare situations.

10.9.2 Macro Parameters

Like procedures, macros allow you to define parameters that let you supply different data on each macro invocation. This lets you write generic macros whose behavior can vary depending on the parameters you supply. By processing these macro parameters at compile time, you can write very sophisticated macros.

Macro parameter declaration syntax is very straight-forward. You simply supply a list of parameter names within parentheses in a macro declaration:

```
#macro neg64( reg32HO, reg32LO );

    neg( reg32HO );
    neg( reg32LO );
    sbb( 0, reg32HO );

#endmacro;
```

Note that you do not associate a data type with a macro parameter like you do procedural parameters. This is because HLA macros are always text objects. The next section will explain the exact mechanism HLA uses to substitute an actual parameter for a formal parameter.

When you invoke a macro, you simply supply the actual parameters the same way you would for a procedure call:

```
neg64( edx, eax );
```

Note that a macro invocation that requires parameters expects you to enclose the parameter list within parentheses.

10.9.2.1 Standard Macro Parameter Expansion

As the previous section explains, HLA automatically associates the type text with macro parameters. This means that during a macro expansion, HLA substitutes the text you supply as the actual parameter everywhere the formal parameter name appears. The semantics of "pass by textual substitution" are a little different than "pass by value" or "pass by reference" so it is worthwhile exploring those differences here.

Consider the following macro invocations, using the neg64 macro from the previous section:

```
neg64( edx, eax );
neg64( ebx, ecx );
```

These two invocations expand into the following code:

```
// neg64(edx, eax );

    neg( edx );
    neg( eax );
    sbb( 0, edx );

// neg64( ebx, ecx );

    neg( ebx );
    neg( ecx );
    sbb( 0, ebx );
```

Note that macro invocations do not make a local copy of the parameters (as pass by value does), nor do they pass the address of the actual parameter to the macro. Instead, a macro invocation of the form "neg64(edx, eax);" is equivalent to the following:

```
?reg32HO: text := "edx";
?reg32LO: text := "eax";

    neg( reg32HO );
    neg( reg32LO );
    sbb( 0, reg32HO );
```

Of course, the text objects immediately expand their string values in-line, producing the former expansion for "neg64(edx, eax);".

Note that macro parameters are not limited to memory, register, or constant operands as are instruction or procedure operands. Any text is fine as long as its expansion is legal wherever you use the formal parameter. Similarly, formal parameters may appear anywhere in the macro body, not just where memory, register, or constant operands are legal. Consider the following macro declaration and sample invocations:

```
#macro chkError( instr, jump, target );

    instr;
    jump target;

#endmacro;


    chkError( cmp( eax, 0 ), jnl, RangeError );    // Example 1
        ...
    chkError( test( 1, bl ), jnz, ParityError );   // Example 2


// Example 1 expands to

    cmp( eax, 0 );
    jnl RangeError;

// Example 2 expands to

    test( 1, bl );
    jnz ParityError;
```

In general, HLA assumes that all text between commas constitutes a single macro parameter. If HLA encounters any opening "bracketing" symbols (left parentheses, left braces, or left brackets), then it will include all text up to the appropriate closing symbol, ignoring any commas that may appear within the bracketing symbols. This is why the chkError invocations above treat "cmp(eax, 0)" and "test(1, bl)" as single parameters rather than as a pair of parameters. Of course, HLA does not consider commas (and bracketing symbols) within a string constant as the end of an actual parameter. So the following macro and invocation is perfectly legal:

```
#macro print( strToPrint );

    stdout.out( strToPrint );

#endmacro;
    .
    .
    .
    print( "Hello, world!" );
```

HLA treats the string "Hello, world!" as a single parameter because the comma appears inside a literal string constant, just as your intuition suggests.

If you are unfamiliar with textual macro parameter expansion in other languages, you should be aware that there are some problems you can run into when HLA expands your actual macro parameters. Consider the following macro declaration and invocation:

```
#macro Echo2nTimes( n, theStr );

    #for( echoCnt := 1 to  n*2 )

        #print( theStr )

    #endfor

#endmacro;
    .
    .
    .
    Echo2nTimes( 3+1, "Hello" );
```

This example displays "Hello" five times during compilation rather than the eight times you might intuitively expect. This is because the #for statement above expands to

```
    #for( echoCnt := 1 to 3+1*2 )
```

The actual parameter for *n* is "3+1"; because HLA expands this text directly in place of *n*, you get the this erroneous text expansion. Of course, at compile time HLA computes "3+1*2" as the value five rather than as the value eight (which you would get had HLA passed this parameter by value rather than by textual substitution).

The common solution to this problem, when passing numeric parameters that may contain compile time expressions, is to surround the formal parameter in the macro with parentheses; e.g., you would rewrite the macro above as follows:

```
#macro Echo2nTimes( n, theStr );

    #for( echoCnt := 1 to  (n)*2 )

        #print( theStr )

    #endfor

#endmacro;
```

The earlier invocation would expand to the following code:

```
    #for( echoCnt := 1 to (3+1)*2 )

        #print( theStr )

    #endfor
```

This version of the macro produces the intuitive result.

If the number of actual parameters does not match the number of formal parameters, HLA will generate a diagnostic message during compilation. Like procedures, the number of actual parameters must agree with the number of formal parameters. If you would like to have optional macro parameters, then keep reading...

10.9.2.2   Macros with a Variable Number of Parameters

You may have noticed by now that some HLA macros don't require a fixed number of parameters. For example, the stdout.put macro in the HLA Standard Library allows one or more actual parameters. HLA uses a special array syntax to tell the compiler that you wish to allow a variable number of parameters in a macro parameter list. If you follow the last macro parameter in the formal parameter list with "[ ]" then HLA will allow a variable number of actual parameters (zero or more) in place of that formal parameter. E.g.,

```
#macro varParms( varying[] );

    << macro body >>

#endmacro;
    .
    .
    .
    varParms( 1 );
    varParms( 1, 2 );
    varParms( 1, 2, 3 );
    varParms();
```

Note the last invocation especially. If a macro has any formal parameters, you must supply parentheses with the macro list after the macro invocation. This is true even if you supply zero actual parameters to a macro with a varying parameter list. Keep in mind this important difference between a macro with no parameters and a macro with a varying parameter list but no actual parameters.

When HLA encounters a formal macro parameter with the "[ ]" suffix (which must be the last parameter in the formal parameter list), HLA creates a constant string array and initializes that array with the text associated with the remaining actual parameters in the macro invocation. You can determine the number of actual parameters assigned to this array using the @elements compile time function. For example, "@elements(varying)" will return some value, zero or greater, that specifies the total number of parameters associated with that parameter. The following declaration for varParms demonstrates how you might use this:

```
#macro varParms( varying[] );

    #for( vpCnt := 0 to @elements( varying ) - 1 )

        #print( varying[ vpCnt ] )

    #endfor

#endmacro;
        .
        .
        .
    varParms( 1 );          // Prints "1" during compilation.
    varParms( 1, 2 );       // Prints "1" and "2" on separate lines.
    varParms( 1, 2, 3 );    // Prints "1", "2", and "3" on separate lines.
    varParms();             // Doesn't print anything.
```

Because HLA doesn't allow arrays of text objects, the varying parameter must be an array of strings. This, unfortunately, means you must treat the varying parameters differently than you handle standard macro parameters. If you want some element of the varying string array to expand as text within the macro body, you can always use the @text function to achieve this. Conversely, if you want to use a non-varying formal parameter as a string object, you can always use the @string(name) function.[7] The following example demonstrates this:

```
#macro ReqAndOpt( Required, optional[] );

    ?@text( optional[0] ) := @string:ReqAndOpt;
    #print( @text( optional[0] ))

#endmacro;
```

---

[7] You could also use @string:name, if you prefer.

```
      .
      .
    ReqAndOpt( i, j );

// The macro invocation above expands to

    ?@text( "j" ) := @string:i;
    #print( "j" )

// The above further expands to

    j := "i";
    #print( j )

// The above simply prints "i" during compilation.
```

Of course, it would be a good idea, in a macro like the above, to verify that there are at least two parameters before attempting to reference element zero of the optional parameter. You can easily do this as follows:

```
#macro ReqAndOpt( Required, optional[] );

    #if( @elements( optional ) > 0 )

        ?@text( optional[0] ) := @string:ReqAndOpt;
        #print( @text( optional[0] ))

    #else

        #error( "ReqAndOpt must have at least two parameters" )

    #endif

#endmacro;
```

10.9.2.3   Required vs. Optional Macro Parameters

As the previous section notes, HLA requires exactly one actual parameter for each non-varying formal macro parameter. If there is no varying macro parameter (and there can be at most one), then the number of actual parameters must exactly match the number of formal parameters. If a varying formal parameter is present, then there must be at least as many actual macro parameters as there are non-varying (or required) formal macro parameters. If there is a single, varying actual parameter, then a macro invocation may have zero or more actual parameters.

There is one big difference between a macro invocation of a macro with no parameters and a macro invocation of a macro with a single, varying parameter that has no actual parameters: The macro with the varying parameter list must have an empty set of parentheses after it, while the macro invocation of the macro without any parameters does not allow this. You can use this fact to your advantage if you wish to write a macro that doesn't have any parameters but you want to follow the macro invocation with "( )" so that it matches the syntax of a procedure call with no parameters. Consider the following macro:

```
#macro neg64( JustForTheParens[] );

    #if( @elements( JustForTheParens ) = 0 )

        neg( edx );
        neg( eax );
        sbb( 0, edx );

    #else

        #error( "Unexpected operand(s)" )

    #endif

#endmacro;
```

The preceding macro allows invocations of the form "neg64();" using the same syntax you would use for a procedure call. This feature is useful if you want the syntax of your parameterless macro invocations to match the syntax of a parameterless procedure call. It's not a bad idea to do this, just in the off-chance you need to convert the macro to a procedure at some point (or vice versa, for that matter).

If, for some reason, it is more convenient to operate on your macro parameters as *string* objects rather than *text* objects, you can specify a single varying parameter for the macro and then use #if and @elements to enforce the number of required actual parameters.

10.9.3   Local Symbols in a Macro

Consider the following macro declaration:

```
macro JZC( target );

            jnz NotTarget;
            jc  target;
    NotTarget:

endmacro;
```

The purpose of this macro is to simulate an instruction that jumps to the specified target location if the zero flag is set *and* the carry flag is set. Conversely, if either the zero flag is clear or the carry flag is clear this macro transfers control to the instruction immediately following the macro invocation.

There is a serious problem with this macro. Consider what happens if you use this macro more than once in your program:

```
JZC( Dest1 );
      .
      .
      .

JZC( Dest2 );
      .
      .
      .
```

The preceding macro invocations expand to the following code:

```
        jnz NotTarget;
        jc Dest1;
NotTarget:
              .
              .
              .

        jnz NotTarget;
        jc Dest2;
NotTarget:
              .
              .
              .
```

The problem with the expansion of these two macro invocations is that they both emit the same label, NotTarget, during macro expansion. When HLA processes this code it will complain about a duplicate symbol definition. Therefore, you must take care when defining symbols inside a macro because multiple invocations of that macro may lead to multiple definitions of that symbol.

HLA's solution to this problem is to allow the use of *local symbols* within a macro. Local macro symbols are unique to a specific invocation of a macro. For example, had NotTarget been a local symbol in the preceding JZC macro invocations, the program would have compiled properly because HLA treats each occurrence of NotTarget as a unique symbol.

HLA does not automatically make internal macro symbol definitions local to that macro.[8] Instead, you must explicitly tell HLA which symbols must be local. You do this in a macro declaration using the following generic syntax:

```
#macro macroname ( optional_parameters ) : optional_list_of_local_names ;
    << macro body >>
#endmacro;
```

---

[8] Sometimes you actually want the symbols to be global.

The list of local names is a sequence of one or more HLA identifiers separated by commas. Whenever HLA encounters this name in a particular macro invocation it automatically substitutes some unique name for that identifier. For each macro invocation, HLA substitutes a different name for the local symbol.

You can correct the problem with the JZC macro by using the following macro code:

```
#macro JZC( target ):NotTarget;

            jnz NotTarget;
            jc  target;
    NotTarget:

#endmacro;
```

Now whenever HLA processes this macro it will automatically associate a unique symbol with each occurrence of NotTarget. This will prevent the duplicate symbol error that occurs if you do not declare NotTarget as a local symbol.

HLA implements local symbols by substituting a symbol of the form "_nnnn_" (where nnnn is a four-digit hexadecimal number) wherever the local symbol appears in a macro invocation. For example, a macro invocation of the form "JZC(SomeLabel);" might expand to

```
        jnz _010A_;
        jc  SomeLabel;
_010A_:
```

For each local symbol appearing within a macro expansion HLA will generate a unique temporary identifier by simply incrementing this numeric value for each new local symbol it needs. As long as you do not explicitly create labels of the form "_nnnn_" (where nnnn is a hexadecimal value) there will never be a conflict in your program. HLA explicitly reserves all symbols that begin and end with a single underscore for its own private use (and for use by the HLA Standard Library). As long as you honor this restriction, there should be no conflicts between HLA local symbol generation and labels in your own programs because all HLA-generated symbols begin and end with a single underscore.

HLA implements local symbols by effectively converting that local symbol to a text constant that expands to the unique symbol HLA generates for the local label. That is, HLA effectively treats local symbol declarations as indicated by the following example:

```
#macro JZC( target );
    ?NotTarget:text := "_010A_";

            jnz NotTarget;
            jc  target;
```

```
        NotTarget:

#endmacro;
```

Whenever HLA expands this macro it will substitute "_010A_" for each occurrence of NotTarget it encounters in the expansion. This analogy isn't perfect because the text symbol NotTarget in this example is still accessible after the macro expansion, whereas this is not the case when defining local symbols within a macro. But this does give you an idea of how HLA implements local symbols.

One important consequence of HLA's implementation of local symbols within a macro is that HLA will produce some puzzling error messages if an error occurs on a line that uses a local symbol. Consider the following (incorrect) macro declaration:

```
#macro LoopZC( TopOfLoop ): ExitLocation;

        jnz ExitLocation;
        jc TopOfLoop;

#endmacro;
```

Note that in this example the macro does not define the ExitLocation symbol, even though there is a jump (jnz) to this label. If you attempt to compile this program, HLA will complain about an undefined statement label, and it will state that the symbol is something like "_010A_" rather than ExitLocation.

Locating the exact source of this problem can be challenging because HLA cannot report this error until the end of the procedure or program in which LoopZC appears (long after you've invoked the macro). If you have lots of macros with lots of local symbols, locating the exact problem is going to be a lot of work; your only option is to carefully analyze the macros you do call (perhaps by commenting them out of your program one by one until the error goes away) to discover the source of the problem. Once you determine the offending macro, the next step is to determine which local symbol is the culprit (if the macro contains more than one local symbol). Because tracking down bugs associated with local symbols can be tough, you should be especially careful when using local symbols within a macro.

10.9.4 Macros as Ccompile Time Procedures

Although programmers typically use macros to expand to some sequence of machine instructions, there is absolutely no requirement that a macro body contain any executable instructions. Indeed, many macros contain only compile time language statements (e.g., #if, #while, #for, "?" assignments, etc.). By placing only compile time language statements in the body of a macro, you can effectively write compile time procedures and functions using macros.

The following unique macro is a good example of a compile time function that returns a string result. Consider the definition of this macro:

```
#macro unique:theSym;

    @string:theSym

#endmacro;
```

Whenever your code references this macro, HLA replaces the macro invocation with the text "@string:theSym" which, of course, expands to some string like "_021F_". Therefore, you can think of this macro as a compile time function that returns a string result.

Be careful that you don't take the function analogy too far. Remember, macros always expand to their body text at the point of invocation. Some expansions may not be legal at any arbitrary point in your programs. Fortunately, most compile time statements are legal anywhere whitespace is legal in your programs. Therefore, macros behave as you would expect functions or procedures to behave during the execution of your compile time programs.

Of course, the only difference between a procedure and a function is that a function returns some explicit value, while procedures simply do some activity. There is no special syntax for specifying a compile time function return value. As the example above indicates, simply specifying the value you wish to return as a statement in the macro body suffices. A compile time procedure, on the other hand, would not contain any non–compile time language statements that expand into some sort of data during macro invocation.

10.9.5 Simulating Function Overloading with Macros

The C++ language supports a nifty feature known as *function overloading*. Function overloading lets you write several different functions or procedures that all have the same name. The difference between these functions is the types of their parameters or the number of parameters. A procedure declaration is unique in C++ if it has a different number of parameters than other functions with the same name, or if the types of its parameters differ from other functions with the same name. HLA does not directly support procedure overloading, but you can use macros to achieve the same result. This section explains how to use HLA's macros and the compile time language to achieve function/procedure overloading.

One good use for procedure overloading is to reduce the number of Standard Library routines you must remember how to use. For example, the HLA Standard Library provides five different "puti" routines that output an integer value: stdout.puti128, stdout.puti64, stdout.puti32, stdout.puti16, and stdout.puti8. The different routines, as their name suggests, output integer values according to the size of their integer parameter. In the C++ language (or another other language supporting procedure/function overloading) the engineer designing the input routines would probably have chosen to name them all stdout.puti and leave it up to the compiler to select the appropriate one based on the operand size.[9] The macro in Listing 10-4 demonstrates how to do this in HLA using the compile time language to figure out the size of the parameter operand.

Listing 10-4: Simple Procedure Overloading Based on Operand Size.

```
// Puti.hla
//
// This program demonstrates procedure overloading via macros.
//
// It defines a "puti" macro that calls stdout.puti8, stdout.puti16,
// stdout.puti32, or stdout.puti64, depending on the size of the operand.


program putiDemo;
#include( "stdlib.hhf" )


// puti-
//
// Automatically decides whether we have a 64-, 32-, 16-, or 8-bit
// operand and calls the appropriate stdout.putiX routine to
// output this value.

macro puti( operand );

    // If we have an eight-byte operand, call puti64:

    #if( @size( operand ) = 8 )

        stdout.puti64( operand );


    // If we have a four-byte operand, call puti32:

    #elseif( @size( operand ) = 4 )

        stdout.puti32( operand );


    // If we have a two-byte operand, call puti16:

    #elseif( @size( operand ) = 2 )

        stdout.puti16( operand );
```

---

[9] By the way, the HLA Standard Library does this as well. Although it doesn't provide stdout.puti, it does provide stdout.put that will choose an appropriate output routine based upon the parameter's type. This is a bit more flexible than a puti routine.

```
        // If we have a one-byte operand, call puti8:

    #elseif( @size( operand ) = 1 )

        stdout.puti8( operand );


        // If it's not an eight-, four-, two-, or one-byte operand,
        // then print an error message:

    #else

        #error( "Expected a 64, 32, 16, or 8-bit operand" )

    #endif

endmacro;


// Some sample variable declarations so we can test the macro above.

static
    i8:     int8    := -8;
    i16:    int16   := -16;
    i32:    int32   := -32;
    i64:    qword;


begin putiDemo;

    // Initialize i64 since we can't do this in the static section.

    mov( -64, (type dword i64 ));
    mov( $FFFF_FFFF, (type dword i64[4]));

    // Demo the puti macro:

    puti( i8  );  stdout.newln();
    puti( i16 );  stdout.newln();
    puti( i32 );  stdout.newln();
    puti( i64 );  stdout.newln();

end putiDemo;
```

The example above simply tests the size of the operand to determine which output routine to use. You can use other HLA compile time functions, like @typename, to do more sophisticated processing. Consider the program in Listing 10-5 that demonstrates a macro that overloads stdout.puti32, stdout.putu32, and stdout.putd depending on the type of the operand.

Listing 10-5: Procedure Overloading Based on Operand Type.

```
// put32.hla
//
// This program demonstrates procedure overloading via macros.
//
// It defines a "put32" macro that calls stdout.puti32, stdout.putu32,
// or stdout.putdw depending on the type of the operand.


program put32Demo;
#include( "stdlib.hhf" )


// put32-
//
// Automatically decides whether we have an int32, uns32, or dword
// operand and calls the appropriate stdout.putX routine to
// output this value.

macro put32( operand );

// If we have an int32 operand, call puti32:

    #if( @typename( operand ) = "int32" )

        stdout.puti32( operand );


    // If we have an uns32 operand, call putu32:

    #elseif( @typename( operand ) = "uns32" )

        stdout.putu32( operand );


    // If we have a dword operand, call putidw:

    #elseif( @typename( operand ) = "dword" )

        stdout.putd( operand );


    // If it's not a 32-bit integer value, report an error:

    #else

        #error( "Expected an int32, uns32, or dword operand" )
```

```
        #endif

endmacro;


// Some sample variable declarations so we can test the macro above.

static
    i32:    int32    := -32;
    u32:    uns32    := 32;
    d32:    dword    := $32;


begin put32Demo;


    // Demo the put32 macro:

    put32( d32 );  stdout.newln();
    put32( u32 );  stdout.newln();
    put32( i32 );  stdout.newln();

end put32Demo;
```

You can easily extend this macro to output 8- and 16-bit operands as well as 32-bit operands. That is left as an exercise.

The number of actual parameters is another way to resolve which overloaded procedure to call. If you specify a variable number of macro parameters (using the "[ ]" syntax, see the discussion earlier in this chapter), you can use the @elements compile time function to determine exactly how many parameters are present and call the appropriate routine. The sample in Listing 10-6 uses this trick to determine whether it should call stdout.puti32 or stdout.puti32Size.

Listing 10-6: Using the Number of Parameters to Resolve Overloaded Procedures.

```
// puti32.hla
//
// This program demonstrates procedure overloading via macros.
//
// It defines a "puti32" macro that calls stdout.puti32 or stdout.puti32size
// depending on the number of parameters present.


program puti32Demo;
#include( "stdlib.hhf" )


// puti32-
//
```

```
// Automatically decides whether we have an int32, uns32, or dword
// operand and calls the appropriate stdout.putX routine to
// output this value.

macro puti32( operand[] );

    // If we have a single operand, call stdout.puti32:

    #if( @elements( operand ) = 1 )

        stdout.puti32( @text(operand[0]) );


    // If we have two operands, call stdout.puti32size and
    // supply a default value of ' ' for the padding character:

    #elseif( @elements( operand ) = 2 )

        stdout.puti32Size( @text(operand[0]), @text(operand[1]), ' ' );


    // If we have three parameters, then pass all three of them
    // along to puti32size:

    #elseif( @elements( operand ) = 3 )

        stdout.puti32Size
        (
            @text(operand[0]),
            @text(operand[1]),
            @text(operand[2])
        );


    // If we don't have one, two, or three operands, report an error:

    #else

        #error( "Expected one, two, or three operands" )

    #endif

endmacro;


// A sample variable declaration so we can test the macro above.

static
    i32:    int32   := -32;
```

```
begin puti32Demo;


    // Demo the put32 macro:

    puti32( i32 );  stdout.newln();
    puti32( i32, 5 );  stdout.newln();
    puti32( i32, 5, '*' );  stdout.newln();

end puti32Demo;
```

All the examples up to this point provide procedure overloading for Standard Library routines (specifically, the integer output routines). Of course, you are not limited to overloading procedures in the HLA Standard Library. You can create your own overloaded procedures as well. All you've got to do is write a set of procedures, all with unique names, and then use a single macro to decide which routine to actually call based on the macro's parameters. Rather than call the individual routines, invoke the common macro and let it decide which procedure to actually call.

10.10   Writing Compile Time "Programs"

The HLA compile time language provides a powerful facility with which to write "programs" that execute while HLA is compiling your assembly language programs. Although it is possible to write some general- purpose programs using the HLA compile time language, the real purpose of the HLA compile time language is to allow you to write short programs *that write other programs*. In particular, the primary purpose of the HLA compile time language is to automate the creation of large or complex assembly language sequences. The following subsections provide some simple examples of such compile time programs.

10.10.1   *Constructing Data Tables at Compile Time*

Earlier, this book suggested that you could write programs to generate large, complex, look-up tables for your assembly language programs (see the discussion of tables in the chapter on advanced arithmetic). That chapter provides examples in HLA but suggests that writing a separate program is unnecessary. This is true; you can generate most look-up tables you'll need using nothing more than the HLA compile time language facilities. Indeed, filling in table entries is one of the principle uses of the HLA compile time language. In this section we will take a look at using the HLA compile time language to construct data tables during compilation.

In the section on generating tables, you saw an example of an HLA program that writes a text file containing a look-up table for the trigonometric *sine* function. The table contains 360 entries with the index into the table specifying an angle in degrees. Each int32 entry in the table contained the value *sin(angle)*1000* where *angle* is equal to the index into the table. The section on generating tables suggests running this program and then including the text output from that program into the actual program that used the resulting table. You can avoid much of this work by using the compile time language. The HLA program in Listing 10-7 includes a short compile time code fragment that constructs this table of sines directly.

Listing 10-7: Generating a SINE Look-up Table with the Compile Time Language.

```
// demoSines.hla
//
// This program demonstrates how to create a look-up table
// of sine values using the HLA compile time language.

program demoSines;
#include( "stdlib.hhf" )

const
    pi :real80 := 3.1415926535897;

readonly
    sines:  int32[ 360 ] :=
            [
                // The following compile time program generates
                // 359 entries (out of 360). For each entry
                // it computes the sine of the index into the
                // table and multiplies this result by 1000
                // in order to get a reasonable integer value.

                ?angle := 0;
                #while( angle < 359 )

                    // Note: HLA's @sin function expects angles
                    // in radians. radians = degrees*pi/180.
                    // the "int32" function truncates its result,
                    // so this function adds 1/2 as a weak attempt
                    // to round the value up.

                    int32( @sin( angle * pi / 180.0 ) * 1000 + 0.5 ),
                    ?angle := angle + 1;

                #endwhile

                // Here's the 360th entry in the table. This code
                // handles the last entry specially because a comma
                // does not follow this entry in the table.

                int32( @sin( 359 * pi / 180.0 ) * 1000 + 0.5 )
            ];
```

```
begin demoSines;

    // Simple demo program that displays all the values in the table.

    for( mov( 0, ebx); ebx<360; inc( ebx )) do

        mov( sines[ ebx*4 ], eax );
        stdout.put
        (
            "sin( ",
            (type uns32 ebx ),
            " )*1000 = ",
            (type int32 eax ),
            nl
        );

    endfor;


end demoSines;
```

Another common use for the compile time language is to build ASCII character look-up tables for use by the xlat instruction at runtime. Common examples include look-up tables for alphabetic case manipulation. The program in Listing 10-8 demonstrates how to construct an upper case conversion table and a lower case conversion table.[10] Note the use of a macro as a compile time procedure to reduce the complexity of the table-generating code:

Listing 10-8: Generating Case Conversion Tables with the Compile Time Language

```
// demoCase.hla
//
// This program demonstrates how to create a look-up table
// of alphabetic case conversion values using the HLA
// compile time language.

program demoCase;
#include( "stdlib.hhf" )

const
    pi :real80 := 3.1415926535897;
```

---

[10] Note that on modern processors, using a look-up table is probably not the most efficient way to convert between alphabetic cases. However, this is just an example of filling in the table using the compile time language. The principles are correct, even if the code is not exactly the best it could be.

```
// emitCharRange-
//
// This macro emits a set of character entries
// for an array of characters. It emits a list
// of values (with a comma suffix on each value)
// from the starting value up to, but not including,
// the ending value.

#macro emitCharRange( start, last ): index;

    ?index:uns8 := start;
    #while( index < last )

        char( index ),
        ?index := index + 1;

    #endwhile

#endmacro;

readonly

    // toUC:
    // The entries in this table contain the value of the index
    // into the table except for indicies #$61..#$7A (those entries
    // whose indicies are the ASCII codes for the lower case
    // characters). Those particular table entries contain the
    // codes for the corresponding upper case alphabetic characters.
    // If you use an ASCII character as an index into this table and
    // fetch the specified byte at that location, you will effectively
    // translate lower case characters to upper case characters and
    // leave all other characters unaffected.

    toUC:   char[ 256 ] :=
            [
                // The following compile time program generates
                // 255 entries (out of 256). For each entry
                // it computes toupper( index ) where index is
                // the character whose ASCII code is an index
                // into the table.

                emitCharRange( 0, uns8('a') )

                // Okay, we've generated all the entries up to
                // the start of the lower case characters. Output
                // upper case characters in place of the lower
                // case characters here.

                emitCharRange( uns8('A'), uns8('Z') + 1 )
```

```
                    // Okay, emit the nonalphabetic characters
                    // through to byte code #$FE:

                    emitCharRange( uns8('z') + 1, $FF )

                    // Here's the last entry in the table. This code
                    // handles the last entry specially because a comma
                    // does not follow this entry in the table.

                    #$FF
                ];


    // The following table is very similar to the one above.
    // You would use this one, however, to translate upper case
    // characters to lower case while leaving everything else alone.
    // See the comments in the previous table for more details.

    TOlc:   char[ 256 ] :=
            [
                emitCharRange( 0, uns8('A') )
                emitCharRange( uns8('a'), uns8('z') + 1 )
                emitCharRange( uns8('Z') + 1, $FF )

                #$FF
            ];


begin demoCase;

    for( mov( uns32( ' ' ), eax ); eax <= $FF; inc( eax )) do

        mov( toUC[ eax ], bl );
        mov( TOlc[ eax ], bh );
        stdout.put
        (
            "toupper( '",
            (type char al),
            "' ) = '",
            (type char bl),
            "'        tolower( '",
            (type char al),
            "' ) = '",
            (type char bh),
            "'",
            nl
        );
```

```
        endfor;


end demoCase;
```

One important thing to note about this sample is the fact that a semicolon does not follow the emitCharRange macro invocations. Macro invocations do not require a closing semicolon. Often, it is legal to go ahead and add one to the end of the macro invocation because HLA is normally very forgiving about having extra semicolons inserted into the code. In this case, however, the extra semicolons are illegal because they would appear between adjacent entries in the TOlc and toUC tables. Keep in mind that macro invocations don't require a semicolon, especially when using macro invocations as compile time procedures.

10.10.2 Unrolling Loops

In the chapter on low level control structures this text points out that you can unravel loops to improve the performance of certain assembly language programs. One problem with unravelling, or unrolling, loops is that you may need to do a lot of extra typing, especially if many iterations are necessary. Fortunately, HLA's compile time language facilities, especially the #while and #for loops, come to the rescue. With a small amount of extra typing plus one copy of the loop body, you can unroll a loop as many times as you please.

If you simply want to repeat the same exact code sequence some number of times, unrolling the code is especially trivial. All you've got to do is wrap an HLA #for..#endfor loop around the sequence and count off a val object the specified number of times. For example, if you wanted to print "Hello World" ten times, you could encode this as follows:

```
#for( count := 1 to 10 )

    stdout.put( "Hello World", nl );

#endfor
```

Although the code above looks very similar to a while (or for) loop you could write in your program, remember the fundamental difference: The preceding code simply consists of ten straight stdout.put calls in the program. Were you to encode this using an HLA for loop, there would be only one call to stdout.put and lots of additional logic to loop back and execute that single call ten times.

Unrolling loops becomes slightly more complicated if any instructions in that loop refer to the value of a loop control variable or another value, which changes with each iteration of the loop. A typical example is a loop that zeros the elements of an integer array:

```
    mov( 0, eax );
    for( mov( 0, ebx ); ebx < 20; inc( ebx )) do
```

```
        mov( eax, array[ ebx*4 ] );

    endfor;
```

In this code fragment the loop uses the value of the loop control variable (in EBX) to index into *array*. Simply copying "mov(eax, array[ebx*4]);" twenty times is not the proper way to unroll this loop. You must substitute an appropriate constant index in the range 0..76 (the corresponding loop indices, times four) in place of "EBX*4" in this example. Correctly unrolling this loop should produce the following code sequence:

```
        mov( eax, array[ 0*4 ] );
        mov( eax, array[ 1*4 ] );
        mov( eax, array[ 2*4 ] );
        mov( eax, array[ 3*4 ] );
        mov( eax, array[ 4*4 ] );
        mov( eax, array[ 5*4 ] );
        mov( eax, array[ 6*4 ] );
        mov( eax, array[ 7*4 ] );
        mov( eax, array[ 8*4 ] );
        mov( eax, array[ 9*4 ] );
        mov( eax, array[ 10*4 ] );
        mov( eax, array[ 11*4 ] );
        mov( eax, array[ 12*4 ] );
        mov( eax, array[ 13*4 ] );
        mov( eax, array[ 14*4 ] );
        mov( eax, array[ 15*4 ] );
        mov( eax, array[ 16*4 ] );
        mov( eax, array[ 17*4 ] );
        mov( eax, array[ 18*4 ] );
        mov( eax, array[ 19*4 ] );
```

You can do this more efficiently using the following compile time code sequence:

```
#for( iteration := 0 to 19 )

    mov( eax, array[ iteration*4 ] );

#endfor
```

If the statements in a loop make use of the loop control variable's value, it is only possible to unroll such loops if those values are known at compile time. You cannot unroll loops when user input (or other run-time information) controls the number of iterations.

10.11　Using Macros in Different Source Files

Unlike procedures, macros do not have a fixed piece of code at some address in memory. Therefore, you cannot create "external" macros and link them with other modules in your program. However, it is very easy to share macros with different source files: Just put the macros you wish to reuse in a header file and include that file using the #include directive. You can make the macro will be available to any source file you choose using this simple trick.

10.12　For More Information

Although this chapter has spent a considerable amount of time describing various features of HLA's macro support and compile time language features, the truth is this chapter has barely described what's possible with HLA. Indeed, this chapter made the claim that HLA's macro facilities are far more powerful than those provided by other assemblers; however, this chapter doesn't do HLA's macros justice. If you've ever used a language with decent macro facilities, you're probably wondering, "What's the big deal?" Well, the really sophisticated stuff is beyond the scope of this chapter. If you're interested in learning more about HLA's powerful macro facilities, please consult the HLA Reference Manual and the electronic editions of *The Art of Assembly Language* on the CD-ROM that accompanies the book. You'll discover that it's actually possible to create your own high level languages using HLA's macro facilities. However, this chapter does not assume the reader has the prerequisite knowledge to do that type of programming (yet!), so this chapter defers that discussion to the material that you'll also find on the CD-ROM.

11

BIT MANIPULATION

11.1 Chapter Overview

Manipulating bits in memory is, perhaps, the feature for which assembly language is most famous. Indeed, one of the reasons people claim that the C programming language is a "medium-level" language rather than a high level language is because of the vast array of bit manipulation operators that C provides. Even with this wide array of bit manipulation operations, the C programming language doesn't provide as complete a set of bit manipulation operations as assembly language.

This chapter will discuss how to manipulate strings of bits in memory and registers using 80x86 assembly language. This chapter begins with a review of the bit manipulation instructions covered thus far and it also introduces a few new instructions. This chapter reviews information on packing and unpacking bit strings in memory because this is the basis for many bit manipulation operations. Finally, this chapter discusses several bit-centric algorithms and their implementation in assembly language.

11.2 What Is Bit Data, Anyway?

Before describing how to manipulate bits, it might not be a bad idea to define exactly what this text means by *bit data*. Most readers probably assume that bit manipulation programs twiddle individual bits in memory. While programs that do this are definitely bit manipulation programs, we're not going to limit our definition to just those programs. For our purposes, "bit manipulation" refers to working with data types that consist of strings of bits that are noncontiguous or are not an even multiple of 8 bits long. Generally, such bit objects will not represent numeric integers, although we will not place this restriction on our bit strings.

A *bit string* is some contiguous sequence of one or more bits (this term even applies if the bit string's length is an even multiple of 8 bits). Note that a bit string does not have to start or end at any special point. For example, a bit string could start in bit 7 of one byte in memory and continue through to bit 6 of the next byte in memory. Likewise, a bit string could begin in bit 30 of EAX, consume the upper 2 bits of EAX, and then continue from bit 0 through bit 17 of EBX. In memory, the bits must be physically contiguous (i.e., the bit numbers are always increasing except when crossing a byte boundary, and at byte boundaries the memory address increases by one byte). In registers, if a bit string crosses a register boundary, the application defines the continuation register, but the bit string always continues in bit zero of that second register.

A *bit set* is a collection of bits, not necessarily contiguous (though they may be contiguous), within some larger data structure. For example, bits 0..3, 7, 12, 24, and 31 from some double word forms a set of bits. Usually, we will limit bit sets to some reasonably sized *container object* (that is, the data structure that encapsulates the bit set), but the definition doesn't specifically limit the size. Normally, we will deal with bit sets that are part of an object no more than about 32 or 64 bits in size, though this limit is completely artificial. Note that bit strings are special cases of bit sets.

A *bit run* is a sequence of bits with all the same value. A *run of zeros* is a bit string that contains all zeros, and a *run of ones* is a bit string containing all ones. The *first set bit* in a bit string is the bit position of the first bit containing a one in a bit string, i.e., the first '1' bit following a possible run of zeros. A similar definition exists for the *first clear bit*. The *last set bit* is the last bit position in a bit string containing that contains '1'; afterward, the remainder of the string forms an uninterrupted run of zeros. A similar definition exists for the *last clear bit*.

A *bit offset* is the number of bits from some boundary position (usually a byte boundary) to the specified bit. As noted in Chapter 2, we number the bits starting from zero at the boundary location. If the offset is less than 32, then the bit offset is the same as the bit number in a byte, word, or double word value.

A *mask* is a sequence of bits that we'll use to manipulate certain bits in another value. For example, the bit string %0000_1111_0000, when it's used with the and instruction, can mask away (clear) all the bits except bits 4 through 7. Likewise, if you use the same value with the or instruction, it can force bits 4 through 7 to ones in the destination operand. The term "mask" comes from the use of these bit strings with the and instruction; in those situations the one and zero bits behave like masking tape when you're painting something; they pass through certain bits unchanged while masking out (clearing) the other bits.

Armed with these definitions, we're ready to start manipulating some bits!

11.3   Instructions That Manipulate Bits

Bit manipulation generally consists of six activities: setting bits, clearing bits, inverting bits, testing and comparing bits, extracting bits from a bit string, and inserting bits into a bit string. By now you should be familiar with most of the instructions we'll use to perform these operations; their introduction started way back in the earliest chapters of this text. Nevertheless, it's worthwhile to review the old instructions here as well as present the few bit manipulation instructions we've yet to consider.

The most basic bit manipulation instructions are the and, or, xor, not, test, and shift and rotate instructions. Indeed, on the earliest 80x86 processors, these were the only instructions available for bit manipulation. The following paragraphs review these instructions, concentrating on how you could use them to manipulate bits in memory or registers.

The and instruction provides the ability to strip away unwanted bits from some bit sequence, replacing the unwanted bits with zeros. This instruction is especially useful for isolating a bit string or a bit set that is merged with other, unrelated data (or, at least, data that is not part of the bit string or bit set). For example, suppose that a bit string consumes bit positions 12 through 24 of the EAX register; we can isolate this bit string by setting all other bits in EAX to zero by using the following instruction:

```
and( %1_1111_1111_1111_0000_0000_0000, eax );
```

Most programs use the and instruction to clear bits that are not part of the desired bit string. In theory, you could use the or instruction to mask all unwanted bits to ones rather than zeros, but later comparisons and operations are often easier if the unneeded bit positions contain zero (see Figure 11-1).

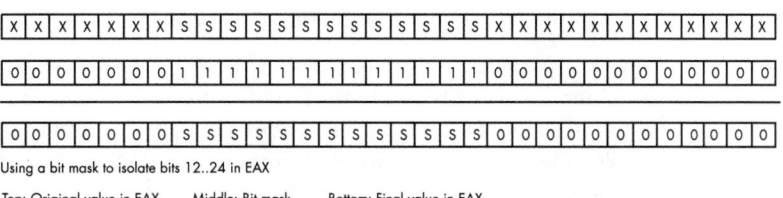

Using a bit mask to isolate bits 12..24 in EAX

Top: Original value in EAX.   Middle: Bit mask.   Bottom: Final value in EAX.

Figure 11-1: Isolating a Bit String Using the AND Instruction.

Once you've cleared the unneeded bits in a set of bits, you can often operate on the bit set in place. For example, to see if the string of bits in positions 12 through 24 of EAX contain $12F3, you could use the following code:

```
and( %1_1111_1111_1111_0000_0000_0000, eax );
cmp( eax, %1_0010_1111_0011_0000_0000_0000 );
```

Here's another solution, using constant expressions, that's a little easier to digest:

```
and( %1_1111_1111_1111_0000_0000_0000, eax );
cmp( eax, $12F3 << 12 );  // "<<12" shifts $12F3 to the left 12 bits.
```

Most of the time, however, you'll want (or need) the bit string aligned with bit zero in EAX prior to any operations you would want to perform. Of course, you can use the shr instruction to properly align the value after you've masked it:

```
and( %1_1111_1111_1111_0000_0000_0000, eax );
shr( 12, eax );
cmp( eax, $12F3 );
<< Other operations that requires the bit string at bit #0 >>
```

Now that the bit string is aligned to bit zero, the constants and other values you use in conjunction with this value are easier to deal with.

You can also use the or instruction to mask unwanted bits around a set of bits. However, the or instruction does not let you clear bits; it allows you to set bits to ones. In some instances setting all the bits around your bit set may be desirable; most software, however, is easier to write if you clear the surrounding bits rather than set them.

The or instruction is especially useful for inserting a bit set into some other bit string. To do this, there are several steps you must go through:

- Clear all the bits surrounding your bit set in the source operand.
- Clear all the bits in the destination operand where you wish to insert the bit set.
- OR the bit set and destination operand together.

For example, suppose you have a value in bits 0..12 of EAX that you wish to insert into bits 12..24 of EBX without affecting any of the other bits in EBX. You would begin by stripping out bits 13 and above from EAX; then you would strip out bits 12..24 in EBX. Next, you would shift the bits in EAX so the bit string occupies bits 12..24 of EAX. Finally, you would or the value in EAX into EBX (see Figure 11-2):

```
and( $1FFF, eax );       // Strip all but bits 0..12 from EAX
and( $1FF_F000, ebx );   // Clear bits 12..24 in EBX.
shl( 12, eax );          // Move bits 0..12 to 12..24 in EAX.
or( eax, ebx );          // Merge the bits into EBX.
```

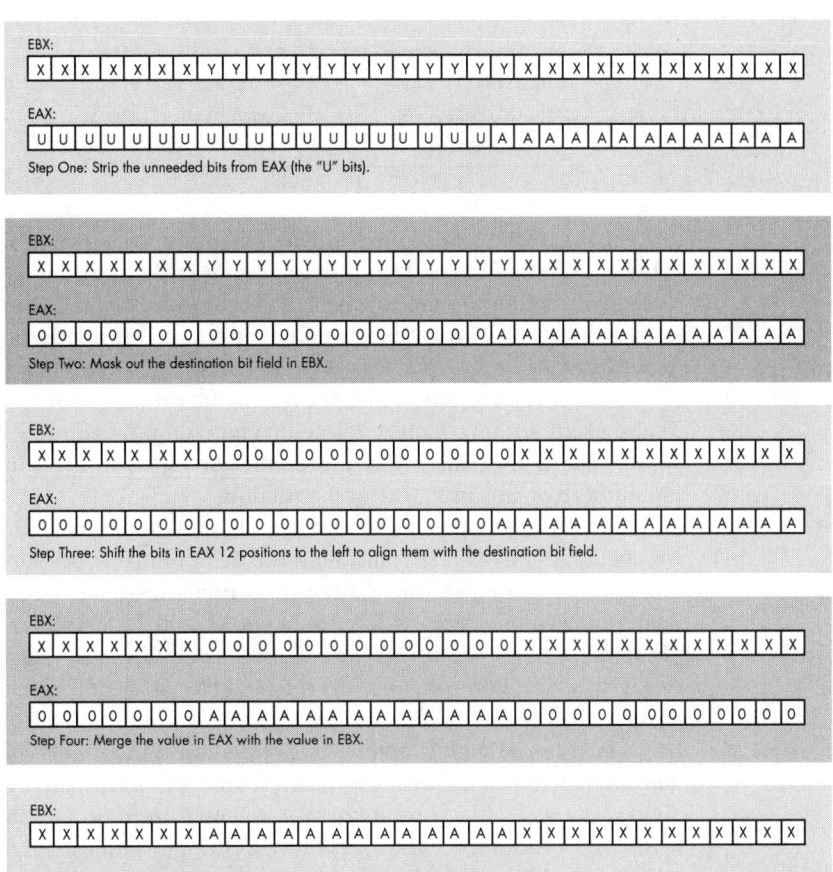

Figure 11-2: Inserting Bits 0..12 of EAX into Bits 12..24 of EBX.

In this example the desired bits (AAAAAAAAAAAAAA) formed a bit string. However, this algorithm still works fine even if you're manipulating a non-contiguous set of bits. All you've got to do is to create an appropriate bit mask you can use for ANDing that has ones in the appropriate places.

When working with bit masks, it is incredibly poor programming style to use literal numeric constants as in the past few examples. You should always create symbolic constants in the HLA const (or val) section for your bit masks. Combined with some constant expressions, you can produce code that is much easier to read and maintain. The current example code is more properly written as:

```
const
    StartPosn:= 12;
    BitMask: dword := $1FFF << StartPosn;    // Mask occupies bits 12..24
    .
    .
```

```
shl( StartPosn, eax );      // Move into position.
and( BitMask, eax );        // Strip all but bits 12..24 from EAX
and( !BitMask, ebx );       // Clear bits 12..24 in EBX.
or( eax, ebx );             // Merge the bits into EBX.
```

Notice the use of the compile time NOT operator ("!") to invert the bit mask in order to clear the bit positions in EBX where the code inserts the bits from EAX. This saves having to create another constant in the program that has to be changed anytime you modify the BitMask constant. Having to maintain two separate symbols whose values are dependent on one another is not a good thing in a program.

Of course, in addition to merging one bit set with another, the or instruction is also useful for forcing bits to one in a bit string. By setting various bits in a source operand to one you can force the corresponding bits in the destination operand to one by using the or instruction.

The xor instruction, as you may recall, gives you the ability to invert selected bits belonging to a bit set. Although the need to invert bits isn't as common as the need to set or clear them, the xor instruction still sees considerable use in bit manipulation programs. Of course, if you want to invert all the bits in some destination operand, the not instruction is probably more appropriate than the xor instruction; however, to invert selected bits while not affecting others, the xor is the way to go.

One interesting fact about xor's operation is that it lets you manipulate known data in just about any way imaginable. For example, if you know that a field contains %1010 you can force that field to zero by XORing it with %1010. Similarly, you can force it to %1111 by XORing it with %0101. Although this might seem like a waste, because you can easily force this 4-bit string to zero or all ones using and/or, the xor instruction has two advantages: (1) you are not limited to forcing the field to all zeros or all ones; you can actually set these bits to any of the 16 valid combinations via xor; and (2) if you need to manipulate other bits in the destination operand at the same time, and/or may not be able to accommodate you. For example, suppose that you know that one field contains %1010 that you want to force to zero and another field contains %1000 and you wish to increment that field by one (i.e., set the field to %1001). You cannot accomplish both operations with a single and or or instruction, but you can do this with a single xor instruction; just XOR the first field with %1010 and the second field with %0001. Remember, however, that this trick only works if you know the current value of a bit set within the destination operand. Of course, while you're adjusting the values of bit fields containing known values, you can invert bits in other fields simultaneously.

In addition to setting, clearing, and inverting bits in some destination operand, the and, or, and xor instructions also affect various condition codes in the flags register. These instructions affect the flags as follows:

- These instructions always clear the carry and overflow flags.

- These instructions set the sign flag if the result has a one in the H.O. bit; they clear it otherwise. I.e., these instructions copy the H.O. bit of the result into the sign flag.

- These instructions set/clear the zero flag depending on whether the result is zero.

- These instructions set the parity flag if there is an even number of set bits in the L.O. byte of the destination operand, they clear the parity flag if there is an odd number of one bits in the L.O. byte of the destination operand.

The first thing to note is that these instructions always clear the carry and overflow flags. This means that you cannot expect the system to preserve the state of these two flags across the execution of these instructions. A very common mistake in many assembly language programs is the assumption that these instructions do not affect the carry flag. Many people will execute an instruction that sets/clears the carry flag, execute an and/or/xor instruction, and then attempt to test the state of the carry from the previous instruction. This simply will not work.

One of the more interesting aspects to these instructions is that they copy the H.O. bit of their result into the sign flag. This means that you can easily test the setting of the H.O. bit of the result by testing the sign flag (using sets/setns, js/jns or using the @s/@ns flags in a boolean expression). For this reason, many assembly language programmers will often place an important boolean variable in the H.O. bit of some operand so they can easily test the state of that bit using the sign flag after a logical operation.

We haven't talked much about the parity flag in this text. We're not going to get into a big discussion of this flag and what you use it for because the primary purpose for this flag has been taken over by hardware.[1] However, because this is a chapter on bit manipulation and parity computation is a bit manipulation operation, it seems only fitting to provide a brief discussion of the parity flag at this time.

Parity is a very simple error-detection scheme originally employed by telegraphs and other serial communication protocols. The idea was to count the number of set bits in a character and include an extra bit in the transmission to indicate whether that character contained an even or odd number of set bits. The receiving end of the transmission would also count the bits and verify that the extra "parity" bit indicated a successful transmission. We're not going to explore the information-theory aspects of this error-checking scheme at this point other than to point out that the purpose of the parity flag is to help compute the value of this extra bit.

The 80x86 and, or, and xor instructions set the parity bit if the L.O. byte of their operand contains an even number of set bits. An important fact bears repeating here: The parity flag only reflects the number of set bits in the L.O. byte of the destination operand; it does not include the H.O. bytes in a word, double word, or other-sized operand. The instruction set only uses the L.O. byte

---

[1] Serial communications chips and other communication hardware that uses parity for error checking normally compute the parity in hardware; you don't have to use software for this purpose.

to compute the parity because communication programs that use parity are typically character-oriented transmission systems (there are better error-checking schemes if you transmit more than 8 bits at a time).

Although the need to know whether the L.O. (or only) byte of some computation has an even or odd number of set bits isn't common in modern programs, it does come in useful once in a great while. Because this is, intrinsically, a bit operation, it's worthwhile to mention the use of this flag and how the and/or/xor instructions affect this flag.

The zero flag setting is one of the more important results the and/or/xor instructions produce. Indeed, programs reference this flag so often after the and instruction that Intel added a separate instruction, test, whose main purpose was to logically AND two results and set the flags without otherwise affecting either instruction operand.

There are three main uses of the zero flag after the execution of an and or test instruction: (1) checking to see if a particular bit in an operand is set; (2) checking to see if at least one of several bits in a bit set is one; and (3) checking to see if an operand is zero. Using (1) is actually a special case of (2) in which the bit set contains only a single bit. We'll explore each of these uses in the following paragraphs.

A common use for the and instruction, and also the original reason for the inclusion of the test instruction in the 80x86 instruction set, is to test to see if a particular bit is set in a given operand. To perform this type of test, you would normally and/test a constant value containing a single set bit with the operand you wish to test. This clears all the other bits in the second operand leaving a zero in the bit position under test if the operand contains a zero in that bit position. ANDing with a one leaves a one in that position if it originally contained a one. Because all of the other bits in the result are zero, the entire result will be zero if that particular bit is zero, the entire result will be non-zero if that bit position contains a one. The 80x86 reflects this status in the zero flag (Z=1 indicates a zero bit, Z=0 indicates a one bit). The following instruction sequence demonstrates how to test to see if bit 4 is set in EAX:

```
test( %1_000, eax );  // Check bit #4 to see if it is 0/1
if( @nz ) then

    << Do this if the bit is set >>

else

    << Do this if the bit is clear >>

endif;
```

You can also use the and/test instructions to see if any one of several bits is set. Simply supply a constant that has one bits in all the positions you want to test (and zeros everywhere else). ANDing such a value with an unknown quantity will produce a non-zero value if one or more of the bits in the operand under test contain a one. The following example tests to see if the value in EAX contains a one in bit positions 1, 2, 4, and 7:

```
test( %1001_0010, eax );
if( @nz ) then // at least one of the bits is set.

    << do whatever needs to be done if one of the bits is set >>

endif;
```

Note that you cannot use a single and or test instruction to see if all the corresponding bits in the bit set are equal to one. To accomplish this, you must first mask out the bits that are not in the set and then compare the result against the mask itself. If the result is equal to the mask, then all the bits in the bit set contain ones. You must use the and instruction for this operation as the test instruction does not mask out any bits. The following example checks to see if all the bits in a bit set (bitMask) are equal to one:

```
and( bitMask, eax );
cmp( eax, bitMask );
if( @e ) then

    << All the bit positions in EAX corresponding to the set >>
    << bits in bitMask are equal to one if we get here.      >>

endif;
```

Of course, once we stick the cmp instruction in there, we don't really have to check to see if all the bits in the bit set contain ones. We can check for any combination of values by specifying the appropriate value as the operand to the cmp instruction.

Note that the test/and instructions will only set the zero flag in the above code sequences if all the bits in EAX (or other destination operand) have zeros in the positions where ones appear in the constant operand. This suggests another way to check for all ones in the bit set: Invert the value in EAX prior to using the and or test instruction. Then if the zero flag is set, you know that there were all ones in the (original) bit set, e.g.,

```
not( eax );
test( bitMask, eax );
if( @z ) then

    << At this point, EAX contained all ones in the bit positions >>
    << occupied by ones in the bitMask constant.                  >>

endif;
```

The paragraphs above all suggest that the bitMask (i.e., source operand) is a constant. This was for purposes of example only. In fact, you can use a variable or other register here, if you prefer. Simply load that variable or register with the appropriate bit mask before you execute the test, and, or cmp instructions in the examples above.

Another set of instructions we've already seen that we can use to manipulate bits are the bit test instructions. These instructions include bt (bit test), bts (bit test and set), btc (bit test and complement), and btr (bit test and reset). We've used these instructions to manipulate bits in HLA character-set variables; we can also use them to manipulate bits in general. The btx instructions allow the following syntactical forms:

```
btx( BitNumber, BitsToTest );


btx( reg16, reg16 );
btx( reg32, reg32 );
btx( constant, reg16 );
btx( constant, reg32 );


btx( reg16, mem16 );
btx( reg32, mem32 );
btx( constant, mem16 );
btx( constant, mem32 );
```

The bt instruction's first operand is a bit number that specifies which bit to check in the second operand. If the second operand is a register, then the first operand must contain a value between zero and the size of the register (in bits) minus one; because the 80x86's largest registers are 32 bits, this value has the maximum value 31 (for 32-bit registers). If the second operand is a memory location, then the bit count is not limited to values in the range 0..31. If the first operand is a constant, it can be any 8-bit value in the range 0..255. If the first operand is a register, it has no limitation.

The bt instruction copies the specified bit from the second operand into the carry flag. For example, the "bt(8, eax);" instruction copies bit number 8 of the EAX register into the carry flag. You can test the carry flag after this instruction to determine whether bit 8 was set or clear in EAX.

The bts, btc, and btr instructions manipulate the bit they test while they are testing it. These instructions are rather slow, and you should avoid them if performance is your primary concern. If performance (versus convenience) is an issue, you should always try two different algorithms — one that uses these instructions, one that uses and/or instructions — and measure the performance difference; then choose the best of the two different approaches.

The shift and rotate instructions are another group of instructions you can use to manipulate and test bits. Of course, all of these instructions move the H.O. (left shift/rotate) or L.O. (right shift/rotate) bits into the carry flag. Therefore, you can test the carry flag after you execute one of these instructions to determine the original setting of the operand's H.O. or L.O. bit (depending on the direction). Of course, the shift and rotate instructions are invaluable for aligning bit strings and packing and unpacking data. Chapter 2 has several examples of this and, of course, some earlier examples in the section also use the shift instructions for this purpose.

11.4   The Carry Flag as a Bit Accumulator

The btx, shift, and rotate instructions all set or clear the carry flag depending on the operation and/or selected bit. Because these instructions place their "bit result" in the carry flag, it is often convenient to think of the carry flag as a 1-bit register or accumulator for bit operations. In this section we will explore some of the operations possible with this bit result in the carry flag.

Instructions that will be useful for manipulating bit results in the carry flag are those that use the carry flag as some sort of input value. The following is a sampling of such instructions:

- adc, sbb
- rcl, rcr
- cmc (we'll throw in clc and stc even though they don't use the carry as input)
- jc, jnc
- setc, setnc

The adc and sbb instructions add or subtract their operands along with the carry flag. So if you've computed some bit result into the carry flag, you can figure that result into an addition or subtraction using these instructions. This isn't a common operation, but it is available if it's useful to you.

To merge a bit result in the carry flag, you most often use the rotate through carry instructions (rcl and rcr). These instructions, of course, move the carry flag into the L.O. or H.O. bits of their destination operand. These instructions are very useful for packing a set of bit results into a byte, word, or double word value.

The cmc (complement carry) instruction lets you easily invert the result of some bit operation. You can also use the clc and stc instructions to initialize the carry flag prior to some string of bit operations involving the carry flag.

Of course, instructions that test the carry flag are going to be very popular after a calculation that leaves a bit result in the carry flag. The jc, jnc, setc, and setnc instructions are quite useful here. You can also use the HLA @c and @nc operands in a boolean expression to test the result in the carry flag.

If you have a sequence of bit calculations and you would like to test to see if the calculations produce a specific set of 1-bit results, the easiest way to do this is to clear a register or memory location and use the rcl or rcr instructions to shift each result into that location. Once the bit operations are complete, then you can compare the register or memory location against a constant value to see if you've obtained a particular result sequence. If you want to test a sequence of results involving conjunction and disjunction (i.e., strings of results involving ANDs and ORs), then you could use the setc and setnc instruction to set a register to zero or one and then use the and/or instructions to merge the results.

11.5 Packing and Unpacking Bit Strings

A common bit operation is inserting a bit string into an operand or extracting a bit string from an operand. Chapter 2 provided simple examples of packing and unpacking such data; now it is time to formally describe how to do this.

For the purposes of the current discussion, we will assume that we're dealing with bit strings — that is, a contiguous sequence of bits. A little later in this chapter we'll take a look at how to extract and insert bit sets in an operand. Another simplification we'll make is that the bit string completely fits within a byte, word, or double word operand. Large bit strings that cross object boundaries require additional processing; a discussion of bit strings that cross double word boundaries appears later in this section.

A bit string has two attributes that we must consider when packing and unpacking that bit string: a starting bit position and a length. The starting bit position is the bit number of the L.O. bit of the string in the larger operand. The length, of course, is the number of bits in the operand. To insert (pack) data into a destination operand, you start with a bit string of the appropriate length that is right-justified (i.e., starts in bit position zero) and is zero extended to 8, 16, or 32 bits. The task is to insert this data at the appropriate starting position in some other operand that is 8, 16, or 32 bits wide. There is no guarantee that the destination bit positions contain any particular value.

The first two steps (which can occur in any order) is to clear out the corresponding bits in the destination operand and shift (a copy of) the bit string so that the L.O. bit begins at the appropriate bit position. After completing these two steps, the third step is to OR the shifted result with the destination operand. This inserts the bit string into the destination operand (see Figure 11-3).

Destination:

| X | X | X | X | X | X | X | D | D | D | D | X | X | X | X | X |

Source:

| 0 | 0 | 0 | 0 | 0 | 0 | 0 | 0 | 0 | 0 | 0 | 0 | Y | Y | Y | Y |

Step One: Insert YYYY into the positions occupied by DDDD in the destination operand. Begin by shifting the source operand to the left 5 bits.

Destination:

| X | X | X | X | X | X | X | D | D | D | D | X | X | X | X | X |

Source:

| 0 | 0 | 0 | 0 | 0 | 0 | 0 | Y | Y | Y | Y | 0 | 0 | 0 | 0 | 0 |

Step Two: Clear out the destination bits using the AND instruction.

Destination:

| X | X | X | X | X | X | X | 0 | 0 | 0 | 0 | X | X | X | X | X |

Source:

| 0 | 0 | 0 | 0 | 0 | 0 | 0 | Y | Y | Y | Y | 0 | 0 | 0 | 0 | 0 |

Step Three: OR the two values together.

Figure 11-3: Inserting a Bit String into a Destination Operand.

It only takes three instructions to insert a bit string of known length into a destination operand. The following three instructions demonstrate how to handle the insertion operation in Figure 11-3. These instructions assume that the source operand is in BX and the destination operand is AX:

```
shl( 5, bx );
and( %111111000011111, ax );
or( bx, ax );
```

If the length and the starting position aren't known when you're writing the program (that is, you have to calculate them at runtime), then bit string insertion is a little more difficult. However, with the use of a look-up table it's still an easy operation to accomplish. Let's assume that we have two 8-bit values: a starting bit position for the field we're inserting and a non-zero 8-bit length value. Also assume that the source operand is in EBX and the destination operand is EAX. The code to insert one operand into another could take the following form:

```
readonly

    // The index into the following table specifies the length of the bit string
    // at each position:

    MaskByLen: dword[ 32 ] :=
        [
            0,  $1,  $3,  $7, $f, $1f, $3f, $7f,
            $ff, $1ff, $3ff, $7ff, $fff, $1fff, $3fff, $7fff, $ffff,
            $1_ffff, $3_ffff, $7_ffff, $f_ffff,
            $1f_ffff, $3f_ffff, $7f_ffff, $ff_ffff,
            $1ff_ffff, $3ff_ffff, $7ff_ffff, $fff_ffff,
            $1fff_ffff, $3fff_ffff, $7fff_ffff, $ffff_ffff
        ];
        .
        .
        .
    movzx( Length, edx );
    mov( MaskByLen[ edx*4 ], edx );
    mov( StartingPosition, cl );
    shl( cl, edx );
    not( edx );
    shl( cl, ebx );
```

```
and( edx, eax );
or( ebx, eax );
```

Each entry in the MaskByLen table contains the number of one bits specified by the index into the table. Using the Length value as an index into this table fetches a value that has as many one bits as the Length value. The code above fetches an appropriate mask, shifts it to the left so that the L.O. bit of this run of ones matches the starting position of the field into which we want to insert the data, then it inverts the mask and uses the inverted value to clear the appropriate bits in the destination operand.

To extract a bit string from a larger operand is just as easy as inserting a bit string into some larger operand. All you've got to do is mask out the unwanted bits and then shift the result until the L.O. bit of the bit string is in bit zero of the destination operand. For example, to extract the 4-bit field starting at bit position five in EBX and leave the result in EAX, you could use the following code:

```
mov( ebx, eax );            // Copy data to destination.
and( %1_1110_0000, ebx );   // Strip unwanted bits.
shr( 5, eax );              // Right justify to bit position zero.
```

If you do not know the bit string's length and starting position when you're writing the program, you can still extract the desired bit string. The code is very similar to insertion (though a tiny bit simpler). Assuming you have the Length and StartingPosition values we used when inserting a bit string, you can extract the corresponding bit string using the following code (assuming source=EBX and dest=EAX):

```
movzx( Length, edx );
mov( MaskByLen[ edx*4 ], edx );
mov( StartingPosition, cl );
mov( ebx, eax );
shr( cl, eax );
and( edx, eax );
```

The examples up to this point all assume that the bit string appears completely within a double word (or smaller) object. This will always be the case if the bit string is less than or equal to 24 bits in length. However, if the length of the bit string plus its starting position (mod eight) within an object is greater than 32, then the bit string will cross a double word boundary within the object. To extract such bit strings requires up to three operations: one operation to extract the start of the bit string (up to the first double word boundary), an operation that copies whole double words (assuming the bit string is so long that it consumes several double words), and a final operation that copies leftover bits in the last double word at the end of the bit string. The actual implementation of this operation is left as an exercise for the reader.

11.6 Coalescing Bit Sets and Distributing Bit Strings

Inserting and extracting bit sets is little different than inserting and extract bit strings if the "shape" of the bit set you're inserting (or resulting bit set you're extracting) is the same as the bit set in the main object. The "shape" of a bit set is the distribution of the bits in the set, ignoring the starting bit position of the set. So a bit set that includes bits zero, four, five, six, and seven has the same shape as a bit set that includes bits 12, 16, 17, 18, and 19 because the distribution of the bits is the same. The code to insert or extract this bit set is nearly identical to that of the previous section; the only difference is the mask value you use. For example, to insert this bit set starting at bit number zero in EAX into the corresponding bit set starting at position 12 in EBX, you could use the following code:

```
and( %1111_0001_0000_0000_0000, ebx );   // Mask out destination bits.
shl( 12, eax );                           // Move source bits into posn.
or( eax, ebx );                           // Merge the bit set into EBX.
```

However, suppose you have 5 bits in bit positions zero through four in EAX and you want to merge them into bits 12, 16, 17, 18, and 19 in EBX. Somehow you've got to distribute the bits in EAX prior to logically ORing the values into EBX. Given the fact that this particular bit set has only two runs of one bits, the process is somewhat simplified. The following code achieves this in a somewhat sneaky fashion:

```
and( %1111_0001_0000_0000_0000, ebx );
shl( 3, eax );    // Spread out the bits: 1-4 goes to 4-7 and 0 to 3.
btr( 3, eax );    // Bit 3->carry and then clear bit 3
rcl( 12, eax );   // Shift in carry and put bits into final position
or( eax, ebx );   // Merge the bit set into EBX.
```

This trick with the btr (bit test and reset) instruction worked well because we only had 1 bit out of place in the original source operand. Alas, had the bits all been in the wrong location relative to one another, this scheme might not have worked quite as well. We'll see a more general solution in just a moment.

Extracting this bit set and collecting ("coalescing") the bits into a bit string is not quite as easy. However, there are still some sneaky tricks we can pull. Consider the following code that extracts the bit set from EBX and places the result into bits 0..4 of EAX:

```
mov( ebx, eax );
and( %1111_0001_0000_0000_0000, eax );  // Strip unwanted bits.
shr( 5, eax );                          // Put bit 12 into bit 7, etc.
shr( 3, ah );                           // Move bits 11..14 to 8..11.
shr( 7, eax );                          // Move down to bit zero.
```

This code moves (original) bit 12 into bit position seven, the H.O. bit of AL. At the same time it moves bits 16..19 down to bits 11..14 (bits 3..6 of AH). Then the code shifts the bits 3..6 in AH down to bit 0. This positions the H.O. bits of the bit set so that they are adjacent to the bit left in AL. Finally, the code shifts all the bits down to bit zero. Again, this is not a general solution, but it shows a clever way to attack this problem if you think about it carefully.

The problem with the coalescing and distribution algorithms above is that they are not general. They apply only to their specific bit sets. In general, specific solutions are going to provide the most efficient solution. A generalized solution (perhaps that lets you specify a mask and the code distributes or coalesces the bits accordingly) is going to be a bit more difficult. The following code demonstrates how to distribute the bits in a bit string according to the values in a bit mask:

```
// EAX- Originally contains some value into which we insert bits from EBX.
// EBX- L.O. bits contain the values to insert into EAX.
// EDX- bitmap with ones indicating the bit positions in EAX to insert.
// CL- Scratchpad register.


            mov( 32, cl );      // Count # of bits we rotate.
            jmp DistLoop;

CopyToEAX:  rcr( 1, ebx );      // Don't use SHR here, must preserve Z-flag.
            rcr( 1, eax );
            jz Done;
DistLoop:   dec( cl );
            shr( 1, edx );
            jc CopyToEAX;
            ror( 1, eax );      // Keep current bit in EAX.
            jnz DistLoop;


Done:       ror( cl, eax );     // Reposition remaining bits.
```

In the code above, if we load EDX with %1100_1001 then this code will copy bits 0..3 to bits 0, 3, 6, and 7 in EAX. Notice the short-circuit test that checks to see if we've exhausted the values in EDX (by checking for a zero in EDX). Note that the rotate instructions do not affect the zero flag while the shift instructions do. Hence the shr instruction above will set the zero flag when there are no more bits to distribute (i.e., when EDX becomes zero).

The general algorithm for coalescing bits is a tad more efficient than distribution. Here's the code that will extract bits from EBX via the bit mask in EDX and leave the result in EAX:

```
// EAX- Destination register.
// EBX- Source register.
// EDX- Bitmap with ones representing bits to copy to EAX.
// EBX and EDX are not preserved.
```

```
            sub( eax, eax );    // Clear destination register.
            jmp ShiftLoop;

ShiftInEAX: rcl( 1, ebx );      // Up here we need to copy a bit from
            rcl( 1, eax );      //   EBX to EAX.
ShiftLoop:  shl( 1, edx );      // Check mask to see if we need to copy a bit.
            jc ShiftInEAX;      // If carry set, go copy the bit.
            rcl( 1, ebx );      // Current bit is uninteresting, skip it.
            jnz ShiftLoop;      // Repeat as long as there are bits in EDX.
```

This sequence takes advantage of one sneaky trait of the shift and rotate instructions: The shift instructions affect the zero flag, while the rotate instructions do not. Therefore, the "shl(1, edx);" instruction sets the zero flag when EDX becomes zero (after the shift). If the carry flag was also set, the code will make one additional pass through the loop in order to shift a bit into EAX, but the next time the code shifts EDX one bit to the left, EDX is still zero and so the carry will be clear. On this iteration, the code falls out of the loop.

Another way to coalesce bits is via table look-up. By grabbing a byte of data at a time (so your tables don't get too large) you can use that byte's value as an index into a look-up table that coalesces all the bits down to bit zero. Finally, you can merge the bits at the low end of each byte together. This might produce a more efficient coalescing algorithm in certain cases. The implementation is left to the reader. . . .

11.7   Packed Arrays of Bit Strings

Although it is far more efficient to create arrays whose elements have an integral number of bytes, it is quite possible to create arrays of elements whose size is not a multiple of 8 bits. The drawback is that calculating the "address" of an array element and manipulating that array element involves a lot of extra work. In this section we'll take a look at a few examples of packing and unpacking array elements in an array whose elements are an arbitrary number of bits long.

Before proceeding, it's probably worthwhile to discuss why you would want to bother with arrays of bit objects. The answer is simple: space. If an object only consumes 3 bits, you can get 2.67 times as many elements into the same space if you pack the data rather than allocating a whole byte for each object. For very large arrays, this can be a substantial savings. Of course, the cost of this space savings is speed: You've got to execute extra instructions to pack and unpack the data, thus slowing down access to the data.

The calculation for locating the bit offset of an array element in a large block of bits is almost identical to the standard array access; it is

```
Element_Address_in_bits = Base_address_in_bits +  index * element_size_in_bits
```

Once you calculate the element's address in bits, you need to convert it to a byte address (because we have to use byte addresses when accessing memory) and extract the specified element. Because the base address of an array element (almost) always starts on a byte boundary, we can use the following equations to simplify this task:

```
Byte_of_1st_bit = Base_Address + (index * element_size_in_bits )/8
Offset_to_1st_bit = (index * element_size_in_bits) % 8     (note "%" = MOD)
```

For example, suppose we have an array of 200 3-bit objects that we declare as follows:

```
static
    AO3Bobjects: byte[ (200*3)/8 + 1 ];  // "+1" handles trucation.
```

The constant expression in the dimension above reserves space for enough bytes to hold 600 bits (200 elements, each 3 bits long). As the comment notes, the expression adds an extra byte at the end to ensure we don't lose any odd bits (that won't happen in this example because 600 is evenly divisible by 8, but in general you can't count on this; one extra byte usually won't hurt things).

Now suppose you want to access the ith 3-bit element of this array. You can extract these bits by using the following code:

```
// Extract the ith group of three bits in AO3Bobjects and leave this value
// in EAX.

        sub( ecx, ecx );      // Put i/8 remainder here.
        mov( i, eax );        // Get the index into the array.
        shrd( 3, eax, ecx );  // EAX/8 -> EAX and EAX mod 8 -> ECX (H.O. bits)
        shr( 3, eax );        // Remember, shrd above doesn't modify eax.
        rol( 3, ecx );        // Put remainder into L.O. three bits of ECX.

        // Okay, fetch the word containing the three bits we want to extract.
        // We have to fetch a word because the last bit or two could wind up
        // crossing the byte boundary (i.e., bit offset six and seven in the
        // byte).

        mov( AO3Bobjecs[eax], eax );
        shr( cl, eax );       // Move bits down to bit zero.
        and( %111, eax );     // Remove the other bits.
```

Inserting an element into the array is a bit more difficult. In addition to computing the base address and bit offset of the array element, you've also got to create a mask to clear out the bits in the destination where you're going to insert the new data. The following code inserts the L.O. 3 bits of EAX into the ith element of the AO3Bobjects array.

```
// Insert the L.O. three bits of AX into the ith element of AO3Bobjects:

readonly
    Masks: word[8] :=
            [
                !%0000_0111,   !%0000_1110,   !%0001_1100, !%0011_1000,
                !%0111_0000,   !%1110_0000,   !%1_1100_0000, !%11_1000_0000
            ];
                    .
                    .
                    .

        sub( ecx, ecx );      // Put remainder here.
        mov( i, ebx );        // Get the index into the array.
        shrd( 3, ebx, ecx );  // i/8 -> EBX, i % 8 -> ECX.
        shr( 3, ebx );
        rol( 3, ecx );

        and( %111, ax );                // Clear unneeded bits from AX.
        mov( Masks[ecx], dx );          // Mask to clear out our array element.
        and( AO3Bobjects[ ebx ], dx );  // Grab the bits and clear those
                                        // we're inserting.
        shl( cl, ax );        // Put our three bits in their proper location.
        or( ax, dx );         // Merge bits into destination.
        mov( dx, AO3Bobjects[ ebx ] ); // Store back into  memory.
```

Notice the use of a look-up table to generate the masks needed to clear out the appropriate position in the array. Each element of this array contains all ones except for three zeros in the position we need to clear for a given bit offset (note the use of the "!" operator to invert the constants in the table).

11.8 Searching for a Bit

A very common bit operation is to locate the end of some run of bits. A very common special case of this operation is to locate the first (or last) set or clear bit in a 16- or 32-bit value. In this section we'll explore ways to accomplish this.

Before describing how to search for the first or last bit of a given value, perhaps it's wise to discuss exactly what the terms "first" and "last" mean in this context. The term "first set bit" means the first bit in a value, scanning from bit zero toward the high order bit, which contains a one. A similar definition exists for the "first clear bit." The "last set bit" is the first bit in a value, scanning from the high order bit toward bit zero, which contains a one. A similar definition exists for the last clear bit.

One obvious way to scan for the first or last bit is to use a shift instruction in a loop and count the number of iterations before you shift out a one (or zero) into the carry flag. The number of iterations specifies the position. Here's some sample code that checks for the first set bit in EAX and returns that bit position in ECX:

```
        mov( -32, ecx );        // Count off the bit positions in ECX.
TstLp:shr( 1, eax );            // Check to see if current bit position contains
        jc Done                 //   a one;  exit loop if it does.
        inc( ecx );             // Bump up our bit counter by one.
        jnz TstLp;              // Exit if we execute this loop 32 times.

Done:   add( 32, cl );          // Adjust loop counter so it holds the bit posn.

// At this point, ECX contains the bit position of the first set bit.
// ECX contains 32 if EAX originally contained zero (no set bits).
```

The only thing tricky about this code is the fact that it runs the loop counter from -32 up to zero rather than 32 down to zero. This makes it slightly easier to calculate the bit position once the loop terminates.

The drawback to this particular loop is that it's expensive. This loop repeats as many as 32 times depending on the original value in EAX. If the values you're checking often have lots of zeros in the L.O. bits of EAX, this code runs rather slow.

Searching for the first (or last) set bit is such a common operation that Intel added a couple of instructions on the 80386 specifically to accelerate this process. These instructions are bsf (bit scan forward) and bsr (bit scan reverse). Their syntax is as follows:

```
        bsr( source, destReg );
        bsf( source, destReg );
```

The source and destinations operands must be the same size, and they must both be 16- or 32-bit objects. The destination operand has to be a register. The source operand can be a register or a memory location.

The bsf instruction scans for the first set bit (starting from bit position zero) in the source operand. The bsr instruction scans for the last set bit in the source operand by scanning from the H.O. bit toward the L.O. bit. If these instructions find a bit that is set in the source operand then they clear the zero flag and put the bit position into the destination register. If the source register contains zero (i.e., there are no set bits) then these instructions set the zero flag and leave an indeterminate value in the destination register. Note that you should test the zero flag immediately after the execution of these instructions to validate the destination register's value. Examples:

```
        mov( SomeValue, ebx );  // Value whose bits we want to check.
        bsf( ebx. eax );        // Put position of first set bit in EAX.
        jz NoBitsSet;           // Branch if SomeValue contains zero.
        mov( eax, FirstBit );   // Save location of first set bit.
            .
            .
            .
```

You use the bsr instruction in an identical fashion except that it computes the bit position of the last set bit in an operand (that is, the first set bit it finds when scanning from the H.O. bit toward the L.O. bit).

The 80x86 CPUs do not provide instructions to locate the first bit containing a zero. However, you can easily scan for a zero bit by first inverting the source operand (or a copy of the source operand if you must preserve the source operand's value). If you invert the source operand, then the first "1" bit you find corresponds to the first zero bit in the original operand value.

The bsf and bsr instructions are complex 80x86 instructions (i.e., they are not a part of the 80x86 "RISC core" instruction set). Therefore, these instructions may be slower than other instructions. Indeed, in some circumstances it may be faster to locate the first set bit using discrete instructions. However, because the execution time of these instructions varies widely from CPU to CPU, you should first test the performance of these instructions prior to using them in time critical code.

Note that the bsf and bsr instructions do not affect the source operand. A common operation is to extract the first (or last) set bit you find in some operand. That is, you might want to clear the bit once you find it. If the source operand is a register (or you can easily move it into a register) and then you can use the btr (or btc) instruction to clear the bit once you've found it. Here's some code that achieves this result:

```
bsf( eax, ecx );      // Locate first set bit in EAX.
if( @nz ) then        // If we found a bit, clear it.

    btr( ecx, eax ); // Clear the bit we just found.

endif;
```

At the end of this sequence, the zero flag indicates whether we found a bit (note that btr does not affect the zero flag). Alternately, you could add an else section to the if statement above that handles the case when the source operand (EAX) contains zero at the beginning of this instruction sequence.

Because the bsf and bsr instructions only support 16- and 32-bit operands, you will have to compute the first bit position of an 8-bit operand a little differently. There are a couple of reasonable approaches. First, of course, you can usually zero extend an 8-bit operand to 16 or 32 bits and then use the bsf or bsr instructions on this operand. Another alternative is to create a look-up table where each entry in the table contains the number of bits in the value you use as an index into the table; then you can use the xlat instruction to "compute" the first bit position in the value (note that you will have to handle the value zero as a special case). Another solution is to use the shift algorithm appearing at the beginning of this section; for an eight-bit operand, this is not an entirely inefficient solution.

One interesting use of the bsf and bsr instructions is to "fill in" a character set with all the values from the lowest-valued character in the set through the highest-valued character. For example, suppose a character set contains the values {'A,' 'M,' 'a'..'n,' 'z'}; if we filled in the gaps in this character set we would have the values {'A'..'z'}. To compute this new set we can use bsf to determine the ASCII code of the first character in the set and bsr to determine the ASCII code of the last character in the set. After doing this, we can feed those two ASCII codes to the cs.rangeChar function to compute the new set.

You can also use the bsf and bsr instructions to determine the size of a run of bits, assuming that you have a single run of bits in your operand. Simply locate the first and last bits in the run (as above) and the compute the difference (plus one) of the two values. Of course, this scheme is only valid if there are no intervening zeros between the first and last set bits in the value.

11.9 Counting Bits

The last example in the previous section demonstrates a specific case of a very general problem: counting bits. Unfortunately, that example has a severe limitation: It only counts a single run of one bits appearing in the source operand. This section discusses a more general solution to this problem.

Hardly a week goes by that someone doesn't ask how to count the number of bits in a register operand on one of the Internet newsgroups. This is a common request, undoubtedly, because many assembly language course instructors assign this task a project to their students as a way to teach them about the shift and rotate instructions. Undoubtedly, the solution these instructors expect is something like the following:

```
// BitCount1:
//
//   Counts the bits in the EAX register, returning the count in EBX.

              mov( 32, cl );      // Count the 32 bits in EAX.
              sub( ebx, ebx );    // Accumulate the count here.
CntLoop:      shr( 1, eax );      // Shift next bit out of EAX and into Carry.
              adc( 0, bl );       // Add the carry into the EBX register.
              dec( cl );          // Repeat 32 times.
              jnz CntLoop
```

The "trick" worth noting here is that this code uses the adc instruction to add the value of the carry flag into the BL register. Because the count is going to be less than 32, the result will fit comfortably into BL.

Tricky code or not, this instruction sequence is not particularly fast. As you can tell with just a small amount of analysis, the loop above always executes 32 times, so this code sequence executes 130 instructions (four instructions per iteration plus two extra instructions). One might ask if there is a more efficient solution; the answer is yes. The following code, taken from the AMD Athlon optimization guide, provides a faster solution (see the comments for a description of the algorithm):

```
// bitCount-
//
//   Counts the number of "1" bits in a dword value.
```

```
        // This function returns the dword count value in EAX.

        procedure bits.cnt( BitsToCnt:dword ); nodisplay;

const
    EveryOtherBit       := $5555_5555;
    EveryAlternatePair  := $3333_3333;
    EvenNibbles         := $0f0f_0f0f;

begin cnt;

    push( edx );
    mov( BitsToCnt, eax );
    mov( eax, edx );

    // Compute sum of each pair of bits
    // in EAX. The algorithm treats
    // each pair of bits in EAX as a two
    // bit number and calculates the
    // number of bits as follows (description
    // is for bits zero and one, it generalizes
    // to each pair):
    //
    // EDX =   BIT1  BIT0
    // EAX =      0  BIT1
    //
    // EDX-EAX =   00 if both bits were zero.
    //             01 if Bit0=1 and Bit1=0.
    //             01 if Bit0=0 and Bit1=1.
    //             10 if Bit0=1 and Bit1=1.
    //
    // Note that the result is left in EDX.

    shr( 1, eax );
    and( EveryOtherBit, eax );
    sub( eax, edx );

    // Now sum up the groups of two bits to
    // produces sums of four bits. This works
    // as follows:
    //
    // EDX = bits 2,3, 6,7, 10,11, 14,15, ..., 30,31
    //       in bit positions 0,1, 4,5, ..., 28,29 with
    //       zeros in the other positions.
    //
    // EAX = bits 0,1, 4,5, 8,9, ... 28,29 with zeros
    //       in the other positions.
    //
    // EDX+EAX produces the sums of these pairs of bits.
```

```
//   The sums consume bits 0,1,2, 4,5,6, 8,9,10, ... 28,29,30
//   in EAX with the remaining bits all containing zero.

mov( edx, eax );
shr( 2, edx );
and( EveryAlternatePair, eax );
and( EveryAlternatePair, edx );
add( edx, eax );

// Now compute the sums of the even and odd nibbles in the
// number. Since bits 3, 7, 11, etc. in EAX all contain
// zero from the above calcuation, we don't need to AND
// anything first, just shift and add the two values.
// This computes the sum of the bits in the four bytes
// as four separate value in EAX (AL contains number of
// bits in original AL, AH contains number of bits in
// original AH, etc.)

mov( eax, edx );
shr( 4, eax );
add( edx, eax );
and( EvenNibbles, eax );

// Now for the tricky part.
// We want to compute the sum of the four bytes
// and return the result in EAX. The following
// multiplication achieves this. It works
// as follows:
//   (1) the $01 component leaves bits 24..31
//       in bits 24..31.
//
//   (2) the $100 component adds bits 17..23
//       into bits 24..31.
//
//   (3) the $1_0000 component adds bits 8..15
//       into bits 24..31.
//
//   (4) the $1000_0000 component adds bits 0..7
//       into bits 24..31.
//
// Bits 0..23 are filled with garbage, but bits
// 24..31 contain the actual sum of the bits
// in EAX's original value. The SHR instruction
// moves this value into bits 0..7 and zeros
// out the H.O. bits of EAX.

intmul( $0101_0101, eax );
shr( 24, eax );
```

```
            pop( edx );


        end cnt;
```

11.10   Reversing a Bit String

Another common programming project instructions assign, and a useful
function in its own right, is a program that reverses the bits in an operand. That
is, it swaps the L.O. bit with the H.O. bit, bit 1 with the next-to-H.O. bit, and so
on. The typical solution an instructor probably expects for this assignment is the
following:

```
// Reverse the 32-bits in EAX, leaving the result in EBX:

                mov( 32, cl );
RvsLoop:        shr( 1, eax );      // Move current bit in EAX to the carry flag.
                rcl( 1, ebx );      // Shift the bit back into EBX, backwards.
                dec( cl );
                jnz RvsLoop
```

As with the previous examples, this code suffers from the fact that it repeats the
loop 32 times for a grand total of 129 instructions. By unrolling the loop you can
get it down to 64 instructions, but this is still somewhat expensive.

As usual, the best solution to an optimization problem is often a better
algorithm rather than attempting to tweak your code by trying to choose faster
instructions to speed up some code. However, a little intelligence goes a long way
when manipulating bits. In the last section, for example, we were able to speed
up counting the bits in a string by substituting a more complex algorithm for the
simplistic "shift and count" algorithm. In the example above, we are once again
faced with a very simple algorithm with a loop that repeats for one bit in each
number. The question is: "Can we discover an algorithm that doesn't execute 129
instructions to reverse the bits in a 32-bit register?" The answer is yes, and the
trick is to do as much work as possible in parallel.

Suppose that all we wanted to do was swap the even and odd bits in a 32-bit
value. We can easily swap the even an odd bits in EAX using the following code:

```
        mov( eax, edx );            // Make a copy of the odd bits in the data.
        shr( 1, eax );              // Move the even bits to the odd positions.
        and( $5555_5555, edx );     // Isolate the odd bits by clearing even bits.
        and( $5555_5555, eax );     // Isolate the even bits (in odd posn now).
        shl( 1, edx );              // Move the odd bits to the even positions.
        or( edx, eax );             // Merge the bits and complete the swap.
```

Of course, swapping the even and odd bits, while somewhat interesting, does not
solve our larger problem of reversing all the bits in the number. But it does take
us part of the way there. For example, if after executing the preceding code

sequence you swap adjacent pairs of bits, you've managed to swap the bits in all the nibbles in the 32-bit value. Swapping adjacent pairs of bits is done in a manner very similar to the above, the code is

```
mov( eax, edx );          // Make a copy of the odd-numbered bit pairs.
shr( 2, eax );            // Move the even bit pairs to the odd posn.
and( $3333_3333, edx );   // Isolate the odd pairs by clearing even pairs.
and( $3333_3333, eax );   // Isolate the even pairs (in odd posn now).
shl( 2, edx );            // Move the odd pairs to the even positions.
or( edx, eax );           // Merge the bits and complete the swap.
```

After completing the preceding sequence you swap the adjacent nibbles in the 32-bit register. Again, the only difference is the bit mask and the length of the shifts. Here's the code:

```
mov( eax, edx );          // Make a copy of the odd-numbered nibbles.
shr( 4, eax );            // Move the even nibbles to the odd position.
and( $0f0f_0f0f, edx );   // Isolate the odd nibbles.
and( $0f0f_0f0f, eax );   // Isolate the even nibbles (in odd posn now).
shl( 4, edx );            // Move the odd pairs to the even positions.
or( edx, eax );           // Merge the bits and complete the swap.
```

You can probably see the pattern developing and can figure out that in the next two steps you have to swap the bytes and then the words in this object. You can use code like the above, but there is a better way: Use the bswap instruction. The bswap (byte swap) instruction uses the following syntax:

```
bswap( reg32 );
```

This instruction swaps bytes zero and three, and it swaps bytes one and two in the specified 32-bit register. The principle use of this instruction is to convert data between the so-called little endian and big-endian data formats.[2] Although you don't specifically need this instruction for this purpose here, the bswap instruction does swap the bytes and words in a 32-bit object exactly the way you want them when reversing bits. Rather than sticking in another 12 instructions to swap the bytes and then the words, you can simply use a "bswap(eax);" instruction to complete the job after the instructions above. The final code sequence is

```
mov( eax, edx );          // Make a copy of the odd bits in the data.
shr( 1, eax );            // Move the even bits to the odd positions.
and( $5555_5555, edx );   // Isolate the odd bits by clearing even bits.
and( $5555_5555, eax );   // Isolate the even bits (in odd posn now).
shl( 1, edx );            // Move the odd bits to the even positions.
or( edx, eax );           // Merge the bits and complete the swap.
```

---

[2] In the little endian system, which is the native 80x86 format, the L.O. byte of an object appears at the lowest address in memory. In the big endian system, which various RISC processors use, the H.O. byte of an object appears at the lowest address in memory. The bswap instruction converts between these two data formats.

```
        mov( eax, edx );            // Make a copy of the odd numbered bit pairs.
        shr( 2, eax );              // Move the even bit pairs to the odd posn.
        and( $3333_3333, edx );     // Isolate the odd pairs by clearing even pairs.
        and( $3333_3333, eax );     // Isolate the even pairs (in odd posn now).
        shl( 2, edx );              // Move the odd pairs to the even positions.
        or( edx, eax );             // Merge the bits and complete the swap.

        mov( eax, edx );            // Make a copy of the odd numbered nibbles.
        shr( 4, eax );              // Move the even nibbles to the odd position.
        and( $0f0f_0f0f, edx );     // Isolate the odd nibbles.
        and( $0f0f_0f0f, eax );     // Isolate the even nibbles (in odd posn now).
        shl( 4, edx );              // Move the odd pairs to the even positions.
        or( edx, eax );             // Merge the bits and complete the swap.

        bswap( eax );               // Swap the bytes and words.
```

This algorithm only requires 19 instructions, and it executes much faster than
the bit-shifting loop appearing earlier. Of course, this sequence does consume a
bit more memory. If you're trying to save memory rather than clock cycles, the
loop is probably a better solution.

11.11   Merging Bit Strings

Another common bit string operation is producing a single bit string by merging,
or interleaving, bits from two different sources. The following example code
sequence creates a 32-bit string by merging alternate bits from two 16-bit strings:

```
// Merge two 16-bit strings into a single 32-bit string.
// AX - Source for even numbered bits.
// BX - Source for odd numbered bits.
// CL - Scratch register.
// EDX- Destination register.

                mov( 16, cl );
MergeLp:        shrd( 1, eax, edx );        // Shift a bit from EAX into EDX.
                shrd( 1, ebx, edx );        // Shift a bit from EBX into EDX.
                dec( cl );
                jne MergeLp;
```

This particular example merged two 16-bit values together, alternating their bits
in the result value. For a faster implementation of this code, unrolling the loop is
probably your best bet because this eliminates half the instructions.

   With a few slight modifications, we could also have merged four 8-bit values
together, or we could have generated the result using other bit sequences; for
example, the following code copies bits 0..5 from EAX, then bits 0..4 from EBX,
then bits 6..11 from EAX, then bits 5..15 from EBX, and finally bits 12..15 from
EAX:

```
            shrd( 6, eax, edx );
            shrd( 5, ebx, edx );
            shrd( 6, eax, edx );
            shrd( 11, ebx, edx );
            shrd( 4, eax, edx );
```

11.12   Extracting Bit Strings

Of course, we can easily accomplish the converse of merging two bit streams; i.e., we can extract and distribute bits in a bit string among multiple destinations. The following code takes the 32-bit value in EAX and distributes alternate bits among the BX and DX registers:

```
                mov( 16, cl );          // Count off the number of loop iterations.
ExtractLp:      shr( 1, eax );          // Extract even bits to (E)BX.
                rcr( 1, ebx );
                shr( 1, eax );          // Extract odd bits to (E)DX.
                rcr( 1, edx );
                dec( cl );              // Repeat 16 times.
                jnz ExtractLp;
                shr( 16, ebx );         // Need to move the results from the H.O.
                shr( 16, edx );         //   bytes of EBX/EDX to the L.O. bytes.
```

This sequence executes 99 instructions. This isn't terrible, but we can probably do a little better by using a better algorithm that extracts bits in parallel. Employing the technique we used to reverse bits in a register, we can come up with the following algorithm that relocates all the even bits to the L.O. word of EAX and all the odd bits to the H.O. word of EAX.

```
// Swap bits at positions (1,2), (5,6), (9,10), (13,14), (17,18),
// (21,22), (25,26), and (29, 30).

        mov( eax, edx );
        and( $9999_9999, eax );     // Mask out the bits we'll keep for now.
        mov( edx, ecx );
        shr( 1, edx );              // Move 1st bits in tuple above to the
        and( $2222_2222, ecx );     //   correct position and mask out the
        and( $2222_2222, edx );     //   unneeded bits.
        shl( 1, ecx );              // Move 2nd bits in tuples above.
        or( edx, ecx );             // Merge all the bits back together.
        or( ecx, eax );

// Swap bit pairs at positions ((2,3), (4,5)),  ((10,11), (12,13)), etc.

        mov( eax, edx );
        and( $c3c3_c3c3, eax );     // The bits we'll leave alone.
        mov( edx, ecx );
        shr( 2, edx );
```

```
        and( $0c0c_0c0c, ecx );
        and( $0c0c_0c0c, edx );
        shl( 2, ecx );
        or( edx, ecx );
        or( ecx, eax );

// Swap nibbles at nibble positions (1,2), (5,6), (9,10), etc.

        mov( eax, edx );
        and( $f00f_f00f, eax );
        mov( edx, ecx );
        shr(4, edx );
        and( $0f0f_0f0f, ecx );
        and( $0f0f_0f0f, ecx );
        shl( 4, ecx );
        or( edx, ecx );
        or( ecx, eax );

// Swap bits at positions 1 and 2.

        ror( 8, eax );
        xchg( al, ah );
        rol( 8, eax );
```

This sequence requires 30 instructions. At first blush it looks like a winner because the original loop executes 64 instructions. However, this code isn't quite as good as it looks. After all, if we're willing to write this much code, why not unroll the loop above 16 times? That sequence only requires 64 instructions. So the complexity of the previous algorithm may not gain much on instruction count. As to which sequence is faster, well, you'll have to time them to figure this out. However, the shrd instructions are not particularly fast and neither are the instructions in the other sequence. This example does not appear here to show you a better algorithm, but rather to demonstrate that writing really tricky code doesn't always provide a big performance boost.

Extracting other bit combinations is left as an exercise for the reader.

11.13   Searching for a Bit Pattern

Another bit-related operation you may need is the ability to search for a particular bit pattern in a string of bits. For example, you might want to locate the bit index of the first occurrence of %1011 starting at some particular position in a bit string. In this section we'll explore some simple algorithms to accomplish this task.

To search for a particular bit pattern we're going to need to know four things: (1) the pattern to search for (the *pattern*), (2) the length of the pattern we're searching for, (3) the bit string that we're going to search through (the *source*), and (4) the length of the bit string to search through. The basic idea behind the search is to create a mask based on the length of the pattern and mask a copy of the source with this value. Then we can directly compare the pattern with the masked source for equality. If they are equal, you're done; if they're not equal, then increment a bit position counter, shift the source one position to the right, and try again. You repeat this operation *length(source) - length(pattern)* times. The algorithm fails if it does not detect the bit pattern after this many attempts (because we will have exhausted all the bits in the source operand that could match the pattern's length). Here's a simple algorithm that searches for a 4-bit pattern throughout the EBX register:

```
            mov( 28, cl );          // 28 attempts because 32-4 = 28 (len(src)-
                                    // len(pat)).
            mov( %1111, ch );       // Mask for the comparison.
            mov( pattern, al );     // Pattern to search for.
            and( ch, al );          // Mask unnecessary bits in AL.
            mov( source, ebx );     // Get the source value.
ScanLp:     mov( bl, dl );          // Make a copy of the L.O. four bits of EBX
            and( ch, dl );          // Mask unwanted bits.
            cmp( dl, al );          // See if we match the pattern.
            jz Matched;
            dec( cl );              // Repeat the specified number of times.
            jnz ScanLp;

    << If we get to this point, we failed to match the bit string >>

        jmp Done;

Matched:
    << If we get to this point, we matched the bit string.  We can >>
    << compute the position in the original source as 28-cl.      >>

Done:
```

Bit string scanning is a special case of string matching. String matching is a well studied problem in computer science, and many of the algorithms you can use for string matching are applicable to bit string matching as well. Such algorithms are a bit beyond the scope of this chapter, but to give you a preview of how this works, you compute some function (like xor or sub) between the pattern and the current source bits and use the result as an index into a look-up table to determine how many bits you can skip. Such algorithms let you skip several bits rather than only shifting once for each iteration of the scanning loop (as is done by the previous algorithm).

11.14   The HLA Standard Library Bits Module

The HLA Standard Library provides the *bits.hhf* module that provides several bit related functions, including built-in functions for many of the algorithms we've studied in this chapter. This section will describe these functions available in the HLA Standard Library.

procedure bits.cnt(b:dword); returns("EAX");

This procedure returns the number of one bits present in the "b" parameter. It returns the count in the EAX register. To count the number of zero bits in the parameter value, invert the value of the parameter before passing it to bits.cnt. If you want to count the number of bits in a 16-bit operand, simply zero extend it to 32 bits prior to calling this function. Here are a couple of examples:

```
// Compute the number of bits in a 16-bit register:

        pushw( 0 );
        push( ax );
        call bits.cnt;

// If you prefer to use a higher-level syntax, try the following:

        bits.cnt( #{ pushw(0); push(ax); }# );

// Compute the number of bits in a 16-bit memory location:

        pushw( 0 );
        push( mem16 );
        bits.cnt;
```

If you want to compute the number of bits in an 8-bit operand it's probably faster to write a simple loop that rotates all the bits in the source operand and adds the carry into the accumulating sum. Of course, if performance isn't an issue, you can zero extend the byte to 32 bits and call the bits.cnt procedure.

procedure bits.distribute(source:dword; mask:dword; dest:dword); returns("EAX");

This function takes the L.O. n bits of source, where n is the number of "1" bits in mask, and inserts these bits into dest at the bit positions specified by the "1" bits in mask (i.e., the same as the distribute algorithm appearing earlier in this chapter). This function does not change the bits in dest that correspond to the zeros in the mask value. This function does not affect the value of the actual dest parameter; it returns the new value in the EAX register.

procedure bits.coalese(source:dword; mask:dword); returns("EAX");

This function is the converse of bits.distribute. It extracts all the bits in source whose corresponding positions in mask contain a one. This function coalesces (right justifies) these bits in the L.O. bit positions of the result and returns the result in EAX.

```
procedure bits.extract( var d:dword ); returns( "EAX" );
    // Really a macro.
```

This function extracts the first set bit in d searching from bit 0 and returns the index of this bit in the EAX register; the function will also return the zero flag clear in this case. This function also clears that bit in the operand. If d contains zero, then this function returns the zero flag set and EAX will contain -1.

Note that HLA actually implements this function as a macro, not a procedure. This means that you can pass any double word operand as a parameter (i.e., a memory or a register operand). However, the results are undefined if you pass EAX as the parameter (because this function computes the bit number in EAX).

```
procedure bits.reverse32( d:dword ); returns( "EAX" );
procedure bits.reverse16( w:word ); returns( "AX" );
procedure bits.reverse8( b:byte ); returns( "AL" );
```

These three routines return their parameter value with the its bits reversed in the accumulator register (AL/AX/EAX). Call the routine appropriate for your data size.

```
procedure bits.merge32( even:dword; odd:dword ); returns( "EDX:EAX" );
procedure bits.merge16( even:word; odd:word ); returns( "EAX" );
procedure bits.merge8( even:byte; odd:byte ); returns( "AX" );
```

These routines merge two streams of bits to produce a value whose size is the combination of the two parameters. The bits from the even parameter occupy the even bits in the result; the bits from the odd parameter occupy the odd bits in the result. Notice that these functions return 16, 32, or 64 bits based on byte, word, and double word parameter values.

```
procedure bits.nibbles32( d:dword ); returns( "EDX:EAX" );
procedure bits.nibbles16( w:word ); returns( "EAX" );
procedure bits.nibbles8( b:byte ); returns( "AX" );
```

These routines extract each nibble from the parameter and place those nibbles into individual bytes. The bits.nibbles8 function extracts the two nibbles from the b parameter and places the L.O. nibble in AL and the H.O. nibble in AH. The bits.nibbles16 function extracts the four nibbles in *w* and places them in each of the four bytes of EAX. You can use the bswap or ro*x* instructions to gain access to the nibbles in the H.O. word of EAX. The bits.nibbles32 function extracts the eight nibbles in EAX and distributes them through the eight bytes in EDX:EAX. Nibble zero winds up in AL and nibble seven winds up in the H.O. byte of EDX. Again, you can use bswap or the rotate instructions to access the upper bytes of EAX and EDX.

11.15   For More Information

The electronic edition of *The Art of Assembly Language* on the accompanying CD-ROM contains some additional information you may find useful when developing bit manipulation algorithms. In particular, the chapter on digital design discusses boolean algebra, a subject that you will find essential when working with bits. The chapter in this text on the MMX instruction set also contains additional information you may find useful when manipulating bits. The HLA Standard Library Reference Manual contains more information about the HLA Standard Library bit manipulation routines. See that documentation on the accompanying CD-ROM for more information about those functions. As noted in the section on bit counting, the AMD Athlon optimization guide contains some useful algorithms for bit-based computations. Finally, to learn more about bit searching algorithms, you should pick up a textbook on Data Structures and Algorithms and study the section on "string matching algorithms."

12

THE STRING INSTRUCTIONS

12.1   Chapter Overview

A *string* is a collection of values stored in contiguous memory locations. Strings are usually arrays of bytes, words, or (on 80386 and later processors) double words. The 80x86 microprocessor family supports several instructions specifically designed to cope with strings. This chapter explores some of the uses of these string instructions.

The 80x86 CPUs can process three types of strings: byte strings, word strings, and double word strings. They can move strings, compare strings, search for a specific value within a string, initialize a string to a fixed value, and do other primitive operations on strings. The 80x86's string instructions are also useful for manipulating arrays, tables, and records. You can easily assign or compare such data structures using the string instructions. Using string instructions may speed up your array manipulation code considerably.

12.2 The 80x86 String Instructions

All members of the 80x86 family support five different string instructions: MOVS*x*, CMPS*x*, SCAS*x*, LODS*x*, and STOS*x*.[1] (*x*= B, W, or D for byte, word, or double word, respectively. This text will generally drop the *x* suffix when talking about these string instructions in a general sense.) They are the string primitives on which you can build most other string operations. How you use these five instructions is the topic of the sections that follow.

```
For MOVS:
    movsb();
    movsw();
    movsd();

For CMPS:
    cmpsb();
    cmpsw();
    cmpsd();

For SCAS:
    scasb();
    scasw();
    scasd();

For STOS:
    stosb();
    stosw();
    stosd();

For LODS:
    lodsb();
    lodsw();
    lodsd();
```

12.2.1 How the String Instructions Operate

The string instructions operate on blocks (contiguous linear arrays) of memory. For example, the movs instruction moves a sequence of bytes from one memory location to another. The cmps instruction compares two blocks of memory. The scas instruction scans a block of memory for a particular value. These string instructions often require three operands, a destination block address, a source block address, and (optionally) an element count. For example, when using the movs instruction to copy a string, you need a source address, a destination address, and a count (the number of string elements to move).

---

[1] The 80x86 processor support two additional string instructions, INS and OUTS, which input strings of data from an input port or output strings of data to an output port. We will not consider these instructions because they are privileged instructions and you cannot execute them in a standard 32-bit OS application.

Unlike other instructions, which operate on memory, the string instructions don't have any explicit operands. The operands for the string instructions are

- the ESI (source index) register
- the EDI (destination index) register
- the ECX (count) register
- the AL/AX/EAX register
- the direction flag in the FLAGS register

For example, one variant of the movs (move string) instruction copies a string from the source address specified by ESI to the destination address specified by EDI, of length ECX. Likewise, the cmps instruction compares the string pointed at by ESI, of length ECX, to the string pointed at by EDI.

Not all string instructions have source and destination operands (only movs and cmps support them). For example, the scas instruction (scan a string) compares the value in the accumulator (AL, AX, or EAX) to values in memory.

12.2.2 The REP/REPE/REPZ and REPNZ/REPNE Prefixes

The string instructions, by themselves, do not operate on strings of data. The movs instruction, for example, will move a single byte, word, or double word. When the movs instruction executes, it ignores the value in the ECX register. The repeat prefixes tell the 80x86 to do a multibyte string operation. The syntax for the repeat prefix is

---

```
For MOVS:
    rep.movsb();
    rep.movsw();
    rep.movsd();

For CMPS:
    repe.cmpsb();    // Note: repz is a synonym for repe.
    repe.cmpsw();
    repe.cmpsd();

    repne.cmpsb();   // Note: repnz is a synonym for repne.
    repne.cmpsw();
    repne.cmpsd();

For SCAS:
    repe.scasb();    // Note: repz is a synonym for repe.
    repe.scasw();
    repe.scasd();

    repne.scasb();   // Note: repnz is a synonym for repne.
    repne.scasw();
    repne.scasd();
```

For STOS:

```
    rep.stosb();
    rep.stosw();
    rep.stosd();
```

You don't normally use the repeat prefixes with the lods instruction.

When specifying the repeat prefix before a string instruction, the string instruction repeats ECX times.[2] Without the repeat prefix, the instruction operates only on a single byte, word, or double word.

You can use repeat prefixes to process entire strings with a single instruction. You can use the string instructions, without the repeat prefix, as string primitive operations to synthesize more powerful string operations.

12.2.3   The Direction Flag

Besides the ESI, EDI, ECX, and AL/AX/EAX registers, one other register controls the operation of the 80x86's string instructions — the flags register. Specifically, the *direction flag* in the flags register controls how the CPU processes strings.

If the direction flag is clear, the CPU increments ESI and EDI after operating upon each string element. For example, executing movs will move the byte, word, or double word at ESI to EDI and will then increment ESI and EDI by one, two, or four. When specifying the rep prefix before this instruction, the CPU increments ESI and EDI for each element in the string (the count in ECX specifies the number of elements). At completion, the ESI and EDI registers will be pointing at the first item beyond the strings.

If the direction flag is set, the 80x86 decrements ESI and EDI after it processes each string element (again, ECX specifies the number of string elements). After a repeated string operation, the ESI and EDI registers will be pointing at the first byte, word, or double word before the strings if the direction flag was set.

You can change the direction flag using the cld (clear direction flag) and std (set direction flag) instructions. When using these instructions inside a procedure, keep in mind that they modify the machine state. Therefore, you may need to save the direction flag during the execution of that procedure. The following example exhibits the kinds of problems you might encounter:

```
procedure Str2; nodisplay;
begin Str2;

        std();
    <Do some string operations>
        .
        .
        .

end Str2;
        .
```

---

[2] Except for the cmps instruction which repeats *at most* the number of times specified in the ECX register.

```
         .
         .
    cld();
<do some operations>
    Str2();
<do some string operations requiring D=0>
```

This code will not work properly. The calling code assumes that the direction flag is clear after Str2 returns. However, this isn't true. Therefore, the string operations executed after the call to Str2 will not function properly.

There are a couple of ways to handle this problem. The first, and probably the most obvious, is always to insert the cld or std instructions immediately before executing a sequence of one or more string instructions. The other alternative is to save and restore the direction flag using the pushfd and popfd instructions. Using these two techniques, the code above would look like this:

Always issuing cld or std before a string instruction:

```
procedure Str2; nodisplay;
begin Str2;

        std();
<Do some string operations>
         .
         .
         .

end Str2;
         .
         .
         .
        cld();
<do some operations>
        Str2();
        cld();
<do some string operations requiring D=0>
```

Saving and restoring the flags register:

```
procedure Str2; nodisplay;
begin Str2;

        pushfd();
        std();
<Do some string operations>
         .
         .
         .
        popfd();
end Str2;
         .
```

```
        .
        .
        .
        cld();
<do some operations>
        Str2();
<do some string operations requiring D=0>
```

If you use the pushfd and popfd instructions to save and restore the flags register, keep in mind that you're saving and restoring all the flags. This makes it somewhat difficult to return information in other flag bits. For example, it's a bit of work to return an error condition in the carry flag if you use pushfd and popfd to preserve the direction flag in the procedure.

A third solution is to always ensure that the direction flag is clear except for the execution of a particular sequence that requires it set. For example, many library calls and some operating systems always assume that the direction flag is clear when you call them. Most standard C library functions work this way, for example. You can follow this convention by always assuming that the direction flag is clear, and then make sure you clear it immediately after a sequence that requires the use of std.

12.2.4   The MOVS Instruction

The movs instruction uses the following syntax:

```
movsb()
movsw()
movsd()
rep.movsb()
rep.movsw()
rep.movsd()
```

The movsb (move string, bytes) instruction fetches the byte at address ESI, stores it at address EDI, and then increments or decrements the ESI and EDI registers by one. If the REP prefix is present, the CPU checks ECX to see if it contains zero. If not, then it moves the byte from ESI to EDI and decrements the ECX register. This process repeats until ECX becomes zero. Especially note that if ECX contains zero upon initial execution, the movs instruction will not copy any data bytes.

The movsw (move string, words) instruction fetches the word at address ESI, stores it at address EDI, and then increments or decrements ESI and EDI by two. If there is a REP prefix, then the CPU repeats this procedure as many times as specified in ECX.

The movsd instruction operates in a similar fashion on double words. It increments or decrements ESI and EDI by four for each data movement.

When you use the rep prefix, the movsb instruction moves the number of bytes you specify in the ECX register. The following code segment copies 384 bytes from CharArray1 to CharArray2:

```
CharArray1: byte[ 384 ];
CharArray2: byte[ 384 ];
        .
        .
        .
    cld();
    lea( esi, CharArray1 );
    lea( edi, CharArray2 );
    mov( 384, ecx );
    rep.movsb();
```

If you substitute movsw for movsb, then the preceding code will move 384 words (768 bytes) rather than 384 bytes:

```
WordArray1: word[ 384 ];
WordArray2: word[ 384 ];
        .
        .
        .
    cld();
    lea( esi, WordArray1 );
    lea( edi, WordArray2 );
    mov( 384, ecx );
    rep.movsw();
```

Remember, the ECX register contains the element count, not the byte count. When using the movsw instruction, the CPU moves the number of words specified in the ECX register. Similarly, movsd moves the number of double words you specify in the ECX register, not the number of bytes.

If you've set the direction flag before executing a movsb/movsw/movsd instruction, the CPU decrements the ESI and EDI registers after moving each string element. This means that the ESI and EDI registers must point at the last element of their respective strings before executing a movsb, movsw, or movsd instruction. For example:

```
CharArray1: byte[ 384 ];
CharArray2: byte[ 384 ];
        .
        .
        .
    cld();
    lea( esi, CharArray1[383] );
    lea( edi, CharArray2[383] );
    mov( 384, ecx );
    rep.movsb();
```

Although there are times when processing a string from tail to head is useful (see the cmps description in the next section), generally you'll process strings in the forward direction because it's more straightforward to do so. There is one class of string operations where being able to process strings in both directions is absolutely mandatory: processing strings when the source and destination blocks overlap. Consider what happens in the following code:

```
CharArray1: byte;
CharArray2: byte[ 384 ];

    .

    .

    .

cld();
lea( esi, CharArray1 );
lea( edi, CharArray2 );
mov( 384, ecx );
rep.movsb();
```

This sequence of instructions treats CharArray1 and CharArray2 as a pair of 384 byte strings. However, the last 383 bytes in the CharArray1 array overlap the first 383 bytes in the CharArray2 array. Let's trace the operation of this code byte by byte.

When the CPU executes the movsb instruction, it copies the byte at ESI (CharArray1) to the byte pointed at by EDI (CharArray2). Then it increments ESI and EDI, decrements ECX by one, and repeats this process. Now the ESI register points at CharArray1+1 (which is the address of CharArray2), and the EDI register points at CharArray2+1. The movsb instruction copies the byte pointed at by ESI to the byte pointed at by EDI. However, this is the byte originally copied from location CharArray1. So the movsb instruction copies the value originally in location CharArray1 to both locations CharArray2 and CharArray2+1. Again, the CPU increments ESI and EDI, decrements ECX, and repeats this operation. Now the movsb instruction copies the byte from location CharArray1+2 (CharArray2+1) to location CharArray2+2. But once again, this is the value that originally appeared in location CharArray1. Each repetition of the loop copies the next element in CharArray1[0] to the next available location in the CharArray2 array. Pictorially, it looks something like Figure 12-1.

The end result is that the movsb instruction replicates X throughout the string. The movsb instruction copies the source operand into the memory location, which will become the source operand for the very next move operation, which causes the replication.

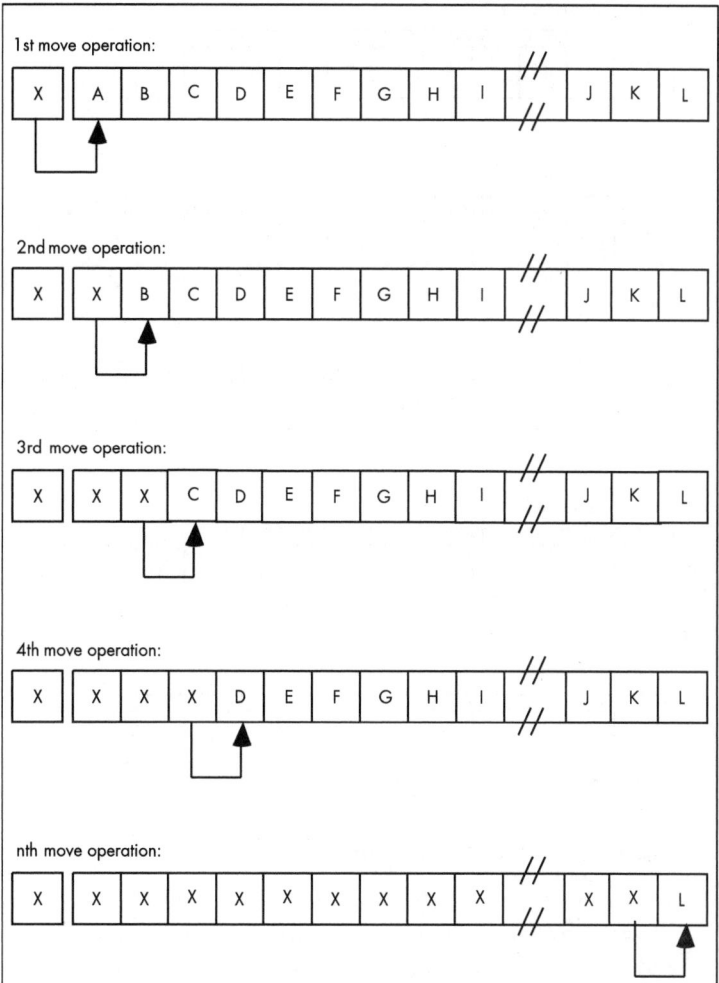

Figure 12-1: Copying Data Between Two Overlapping Arrays (Forward Direction).

If you really want to move one array into another when they overlap, you should move each element of the source string to the destination string starting at the end of the two strings, as shown in Figure 12-2.

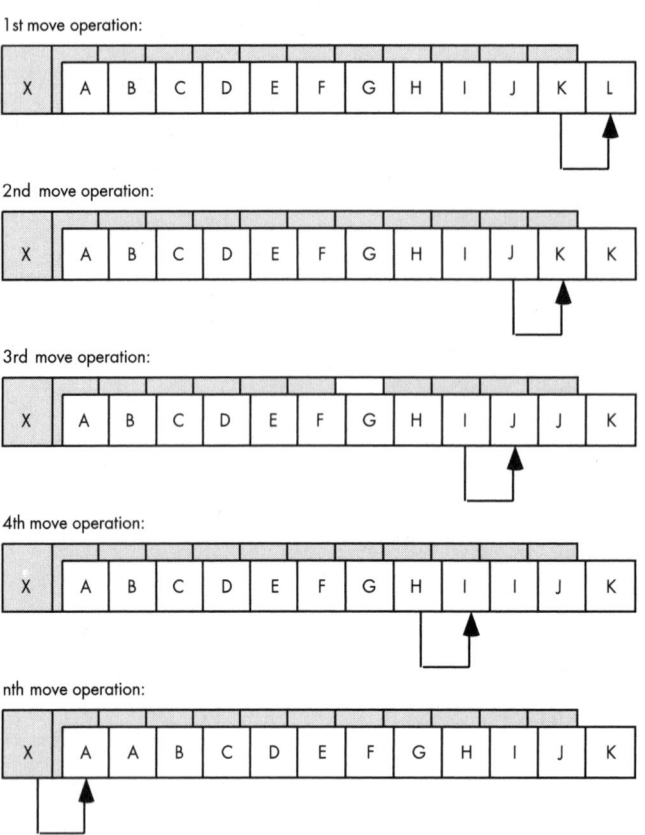

Figure 12-2: Using a Backward Copy to Copy Data in Overlapping Arrays.

Setting the direction flag and pointing ESI and EDI at the end of the strings will allow you to (correctly) move one string to another when the two strings overlap and the source string begins at a lower address than the destination string. If the two strings overlap and the source string begins at a higher address than the destination string, then clear the direction flag and point ESI and EDI at the beginning of the two strings.

If the two strings do not overlap, then you can use either technique to move the strings around in memory. Generally, operating with the direction flag clear is the easiest, so that makes the most sense in this case.

You shouldn't use the movs*x* instruction to fill an array with a single byte, word, or double word value. Another string instruction, stos, is much better for this purpose.[3] However, for arrays whose elements are larger than four bytes, you can use the movs instruction to initialize the entire array to the content of the first element.

The movs instruction is sometimes more efficient when copying double words than it is copying bytes or words. On some systems, it typically takes the same amount of time to copy a byte using movsb as it does to copy a double word using

---

[3] From a performance point of view, this is not true; but if you want to quickly fill an array with a set value, the string instructions are probably not the fastest way to do this.

movsd. Therefore, if you are moving a large number of bytes from one array to another, the copy operation will be faster if you can use the movsd instruction rather than the movsb instruction. Of course, if the number of bytes you wish to move is an even multiple of four, this is a trivial change; just divide the number of bytes to copy by four, load this value into ECX, and then use the movsb instruction. If the number of bytes is not evenly divisible by four, then you can use the movsd instruction to copy all but the last one, two, or three bytes of the array (that is, the remainder after you divide the byte count by four). For example, if you want to efficiently move 4099 bytes, you can do so with the following instruction sequence:

```
lea( esi, Source );
lea( edi, Destination );
mov( 1024, ecx );          // Copy 1024 dwords = 4096 bytes
rep.movsd();
movsw();                   // Copy bytes 4097 and 4098.
movsb();                   // Copy the last byte.
```

Using this technique to copy data never requires more than three movs*x* instructions because you can copy one, two, or three bytes with no more than two movsb and movsw instructions. The scheme above is most efficient if the two arrays are aligned on double word boundaries. If not, you might want to move the movsb or movsw instruction (or both) before the movsd so that the movsd instruction works with double word-aligned data.

If you do not know the size of the block you are copying until the program executes, you can still use code like the following to improve the performance of a block move of bytes:

```
lea( esi, Source );
lea( edi, Dest );
mov( Length, ecx );
shr( 2, ecx );         // divide by four.
if( @nz ) then         // Only execute MOVSD if four or more bytes.

    rep.movsd();       // Copy the dwords.

endif;
mov( Length, ecx );
and( %11, ecx );       // Compute (Length mod 4).
if( @nz ) then         // Only execute MOVSB if #bytes/4 <> 0.

    rep.movsb();       // Copy the remaining one, two, or three bytes.

endif;
```

On many computer systems, the movsd instruction provides about the fastest way to copy bulk data from one location to another. While there are, arguably, faster ways to copy the data on certain CPUs, ultimately the memory bus performance is the limiting factor and the CPUs are generally much faster than the memory bus. Therefore, unless you have a special system, writing fancy code to improve memory-to-memory transfers is probably a waste of time. Also note that Intel has improved the performance of the movsx instructions on later processors so that movsb operates almost as efficiently as movsw and movsd when copying the same number of bytes. Therefore, when working on a later 80x86 processor, it may be more efficient to simply use movsb to copy the specified number of bytes rather than go through all the complexity outlined above. The bottom line is this: If the speed of a block move matters to you, try it several different ways and pick the fastest (or the simplest, if they all run the same speed, which is likely).

12.2.5 The CMPS Instruction

The cmps instruction compares two strings. The CPU compares the string referenced by EDI to the string pointed at by ESI. ECX contains the length of the two strings (when using the repe or repne prefix). Like the movs instruction, HLA allows several different forms of this instruction:

```
cmpsb();
cmpsw();
cmpsd();

repe.cmpsb();
repe.cmpsw();
repe.cmpsd();

repne.cmpsb();
repne.cmpsw();
repne.cmpsd();
```

Like the movs instruction you specify the actual operand addresses in the ESI and EDI registers.

Without a repeat prefix, the cmps instruction subtracts the value at location EDI from the value at ESI and updates the flags. Other than updating the flags, the CPU doesn't use the difference produced by this subtraction. After comparing the two locations, cmps increments or decrements the ESI and EDI registers by one, two, or four (for cmpsb/cmpsw/cmpsd, respectively). cmps increments the ESI and EDI registers if the direction flag is clear and decrements them otherwise.

Of course, you will not tap the real power of the cmps instruction using it to compare single bytes, words, or double words in memory. This instruction shines when you use it to compare whole strings. With cmps, you can compare consecutive elements in a string until you find a match or until consecutive elements do not match.

To compare two strings to see if they are equal or not equal, you must compare corresponding elements in a string until they don't match. Consider the following strings:

```
"String1"
"String1"
```

The only way to determine that these two strings are equal is to compare each character in the first string to the corresponding character in the second. After all, the second string could have been "String2," which definitely is not equal to "String1." Of course, once you encounter a character in the destination string which does not equal the corresponding character in the source string, the comparison can stop. You needn't compare any other characters in the two strings.

The repe prefix accomplishes this operation. It will compare successive elements in a string as long as they are equal and ECX is greater than zero. We could compare the two strings above using the following 80x86 assembly language code:

```
cld();
mov( AdrsString1, esi );
mov( AdrsString2, edi );
mov( 7, ecx );
repe.cmpsb();
```

After the execution of the cmpsb instruction, you can test the flags using the standard (unsigned) conditional jump instructions. This lets you check for equality, inequality, less than, greater than, and so on.

Character strings are usually compared using *lexicographical ordering*. In lexicographical ordering, the least significant element of a string carries the most weight. This is in direct contrast to standard integer comparisons where the most significant portion of the number carries the most weight. Furthermore, the length of a string affects the comparison only if the two strings are identical up to the length of the shorter string. For example, "Zebra" is less than "Zebras," because it is the shorter of the two strings; however, "Zebra" is greater than "AAAAAAAAAH!" even though it is shorter. Lexicographical comparisons compare corresponding elements until encountering a character, that doesn't match or until encountering the end of the shorter string. If a pair of corresponding characters do not match, then this algorithm compares the two strings based on that single character. If the two strings match up to the length of the shorter string, we must compare their length. The two strings are equal if and only if their lengths are equal and each corresponding pair of characters in the two strings is identical. Lexicographical ordering is the standard alphabetical ordering you've grown up with.

For character strings, use the cmps instruction in the following manner:

- The direction flag must be cleared before comparing the strings.

- Use the cmpsb instruction to compare the strings on a byte-by-byte basis. Even if the strings contain an even number of characters, you cannot use the cmpsw or cmpsd instructions. They do not compare strings in lexicographical order.

- You must load the ECX register with the length of the smaller string.

- Use the repe prefix.
- The ESI and EDI registers must point at the very first character in the two strings you want to compare.

After the execution of the cmps instruction, if the two strings were equal, their lengths must be compared in order to finish the comparison. The following code compares a couple of character strings:

```
mov( AdrsStr1, esi );
mov( AdrsStr2, edi );
mov( LengthSrc, ecx );
if( ecx > LengthDest ) then   // Put the length of the shorter string in ECX.

    mov( LengthDest, ecx );

endif;
repe.cmpsb();
if( @z ) then   // If equal to the length of the shorter string, cmp lengths.

    mov( LengthSrc, ecx );
    cmp( ecx, LengthDest );

endif;
```

If you're using bytes to hold the string lengths, you should adjust this code appropriately (i.e., use a movzx instruction to load the lengths into ECX). Of course, HLA strings use a double word to hold the current length value, so this isn't an issue when using HLA strings.

You can also use the cmps instruction to compare multiword integer values (that is, extended precision integer values). Because of the amount of setup required for a string comparison, this isn't practical for integer values less than six or eight double words in length, but for large integer values, it's an excellent way to compare such values. Unlike character strings, we cannot compare integer strings using a lexicographical ordering. When comparing strings, we compare the characters from the least significant byte to the most significant byte. When comparing integers, we must compare the values from the most significant byte (or word/double word) down to the least significant byte, word, or double word. So, to compare two 32-byte (256-bit) integer values, use the following code on the 80x86:

```
std();
lea( esi, SourceInteger[28] );
lea( edi, DestInteger[28] );
mov( 8, ecx );
rep.cmpsd();
```

This code compares the integers from their most significant word down to the least significant word. The cmpsd instruction finishes when the two values are unequal or upon decrementing ECX to zero (implying that the two values are equal). Once again, the flags provide the result of the comparison.

The repne prefix will instruct the cmps instruction to compare successive string elements as long as they do not match. The 80x86 flags are of little use after the execution of this instruction. Either the ECX register is zero (in which case the two strings are totally different), or it contains the number of elements compared in the two strings until a match. While this form of the cmps instruction isn't particularly useful for comparing strings, it is useful for locating the first pair of matching items in a couple of byte, word, or double word arrays. In general, though, you'll rarely use the repne prefix with cmps.

One last thing to keep in mind with using the cmps instruction: The value in the ECX register determines the number of elements to process, not the number of bytes. Therefore, when using cmpsw, ECX specifies the number of words to compare. This, of course, is twice the number of bytes to compare. Likewise, for cmpsd, ECX contains the number of double words to process.

12.2.6 The SCAS Instruction

The cmps instruction compares two strings against one another. You do not use it to search for a particular element within a string. For example, you could not use the cmps instruction to quickly scan for a zero throughout some other string. You can use the scas (scan string) instruction for this task.

Unlike the movs and cmps instructions, the scas instruction only requires a destination string (pointed at by EDI) rather than both a source and destination string. The source operand is the value in the AL (scasb), AX (scasw), or EAX (scasd) register. The scas instruction compares the value in the accumulator (AL, AX, or EAX) against the value pointed at by EDI and then increments (or decrements) EDI by one, two, or four. The CPU sets the flags according to the result of the comparison. While this might be useful on occasion, scas is a lot more useful when using the repe and repne prefixes.

With the repe prefix (repeat while equal), scas scans the string searching for an element, which does not match the value in the accumulator. When using the repne prefix (repeat while not equal), scas scans the string searching for the first string element which is equal to the value in the accumulator.

You're probably wondering, "Why do these prefixes do exactly the opposite of what they ought to do?" The preceding paragraphs haven't quite phrased the operation of the scas instruction properly. When using the repe prefix with SCAS, the 80x86 scans through the string while the value in the accumulator is equal to the string operand. This is equivalent to searching through the string for the first element, which does not match the value in the accumulator. The scas instruction with repne scans through the string while the accumulator is not equal to the string operand. Of course, this form searches for the first value in the string, which matches the value in the accumulator register. The scas instructions take the following forms:

```
scasb()
scasw()
scasd()

repe.scasb()
repe.scasw()
repe.scasd()

repne.scasb()
repne.scasw()
repne.scasd()
```

Like the cmps and movs instructions, the value in the ECX register specifies the number of elements to process, not bytes, when using a repeat prefix.

12.2.7   The STOS Instruction

The stos instruction stores the value in the accumulator at the location specified by EDI. After storing the value, the CPU increments or decrements EDI depending upon the state of the direction flag. Although the stos instruction has many uses, its primary use is to initialize arrays and strings to a constant value. For example, if you have a 256-byte array you want to clear out with zeros, use the following code:

```
cld();
lea( edi, DestArray );
mov( 64, ecx );      // 64 double words = 256 bytes.
xor( eax, eax );     // Zero out EAX.
rep.stosd();
```

This code writes 64 double words rather than 256 bytes because a single stosd operation is faster than four stosb operations.

The stos instructions take four forms. They are

```
stosb();
stosw();
stosd();

rep.stosb();
rep.stosw();
rep.stosd();
```

The stosb instruction stores the value in the AL register into the specified memory location(s), the stosw instruction stores the AX register into the specified memory location(s), and the stosd instruction stores EAX into the specified location(s).

Keep in mind that the stos instruction is useful only for initializing a byte, word, or double word array to a constant value. If you need to initialize an array with elements that have different values, you cannot use the stos instruction.

12.2.8 The LODS Instruction

The lods instruction is unique among the string instructions. You will probably never use a repeat prefix with this instruction. The lods instruction copies the byte, word, or double word pointed at by ESI into the AL, AX, or EAX register, after which it increments or decrements the ESI register by one, two, or four. Repeating this instruction via the repeat prefix would serve no purpose whatsoever because the accumulator register will be overwritten each time the lods instruction repeats. At the end of the repeat operation, the accumulator will contain the last value read from memory.

Instead, use the lods instruction to fetch bytes (lodsb), words (lodsw), or double words (lodsd) from memory for further processing. By using the stos instruction, you can synthesize powerful string operations.

Like the stos instruction, the lods instructions take four forms:

```
lodsb();
lodsw();
lodsd();

rep.lodsb();
rep.lodsw();
rep.lodsd();
```

As mentioned earlier, you'll rarely, if ever, use the rep prefixes with these instructions.[4] The 80x86 increments or decrements ESI by one, two, or four depending on the direction flag and whether you're using the lodsb, lodsw, or lodsd instruction.

12.2.9 Building Complex String Functions from LODS and STOS

The 80x86 supports only five different string instructions: movs, cmps, scas, lods, and stos.[5] These certainly aren't the only string operations you'll ever want to use. However, you can use the lods and stos instructions to easily generate any particular string operation you like. For example, suppose you wanted a string operation that converts all the upper case characters in a string to lower case. You could use the following code:

---

[4] They appear here simply because they are allowed. They're not very useful, but they are allowed. About the only use for this form of the instruction is to "touch" items in the cache so they are preloaded into the cache. However, there are better ways to accomplish this.

[5] Not counting INS and OUTS, which we're ignoring here.

```
mov( StringAddress, esi );  // Load string address into ESI.
mov( esi, edi );            // Also point EDI here.
mov( (type str.strrec [esi].length, ecx );

repeat

    lodsb();                // Get the next character in the string.
    if( al in 'A'..'Z' ) then

        or( $20, al );  // Convert upper case character to lower case.

    endif;
    stosb();                // Store converted character back into string.
    dec( ecx );

until( @z );                // Zero flag is set when ECX decrements to zero.
```

Because the lods and stos instructions use the accumulator as an intermediary, you can use any accumulator operation to quickly manipulate string elements.

12.3 Performance of the 80x86 String Instructions

In the early 80x86 processors, the string instructions provided the most efficient way to manipulate strings and blocks of data. However, these instructions are not part of Intel's "RISC Core" instruction set and, as such, they can be slower than doing the same operations using discrete instructions. Intel has optimized the movs instruction on later processors so that it operates about as rapidly as possible, but the other string instructions can be fairly slow. As always, it's a good idea to implement performance-critical algorithms using different algorithms (with and without the string instructions) and compare their performance to determine which solution to use.

Keep in mind that the string instructions run at different speeds relative to other instructions depending on which processor you're using. So the fact that you "prove" one way is faster than another on a given processor really doesn't prove much. The reverse could be true on a different processor. Therefore, it's a good idea to try your experiments on the processors where you expect your code to run. Note that on most processors, the movs instruction is faster than the corresponding discrete instructions. Intel has worked hard to keep movs optimized because so much performance-critical code uses it.

Although the string instructions can be slower than discrete instructions, there is no question that the string instructions are generally more compact than the discrete code that achieves the same result.

12.4 For More Information

The HLA Standard Library contains dozens of string and pattern matching functions you may find useful. All of this appears in source form on the CD-ROM accompanying this text; you should check out some of that source code if you want to see some examples of string instructions in action. Note also that some of the HLA Standard Library routines use discrete instructions to implement certain high-performance algorithms. You may want to look at that code as an example of such code. The 16-bit edition of this book (that appears on the CD-ROM) discusses the implementation of several character-string functions using the 80x86 string instructions. Check out that edition for additional examples (those examples do not appear here because of the performance problems with the string instructions). Finally, for general information about string functions, check out the HLA Standard Library Reference Manual. It explains the operation of the string and pattern matching functions found in the HLA Standard Library.

13

THE MMX INSTRUCTION SET

13.1 Chapter Overview

While working on the Pentium and Pentium Pro processors, Intel was also developing an instruction set architecture extension for multimedia applications. By studying several existing multimedia applications, by developing lots of multimedia related algorithms, and through simulation, Intel developed 57 instructions that would greatly accelerate the execution of multimedia applications. The end result was the multimedia extensions to the Pentium processor that Intel calls the MMX Technology Instructions.

Prior to the invention of the MMX enhancements, good-quality multimedia systems required separate digital signal processors and special electronics to handle much of the multimedia workload.[1] The introduction of the MMX instruction set allowed later Pentium processors to handle these multimedia tasks without these expensive digital signal processors (DSPs), thus lowering the cost of multimedia systems. So later Pentium, Pentium II, Pentium III, and Pentium IV processors all have the MMX instruction set. Earlier Pentiums (and CPUs prior to the Pentium)

---

[1] A good example was the Apple Quadra 660AV and 840AV computer systems; they were built around the Motorola 68040 processor rather than a Pentium, but the 68040 was no more capable of handling multimedia applications than the Pentium. However, an on-board DSP (digital signal processor) CPU allowed the Quadras to easily handle audio applications that the 68040 could not.

and the Pentium Pro do not have these instructions available. Because the instruction set has been available for quite some time, you can probably use the MMX instructions without worrying about your software failing on many machines.

In this chapter we will discuss the MMX Technology Instructions and how to use them in your assembly language programs. The use of MMX instructions, while not completely limited to assembly language, is one area where assembly language truly shines because most high level languages do not make good use of MMX instructions except in library routines. Therefore, writing fast code that uses MMX instructions is mainly the domain of the assembly language programmer. Hence, it's a good idea to learn these instructions if you're going to write much assembly code.

13.2   Determining Whether a CPU Supports the MMX Instruction Set

While it's almost a given that any modern CPU your software will run on will support the MMX extended instruction set, there may be times when you want to write software that will run on a machine even in the absence of MMX instructions. There are two ways to handle this problem: Either provide two versions of the program, one with MMX support and one without (and let the user choose which program they wish to run), or have the program dynamically determine whether a processor supports the MMX instruction set and skip the MMX instructions if they are not available.

The first situation, providing two different programs, is the easiest solution from a software development point of view. You don't actually create two source files, of course; what you do is use conditional compilation statements (i.e., #if..#else..#endif) to selectively compile MMX or standard instructions depending on the presence of an identifier or value of a boolean constant in your program. See the chapter about macros for more details.

Another solution is to dynamically determine the CPU type at runtime and use program logic to skip over the MMX instructions and execute equivalent standard code if the CPU doesn't support the MMX instruction set. If you're expecting the software to run on an Intel Pentium or later CPU, you can use the cpuid instruction to determine whether the processor supports the MMX instruction set. If MMX instructions are available, the cpuid instruction will return bit 23 as a one in the feature flags return result.

The following code illustrates how to use the cpuid instruction. This example does not demonstrate the entire cpuid sequence, but shows the portion used for detection of MMX technology:

```
// For a perfectly general routine, you should determine if this
// is a Pentium or later processor.  We'll assume at least a Pentium
// for now, since most OSes expect a Pentium or better processor.

        mov( 1, eax );          // Request for CPUID feature flags.
        CPUID();                // Get the feature flags into EDX.
        test( $80_0000, edx );  // Is bit 23 set?
        jnz HasMMX;
```

This code assumes at least the presence of a Pentium Processor. If your code
needs to run on a 486 or 386 processor, you will have to detect that the system is
using one of these processors. There is tons of code on the Internet that detects
different processors, but most of it will not run under 32-bit OSes because the
code typically uses protected (non–user-mode) instructions. Some operating
systems provide a system call or environment variable that will specify the CPU.
We'll not go into the details here because 99% of the users out there that are
running modern operating systems have a CPU that supports the MMX
instruction set or, at least, the cpuid instruction.

13.3   The MMX Programming Environment

The MMX architecture extends the Pentium architecture by adding the
following:

- Eight MMX registers (MM0..MM7)
- Four MMX data types (packed bytes, packed words, packed double words,
  and quad words)
- 57 MMX instructions

13.3.1   The MMX Registers

The MMX architecture adds eight 64-bit registers to the Pentium. The MMX
instructions refer to these registers as MM0, MM1, MM2, MM3, MM4, MM5,
MM6, and MM7. These are strictly data registers; you cannot use them to hold
addresses nor are they suitable for calculations involving addresses.

Although MM0..MM7 appear as separate registers in the Intel architecture,
the Pentium processors alias these registers with the FPU's registers (ST0..ST7).
Each of the eight MMX 64-bit registers is physically equivalent to the L.O. 64 bits
of each of the FPU's registers (see Figure 13-1). The MMX registers overlay the
FPU registers in much the same way that the 16-bit general purpose registers
overlay the 32-bit general purpose registers.

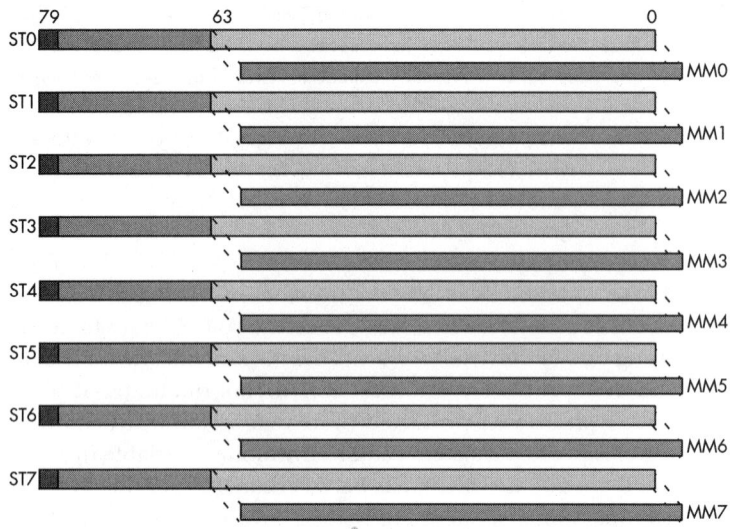

Figure 13-1: MMX and FPU Register Aliasing.

Because the MMX registers overlay the FPU registers, you cannot mix FPU and MMX instructions in the same computation sequence. You can begin executing an MMX instruction sequence at any time; however, once you execute an MMX instruction you cannot execute another FPU instruction until you execute a special MMX instruction, emms (Exit MMX Machine State). This instruction resets the FPU so you may begin a new sequence of FPU calculations. The CPU does not save the FPU state across the execution of the MMX instructions; executing emms clears all the FPU registers. Because saving the FPU state is very expensive, and the emms instruction is quite slow, it's not a good idea to frequently switch between MMX and FPU calculations. Instead, you should attempt to execute the MMX and FPU instructions at different times during your program's execution.

You're probably wondering why Intel chose to alias the MMX registers with the FPU registers. Intel, in its literature, brags constantly about what a great idea this was. You see, by aliasing the MMX registers with the FPU registers, Microsoft and other multitasking OS vendors did not have to write special code to save the MMX state when the CPU switched from one process to another. The fact that the OS automatically saved the FPU state means that the CPU would automatically save the MMX state as well. This meant that the new Pentium chips with MMX technology that Intel created were automatically compatible with Windows 95, Windows NT, and Linux without any changes to the operating system code.

Of course, those operating systems have long since been upgraded and Microsoft (and Linux developers) could have easily provided a "service pack" to handle the new registers (had Intel chosen not to alias the FPU and MMX registers). So while aliasing MMX with the FPU provided a very short-lived and temporary benefit, in retrospect Intel made a big mistake with this decision. It has obviously realized its mistake, because as it has introduced new "streaming" instructions (the floating point equivalent of the MMX instruction set), it has added new registers (XMM0..XMM7). It's too bad it doesn't fix the problem in its current CPUs (there is no technical reason why it can't create separate MMX and FPU registers at this point). Oh well, you'll just have to live with the fact that you can't execute interleaved FPU and MMX instructions.

13.3.2 The MMX Data Types

The MMX instruction set supports four different data types: an eight-byte array, a four-word array, a two-element double word array, and a quad word object. Each MMX register processes one of these four data types (see Figure 13-2).

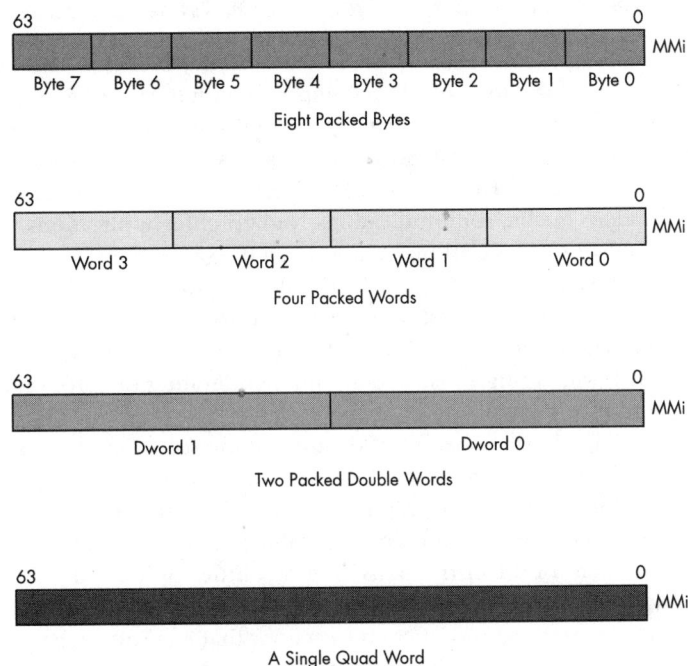

Figure 13-2: The MMX Data Types.

Despite the presence of 64-bit registers, the MMX instruction set does not extend the 32-bit Pentium processor to 64 bits. Instead, after careful study Intel added only those 64-bit instructions that were useful for multimedia operations. For example, you cannot add or subtract two 64-bit integers with the MMX instruction set. In fact, only the logical and shift operations directly manipulate 64 bits.

The MMX instruction set was not designed to provide general 64-bit capabilities to the Pentium. Instead, the MMX instruction set provides the Pentium with the capability of performing multiple 8-, 16-, or 32-bit operations simultaneously. In other words, the MMX instructions are generally SIMD (Single Instruction Multiple Data) instructions (see the electronic version of *The Art of Assembly Language* on the accompanying CD-ROM for details about SIMD architectures). For example, a single MMX instruction can add eight separate pairs of byte values together. This is not the same as adding two 64-bit values because the overflow from the individual bytes does not carry over into the higher order bytes. This can accelerate a program that needs to add a long string of bytes together because a single MMX instruction can do the work of eight regular Pentium instructions. This is how the MMX instruction set speeds up multimedia applications — by processing multiple data objects in parallel with a single instruction. Given the data types the MMX instruction set supports, you can process up to eight byte objects in parallel, four word objects in parallel, or two double words in parallel so the CPU should be capable of executing code up to eight times faster than without the MMX extensions.

13.4   The Purpose of the MMX Instruction Set

The Single Instruction Multiple Data (SIMD) model the MMX architecture supports may not look all that impressive when viewed with a SISD (Single Instruction Single Data) bias. Once you've mastered the basic integer instructions on the 80x86, it's difficult to see the application of the MMX's SIMD instruction set. However, the MMX instructions directly address the needs of modern media, communications, and graphics applications, which often use sophisticated algorithms that perform the same operations on a large number of small data types (bytes, words, and double words).

For example, most programs use a stream of bytes or words to represent audio and video data. The MMX instructions can operate on eight bytes or four words with a single instruction, thus accelerating the program by almost a factor of four or eight.

One drawback to the MMX instruction set is that it is not general purpose. Intel's research that led to the development of these new instructions specifically targeted audio, video, graphics, and another multimedia applications. Although some of the instructions are applicable in many general programs, you'll find that many of the instructions have very little application outside their limited domain. Although, with a lot of deep thought, you can probably dream up some novel uses of many of these instructions that have nothing whatsoever at all to do with multimedia, you shouldn't get too frustrated if you cannot figure out why you would want to use a particular instruction; that instruction probably has a specific purpose and if you're not trying to code a solution for that problem, you may not be able to use the instruction. If you're questioning why Intel would put such limited instructions in their instruction set, just keep in mind that although you can use the instruction(s) for lots of different purposes, they are invaluable for the few purposes they are uniquely suited.

13.5   Saturation Arithmetic and Wrap-Around Mode

The MMX instruction set supports saturating arithmetic (see Chapter 2 for details). When manipulating standard integer values and an overflow occurs, the standard integer instructions maintain the correct L.O. bits of the value in the integer while truncating any overflow.[2] This form of arithmetic is known as *wraparound* mode because the L.O. bits wrap back around to zero. For example,

---

[2] Typically you would merge in a fourth byte of zero and then store the resulting double word every three bytes in memory to overwrite the zeros.

if you add the two 8-bit values $02 and $FF you wind up with a carry and the result $01. The actual sum is $101, but the operation truncates the ninth bit and the L.O. byte wraps around to $01.

In saturation mode, results of an operation that overflow or underflow are clipped (saturated) to some maximum or minimum value depending on the size of the object and whether it is signed or unsigned. The result of an operation that exceeds the range of a data type saturates to the maximum value of the range. A result that is less than the range of a data type saturates to the minimum value of the range.

For example, as you can see in Table 13-1, when the result exceeds the data range limit for signed bytes, it is saturated to $7f; if a value is less than the data range limit, it is saturated to $80 for signed bytes. If a value exceeds the range for unsigned bytes, it is saturated to $ff or $00.

Table 13-1: Ranges for Decimal and Hexidecimal Values

Data Type	Decimal		Hexadecimal	
	Lower Limit	Upper Limit	Lower Limit	Upper Limit
Signed Byte	-128	+127	$80	$7f
Unsigned Byte	0	255	$00	$ff
Signed Word	-32768	+32767	$8000	$7fff
Unsigned Word	0	65535	0	$ffff

This saturation effect is very useful for audio and video data. For example, if you are amplifying an audio signal by multiplying the words in the CD-quality 44.1 kHz audio stream by 1.5, then clipping the value at +32767 (while introducing distortion) sounds far better than allowing the waveform to wrap around to -32768. Similarly, if you are mixing colors in a 24-bit graphic or video image, saturating to white produces much more meaningful results than wraparound.

Because Intel created the MMX architecture to support audio, graphics, and video, it should come as no surprise that the MMX instruction set supports saturating arithmetic. For those applications that require saturating arithmetic, having the CPU automatically handle this process (rather than having to explicitly check after each calculation) is another way the MMX architecture speeds up multimedia applications.

13.6   MMX Instruction Operands

Most MMX instructions operate on two operands, a source and a destination operand. A few instructions have three operands with the third operand being a small immediate (constant) value. In this section we'll take a look at the common MMX instruction operands.

The destination operand is almost always an MMX register. In fact, the only exceptions are those instructions that store an MMX register into memory. The MMX instructions always leave the result of MMX calculations in an MMX register.

The source operand can be an MMX register or a memory location. The memory location is usually a quad word entity, but certain instructions operate on double word objects. Note that, in this context, "quad word" and "double word" mean eight or four consecutive bytes in memory; they do not necessarily imply that the MMX instruction is operating on a qword or dword object. For example, if you add eight bytes together using the paddb (packed add bytes) instruction, paddb references a qword object in memory, but actually adds together eight separate bytes.

For most MMX instructions, the generic HLA syntax is the following:

```
    mmxInstr( source, dest );
```

The specific forms are

```
    mmxInstr( mmi, mmi );    // i=0..7
    mmxInstr( mem, mmi );    // i=0..7
```

MMX instructions access memory using the same addressing modes as the standard integer instructions. Therefore, any legal 80x86 addressing mode is usable in an MMX instruction. For those instructions that reference a 64-bit memory location, HLA requires that you specify an anonymous memory object (e.g., "[ebx]" or "[ebp+esi*8+6]") as a qword variable.

A few instructions require a small immediate value (or constant). For example, the shift instructions let you specify a shift count as an immediate value in the range 0..63. Another instruction uses the immediate value to specify a set of four different count values in the range 0..3 (i.e., four 2-bit count values). These instructions generally take the following form:

```
    mmxInstr( imm₈, source, dest );
```

Note that, in general, MMX instructions do not allow you to specify immediate constants as operands except for a few special cases (such as shift counts). In particular, the source operand to an MMX instruction has to be a register or a quad word variable; it cannot be a 64-bit constant. To achieve the same effect as specifying a constant as the source operand, you must initialize a quad word variable in the readonly (or static) section of your program and specify this variable as the source operand.

Although HLA allows you to declare initialized 64-bit variables using the uns64, int64, and qword types, you'll discover that very few MMX instructions actually operate on 64-bit data operands; instead, they typically operate on an array of bytes, words, or double words. Because HLA provides good support for byte, word, and double word constant expressions, specifying a 64-bit MMX memory operand as a short array of objects is probably the best way to create this data. However, the MMX instructions that fetch a source value from memory expect a 64-bit operand. Therefore, you must declare such objects as qword variables. You can easily declare the objects as quad words and initialize them with bytes, words, and double words using the @nostorage attribute, e.g.,

```
static
    mmxDVar: qword; @nostorage;
        dword $1234_5678, $90ab_cdef;
```

Note that the dword directive above stores the double word constants in successive memory locations. Therefore, $1234_5678 will appear in the L.O. double word of the 64-bit value and $90ab_cdef will appear in the H.O. double word of the 64-bit value. Always keep in mind that the L.O. objects come first in the list following the dword (or byte, or word, or ???) directive; this is opposite of the way you're used to reading 64-bit values.

The example above used a dword directive to provide the initialization constant. However, you can use any data declaration directive, or even a combination of directives, as long as you allocate at least eight bytes (64-bits) for each qword constant. The following data declaration, for example, initializes eight 8-bit constants for an MMX operand; this would be perfect for a paddb instruction or some other instruction that operates on eight bytes in parallel:

```
static
    eightBytes: qword; @nostorage;
        byte 0, 1, 2, 3, 4, 5, 6, 7;
```

Although most MMX instructions operate on small arrays of bytes, words, or double words, a few actually do operate on 64-bit quantities. For such memory operands you would probably prefer to specify a 64-bit constant rather than break it up into its constituent double word values. This way, you don't have to remember to put the L.O. double word first and perform other mental adjustments. Of course, HLA fully supports 64-bit (and even 128-bit) numeric constants as initializers, so this is a trivial issue in HLA. Example:

```
static
    anotherEightBytes: qword := $1234_5678_9abc_def0;
```

13.7   MMX Technology Instructions

The following subsections describe each of the MMX instructions in detail. The organization is as follows:

- Data Transfer Instructions
- Conversion Instructions
- Packed Arithmetic Instructions
- Logical Instructions
- Comparison Instructions
- Shift and Rotate Instructions
- EMMS Instruction

These sections describe *what* these instructions do, not *how* you would use them. Later sections will provide examples of how you can use several of these instructions.

13.7.1 MMX Data Transfer Instructions

```
movd( reg32, mmi );
movd( mem32, mmi );
movd( mmi, reg32 );
movd( mmi, mem32 );


movq( mem64, mmi );
movq( mmi, mem64 );
movq( mmi, mmi );
```

The movd (move double word) instruction copies data between a 32-bit integer register or double word memory location and an MMX register. If the destination is an MMX register, this instruction zero extends the value while moving it. If the destination is a 32-bit register or memory location, this instruction copies the L.O. 32 bits of the MMX register to the destination.

The movq (move quad word) instruction copies data between two MMX registers or between an MMX register and memory. If either the source or destination operand is a memory object, it must be a qword variable or HLA will complain.

13.7.2 MMX Conversion Instructions

```
packssdw( mem64, mmi );        // i=0..7
packssdw( mmi, mmi );


packsswb( mem64, mmi );
packsswb( mmi, mmi );


packusdw( mem64, mmi );
packusdw( mmi, mmi );


packuswb( mem64, mmi );
packuswb( mmi, mmi );


punpckhbw( mem64, mmi );
punpckhbw( mmi, mmi );


punpckhdq( mem64, mmi );
punpckhdq( mmi, mmi );


punpckhwd( mem64, mmi );
punpckhwd( mmi, mmi );
```

```
punpcklbw( mem64, mmi );
punpcklbw( mmi, mmi );

punpckldq( mem64, mmi );
punpckldq( mmi, mmi );

punpcklwd( mem64, mmi );
punpcklwd( mmi, mmi );
```

The packssxx instructions pack and saturate signed values. They convert a sequence of larger values to a sequence of smaller values via saturation. Those instructions with the *dw* suffix pack four double words into four words; those with the *wb* suffix saturate and pack eight signed words into eight signed bytes.

The packssdw instruction takes the two double words in the source operand and the two double words in the destination operand and converts these to four signed words via saturation. The instruction packs these four words together and stores the result in the destination MMX register. See Figure 13-3 for details.

The packsswb instruction takes the four words from the source operand and the four signed words from the destination operand and converts, via signed saturation, these values to eight signed bytes. This instruction leaves the eight bytes in the destination MMX register. See Figure 13-4 on the next page for details.

One application for these pack instructions is to convert UNICODE to ASCII (ANSI). You can convert UNICODE (16-bit) character to ANSI (8-bit) character if the H.O. 8 bits of each UNICODE character is zero. The packuswb instruction will take eight UNICODE characters and pack them into a string that is eight bytes long with a single instruction. If the H.O. byte of any UNICODE character contains a non-zero value, then the packuswb instruction will store $FF in the respective byte; therefore, you can use $FF as a conversion error indication.

Another use for the packsswb instruction is to translate a 16-bit audio stream to an 8-bit stream. Assuming you've scaled your 16-bit values to produce a sequence of values in the range -128..+127, you can use the packsswb instruction to convert that sequence of 16-bit values into a packed sequence of 8-bit values.

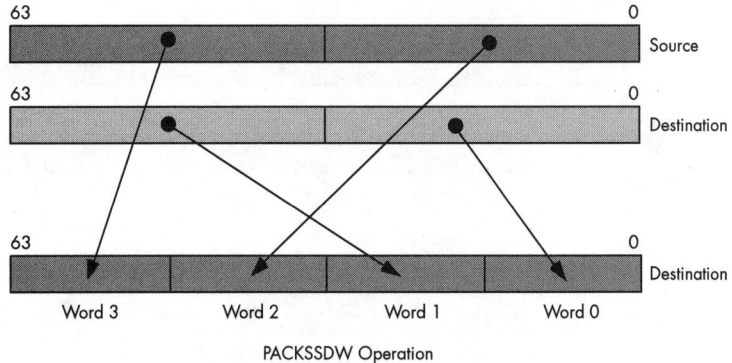

PACKSSDW Operation

Figure 13-3: PACKSSDW Instruction.

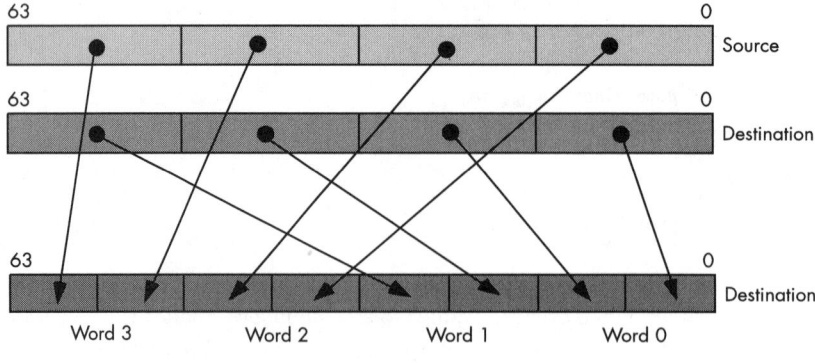

PACKSSWB Operation

Figure 13-4: PACKSSWB Instruction.

The unpack instructions (punpckxxx) provide the converse operation to the pack instructions. The unpack instructions take a sequence of smaller, packed values and translate them into larger values. There is one problem with this conversion, however. Unlike the pack instructions, where it took two 64-bit operands to generate a single 64-bit result, the unpack operations will produce a 64-bit result from a single 32-bit result. Therefore, these instructions cannot operate directly on full 64-bit source operands. To overcome this limitation, there are two sets of unpack instructions: One set unpacks the data from the L.O. double word of a 64-bit object, the other set of instructions unpacks the H.O. double word of a 64-bit object. By executing one instruction from each set you can unpack a 64-bit object into a 128-bit object.

The punpcklbw, punpcklwd, and punpckldq instructions merge (unpack) the L.O. double words of their source and destination operands and store the 64-bit result into their destination operand.

The punpcklbw instruction unpacks and interleaves the low-order four bytes of the source (first) and destination (second) operands. It places the L.O. four bytes of the destination operand at the even byte positions in the destination, and it places the L.O. four bytes of the source operand in the odd byte positions of the destination operand (see Figure 13-5).

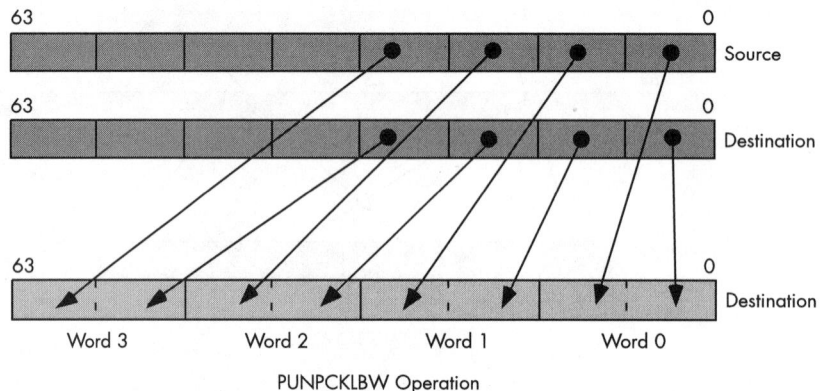

PUNPCKLBW Operation

Figure 13-5: PUNPCKLBW Instruction.

The `punpcklwd` instruction unpacks and interleaves the low-order two words of the source (first) and destination (second) operands. It places the L.O. two words of the destination operand at the even word positions in the destination, and it places the L.O. words of the source operand in the odd word positions of the destination operand (see Figure 13-6).

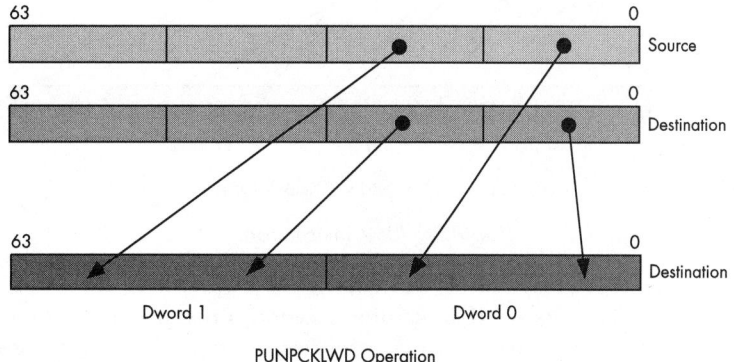

PUNPCKLWD Operation

Figure 13-6: PUNPCKLWD Instruction.

The `punpckdq` instruction copies the L.O. dword of the source operand to the L.O. dword of the destination operand, and it copies the (original) L.O. dword of the destination operand to the L.O. dword of the destination (i.e., it doesn't change the L.O. dword of the destination, as shown in Figure 13-7).

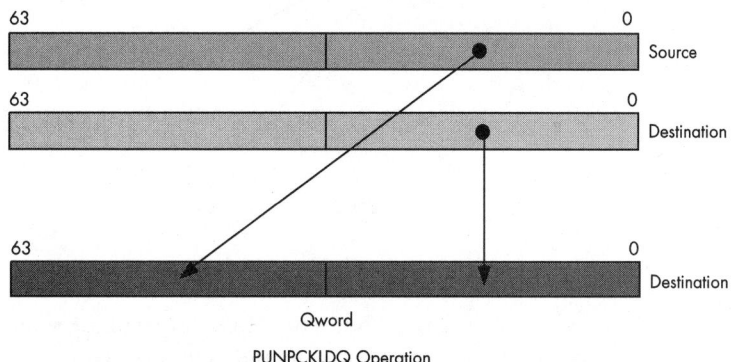

PUNPCKLDQ Operation

Figure 13-7: PUNPCKLDQ Instruction.

The `punpckhbw` instruction is quite similar to the `punpcklbw` instruction. The difference is that it unpacks and interleaves the high order four bytes of the source (first) and destination (second) operands. It places the H.O. four bytes of the destination operand at the even byte positions in the destination, and it places the H.O. four bytes of the source operand in the odd byte positions of the destination operand (see Figure 13-8 on the following page).

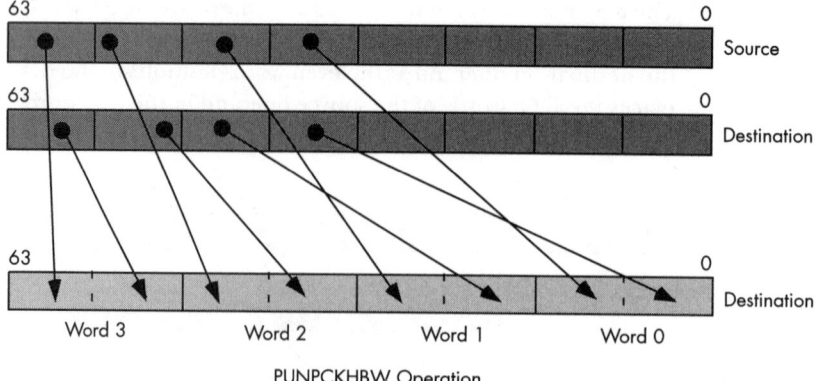

PUNPCKHBW Operation

Figure 13-8: PUNPCKHBW Instruction.

The punpckhwd instruction unpacks and interleaves the low-order two words of the source (first) and destination (second) operands. It places the L.O. two words of the destination operand at the even word positions in the destination, and it places the L.O. words of the source operand in the odd word positions of the destination operand (see Figure 13-9).

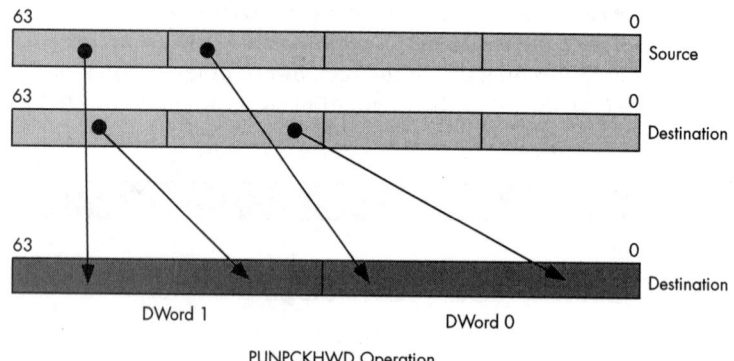

PUNPCKHWD Operation

Figure 13-9: PUNPCKHWD Instruction.

The punpckhdq instruction copies the H.O. dword of the source operand to the H.O. dword of the destination operand, and it copies the (original) H.O. dword of the destination operand to the L.O. dword of the destination (see Figure 13-10).

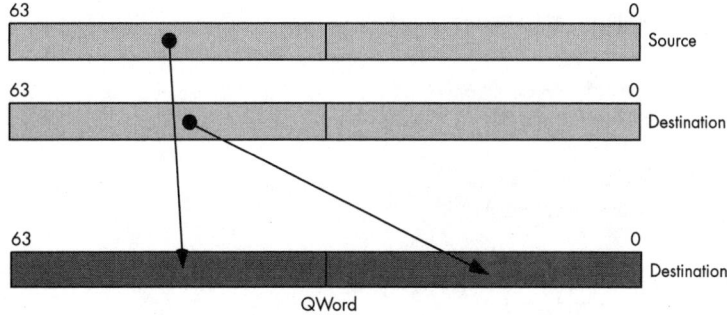

QWord

PUNPCKHDQ Operation

Figure 13-10: PUNPCKDQ Instruction.

Because the unpack instructions provide the converse operation of the pack instructions, it should come as no surprise that you can use these instructions to perform the inverse algorithms of the examples given earlier for the pack instructions. For example, if you have a string of 8-bit ANSI characters, you can convert them to their UNICODE equivalents by setting one MMX register (the source) to all zeros. You can convert each four characters of the ANSI string to UNICODE by loading those four characters into the L.O. double word of an MMX register and executing the punpcklbw instruction. This will interleave each of the characters with a zero byte, thus converting them from ANSI to UNICODE.

Of course, the unpack instructions are quite valuable any time you need to interleave data. For example, if you have three separate images containing the blue, red, and green components of a 24-bit image, it is possible to merge these three bytes together using the punpcklbw instruction.[3]

13.7.3 MMX Packed Arithmetic Instructions

```
paddb( mem64, mmi );        // i=0..7
paddb( mmi, mmi );

paddw( mem64, mmi );
paddw( mmi, mmi );

paddd( mem64, mmi );
paddd( mmi, mmi );

paddsb( mem64, mmi );
paddsb( mmi, mmi );

paddsw( mem64, mmi );
paddsw( mmi, mmi );
```

---

[3] Actually, the code could be rewritten easily enough to use only one MMX register.

```
paddusb( mem_64, mmi );
paddusb( mmi, mmi );

paddusw( mem_64, mmi );
paddusw( mmi, mmi );

psubb( mem_64, mmi );
psubb( mmi, mmi );

psubw( mem_64, mmi );
psubw( mmi, mmi );

psubd( mem_64, mmi );
psubd( mmi, mmi );

psubsb( mem_64, mmi );
psubsb( mmi, mmi );

psubsw( mem_64, mmi );
psubsw( mmi, mmi );

psubusb( mem_64, mmi );
psubusb( mmi, mmi );

psubusw( mem_64, mmi );
psubusw( mmi, mmi );

pmulhuw( mem_64, mmi );
pmulhuw( mmi, mmi );

pmulhw( mem_64, mmi );
pmulhw( mmi, mmi );

pmullw( mem_64, mmi );
pmullw( mmi, mmi );

pmaddwd( mem_64, mmi );
pmaddwd( mmi, mmi );
```

The packed arithmetic instructions operate on a set of bytes, words, or double words within a 64-bit block. For example, the paddw instruction computes four 16-bit sums of two operands simultaneously. None of these instructions affect the CPU's FLAGs register. Therefore, there is no indication of overflow, underflow, zero result, negative result, and so on. If you need to test a result after a packed arithmetic computation, you will need to use one of the packed compare instructions.

The paddb, paddw, and paddd instructions add the individual bytes, words, or double words in the two 64-bit operands using a wrap-around (i.e., non-saturating) addition. Any carry out of a sum is lost; it is your responsibility to ensure that overflow never occurs. As for the integer instructions, these packed add instructions add the values in the source operand to the destination operand, leaving the sum in the destination operand. These instructions produce correct results for signed or unsigned operands (assuming overflow / underflow does not occur).

The paddsb and paddsw instructions add the eight 8-bit or four 16-bit operands in the source and destination locations together using signed saturation arithmetic. The paddusb and paddusw instructions add their eight 8-bit or four 16-bit operands together using unsigned saturation arithmetic. Notice that you must use different instructions for signed and unsigned values since saturation arithmetic is different depending upon whether you are manipulating signed or unsigned operands. Also note that the instruction set does not support the saturated addition of double word values.

The psubb, psubw, and psubd instructions work just like their addition counterparts, except of course, they compute the wrap-around difference rather than the sum. These instructions compute dest=dest-src. Likewise, the psubsb, psubsw, psubusb, and psubusw instruction compute the difference of the destination and source operands using saturation arithmetic.

While addition and subtraction can produce a one-bit carry or borrow, multiplication of two n-bit operands can produce as large as a $2*n$ bit result. Because overflow is far more likely in multiplication than in addition or subtraction, the MMX packed multiply instructions work a little differently than their addition and subtraction counterparts. To successfully multiply two packed values requires two instructions — one to compute the L.O. component of the result and one to produce the H.O. component of the result. The pmullw, pmulhw, and pmulhuw instructions handle this task.

The pmullw instruction multiplies the four words of the source operand by the four words of the destination operand and stores the four L.O. words of the four double word results into the destination operand. This instruction ignores the H.O. words of the results. Used by itself, this instruction computes the wrap-around product of an unsigned or signed set of operands; this is also the L.O. words of the four products.

The pmulhw and pmulhuw instructions complete the calculation started with pmullw. After computing the L.O. words of the four products with the pmullw instruction, you use either the pmulhw or pmulhuw instruction to compute the H.O. words of the products. These two instruction multiply the four words in the source by the four words in the destination and then store the H.O. words of the results in the destination MMX register. The difference between the two is that you use pmulhw for signed operands and pmulhuw for unsigned operands. If you compute the full product by using a pmullw and a pmulhw (or pmulhuw) instruction pair, then there is no overflow possible, hence you don't have to worry about wrap-around or saturation arithmetic.

The pmaddwd instruction multiplies the four words in the source operand by the four words in the destination operand to produce four double word products. Then it adds the two L.O. double words together and stores the result in the L.O. double word of the destination MMX register; it also adds together the two H.O. double words and stores their sum in the H.O. word of the destination MMX register.

13.7.4 MMX Logical Instructions

```
pand( mem64, mmi );          // i=0..7
pand( mmi, mmi );

pandn( mem64, mmi );
pandn( mmi, mmi );

por( mem64, mmi );
por( mmi, mmi );

pxor( mem64, mmi );
pxor( mmi, mmi );
```

The packed logical instructions are some examples of MMX instructions that actually operate on 64-bit values. There are not packed byte, packed word, or packed double word versions of these instructions. Of course, there is no need for special byte, word, or double word versions of these instructions because they would all be equivalent to the 64-bit logical instructions. Hence, if you want to logically AND eight bytes together in parallel, you use the pand instruction; likewise, if you want to logically AND four words or two double words together, you just use the pand instruction.

The pand, por, and pxor instructions do the same thing as their 32-bit integer instruction counterparts (and, or, xor) except, of course, they operate on two 64-bit MMX operands. Hence, no further discussion of these instructions is really necessary here. The pandn (AND NOT) instruction is a new logic instruction, so it bears a little bit of a discussion. The pandn instruction computes the following result:

```
dest := dest and (not source);
```

If you're wondering why Intel chose to include such a weird function in the MMX instruction set, well, this instruction has one very useful property: It forces bits to zero in the destination operand everywhere there is a one bit in the source operand. This is an extremely useful function for merging to 64-bit quantities together. The following code sequence demonstrates this:

```
readonly
    AlternateNibbles: qword := $F0F0_F0F0_F0F0_F0F0;  //
           .
           .
           .

// Create a 64-bit value in MM0 containing the Odd nibbles from MM1 and
// the even nibbles from MM0:

    pandn( AlternateNibbles, mm0 );   // Clear the odd-numbered nibbles.
    pand( AlternateNibbles, mm1 );    // Clear the even-numbered nibbles.
    por( mm1, mm0 );                  // Merge the two.
```

The pandn operation is also useful for computing the set difference of two character sets. You could implement the cs.difference function using only six MMX instructions:

```
// Compute csdest := csdest - cssrc;

    movq( (type qword csdest), mm0 );
    pandn( (type qword cssrc), mm0 );
    movq( mm0, (type qword csdest ));
    movq( (type qword csdest[8]), mm0 );
    pandn( (type qword cssrc[8]), mm0 );
    movq( mm0, (type qword csdest[8] ));
```

Of course, if you want to improve the performance of the HLA Standard Library character set functions, you can use the MMX logic instructions throughout that module, not just for the cs.diffference function.

13.7.5 MMX Comparison Instructions

```
pcmpeqb( mem64, mmi );        // i=0..7
pcmpeqb( mmi, mmi );


pcmpeqw( mem64, mmi );
pcmpeqw( mmi, mmi );


pcmpeqd( mem64, mmi );
pcmpeqd( mmi, mmi );


pcmpgtb( mem64, mmi );
pcmpgtb( mmi, mmi );


pcmpgtw( mem64, mmi );
pcmpgtw( mmi, mmi );
```

```
pcmpgtd( mem₆₄, mmi );
pcmpgtd( mmi, mmi );
```

The packed comparison instructions compare the destination (second) operand to the source (first) operand to test for equality or greater than. These instructions compare eight pairs of bytes (pcmpeqb, pcmpgtb), four pairs of words (pcmpeqw, pcmpgtw), or two pairs of double words (pcmpeqd, pcmpgtd).

The first big difference to notice about these packed comparison instructions is that they compare the second operand to the first operand. This is exactly opposite of the standard cmp instruction (that compares the first operand to the second operand). The reason for this will become clear in a moment. If this ordering bothers you, you can create macros to reverse the operands; we will explore this possibility a little later in this section.

The second big difference between the packed comparisons and the standard integer comparison is that these instructions test for a specific condition (equality or greater than) rather than doing a generic comparison. This is because these instructions, like the other MMX instructions, do not affect any condition code bits in the FLAGs register. This may seem contradictory; after all the whole purpose of the cmp instruction is to set the condition code bits. However, keep in mind that these instructions simultaneously compare two, four, or eight operands; that implies that you would need two, four, or eight sets of condition code bits to hold the results of the comparisons. Because the FLAGs register maintains only one set of condition code bits, it is not possible to reflect the comparison status in the FLAGs. This is why the packed comparison instructions test a specific condition — so they can return true or false to indicate the result of their comparison.

Okay, so where do these instructions return their true or false values? In the destination operand, of course. This is the third big difference between the packed comparisons and the standard integer cmp instruction: The packed comparisons modify their destination operand. Specifically, the pcmpeqb and pcmpgtb instructions compare each pair of bytes in the two operands and write false ($00) or true ($FF) to the corresponding byte in the destination operand, depending on the result of the comparison. For example, the instruction "pcmpgtb(MM1, MM0);" compares the L.O. byte of MM0 (A) with the L.O. byte of MM1 (B) and writes $00 to the L.O. byte of MM0 if A is not greater than B. It writes $FF to the L.O. byte of MM0 if A is greater than B (see Figure 13-11).

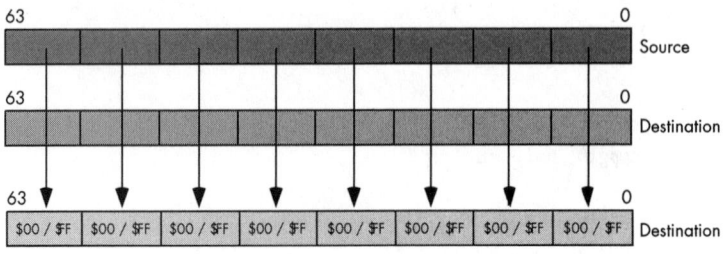

PCMPEQB/PCMPGTB Operation

Figure 13-11: PCMPEQB and PCMPGTB Instructions.

The `pcmpeqw`, `pcmpgtw`, `pcmpeqd`, and `pcmpgtd` instructions work in an analogous fashion except, of course, they compare words and double words rather than bytes (see Figures 13-12 and 13-13).

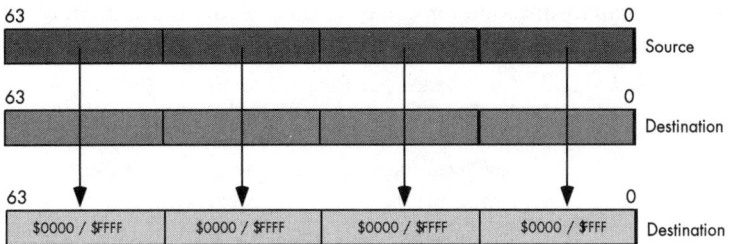

PCMPEQW/PCMPGTW Operation

Figure 13-12: PCMPEQW and PCMPGTW Instructions.

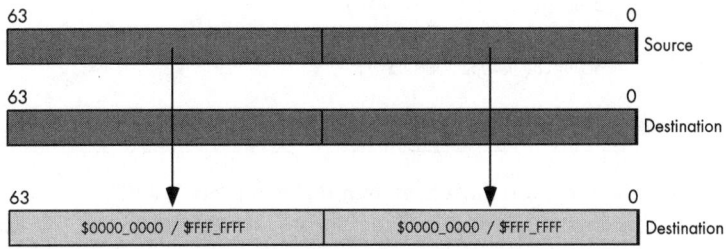

PCMPEQD/PCMPGTD Operation

Figure 13-13: PCMPEQD and PCMPGTD Instructions.

You've probably already noticed that there isn't a set of `pcmpltx` instructions. Intel chose not to provide these instructions because you can simulate them with the `pcmpgtx` instructions by reversing the operands. That is, A>B implies B<A. Therefore, if you want to do a concurrent comparison of multiple operands for less than, you can use the `pcmpgtx` instructions to do this by simply reversing the operands. The only time this isn't directly possible is if your source operand is a memory operand; because the destination operand of the packed comparison instructions has to be an MMX register, you would have to move the memory operand into an MMX register before comparing them.

In addition to the lack of a packed less than comparison, you're also missing the not equals, less than or equal, and greater than or equal comparisons. You can easily synthesize these comparisons by executing a `pxor` or `por` instruction after the packed comparison.

To simulate a `pcmpnex` instruction, all you've got to do is invert all the bits in the destination operand after executing a `pcmpeqx` instruction, e.g.,

```
pcmpeqb( mm1, mm0 );
pxor( AllOnes, mm0 );   // Assumption: AllOnes is a qword variable
                        // containing $FFFF_FFFF_FFFF_FFFF.
```

Of course, you can save the execution of the pxor instruction by testing for zeros in the destination operand rather than ones (that is, use your program's logic to invert the result rather than actually computing the inverse).

To simulate the pcmpgex and pcmplex instructions, you must do two comparisons, one for equality and one for greater than or less than, and then logically OR the results. Here's an example that computes MM0 <= MM1:

```
movq( mm1, mm2 );          // Need a copy of destination operand.
pcmpgtb( mm0, mm1 );       // Remember: A<B is equal to B>A, so we're
pcmpeqb( mm0, mm2 );       //   MM0<MM1 and MM0=MM1 here.
por( mm2, mm1 );           // Leaves boolean results in MM1.
```

If it really bothers you to have to reverse the operands, you can create macros to create your own pcmpltx instructions. The following example demonstrates how to create the pcmpltb macro:

```
#macro pcmpltb( mmOp1, mmOp2 );

    pcmpgtb( mmOp2, mmOp1 );

#endmacro
```

Of course, you must keep in mind that there are two very big differences between this pcmpltb "instruction" and a true pcmpltb instruction. First, this form leaves the result in the first operand, not the second operand; therefore, the semantics of this "instruction" are different than the other packed comparisons. Second, the first operand has to be an MMX register while the second operand can be an MMX register or a quad word variable — again, just the opposite of the other packed instructions. The fact that this instruction's operands behave differently than the pcmpgtb instruction may create some problems. So you will have to carefully consider whether you really want to use this scheme to create a pcmpltb "instruction" for use in your programs. If you decide to do this, it would help tremendously if you always comment each invocation of the macro to point out that the first operand is the destination operand, e.g.,

```
pcmpltb( mm0, mm1 );  // Computes mm0 := mm1<mm0!
```

If the fact that the packed comparison instruction's operands are reversed bothers you, you can also use macros to swap those operands. The following example demonstrates how to write such macros for the peqb (pcmpeqb), pgtb (pcmpgtb), and pltb (packed less than, byte) instructions.

```
#macro peqb( leftOp, rightOp );

    pcmpeqb( rightOp, leftOp );

#endmacro
```

```
#macro pgtb( leftOp, rightOp );

    pcmpgtb( rightOp, leftOp );

#endmacro

#macro pltb( leftOp, rightOp );

    pcmpgtb( leftOp, rightOp );

#endmacro
```

Note that these macros don't solve the pltb problem of having the wrong operand as the destination. However, these macros do compare the first operand to the second operand, just like the standard cmp instruction.

Of course, once you obtain a boolean result in an MMX register, you'll probably want to test the results at one point or another. Unfortunately, the MMX instructions only provide a couple of ways to move comparison information in and out of the MMX processor: You can store an MMX register value into memory or you can copy 32 bits of an MMX register to a general purpose integer register. Because the comparison instructions produce a 64-bit result, writing the destination of a comparison to memory is the easiest way to gain access to the comparison results in your program. Typically, you'd use an instruction sequence like the following:

```
        pcmpeqb( mm1, mm0 );            // Compare 8 bytes in mm1 to mm0.
        movq( mm0, qwordVar );          // Write comparison results to memory.
        if((type boolean qwordVar )) then

            << do this if byte #0 contained true ($FF, which is non-zero). >>

        endif;
        if((type boolean qwordVar[1])) then

            << do this if byte #1 contained true. >>

        endif;
        etc.
```

13.7.6 MMX Shift Instructions

```
psllw( mmi, mmi );       // i=0..7
psllw( imm8, mmi );

pslld( mmi, mmi );
pslld( imm8, mmi );
```

```
psllq( mmi, mmi );
psllq( imm8, mmi );

pslrw( mmi, mmi );
pslrw( imm8, mmi );

psrld( mmi, mmi );
psrld( imm8, mmi );

pslrq( mmi, mmi );
pslrq( imm8, mmi );

psraw( mmi, mmi );
psraw( imm8, mmi );

psrad( mmi, mmi );
psrad( imm8, mmi );
```

The MMX shift instructions, like the arithmetic instructions, allow you to simultaneously shift several different values in parallel. The psllx instructions perform a packed shift-left logical operation, the pslrx instructions do a packed logical shift-right operation, and the psrax instructions do a packed arithmetic shift-right operation. These instructions operate on word, double word, and quad word operands. Note that Intel does not provide a version of these instructions that operates on bytes.

The first operand to these instructions specifies a shift count. This should be an unsigned integer value in the range 0..15 for word shifts, 0..31 for double word operands, and 0..63 for quad word operands. If the shift count is outside these ranges, then these instructions set their destination operands to all zeros. If the count (first) operand is not an immediate constant, then it must be an MMX register.

The psllw instruction simultaneously shifts the four words in the destination MMX register to the left the number of bit positions specified by the source operand. The instruction shifts zero into the L.O. bit of each word and the bit shifted out of the H.O. bit of each word is lost. There is no carry from one word to the other (because that would imply a larger shift operation). This instruction, like all the other MMX instructions, does not affect the FLAGs register (including the carry flag).

The pslld instruction simultaneously shifts the two double words in the destination MMX register to the left one bit position. Like the psllw instruction, this instruction shifts zeros into the L.O. bits and any bits shifted out of the H.O. positions are lost.

The psllq is one of the few MMX instructions that operate on 64-bit quantities. This instruction shifts the entire 64-bit destination register to the left the number of bits specified by the count (source) operand. In addition to allowing you to manipulate 64-bit integer quantities, this instruction is especially useful for moving data around in MMX registers so you can pack or unpack data as needed.

Although there is no psllb instruction to shift bits, you can simulate this instruction using a psllw and a pandn instruction. After shifting the word values to the left the specified number of bits, all you've got to do is clear the L.O. *n* bits of each byte, where *n* is the shift count. For example, to shift the bytes in MM0 to the left three positions you could use the following two instructions:

```
static
    ThreeBitsZero: byte; @nostorage;
        byte $F8, $F8, $F8, $F8, $F8, $F8, $F8, $F8;
            .
            .
            .
        psllw( 3, mm0 );
        pandn( ThreeBitsZero, mm0 );
```

The pslrw, pslrd, and pslrq instructions work just like their left shift counterparts except that these instructions shift their operands to the right rather than to the left. They shift zeros into the vacated H.O. positions of the destination values, and bits they shift out of the L.O. positions are lost. As with the shift-left instructions, there is no pslrb instruction, but you can easily simulate this with a pslrw and a pandn instruction.

The psraw and psrad instructions do an arithmetic shift-right operation on the words or double words in the destination MMX register. Note that there isn't a psraq instruction. While shifting data to the right, these instructions replicate the H.O. bit of each word, double word, or quad word rather than shifting in zeros. As for the logical shift right instructions, bits that these instructions shift out of the L.O. position are lost forever.

The psllq and pslrq instructions provide a convenient way to shift a quad word to the left or right. However, the MMX shift instructions are not generally useful for extended precision shifts because all data shifted out of the operands is lost. If you need to do an extended precision shift other than 64 bits, you should stick with the shld and shrd instructions. The MMX shift instructions are mainly useful for shifting several values in parallel or (psllq and pslrq) repositioning data in an MMX register.

13.7.7   The EMMS Instruction

```
emms();
```

The emms (Empty MMX Machine State) instruction restores the FPU status on the CPU so that it can begin processing FPU instructions again after an MMX instruction sequence. You should always execute the EMMS instruction once you complete some MMX sequence. Failure to do so may cause any following floating point instructions to fail.

When an MMX instruction executes, the floating point tag word is marked valid (00s). Subsequent floating point instructions that will be executed may produce unexpected results because the floating point stack seems to contain valid data. The emms instruction marks the floating point tag word as empty. This must occur before the execution of any following floating point instructions.

Of course, you don't have to execute the emms instruction immediately after an MMX sequence if you're going to execute some additional MMX instructions prior to executing any FPU instructions, but you must take care to execute this instruction if

- you call any library routines or OS APIs (that might possibly use the FPU).

- you switch tasks in a cooperative fashion.

- you execute any FPU instructions.

If you do not execute the emms instruction prior to a floating point instruction sequence (after an MMX instruction sequence), the following may occur:

- Depending on the exception mask bits of the floating point control word, a floating point exception event may be generated.

- A "soft exception" may occur. In this case floating point code continues to execute, but generates incorrect results.

The emms instruction is rather slow, so you don't want to unnecessarily execute it, but it is critical that you execute it at the appropriate times. Of course, better safe than sorry; if you're not sure you're going to execute more MMX instructions before any FPU instructions, then go ahead and execute the emms instruction to clear the state.

13.8   The MMX Programming Paradigm

In general, you don't learn scalar (non-MMX) 80x86 assembly language programming and then use that same mindset when writing programs using the MMX instruction set. While it is possible to directly use various MMX instructions the same way you would the general purpose integer instructions, one phrase comes to mind when working with MMX: think parallel. This text has spent many hundreds of pages up to this point attempting to get you to think in assembly language; to think that this small section can teach you how to design optimal MMX sequence would be ludicrous. Nonetheless, a few simple examples are useful to help start you thinking about how to use the MMX instructions to your benefit in your programs. This section will begin by presenting some fairly obvious uses for the MMX instruction set, and then it will attempt to present some examples that exploit the inherent parallelism of the MMX instructions.

Because the MMX registers are 64 bits wide, you can double the speed of certain data movement operations by using MMX registers rather than the 32-bit general purpose registers. For example, consider the code in Listing 13-1 that replaces the cs.cpy function in the HLA Standard Library that copies one character set object to another.

Listing 13-1: HLA Standard Library cs.cpy Routine.

```
procedure cs.cpy( src:cset; var dest:cset ); nodisplay;
begin cpy;

    push( eax );
    push( ebx );
    mov( dest, ebx );
    mov( (type dword src), eax );
    mov( eax, [ebx] );
    mov( (type dword src[4]), eax );
    mov( eax, [ebx+4] );
    mov( (type dword src[8]), eax );
    mov( eax, [ebx+8] );
    mov( (type dword src[12]), eax );
    mov( eax, [ebx+12] );
    pop( ebx );
    pop( eax );

end cpy;
```

This is a relatively simple code sequence. Indeed, a fair amount of the execution time is spent copying the parameters (20 bytes) onto the stack, calling the routine, and returning from the routine. We can reduce this entire sequence to the following four MMX instructions:

```
movq( (type qword src), mm0 );
movq( (type qword src[8]), mm1 );
movq( mm0, (type qword dest));
movq( mm1, (type qword dest[8]));
```

Of course, this sequence assumes two things: (1) it's okay to wipe out the values in MM0 and MM1, and (2) you'll execute the emms instruction a little later after the execution of some other MMX instructions. If either, or both, of these assumptions is incorrect, the performance of this sequence won't be quite as good (though probably still better than the cs.cpy routine). However, if these two assumptions do hold, then it's relatively easy to implement the cs.cpy routine as an in-line function (i.e., a macro) and have it run much faster. If you really need this operation to occur inside a procedure and you need to preserve the MMX registers, and you don't know if any MMX instructions will execute shortly thereafter (i.e., you'll need to execute emms), then it's doubtful that using the MMX instructions will help here. However, in those cases when you can put the code in-line, using the MMX instructions will be faster.

Warning: Don't get too carried away with the MMX movq instruction. Several programmers have gone to great extremes to use this instruction as part of a high-performance movsd replacement. However, except in very special cases on very well designed systems, the limiting factor for a block move is the speed of memory. Because Intel has optimized the operation of the movsd instruction, you're best off using the movsd instructions when moving blocks of memory around.

Earlier, this chapter used the cs.difference function as an example when discussing the pandn instruction. Listing 13-2 provides the original HLA Standard Library implementation of this function.

Listing 13-2: HLA Standard Library cs.difference Routine.

```
procedure cs.difference( src:cset; var dest:cset ); nodisplay;
begin difference;

    push( eax );
    push( ebx );
    mov( dest, ebx );
    mov( (type dword src), eax );
    not( eax );
    and( eax, [ebx] );
    mov( (type dword src[4]), eax );
    not( eax );
    and( eax, [ebx+4] );
    mov( (type dword src[8]), eax );
    not( eax );
    and( eax, [ebx+8] );
    mov( (type dword src[12]), eax );
    not( eax );
    and( eax, [ebx+12] );
    pop( ebx );
    pop( eax );

end difference;
```

Once again, the high level nature of HLA is hiding the fact that calling this function is somewhat expensive. A typical call to cs.difference emits five or more instructions just to push the parameters (it takes four 32-bit push instructions to pass the src character set because it is a value parameter). If you're willing to wipe out the values in MM0 and MM1, and you don't need to execute an emms instruction right away, it's possible to compute the set difference with only six instructions. That's about the same number of instructions (and often fewer) than are needed to call this routine, much less do the actual work. Here are those six instructions:

```
        movq( (type qword dest), mm0 );
        movq( (type qword dest[8]), mm1 );
        pandn( (type qword src), mm0 );
        pandn( (type qword src[8]), mm1 );
        movq( mm0, (type qword dest) );
        movq( mm1, (type qword dest[8]) );
```

These six instructions replace 12 of the instructions in the body of the function. The sequence is sufficiently short that it's reasonable to code it in-line rather than in a function. However, were you to bury this code in the cs.difference routine, you needed to preserve MM0 and MM1,[4] and you needed to execute emms afterwards, this would cost more than it's worth. As an in-line macro, however, it is going to be significantly faster because it avoids passing parameters and the call/return sequence.

If you want to compute the intersection of two character sets, the instruction sequence is identical to the above except you substitute pand for pandn. Similarly, if you want to compute the union of two character sets, use the code sequence above substituting por for pandn. Again, both approaches pay off handsomely if you insert the code in-line rather than burying it in a procedure and you don't need to preserve MMX registers or execute emms afterward.

We can continue with this exercise of working our way through the HLA Standard Library character set (and other) routines substituting MMX instructions in place of standard integer instructions. As long as we don't need to preserve the MMX machine state (i.e., registers) and we don't have to execute emms, most of the character set operations will be short enough to code in-line. Unfortunately, we're not buying that much over code the standard implementations of these functions in-line from a performance point of view (though the code would be quite a bit shorter). The problem here is that we're not "thinking in MMX." We're still thinking in scalar (non-parallel mode) and the fact that the MMX instruction set requires a lot of setup (well, "tear-down" actually) negates many of the advantages of using MMX instructions in our programs.

The MMX instructions are most appropriate when you compute multiple results in parallel. The problem with the character set examples above is that we're not even processing a whole data object with a single instruction; we're actually only processing a half of a character set with a sequence of three MMX instructions (i.e., it requires six instructions to compute the intersection, union, or difference of two character sets). At best, we can only expect the code to run about twice as fast because we're processing 64 bits at a time instead of 32 bits. Executing emms (and having to preserve MMX registers) negates much of what we might gain by using the MMX instructions. Again, we're only going to see a speed improvement if we process multiple objects with a single MMX instruction. We're not going to do that manipulating large objects like character sets.

One data type that will let us easily manipulate up to eight objects at one time is a character string. We can speed up many character string operations by operating on eight characters in the string at one time. Consider the HLA Standard Library str.uppercase procedure. This function steps through each character of a string, tests to see if it's a lower case character, and if so, converts the lower case character to upper case. A good question to ask is, "Can we process eight characters at a time using the MMX instructions?" The answer turns out to be yes, and the MMX implementation of this function provides an interesting perspective on writing MMX code.

---

[4] For some instructions the overflow may appear in another register or the carry flag, but in the destination register the high order bits are lost.

At first glance it might seem impractical to use the MMX instructions to test for lower case characters and convert them to upper case. Consider the typical scalar approach that tests and converts a single character at a time:

```
<< Get character to convert into the AL register >>

            cmp( al, 'a' );
            jb noConversion;
            cmp( al, 'z' );
            ja noConversion;
            sub( $20, al );      // Could also use AND($5f, al); here.
noConversion:
```

This code first checks the value in AL to see if it's actually a lower case character (that's the cmp and Jcc instructions in the code above). If the character is outside the range 'a'..'z' then this code skips over the conversion (the sub instruction); however, if the code is in the specified range, then the sequence above drops through to the sub instruction and converts the lower case character to upper case by subtracting $20 from the lower case character's ASCII code (because lower case characters always have bit #5 set, subtracting $20 always clears this bit).

Any attempt to convert this code directly to an MMX sequence is going to fail. Comparing and branching around the conversion instruction only works if you're converting one value at a time. When operating on eight characters simultaneously, any mixture of the eight characters may or may not require conversion from lower case to upper case. Hence, we need to be able to perform some calculation that is benign if the character is not lower case (i.e., doesn't affect the character's value), while converting the character to upper case if it was lower case to begin with. Worse, we have to do this with pure computation because flow of control isn't going to be particularly effective here (if we test each individual result in our MMX register we won't really save anything over the scalar approach). To save you some suspense, yes, such a calculation does exist.

Consider the following algorithm that converts lower case characters to upper case:

```
            << Get character to test into AL >>
            cmp( al, 'a' );
            setae( bl );      // bl := al >= 'a'
            cmp( al, 'z' );
            setbe( bh );      // bh := al <= 'z'
            and( bh, bl );    // bl := (al >= 'a') && (al <= 'z' );
            dec( bl );        // bl := $FF/$00 if false/true.
            not( bl );        // bl := $FF/$00 if true/false.
            and( $20, bl );   // bl := $20/$00 if true/false.
            sub( bl, al );    // subtract $20 if al was lowercase.
```

This code sequence is fairly straight-forward up until the dec instruction above. It computes true/false in BL depending on whether AL is in the range 'a'..'z'. At the point of the dec instruction, BL contains one if AL is a lower case character; it contains zero if AL's value is not lower case. After the dec instruction, BL contains $FF for false (AL is not lower case) and $00 for true (AL is lowercase). The code is going to use this as a mask a little later, but it really needs true to be $FF and false $00, hence the not instruction that follows. The (second) and instruction above converts true to $20 and false to $00, and the final sub instruction subtracts $20 if AL contained lower case; it subtracts $00 from AL if AL did not contain a lower case character (subtracting $20 from a lower case character will convert it to upper case).

Whew! This sequence probably isn't very efficient when compared to the simpler code given previously. Certainly there are more instructions in this version (nearly twice as many). Whether this code without any branches runs faster or slower than the earlier code with two branches is a good question. The important thing to note here, though, is that we converted the lower case characters to upper case (leaving other characters unchanged) using only a calculation; no program flow logic is necessary. This means that the code sequence above is a good candidate for conversion to MMX. Even if the code sequence above is slower than the previous algorithm when converting one character at a time to upper case, it's positively going to scream when it converts eight characters at a shot (because you'll only need to execute the sequence one-eighth as many times).

The following is the code sequence that will convert the eight characters starting at location [EDI] in memory to upper case:

```
static
    A:qword; @nostorage;
        byte $60, $60, $60, $60, $60, $60, $60, $60; // Note: $60 = 'a'-1.
    Z:qword; @nostorage;
        byte $7B, $7B, $7B, $7B, $7B, $7B, $7B, $7B; // Note: $7B = 'z' + 1.
    ConvFactor:qword; @nostorage;
        byte $20, $20, $20, $20, $20, $20, $20, $20; // Magic value for lc->UC.
        .
        .
        .

    movq( ConvFactor, mm4 ); // Eight copies of conversion value.
    movq( A, mm2 );          // Put eight "a" characters in mm2.
    movq( Z, mm3 );          // Put eight "z" characters in mm3.
    movq( [edi], mm0 );      // Get next eight characters of our string.
    movq( mm0, mm1 );        // We need two copies.
    pcmpgtb( mm2, mm1 );     // Generate 1s in MM1 everywhere chars >= 'a'
    pcmpgtb( mm0, mm3 );     // Generate 1s in MM3 everywhere chars <= 'z'
    pand( mm3, mm1 );        // Generate 1s in MM1 when 'a'<=chars<='z'
    pand( mm4, mm1 );        // Generates $20 in each spot we have a l.c. char
    psubb( mm1, mm0 );       // Convert l.c. chars to U.C. by adding $20.
    movq( mm0, [edi]);
```

Note how this code compares the characters that [EDI] points at to 'a'-1 and 'z'+1, because we only have a greater than comparison rather than a greater or equal comparison (this saves a few extra instructions). Other than setting up the

MMX registers and taking advantage of the fact that the `pcmpgtb` instructions automatically produce $FF for true and $00 for false, this is a faithful reproduction of the previous algorithm except it operates on eight bytes simultaneously. So if we put this code in a loop and execute it once for each eight characters in the string, there will be one-eighth the iterations of a similar loop using the scalar instructions.

Of course, there is one problem with this code. Not all strings have lengths that are an even multiple of eight bytes. Therefore, we've got to put some special case code into our algorithm to handle strings that are less than eight characters long and handle strings whose length is not an even multiple of eight characters. In Listing 13-3, the `mmxupper` function simply borrows the scalar code from the HLA Standard Library's `str.upper` procedure to handle the leftover characters. The following example program provides both an MMX and a scalar solution with a main program that compares the running time of both. If you're wondering, the MMX version is about three times faster (on a Pentium III) for strings around 35 characters long, containing mostly lower case (mostly lower case favors the scalar algorithm because fewer branches are taken with lower case characters; longer strings favor the MMX algorithm because it spends more time in the MMX code compared to the scalar code at the end).

Listing 13-3: MMX Implementation of the HLA Standard Library str.upper Procedure.

```
program UpperCase;
#include( "stdlib.hhf" )


// The following code was stolen from the
// HLA Standard Library's str.upper function.
// It is not optimized, but then none of this
// code is optimized other than to use the MMX
// instruction set (later).

procedure strupper( dest: string ); @nodisplay;
begin strupper;

    push( edi );
    push( eax );

    mov( dest, edi );
    if( edi = 0 ) then

        raise( ex.AttemptToDerefNULL );

    endif;

    // Until we encounter a zero byte, convert any lower
    // case characters to upper case.
```

```
    forever

        mov( [edi], al );
        breakif( al = 0 );        // Quit when we find a zero byte.

        // If a lower case character, convert it to upper case
        // and store the result back into the destination string.

        if
        (#{
            cmp( al, 'a' );
            jb false;
            cmp( al, 'z' );
            ja false;
        }#) then

            and( $5f, al );        // Magic lc->UC translation.
            mov( al, [edi] );      // Save result.

        endif;

        // Move on to the next character.

        inc( edi );

    endfor;

    pop( edi );
    pop( eax );

end strupper;




procedure mmxupper( dest: string ); @nodisplay;
const
    zCh:char := char( uns8( 'z') + 1 );
    aCh:char := char( uns8( 'a') - 1 );

static

    // Create eight copies of the A-1 and Z+1 characters
    // so we can compare eight characters at once:

    A:qword; @nostorage;
        byte aCh, aCh, aCh, aCh, aCh, aCh, aCh, aCh;


    Z:qword; @nostorage;
```

```
                byte zCh, zCh, zCh, zCh, zCh, zCh, zCh, zCh;

        // Conversion factor: UC := LC - $20.

        ConvFactor: qword; @nostorage;
                byte $20, $20, $20, $20, $20, $20, $20, $20;

begin mmxupper;

        push( edi );
        push( eax );

        mov( dest, edi );
        if( edi = 0 ) then

            raise( ex.AttemptToDerefNULL );

        endif;

        // Some invariant operations (things that don't
        // change on each iteration of the loop):

        movq( A, mm2 );
        movq( ConvFactor, mm4 );

        // Get the string length from the length field:

        mov( (type str.strRec [edi]).length, eax );

        // Process the string in blocks of eight characters:

        while( (type int32 eax) >= 8 ) do

            movq( [edi], mm0 );    // Get next eight characters of our string.
            movq( mm0, mm1 );      // We need two copies.
            movq( Z, mm3 );        // Need to refresh on each loop.
            pcmpgtb( mm2, mm1 );   // Generate 1s in MM1 everywhere chars >= 'a'
            pcmpgtb( mm0, mm3 );   // Generate 1s in MM3 everywhere chars <= 'z'
            pand( mm3, mm1 );      // Generate 1s in MM1 when 'a'<=chars<='z'
            pand( mm4, mm1 );      // Generates $20 in each spot we have a l.c. char
            psubb( mm1, mm0 );     // Convert l.c. chars to u.c. by adding $20.
            movq( mm0, (type qword [edi]));

            // Move on to the next eight characters in the string.

            sub( 8, eax );
            add( 8, edi );

        endwhile;
```

```
            // If we're processing less than eight characters, do it the old-fashioned
            // way (one character at a time). This also handles the last 1..7 chars
            // if the number of characters is not an even multiple of eight. This
            // code was swiped directly from the HLA str.upper function (above).

        if( eax != 0 ) then

            forever

                mov( [edi], al );
                breakif( al = 0 );       // Quit when we find a zero byte.

                // If a lower case character, convert it to upper case
                // and store the result back into the destination string.

                if
                (#{
                    cmp( al, 'a' );
                    jb false;
                    cmp( al, 'z' );
                    ja false;
                }#) then

                    and( $5f, al );      // Magic lc->UC translation.
                    mov( al, [edi] );    // Save result.

                endif;

                // Move on to the next character.

                inc( edi );

            endfor;

        endif;
        emms(); // Clean up MMX state.


        pop( edi );
        pop( eax );

end mmxupper;



static
    MyStr: string := "Hello There, MMX Uppercase Routine!";
    destStr:string;
```

```
        mmxCycles:qword;
        strCycles:qword;

    begin UpperCase;

        // Charge up the cache (prefetch the code and data
        // to avoid cache misses later).

        mov( str.a_cpy( MyStr ), destStr );
        mmxupper( destStr );
        strupper( destStr );


        // Okay, time the execution of the MMX version:

        mov( str.a_cpy( MyStr ), destStr );

        rdtsc();
        mov( eax, (type dword mmxCycles));
        mov( edx, (type dword mmxCycles[4]));
        mmxupper( destStr );
        rdtsc();
        sub( (type dword mmxCycles), eax );
        sbb( (type dword mmxCycles[4]), edx );
        mov( eax, (type dword mmxCycles));
        mov( edx, (type dword mmxCycles[4]));

        stdout.put( "Dest String = '", destStr, "'", nl );


        // Okay, time the execution of the HLA version:

        mov( str.a_cpy( MyStr ), destStr );

        rdtsc();
        mov( eax, (type dword strCycles));
        mov( edx, (type dword strCycles[4]));
        strupper( destStr );
        rdtsc();
        sub( (type dword strCycles), eax );
        sbb( (type dword strCycles[4]), edx );
        mov( eax, (type dword strCycles));
        mov( edx, (type dword strCycles[4]));

        stdout.put( "Dest String(2) = '", destStr, "'", nl );

        stdout.put( "MMX cycles:" );
        stdout.puti64( mmxCycles );
        stdout.put( nl "HLA cycles: " );
```

```
        stdout.puti64( strCycles );
        stdout.newln();


end UpperCase;
```

Other string functions, like a case-insensitive string comparison, can greatly benefit from the use of parallel computation via the MMX instruction set. Implementation of other string functions is left as an exercise to the reader; interested readers should consider converting string functions that involve calculations and tests on each individual character in a string as candidates for optimization via MMX.

13.9   For More Information

Intel's online documentation discusses the MMX instruction set in greater detail. You can find this documentation by visiting www.intel.com. This chapter discusses only the integer MMX instruction set. Since the development of the MMX instruction set, Intel has also developed the SSE and SSE2 instruction extensions (that provide SIMD floating point instructions). Please see the Intel documentation for information about these additional instructions.

14

CLASSES AND OBJECTS

14.1 Chapter Overview

Many modern high level languages support the notion of classes and objects. C++ (an object version of C), Java, and Delphi/Kylix (object versions of Pascal) are good examples. Of course, these high level language compilers translate their source code into low level machine code, so it should be pretty obvious that some mechanism exists in machine code for implementing classes and objects.

Although it has always been possible to implement classes and objects in machine code, most assemblers provide poor support for writing object-oriented assembly language programs. Of course, HLA does not suffer from this drawback, as it provides good support for writing object-oriented assembly language programs. This chapter discusses the general principles behind object-oriented programming (OOP) and how HLA supports OOP.

14.2   General Principles

Before discussing the mechanisms behind OOP, it is probably a good idea to take a step back and explore the benefits of using OOP (especially in assembly language programs). Most texts that describe the benefits of OOP will mention buzzwords like "code reuse," "abstract data types," "improved development efficiency," and so on. While all of these features are nice and are good attributes for a programming paradigm, a good software engineer would question the use of assembly language in an environment where "improved development efficiency" is an important goal. After all, you can probably obtain far better efficiency by using a high level language (even in a non-OOP fashion) than you can by using objects in assembly language. If the purported features of OOP don't seem to apply to assembly language programming, why bother using OOP in assembly? This section will explore some of those reasons.

The first thing you should realize is that the use of assembly language does not negate the aforementioned OOP benefits. OOP in assembly language does promote code reuse; it provides a good method for implementing abstract data types, and it can improve development efficiency *in assembly language*. In other words, if you're dead set on using assembly language, there are benefits to using OOP.

To understand one of the principle benefits of OOP, consider the concept of a global variable. Most programming texts strongly recommend against the use of global variables in a program (as does this text). Interprocedural communication through global variables is dangerous because it is difficult to keep track of all the possible places in a large program that modify a given global object. Worse, it is very easy when making enhancements to accidentally reuse a global object for something other than its intended purpose; this tends to introduce defects into the system.

Despite the well-understood problems with global variables, the semantics of global objects (extended lifetimes and accessibility from different procedures) are absolutely necessary in various situations. Objects solve this problem by letting the programmer decide on the lifetime of an object[1] as well as allowing access to data fields from different procedures. Objects have several advantages over simple global variables insofar as objects can control access to their data fields (making it difficult for procedures to accidentally access the data), and you can also create multiple instances of an object allowing separate sections of your program to use their own unique "global" object without interference from other sections.

Of course, objects have many other valuable attributes. One could write several volumes on the benefits of objects and OOP; this single chapter cannot do the subject justice. The remainder of this chapter presents objects with an eye toward using them in HLA/assembly programs. However, if you are new to OOP or wish more information about the object-oriented paradigm, you should consult other texts on this subject.

---

[1] That is, the time during which the system allocates memory for an object.

An important use for classes and objects is to create *abstract data types* (ADTs). An abstract data type is a collection of data objects and the functions (which we'll call *methods*) that operate on the data. In a pure abstract data type, the ADT's methods are the only code that has access to the data fields of the ADT; external code may only access the data using function calls to get or set data field values (these are the ADT's *accessor* methods). In real life, for efficiency reasons, most languages that support ADTs allow, at least, limited access to the data fields of an ADT by external code.

Assembly language is not a language most people associate with ADTs. Nevertheless, HLA provides several features to allow the creation of rudimentary ADTs. While some might argue that HLA's facilities are not as complete as those in a language such as C++ or Java, keep in mind that these differences exist because HLA is an assembly language.

True ADTs should support *information hiding*. This means that the ADT does not allow the user of an ADT access to internal data structures and routines, which manipulate those structures. In essence, information hiding restricts access to an ADT only the access via the ADT's accessor methods. Assembly language, of course, provides very few restrictions. If you are dead set on accessing an object directly, there is very little HLA can do to prevent you from doing this. However, HLA has some facilities, which will provide a limited form of information hiding. Combined with some care on your part, you will be able to enjoy many of the benefits of information hiding within your programs.

The primary facilities HLA provide to support information hiding are separate compilation, linkable modules, and the #include/#includeonce directives. For our purposes, an abstract data type definition will consist of two sections: an *interface* section and an *implementation* section.

The interface section contains the definitions that must be visible to the application program. In general, it should not contain any specific information that would allow the application program to violate the information-hiding principle, but this is often impossible given the nature of assembly language. Nevertheless, you should attempt to only reveal what is absolutely necessary within the interface section.

The implementation section contains the code, data structures, and so on to actually implement the ADT. While some of the methods and data types appearing in the implementation section may be public (by virtue of appearance within the interface section), many of the subroutines, data items, and so on will be private to the implementation code. The implementation section is where you hide all the details from the application program.

If you wish to modify the abstract data type at some point in the future, you will only have to change the interface and implementation sections. Unless you delete some previously visible object that the applications use, there will be no need to modify the applications at all.

Although you could place the interface and implementation sections directly in an application program, this would not promote information hiding or maintainability, especially if you have to include the code in several different applications. The best approach is to place the implementation section in an include file that any interested application reads using the HLA #include directive and to place the implementation section in a separate module that you link with your applications.

The include file would contain @external directives, any necessary macros, and other definitions you want made public. It generally would not contain 80x86 code except, perhaps, in some macros. When an application wants to make use of an ADT it would include this file.

The separate assembly file containing the implementation section would contain all the procedures, functions, data objects, and so on to actually implement the ADT. Those names that you want to be public should appear in the interface include file and have the @external attribute. You should also include the interface include file in the implementation file so you do not have to maintain two sets of @external directives.

One problem with using procedures for data access methods is the fact that many accessor methods are especially trivial (e.g., just a mov instruction), and the overhead of the call and return instructions is expensive for such trivial operations. For example, suppose you have an ADT whose data object is a structure, but you do not want to make the field names visible to the application and you really do not want to allow the application to access the fields of the data structure directly (because the data structure may change in the future). The normal way to handle this is to supply a GetField method that returns the value of the desired field. However, as pointed out above, this can be very slow. An alternative for simple access methods is to use a macro to emit the code to access the desired field. Although code to directly access the data object appears in the application program (via macro expansion), it will be automatically updated if you ever change the macro in the interface section by simply reassembling your application.

Although it is quite possible to create ADTs using nothing more than separate compilation and, perhaps, records, HLA does provide a better solution: the class. Read on to find out about HLA's support for classes and objects as well as how to use these to create ADTs.

14.3   Classes in HLA

HLA's classes provide a good mechanism for creating abstract data types. Fundamentally, a class is little more than a record declaration that allows the definition of non-data fields (e.g., procedures, constants, and macros). The inclusion of other objects in the class definition dramatically expands the capabilities of a class over that of a record. For example, with a class it is now possible to easily define an ADT because classes may include data and methods (procedures) that operate on that data.

The principle way to create an abstract data type in HLA is to declare a class data type. Classes in HLA always appear in the type section and use the following syntax:

```
classname : class

        << Class declaration section >>

        endclass;
```

The class declaration section is very similar to the local declaration section for a procedure insofar as it allows const, val, var, and static variable declaration sections. Classes also let you define macros and specify procedure, iterator,[2] and *method* prototypes (method declarations are legal only in classes). Conspicuously absent from this list is the type declaration section. You cannot declare new types within a class.

A method is a special type of procedure that appears only within a class. A little later you will see the difference between procedures and methods; for now you can treat them as being one and the same. Other than a few subtle details regarding class initialization and the use of pointers to classes, their semantics are identical.[3] Generally, if you don't know whether to use a procedure or method in a class, the safest bet is to use a method.

You do not place procedure/iterator/method code within a class. Instead you simply supply *prototypes* for these routines. A routine prototype consists of the procedure, iterator, or method reserved word, the routine name, any parameters, and a couple of optional procedure attributes (@use, @returns, and @external). The actual routine definition (i.e., the body of the routine and any local declarations it needs) appears outside the class.

The following example demonstrates a typical class declaration appearing in the type section:

```
TYPE
    TypicalClass:      class

        const
            TCconst := 5;

        val
            TCval := 6;

        var
            TCvar : uns32;              // Private field used only by TCproc.

        static
            TCstatic : int32;

        procedure TCproc( u:uns32 ); @returns( "eax" );
        iterator TCiter( i:int32 ); @external;
```

---

[2] This text does not discuss iterators. See the HLA Reference Manual for details on this type of function.

[3] Note, however, that the difference between procedures and methods makes all the difference in the world to the object-oriented programming paradigm. Hence the inclusion of methods in HLA's class definitions.

```
        method TCmethod( c:char );

    endclass;
```

As you can see, classes are very similar to records in HLA. Indeed, you can think of a record as being a class that only allows var declarations. HLA implements classes in a fashion quite similar to records insofar as it allocates sequential data fields in sequential memory locations. In fact, with only one minor exception, there is almost no difference between a record declaration and a class declaration that only has a var declaration section. Later you'll see exactly how HLA implements classes, but for now you can assume that HLA implements them the same as it does records and you won't be too far off the mark.

You can access the TCvar and TCstatic fields (in the class above) just like a record's fields. You access the const and val fields in a similar manner. If a variable of type TypicalClass has the name obj, you can access the fields of obj as follows:

```
    mov ( obj.TCconst, eax );
    mov( obj.TCval, ebx );
    add( obj.TCvar, eax );
    add( obj.TCstatic, ebx );
    obj.TCproc( 20 );        // Calls the TCproc procedure in TypicalClass.
    etc.
```

If an application program includes the class declaration above, it can create variables using the TypicalClass type and perform operations using the mentioned methods. Unfortunately, the application program can also access the fields of the *ADT* data type with impunity. For example, if a program created a variable MyClass of type TypicalClass, then it could easily execute instructions like "mov(MyClass.TCvar, eax);" even though this field might be private to the implementation section. Unfortunately, if you are going to allow an application to declare a variable of type TypicalClass, the field names will have to be visible. While there are some tricks we could play with HLA's class definitions to help hide the private fields, the best solution is to thoroughly comment the private fields and then exercise some restraint when accessing the fields of that class. Specifically, this means that ADTs you create using HLA's classes cannot be "pure" ADTs because HLA allows direct access to the data fields. However, with a little discipline, you can simulate a pure ADT by simply electing not to access such fields outside the class's methods, procedures, and iterators.

Prototypes appearing in a class are effectively forward declarations. Like normal forward declarations, all procedures, iterators, and methods you define in a class must have an actual implementation later in the code. Alternately, you may attach the @external option to the end of a procedure, iterator, or method declaration within a class to inform HLA that the actual code appears in a separate module. As a general rule, class declarations appear in header files and represent the interface section of an ADT. The procedure, iterator, and method bodies appear in the implementation section, which is usually a separate source file that you compile separately and link with the modules that use the class.

The following is an example of a sample class procedure implementation:

```
procedure TypicalClass.TCproc( u:uns32 ); @nodisplay;
    << Local declarations for this procedure >>
begin TCproc;

    << Code to implement whatever this procedure does >>

end TCProc;
```

There are several differences between a standard procedure declaration and a class procedure declaration. First, and most obvious, the procedure name includes the class name (e.g., TypicalClass.TCproc). This differentiates this class procedure definition from a regular procedure that just happens to have the name TCproc. Note, however, that you do not have to repeat the class name before the procedure name in the begin and end clauses of the procedure (this is similar to procedures you define in HLA namespaces).

A second difference between class procedures and non-class procedures is not obvious. Some procedure attributes (@use, @external, @returns, @cdecl, @pascal, and @stdcall) are legal only in the prototype declaration appearing within the class while other attributes (@noframe, @nodisplay, @noalignstack, and @align) are legal only within the procedure definition and not within the class. Fortunately, HLA provides helpful error messages if you stick the option in the wrong place, so you don't have to memorize this rule.

If a class routine's prototype does not have the @external option, the compilation unit (that is, the program or unit) containing the class declaration must also contain the routine's definition or HLA will generate an error at the end of the compilation. For small, local classes (i.e., when you're embedding the class declaration and routine definitions in the same compilation unit) the convention is to place the class's procedure, iterator, and method definitions in the source file shortly after the class declaration. For larger systems (i.e., when separately compiling a class's routines), the convention is to place the class declaration in a header file by itself and place all the procedure, iterator, and method definitions in a separate HLA unit and compile them by themselves.

14.4 Objects

Remember, a class definition is just a type. Therefore, when you declare a class type you haven't created a variable whose fields you can manipulate. An *object* is an *instance* of a class; that is, an object is a variable that is some class type. You declare objects (i.e., class variables) the same way you declare other variables: in a var, static, or storage section.[4] Here is a pair of sample object declarations:

```
var
    T1: TypicalClass;
    T2: TypicalClass;
```

[4] Technically, you could also declare an object in a readonly section, but HLA does not allow you to define class constants, so there is little utility in declaring class objects in the readonly section.

For a given class object, HLA allocates storage for each variable appearing in the var section of the class declaration. If you have two objects, T1 and T2, of type TypicalClass then T1.TCvar is unique as is T2.TCvar. This is the intuitive result (similar to record declarations); most data fields you define in a class will appear in the var declaration section of the class.

Static data objects (e.g., those you declare in the static or storage sections of a class declaration) are not unique among the objects of that class; that is, HLA allocates only a single static variable that all variables of that class share. For example, consider the following (partial) class declaration and object declarations:

```
type
    sc: class

        var
            i:int32;

        static
            s:int32;
            .
            .
            .
    endclass;

var
    s1: sc;
    s2: sc;
```

In this example, s1.i and s2.i are different variables. However, s1.s and s2.s are aliases of one another. Therefore, an instruction like "mov(5, s1.s);" also stores five into s2.s. Generally you use static class variables to maintain information about the whole class while you use class var objects to maintain information about the specific object. Because keeping track of class information is relatively rare, you will probably declare most class data fields in a var section.

You can also create dynamic instances of a class and refer to those dynamic objects via pointers. In fact, this is probably the most common form of object storage and access. The following code shows how to create pointers to objects and how you can dynamically allocate storage for an object:

```
var
    pSC: pointer to sc;
        .
        .
        .
    malloc( @size( sc ) );
    mov( eax, pSC );
```

```
            .
            .
            .
    mov( pSC, ebx );
    mov( (type sc [ebx]).i, eax );
```

Note the use of type coercion to cast the pointer in EBX as type sc.

14.5   Inheritance

Inheritance is one of the most fundamental ideas behind object-oriented
programming. The basic idea is that a class inherits, or copies, all the fields from
some class and then possibly expands the number of fields in the new data type.
For example, suppose you created a data type point that describes a point in the
planar (two dimensional) space. The class for this point might look like the
following:

```
type
    point: class

        var
            x:int32;
            y:int32;

        method distance;

    endclass;
```

Suppose you want to create a point in 3D space rather than 2D space. You can
easily build such a data type as follows:

```
type
    point3D: class inherits( point )

        var
            z:int32;

    endclass;
```

The inherits option on the class declaration tells HLA to insert the fields of point
at the beginning of the class. In this case, point3D inherits the fields of point. HLA
always places the inherited fields at the beginning of a class object. The reason
for this will become clear a little later. If you have an instance of point3D, which
you call P3, then the following 80x86 instructions are all legal:

```
mov( P3.x, eax );
add( P3.y, eax );
mov( eax, P3.z );
P3.distance();
```

Note that the p3.distance method invocation in this example calls the point.distance method. You do not have to write a separate distance method for the point3D class unless you really want to do so (see the next section for details). Just like the x and y fields, point3D objects inherit point's methods.

14.6 Overriding

Overriding is the process of replacing an existing method in an inherited class with one more suitable for the new class. In the point and point3D examples appearing in the previous section, the distance method (presumably) computes the distance from the origin to the specified point. For a point on a two-dimensional plane, you can compute the distance using the function:

$$\text{dist} = \sqrt{x^2 + y^2}$$

However, the distance for a point in 3D space is given by the equation:

$$\text{dist} = \sqrt{x^2 + y^2 + z^2}$$

Clearly, if you call the distance function for point for a point3D object you will get an incorrect answer. In the previous section, however, you saw that the P3 object calls the distance function inherited from the point class. Therefore, this would produce an incorrect result.

In this situation the point3D data type must override the distance method with one that computes the correct value. You cannot simply redefine the point3D class by adding a distance method prototype:

```
type
    point3D:                    class inherits( point )

        var
            z:int32;
```

```
        method distance;    // This doesn't work!

    endclass;
```

The problem with the distance method declaration above is that point3D already has a distance method — the one that it inherits from the point class. HLA will complain because it doesn't like two methods with the same name in a single class.

To solve this problem, we need some mechanism by which we can override the declaration of point.distance and replace it with a declaration for point3D.distance. To do this, you use the override keyword before the method declaration:

```
type
    point3D:      class inherits( point )

        var
            z:int32;

        override method distance;    // This will work!

    endclass;
```

The override prefix tells HLA to ignore the fact that point3D inherits a method named distance from the point class. Now, any call to the distance method via a point3D object will call the point3D.distance method rather than point.distance. Of course, once you override a method using the override prefix, you must supply the method in the implementation section of your code, e.g.,

```
method point3D.distance; @ no display ;

    << local declarations for the distance function>>

begin distance;

    << Code to implement the distance function >>

end distance;
```

14.7   Virtual Methods vs. Static Procedures

A little earlier, this chapter suggested that you could treat class methods and class procedures the same. There are, in fact, some major differences between the two (after all, why have methods if they're the same as procedures?). As it turns out, the differences between methods and procedures are crucial if you want to develop object-oriented programs. Methods provide the second feature necessary to support true polymorphism: virtual procedure calls.[5] A virtual procedure call is just a fancy name for an indirect procedure call (using a pointer associated with the object). The key benefit of virtual procedures is that the system automatically calls the right method when using pointers to generic objects.

Consider the following declarations using the *point* class from the previous sections:

```
var
     P2: point;
     P: pointer to point;
```

Given the declarations above, the following assembly statements are all legal:

```
mov( P2.x, eax );
mov( P2.y, ecx );
P2.distance();                          // Calls point3D.distance.

lea( ebx, P2 );                         // Store address of P2 into P.
mov( ebx, P );
P.distance();                           // Calls point.distance.
```

Note that HLA lets you call a method via a pointer to an object rather than directly via an object variable. This is a crucial feature of objects in HLA and a key to implementing *virtual method calls*.

The magic behind polymorphism and inheritance is that object pointers are *generic*. In general, when your program references data indirectly through a pointer, the value of the pointer should be the address of some value of the underlying data type associated with that pointer. For example, if you have a pointer to a 16-bit unsigned integer, you wouldn't normally use that pointer to access a 32-bit signed integer value. Similarly, if you have a pointer to some record, you would not normally cast that pointer to some other record type and access the fields of that other type.[6] With pointers to class objects, however, we can lift this restriction a bit. Pointers to objects may legally contain the address of the object's type *or the address of any object that inherits the fields of that type.* Consider the following declarations that use the point and point3D types from the previous examples:

```
var
     P2: point;
     P3: point3D;
     p: pointer to point;

          .
          .
          .

     lea( ebx, P2 );
```

---

[5] Polymorphism literally means "many-faced." In the context of object-oriented programming polymorphism means that the same method name, e.g., *distance*, and refer to one of several different methods.

[6] Of course, assembly language programmers break rules like this all the time. For now, let's assume we're playing by the rules and only access the data using the data type associated with the pointer.

```
        mov( ebx, p );
        p.distance();                       // Calls the point.distance method.
            .
            .
            .
        lea( ebx, P3 );
        mov( ebx, p );                       // Yes, this is semantically legal.
        p.distance();                        // Surprise, this calls point3D.distance.
```

Because p is a pointer to a point object, it might seem intuitive for p.distance to call the point.distance method. However, methods are *polymorphic*. If you've got a pointer to an object and you call a method associated with that object, the system will call the actual (overridden) method associated with the object, not the method specifically associated with the pointer's class type.

Class procedures behave differently than methods with respect to overridden procedures. When you call a class procedure indirectly through an object pointer, the system will always call the procedure associated with the underlying class. So had distance been a procedure rather than a method in the previous examples, the "p.distance();" invocation would always call point.distance, even if p is pointing at a point3D object. The section on object initialization, later in this chapter, explains why methods and procedures are different.

14.8 Writing Class Methods and Procedures

For each class procedure and method prototype appearing in a class definition, there must be a corresponding procedure or method appearing within the program (for the sake of brevity, this section will use the term *routine* to mean procedure or method from this point forward). If the prototype does not contain the @external option, then the code must appear in the same compilation unit as the class declaration. If the @external option does follow the prototype, then the code may appear in the same compilation unit or a different compilation unit (as long as you link the resulting object file with the code containing the class declaration). Like external (non-class) procedures, if you fail to provide the code the linker will complain when you attempt to create an executable file. To reduce the size of the following examples, they will all define their routines in the same source file as the class declaration.

HLA class routines must always follow the class declaration in a compilation unit. If you are compiling your routines in a separate unit, the class declarations must still precede the implementation of the routines from the class (usually via an #include file). If you haven't defined the class by the time you define a routine like point.distance, HLA doesn't know that point is a class and, therefore, doesn't know how to handle the routine's definition.

Consider the following declarations for a point2D class:

```
type
    point2D: class
```

```
const
    UnitDistance: real32 := 1.0;

var
    x: real32;
    y: real32;

static
    LastDistance: real32;

method distance( fromX: real32;  fromY:real32 ); returns( "st0" );
procedure InitLastDistance;

endclass;
```

The distance function for this class should compute the distance from the object's point to (fromX,fromY). The following formula describes this computation:

$$\sqrt{(x - fromX)^2 + (y - fromY)^2}$$

A first pass at writing the distance method might produce the following code:

```
method point2D.distance( fromX:real32; fromY:real32 ); nodisplay;
begin distance;

    fld( x );                       // Note: this doesn't work!
    fld( fromX );                   // Compute (x-fromX)
    fsub();
    fld( st0 );                     // Duplicate value on TOS.
    fmul();                         // Compute square of difference.

    fld( y );                       // This doesn't work either.
    fld( fromY );                   // Compute (y-fromY)
    fsub();
    fld( st0 );                     // Compute the square of the difference.
    fmul();

    fsqrt();

end distance;
```

This code probably looks like it should work to someone who is familiar with an object-oriented programming language like C++ or Delphi. However, as the comments indicate, the instructions that push the x and y variables onto the FPU stack don't work; HLA doesn't automatically define the symbols associated with the data fields of a class within that class's routines.

To learn how to access the data fields of a class within that class's routines, we need to back up a moment and discover some very important implementation details concerning HLA's classes. To do this, consider the following variable declarations:

```
var
    Origin: point2D;
    PtInSpace: point2D;
```

Remember, whenever you create two objects like Origin and PtInSpace, HLA reserves storage for the x and y data fields for both of these objects. However, there is only one copy of the point2D.distance method in memory. Therefore, were you to call Origin.distance and PtInSpace.distance, the system would call the same routine for both method invocations. Once inside that method, one has to wonder what an instruction like "fld(x);" would do. How does it associate *x* with Origin.x or PtInSpace.x? Worse still, how would this code differentiate between the data field x and a global object x? In HLA, the answer is it doesn't. You do not specify the data field names within a class routine by simply using their names as though they were common variables.

To differentiate Origin.x from PtInSpace.x within class routines, HLA automatically passes a pointer to an object's data fields whenever you call a class routine. Therefore, you can reference the data fields indirectly off this pointer. HLA passes this object pointer in the ESI register. This is one of the few places where HLA-generated code will modify one of the 80x86 registers behind your back: **Anytime you call a class routine, HLA automatically loads the ESI register with the object's address**. Obviously, you cannot count on ESI's value being preserved across class routine calls nor can you pass parameters to the class routine in the ESI register (though it is perfectly reasonable to specify "@use esi;" to allow HLA to use the ESI register when setting up other parameters). For class methods (but not procedures), HLA will also load the EDI register with the address of the classes's *virtual method table*. While the virtual method table address isn't as interesting as the object address, keep in mind that **HLA-generated code will overwrite any value in the EDI register when you call a class method or an iterator**. Again, "EDI" is a good choice for the @use operand for methods because HLA will wipe out the value in EDI anyway.

Upon entry into a class routine, ESI contains a pointer to the (non-static) data fields associated with the class. Therefore, to access fields like x and y (in our point2D example), you could use an address expression like the following:

```
(type point2D [esi]).x
```

Because you use ESI as the base address of the object's data fields, it's a good idea not to disturb ESI's value within the class routines (or, at least, preserve ESI's value across the code where you must use ESI for some other purpose). Note that if you call a method you do not have to preserve EDI (unless, for some reason, you need access to the virtual method table, which is unlikely).

Accessing the fields of a data object within a class's routines is such a common operation that HLA provides a shorthand notation for casting ESI as a pointer to the class object: this. Within a class in HLA, the reserved word this automatically expands to a string of the form "(type *classname* [esi])" substituting, of course, the appropriate class name for *classname*. Using the this keyword, we can (correctly) rewrite the previous distance method as follows:

```
method point2D.distance( fromX:real32; fromY:real32 ); nodisplay;
begin distance;

        fld( this.x );
        fld( fromX );                   // Compute (x-fromX)
        fsub();
        fld( st0 );                     // Duplicate value on TOS.
        fmul();                         // Compute square of difference.

        fld( this.y );
        fld( fromY );                   // Compute (y-fromY)
        fsub();
        fld( st0 );                     // Compute the square of the difference.
        fmul();

        fsqrt();

end distance;
```

Don't forget that calling a class routine wipes out the value in the ESI register. This isn't obvious from the syntax of the routine's invocation. It is especially easy to forget this when calling some class routine from inside some other class routine; don't forget that if you do this the internal call wipes out the value in ESI and on return from that call ESI no longer points at the original object. Always push and pop ESI (or otherwise preserve ESI's value) in this situation. For example:

```
        .
        .
        .
        fld( this.x );              // ESI points at current object.
        .
        .
        .
        push( esi );                // Preserve ESI across this method call.
        SomeObject.SomeMethod();
        pop( esi );
        .
        .
        .
        lea( ebx, this.x );         // ESI points at original object here.
```

The this keyword provides access to the class variables you declare in the var section of a class. You can also use this to call other class routines associated with the current object, e.g.,

```
this.distance( 5.0, 6.0 );
```

To access class constants and static data fields, you generally do not use the this pointer. HLA associates constant and static data fields with the whole class, not a specific object (just like static fields in a class). To access these class members, use the class name in place of the object name. For example, to access the unitdistance constant in the point2d class you could use a statement like the following:

```
fld( point2D.UnitDistance );
```

As another example, if you wanted to update the LastDistance field in the point2D class each time you computed a distance, you could rewrite the point2D.distance method as follows:

```
method point2D.distance( fromX:real32; fromY:real32 ); nodisplay;
begin distance;

    fld( this.x );
    fld( fromX );                    // Compute (x-fromX)
    fsub();
    fld( st0 );                          // Duplicate value on TOS.
    fmul();                              // Compute square of difference.

    fld( this.y );
    fld( fromY );                    // Compute (y-fromY)
    fsub();
    fld( st0 );                          // Compute the square of the difference.
    fmul();

    fsqrt();

    fst( point2D.LastDistance );     // Update shared (STATIC) field.

end distance;
```

To understand why you use the class name when referring to constants and static objects but you use this to access var objects, check out the next section.

Class procedures are also static objects, so it is possible to call a class procedure by specifying the class name rather than an object name in the procedure invocation; e.g., both of the following are legal:

```
        Origin.InitLastDistance();
        point2D.InitLastDistance();
```

There is, however, a subtle difference between these two class procedure calls. The first call above loads ESI with the address of the origin object prior to actually calling the initlastdistance procedure. The second call, however, is a direct call to the class procedure without referencing an object; therefore, HLA doesn't know what object address to load into the ESI register. In this case, HLA loads NULL (zero) into ESI prior to calling the InitLastDistance procedure. Because you can call class procedures in this manner, it's always a good idea to check the value in ESI within your class procedures to verify that HLA contains a valid object address. Checking the value in ESI is a good way to determine which calling mechanism is in use. Later, this chapter will discuss constructors and object initialization; there you will see a good use for static procedures and calling those procedures directly (rather than through the use of an object).

14.9   Object Implementation

In a high level object-oriented language like C++ or Delphi, it is quite possible to master the use of objects without really understanding how the machine implements them. One of the reasons for learning assembly language programming is to fully comprehend low level implementation details so you can make educated decisions concerning the use of programming constructs like objects. Further, because assembly language allows you to poke around with data structures at a very low level, knowing how HLA implements objects can help you create certain algorithms that would not be possible without a detailed knowledge of object implementation. Therefore, this section and its corresponding subsections explain the low level implementation details you will need to know in order to write object-oriented HLA programs.

HLA implements objects in a manner quite similar to records. In particular, HLA allocates storage for all var objects in a class in a sequential fashion, just like records. Indeed, if a class consists of only var data fields, the memory representation of that class is nearly identical to that of a corresponding record declaration. Consider the Student record declaration taken from Chapter 4 and the corresponding class (see Figures 14-1 and 14-2, respectively):

```
type
    student: record
                Name: char[65];
                Major: int16;
                SSN:    char[12];
                Midterm1: int16;
                Midterm2: int16;
                Final: int16;
                Homework: int16;
                Projects: int16;
            endrecord;
```

```
student2: class
     var
          Name: char[65];
          Major: int16;
          SSN:   char[12];
          Midterm1: int16;
          Midterm2: int16;
          Final: int16;
          Homework: int16;
          Projects: int16;
endclass;
```

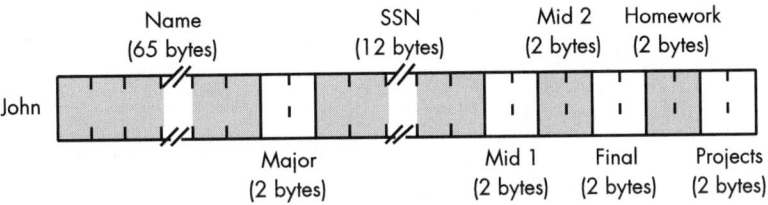

Figure 14-1: Student RECORD Implementation in Memory.

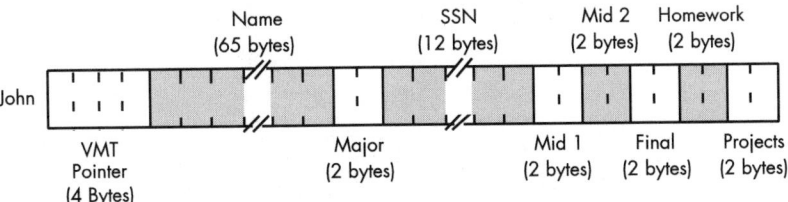

Figure 14-2: Student CLASS Implementation in Memory.

If you look carefully at Figures 14-1 and 14-2, you'll discover that the only difference between the class and the record implementations is the inclusion of the VMT (virtual method table) pointer field at the beginning of the class object. This field, which is always present in a class, contains the address of the class's virtual method table that, in turn, contains the addresses of all the class's methods and iterators. The VMT field, by the way, is present even if a class doesn't contain any methods or iterators.

As pointed out in previous sections, HLA does not allocate storage for static objects within the object. Instead, HLA allocates a single instance of each static data field that all objects share. As an example, consider the following class and object declarations:

```
type
     tHasStatic: class

          var
                i:int32;
```

```
            j:int32;
            r:real32;

        static
            c:char[2];
            b:byte;

    endclass;

var
    hs1: tHasStatic;
    hs2: tHasStatic;
```

Figure 14-3 shows the storage allocation for these two objects in memory.

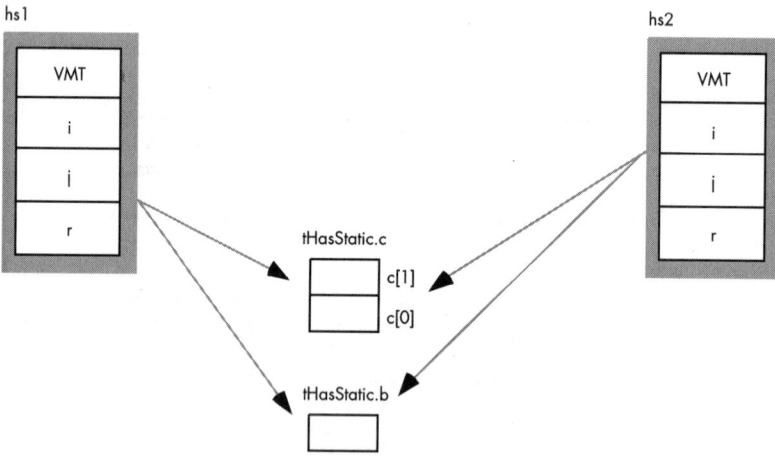

Figure 14-3: Object Allocation with Static Data Fields.

Of course, const, val, and #macro objects do not have any run-time memory requirements associated with them, so HLA does not allocate any storage for these fields. Like the static data fields, you may access const, val, and #macro fields using the class name as well as an object name. Hence, even if tHasStatic has these types of fields, the memory organization for tHasStatic objects would still be the same as shown in Figure 14-3.

Other than the presence of the virtual method table (VMT) pointer, the presence of methods and procedures has no impact on the storage allocation of an object. Of course, the machine instructions associated with these routines do appear somewhere in memory. So in a sense the code for the routines is quite similar to static data fields insofar as all the objects share a single instance of the routine.

14.9.1   Virtual Method Tables

When HLA calls a class procedure, it directly calls that procedure using a `call` instruction, just like any normal procedure call. Methods are another story altogether. Each object in the system carries a pointer to a virtual method table, which is an array of pointers to all the methods and iterators appearing within the object's class (see Figure 14-4).

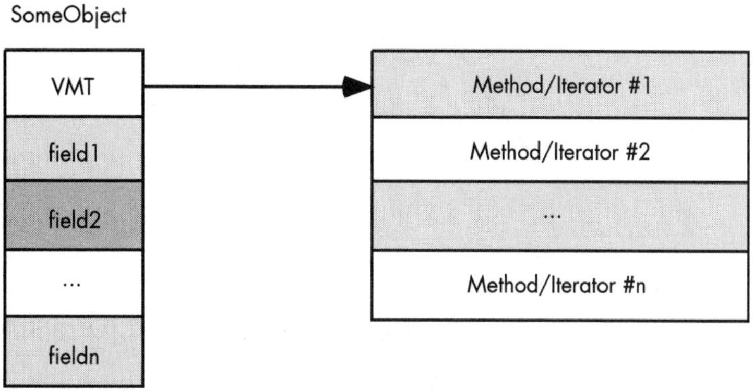

SomeObject

Figure 14-4: Virtual Method Table Organization.

Each iterator or method you declare in a class has a corresponding entry in the virtual method table. That double word entry contains the address of the first instruction of that iterator or method. Calling a class method or iterator is a bit more work than calling a class procedure (it requires one additional instruction plus the use of the EDI register). Here is a typical calling sequence for a method:

```
mov( ObjectAdrs, ESI );         // All class routines do this.
mov( [esi], edi );              // Get the address of the VMT into EDI
call( (type dword [edi+n]));    // "n" is the offset of the method's
                                // entry in the VMT.
```

For a given class there is only one copy of the VMT in memory. This is a static object so all objects of a given class type share the same VMT. This is reasonable since all objects of the same class type have exactly the same methods and iterators (see Figure 14-5).

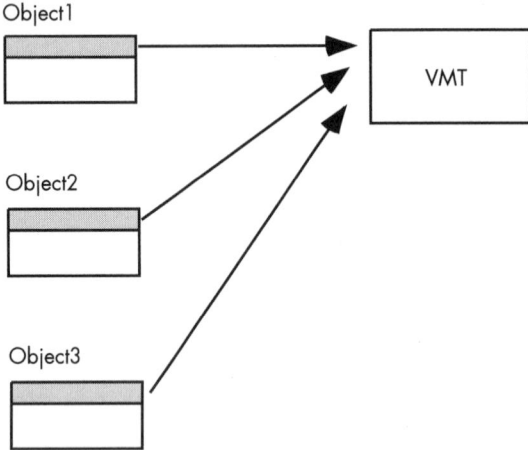

Note: Objects are all the same class type.

Figure 14-5: All Objects That Are the Same Class Type Share the Same VMT.

Although HLA builds the VMT record structure as it encounters methods and iterators within a class, HLA does not automatically create the virtual method table for you. You must explicitly declare this table in your program. To do this, you include a statement like the following in a static or readonly declaration section of your program, e.g.,

```
readonly
    VMT( classname );
```

Because the addresses in a virtual method table should never change during program execution, the readonly section is probably the best choice for declaring VMTs. It should go without saying that changing the pointers in a VMT is, in general, a really bad idea. So putting VMTs in a static section is usually not a good idea.

A declaration like the one above defines the variable classname._VMT_. In the section on constructors coming up later this chapter, you will see that you need this name when initializing object variables. The class declaration automatically defines the classname._VMT_ symbol as an external static variable. The declaration above just provides the actual definition for this external symbol.

The declaration of a VMT uses a somewhat strange syntax because you aren't actually declaring a new symbol with this declaration; you're simply supplying the data for a symbol that you previously declared implicitly by defining a class. That is, the class declaration defines the static table variable classname._VMT_; all you're doing with the VMT declaration is telling HLA to emit the actual data for the table. If, for some reason, you would like to refer to this table using a name other than classname._VMT_, HLA does allow you to prefix the declaration above with a variable name, e.g.,

```
readonly
    myVMT: VMT( classname );
```

In this declaration, myVMT is an alias of classname._VMT_. As a general rule, you should avoid aliases in a program because they make the program more difficult to read and understand. Therefore, it is unlikely that you would ever really need to use this type of declaration.

Like any other global static variable, there should be only one instance of a VMT for a given class in a program. The best place to put the VMT declaration is in the same source file as the class's method, iterator, and procedure code (assuming they all appear in a single file). This way you will automatically link in the VMT whenever you link in the routines for a given class.

14.9.2 Object Representation with Inheritance

Up to this point, the discussion of the implementation of class objects has ignored the possibility of inheritance. Inheritance only affects the memory representation of an object by adding fields that are not explicitly stated in the class declaration.

Adding inherited fields from a *base class* to another class must be done carefully. Remember, an important attribute of a class that inherits fields from a base class is that you can use a pointer to the base class to access the inherited fields from that base class, even if the pointer contains the address of some other class (that inherits the fields from the base class). As an example, consider the following classes:

```
type
    tBaseClass: class
        var
            i:uns32;
            j:uns32;
            r:real32;

        method mBase;
    endclass;

    tChildClassA: class inherits( tBaseClass )
        var
            c:char;
            b:boolean;
            w:word;

        method mA;
    endclass;

    tChildClassB: class inherits( tBaseClass )
        var
            d:dword;
            c:char;
            a:byte[3];
    endclass;
```

Because both tChildClassA and tChildClassB inherit the fields of tBaseClass, these two child classes include the i, j, and r fields as well as their own specific fields. Furthermore, whenever you have a pointer variable whose base type is tBaseClass, it is legal to load this pointer with the address of any child class of tBaseClass; therefore, it is perfectly reasonable to load such a pointer with the address of a tChildClassA or tChildClassB variable. For example:

```
var
      B1: tBaseClass;
      CA: tChildClassA;
      CB: tChildClassB;
      ptr: pointer to tBaseClass;
               .
               .
               .

      lea( ebx, B1 );
      mov( ebx, ptr );
      << Use ptr >>
               .
               .
               .

      lea( eax, CA );
      mov( ebx, ptr );
      << Use ptr >>
               .
               .
               .

      lea( eax, CB );
      mov( eax, ptr );
      << Use ptr >>
```

Because ptr points at an object of type tBaseClass, you may legally (from a semantic sense) access the i, j, and r fields of the object where ptr is pointing. It is not legal to access the c, b, w, or d fields of the tChildClassA or tChildClassB objects because at any one given moment the program may not know exactly what object type ptr references.

In order for inheritance to work properly, the i, j, and r fields must appear at the same offsets in all child classes as they do in tBaseClass. This way, an instruction of the form "mov((type tBaseClass [ebx]).i, eax);" will correct access the i field even if EBX points at an object of type tChildClassA or tChildClassB. Figure 14-6 shows the layout of the child and base classes:

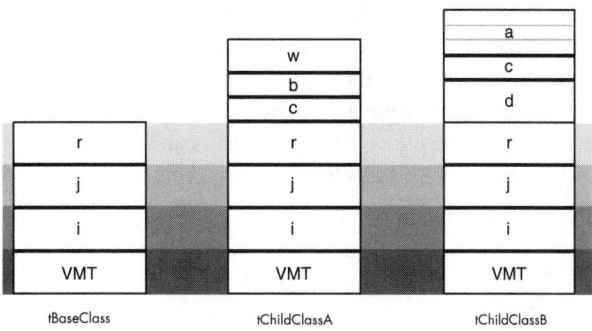

Derived (child) classes locate their inherited fields at the same offsets as
those fields in the base class.

Figure 14-6: Layout of Base and Child Class Objects in Memory.

Note that the new fields in the two child classes bear no relation to one another,
even if they have the same name (e.g., the c fields in the two child classes do not
lie at the same offset). Although the two child classes share the fields they inherit
from their common base class, any new fields they add are unique and separate.
Two fields in different classes share the same offset only by coincidence if those
fields are not inherited from a common base class.

All classes (even those that aren't related to one another) place the pointer
to the virtual method table at offset zero within the object. There is a single VMT
associated with each class in a program; even classes that inherit fields from some
base class have a VMT that is (generally) different than the base class's VMT. Figure
14-7 shows how objects of type tBaseClass, tChildClassA, and tChildClassB point at
their specific VMTs:

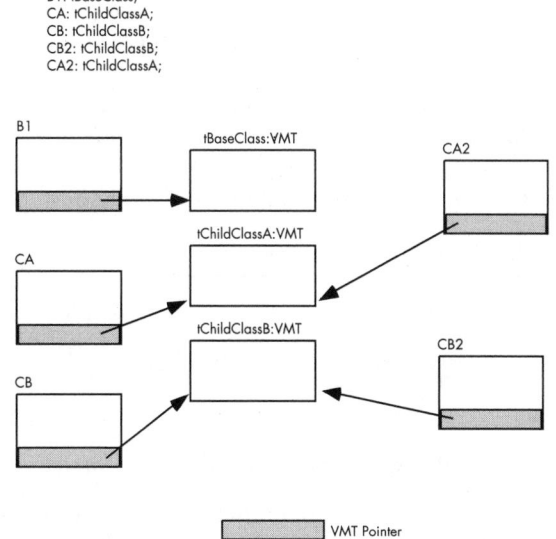

Figure 14-7: Virtual Method Table References from Objects.

A virtual method table is nothing more than an array of pointers to the methods and iterators associated with a class. The address of the first method or iterator that appears in a class is at offset zero, the address of the second appears at offset four, and so on. You can determine the offset value for a given iterator or method by using the @offset function. If you want to call a method directly (using 80x86 syntax rather than HLA's high level syntax), you could use code like the following:

```
var
    sc: tBaseClass;
        .
        .
        .
    lea( esi, sc );                 // Get the address of the object (& VMT).
    mov( [esi], edi );              // Put address of VMT into EDI.
    call( (type dword [edi+@offset( tBaseClass.mBase )] );
```

Of course, if the method has any parameters, you must push them onto the stack before executing the code above. Don't forget when making direct calls to a method you must load ESI with the address of the object. Any field references within the method will probably depend upon ESI containing this address. The choice of EDI to contain the VMT address is nearly arbitrary. Unless you're doing something tricky (like using EDI to obtain run-time type information), you could use any register you please here. As a general rule, you should use EDI when simulating class method calls because this is the convention that HLA employs and most programmers will expect this.

Whenever a child class inherits fields from some base class, the child class's VMT also inherits entries from the base class's VMT. For example, the VMT for class tBaseClass contains only a single entry — a pointer to method tBaseClass.mBase. The VMT for class tChildClassA contains two entries: a pointer to tBaseClass.mBase and tChildClassA.mA. Because tChildClassB doesn't define any new methods or iterators, tChildClassB's VMT contains only a single entry, a pointer to the tBaseClass.mBase method. Note that tChildClassB's VMT is identical to tBaseclass's VMT. Nevertheless, HLA produces two distinct VMTs. This is a critical fact that we will make use of a little later. Figure 14-8 shows the relationship between these VMTs.

Virtual Method Tables for Derived (Inherited) Classes

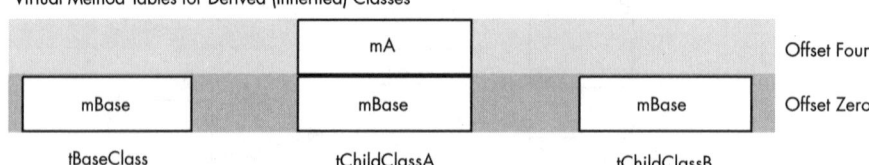

Figure 14-8: Virtual Method Tables for Inherited Classes.

Although the VMT always appears at offset zero in an object (and, therefore, you can access the VMT using the address expression "[ESI]" if ESI points at an object), HLA actually inserts a symbol into the symbol table so you may refer to the VMT symbolically. The symbol _pVMT_ (pointer to virtual methodtable) provides this capability. So a more readable way to access the VMT pointer (as in the previous code example) is

```
lea( esi, sc );
mov( (type tBaseClass [esi])._pVMT_, edi );
call( (type dword [edi+@offset( tBaseClass.mBase )] ) );
```

If you need to access the VMT directly, there are a couple ways to do this. Whenever you declare a class object, HLA automatically includes a field named _VMT_ as part of that class. _VMT_ is a static array of double word objects. Therefore, you may refer to the VMT using an identifier of the form classname._VMT_. Generally, you shouldn't access the VMT directly, but as you'll see shortly, there are some good reasons why you need to know the address of this object in memory.

14.10   Constructors and Object Initialization

If you've tried to get a little ahead of the game and write a program that uses objects prior to this point, you've probably discovered that the program inexplicably crashes whenever you attempt to run it. We've covered a lot of material in this chapter thus far, but you are still missing one crucial piece of information — how to properly initialize objects prior to use. This section will put the final piece into the puzzle and allow you to begin writing programs that use classes.

Consider the following object declaration and code fragment:

```
var
    bc: tBaseClass;
        .
        .
        .
    bc.mBase();
```

Remember that variables you declare in the var section are uninitialized at run-time. Therefore, when the program containing these statements gets around to executing bc.mBase, it executes the three-statement sequence you've seen several times already:

```
lea( esi, bc);
mov( [esi], edi );
call( (type dword [edi+@offset( tBaseClass.mBase )] ) );
```

The problem with this sequence is that it loads EDI with an undefined value assuming you haven't previously initialized the bc object. Because EDI contains a garbage value, attempting to call a subroutine at address "[EDI+@offset(tBaseClass.mBase)]" will likely crash the system. Therefore, before using an object, you must initialize the _pVMT_ field with the address of that object's VMT. One easy way to do this is with the following statement:

```
mov( &tBaseClass._VMT_, bc._pVMT_ );
```

Always remember, before using an object, be sure to initialize the virtual method table pointer for that object.

Although you must initialize the virtual method table pointer for all objects you use, this may not be the only field you need to initialize in those objects. Each specific class may have its own application-specific initialization that is necessary. Although the initialization may vary by class, you need to perform the same initialization on each object of a specific class that you use. If you ever create more than a single object from a given class, it is probably a good idea to create a procedure to do this initialization for you. This is such a common operation that object-oriented programmers have given these initialization procedures a special name: *constructors*.

Some object-oriented languages (e.g., C++) use a special syntax to declare a constructor. Others (e.g., Delphi) simply use existing procedure declarations to define a constructor. One advantage to employing a special syntax is that the language knows when you define a constructor and can automatically generate code to call that constructor for you (whenever you declare an object). Languages, like Delphi, require that you explicitly call the constructor; this can be a minor inconvenience and a source of defects in your programs. HLA does not use a special syntax to declare constructors: You define constructors using standard class procedures. As such, you will need to explicitly call the constructors in your program; however, you'll see an easy method for automating this in a later section of this chapter.

Perhaps the most important fact you must remember is that **constructors must be class procedures**. You must not define constructors as methods. The reason is quite simple: One of the tasks of the constructor is to initialize the pointer to the virtual method table, and you cannot call a class method or iterator until after you've initialized the VMT pointer. Because class procedures don't use the virtual method table, you can call a class procedure prior to initializing the VMT pointer for an object.

By convention, HLA programmers use the name *Create* for the class constructor. There is no requirement that you use this name, but by doing so you will make your programs easier to read and follow by other programmers.

As you may recall, you can call a class procedure via an object reference or a class reference. E.g., if clsProc is a class procedure of class tClass and Obj is an object of type tClass, then the following two class procedure invocations are both legal:

```
tClass.clsProc();
Obj.clsProc();
```

There is a big difference between these two calls. The first one calls clsProc with ESI containing zero (NULL) while the second invocation loads the address of Obj into ESI before the call. We can use this fact to determine within a method the particular calling mechanism.

14.10.1   Dynamic Object Allocation Within the Constructor

As it turns out, most programs allocate objects dynamically using malloc and refer to those objects indirectly using pointers. This adds one more step to the initialization process — allocating storage for the object. The constructor is the perfect place to allocate this storage. Because you probably won't need to allocate all objects dynamically, you'll need two types of constructors: one that allocates storage and then initializes the object, and another that simply initializes an object that already has storage.

Another constructor convention is to merge these two constructors into a single constructor and differentiate the type of constructor call by the value in ESI. On entry into the class's Create procedure, the program checks the value in ESI to see if it contains NULL (zero). If so, the constructor calls malloc to allocate storage for the object and returns a pointer to the object in ESI. If ESI does not contain NULL upon entry into the procedure, then the constructor assumes that ESI points at a valid object and skips over the memory allocation statements. At the very least, a constructor initializes the pointer to the VMT; therefore, the minimalist constructor will look like the following:

```
procedure tBaseClass.mBase; @nodisplay;
begin mBase;

    if( ESI = 0 ) then

        push( eax );        // Malloc returns its result here, so save it.
        malloc( @size( tBaseClass ));
        mov( eax, esi );  // Put pointer into ESI;
        pop( eax );

    endif;

    // Initialize the pointer to the VMT:
    // (remember, "this" is shorthand for (type tBaseClass [esi])"

    mov( &tBaseClass._VMT_, this._pVMT_ );

    // Other class initialization would go here.

end mBase;
```

After you write a constructor like the preceding, you choose an appropriate calling mechanism based on whether your object's storage is already allocated. For preallocated objects (i.e., those you've declared in var, static, or storage sections[7] or those you've previously allocated storage for via malloc) you simply load the address of the object into ESI and call the constructor. For those objects you declare as a variable, this is very easy: Just call the appropriate Create constructor:

---

[7] You generally do not declare objects in readonly sections because you cannot initialize them.

```
var
    bc0: tBaseClass;
    bcp: pointer to tBaseClass;
        .
        .
        .
    bc0.Create();  // Initializes preallocated bc0 object.
        .
        .
        .
    malloc( @size( tBaseClass ));  // Allocate storage for bcp object.
    mov( eax, bcp );
        .
        .
        .
    bcp.Create();  // Initializes preallocated bcp object.
```

Note that although bcp is a pointer to a tBaseClass object, the Create method does not automatically allocate storage for this object. The program already allocates the storage earlier. Therefore, when the program calls *bcp.Create* it loads ESI with the address contained within bcp; because this is not NULL, the tBaseClass.Create procedure does not allocate storage for a new object. By the way, the call to bcp.Create emits the following sequence of machine instructions:

```
    mov( bcp, esi );
    call tBaseClass.Create;
```

Until now, the code examples for a class procedure call always began with an lea instruction. This is because all the examples to this point have used object variables rather than pointers to object variables. Remember, a class procedure (method) call passes the address of the object in the ESI register. For object variables HLA emits an lea instruction to obtain this address. For pointers to objects, however, the actual object address is the *value* of the pointer variable; therefore, to load the address of the object into ESI, HLA emits a mov instruction that copies the value of the pointer into the ESI register.

In the preceding example, the program preallocates the storage for an object prior to calling the object constructor. While there are several reasons for preallocating object storage (e.g., you're creating a dynamic array of objects), you can achieve most simple object allocations like the one above by calling a standard Create procedure (i.e., one that allocates storage for an object if ESI contains NULL). The following example demonstrates this:

```
var
    bcp2: pointer to tBaseClass;
        .
        .
        .
```

```
        tBaseClass.Create();    // Calls Create with ESI=NULL.
        mov( esi, bcp2 );       // Save pointer to new class object in bcp2.
```

Remember, a call to a tBaseClass.Create constructor returns a pointer to the new
object in the ESI register. It is the caller's responsibility to save the pointer this
function returns into the appropriate pointer variable; the constructor does not
automatically do this for you. Likewise, it is the caller's responsibility to free the
storage associated with this object when the application is done using the object
(see the discussion of destructors a little later in this chapter).

14.10.2 Constructors and Inheritance

Constructors for derived (child) classes that inherit fields from a base class
represent a special case. Each class must have its own constructor but needs the
ability to call the base class constructor. This section explains the reasons for this
and how to do this.

A derived class inherits the Create procedure from its base class. However,
you must override this procedure in a derived class because the derived class
probably requires more storage than the base class and, therefore, you will
probably need to use a different call to malloc to allocate storage for a dynamic
object. Hence, it is very unusual for a derived class not to override the definition
of the Create procedure.

However, overriding a base class's Create procedure has problems of its own.
When you override the base class's Create procedure, you take the full
responsibility of initializing the (entire) object, including all the initialization
required by the base class. At the very least, this involves putting duplicate code
in the overridden procedure to handle the initialization usually done by the base
class constructor. In addition to make your program larger (by duplicating code
already present in the base class constructor), this also violates information
hiding principles because the derived class must be aware of all the fields in the
base class (including those that are logically private to the base class). What we
need here is the ability to call a base class's constructor from within the derived
class's destructor and let that call do the lower-level initialization of the base
class's fields. Fortunately, this is an easy thing to do in HLA.

Consider the following class declarations (which do things the hard way):

```
type
    tBase: class
        var
            i:uns32;
            j:int32;

        procedure Create(); returns( "esi" );
    endclass;

    tDerived: class inherits( tBase );
        var
            r: real64;
```

```hla
        override procedure Create(); returns( "esi" );
    endclass;

    procedure tBase.Create; @nodisplay;
    begin Create;

        if( esi = 0 ) then

            push( eax );
            mov( malloc( @size( tBase )), esi );
            pop( eax );

        endif;
        mov( &tBase._VMT_, this._pVMT_ );
        mov( 0, this.i );
        mov( -1, this.j );

    end Create;

    procedure tDerived.Create; @nodisplay;
    begin Create;

        if( esi = 0 ) then

            push( eax );
            mov( malloc( @size( tDerived )), esi );
            pop( eax );

        endif;

        // Initialize the VMT pointer for this object:

        mov( &tDerived._VMT_, this._pVMT_ );

        // Initialize the "r" field of this particular object:

        fldz();
        fstp( this.r );

        // Duplicate the initialization required by tBase.Create:

        mov( 0, this.i );
        mov( -1, this.j );

    end Create;
```

Let's take a closer look at the tDerived.Create procedure above. Like a conventional constructor, it begins by checking ESI and allocates storage for a new object if ESI contains NULL. Note that the size of a tDerived object includes the size required by the inherited fields, so this properly allocates the necessary storage for all fields in a tDerived object.

Next, the tDerived.Create procedure initializes the VMT pointer field of the object. Remember, each class has its own VMT and, specifically, derived classes do not use the VMT of their base class. Therefore, this constructor must initialize the _pVMT_ field with the address of the tDerived VMT.

After initializing the VMT pointer, the tDerived constructor initializes the value of the r field to 0.0 (remember, FLDZ loads zero onto the FPU stack). This concludes the tDerived-specific initialization.

The remaining instructions in tDerived.Create are the problem. These statements duplicate some of the code appearing in the *tBase.Create* procedure. The problem with code duplication becomes really apparent when you decide to modify the initial values of these fields; if you've duplicated the initialization code in derived classes, you will need to change the initialization code in more than one Create procedure. More often than not, however, this results in defects in the derived class Create procedures, especially if those derived classes appear in different source files than the base class.

Another problem with burying base class initialization in derived class constructors is the violation of the information hiding principle. Some fields of the base class may be *logically private.* Although HLA does not explicitly support the concept of public and private fields in a class (as, say, C++ does), well-disciplined programmers will still partition the fields as private or public and then only use the private fields in class routines belonging to that class. Initializing these private fields in derived classes is not acceptable to such programmers. Doing so will make it very difficult to change the definition and implementation of some base class at a later date.

Fortunately, HLA provides an easy mechanism for calling the inherited constructor within a derived class's constructor. All you have to do is call the base constructor using the classname syntax, e.g., you could call tBase.Create directly from within tDerived.Create. By calling the base class constructor, your derived class constructors can initialize the base class fields without worrying about the exact implementation (or initial values) of the base class.

Unfortunately, there are two types of initialization that every (conventional) constructor does that will affect the way you call a base class constructor: all conventional constructors allocate memory for the class if ESI contains zero and all conventional constructors initialize the VMT pointer. Fortunately, it is very easy to deal with these two problems

The memory required by an object of some most base class is usually less than the memory required for an object of a class you derive from that base class (because the derived classes usually add more fields). Therefore, you cannot allow the base class constructor to allocate the storage when you call it from inside the derived class's constructor. This problem is easily solved by checking ESI within the derived class constructor and allocating any necessary storage for the object *before* calling the base class constructor.

The second problem is the initialization of the VMT pointer. When you call the base class's constructor, it will initialize the VMT pointer with the address of the base class's virtual method table. A derived class object's _pVMT_ field, however, must point at the virtual method table for the derived class. Calling the base class constructor will always initialize the _pVMT_ field with the wrong pointer; to properly initialize the _pVMT_ field with the appropriate value, the derived class constructor must store the address of the derived class's virtual method table into the _pVMT_ field *after* the call to the base class constructor (so that it overwrites the value written by the base class constructor).

The tDerived.Create constructor, rewritten to call the tBase.Create constructors, follows:

```
procedure tDerived.Create; @nodisplay;
begin Create;

    if( esi = 0 ) then

        push( eax );
        mov( malloc( @size( tDerived )), esi );
        pop( eax );

    endif;

    // Call the base class constructor to do any initialization
    // needed by the base class. Note that this call must follow
    // the object allocation code above (so ESI will always contain
    // a pointer to an object at this point and tBase.Create will
    // never allocate storage).

    tBase.Create();

    // Initialize the VMT pointer for this object. This code
    // must always follow the call to the base class constructor
    // because the base class constructor also initializes this
    // field and we don't want the initial value supplied by
    // tBase.Create.

    mov( &tDerived._VMT_, this._pVMT_ );

    // Initialize the "r" field of this particular object:

    fldz();
    fstp( this.r );

end Create;
```

This solution solves all the above concerns with derived class constructors.

14.10.3　Constructor Parameters and Procedure Overloading

All the constructor examples to this point have not had any parameters. However, there is nothing special about constructors that prevents the use of parameters. Constructors are procedures; therefore, you can specify any number and types of parameters you choose. You can use these parameter values to initialize certain fields or control how the constructor initializes the fields. Of course, you may use constructor parameters for any purpose you'd use parameters in any other procedure. In fact, about the only issue you need concern yourself with is the use of parameters whenever you have a derived class. This section deals with those issues.

The first, and probably most important, problem with parameters in derived class constructors actually applies to all overridden procedures and methods: The parameter list of an overridden routine must exactly match the parameter list of the corresponding routine in the base class. In fact, HLA doesn't even give you the chance to violate this rule because override routine prototypes don't allow parameter list declarations: They automatically inherit the parameter list of the base routine. Therefore, you cannot use a special parameter list in the constructor prototype for one class and a different parameter list for the constructors appearing in base or derived classes. Sometimes it would be nice if this weren't the case, but there are some sound and logical reasons why HLA does not support this.[8]

Some languages, like C++, support function overloading letting you specify several different constructors whose parameter list specifies which constructor to use. HLA does not directly support procedure overloading in this manner, but you can use macros to simulate this language feature (see the chapter on macros and the HLA compile time language). To use this trick with constructors you would create a macro with the name Create. The actual constructors could have names that describe their differences (e.g., createdefault, createsetij, and so on). The Create macro would parse the actual parameter list to determine which routine to call.

HLA does not support macro overloading. Therefore, you cannot override a macro in a derived class to call a constructor unique to that derived class. In certain circumstances you can create a small work-around by defining empty procedures in your base class that you intend to override in some derived class (this is similar to an abstract method; see the discussion of abstract methods a little later in this chapter). Presumably, you would never call the procedure in the base class (in fact, you would probably want to put an error message in the body of the procedure just in case you accidentally call it). By putting the empty procedure declaration in the base class, the macro that simulates function overloading can refer to that procedure, and you can use that in derived classes later on.

---

[8] Calling virtual methods and iterators would be a real problem because you don't really know which routine a pointer references. Therefore, you couldn't know the proper parameter list. While the problems with procedures aren't quite as drastic, there are some subtle problems that could creep into your code if base or derived classes allowed overridden procedures with different parameter lists.

14.11 Destructors

A *destructor* is a class routine that cleans up an object once a program finishes using that object. Like constructors, HLA does not provide a special syntax for creating destructors nor does HLA automatically call a destructor; unlike constructors, a destructor is usually a method rather than a procedure (because virtual destructors make a lot of sense while virtual constructors do not).

A typical destructor will close any files opened by the object, free the memory allocated during the use of the object, and, finally, free the object itself if it was created dynamically. The destructor also handles any other cleanup chores the object may require before it ceases to exist.

By convention, most HLA programmers name their destructors Destroy. Destructors generally do not have any parameters, so the issue of overloading the parameter list rarely arises. About the only code that most destructors have in common is the code to free the storage associated with the object. The following destructor demonstrates how to do this:

```
procedure tBase.Destroy; @nodisplay;
begin Destroy;

    push( eax );    // isInHeap uses this

    // Place any other cleanup code here.
    // The code to free dynamic objects should always appear last
    // in the destructor.

    /************/

    // The following code assumes that ESI still contains the address
    // of the object.

    if( isInHeap( esi )) then

        free( esi );

    endif;
    pop( eax );

end Destroy;
```

The HLA Standard Library routine isInHeap returns true if its parameter is an address that malloc returned. Therefore, this code automatically frees the storage associated with the object if the program originally allocated storage for the object by calling malloc. Obviously, on return from this method call, ESI will no longer point at a legal object in memory if you allocated it dynamically. Note that this code will not affect the value in ESI nor will it modify the object if the object wasn't one you've previously allocated via a call to malloc.

14.12 HLA's "_initialize_" and "_finalize_" Strings

Although HLA does not automatically call constructors and destructors associated with your classes, HLA does provide a mechanism whereby you can force HLA to automatically emit these calls: by using the _initialize_ and _finalize_ compile time string variables (i.e., val constants) HLA automatically declares in every procedure.

Whenever you write a procedure, iterator, or method, HLA automatically declares several local symbols in that routine. Two such symbols are _initialize_ and _finalize_. HLA declares these symbols as follows:

```
val
    _initialize_: string := "";
    _finalize_: string := "";
```

HLA emits the _initialize_ string as text at the very beginning of the routine's body, i.e., immediately after the routine's begin clause.[9] Similarly, HLA emits the _finalize_ string at the very end of the routine's body, just before the end clause. This is comparable to the following:

```
procedure SomeProc;
    << declarations >>
begin SomeProc;

    @text( _initialize_ );

        << procedure body >>

    @text( _finalize_ );

end SomeProc;
```

Because _initialize_ and _finalize_ initially contain the empty string, these expansions have no effect on the code that HLA generates unless you explicitly modify the value of _initialize_ prior to the begin clause or you modify _finalize_ prior to the end clause of the procedure. So if you modify either of these string objects to contain a machine instruction, HLA will compile that instruction at the beginning or end of the procedure. The following example demonstrates how to use this technique:

```
procedure SomeProc;
    ?_initialize_ := "mov( 0, eax );";
    ?_finalize_ := "stdout.put( eax );"
begin SomeProc;

    // HLA emits "mov( 0, eax );" here in response to the _initialize_
    // string constant.
```

---

[9] If the routine automatically emits code to construct the activation record, HLA emits _initialize_'s text after the code that builds the activation record.

```
        add( 5, eax );

        // HLA emits "stdout.put( eax );" here.

end SomeProc;
```

Of course, these examples don't save you much. It would be easier to type the actual statements at the beginning and end of the procedure than assign a string containing these statements to the _initialize_ and _finalize_ compile time variables. However, if we could automate the assignment of some string to these variables, so that you don't have to explicitly assign them in each procedure, then this feature might be useful. In a moment, you'll see how we can automate the assignment of values to the _initialize_ and _finalize_ strings. For the time being, consider the case where we load the name of a constructor into the _initialize_ string and we load the name of a destructor in to the _finalize_ string. By doing this, the routine will "automatically" call the constructor and destructor for that particular object.

The previous example has a minor problem. If we can automate the assignment of some value to _initialize_ or _finalize_, what happens if these variables already contain some value? For example, suppose we have two objects we use in a routine, and the first one loads the name of its constructor into the _initialize_ string; what happens when the second object attempts to do the same thing? The solution is simple: Don't directly assign any string to the _initialize_ or _finalize_ compile time variables; instead, always concatenate your strings to the end of the existing string in these variables. The following is a modification to the above example that demonstrates how to do this:

```
procedure SomeProc;
    ?_initialize_  :=  _initialize_  + "mov( 0, eax );";
    ?_finalize_    :=  _finalize_ + "stdout.put( eax );"
begin SomeProc;

    // HLA emits "mov( 0, eax );" here in response to the _initialize_
    // string constant.

    add( 5, eax );

    // HLA emits "stdout.put( eax );" here.

end SomeProc;
```

When you assign values to the _initialize_ and _finalize_ strings, HLA almost guarantees that the _initialize_ sequence will execute upon entry into the routine. Sadly, the same is not true for the _finalize_ string upon exit. HLA simply emits the code for the _finalize_ string at the end of the routine, immediately before the code that cleans up the activation record and returns. Unfortunately, "falling off the end of the routine" is not the only way that one could return from that routine. One could explicitly return from somewhere in the middle of the code by executing a ret instruction. Because HLA only emits the _finalize_ string at the very end of the routine, returning from that routine in this manner bypasses the _finalize_ code. Unfortunately, other than manually emitting the _finalize_ code, there is nothing you can do about this.[10] Fortunately, this mechanism for exiting a routine is completely under your control; if you never exit a routine except by "falling off the end" then you won't have to worry about this problem (note that you can use the exit control structure to transfer control to the end of a routine if you really want to return from that routine from somewhere in the middle of the code).

Another way to prematurely exit a routine, over which, unfortunately, you don't have any control, is by raising an exception. Your routine could call some other routine (e.g., a Standard Library routine) that raises an exception and then transfers control immediately to whomever called your routine. Fortunately, you can easily trap and handle exceptions by putting a try..endtry block in your procedure. Here is an example that demonstrates this:

```
procedure SomeProc;
    << declarations that  modify _initialize_ and _finalize_ >>
begin SomeProc;

    << HLA emits the code for the _initialize_ string here. >>

    try    // Catch any exceptions that occur:

        << Procedure Body Goes Here >>

      anyexception

        push( eax );    // Save the exception #.
        @text( _finalize_ );  // Execute the _finalize_ code here.
        pop( eax );           // Restore the exception #.
        raise( eax );         // Reraise the exception.

    endtry;

    // HLA automatically emits the _finalize_ code here.

end SomeProc;
```

Although the previous code handles some problems that exist with _finalize_, by no means does it handle every possible case. Always be on the look out for ways your program could inadvertently exit a routine without executing the code found in the _finalize_ string. You should explicitly expand _finalize_ if you encounter such a situation.

---

[10] Note that you can manually emit the _finalize_ code using the statement "@text(_finalize_);".

There is one important place you can get into trouble with respect to exceptions: within the code the routine emits for the _initialize_ string. If you modify the _initialize_ string so that it contains a constructor call and the execution of that constructor raises an exception, this will probably force an exit from that routine without executing the corresponding _finalize_ code. You could bury the try..endtry statement directly into the _initialize_ and _finalize_ strings, but this approach has several problems, not the least of which is the fact that one of the first constructors you call might raise an exception that transfers control to the exception handler that calls the destructors for all objects in that routine (including those objects whose constructors you have yet to call). Although no single solution that handles all problems exists, probably the best approach is to put a try..endtry block within each constructor call if it is possible for that constructor to raise some exception that is possible to handle (i.e., doesn't require the immediate termination of the program).

Thus far this discussion of _initialize_ and _finalize_ has failed to address one important point: Why use this feature to implement the "automatic" calling of constructors and destructors because it apparently involves more work that simply calling the constructors and destructors directly? Clearly there must be a way to automate the assignment of the _initialize_ and _finalize_ strings or this section wouldn't exist. The way to accomplish this is by using a macro to define the class type. So now it's time to take a look at another HLA feature that makes is possible to automate this activity: the forward keyword.

You've seen how to use the forward reserved word to create procedure prototypes (see the discussion in the chapter on procedures), it turns out that you can declare forward const, val, type, and variable declarations as well. The syntax for such declarations takes the following form:

```
ForwardSymbolName: forward( undefinedID );
```

This declaration is completely equivalent to the following:

```
?undefinedID: text := "ForwardSymbolName";
```

Especially note that this expansion does not actually define the symbol ForwardSymbolName. It just converts this symbol to a string and assigns this string to the specified text object (undefinedID in this example).

Now you're probably wondering how something like the above is equivalent to a forward declaration. The truth is, it isn't. However, forward declarations let you create macros that simulate type names by allowing you to defer the actual declaration of an object's type until some later point in the code. Consider the following example:

```
type
    myClass: class
        var
            i:int32;

        procedure Create; returns( "esi" );
```

```
            procedure Destroy;
        endclass;

#macro _myClass: varID;
        forward( varID );
        ?_initialize_ := _initialize_ + @string:varID + ".Create(); ";
        ?_finalize_ := _finalize_ + @string:varID + ".Destroy(); ";
        varID: myClass
#endmacro;
```

Note, and this is very important, that a semicolon does not follow the "varID: myClass" declaration at the end of this macro. You'll find out why this semicolon is missing in a little bit.

If you have the class and macro declarations above in your program, you can now declare variables of type _myClass that automatically invoke the constructor and destructor upon entry and exit of the routine containing the variable declarations. To see how, take a look at the following procedure shell:

```
procedure HasmyClassObject;
var
        mco: _myClass;
begin HasmyClassObject;

        << do stuff with mco here >>

end HasmyClassObject;
```

Since _myClass is a macro, the procedure above expands to the following text during compilation:

```
procedure HasmyClassObject;
var
        mco:                    // Expansion of the _myClass macro:
            forward( _0103_ );  // _0103_ symbol is an HLA-supplied text symbol
                                // that expands to "mco".

        ?_initialize_ := _initialize_ + "mco" + ".Create(); ";
        ?_finalize_ := _finalize_ + "mco" + ".Destroy(); ";
        mco: myClass;

begin HasmyClassObject;

        mco.Create();           // Expansion of the _initialize_ string.

        << do stuff with mco here >>

        mco.Destroy();          // Expansion of the _finalize_ string.
```

```
end HasmyClassObject;
```

You might notice that a semicolon appears after "mco: myClass" declaration in the example above. This semicolon is not actually a part of the macro; instead it is the semicolon that follows the "mco: _myClass;" declaration in the original code.

If you want to create an array of objects, you could legally declare that array as follows:

```
var
    mcoArray: _myClass[10];
```

Because the last statement in the _myClass macro doesn't end with a semicolon, the declaration above will expand to something like the following (almost correct) code:

```
mcoArray:                        // Expansion of the _myClass macro:
    forward( _0103_ );  // _0103_ symbol is an HLA-supplied text symbol
                        // that expands to "mcoArray".

?_initialize_ := _initialize_ + "mcoArray" + ".Create(); ";
?_finalize_ := _finalize_ + "mcoArray" + ".Destroy(); ";
mcoArray: myClass[10];
```

The only problem with this expansion is that it only calls the constructor for the first object of the array. There are several ways to solve this problem; one is to append a macro name to the end of _initialize_ and _finalize_ rather than the constructor name. That macro would check the object's name (mcoArray in this example) to determine if it is an array. If so, that macro could expand to a loop that calls the constructor for each element of the array.

Another solution to this problem is to use a macro parameter to specify the dimensions for arrays of myClass. This scheme is easier to implement than the one above, but it does have the drawback of requiring a different syntax for declaring object arrays (you have to use parentheses around the array dimension rather than square brackets).

The forward directive is quite powerful and lets you achieve all kinds of tricks. However, there are a few problems of which you should be aware. First, because HLA emits the _initialize_ and _finalize_ code transparently, you can be easily confused if there are any errors in the code appearing within these strings. If you start getting error messages associated with the begin or end statements in a routine, you might want to take a look at the _initialize_ and _finalize_ strings within that routine. The best defense here is to always append very simple statements to these strings so that you reduce the likelihood of an error.

Fundamentally, HLA doesn't support automatic constructor and destructor calls. This section has presented several tricks to attempt to automate the calls to these routines. However, the automation isn't perfect and, indeed, the aforementioned problems with the _finalize_ strings limit the applicability of this approach. The mechanism this section presents is probably fine for simple classes and simple programs. One piece of advice is probably worth following: If your code is complex or correctness is critical, it's probably a good idea to explicitly call the constructors and destructors manually.

14.13　Abstract Methods

An *abstract base class* is one that exists solely to supply a set of common fields to its derived classes. You never declare variables whose type is an abstract base class; you always use one of the derived classes. The purpose of an abstract base class is to provide a template for creating other classes, nothing more. As it turns out, the only difference in syntax between a standard base class and an abstract base class is the presence of at least one *abstract method* declaration. An abstract method is a special method that does not have an actual implementation in the abstract base class. Any attempt to call that method will raise an exception. If you're wondering what possible good an abstract method could be, well, keep on reading. . . .

Suppose you want to create a set of classes to hold numeric values. One class could represent unsigned integers, another class could represent signed integers, a third could implement BCD values, and a fourth could support real64 values. While you could create four separate classes that function independently of one another, doing so passes up an opportunity to make this set of classes more convenient to use. To understand why, consider the following possible class declarations:

```
type
    uint: class
        var
            TheValue: dword;

        method put;
        << other methods for this class >>
    endclass;

    sint: class
        var
            TheValue: dword;

        method put;
        << other methods for this class >>
    endclass;

    r64: class
        var
            TheValue: real64;

        method put;
```

```
        << other methods for this class >>
    endclass;
```

The implementation of these classes is not unreasonable. They have fields for the data and they have a put method (which, presumably, writes the data to the standard output device), Presumably they have other methods and procedures in implement various operations on the data. There are, however, two problems with these classes, one minor and one major, both occurring because these classes do not inherit any fields from a common base class.

The first problem, which is relatively minor, is that you have to repeat the declaration of several common fields in these classes. For example, the put method declaration appears in each of these classes.[11] This duplication of effort involves results in a harder-to-maintain program because it doesn't encourage you to use a common name for a common function because it's easy to use a different name in each of the classes.

A bigger problem with this approach is that it is not generic. That is, you can't create a generic pointer to a "numeric" object and perform operations like addition, subtraction, and output on that value (regardless of the underlying numeric representation).

We can easily solve these two problems by turning the previous class declarations into a set of derived classes. The following code demonstrates an easy way to do this:

```
type
    numeric: class
        procedure put;
        << Other common methods shared by all the classes >>
    endclass;

    uint: class inherits( numeric )
        var
            TheValue: dword;

        override method put;
        << other methods for this class >>
    endclass;

    sint: class inherits( numeric )
        var
            TheValue: dword;

        override method put;
        << other methods for this class >>
    endclass;

    r64: class inherits( numeric )
        var
```

[11] Note, by the way, that TheValue is not a common field because this field has a different type in the r64 class.

```
        TheValue: real64;

    override method put;
    << other methods for this class >>
endclass;
```

This scheme solves both the problems. First, by inheriting the put method from numeric, this code encourages the derived classes to always use the name *put,* thereby making the program easier to maintain. Second, because this example uses derived classes, it's possible to create a pointer to the numeric type and load this pointer with the address of a uint, sint, or r64 object. That pointer can invoke the methods found in the numeric class to do functions like addition, subtraction, or numeric output. Therefore, the application that uses this pointer doesn't need to know the exact data type, it only deals with numeric values in a generic fashion.

One problem with this scheme is that it's possible to declare and use variables of type numeric. Unfortunately, such numeric variables don't have the ability to represent any type of number (notice that the data storage for the numeric fields actually appears in the derived classes). Worse, because you've declared the put method in the numeric class, you've actually got to write some code to implement that method even though one should never really call it; the actual implementation should only occur in the derived classes. While you could write a dummy method that prints an error message (or, better yet, raises an exception), there shouldn't be any need to write "dummy" procedures like this. Fortunately, there is no reason to do so — if you use *abstract* methods.

The @abstract keyword, when it follows a method declaration, tells HLA that you are not going to provide an implementation of the method for this class. Instead, it is the responsibility of all derived class to provide a concrete implementation for the abstract method. HLA will raise an exception if you attempt to call an abstract method directly. The following is the modification to the numeric class to convert put to an abstract method:

```
type
    numeric: class
        method put; @abstract;
        << Other common methods shared by all the classes >>
    endclass;
```

An abstract base class is a class that has at least one abstract method. Note that you don't have to make all methods abstract in an abstract base class; it is perfectly legal to declare some standard methods (and, of course, provide their implementation) within the abstract base class.

Abstract method declarations provide a mechanism by which a base class can specify some generic methods that the derived classes must implement. In theory, all derived classes must provide concrete implementations of all abstract methods, or those derived classes are themselves abstract base classes. In practice, it's possible to bend the rules a little and use abstract methods for a slightly different purpose.

A little earlier, you read that one should never create variables whose type is an abstract base class. For if you attempt to execute an abstract method the program would immediately raise an exception to complain about this illegal method call. In practice, you actually can declare variables of an abstract base type and get away with this as long as you don't call any abstract methods. We can use this fact to provide a better form of method overloading (that is, providing several different routines with the same name but different parameter lists). Remember, the standard trick in HLA to overload a routine is to write several different routines and then use a macro to parse the parameter list and determine which actual routine to call. The problem with this technique is that you cannot override a macro definition in a class, so if you want to use a macro to override a routine's syntax, then that macro must appear in the base class. Unfortunately, you may not need a routine with a specific parameter list in the base class (for that matter, you may only need that particular version of the routine in a single derived class), so implementing that routine in the base class and in all the other derived classes is a waste of effort. This isn't a big problem. Just go ahead and define the abstract method in the base class and only implement it in the derived class that needs that particular method. As long as you don't call that method in the base class or in the other derived classes that don't override the method, everything will work fine.

One problem with using abstract methods to support overloading is that this trick does not apply to procedures — only methods. However, you can achieve the same effect with procedures by declaring a (non-abstract) procedure in the base class and overriding that procedure only in the class that actually uses it. You will have to provide an implementation of the procedure in the base class, but that is a minor issue (the procedure's body, by the way, should simply raise an exception to indicate that you should have never called it).

14.14   Run-Time Type Information (RTTI)

When working with an object variable (as opposed to a pointer to an object), the type of that object is obvious: It's the variable's declared type. Therefore, at both compile time and runtime the program trivially knows the type of the object. When working with pointers to objects you cannot, in the general case, determine the type of an object a pointer references. However, at runtime it is possible to determine the object's actual type. This section discusses how to detect the underlying object's type and how to use this information.

If you have a pointer to an object and that pointer's type is some base class, at runtime the pointer could point at an object of the base class or any derived type. At compile time it is not possible to determine the exact type of an object at any instant. To see why, consider the following short example:

```
ReturnSomeObject();              // Returns a pointer to some class in ESI.
mov( esi, ptrToObject );
```

The routine ReturnSomeObject returns a pointer to an object in ESI. This could be the address of some base class object or a derived class object. At compile time there is no way for the program to know what type of object this function returns.

For example, `ReturnSomeObject` could ask the user what value to return so the exact type could not be determined until the program actually runs and the user makes a selection.

In a perfectly designed program, there probably is no need to know a generic object's actual type. After all, the whole purpose of object-oriented programming and inheritance is to produce general programs that work with lots of different objects without having to make substantial changes to the program. In the real world, however, programs may not have a perfect design and sometimes it's nice to know the exact object type a pointer references. Run-time type information, or RTTI, gives you the capability of determining an object's type at runtime, even if you are referencing that object using a pointer to some base class of that object.

Perhaps the most fundamental RTTI operation you need is the ability to ask if a pointer contains the address of some specific object type. Many object-oriented languages (e.g., Delphi) provide an *IS* operator that provides this functionality. *IS* is a boolean operator that returns true if its left operand (a pointer) points at an object whose type matches the right operand (which must be a type identifier). The typical syntax is generally the following:

```
ObjectPointerOrVar  is ClassType
```

This operator would return true if the variable is of the specified class; it returns false otherwise. Here is a typical use of this operator (in the Delphi language)

```
    if( ptrToNumeric is uint ) then begin
      .
      .
      .
    end;
```

It's actually quite simple to implement this functionality in HLA. As you may recall, each class is given its own virtual method table. Whenever you create an object, you must initialize the pointer to the VMT with the address of that class's VMT. Therefore, the VMT pointer field of all objects of a given class type contains the same pointer value, and this pointer value is different from the VMT pointer field of all other classes. We can use this fact to see if an object is some specific type. The following code demonstrates how to implement the Delphi statement above in HLA:

```
    mov( ptrToNumeric, esi );
    if( (type uint [esi])._pVMT_ = &uint._VMT_  ) then
      .
      .
      .
    endif;
```

This if statement simply compares the object's _pVMT_ field (the pointer to the VMT) against the address of the desired classes' VMT. If they are equal, then the ptrToNumeric variable points at an object of type uint.

Within the body of a class method or iterator, there is a slightly easier way to see if the object is a certain class. Remember, upon entry into a method or an iterator, the EDI register contains the address of the virtual method table. Therefore, assuming you haven't modified EDI's value, you can easily test to see if this (ESI) is a specific class type using an if statement like the following:

```
if( EDI = &uint._VMT_ ) then
       .
       .
       .
endif;
```

Remember, however, that EDI will only contain a pointer to the VMT when you call a class method. This is not the case when calling a class procedure.

14.15   Calling Base Class Methods

In the section on constructors you saw that it is possible to call an ancestor class's procedure within the derived class's overridden procedure. To do this, all you needed to do was to invoke the procedure using the call "classname.procedureName(parameters);". On occasion you may want to do this same operation with a class's methods as well as its procedures (that is, have an overridden method call the corresponding base class method in order to do some computation you'd rather not repeat in the derived class's method). Unfortunately, HLA does not let you directly call methods as it does procedures. You will need to use an indirect mechanism to achieve this; specifically, you will have to call the method using the address in the base class's virtual method table. This section describes how to do this.

Whenever your program calls a method it does so indirectly, using the address found in the virtual method table for the method's class. The virtual method table is nothing more than an array of 32-bit pointers with each entry containing the address of one of that class's methods. So to call a method, all you need is the index into this array (or, more properly, the offset into the array) of the address of the method you wish to call. The HLA compile time function @offset comes to the rescue: It will return the offset into the virtual method table of the method whose name you supply as a parameter. Combined with the call instruction, you can easily call any method associated with a class. Here's an example of how you would do this:

```
type
    myCls: class
       .
       .
       .
        method m;
```

```
        .
        .
        .
   endclass;
        .
        .
        .
   call( myCls._VMT_[ @offset( myCls.m )]);
```

The call instruction above calls the method whose address appears at the specified entry in the virtual method table for myCls. The @offset function call returns the offset (i.e., index times four) of the address of myCls.m within the virtual method table. Hence, this code indirectly calls the m method by using the virtual method table entry for m.

There is one major drawback to calling methods using this scheme: you don't get to use the high level syntax for procedure/method calls. Instead, you must use the low level call instruction. In the example above, this isn't much of an issue because the m procedure doesn't have any parameters. If it did have parameters, you would have to manually push those parameters onto the stack yourself. Fortunately, you'll rarely need to call ancestor class methods from a derived class, so this won't be much of an issue in real-world programs.

14.16 For More Information

The HLA Reference Manual on the accompanying CD-ROM contains additional information about HLA's class implementation. Check out this document for additional low level implementation features. This chapter hasn't really attempted to teach the object-oriented programming paradigm. Please see a generic text on object-oriented design for more details about this subject.

15

MIXED LANGUAGE PROGRAMMING

15.1 Chapter Overview

Most assembly language code doesn't appear in a stand-alone assembly language program. Instead, most assembly code is actually part of a library package that programs written in a high level language wind up calling. Although HLA makes it really easy to write stand-alone assembly applications, at one point or another you'll probably want to call an HLA procedure from some code written in another language, or you may want to call code written in another language from HLA. This chapter discusses the mechanisms for doing this in three languages: low level assembly (i.e., MASM or Gas), C/C++, and Delphi/Kylix. The mechanisms for other languages are usually similar to one of these three, so the material in this chapter will still apply even if you're using some other language.

15.2 Mixing HLA and MASM/Gas Code in the Same Program

It may seem kind of weird to mix MASM or Gas and HLA code in the same program. After all, they're both assembly languages, and almost anything you can do with MASM or Gas can be done in HLA. So why bother trying to mix the two in the same program? Well, there are three reasons:

- You already have a lot of code written in MASM or Gas and you don't want to convert it to HLA's syntax.

- There are a few things MASM and Gas do that HLA cannot, and you happen to need to do one of those things.

- Someone else has written some MASM or Gas code and s/he wants to be able to call code you've written using HLA.

In this section, we'll discuss two ways to merge MASM/Gas and HLA code in the same program: via in-line assembly code and through linking object files.

15.2.1 In-Line (MASM/Gas) Assembly Code in Your HLA Programs

As you're probably aware, the HLA compiler doesn't actually produce machine code directly from your HLA source files. Instead, it first compiles the code to a MASM or Gas-compatible assembly language source file and then it calls MASM or Gas to assemble this code to object code. If you're interested in seeing the MASM- or Gas output HLA produces, just edit the *filename.asm* file that HLA creates after compiling your *filename.hla* source file. The output assembly file isn't amazingly readable, but it is fairly easy to correlate the assembly output with the HLA source file.

HLA provides two mechanisms that let you inject raw MASM or Gas code directly into the output file it produces: the #asm..#endasm sequence and the #emit statement. The #asm..#endasm sequence copies all text between these two clauses directly to the assembly output file, e.g.,

```
#asm

    mov eax, 0      ;MASM/Gas syntax for MOV( 0, EAX );
    add eax, ebx    ; "      "    "  ADD( ebx, eax );

#endasm
```

The #asm..#endasm sequence is how you inject in-line (MASM or Gas) assembly code into your HLA programs. For the most part there is very little need to use this feature, but in a few instances it is invaluable. Note, when using Gas, that HLA specifies the ".intel_syntax" directive, so you should use Intel syntax when supplying Gas code between #asm and #endasm.

For example, if you're writing structured exception handling code under Windows, you'll need to access the double word at address FS:[0] (offset zero in the segment pointed at by the 80x86's FS segment register). You can drop into MASM for a statement or two to handle memory accesses as follows:

```
#asm
     mov ebx, fs:[0]     ; Loads process pointer into EBX
#endasm
```

At the end of this instruction sequence, EBX will contain the pointer to the process information structure that Windows maintains.

HLA blindly copies all text between the #asm and #endasm clauses directly to the assembly output file. HLA does not check the syntax of this code or otherwise verify its correctness. If you introduce an error within this section of your program, the assembler will report the error when HLA assembles your code by calling MASM or Gas.

The #emit statement also writes text directly to the assembly output file. However, this statement does not simply copy the text from your source file to the output file; instead, this statement copies the value of a (constant) string expression to the output file. The syntax for this statement is

```
#emit( string_expression );
```

This statement evaluates the expression and verifies that it's a string expression. Then it copies the string data to the output file. Like the #asm/#endasm statement, the #emit statement does not check the syntax of the MASM/Gas statement it writes to the assembly file. If there is a syntax error, MASM or Gas will catch it later on when the assembler processes the output file.

One advantage of the #emit statement is that it lets you construct MASM or Gas statements under (compile time) program control. You can write an HLA compile time program that generates a sequence of strings and emits them to the assembly file via the #emit statement. The compile time program has access to the HLA symbol table; this means that you can extract the identifiers that HLA emits to the assembly file and use these directly, even if they aren't external objects.

When HLA compiles your programs into assembly language, it does not use the same symbols in the assembly language output file that you use in the HLA source files. There are several technical reasons for this, but the bottom line is this: You cannot easily reference your HLA identifiers in your in-line assembly code. The only exception to this rule is external identifiers. HLA external identifiers use the same name in the assembly file as in the HLA source file. Therefore, you can refer to external objects within your in-line assembly sequences or in the strings you output via #emit.

The @staticname compile time function returns the name that HLA uses to refer to most static objects in your program. The program in Listing 15-1 demonstrates a simple use of this compile time function to obtain the assembly name of an HLA procedure.

Listing 15-1: Using the @StaticName Compile Time Function.

```
program emitDemo;
#include( "stdlib.hhf" )

    procedure myProc;
```

```
    begin myProc;

        stdout.put( "Inside MyProc" nl );

    end myProc;

begin emitDemo;

    ?stmt:string := "call " + @StaticName( myProc );
    #emit( stmt );

end emitDemo;
```

This example creates a string value (stmt) that contains something like "call ?741_myProc" and emits this assembly instruction directly to the source file ("?741_myProc" is typical of the type of name mangling that HLA does to static names it writes to the output file). If you compile and run this program, it should display "Inside MyProc" and then quit. If you look at the assembly file that HLA emits, you will see that it has given the myProc procedure the same name it appends to the call instruction.[1]

The @StaticName function is only valid for static symbols. This includes static, readonly, and storage variables, and procedures. It does not include var objects, constants, macros, or methods.

You can access var variables by using the [EBP+offset] addressing mode, specifying the offset of the desired local variable. You can use the @offset compile time function to obtain the offset of a var object or a parameter. Listing 15-2 demonstrates how to do this:

Listing 15-2: Using the @Offset Compile Time Function.

```
program offsetDemo;
#include( "stdlib.hhf" )

var
    i:int32;

begin offsetDemo;

    mov( -255, i );
    ?stmt := "mov eax, [ebp+(" + string( @offset( i )) + ")]";
    #print( "Emitting '", stmt, "'" )
    #emit( stmt );
    stdout.put( "eax = ", (type int32 eax), nl );

end offsetDemo;
```

---

[1] HLA may assign a different name than "?741_myProc" when you compile the program. The exact symbol HLA chooses varies from version to version of the assembler (it depends on the number of symbols defined prior to the definition of *myProc*. In this example, there were 741 static symbols defined in the HLA Standard Library before the definition of *myProc*.

This example emits the statement "mov eax, [ebp+(-8)]" to the assembly language source file. It turns out that -8 is the offset of the i variable in the *offsetDemo* program's activation record.

Of course, the examples of #emit up to this point have been somewhat ridiculous because you can achieve the same results by using HLA statements. One very useful purpose for the #emit statement, however, is to create some instructions that HLA does not support. For example, at one time HLA did not support the les instruction because you can't really use it under most 32-bit operating systems.[2] However, if you found a need for this instruction, you could easily write a macro to emit this instruction and appropriate operands to the assembly source file. Using the #emit statement gives you the ability to reference HLA objects, something you cannot do with the #asm. .#endasm sequence.

15.2.2 *Linking MASM/Gas-Assembled Modules with HLA Modules*

Although you can do some interesting things with HLA's in-line assembly statements, you'll probably never use them. Further, future versions of HLA may not even support these statements, so you should avoid them as much as possible even if you see a need for them. Of course, HLA does most of the stuff you'd want to do with the #asm/#endasm and #emit statements anyway, so there is very little reason to use them at all. If you're going to combine MASM/Gas (or other assembler) code and HLA code together in a program, most of the time this will occur because you've got a module or library routine written in some other assembly language and you would like to take advantage of that code in your HLA programs. Rather than convert the other assembler's code to HLA, the easy solution is to simply assemble that other code to an object file and link it with your HLA programs.

Once you've compiled or assembled a source file to an object file, the routines in that module are callable from almost any machine code that can handle the routines' calling sequences. If you have an object file that contains a sqrt function, for example, it doesn't matter whether you compiled that function with HLA, MASM, TASM, NASM, Gas, or even a high level language; if it's object code and it exports the proper symbols, you can call it from your HLA program.

Compiling a module in MASM or Gas and linking that with your HLA program is little different than linking other HLA modules with your main HLA program. In the assembly source file, you will have to export some symbols (using the PUBLIC directive in MASM or the .GLOBAL directive in Gas), and in your HLA program you have to tell HLA that those symbols appear in a separate module (using the @external option).

Because the two modules are written in assembly language, there is very little language-imposed structure on the calling sequence and parameter passing mechanisms. If you're calling a function written in MASM or Gas from your HLA program, then all you've got to do is to make sure that your HLA program passes parameters in the same locations where the MASM/Gas function is expecting them.

---

[2] Support was added for this instruction in HLA 1.33; we'll pretend for the sake of example that HLA still does not support this instruction.

About the only issue you've got to deal with is the case of identifiers in the two programs. By default, Gas is case sensitive and MASM is case insensitive. HLA, on the other hand, enforces case neutrality (which, essentially, means that it is case sensitive). If you're using MASM, there is a MASM command line option ("/Cp") that tells MASM to preserve case in all public symbols. It's a real good idea to use this option when assembling modules you're going to link with HLA so that MASM doesn't mess with the case of your identifiers during assembly.

Of course, because MASM and Gas process symbols in a case-sensitive manner, it's possible to create two separate identifiers that are the same except for alphabetic case. HLA enforces case neutrality so it won't let you (directly) create two different identifiers that differ only in case. In general, this is such a bad programming practice that one would hope you never encounter it (and God forbid you actually do this yourself). However, if you inherit some MASM or Gas code written by a C hacker, it's quite possible the code uses this technique. The way around this problem is to use two separate identifiers in your HLA program and use the extended form of the @external directive to provide the external names. For example, suppose that in MASM you have the following declarations:

```
           public  AVariable
           public  avariable
               .
               .
               .
           .data
AVariable  dword    ?
avariable  byte     ?
```

If you assemble this code with the "/Cp" or "/Cx" (total case sensitivity) command line options, MASM will emit these two external symbols for use by other modules. Of course, were you to attempt to define variables by these two names in an HLA program, HLA would complain about the duplicate-symbol definition. However, you can connect two different HLA variables to these two identifiers using code like the following:

```
static
    AVariable: dword; external( "AVariable" );
    AnotherVar: byte; external( "avariable" );
```

HLA does not check the strings you supply as parameters to the @external clause. Therefore, you can supply two names that are the same except for case, and HLA will not complain. Note that when HLA calls MASM to assemble its output file, HLA specifies the "/Cp" option that tells MASM to preserve case in public and global symbols. Of course, you would use this same technique in Gas if the Gas programmer has exported two symbols that are identical except for case.

The programs in Listings 15-3 and 15-4, respectively, demonstrate how to call a MASM subroutine from an HLA main program:

Listing 15-3: Main HLA Program to Link with a MASM Program.

```
// To compile this module and the attendant MASM file, use the following
// command line:
//
//      ml -c masmupper.masm
//      hla masmdemo1.hla masmupper.obj

program MasmDemo1;
#include( "stdlib.hhf" )

    // The following external declaration defines a function that
    // is written in MASM to convert the character in AL from
    // lower case to upper case.

    procedure masmUpperCase( c:char in al ); @external( "masmUpperCase" );

static
    s: string := "Hello World!";

begin MasmDemo1;

    stdout.put( "String converted to uppercase: '" );
    mov( s, edi );
    while( mov( [edi], al ) <> #0 ) do

        masmUpperCase( al );
        stdout.putc( al );
        inc( edi );

    endwhile;
    stdout.put( "'" nl );


end MasmDemo1;
```

Listing 15-4: Calling a MASM Procedure from an HLA Program: MASM Module.

```
; MASM source file to accompany the MasmDemo1.HLA source
; file. This code compiles to an object module that
; gets linked with an HLA main program. The function
; below converts the character in AL to upper case if it
; is a lower case character.

                .586
                .model  flat, pascal

                .code
```

```
                  public  masmUpperCase
masmUpperCase     proc    near32
                  .if al >= 'a' && al <= 'z'
                  and al, 5fh
                  .endif
                  ret
masmUpperCase     endp
                  end
```

It is also possible to call an HLA procedure from a MASM or Gas program (this should be obvious because HLA compiles its source code to an assembly source file and that assembly source file can call HLA procedures such as those found in the HLA Standard Library). There are a few restrictions when calling HLA code from some other language. First of all, you can't easily use HLA's exception handling facilities in the modules you call from other languages (including MASM or Gas). The HLA main program initializes the exception handling system. This initialization is probably not done by your non-HLA assembly programs. Further, the HLA main program exports a couple of important symbols needed by the exception handling subsystem; again, it's unlikely your non-HLA main assembly program provides these public symbols. Until you get to the point you can write code in MASM or Gas to properly set up the HLA exception handling system, you should not execute any code that uses the try..endtry, raise, or any other exception handling statements.

CAUTION *A large percentage of the HLA Standard Library routines include exception handling statements or call other routines that use exception handling statements. Unless you've set up the HLA exception handling subsystem properly, you should not call any HLA Standard Library routines from non-HLA programs.*

Other than the issue of exception handling, calling HLA procedures from standard assembly code is really easy. All you've got to do is put an @external prototype in the HLA code to make the symbol you wish to access public and then include an EXTERN (or EXTERNDEF) statement in the MASM/Gas source file to provide the linkage. Then just compile the two source files and link them together.

About the only issue you need concern yourself with when calling HLA procedures from assembly is the parameter passing mechanism. Of course, if you pass all your parameters in registers (the best place), then communication between the two languages is trivial. Just load the registers with the appropriate parameters in your MASM/Gas code and call the HLA procedure. Inside the HLA procedure, the parameter values will be sitting in the appropriate registers (sort of the converse of what happened in Listing 15-4).

If you decide to pass parameters on the stack, note that HLA normally uses the Pascal language-calling model. Therefore, you push parameters on the stack in the order they appear in a parameter list (from left to right), and it is the called procedure's responsibility to remove the parameters from the stack. Note that you can specify the Pascal calling convention for use with MASM's INVOKE statement using the ".model" directive. For example:

```
            .586
            .model  flat, pascal
                  .
                  .
                  .
```

Of course, if you manually push the parameters on the stack yourself, then the specific language model doesn't really matter. Gas users, of course, don't have the INVOKE statement, so they have to manually push the parameters themselves anyway.

This section is not going to attempt to go into gory details about MASM or Gas syntax. Presumably, you already know that syntax if you're wanting to combine HLA with MASM or Gas code. An alternative is to read a copy of the DOS/16-bit edition of this text (available on the accompanying CD-ROM) that uses the MASM assembler. That text describes MASM syntax in much greater detail, albeit from a 16-bit perspective. Finally, this section isn't going to go into any further detail because, quite frankly, the need to call MASM or Gas code from HLA (or vice versa) just isn't that great. After all, most of the stuff you can do with MASM and Gas can be done directly in HLA so there really is little need to spend much more time on this subject. Better to move on to more important questions, such as, "How do you call HLA routines from C or Pascal?"

15.3   Programming in Delphi/Kylix and HLA

Delphi is a marvelous language for writing Win32 GUI-based applications. Kylix is the companion product that runs under Linux. Their support for Rapid Application Design (RAD) and visual programming is superior to almost every other Windows or Linux programming approach available. However, being Pascal based, there are some things that just cannot be done in Delphi/Kylix and many things that cannot be done as efficiently in Delphi/Kylix as in assembly language. Fortunately, Delphi/Kylix lets you call assembly language procedures and functions so you can overcome their limitations.

Delphi/Kylix provides two ways to use assembly language in the Pascal code: via a built-in assembler (BASM) or by linking in separately compiled assembly language modules. The built-in Borland Assembler (BASM) is a very weak Intel-syntax assembler. It is suitable for injecting a few instructions into your Pascal source code or perhaps writing a very short assembly language function or procedure. It is not suitable for serious assembly language programming. If you know Intel syntax and you only need to execute a few machine instructions, then BASM is perfect. However, because this is a text on assembly language programming, the assumption here is that you want to write some serious assembly code to link with your Pascal/Kylix code. To do that, you will need to write the assembly code and compile it with a different assembler (e.g., HLA) and link the code into your Delphi/Kylix application. That is the approach this section will concentrate on. For more information about BASM, check out the Delphi/Kylix documentation.

Before we get started discussing how to write HLA modules for your Delphi/Kylix programs, you must understand two very important facts:

- HLA's exception handling facilities are not directly compatible with Delphi/Kylix's. This means that you cannot use the try..endtry and raise statements in the HLA code you intend to link to a Delphi/Kylix program. This also means that you cannot call library functions that contain such statements. Because the HLA Standard Library modules use exception handling statements all over the place, this effectively prevents you from calling HLA Standard Library routines from the code you intend to link with Delphi/Kylix.[3]

- Although you can write console applications with Delphi/Kylix, 99 percent of Delphi/Kylix applications are GUI applications. You cannot call console-related functions (e.g., stdin.xxxx or stdout.xxxx) from a GUI application. Even if HLA's console and standard input/output routines didn't use exception handling, you wouldn't be able to call them from a standard Delphi/Kylix application.

Given the rich set of language features that Delphi/Kylix supports, it should come as no surprise that the interface between Delphi/Kylix's Object Pascal language and assembly language is somewhat complex. Fortunately there are two facts that reduce this problem. First, HLA uses many of the same calling conventions as Pascal; so much of the complexity is hidden from sight by HLA. Second, the other complex stuff you won't use very often, so you may not have to bother with it.

NOTE *The following sections assume you are already familiar with Delphi/Kylix programming. They make no attempt to explain Delphi/Kylix syntax or features other than as needed to explain the Delphi/Kylix assembly language interface. If you're not familiar with Delphi/Kylix, you will probably want to skip this section.*

15.3.1 Linking HLA Modules with Delphi/Kylix Programs

The basic unit of interface between a Delphi/Kylix program and assembly code is the procedure or function. That is, to combine code between the two languages you will write procedures in HLA (that correspond to procedures or functions in Delphi/Kylix) and call these procedures from the Delphi/Kylix program. Of course, there are a few mechanical details you've got to worry about. The following section will cover those.

To begin with, when writing HLA code to link with a Delphi/Kylix program you've got to place your HLA code in an HLA unit. An HLA program module contains start-up code and other information that the operating system uses to determine where to begin program execution when it loads an executable file from disk. However, the Delphi/Kylix program also supplies this information and specifying two starting addresses confuses the linker; therefore, you must place all your HLA code in a unit rather than a program module.

---

[3] Note that the HLA Standard Library source code is available; feel free to modify the routines you want to use and remove any exception handling statements contained therein.

Within the HLA unit you must create @external procedure prototypes for each procedure you wish to call from Delphi/Kylix. If you prefer, you can put these prototype declarations in a header file and #include them in the HLA code, but because you'll probably only reference these declarations from this single file, it's okay to put the @external prototype declarations directly in the HLA unit module. These @external prototype declarations tell HLA that the associated functions will be public so that Delphi/Kylix can access their names during the link process. Here's a typical example:

```
unit LinkWithKylix;

    procedure prototype; @external;

    procedure prototype;
    begin prototype;

        << Code to implement prototype's functionality >>

    end prototype;

end LinkWithKylix;
```

After creating the module above, you'd compile it using HLA's "-s" (compile to assembly only) command line option. This will produce an ASM file. Were this just about any other language, under Windows you'd then assemble the ASM file with MASM. Unfortunately, Delphi doesn't like the OBJ files that MASM produces. For all but the most trivial of assembly modules, Delphi will reject MASM's output. Borland Delphi expects external assembly modules to be written with Borland's assembler, *tasm32.exe* (the 32-bit Turbo Assembler). Fortunately, because HLA 1.26, HLA provides an option to produce TASM output that is compatible with TASM 5.3 and later. Unfortunately, Borland doesn't really sell TASM anymore; the only way to get a copy of TASM 5.3 is to obtain a copy of Borland's C++ Builder Professional system, which includes TASM32 5.3. If you don't own Borland C++ and really have no interest in using C++ Builder, Borland has produced an evaluation disk for C++ Builder that includes TASM 5.3, so order the evaluation disk to get a copy of TASM 5.3. Note that earlier versions of TASM32 (e.g., 5.0) do not support MMX and other Pentium-only instructions. You really need TASM 5.3 if you want to link HLA programs containing such code with Delphi programs.

Here is the Windows command that will compile and assemble the module given earlier:

```
hla -c -tasm -o:omf LinkWithDelphi.hla
```

Of course, if you don't like typing this long command to compile and assemble your HLA code, you can always create a make file or a batch file that will let you do both operations with a single command.

After creating the module above, you'd compile it using HLA's "-c" (compile to object only) command line option. This will produce an object (".obj") file.

Linux/Kylix users have it a little easier. Under Linux, Borland's Kylix program handles ELF object code (the stuff Gas emits) just fine. Therefore, the following is all you need to do when compiling an HLA program to link with Kylix:

```
hla -c LinkWithKylix.hla
```

Once you've created the HLA code and compiled it to an object file, the next step is to tell Delphi/Kylix that it needs to call the HLA/assembly code. There are two steps needed to achieve this: You've got to inform Delphi/Kylix that a procedure (or function) is written in assembly language (rather than Pascal), and you've got to tell Delphi/Kylix to link in the object file you've created when compiling the Delphi/Kylix code.

The second step above, telling Delphi/Kylix to include the HLA object module, is the easiest task to achieve. All you've got to do is insert a compiler directive of the form "{$L *objectFileName*.obj }" in the Delphi/Kylix program before declaring and calling your object module. A good place to put this is after the **implementation** reserved word in the module that calls your assembly procedure. The code examples a little later in this section will demonstrate this.

The next step is to tell Delphi/Kylix that you're supplying an external procedure or function. This is done using the Delphi/Kylix EXTERNAL directive on a procedure or function prototype. For example, a typical external declaration for the *prototype* procedure appearing earlier is

```
procedure prototype; external;   // This may look like HLA code, but it's
                                 // really Kylix code!
```

As you can see here, Delphi/Kylix's syntax for declaring external procedures is nearly identical to HLA's. This is not an accident; much of HLA's syntax was borrowed directly from Pascal.

The next step is to call the assembly procedure from the Delphi/Kylix code. This is easily accomplished using standard Pascal procedure calling syntax. Listings 15-5 and 15-6, respectively, provide a complete, working example of an HLA procedure that a Delphi/Kylix program can call. This program doesn't accomplish very much other than to demonstrate how to link in an assembly procedure. The Delphi/Kylix program contains a form with a single button on it. Pushing the button calls the HLA procedure, whose body is empty and therefore returns immediately to the Delphi/Kylix code without any visible indication that it was ever called. Nevertheless, this code does provide all the syntactical elements necessary to create and call an assembly language routine from a Delphi/Kylix program.

Listing 15-5: CalledFromDelphi.HLA Module Containing the Assembly Code.

```
unit LinkWithDelphi; // Or LinkWithKylix for Linux users.
```

```
    procedure CalledFromDelphi; @external;

    procedure CalledFromDelphi;
    begin CalledFromDelphi;
    end CalledFromDelphi;

end LinkWithDelphi;
```

Listing 15-6: DelphiEx1: Delphi Source Code That Calls an Assembly Procedure.

```
unit DelphiEx1;

interface

uses
  Windows, Messages, SysUtils, Classes, Graphics, Controls, Forms, Dialogs,
  StdCtrls;

type
  TDelphiEx1Form = class(TForm)
    Button1: TButton;
    procedure Button1Click(Sender: TObject);
  private
    { Private declarations }
  public
    { Public declarations }
  end;

var
  DelphiEx1Form: TDelphiEx1Form;

implementation

{$R *.DFM}
{$L CalledFromDelphi.obj }

procedure CalledFromDelphi; external;

procedure TDelphiEx1Form.Button1Click(Sender: TObject);
begin

    CalledFromDelphi();

end;

end.
```

The full Delphi (for Windows), Kylix (for Linux), and HLA source code for the programs appearing in Listings 15-5 and 15-6 appear on the accompanying CD-ROM. If you've got a copy of Delphi/Kylix 5 or later, you might want to load this module and try compiling it. To compile the HLA code for this example, you would use the following commands from the command prompt:

```
hla -tasm -c -o:omf -tasm CalledFromDelphi.hla   (for Windows users)


hla -c CalledFromKylix.hla  (for Linux users)
```

After producing the *CalledFromDelphi* or *CalledFromKylix* object module (depending on your OS) with the appropriate command, you'd enter the Delphi/Kylix Integrated Development Environment and tell it to compile the DelphiEx1/KylixEx1 code (i.e., you'd load the DelphiEx1Project/KylixEx1Project file into Delphi/Kylix and the compile the code). This process automatically links in the HLA code, and when you run the program you can call the assembly code by simply pressing the single button on the Delphi/Kylix form.

15.3.2 *Register Preservation*

Delphi/Kylix code expects all procedures to preserve the EBX, ESI, EDI, and EBP registers. Routines written in assembly language may freely modify the contents of EAX, ECX, and EDX without preserving their values. The HLA code will have to modify the ESP register to remove the activation record (and, possibly, some parameters). Of course, HLA procedures (unless you specify the @noframe option) automatically preserve and set up EBP for you, so you don't have to worry about preserving this register's value; of course, you will not usually manipulate EBP's value because it points at your procedure's parameters and local variables.

Although you can modify EAX, ECX, and EDX to your heart's content and not have to worry about preserving their values, don't get the idea that these registers are available for your procedure's exclusive use. In particular, Delphi/Kylix may pass parameters into a procedure within these registers and you may need to return function results in some of these registers. Details on the further use of these registers appear in later sections of this chapter.

Whenever Delphi/Kylix calls a procedure, that procedure can assume that the direction flag is clear. On return, all procedures must ensure that the direction flag is still clear. So if you manipulate the direction flag in your assembly code (or call a routine that might set the direction flag), be sure to clear the direction flag before returning to the Kylix code.

If you use any MMX instructions within your assembly code, be sure to execute the emms instruction before returning. Delphi/Kylix code assumes that it can manipulate the floating point stack without running into problems.

Although the Delphi/Kylix documentation doesn't explicitly state this, experiments with Delphi/Kylix code seem to suggest that you don't have to preserve the FPU (or MMX) registers across a procedure call other than to ensure that you're in FPU mode (versus MMX mode) upon return to Delphi/Kylix.

15.3.3 Function Results

Delphi/Kylix generally expects functions to return their results in a register. For ordinal return results, a function should return a byte value in AL, a word value in AX, or a double word value in EAX. Functions return pointer values in EAX. Functions return real values in ST0 on the FPU stack. The code example in this section demonstrates each of these parameter return locations.

For other return types (e.g., arrays, sets, records, and so on), Delphi/Kylix generally passes an extra reference (var) parameter containing the address of the location where the function should store the return result. We will not consider such return results in this text; see the Delphi/Kylix documentation for more details.

The Delphi/HLA program in Listings 15-7 through 15-12, respectively, demonstrates how to return different types of scalar (ordinal and real) parameters to a Delphi program from an assembly language function. The HLA functions return boolean (one-byte) results, word results, double word results, a pointer (PChar) result, and a floating point result when you press an appropriate button on the form. See the DelphiEx2/KylixEx2 example code on the CD-ROM for the full project. (Linux users: The Kylix code is slightly different, but the functionality is the same; there is no difference between the way Delphi and Kylix interface with assembly language.)

Note that the following code doesn't really do anything useful other than demonstrate how to return function results in EAX and ST0.

Listing 15-7: DelphiEx2: Pascal Code for Assembly Return Results Example.

```
unit DelphiEx2;

interface

uses
  Windows, Messages, SysUtils, Classes, Graphics, Controls, Forms, Dialogs,
  StdCtrls;

type
  TDelphiEx2Form = class(TForm)
    BoolBtn: TButton;
    BooleanLabel: TLabel;
    WordBtn: TButton;
    WordLabel: TLabel;
    DWordBtn: TButton;
    DWordLabel: TLabel;
    PtrBtn: TButton;
```

```
      PCharLabel: TLabel;
      FltBtn: TButton;
      RealLabel: TLabel;
      procedure BoolBtnClick(Sender: TObject);
      procedure WordBtnClick(Sender: TObject);
      procedure DWordBtnClick(Sender: TObject);
      procedure PtrBtnClick(Sender: TObject);
      procedure FltBtnClick(Sender: TObject);
    private
      { Private declarations }
    public
      { Public declarations }
    end;

var
  DelphiEx2Form: TDelphiEx2Form;

implementation

{$R *.DFM}

// Here are the directives that tell Delphi to link in our
// HLA code.

{$L ReturnBoolean.obj }
{$L ReturnWord.obj }
{$L ReturnDWord.obj }
{$L ReturnPtr.obj }
{$L ReturnReal.obj }

// Here are the external function declarations:

function ReturnBoolean:boolean; external;
function ReturnWord:smallint; external;
function ReturnDWord:integer; external;
function ReturnPtr:pchar; external;
function ReturnReal:real; external;


// Demonstration of calling an assembly language
// procedure that returns a byte (boolean) result.

procedure TDelphiEx2Form.BoolBtnClick(Sender: TObject);
var
    b:boolean;

begin
```

```
    // Call the assembly code and return its result:

    b := ReturnBoolean;

    // Display "true" or "false" depending on the return result.

    if( b ) then

        booleanLabel.caption := 'Boolean result = true '

    else

        BooleanLabel.caption := 'Boolean result = false';

end;


// Demonstrate calling an assembly language function that
// returns a word result.

procedure TDelphiEx2Form.WordBtnClick(Sender: TObject);
var
    si:smallint;    // Return result here.
    strVal:string;  // Used to display return result.
begin

    si := ReturnWord();     // Get result from assembly code.
    str( si, strVal );      // Convert result to a string.
    WordLabel.caption := 'Word Result = ' + strVal;

end;

// Demonstration of a call to an assembly language routine
// that returns a 32-bit result in EAX:

procedure TDelphiEx2Form.DWordBtnClick(Sender: TObject);
var
    i:integer;          // Return result goes here.
    strVal:string;      // Used to display return result.
begin

    i := ReturnDWord(); // Get result from assembly code.
    str( i, strVal );   // Convert that value to a string.
    DWordLabel.caption := 'Double Word Result = ' + strVal;

end;
```

```
// Demonstration of a routine that returns a pointer
// as the function result. This demo is kind of lame
// because we can't initialize anything inside the
// assembly module, but it does demonstrate the mechanism
// even if this example isn't very practical.

procedure TDelphiEx2Form.PtrBtnClick(Sender: TObject);
var
    p:pchar;    // Put returned pointer here.
begin

    // Get the pointer (to a zero byte) from the assembly code.

    p := ReturnPtr();

    // Display the empty string that ReturnPtr returns.

    PCharLabel.caption := 'PChar Result = "' + p + '"';

end;



// Quick demonstration of a function that returns a
// floating point value as a function result.

procedure TDelphiEx2Form.FltBtnClick(Sender: TObject);
var
    r:real;
    strVal:string;
begin

    // Call the assembly code that returns a real result.

    r := ReturnReal();      // Always returns 1.0

    // Convert and display the result.

    str( r:13:10, strVal );
    RealLabel.caption := 'Real Result = ' + strVal;

end;

end.
```

Listing 15-8: ReturnBoolean: Demonstrates Returning a Byte Value in AL.

```
// ReturnBooleanUnit-
//
// Provides the ReturnBoolean function for the DelphiEx2 program.
```

```
unit  ReturnBooleanUnit;

// Tell HLA that ReturnBoolean is a public symbol:

procedure ReturnBoolean; @external;

// Demonstration of a function that returns a byte value in AL.
// This function simply returns a boolean result that alternates
// between true and false on each call.

procedure ReturnBoolean;  @nodisplay; @noalignstack; @noframe;
static b:boolean:=false;
begin ReturnBoolean;

    xor( 1, b );    // Invert boolean status
    and( 1, b );    // Force to zero (false) or one (true).
    mov( b, al );   // Function return result comes back in AL.
    ret();

end ReturnBoolean;


end ReturnBooleanUnit;
```

Listing 15-9: ReturnWord: Demonstrates Returning a Word Value in AX.

```
// ReturnWordUnit-
//
//  Provides the ReturnWord function for the DelphiEx2 program.


unit  ReturnWordUnit;

procedure ReturnWord; @external;

procedure ReturnWord;  @nodisplay; @noalignstack; @noframe;
static w:int16 := 1234;
begin ReturnWord;

    // Increment the static value by one on each
    // call and return the new result as the function
    // return value.

    inc( w );
    mov( w, ax );
    ret();
```

```
end ReturnWord;


end ReturnWordUnit;
```

Listing 15-10: ReturnDWord: Demonstrates Returning a Dword Value in EAX.

```
// ReturnDWordUnit-
//
//  Provides the ReturnDWord function for the DelphiEx2 program.

unit  ReturnDWordUnit;

procedure ReturnDWord; @external;

// Same code as ReturnWord except this one returns a 32-bit value
// in EAX rather than a 16-bit value in AX.

procedure ReturnDWord;  @nodisplay; @noalignstack; @noframe;
static
    d:int32 := -7;
begin ReturnDWord;

    inc( d );
    mov( d, eax );
    ret();

end ReturnDWord;


end ReturnDWordUnit;
```

Listing 15-11: ReturnPtr: Demonstrates Returning a 32-Bit Address in EAX.

```
// ReturnPtrUnit-
//
//  Provides the ReturnPtr function for the DelphiEx2 program.

unit  ReturnPtrUnit;

procedure ReturnPtr; @external;

// This function, which is lame, returns a pointer to a zero
// byte in memory (i.e., an empty pchar string). Although
// not particularly useful, this code does demonstrate how
// to return a pointer in EAX.

procedure ReturnPtr;  @nodisplay; @noalignstack; @noframe;
static
```

```
        stringData: byte; @nostorage;
                byte "Pchar object", 0;

begin ReturnPtr;

    lea( eax, stringData );
    ret();

end ReturnPtr;


end ReturnPtrUnit;
```

Listing 15-12: ReturnReal: Demonstrates Returning a Real Value in STO.

```
// ReturnRealUnit-
//
//  Provides the ReturnReal function for the DelphiEx2 program.

unit  ReturnRealUnit;

procedure ReturnReal; @external;
procedure ReturnReal;  @nodisplay; @noalignstack; @noframe;
static
    realData: real80 := 1.234567890;

begin ReturnReal;

    fld( realData );
    ret();

end ReturnReal;


end ReturnRealUnit;
```

15.3.4   Calling Conventions

Delphi/Kylix supports five different calling mechanisms for procedures and
functions: register, pascal, cdecl, stdcall, and safecall. The register and pascal
calling methods are very similar except that the pascal parameter passing scheme
always passes all parameters on the stack while the register calling mechanism
passes the first three parameters in CPU registers. We'll return to these two
mechanisms shortly because they are the primary mechanisms we'll use. The
cdecl calling convention uses the C/C++ programming language calling
convention. We'll study this scheme more in the section on interfacing C/C++
with HLA. There is no need to use this scheme when calling HLA procedures
from Delphi/Kylix. If you must use this scheme, then see the section on the

C/C++ languages for details. The stdcall convention is used to call Windows API functions. Again, there really is no need to use this calling convention, so we will ignore it here. See the Delphi/Kylix documentation for more details. Safecall is another specialized calling convention that we will not use. See, we've already reduced the complexity from five mechanisms to two! Seriously, though, when calling assembly language routines from Delphi/Kylix code that you're writing, you only need to use the pascal and register conventions.

The calling convention options specify how Delphi/Kylix passes parameters between procedures and functions as well as who is responsible for cleaning up the parameters when a function or procedure returns to its caller. The pascal calling convention passes all parameters on the stack and makes it the procedure or function's responsibility to remove those parameters from the stack. The pascal calling convention mandates that the caller push parameters in the order the compiler encounters them in the parameter list (i.e., left to right). This is exactly the calling convention that HLA uses (assuming you don't use the "IN register" parameter option). Here's an example of a Delphi/Kylix external procedure declaration that uses the pascal calling convention:

```
procedure UsesPascal( parm1:integer; parm2:integer; parm3:integer );
```

The program in Listings 15-13 and 15-14, respectively, provides a quick example of a Delphi program that calls an HLA procedure (function) using the pascal calling convention (the Kylix code is almost identical).

Listing 15-13: DelphiEx3: Sample Program That Demonstrates the Pascal Calling Convention.

```
unit DelphiEx3;

interface

uses
  Windows, Messages, SysUtils, Classes, Graphics, Controls, Forms, Dialogs,
  StdCtrls;

type
  TForm1 = class(TForm)
    callUsesPascalBtn: TButton;
    UsesPascalLabel: TLabel;
    procedure callUsesPascalBtnClick(Sender: TObject);
  private
    { Private declarations }
  public
    { Public declarations }
  end;

var
  Form1: TForm1;
```

```
implementation

{$R *.DFM}
{$L usespascal.obj}

function UsesPascal
(
    parm1:integer;
    parm2:integer;
    parm3:integer
):integer; pascal; external;

procedure TForm1.callUsesPascalBtnClick(Sender: TObject);
var
    i:      integer;
    strVal: string;
begin

    i := UsesPascal( 5, 6, 7 );
    str( i, strVal );
    UsesPascalLabel.caption := 'Uses Pascal = ' + strVal;

end;

end.
```

Listing 15-14: UsesPascal: HLA Function the Previous Delphi/Kylix Code Will Call.

```
// UsesPascalUnit-
//
//  Provides the UsesPascal function for the DelphiEx3 program.

unit  UsesPascalUnit;

// Tell HLA that UsesPascal is a public symbol:

procedure UsesPascal( parm1:int32; parm2:int32; parm3:int32 ); @external;

// Demonstration of a function that uses the PASCAL calling convention.
// This function simply computes parm1+parm2-parm3 and returns the
// result in EAX. Note that this function does not have the
// "NOFRAME" option because it needs to build the activation record
// (stack frame) in order to access the parameters. Furthermore, this
// code must clean up the parameters upon return (another chore handled
// automatically by HLA if the "NOFRAME" option is not present).
```

```
procedure UsesPascal( parm1:int32; parm2:int32; parm3:int32 );
    @nodisplay; @noalignstack;

begin UsesPascal;

    mov( parm1, eax );
    add( parm2, eax );
    sub( parm3, eax );

end UsesPascal;


end UsesPascalUnit;
```

To compile the HLA code under Windows, you would use the following two commands in a command window:

```
hla -st UsesPascal.hla
tasm32 -mx -m9 UsesPascal.asm
```

To compile the HLA code under Linux, you would use the following command from the shell:

```
hla -c UsesPascal.hla
```

Once you produce the object file with the above two command sequences, you can get into Delphi/Kylix and compile the Pascal code.

The register calling convention also processes parameters from left to right and requires the procedure/function to clean up the parameters upon return; the difference is that procedures and functions that use the register calling convention will pass their first three (ordinal) parameters in the EAX, EDX, and ECX registers (in that order) rather than on the stack. You can use HLA's "IN *register*" syntax to specify that you want the first three parameters passed in this registers, e.g.,

```
procedure UsesRegisters
(
    parm1:int32 in EAX;
    parm2:int32 in EDX;
    parm3:int32 in ECX
);
```

If your procedure had four or more parameters, you would not specify registers for any parameters beyond the third. Instead, you'd access those parameters on the stack. Because most procedures have three or fewer parameters, the register calling convention will typically pass all of a procedure's parameters in the registers.

Although you can use the register keyword just like pascal to force the use of the register calling convention, the register calling convention is the default mechanism in Delphi/Kylix. Therefore, a Delphi/Kylix declaration like the following will automatically use the register calling convention:

```
procedure UsesRegisters
(
    parm1:integer;
    parm2:integer;
    parm3:integer
); external;
```

The program in Listings 15-15 and 15-16 is a modification of the previous program in this section that uses the register calling convention rather than the pascal calling convention.

Listing 15-15: DelphiEx4: Using the register Calling Convention.

```
unit DelphiEx4;

interface

uses
  Windows, Messages, SysUtils, Classes, Graphics, Controls, Forms, Dialogs,
  StdCtrls;

type
  TForm1 = class(TForm)
    callUsesRegisterBtn: TButton;
    UsesRegisterLabel: TLabel;
    procedure callUsesRegisterBtnClick(Sender: TObject);
  private
    { Private declarations }
  public
    { Public declarations }
  end;

var
  Form1: TForm1;

implementation

{$R *.DFM}
{$L usesregister.obj}

function UsesRegister
(
    parm1:integer;
    parm2:integer;
```

```
        parm3:integer;
        parm4:integer
    ):integer; external;


procedure TForm1.callUsesRegisterBtnClick(Sender: TObject);
var
    i:      integer;
    strVal: string;
begin

    i := UsesRegister( 5, 6, 7, 3 );
    str( i, strVal );
    UsesRegisterLabel.caption := 'Uses Register = ' + strVal;

end;


end.
```

Listing 15-16: HLA Code to Support the DelphiEx4 Program.

```
// UsesRegisterUnit-
//
//  Provides the UsesRegister function for the DelphiEx4 program.

unit  UsesRegisterUnit;

// Tell HLA that UsesRegister is a public symbol:

procedure UsesRegister
(
    parm1:int32 in eax;
    parm2:int32 in edx;
    parm3:int32 in ecx;
    parm4:int32
);  @external;


// Demonstration of a function that uses the REGISTER calling convention.
// This function simply computes (parm1+parm2-parm3)*parm4 and returns the
// result in EAX. Note that this function does not have the
// "NOFRAME" option because it needs to build the activation record
// (stack frame) in order to access the fourth parameter.  Furthermore, this
// code must clean up the fourth parameter upon return (another chore handled
// automatically by HLA if the "NOFRAME" option is not present).

procedure UsesRegister
(
    parm1:int32 in eax;
    parm2:int32 in edx;
    parm3:int32 in ecx;
```

```
        parm4:int32
); @nodisplay; @noalignstack;

begin UsesRegister;

    mov( parm1, eax );
    add( parm2, eax );
    sub( parm3, eax );
    intmul( parm4, eax );

end UsesRegister;


end UsesRegisterUnit;
```

To compile the HLA code under Windows, you would use the following two commands in a command window:

```
hla -st UsesRegister.hla
tasm32 -mx -m9 UsesRegister.hla
```

Once you produce the OBJ file with the preceding command, you can get into Delphi and compile the Pascal code.

To compile the HLA code under Linux, you would use the following shell command:

```
hla -c UsesRegister.hla
```

Once you produce the .o file with the preceding command, you can get into Kylix and compile the Pascal code.

15.3.5   Pass by Value, Reference, CONST, and OUT in Kylix

A Delphi/Kylix program can pass parameters to a procedure or function using one of four different mechanisms:

- pass by value
- pass by reference
- CONST parameters
- OUT parameters

The examples up to this point in this chapter have all used Delphi/Kylix's (and HLA's) default pass by value mechanism. In this section we'll look at the other parameter passing mechanisms.

HLA and Delphi/Kylix also share a (mostly) common syntax for pass by reference parameters. The following two lines provide an external declaration in Delphi/Kylix and the corresponding external (public) declaration in HLA for a pass by reference parameter using the pascal calling convention:

```
procedure HasRefParm( var refparm: integer ); pascal; external;   // Delphi/Kylix
procedure HasRefParm( var refparm: int32 ); @external;           // HLA
```

Like HLA, Delphi/Kylix will pass the 32-bit address of whatever actual parameter
you specify when calling the HasRefParm procedure. Don't forget, inside the HLA
code, that you must dereference this pointer to access the actual parameter data.
See the chapter on procedures for more details.

The Delphi/Kylix CONST and OUT parameter passing mechanisms are
virtually identical to pass by reference. Like pass by reference these two schemes
pass a 32-bit address of their actual parameter. The difference is that the
procedure is not supposed to write to CONST objects because they're,
presumably, constant. Conversely, the procedure is supposed to write to an OUT
parameter (and not assume that it contains any initial value of consequence)
because the whole purpose of an OUT parameter is to return data from a
procedure or function. Other than the fact that the Delphi/Kylix compiler will
check procedures and functions for compliance with these rules, there is no
difference between CONST, OUT, and reference parameters. Delphi/Kylix
passes all such parameters by reference to the procedure or function. Note that
in HLA you would declare all CONST and OUT parameters as pass by reference
parameters. HLA does not enforce the read-only attribute of the CONST object
nor does it check for an attempt to access an uninitialized OUT parameter; those
checks are the responsibility of the assembly language programmer.

As you've learned in the previous section, by default Delphi/Kylix uses the
register calling convention. If you pass one of the first three parameters by
reference to a procedure or function, Delphi/Kylix will pass the address of that
parameter in the EAX, EDX, or ECX register. This is very convenient as you can
immediately apply the register indirect addressing mode without first loading the
parameter into a 32-bit register.

Like HLA, Delphi/Kylix lets you pass untyped parameters by reference (or
by CONST or OUT). The syntax to achieve this in Delphi/Kylix is the following:

```
procedure UntypedRefParm( var parm1; const parm2; out parm3 ); external;
```

Note that you do not supply a type specification for these parameters.
Delphi/Kylix will compute the 32-bit address of these objects and pass them on
to the UntypedRefParm procedure without any further type checking. In HLA, you
can use the var keyword as the data type to specify that you want an untyped
reference parameter. Here's the corresponding prototype for the *UntypedRefParm*
procedure in HLA:

```
procedure UntypedRefParm( var parm1:var; var parm2:var; var parm3:var );
@external;
```

As noted above, you use the var keyword (pass by reference) when passing
CONST and OUT parameters. Inside the HLA procedure it's your responsibility
to use these pointers in a manner that is reasonable given the expectations of the
Delphi/Kylix code.

15.3.6 Scalar Data Type Correspondence Between Delphi/Kylix and HLA

When passing parameters between Delphi/Kylix and HLA procedures and functions, it's very important that the calling code and the called code agree on the basic data types for the parameters. In this section we will draw a correspondence between the Delphi/Kylix scalar data types and the HLA (1.*x*) data types.[4]

Assembly language supports any possible data format, so HLA's data type capabilities will always be a superset of Kylix's. Therefore, there may be some objects you can create in HLA, which have no counterpart in Kylix, but the reverse is not true. Because the assembly functions and procedures you write are generally manipulating data that Kylix provides, you don't have to worry about not being able to process some data passed to an HLA procedure by Kylix.[5]

Delphi/Kylix provides a wide range of different integer data types. Table 15-1 lists the Delphi/Kylix types and their HLA equivalents.

Table 15-1: Kylix and HLA Integer Types

Kylix	HLA Equivalent	Range	
		Minimum	Maximum
integer	int32[1]	-2147483648	2147483647
cardinal	uns32[2]	0	4294967295
shortint	int8	-128	127
smallint	int16	-32768	32767
longint	int32	-2147483648	2147483647
int64	int64	-2^{63}	$(2^{63}-1)$
byte	uns8	0	255
word	uns16	0	65535
longword	uns32	0	4294967295
subrange types	Depends on range	Minimum range value	Maximum range value

1. Int32 is the implementation of integer in Delphi/Kylix, though this may change in later releases.
2. Uns32 is the implementation of cardinal in Delphi/Kylix, though this may change in later releases.

In addition to the integer values, Delphi/Kylix supports several non-integer ordinal types. Table 15-2 provides their HLA equivalents.

Table 15-2: Non-integer Ordinal Types in Kylix and HLA

Kylix	HLA	Range	
		Minimum	Maximum
char	char	#0	#255
widechar	wchar	#0	#65535
boolean	boolean	false (0)	true(1)
bytebool	byte	0(false)	255 (non-zero is true)

---

[4] Scalar data types are the ordinal, pointer, and real types. They do not include strings or other composite data types.

[5] Delphi/Kylix string objects are an exception. For reasons that have nothing to do with data representation, you should not manipulate string parameters passed in from Delphi/Kylix to an HLA routine. This section will explain the problems more fully a little later.

Table 15-2: Non-integer Ordinal Types in Kylix and HLA

Kylix	HLA	Range	
wordbool	word	0 (false)	65535 (non-zero is true)
longbool	dword	0 (false)	4294967295 (non-zero is true)
enumerated types	enum, byte, or word	0	Depends on number of items in the enumeration list. Usually the upper limit is 256 symbols.

Like the integer types, Delphi/Kylix supports a wide range of real numeric formats. Table 15-3 presents these types and their HLA equivalents.

Table 15-3: Real Types in Kylix and HLA

Kylix	HLA	Range	
		Minimum	Maximum
real	real64	5.0 E-324	1.7 E+308
single	real32	1.5 E-45	3.4 E+38
double	real64	5.0 E-324	1.7 E+308
extended	real80	3.6 E-4951	1.1 E+4932
comp	real80	$-2^{63}+1$	$2^{63}-1$
currency	real80	-922337203685477.5808	922337203685477.5807
real48[1]	byte[6]	2.9 E-39	1.7 E+38

1. real48 is an obsolete type that depends upon a software floating point library. You should never use this type in assembly code. If you do, you are responsible for writing the necessary floating point subroutines to manipulate the data.

The last scalar type of interest is the pointer type. Both HLA and Delphi/Kylix use a 32-bit address to represent pointers, so these data types are completely equivalent in both languages.

15.3.7   Passing String Data Between Delphi/Kylix and HLA Code

Delphi/Kylix supports a couple of different string formats. The native string format is actually very similar to HLA's string format. A string object is a pointer that points at a zero terminated sequence of characters. In the four bytes preceding the first character of the string, Delphi/Kylix stores the current dynamic length of the string (just like HLA). In the four bytes before the length, Delphi/Kylix stores a reference count (unlike HLA, which stores a maximum length value in this location). Delphi/Kylix uses the reference count to keep track of how many different pointers contain the address of this particular string object. Delphi/Kylix will automatically free the storage associated with a string object when the reference count drops to zero (this is known as *garbage collection*).

The Delphi/Kylix string format is just close enough to HLA's to tempt you to use some HLA string functions in the HLA Standard Library. This will fail for two reasons: (1) many of the HLA Standard Library string functions check the maximum length field, so they will not work properly when they access Delphi/Kylix's reference count field; (2) HLA Standard Library string functions have a habit of raising string overflow (and other) exceptions if they detect a problem (such as exceeding the maximum string length value). Remember, the HLA exception handling facility is not directly compatible with Delphi/Kylix's, so you should never call any HLA code that might raise an exception.

Of course, you can always grab the source code to some HLA Standard Library string function and strip out the code that raises exceptions and checks the maximum length field (this is usually the same code that raises exceptions). However, you could still run into problems if you attempt to manipulate some Delphi/Kylix string. In general, it's okay to read the data from a string parameter that Delphi/Kylix passes to your assembly code, but you should never change the value of such a string. To understand the problem, consider the following HLA code sequence:

```
static
    s:string := "Hello World";
    sref:string;
    scopy:string;
        .
        .
        .
    str.a_cpy( s, scopy );   // scopy has its own copy of "Hello World"

    mov( s, eax );           // After this sequence, s and sref point at
    mov( eax, sref );        // the same character string in memory.
```

After the code sequence above, any change you would make to the scopy string would affect only scopy because it has its own copy of the "Hello World" string. On the other hand, if you make any changes to the characters that s points at, you'll also be changing the string that sref points at because sref contains the same pointer value as s; in other words, s and sref are aliases of the same data. Although this aliasing process can lead to the creation of some killer defects in your code, there is a big advantage to using copy by reference rather than copy by value: copy by reference is much quicker because it only involves copying a single four-byte pointer. If you rarely change a string variable after you assign one string to that variable, copy by reference can be very efficient.

What happens if you use copy by reference to copy s to sref and then you want to modify the string that sref points at without changing the string that s points at? One way to do this is to make a copy of the string at the time you want to change sref and then modify the copy. This is known as *copy on write semantics*. In the average program, copy on write tends to produce faster running programs because the typical program tends to assign one string to another without modification more often that it assigns a string value and then modifies it later. Of course, the real problem is, how do you know whether multiple string variables are pointing at the same string in memory? After all, if only one string variable is pointing at the string data, you don't have to make a copy of the data, you can manipulate the string data directly. The *reference counter field* that

Delphi/Kylix attaches to the string data solves this problem. Each time a Delphi/Kylix program assigns one string variable to another, the Delphi/Kylix code simply copies a pointer and then increments the reference counter. Similarly, if you assign a string address to some Delphi/Kylix string variable and that variable was previously pointing at some other string data, Delphi/Kylix decrements the reference counter field of that previous string value. When the reference count hits zero, Delphi/Kylix automatically deallocates storage for the string (this is the garbage collection operation).

Note that Delphi/Kylix strings don't need a maximum length field because Delphi/Kylix dynamically allocates (standard) strings whenever you create a new string. Hence, string overflow doesn't occur and there is no need to check for string overflow (and, therefore, no need for the maximum length field). For literal string constants (which the compiler allocates statically, not dynamically on the heap), Delphi/Kylix uses a reference count field of -1 so that the compiler will not attempt to deallocate the static object.

It wouldn't be that hard to take the HLA Standard Library strings module and modify it to use Delphi/Kylix's dynamically allocated string format. There is, however, one problem with this approach: Borland has not published the internal string format for Delphi/Kylix strings (the information appearing above is the result of sleuthing through memory with a debugger). They have probably withheld this information because they want the ability to change the internal representation of their string data type without breaking existing Delphi/Kylix programs. So if you poke around in memory and modify Delphi/Kylix string data (or allocate or deallocate these strings on your own), don't be surprised if your program malfunctions when a later version of Delphi/Kylix appears (indeed, this information may already be obsolete).

Like HLA strings, a Delphi/Kylix string is a pointer that happens to contain the address of the first character of a zero terminated string in memory. As long as you don't modify this pointer, you don't modify any of the characters in that string, and you don't attempt to access any bytes before the first character of the string or after the zero terminating byte, you can safely access the string data in your HLA programs. Just remember that you cannot use any Standard Library routines that check the maximum string length or raise any exceptions. If you need the length of a Delphi/Kylix string that you pass as a parameter to an HLA procedure, it would be wise to use the Delphi/Kylix *Length* function to compute the length and pass this value as an additional parameter to your procedure. This will keep your code working should Borland ever decide to change their internal string representation.

Delphi/Kylix also supports a *ShortString* data type. This data type provides backward compatibility with older versions of Borland's Turbo Pascal (Borland Object Pascal) product. *ShortString* objects are traditional length prefixed strings (see Chapter 4). A short string variable is a sequence of 1 to 256 bytes in which the first byte contains the current dynamic string length (a value in the range 0..255) and the following n bytes hold the actual characters in the string (n being the value found in the first byte of the string data). If you need to manipulate the value of a string variable within an assembly language module, you should pass that parameter as a *ShortString* variable (assuming, of course, that you don't need to handle strings longer than 256 characters). For efficiency reasons, you should always pass *ShortString* variables by reference (or CONST or OUT) rather than by value. If you pass a short string by value, Delphi/Kylix must copy all the characters allocated for that string (even if the current length is shorter) into the procedure's activation record. This can be very slow. If you pass a *ShortString* by reference, then Delphi/Kylix will only need to pass a pointer to the string's data; this is very efficient.

Note that *ShortString* objects do not have a zero terminating byte following the string data. Therefore, your assembly code must use the length prefix byte to determine the end of the string. It should not search for a zero byte in the string.

If you need the maximum length of a *ShortString* object, you can use the Delphi/Kylix *high* function to obtain this information and pass it to your HLA code as another parameter. Note that the *high* function is a compiler-intrinsic function much like HLA's @size function. Delphi/Kylix simply replaces this "function call" with the equivalent constant at compile time; this isn't a true function you can call. This maximum size information is not available at runtime (unless you've used the Delphi/Kylix *high* function) and you cannot compute this information within your HLA code.

15.3.8 *Passing Record Data Between HLA and Kylix*

Records in HLA are (mostly) compatible with Delphi/Kylix records. Syntactically their declarations are very similar, and if you've specified the correct Delphi/Kylix compiler options you can easily translate a Delphi/Kylix record to an HLA record. In this section we'll explore how to do this and learn about the incompatibilities that exist between HLA records and Delphi/Kylix records.

For the most part, translating Delphi/Kylix records to HLA is a no-brainer. The two record declarations are so similar syntactically that conversion is trivial. The only time you really run into a problem in the conversion process is when you encounter case variant records in Delphi/Kylix; fortunately, these don't occur very often and when they do, HLA's anonymous unions within a record come to the rescue.

Consider the following Pascal record type declaration:

```
type
    recType =
        record

            day: byte;
            month:byte;
            year:integer;
            dayOfWeek:byte;

        end;
```

The translation to an HLA record is, for the most part, very straight-forward. Just translate the field types accordingly and use the HLA record syntax and you're in business. The translation is the following:

```
type
    recType:
        record

            day: byte;
            month: byte;
            year:int32;
            dayOfWeek:byte;


        endrecord;
```

There is one minor problem with this example: data alignment. By default
Delphi/Kylix aligns each field of a record on the size of that object and pads the
entire record so its size is an even multiple of the largest (scalar) object in the
record. This means that the Delphi/Kylix declaration above is really equivalent
to the following HLA declaration:

```
type
    recType:
        record

            day: byte;
            month: byte;
            padding:byte[2];       // Align year on a four-byte boundary.
            year:int32;
            dayOfWeek:byte;
            morePadding: byte[3]; // Make record an even multiple of four bytes.


        endrecord;
```

Of course, a better solution is to use HLA's align directive to automatically align
the fields in the record:[6]

```
type
    recType:
        record

            day: byte;
            month: byte;
            align( 4 );       // Align year on a four-byte boundary.
            year:int32;
            dayOfWeek:byte;
            align(4);         // Make record an even multiple of four bytes.


        endrecord;
```

---

[6] Actually, an even better solution is to use HLA's record field alignment options. See the HLA
Reference Manual on the accompanying CD-ROM for more details.

Alignment of the fields is good insofar as access to the fields is faster if they are aligned appropriately. However, aligning records in this fashion does consume extra space (five bytes in the examples above), and that can be expensive if you have a large array of records whose fields need padding for alignment.

Table 15-4 lists how the alignment parameters for an HLA record appear.

Table 15-4: Alignment of Record Fields

Data Type	Alignment
Ordinal types	Size of the type: 1, 2, or 4 bytes
Real types	2 for real48 and extended, 4 bytes for other real types
ShortString	1
Arrays	Same as the element size
Records	Same as the largest alignment of all the fields
Sets	1 or two if the set has fewer than 8 or 16 elements, 4 otherwise
All other types	4

Another possibility is to tell Delphi/Kylix not to align the fields in the record. There are two ways to do this: use the "packed" reserved word or use the {$A-} compiler directive.

The packed keyword tells Delphi/Kylix not to add padding to a specific record. For example, you could declare the original Delphi/Kylix record as follows:

```
type
    recType =
        packed record

            day: byte;
            month:byte;
            year:integer;
            dayOfWeek:byte;

        end;
```

With the packed reserved word present, Delphi/Kylix does not add any padding to the fields in the record. The corresponding HLA code would be the original record declaration above. For example:

```
type
    recType:
        record

            day: byte;
            month: byte;
```

```
        year:int32;
        dayOfWeek:byte;


    endrecord;
```

The nice thing about the packed keyword is that it lets you explicitly state whether you want data alignment/padding in a record. On the other hand, if you've got a lot of records and you don't want field alignment on any of them, you'll probably want to use the "{$A-}" (turn data alignment off) option rather than add the packed reserved word to each record definition. Note that you can turn data alignment back on with the "{$A+}" directive if you want a sequence of records to be packed and the rest of them to be aligned.

While it's far easier (and syntactically safer) to used packed records when passing record data between assembly language and Delphi/Kylix, you will have to determine on a case-by-case basis whether you're willing to give up the performance gain in exchange for using less memory (and a simpler interface). It is certainly the case that packed records are easier to maintain in HLA than aligned records (because you don't have to carefully place align directives throughout the record in the HLA code). Furthermore, on new 80x86 processors most misaligned data accesses aren't particularly expensive (the cache takes care of this). However, if performance really matters you will have to measure the performance of your program and determine the cost of using packed records.

Case variant records in Delphi/Kylix let you add mutually exclusive fields to a record with an optional tag field. Here are two examples:

```
type
    r1=
        record

            stdField: integer;
            case choice:boolean of
                true:( i:integer );
                false:( r:real );
        end;


    r2=
        record
            s2:real;
            case boolean of // Notice no tag object here.
                true:( s:string );
                false:( c:char );
        end;
```

HLA does not support the case variant syntax, but it does support anonymous unions in a record that let you achieve the same semantics. The two preceding examples, converted to HLA (assuming "{A-}") are:

```
type
    r1:
        record

            stdField: int32;
            choice: boolean;    // Notice that the tag field is just another field
            union

                i:int32;
                r:real64;

            endunion;

        endrecord;

    r2:
        record

            s2:real64;
            union

                s: string;
                c: char;

            endunion;

        endrecord;
```

Again, you should insert appropriate align directives if you're not creating a packed record. Note that you shouldn't place any align directives inside the anonymous union section; instead, place a single align directive before the union reserved word that specifies the size of the largest (scalar) object in the union.

In general, if the size of a record exceeds about 16 to 32 bytes, you should pass the record by reference rather than by value.

15.3.9 Passing Set Data Between Delphi/Kylix and HLA

Sets in Delphi/Kylix can have between 1 and 256 elements. Delphi/Kylix implements sets using an array of bits, exactly as HLA implements character sets. Delphi/Kylix reserves one to 32 bytes for each set; the size of the set (in bytes) is (Number_of_elements + 7) div 8. Like HLA's character sets, Delphi/Kylix uses a set bit to indicate that a particular object is a member of the set and a zero bit indicates absence from the set. You can use the bit test (and set/complement/reset) instructions and all the other bit manipulation operations to manipulate character sets. Furthermore, the MMX instructions might provide a little added performance boost to your set operations. For more details on the possibilities, consult the Delphi/Kylix documentation and the chapters on character sets and the MMX instructions in this text.

Generally, sets are sufficiently short (maximum of 32 bytes) that passing them by value isn't totally horrible. However, you will get slightly better performance if you pass larger sets by reference. Note that HLA often passes character sets by value (16 bytes per set) to various Standard Library routines, so don't be totally afraid of passing sets by value.

15.3.10 *Passing Array Data Between HLA and Delphi/Kylix*

Passing array data between some procedures written in Delphi/Kylix and HLA is little different than passing array data between two HLA procedures. Generally, if the arrays are large, you'll want to pass the arrays by reference rather than value. Other than that, you should declare an appropriate array type in HLA to match the type you're passing in from Delphi/Kylix and have at it. The following code fragments provide a simple example:

```
type
      PascalArray = array[0..127, 0..3] of integer;

procedure PassedArrray( var ary: PascalArray ); external;

Corresponding HLA code:
type
      PascalArray: int32[ 128, 4 ];

procedure PassedArray( var ary: PascalArray ); @external;
```

As the above examples demonstrate, Delphi/Kylix's array declarations specify the starting and ending indices while HLA's array bounds specify the number of elements for each dimension. Other than this difference, however, you can see that the two declarations are very similar.

Delphi/Kylix uses row major ordering for arrays. So if you're accessing elements of a Delphi/Kylix multidimensional array in HLA code, be sure to use the row major order computation (see Chapter 4 for details).

15.3.11 *Referencing Delphi/Kylix Objects from HLA Code*

Symbols you declare in the INTERFACE section of a Delphi/Kylix program are public. Therefore, you can access these objects from HLA code if you declare those objects as external in the HLA program. The sample program in Listings 15-17 and 15-18, respectively, demonstrate this fact by declaring a structured constant (y) and a function (callme) that the HLA code uses when you press the button on a form. The HLA code calls the callme function (which returns the value 10), and then the HLA code stores the function return result into the y structured constant (which is really just a static variable).

Listing 15-17: DelphiEx5: Static Data and Delphi Public Symbols Demonstration.

```delphi
unit DelphiEx5;

interface

uses
  Windows, Messages, SysUtils, Classes, Graphics, Controls, Forms, Dialogs,
  StdCtrls;

type
  TDataTable = class(TForm)
    GetDataBtn: TButton;
    DataLabel: TLabel;
    procedure GetDataBtnClick(Sender: TObject);
  private
    { Private declarations }
  public
    { Public declarations }
  end;

 // Here's a static variable that we will export to
 // the HLA source code (in Delphi, structured constants
 // are initialized static variables).

const
    y:integer = 12345;

var
  DataTable: TDataTable;

  // Here's the function we will export to the HLA code:

  function callme:integer;

implementation

{$R *.DFM}
{$L TableData.obj }

function TableData:integer; external;

// This function will simply return 10 as the function
// result (remember, function results come back in EAX).

function callme;
begin

    callme := 10;
```

```
end;


procedure TDataTable.GetDataBtnClick(Sender: TObject);
var
    strVal: string;
    yVal:   string;
begin

    // Display the value that TableData returns.
    // Also display the value of y, which TableValue modifies

    str( TableData(), strVal );
    str( y, yVal );
    DataLabel.caption := 'Data = ' + strVal + ' y=' + yVal;

end;

end.
```

Listing 15-18: HLA Code for DelphiEx5 Example.

```
unit TableDataUnit;

static
    y:int32; @external;        // Static object from Delphi code

    index: dword := -1;        // index initial value;
    TheTable: dword[12] :=
        [ -5, -4, -3, -2, -1, 0, 1, 2, 3, 4, 5, 6]; // TheTable values.



// Interface to "callme" procedure found in the Delphi code:

procedure callme; @external;


// Declare the procedure we're supplying to the Delphi code:

procedure TableData; @external;
procedure TableData; @nodisplay; @noalignstack; @noframe;
begin TableData;

    callme();          // Call Delphi code.
    mov( eax, y );     // Store return result in Y.

    // Okay, on each successive call to this function, return
```

```
    // the next element (or wraparound to the first element) from
    // the "TheTable" array:

    inc( index );
    mov( index, eax );
    if( eax > 11 ) then

        xor( eax, eax );
        mov( eax, index );

    endif;
    mov( TheTable[ eax*4 ], eax );
    ret();

end TableData;


end TableDataUnit;
```

15.4   Programming in C/C++ and HLA

Without question, the most popular language used to develop applications is, uh, Visual Basic. We're not going to worry about interfacing Visual Basic to assembly in this text for two reasons: (1) Visual Basic programmers will get better control and performance from their code if they learn Delphi/Kylix, and (2) Visual Basic's interface to assembly is via dynamic linked libraries (which is just beyond the scope of this text, because DLLs are very OS specific). Coming in second as the development language of choice is C/C++. The C/C++ interface to assembly language is a bit different than Pascal/Kylix. That's why this section appears in this text.

Unlike Pascal/Kylix, that has only a single vendor, there are many different C/C++ compilers available on the market. Each vendor (Microsoft, Borland, Watcom, GNU, and so on) has its own ideas about how C/C++ should interface to external code. Many vendors have their own extensions to the C/C++ language to aid in the interface to assembly and other languages. For example, Borland provides a special keyword to let Borland C++ (and C++ Builder) programmers call Pascal code (or, conversely, allow Pascal code to call the C/C++ code). Microsoft, which stopped making Pascal compilers years ago, no longer supports this option. This is unfortunate because HLA, by default, uses the Pascal calling conventions. Fortunately, HLA provides a special interface to code that C/C++ systems generate.

Before we get started discussing how to write HLA modules for your C/C++ programs, you must understand two very important facts:

1. HLA's exception handling facilities are not directly compatible with C/C++'s exception handling facilities. This means that you cannot use the try..endtry and raise statements in the HLA code you intend to link to a C/C++ program. This also means that you cannot call library functions that contain such statements. Because the HLA Standard Library modules use exception handling statements all over the place, this effectively prevents you from calling HLA Standard Library routines from the code you intend to link with C/C++.[7]

2. You cannot call console-related functions (e.g., stdin.xxxx or stdout.xxxx) from a GUI application (Windows or Linux). Even if HLA's console and standard input/output routines didn't use exception handling, you wouldn't be able to call them from a GUI C/C++ application. Even if you are writing a console application in C/C++, you still shouldn't call the stdin.xxxx or stdout.xxx routines because they could raise an HLA exception.

Given the rich set of language features that C/C++ supports, it should come as no surprise that the interface between the C/C++ language and assembly language is somewhat complex. Fortunately there are two facts that reduce this problem. First, HLA (1.26 and later) supports C/C++'s calling conventions. Second, the other complex stuff you won't use very often, so you may not have to bother with it.

NOTE *The following sections assume you are already familiar with C/C++ programming. They make no attempt to explain C/C++ syntax or features other than as needed to explain the C/C++ assembly language interface. If you're not familiar with C/C++, you will probably want to skip this section.*

NOTE *Although this text uses the generic term "C/C++" when describing the interface between HLA and various C/C++ compilers, the truth is that you're really interfacing HLA with the C language. There is a fairly standardized interface between C and assembly language that most vendors follow. No such standard exists for the C++ language and every vendor, if it even supports an interface between C++ and assembly, uses a different scheme. In this text we will stick to interfacing HLA with the C language. Fortunately, all popular C++ compilers support the C interface to assembly, so this isn't much of a problem.*

The examples in this text will use the Borland C++ compiler, GNU C++, and Microsoft's Visual C++ compiler. There may be some minor adjustments you need to make if you're using some other C/C++ compiler; please see the vendor's documentation for more details. This text will note differences between Borland's, GNU/FSF's, and Microsoft's offerings, as necessary.

---

[7] Note that the HLA Standard Library source code is available; feel free to modify the routines you want to use and remove any exception handling statements contained therein.

15.4.1 Linking HLA Modules with C/C++ Programs

One big advantage of C/C++ over Pascal/Kylix is that (most) C/C++ compiler vendors' products emit standard object files. So, working with object files and a true linker is much nicer than having to deal with Delphi/Kylix's built-in linker. As nice as the Pascal/Kylix system is, interfacing with assembly language is much easier in C/C++ than in Kylix.

Under Windows, the Visual C++ compiler works with COFF object files, and the Borland C++ compiler works with OMF object files. Both forms of object files use the OBJ extension, so you can't really tell by looking at a directory listing which form you've got. Fortunately, if you need to create a single OBJ file that will work with both, the Visual C++ compiler will also accept OMF files and convert them to a COFF file during the link phase. Of course, most of the time you will not be using both compilers, so you can pick whichever OBJ file format you're comfortable with and use that. Linux users have it a little easier because most Linux compilers work strictly with ELF object files.

By default, HLA tells MASM to produce a COFF file when assembling the HLA output. This means that if you compile an HLA program using a command line like the following, you will not be able to directly link the code with Borland C++ code:

```
hla -c filename.hla      // The "-c" option tells HLA to compile and assemble.
```

If you want to create an OMF file rather than a COFF file, you can do so by using the following command:

```
hla -o:omf filename.hla      // The "-o:omf" option tells HLA to compile to OMF.
```

The execution of this command produces an OMF object file that both VC++ and BCC (Borland C++) will accept (though VC++ prefers COFF, it accepts OMF).

Both BCC and VC++ look at the extension of the source filenames you provide on the command line to determine whether they are compiling a C or a C++ program. There are some minor syntactical differences between the external declarations for a C and a C++ program. This text assumes that you are compiling C++ programs that have a ".cpp" extension. The difference between a C and a C++ compilation occurs in the external declarations for the functions you intend to write in assembly language. For example, in a C source file you would simply write:

```
extern char* RetHW( void );
```

However, in a C++ environment, you would need the following external declaration:

```
extern "C"
{
    extern char* RetHW( void );
};
```

The 'extern "C"' clause tells the compiler to use standard C linkage even though the compiler is processing a C++ source file (C++ linkage is different than C and definitely far more complex; this text will not consider pure C++ linkage because it varies so much from vendor to vendor). If you're going to compile C source files with VC++ or BCC (i.e., files with a ".c" suffix), simply drop the 'extern "C"' and the curly braces from around the external declarations. GNU GCC users should always use the "extern" option.

Listing 15-19 demonstrates this external linkage mechanism by writing a short HLA program that returns the address of a string ("Hello World") in the EAX register (like Pascal/Kylix, C/C++ expects functions to return their results in EAX). Then the main C/C++ program prints this string to the console device, as shown in Listing 15-20.

Listing 15-19: Cex1: A Simple Example of a Call to an Assembly Function from C++.

```
#include <stdlib.h>
#include "ratc.h"

extern "C"
{
    extern char* ReturnHW( void );
};

int main()
_begin( main )

    printf( "%s\n", ReturnHW() );
    _return 0;

_end( main )
```

Listing 15-20: RetHW.hla: Assembly Code That Cex1 Calls.

```
unit ReturnHWUnit;

    procedure ReturnHW; @external( "_ReturnHW" ); // Drop string for GCC.
    procedure ReturnHW; nodisplay; noframe; noalignstk;
    begin ReturnHW;

        lea( eax, "Hello World" );
```

```
        ret();

    end ReturnHW;

end ReturnHWUnit;
```

There are several new things in both the C/C++ and HLA code that might confuse you at first glance, so let's discuss these things real quick here.

The first strange thing you will notice in the C++ code is the #include "ratc.h" statement. RatC is a C/C++ macro library that adds new features to the C++ language. RatC adds several interesting features and capabilities to the C/C++ language, but a primary purpose of RatC is to help make C/C++ programs a little more readable. Of course, if you've never seen RatC before, you'll probably argue that it's not as readable as pure C/C++, but even someone who has never seen RatC before can figure out 80 percent of RatC within a few minutes. In the preceding example, the _begin and _end clauses clearly map to the "{" and "}" symbols (notice how the use of _begin and _end make it clear what function or statement associates with the braces; unlike the guesswork you've got in standard C). The _return statement is clearly equivalent to the C return statement. As you'll quickly see, all of the standard C control structures are improved slightly in RatC. You'll have no trouble recognizing them because they use the standard control structure names with an underscore prefix. This text promotes the creation of readable programs, hence the use of RatC in the examples appearing in this chapter.[8] The RatC macro package appears on the accompanying CD-ROM.

The C/C++ program isn't the only source file to introduce something new. If you look at the HLA code you'll notice that the lea instruction appears to be illegal. It takes the following form:

```
    lea( eax, "Hello World" );
```

The lea instruction is supposed to have a memory and a register operand. This example has a register and a constant; what is the address of a constant, anyway? Well, this is a syntactical extension that HLA provides to 80x86 assembly language. If you supply a constant instead of a memory operand to lea, HLA will create a static (readonly) object initialized with that constant and the lea instruction will return the address of that object. In this example, HLA will output the string data to the constants segment and then load EAX with the address of the first character of that string. Since HLA strings always have a zero terminating byte, EAX will contain the address of a zero terminated string which is exactly what C++ wants. If you look back at the original C++ code, you will see that rethw returns a *char** object and the main C++ program displays this result on the console device.

If you haven't figured it out yet, this is a roundabout version of the venerable "Hello World" program.

---

[8] If RatC really annoys you, just keep in mind that you've only got to look at a few RatC programs in this chapter. Then you can go back to the old-fashioned C code and hack to your heart's content!

Microsoft VC++ users can compile this program from the command line by using the following commands:[9]

```
hla -c RetHW.hla          // Compiles and assembles RetHW.hla to RetHW.obj
cl Cex1.cpp RetHW.obj     // Compiles C++ code and links it with RetHW.obj
```

If you are a Borland C++ user, you would use the following command sequence:

```
hla -o:omf RetHW.hla         // Compile HLA file to an OMF file.
bcc32i Cex1.cpp RetHW.obj    // Compile and link C++ and assembly code.
                             // Could also use the BCC32 compiler.
```

GCC users can compile this program from the command line by using the following commands:

```
hla -c RetHW.hla         // Compile HLA file to an ELF file.
gcc Cex1.cpp RetHW.o     // Compile and link C++ and assembly code.
                         // Could also use the BCC32 compiler.
```

15.4.2 Register Preservation

For C/C++ compilers, there is no single list of registers that you can freely use as scratchpad values within an assembly language function. The list changes by vendor and even changes between versions from the same vendor. However, you can safely assume that EAX is available for scratchpad use because C functions return their result in the EAX register. You should probably preserve everything else. Note that Intel has a standard called the Intel ABI (application binary interface). This standard specifies that procedures may freely use EAX, ECX, and EDX without preservation, but procedures must preserve all other registers across the call. Most C/C++ compilers conform to this ABI. However, there are some compilers that do not, so be sure to check your compiler vendor's documentation to verify this.

15.4.3 Function Results

C/C++ compilers universally seem to return ordinal and pointer function results in AL, AX, or EAX depending on the operand's size. The compilers probably return floating point results on the top of the FPU stack as well. Other than that, check your C/C++ vendor's documentation for more details on function return locations.

15.4.4 Calling Conventions

The standard C/C++ calling convention is probably the biggest area of contention between the C/C++ and HLA languages. VC++ and BCC both support multiple calling conventions. BCC even supports the Pascal calling convention that HLA uses, making it trivial to write HLA functions for BCC

---

[9] This text assumes you've executed the VCVARS32.BAT file that sets up the system to allow the use of VC++ from the command line.

programs. However, before we get into the details of these other calling conventions, it's probably a wise idea to first discuss the standard C/C++ calling convention.

Both VC++ and BCC *decorate* the function name when you declare an external function. For external "C" functions, the decoration consists of an underscore. If you look back at Listing 15–20 you'll notice that the external name the HLA program actually uses is "_RetHW" rather than simply "RetHW". The HLA program itself, of course, uses the symbol "RetHW" to refer to the function, but the external name (as specified by the optional parameter to the @external option) is "_RetHW". In the C/C++ program (Listing 15-19) there is no explicit indication of this decoration; you simply have to read the compiler documentation to discover that the compiler automatically prepends this character to the function name.[10] Fortunately, HLA's @external option syntax allows us to *undecorate* the name, so we can refer to the function using the same name as the C/C++ program. Name decoration is a trivial matter, easily fixed by HLA.

Linux users should note that GCC does not, by default, require the prepended underscore decoration. If you're writing code that needs to link with code any of these three C/C++ compilers, you might consider doing the following:

```
const
    cPrefix :text := "_"; // Set to the empty string for GCC.
        .
        .
        .

procedure someProc; @external( cPrefix "someProc" );
```

Remember, when HLA sees two string constants adjacent to one another (as it will once HLA expands the text constant to either "" or "_") it simply concatenates the two strings. By sticking the cPrefix string constant before the procedure's name in all the @external options in your code, you can easily decorate or not decorate all the external names by simply changing one line of code in your program (the constant declaration for cPrefix).

A big problem is the fact that C/C++ pushes parameters on the stack in the opposite direction of just about every other (non–C-based) language on the planet; specifically, C/C++ pushes actual parameters on the stack from right to left instead of the more common left to right. This means that you cannot declare a C/C++ function with two or more parameters and use a simple translation of the C/C++ external declaration as your HLA procedure declaration, i.e., the following are not equivalent:

```
extern void CToHLA( int p, unsigned q, double r );
procedure CToHLA( p:int32; q:uns32; r:real64 ); @external( cPrefix "CToHLA" );
```

---

[10] Most compilers provide an option to turn this off if you don't want this to occur. We will assume that this option is active in this text because that's the standard for external C names.

Were you to call CToHLA from the C/C++ program, the compiler would push the r parameter first, the q parameter second, and the p parameter third — exactly the opposite order that the HLA code expects. As a result, the HLA code would use the L.O. double word of r as p's value, the H.O. double word of r as q's value, and the combination of p and q's values as the value for r. Obviously, you'd most likely get an incorrect result from this calculation. Fortunately, there's an easy solution to this problem: use the @cdecl procedure option in the HLA code to tell it to reverse the parameters:

```
procedure CToHLA( p:int32; q:uns32; r:real64 );
    @cdecl;
    @external( cPrefix "CToHLA" );
```

Now when the C/C++ code calls this procedure, it pushes the parameters on the stack, and the HLA code will retrieve them in the proper order.

There is another big difference between the C/C++ calling convention and HLA: HLA procedures automatically clean up after themselves by removing all parameters pass to a procedure prior to returning to the caller. C/C++, on the other hand, requires the caller, not the procedure, to clean up the parameters. This has two important ramifications: (1) if you call a C/C++ function (or one that uses the C/C++ calling sequence), then your code has to remove any parameters it pushed upon return from that function; (2) your HLA code cannot automatically remove parameter data from the stack if C/C++ code calls it. The @cdecl procedure option tells HLA not to generate the code that automatically removes parameters from the stack upon return. Of course, if you use the @noframe option, you must ensure that you don't remove these parameters yourself when your procedures return to their caller.

One thing HLA cannot handle automatically for you is removing parameters from the stack when you call a procedure or function that uses the @cdecl calling convention; for example, you must manually pop these parameters whenever you call a C/C++ function from your HLA code.

Removing parameters from the stack when a C/C++ function returns to your code is very easy, just execute an "add(constant, esp);" instruction where constant is the number of parameter bytes you've pushed on the stack. For example, the CToHLA function has 16 bytes of parameters (two int32 objects and one real64 object) so the calling sequence (in HLA) would look something like the following:

```
        CToHLA( pVal, qVal, rVal );  // Assume this is the macro version.
        add( 16, esp );              // Remove parameters from the stack.
```

Cleaning up after a call is easy enough. However, if you're writing the function that must leave it up to the caller to remove the parameters from the stack, then you've got a tiny problem — by default, HLA procedures always clean up after themselves. If you use the @cdecl option and don't specify the @noframe option, then HLA automatically handles this for you. However, if you use the @noframe option, then you've got to ensure that you leave the parameter data on the stack when returning from a function/procedure that uses the @cdecl calling convention.

If you want to leave the parameters on the stack for the caller to remove, then you must write the standard entry and exit sequences for the procedure that build and destroy the activation record (for details, see the chapter on procedures). This means you've got to use the @noframe and @nodisplay options on your procedures that C/C++ will call. Here's a sample implementation of the CToHLA procedure that builds and destroys the activation record:

```
procedure _CToHLA( rValue:real64; q:uns32; p:int32 ); @nodisplay; @noframe;
begin _CToHLA;

    push( ebp );            // Standard Entry Sequence
    mov( esp, ebp );
    // sub( _vars_, esp );  // Needed if you have local variables.
        .
        .           // Code to implement the function's body.
        .
    mov( ebp, esp );        // Restore the stack pointer.
    pop( ebp );             // Restore link to previous activation record.
    ret();                  // Note that we don't remove any parameters.

end _CToHLA;
```

If you're willing to use some vendor extensions to the C/C++ programming language, then you can make the interface to HLA much simpler. For example, if you're using Borland's C++ product, it has an option you can apply to function declarations to tell the compiler to use the Pascal calling convention. Because HLA uses the Pascal calling convention, specifying this option in your BCC programs will make the interface to HLA trivial. In Borland C++ you can specify the Pascal calling convention for an external function using the following syntax:

```
extern type _pascal funcname( parameters )
```

Example:

```
extern void _pascal CToHLA( int p, unsigned q, double r );
```

The Pascal calling convention does not decorate the name, so the HLA name would not have a leading underscore. The Pascal calling convention uses case-insensitive names; BCC achieves this by converting the name to all uppercase. Therefore, you'd probably want to use an HLA declaration like the following:

```
procedure CToHLA( p:int32; q:uns32; r:real64 ); @external( "CTOHLA" );
```

Procedures using the Pascal calling convention push their parameters from left to right and leave it up to the procedure to clean up the stack upon return, exactly what HLA does by default. When using the Pascal calling convention, you could write the CToHLA function as follows:

```
procedure CToHLA( rValue:real64; q:uns32; p:int32 ); @external( "CTOHLA" );

procedure CToHLA( rValue:real64; q:uns32; p:int32 ); @nodisplay; @noalignstack;
begin CToHLA;

        .
        .       // Code to implement the function's body.
        .

end CToHLA;
```

Note that you don't have to supply the standard entry and exit sequences. HLA provides those automatically.

Of course, Microsoft isn't about to support the Pascal calling sequence because they don't have a Pascal compiler. So this option isn't available to VC++ users.

Both Borland and Microsoft (and HLA) support the so-called StdCall calling convention. This is the calling convention that Windows uses, so nearly every language that operates under Windows provides this calling convention. The StdCall calling convention is a combination of the C and Pascal calling conventions. Like C, the functions need to have their parameters pushed on the stack in a right to left order; like Pascal, it is the caller's responsibility to clean up the parameters when the function returns; like C, the function name is case sensitive; like Pascal, the function name is not decorated (i.e., the external name is the same as the function declaration). The syntax for a StdCall function is the same in both VC++ and BCC; it is the following:

```
extern void _stdcall CToHLA( int p, unsigned q, double r );
```

HLA supports the StdCall convention using the @stdcall procedure option.. Because the name is undecorated, you could use a prototype and macro like the following:

```
procedure CToHLA( p:int32; q:uns32; r:real64 ); @stdcall; @external( "CTOHLA" );
procedure CToHLA( p:int32; q:uns32; r:real64  );  @nodisplay; @noalignstack;
begin CToHLA;

    .
    .  // Function body
    .

end CToHLA;

    .
    .
    .

CToHLA( pValue, qValue, rValue );  // Demo of a call to CToHLA.
```

15.4.5 Pass by Value and Reference in C/C++

A C/C++ program can pass parameters to a procedure or function using one of two different mechanisms: pass by value and pass by reference. Because pass by reference parameters use pointers, this parameter passing mechanism is completely compatible between HLA and C/C++. The following two lines provide an external declaration in C++ and the corresponding external (public) declaration in HLA for a pass by reference parameter using the calling convention:

```
extern void HasRefParm( int& refparm );                    // C++
procedure HasRefParm( var refparm: int32 ); @external;     // HLA
```

Like HLA, C++ will pass the 32-bit address of whatever actual parameter you specify when calling the HasRefParm procedure. Don't forget that inside the HLA code, you must dereference this pointer to access the actual parameter data. See the chapter on procedures for more details.

Like HLA, C++ lets you pass untyped parameters by reference. The syntax to achieve this in C++ is the following:

```
extern void UntypedRefParm( void* parm1 );
```

Actually, this is not a reference parameter, but a value parameter with an untyped pointer.

In HLA, you can use the var keyword as the data type to specify that you want an untyped reference parameter. Here's the corresponding prototype for the UntypedRefParm procedure in HLA:

```
procedure UntypedRefParm( var parm1:var );
    @external;
```

15.4.6 Scalar Data Type Correspondence Between C/C++ and HLA

When passing parameters between C/C++ and HLA procedures and functions, it's very important that the calling code and the called code agree on the basic data types for the parameters. In this section we will draw a correspondence between the C/C++ scalar data types and the HLA (1.x) data types.

Assembly language supports any possible data format, so HLA's data type capabilities will always be a superset of C/C++'s. Therefore, there may be some objects you can create in HLA that have no counterpart in C/C++, but the reverse is not true. Because the assembly functions and procedures you write are generally manipulating data that C/C++ provides, you don't have to worry too much about not being able to process some data passed to an HLA procedure by C/C++.

C/C++ provides a wide range of different integer data types. Unfortunately, the exact representation of these types is implementation specific. Table 15-5 lists the C/C++ types as currently implemented by Borland C++, GNU's GCC, and Microsoft VC++. These types may very well change as 64-bit compilers become available.

Table 15-5: C/C++ and HLA Integer Types

C/C++	HLA Equivalent	Range	
		Minimum	Maximum
int	int32	-2147483648	2147483647
unsigned	uns32	0	4294967295
signed char	int8	-128	127
short	int16	-32768	32767
long	int32	-2147483648	2147483647
unsigned char	uns8	0	255
unsigned short	uns16	0	65535

In addition to the integer values, C/C++ supports several non-integer ordinal types. Table 15-6 provides their HLA equivalents.

Table 15-6: Non-integer Ordinal Types in C/C++ and HLA

C/C++	HLA	Range	
		Minimum	Maximum
wchar, TCHAR	wchar	#0	#65535
BOOL	boolean	false (0)	true (not zero)

Like the integer types, C/C++ supports a wide range of real numeric formats. Table 15-7 presents these types and their HLA equivalents.

Table 15-7: Real Types in C/C++ and HLA

C/C++	HLA	Range	
		Minimum	Maximum
double	real64	5.0 E-324	1.7 E+308
float	real32	1.5 E-45	3.4 E+38
long double[1]	real80	3.6 E-4951	1.1 E+4932

1. This data type is 80 bits only in BCC. GCC and VC++ uses 64 bits for the long double type.

The last scalar type of interest is the pointer type. Both HLA and C/C++ use a 32-bit address to represent pointers, so these data types are completely equivalent in both languages.

15.4.7 Passing String Data Between C/C++ and HLA Code

C/C++ uses zero terminated strings. Algorithms that manipulate zero terminated strings are not as efficient as functions that work on length prefixed strings; on the plus side, however, zero terminated strings are very easy to work with. HLA's strings are downward compatible with C/C++ strings because HLA places a zero byte at the end of each HLA string. Because you'll probably not be calling HLA Standard Library string routines, the fact that C/C++ strings are not upward compatible with HLA strings generally won't be a problem. If you do decide to modify some of the HLA string functions so that they don't raise exceptions, you can always translate the str.cStrToStr function that translates zero terminated C/C++ strings to HLA strings.

A C/C++ string variable is typically a char* object or an array of characters. In either case, C/C++ will pass the address of the first character of the string to an external procedure whenever you pass a string as a parameter. Within the procedure, you can treat the parameter as an indirect reference and dereference to pointer to access characters within the string.

15.4.8 Passing Record/Structure Data Between HLA and C/C++

Records in HLA are (mostly) compatible with C/C++ structs. You can easily translate a C/C++ struct to an HLA record. In this section we'll explore how to do this and learn about the incompatibilities that exist between HLA records and C/C++ structures.

For the most part, translating C/C++ records to HLA is a no-brainer. Just grab the "guts" of a structure declaration and translate the declarations to HLA syntax within a record..endrecord block and you're done.

Consider the following C/C++ structure type declaration:

```
typedef struct
{
    unsigned char day;
    unsigned char month;
    int year;
    unsigned char dayOfWeek;
} dateType;
```

The translation to an HLA record is, for the most part, very straight-forward. Just translate the field types accordingly and use the HLA record syntax and you're in business. The translation is the following:

```
type
    recType:
        record

                day: byte;
                month: byte;
                year:int32;
                dayOfWeek:byte;
```

```
        endrecord;
```

There is one minor problem with this example: data alignment. Depending on your compiler and whatever defaults it uses, C/C++ might not pack the data in the structure as compactly as possible. Most C/C++ compilers will attempt to align the fields on double word or other boundaries. With double word alignment of objects larger than a byte, the previous C/C++ typedef statement is probably better modeled by:

```
type
    recType:
        record

            day: byte;
            month: byte;
            padding:byte[2];        // Align year on a four-byte boundary.
            year:int32;
            dayOfWeek:byte;
            morePadding: byte[3]; // Make record an even multiple of four bytes.

        endrecord;
```

Of course, a better solution is to use HLA's align directive to automatically align the fields in the record:

```
type
    recType:
        record

            day: byte;
            month: byte;
            align( 4 );        // Align year on a four-byte boundary.
            year:int32;
            dayOfWeek:byte;
            align(4);          // Make record an even multiple of four bytes.

        endrecord;
```

Alignment of the fields is good insofar as access to the fields is faster if they are aligned appropriately. However, aligning records in this fashion does consume extra space (five bytes in the preceding examples) and that can be expensive if you have a large array of records whose fields need padding for alignment.

You will need to check your compiler vendor's documentation to determine whether it packs or pads structures by default. Most compilers give you several options for packing or padding the fields on various boundaries. Padded structures might be a bit faster, while packed structures (i.e., no padding) are going to be more compact. You'll have to decide which is more important to you and then adjust your HLA code accordingly.

Since HLA 1.37 became available, HLA has provided some additional features making it possible for HLA to automatically align fields of a record on various boundaries. These new features in HLA were added specifically to make HLA easier to use with a wide variety of C/C++ compilers. The syntax that supports automatic field alignment is the following:

```
type
    rType    :record [ maxAlign : minAlign ];
        << fields >>
    endrecord;
```

The maxalign and minalign items are constant expressions. HLA will compare the size of each field with these two values. If the size of a particular field is less than minAlign, then HLA will automatically align that field on a boundary that is an even multiple of minAlign. If the size of the field is greater than maxAlign, then HLA will align that field on a boundary that is an even multiple of maxAlign. If the size of the field is between minAlign and maxAlign, then HLA will align the field on a boundary that is an even multiple of the field's size. This is usually sufficient to match the alignment that any given C/C++ compiler will use. For more details on record field alignment, please see the HLA Reference Manual on the accompanying CD-ROM.

Note that by default, C/C++ passes structures by value. A C/C++ program must explicitly take the address of a structure object and pass that address in order to simulate pass by reference. In general, if the size of a structure exceeds about 16 bytes, you should pass the structure by reference rather than by value.

15.4.9   Passing Array Data Between HLA and C/C++

Passing array data between some procedures written in C/C++ and HLA is little different than passing array data between two HLA procedures. First of all, C/C++ can only pass arrays by reference, never by value. Therefore, you must always use pass by reference inside the HLA code. The following code fragments provide a simple example:

```
    int CArray[128][4];

extern void PassedArrray( int array[128][4] );
```

Corresponding HLA code:

```
type
    CArray: int32[ 128, 4];

procedure PassedArray( var ary: CArray ); @external;
```

As the above examples demonstrate, C/C++'s array declarations are similar to HLA's insofar as you specify the bounds of each dimension in the array.

C/C++ uses row major ordering for arrays. So if you're accessing elements of a C/C++ multidimensional array in HLA code, be sure to use the row major order computation.

15.5   For More Information

The best source of information concerning the interface between assembly and high level languages is the documentation that comes with your compiler. Most compiler reference manuals go into great detail, discussing the interface between assembly language and the high level language.

ASCII CHARACTER SET

Binary	Hex	Decimal	Character
0000_0000	00	0	NULL
0000_0001	01	1	CTRL A
0000_0010	02	2	CTRL B
0000_0011	03	3	CTRL C
0000_0100	04	4	CTRL D
0000_0101	05	5	CTRL E
0000_0110	06	6	CTRL F
0000_0111	07	7	bell
0000_1000	08	8	backspace
0000_1001	09	9	TAB
0000_1010	0A	10	line feed
0000_1011	0B	11	CTRL K
0000_1100	0C	12	form feed
0000_1101	0D	13	RETURN
0000_1110	0E	14	CTRL N
0000_1111	0F	15	CTRL O
0001_0000	10	16	CTRL P
0001_0001	11	17	CTRL Q
0001_0010	12	18	CTRL R

Binary	Hex	Decimal	Character
0001_0011	13	19	CTRL S
0001_0100	14	20	CTRL T
0001_0101	15	21	CTRL U
0001_0110	16	22	CTRL V
0001_0111	17	23	CTRL W
0001_1000	18	24	CTRL X
0001_1001	19	25	CTRL Y
0001_1010	1A	26	CTRL Z
0001_1011	1B	27	CTRL [
0001_1100	1C	28	CTRL \
0001_1101	1D	29	ESC
0001_1110	1E	30	CTRL ^
0001_1111	1F	31	CTRL _
0010_0000	20	32	space
0010_0001	21	33	!
0010_0010	22	34	"
0010_0011	23	35	#
0010_0100	24	36	$
0010_0101	25	37	%
0010_0110	26	38	&
0010_0111	27	39	'
0010_1000	28	40	(
0010_1001	29	41	)
0010_1010	2A	42	*
0010_1011	2B	43	+
0010_1100	2C	44	,
0010_1101	2D	45	-
0010_1110	2E	46	.
0010_1111	2F	47	/
0011_0000	30	48	0
0011_0001	31	49	1
0011_0010	32	50	2
0011_0011	33	51	3
0011_0100	34	52	4
0011_0101	35	53	5
0011_0110	36	54	6
0011_0111	37	55	7
0011_1000	38	56	8
0011_1001	39	57	9
0011_1010	3A	58	:

Binary	Hex	Decimal	Character
0011_1011	3B	59	;
0011_1100	3C	60	<
0011_1101	3D	61	=
0011_1110	3E	62	>
0011_1111	3F	63	?
0100_0000	40	64	@
0100_0001	41	65	A
0100_0010	42	66	B
0100_0011	43	67	C
0100_0100	44	68	D
0100_0101	45	69	E
0100_0110	46	70	F
0100_0111	47	71	G
0100_1000	48	72	H
0100_1001	49	73	I
0100_1010	4A	74	J
0100_1011	4B	75	K
0100_1100	4C	76	L
0100_1101	4D	77	M
0100_1110	4E	78	N
0100_1111	4F	79	O
0101_0000	50	80	P
0101_0001	51	81	Q
0101_0010	52	82	R
0101_0011	53	83	S
0101_0100	54	84	T
0101_0101	55	85	U
0101_0110	56	86	V
0101_0111	57	87	W
0101_1000	58	88	X
0101_1001	59	89	Y
0101_1010	5A	90	Z
0101_1011	5B	91	[
0101_1100	5C	92	\
0101_1101	5D	93	]
0101_1110	5E	94	^
0101_1111	5F	95	_
0110_0000	60	96	`
0110_0001	61	97	a
0110_0010	62	98	b

Binary	Hex	Decimal	Character
0110_0011	63	99	c
0110_0100	64	100	d
0110_0101	65	101	e
0110_0110	66	102	f
0110_0111	67	103	g
0110_1000	68	104	h
0110_1001	69	105	i
0110_1010	6A	106	j
0110_1011	6B	107	k
0110_1100	6C	108	l
0110_1101	6D	109	m
0110_1110	6E	110	n
0110_1111	6F	111	o
0111_0000	70	112	p
0111_0001	71	113	q
0111_0010	72	114	r
0111_0011	73	115	s
0111_0100	74	116	t
0111_0101	75	117	u
0111_0110	76	118	v
0111_0111	77	119	w
0111_1000	78	120	x
0111_1001	79	121	y
0111_1010	7A	122	z
0111_1011	7B	123	{
0111_1100	7C	124	|
0111_1101	7D	125	}
0111_1110	7E	126	~
0111_1111	7F	127	

THE 80x86 INSTRUCTION SET

The following three tables discuss the integer/control, floating point, and MMX instruction sets. This document uses the following abbreviations:

imm	A constant value; must be appropriate for the operand size.
imm8	An 8-bit immediate constant. Some instructions limit the range of this value to less than 0..255.
immL	A 16- or 32-bit immediate constant.
immH	A 16- or 32-bit immediate constant.
reg	A general purpose integer register.
reg8	A general purpose 8-bit register.
reg16	A general purpose 16-bit register.
reg32	A general purpose 32-bit register.
mem	An arbitrary memory location using any of the available addressing modes.
mem16	A word variable using any legal addressing mode.
mem32	A dword variable using any legal addressing mode.
mem64	A qword variable using any legal addressing mode.
label	A statement label in the program.
ProcedureName	The name of a procedure in the program.

Instructions that have two source operands typically use the first operand as a source operand and the second operand as a destination operand. For exceptions and other formats, please see the description for the individual instruction.

Note that this appendix only lists those instructions that are generally useful for application programming. HLA actually supports some additional instructions that are useful for OS kernel developers; please see the HLA documentation for more details on those instructions.

Table B-1: 80x86 Integer and Control Instruction Set

Instruction Syntax	Description
aaa();	ASCII Adjust after Addition. Adjusts value in AL after a decimal addition operation.
aad();	ASCII Adjust before Division. Adjusts two unpacked values in AX prior to a decimal division.
aam();	ASCII Adjust AX after Multiplication. Adjusts the result in AX for a decimal mulitply.
aas();	ASCII Adjust AL after Subtraction. Adjusts the result in AL for a decimal subtraction.
adc(imm, reg); adc(imm, mem); adc(reg, reg); adc(reg, mem); adc(mem, reg);	Add with carry. Adds the source operand plus the carry flag to the destination operand.
add(imm, reg); add(imm, mem); add(reg, reg); add(reg, mem); add(mem, reg);	Add. Adds the source operand to the destination operand.
and(imm, reg); and(imm, mem); and(reg, reg); and(reg, mem); and(mem, reg);	Bitwise AND. Logically ANDs the source operand into the destination operand. Clears the carry and overflow flags and sets the sign and zero flags according to the result.
bound(reg, mem); bound(reg, immL, immH);	Bounds check. Reg and memory operands must be the same size and they must be 16- or 32-bit values. This instruction compares the register operand against the value at the specified memory location and raises an exception if the register's value is less than the value in the memory location. If greater or equal, then this instruction compares the register to the next word or dword in memory and raises an exception if the register's value is greater. The second form of this instruction is an HLA extended syntax instruction. HLA encodes the constants as two memory locations and then emits the first form of this instruction using these newly created memory locations. For the second form, the constant values must not exceed the 16-bit or 32-bit register size.

Table B-1: 80x86 Integer and Control Instruction Set

Instruction Syntax	Description
bsf(reg, reg); bsf(mem, reg);	Bit Scan Forward. The two operands must be the same size and they must be 16-bit or 32-bit operands. This instruction locates the first set bit in the source operand and stores the bit number into the destination operand and clears the zero flag. If the source operand does not have any set bits, then this instruction sets the zero flag and the dest register value is undefined.
bsr(reg, reg); bsr(mem, reg);	Bit Scan Reverse. The two operands must be the same size and they must be 16-bit or 32-bit operands. This instruction locates the last set bit in the source operand and stores the bit number into the destination operand and clears the zero flag. If the source operand does not have any set bits, then this instruction sets the zero flag and the dest register value is undefined.
bswap(reg32);	Byte Swap. This instruction reverses the order of the bytes in a 32-bit register. It swaps bytes zero and three and it swaps bytes one and two. This effectively converts data between the little endian (used by Intel) and big endian (used by some other CPUs) formats.

bt(reg, mem);
bt(reg, reg);
bt(imm8, reg);
bt(imm8, mem);
	Register and memory operands must be 16- or 32-bit values. 8-bit immediate values must be in the range 0..15 for 16-bit registers, 0..31 for 32-bit registers, and 0..255 for memory operands. Source register must be in the range 0..15 or 0..31 for registers. Any value is legal for the source register if the destination operand is a memory location. This instruction copies the bit in the second operand, whose bit position the first operand specifies, into the carry flag.

btc(reg, mem);
btc(reg, reg);
btc(imm8, reg);
btc(imm8, mem);
	Bit test and complement. As above, except this instruction also complements the value of the specified bit in the second operand. Note that this instruction first copies the bit to the carry flag, then complements it. To support atomic operations, the memory-based forms of this instruction are always "memory locked" and they always directly access main memory; the CPU does not use the cache for this result. Hence, this instruction always operates at memory speeds (i.e., slow).

btr(reg, mem);
btr(reg, reg);
btr(imm8, reg);
btr(imm8, mem);
	Bit test and reset. Same as BTC except this instruction tests and resets (clears) the bit.

bts(reg, mem);
bts(reg, reg);
bts(imm8, reg);
bts(imm8, mem);
	Bit test and set. Same as BTC except this instruction tests and sets the bit.

call label;
call(label);
call(reg32);
call(mem32);
	Pushes a return address onto the stack and calls the subroutine at the address specified. Note that the first two forms are the same instruction. The other two forms provide indirect calls via a register or a pointer in memory.

cbw();	Convert Byte to Word. Sign extends AL into AX.
cdq();	Convert double word to quad word. Sign extends EAX into EDX:EAX.
clc();	Clear Carry.
cld();	Clear direction flag. When the direction flag is clear the string instructions increment ESI and/or EDI after each operation.

Table B-1: 80x86 Integer and Control Instruction Set

Instruction Syntax	Description
cli();	Clear the interrupt enable flag.
cmc();	Complement (invert) Carry.

cmova(mem, reg);
cmova(reg, reg);
cmova(reg, mem);
	Conditional Move (if above). Copies the source operand to the destination operand if the previous comparison found the left operand to be greater than (unsigned) the right operand (c=0, z=0). Register and memory operands must be 16-bit or 32-bit values; 8-bit operands are illegal. Does not affect the destination operand if the condition is false.

cmovae(mem, reg);
cmovae(reg, reg);
cmovae(reg, mem);
	Conditional move if above or equal to (see cmova for details).

cmovb(mem, reg);
cmovb(reg, reg);
cmovb(reg, mem);
	Conditional move if below (see cmova for details).

cmovbe(mem, reg);
cmovbe(reg, reg);
cmovbe(reg, mem);
	Conditional move if below or equal to (see cmova for details).

cmovc(mem, reg);
cmovc(reg, reg);
cmovc(reg, mem);
	Conditional move if carry set (see cmova for details).

cmove(mem, reg);
cmove(reg, reg);
cmove(reg, mem);
	Conditional move if equal to (see cmova for details).

cmovg(mem, reg);
cmovg(reg, reg);
cmovg(reg, mem);
	Conditional move if (signed) greater than (see cmova for details).

cmovge(mem, reg);
cmovge(reg, reg);
cmovge(reg, mem);
	Conditional move if (signed) greater than or equal to (see cmova for details).

cmovl(mem, reg);
cmovl(reg, reg);
cmovl(reg, mem);
	Conditional move if (signed) less than (see cmova for details).

cmovle(mem, reg);
cmovle(reg, reg);
cmovle(reg, mem);
	Conditional move if (signed) less than or equal to (see cmova for details).

cmovna(mem, reg);
cmovna(reg, reg);
cmovna(reg, mem);
	Conditional move if (unsigned) not greater than (see cmova for details).

cmovnae(mem, reg);
cmovnae(reg, reg);
cmovnae(reg, mem);
	Conditional move if (unsigned) not greater than or equal to (see cmova for details).

cmovnb(mem, reg);
cmovnb(reg, reg);
cmovnb(reg, mem);
	Conditional move if (unsigned) not less than (see cmova for details).

cmovnbe(mem, reg);
cmovnbe(reg, reg);
cmovnbe(reg, mem);
	Conditional move if (unsigned) not less than or equal to (see cmova for details).

cmovnc(mem, reg);
cmovnc(reg, reg);
cmovnc(reg, mem);
	Conditional move if no carry/carry clear (see cmova for details).

Table B-1: 80x86 Integer and Control Instruction Set

Instruction Syntax	Description

cmovne(mem, reg);
cmovne(reg, reg);
cmovne(reg, mem);
	Conditional move if not equal to (see cmova for details).

cmovng(mem, reg);
cmovng(reg, reg);
cmovng(reg, mem);
	Conditional move if (signed) not greater than (see cmova for details).

cmovnge(mem, reg);
cmovnge(reg, reg);
cmovnge(reg, mem);
	Conditional move if (signed) not greater than or equal to (see cmova for details).

cmovnl(mem, reg);
cmovnl(reg, reg);
cmovnl(reg, mem);
	Conditional move if (signed) not less than (see cmova for details).

cmovnle(mem, reg);
cmovnle(reg, reg);
cmovnle(reg, mem);
	Conditional move if (signed) not less than or equal to (see cmova for details).

cmovno(mem, reg);
cmovno(reg, reg);
cmovno(reg, mem);
	Conditional move if no overflow / overflow flag = 0 (see cmova for details).

cmovnp(mem, reg);
cmovnp(reg, reg);
cmovnp(reg, mem);
	Conditional move if no parity / parity flag = 0 / odd parity (see cmova for details).

cmovns(mem, reg);
cmovns(reg, reg);
cmovns(reg, mem);
	Conditional move if no sign / sign flag = 0 (see cmova for details).

cmovnz(mem, reg);
cmovnz(reg, reg);
cmovnz(reg, mem);
	Conditional move if not zero (see cmova for details).

cmovo(mem, reg);
cmovo(reg, reg);
cmovo(reg, mem);
	Conditional move if overflow / overflow flag = 1 (see cmova for details).

cmovp(mem, reg);
cmovp(reg, reg);
cmovp(reg, mem);
	Conditional move if parity flag = 1 (see cmova for details).

cmovpe(mem, reg);
cmovpe(reg, reg);
cmovpe(reg, mem);
	Conditional move if even parity / parity flag = 1 (see cmova for details).

cmovpo(mem, reg);
cmovpo(reg, reg);
cmovpo(reg, mem);
	Conditional move if odd parity / parity flag = 0 (see cmova for details).

cmovs(mem, reg);
cmovs(reg, reg);
cmovs(reg, mem);
	Conditional move if sign flag = 1 (see cmova for details).

cmovz(mem, reg);
cmovz(reg, reg);
cmovz(reg, mem);
	Conditional move if zero flag = 1 (see cmova for details).

cmp(imm, reg);
cmp(imm, mem);
cmp(reg, reg);
cmp(reg, mem);
cmp(mem, reg);
	Compare. Compares the first operand against the second operand. The two operands must be the same size. This instruction sets the condition code flags as appropriate for the condition jump and set instructions. This instruction does not change the value of either operand.

Table B-1: 80x86 Integer and Control Instruction Set

Instruction Syntax	Description

cmpsb();
repe.cmpsb();
repne.cmpsb();
	Compare string of bytes. Compares the byte pointed at byte ESI with the byte pointed at by EDI and then adjusts ESI and EDI by ±1 depending on the value of the direction flag. Sets the flags according to the result. With the REPNE (repeat while not equal) flag, this instruction compares corresponding characters in the two strings until it finds two characters that are equal, or it compares the number of characters specified by ECX. With the REPE (repeat while equal) prefix, this instruction compares two strings up to the first byte that is different. See Chapter 12, "The String Instructions," for more details.

cmpsw()
repe.cmpsw();
repne.cmpsw();
	Compare a string of words. Like cmpsb except this instruction compares words rather than bytes and adjusts ESI/EDI by ±2.

cmpsd()
repe.cmpsd();
repne.cmpsd();
	Compare a string of double words. Like cmpsb except this instruction compares double words rather than bytes and adjusts ESI/EDI by ±4.

cmpxchg(reg, mem); cmpxchg(reg, reg);	Reg and mem must be the same size. They can be 8-, 16-, or 32-bit objects. This instruction compares the value in the accumulator (al, ax, or eax) against the second operand. If the two values are equal, this instruction copies the source (first) operand to the destination (second) operand. Otherwise, this instruction copies the second operand into the accumulator.
cmpxchg8b(mem64);	Compares the 64-bit value in EDX:EAX with the memory operand. If the values are equal, then this instruction stores the 64-bit value in ECX:EBX into the memory operand and sets the zero flag. Otherwise, this instruction copies the 64-bit memory operand into the EDX:EAX registers and clears the zero flag.
cpuid();	CPU Identification. This instruction identifies various features found on the different Pentium processors. See the Intel documentation on this instruction for more details.
cwd();	Convert Word to Double. Sign extends AX to DX:AX.
cwde();	Convert Word to Double Word Extended. Sign extends AX to EAX.
daa();	Decimal Adjust after Addition. Adjusts value in AL after a decimal addition.
das();	Decimal Adjust after Subtraction. Adjusts value in AL after a decimal subtraction.
dec(reg); dec(mem);	Decrement. Subtracts one from the destination memory location or register.

Table B-1: 80x86 Integer and Control Instruction Set

Instruction Syntax	Description

div(reg);
div(reg8, ax);
div(reg16, dx:ax);
div(reg32, edx:eax);
div(mem)
div(mem8, ax);
div(mem16, dx:ax);
div(mem32, edx:eax);
div(imm8, ax);
div(imm16, dx:ax);
div(imm32, edx:eax);
	Divides accumulator or extended accumulator (dx:ax or edx:eax) by the source operand. Note that the instructions involving an immediate operand are HLA extensions. HLA creates a memory object holding these constants and then divides the accumulator or extended accumulator by the contents of this memory location. Note that the accumulator operand is twice the size of the source (divisor) operand. This instruction computes the quotient and places it in AL, AX, or EAX and it computes the remainder and places it in AH, DX, or EDX (depending on the divisor's size). This instruction raises an exception if you attempt to divide by zero or if the quotient doesn't fit in the destination register (AL, AX, or EAX).
	This instruction performs an unsigned division.

enter(imm16, imm8);	Enter a procedure. Creates an activation record for a procedure. The first constant specifies the number of bytes of local variables. The second parameter (in the range 0..31) specifies the static nesting level (lex level) of the procedure.

idiv(reg);
idiv(reg8, ax);
idiv(reg16, dx:ax);
idiv(reg32, edx:eax);
idiv(mem);
idiv(mem8, ax);
idiv(mem16, dx:ax);
idiv(mem32, edx:eax);
idiv(imm8, ax);
idiv(imm16, dx:ax);
idiv(imm32, edx:eax);
	Divides accumulator or extended accumulator (dx:ax or edx:eax) by the source operand. Note that the instructions involving an immediate operand are HLA extensions. HLA creates a memory object holding these constants and then divides the accumulator or extended accumulator by the contents of this memory location. Note that the accumulator operand is twice the size of the source (divisor) operand. This instruction computes the quotient and places it in AL, AX, or EAX and it computes the remainder and places it in AH, DX, or EDX (depending on the divisor's size). This instruction raises an exception if you attempt to divide by zero or if the quotient doesn't fit in the destination register (AL, AX, or EAX).
	This instruction performs a signed division. The condition code bits are undefined after executing this instruction.

imul(reg);
imul(reg8, al);
imul(reg16, ax);
imul(reg32, eax);
imul(mem);
imul(mem8, al);
imul(mem16, ax);
imul(mem32, eax);
imul(imm8, al);
imul(imm16, ax);
imul(imm32, eax);
	Multiplies the accumulator (AL, AX, or EAX) by the source operand. The source operand will be the same size as the accumulator. The product produces an operand that is twice the size of the two operands with the product winding up in AX, DX:AX, or EDX:EAX. Note that the instructions involving an immediate operand are HLA extensions. HLA creates a memory object holding these constants and then multiplies the accumulator by the contents of this memory location.
	This instruction performs a signed multiplication. Also see INTMUL.
	This instruction sets the carry and overflow flag if the H.O. portion of the result (AH, DX, EDX) is not a sign extension of the L.O. portion of the product. The sign and zero flags are undefined after the execution of this instruction.

in(imm8, al);
in(imm8, ax);
in(imm8, eax);
in(dx, al);
in(dx, ax);
in(dx, eax);
	Input data from a port. These instructions read a byte, word, or double word from an input port and place the input data into the accumulator register. Immediate port constants must be in the range 0..255. For all other port addresses you must use the DX register to hold the 16-bit port number. Note that this is a privileged instruction that will raise an exception in many Win32 Operating Systems.

Table B-1: 80x86 Integer and Control Instruction Set

Instruction Syntax	Description
inc(reg); inc(mem);	Increment. Adds one to the specified memory or register operand. Does not affect the carry flag. Sets the overflow flag if there was signed overflow. Sets the zero and sign flags according to the result. Note that Z=1 indicates an unsigned overflow.
int(imm8);	Call an interrupt service routine specified by the immediate operand. Note that Windows does not use this instruction for system calls, so you will probably never use this instruction under Windows. Note that INT(3); is the user breakpoint instruction (that raises an appropriate exception). INT(0) is the divide error exception. INT(4) is the overflow exception. However, it's better to use the HLA RAISE statement than to use this instruction for these exceptions.

intmul(imm, reg);
 intmul(imm, reg, reg);
 intmul(imm, mem, reg);
 intmul(reg, reg);
 intmul(mem, reg);
	Integer mutiply. Multiplies the destination (last) operand by the source operand (if there are only two operands); or it multiplies the two source operands together and stores the result in the destination operand (if there are three operands). The operands must all be 16- or 32-bit operands and they must all be the same size.
	 This instruction computes a signed product. This instruction sets the overflow and carry flags if there was a signed arithmetic overflow; the zero and sign flags are undefined after the execution of this instruction.

into();	Raises an exception if the overflow flag is set. Note: The HLA pseudo-variable "@into" controls the code generation for this instruction. If @into is false, HLA ignores this instruction; if @into is true (default), then HLA emits the object code for this instruction. Note that if the overflow flag is set, this instruction behaves like the "INT(4);" instruction.
iret();	Return from an interrupt. This instruction is not generally usable from an application program. It is for use in interrupt service routines only.
ja *label*;	Conditional jump if (unsigned) above. You would generally use this instruction immediately after a CMP instruction to test to see if one operand is greater than another using an unsigned comparison. Control transfers to the specified label if this condition is true, control falls through to the next instruction if the condition is false.
jae *label*;	Conditional jump if (unsigned) above or equal to. See JA above for details.
jb *label*;	Conditional jump if (unsigned) below. See JA above for details.
jbe *label*;	Conditional jump if (unsigned) below or equal to. See JA above for details.
jc *label*;	Conditional jump if carry is one. See JA above for details.
je *label*;	Conditional jump if equal to. See JA above for details.
jg *label*;	Conditional jump if (signed) greater than. See JA above for details.
jge *label*;	Conditional jump if (signed) greater than or equal to. See JA above for details.
jl *label*;	Conditional jump if (signed) less than. See JA above for details.

Table B-1: 80x86 Integer and Control Instruction Set

Instruction Syntax	Description
jle *label*;	Conditional jump if (signed) less than or equal to. See JA above for details.
jna *label*;	Conditional jump if (unsigned) not above. See JA above for details.
jnae *label*;	Conditional jump if (unsigned) not above or equal to. See JA above for details.
jnb *label*;	Conditional jump if (unsigned) below. See JA above for details.
jnbe *label*;	Conditional jump if (unsigned) below or equal to. See JA above for details.
jnc *label*;	Conditional jump if carry flag is clear (no carry). See JA above for details.
jne *label*;	Conditional jump if not equal to. See JA above for details.
jng *label*;	Conditional jump if (signed) not greater than. See JA above for details.
jnge *label*;	Conditional jump if (signed) not greater than or equal to. See JA above for details.
jnl *label*;	Conditional jump if (signed) not less than. See JA above for details.
jnle *label*;	Conditional jump if (signed) not less than or equal to. See JA above for details.
jno *label*;	Conditional jump if no overflow (overflow flag = 0). See JA above for details.
jnp *label*;	Conditional jump if no parity/parity odd (parity flag = 0). See JA above for details.
jns *label*;	Conditional jump if no sign (sign flag = 0). See JA above for details.
jnz *label*;	Conditional jump if not zero (zero flag = 0). See JA above for details.
jo *label*;	Conditional jump if overflow (overflow flag = 1). See JA above for details.
jp *label*;	Conditional jump if parity (parity flag = 1). See JA above for details.
jpe *label*;	Conditional jump if parity even (parity flag = 1). See JA above for details.
jpo *label*;	Conditional jump if parity odd (parity flag = 0). See JA above for details.
js *label*;	Conditional jump if sign (sign flag = 0). See JA above for details.
jz *label*;	Conditional jump if zero (zero flag = 0). See JA above for details.
jcxz *label*;	Conditional jump if CX is zero. See JA above for details. Note: The range of this branch is limited to ±128 bytes around the instruction. HLA does not check for this (MASM reports the error when it assembles HLA's output). Since this instruction is slower than comparing CX to zero and using JZ, you probably shouldn't even use this instruction. If you do, be sure that the target label is nearby in your code.

Table B-1: 80x86 Integer and Control Instruction Set

Instruction Syntax	Description
jecxz *label*;	Conditional jump if ECX is zero. See JA above for details. Note: The range of this branch is limited to ±128 bytes around the instruction. HLA does not check for this (MASM reports the error when it assembles HLA's output). Since this instruction is slower than comparing ECX to zero and using JZ, you probably shouldn't even use this instruction. If you do, be sure that the target label is nearby in your code.

jmp *label*;
jmp(*label*);
jmp *ProcedureName*;
jmp(mem32);
jmp(reg32);
	Jump instruction. This instruction unconditionally transfers control to the specified destination operand. If the operand is a 32-bit register or memory location, the JMP instruction transfers control to the instruction whose address appears in the register or the memory location.
	
	Note: You should exercise great care when jumping to a procedure label. The JMP instruction does not push a return address or any other data associated with a procedure's activation record. Hence, when the procedure attempts to return, it will use data on the stack that was pushed prior to the execution of the JMP instruction; it is your responsibility to ensure such data is present on the stack when using JMP to transfer control to a procedure.

lahf();	Load AH from flags. This instruction loads the AH register with the L.O. eight bits of the flags register. See SAHF for the flag layout.
lea(reg32, mem); lea(mem, reg32);	Load Effective Address. These instructions, which are semantically identical, load the 32-bit register with the address of the specified memory location. The memory location does not need to be a double word object. Note that there is never any ambiguity in this instruction since the register is always the destination operand and the memory location is always the source.
leave();	Leave procedure. This instruction cleans up the activation record for a procedure prior to returning from the procedure. You would normally use this instruction to clean up the activation record created by the ENTER instruction.

Table B-1: 80x86 Integer and Control Instruction Set

Instruction Syntax	Description

lock prefix	The lock prefix asserts a special pin on the processor during the execution of the following instruction. In a multiprocessor environment, this ensures that the processor has exclusive use of a shared memory object while the instruction executes. The lock prefix may only precede one of the following instructions: ADD, ADC, AND BTC, BTR, BTS, CMPXCHG, DEC, INC NEG, NOT, OR, SBB, SUB, XOR, XADD, and XCHG. Furthermore, this prefix is only valid for the forms that have a memory operand as their destination operand. Any other instruction or addressing mode will raise an undefined opcode exception. HLA does not directly support the LOCK prefix on these instructions (if it did, you would normally write instructions like "lock.add();" and "lock.bts();". However, you can easily add this instruction to HLA's instruction set through the use of the following macro:
	
	#macro lock;
	byte $F0; // $F0 is the opcode for the lock prefix.
	#endmacro;
	
	To use this macro, simply precede the instruction you wish to lock with an invocation of the macro, e.g.,
	
	lock add(al, mem);
	
	Note that a LOCK prefix will dramatically slow an instruction down since it must access main memory (i.e., no cache) and it must negotiate for the use of that memory location with other processors in a multiprocessor system. The LOCK prefix has very little value in single processor systems.

lodsb();	Load String Byte. Loads AL with the byte whose address appears in ESI. Then it increments or decrements ESI by one depending on the value of the direction flag. See Chapter 12 for more details. Note: HLA does not allow the use of any repeat prefix with this instruction.
lodsw();	Load String Word. Loads AX from [ESI] and adds ±2 to ESI. See LODSB for more details.
lodsd();	Load String Double Word. Loads EAX from [ESI] and adds ±4 to ESI. See LODSB for more details.
loop *label*;	Decrements ECX and jumps to the target label if ECX is not zero. See JA for more details. Like JECX, this instruction is limited to a range of ±128 bytes around the instruction and only MASM will catch the range error. Since this instruction is actually slower than a DEC/JNZ pair, you should probably avoid using this instruction.
loope *label*;	Check the zero flag, decrement ECX, and branch if the zero flag was set and ECX did not become zero. Same limitations as LOOP. See LOOP above for details.
loopne *label*;	Check the zero flag, decrement ECX, and branch if the zero flag was clear and ECX did not become zero. Same limitations as LOOP. See LOOP above for details.
loopnz *label*;	Same instruction as LOOPNE.
loopz *label*;	Same instruction as LOOPE.

Table B-1: 80x86 Integer and Control Instruction Set

Instruction Syntax	Description

mov(imm, reg);
mov(imm, mem);
mov(reg, reg);
mov(reg, mem);
mov(mem, reg);
mov(mem16, mem16);
mov(mem32, mem32);
	Move. Copies the data from the source (first) operand to the destination (second) operand. The operands must be the same size. Note that the memory to memory moves are an HLA extension. HLA compiles these statements into a push(source)/pop(dest) instruction pair.

movsb(); rep.movsb();	Move string of bytes. Copies the byte pointed at by ESI to the byte pointed at by EDI and then adjusts ESI and EDI by ±1 depending on the value of the direction flag. With the REP (repeat) prefix, this instruction moves ECX bytes. See Chapter 12 for more details.
movsw(); rep.movsw();	Move string of words. Like MOVSB above except it copies words and adjusts ESI/EDI by ±2.
movsd(); rep.movsd();	Move string of words. Like MOVSB above except it copies double words and adjusts ESI/EDI by ±4.
movsx(reg, reg); movsx(mem, reg);	Move with sign extension. Copies the (smaller) source operand to the (larger) destination operand and sign extends the value to the size of the larger operand. The source operand must be smaller than the destination operand.
movzx(reg, reg); movzx(mem, reg);	Move with zero extension. Copies the (smaller) source operand to the (larger) destination operand and zero extends the value to the size of the larger operand. The source operand must be smaller than the destination operand.

mul(reg);
mul(reg8, al);
mul(reg16, ax);
mul(reg32, eax);
mul(mem);
mul(mem8, al);
mul(mem16, ax);
mul(mem32, eax);
mul(imm8, al);
mul(imm16, ax);
mul(imm32, eax);
	Multiplies the accumulator (AL, AX, or EAX) by the source operand. The source operand will be the same size as the accumulator. The product produces an operand that is twice the size of the two operands with the product winding up in AX, DX:AX, or EDX:EAX. Note that the instructions involving an immediate operand are HLA extensions. HLA creates a memory object holding these constants and then multiplies the accumulator by the contents of this memory location.
	This instruction performs a signed multiplication. Also see INTMUL. The carry and overflow flags are cleared if the H.O. portion of the result is zero, they are set otherwise. The sign and zero flags are undefined after this instruction.

neg(reg); neg(mem);	Negate. Computes the two's complement of the operand and leaves the result in the operand. This instruction clears the carry flag if the result is zero, it sets the carry flag otherwise. It sets the overflow flag if the original value was the smallest possible negative value (which has no positive counterpart). It sets the sign and zero flags according to the result obtained.
nop();	No Operation. Consumes space and time but does nothing else. Same instruction as "xchg(eax, eax);".
not(reg); not(mem);	Bitwise NOT. Inverts all the bits in its operand. Note: This instruction does not affect any flags.

Table B-1: 80x86 Integer and Control Instruction Set

Instruction Syntax	Description

or(imm, reg);
or(imm, mem);
or(reg, reg);
or(reg, mem);
or(mem, reg);
	Bitwise OR. Logically ORs the source operand with the destination operand and leaves the result in the destination. The two operands must be the same size. Clears the carry and overflow flags and sets the sign and zero flags according to the result.

out(al, imm8);
out(ax, imm8);
out(eax, imm8);
out(al, dx);
out(ax, dx);
out(eax, dx);
	Outputs the accumulator to the specified port. See the IN instruction for limitations under Win32.

pop(reg); pop(mem);	Pop a value off the stack. Operands must be 16 or 32 bits.
popa();	Pops all the 16-bit registers off the stack. The popping order is DI, SI, BP, SP, BX, DX, CX, AX.
popad();	Pops all the 32-bit registers off the stack. The popping order is EDI, ESI, EBP, ESP, EBX, EDX, ECX, EAX.
popf();	Pops the 16-bit flags register off the stack. Note that in user (application) mode, this instruction ignores the interrupt disable flag value it pops off the stack.
popfd();	Pops the 32-bit eflags register off the stack. Note that in user (application) mode, this instruction ignores many of the bits it pops off the stack.
push(reg); push(mem);	Pushes the specified 16-bit or 32-bit register or memory location onto the stack. Note that you cannot push 8-bit objects.
pusha();	Pushes all the 16-bit general purpose registers onto the stack in the order AX, CX, DX, BX, SP, BP, SI, DI.
pushad();	Pushes all the 32-bit general purpose registers onto the stack in the order EAX, ECX, EDX, EBX, ESP, EBP, ESI, EDI.

pushd(imm);
pushd(reg);
pushd(mem);
	Pushes the 32-bit operand onto the stack. Generally used to push constants or anonymous variables. Note that this is a synonym for PUSH if you specify a register or typed memory operand.

pushf();	Pushes the value of the 16-bit flags register onto the stack.
pushfd();	Pushes the value of the 32-bit flags register onto the stack.

pushw(imm);
pushw(reg);
pushw(mem);
	Pushes the 16-bit operand onto the stack. Generally used to push constants or anonymous variables. Note that this is a synonym for PUSH if you specify a register or typed memory operand.

rcl(imm, reg);
rcl(imm, mem);
rcl(cl, reg);
rcl(cl, mem);
	Rotate through carry, left. Rotates the destination (second) operand through the carry the number of bits specified by the first operand, shifting the bits from the L.O. to the H.O. position (i.e., rotate left). The carry flag contains the last bit shifted into it. The overflow flag, which is valid only when the shift count is one, is set if the sign changes as a result of the rotate. This instruction does not affect the other flags. In particular, **note that this instruction does not affect the sign or zero flags.**

Table B-1: 80x86 Integer and Control Instruction Set

Instruction Syntax	Description

rcr(imm, reg);
rcr(imm, mem);
rcr(cl, reg);
rcr(cl, mem);
	Rotate through carry, right. Rotates the destination (second) operand through the carry the number of bits specified by the first operand, shifting the bits from the H.O. to the L.O. position (i.e., rotate right). The carry flag contains the last bit shifted into it. The overflow flag, which is valid only when the shift count is one, is set if the sign changes as a result of the rotate. This instruction does not affect the other flags. In particular, **note that this instruction does not affect the sign or zero flags.**

rdtsc();	Read Time Stamp Counter. Returns in EDX:EAX the number of clock cycles that have transpired since the last reset of the processor. You can use this instruction to time events in your code (i.e., to determine whether one instruction sequence takes more time than another).
ret(); ret(imm16);	Return from subroutine. Pops a return address off the stack and transfers control to that location. The second form of the instruction adds the immediate constant to the ESP register to remove the procedure's parameters from the stack.

rol(imm, reg);
rol(imm, mem);
rol(cl, reg);
rol(cl, mem);
	Rotate left. Rotates the destination (second) operand the number of bits specified by the first operand, shifting the bits from the L.O. to the H.O. position (i.e., rotate left). The carry flag contains the last bit shifted into it. The overflow flag, which is valid only when the shift count is one, is set if the sign changes as a result of the rotate. This instruction does not affect the other flags. In particular, **note that this instruction does not affect the sign or zero flags.**

ror(imm, reg);
ror(imm, mem);
ror(cl, reg);
ror(cl, mem);
	Rotate right. Rotates the destination (second) operand the number of bits specified by the first operand, shifting the bits from the H.O. to the L.O. position (i.e., rotate right). The carry flag contains the last bit shifted into it. The overflow flag, which is valid only when the shift count is one, is set if the sign changes as a result of the rotate. This instruction does not affect the other flags. In particular, **note that this instruction does not affect the sign or zero flags.**

sahf();	Store AH into flags. Copies the value in AH into the L.O. eight bits of the flags register. Note that this instruction will not affect the interrupt disable flag when operating in user (application) mode. Bit #7 of AH goes into the Sign flag, bit #6 goes into the zero flag, bit #4 goes into the auxilary carry (BCD carry) flag, bit #2 goes into the parity flag, and bit #0 goes into the carry flag. This instruction also clears bits 1, 3, and 5 of the flags register. It does not affect any other bits in flags or eflags.

sal(imm, reg);
sal(imm, mem);
sal(cl, reg);
sal(cl, mem);
	Shift Arithmetic Left. Same instruction as SHL. See SHL for details.

sar(imm, reg);
sar(imm, mem);
sar(cl, reg);
sar(cl, mem);
	Shift Arithmetic Right. Shifts the destination (second) operand to the right the specified number of bits using an arithmetic shift right algorithm. The carry flag contains the value of the last bit shifted out of the second operand. The overflow flag is only defined when the bit shift count is one; this instruction always clears the overflow flag. The sign and zero flags are set according to the result.

Table B-1: 80x86 Integer and Control Instruction Set

Instruction Syntax	Description

sbb(imm, reg);
sbb(imm, mem);
sbb(reg, reg);
sbb(reg, mem);
sbb(mem, reg);
	Subtract with borrow. Subtracts the source (first) operand and the carry from the destination (second) operand. Sets the condition code bits according to the result it computes. This instruction sets the flags the same way as the SUB instruction. See SUB for details.

scasb();
repe.scasb();
repne.scasb();
	Scan string byte. Compares the value in AL against the byte that EDI points at and sets the flags accordingly (same as the CMP instruction). Adds ±1 to EDI after the comparison (based on the setting of the direction flag). With the REPE (repeat while equal) prefix, this instruction will search through the next n characters (n in ECX), starting at location EDI, for the first character that is not equal to the value in AL. With the REPNE (repeat while not equal) prefix, this instruction will search through the next n characters (n in ECX), starting at location EDI, for the first character that is equal to the value in AL. See Chapter 12 for more details.

scasw();
repe.scasw();
repne.scasw();
	Scan String Word. Compares the value in AX against the word that EDI points at and set the flags. Adds ±2 to EDI after the operation. Also supports the REPE and REPNE prefixes (see SCASB above).

scasd();
repe.scasd();
repne.scasd();
	Scan String Double Word. Compares the value in EAX against the double word that EDI points at and set the flags. Adds ±4 to EDI after the operation. Also supports the REPE and REPNE prefixes (see SCASB above).

seta(reg); seta(mem);	Conditional set if (unsigned) above (Carry=0 and Zero=0). Stores a one in the destination operand if the result of the previous comparison found the first operand to be greater than the second using an unsigned comparison. Stores a zero into the destination operand otherwise.
setae(reg); setae(mem);	Conditional set if (unsigned) above or equal to (Carry=0). See SETA for details.
setb(reg); setb(mem);	Conditional set if (unsigned) below (Carry=1). See SETA for details.
setbe(reg); setbe(mem);	Conditional set if (unsigned) below or equal to (Carry=1 or Zero=1). See SETA for details.
setc(reg); setc(mem);	Conditional set if carry set (Carry=1). See SETA for details.
sete(reg); sete(mem);	Conditional set if equal to (Zero=1). See SETA for details.
setg(reg); setg(mem);	Conditional set if (signed) greater than (Sign=Overflow and Zero=0). See SETA for details.
setge(reg); setge(mem);	Conditional set if (signed) greater than or equal to (Sign=Overflow or Zero=1). See SETA for details.
setl(reg); setl(mem);	Conditional set if (signed) less than (Sign<>Overflow). See SETA for details.
setle(reg); setle(mem);	Conditional set if (signed) less than or equal to (Sign<>Overflow or Zero = 1). See SETA for details.
setna(reg); setna(mem);	Conditional set if (unsigned) not above (Carry=1 or Zero=1). See SETA for details.
setnae(reg); setnae(mem);	Conditional set if (unsigned) not above or equal to (Carry=1). See SETA for details.

Table B-1: 80x86 Integer and Control Instruction Set

Instruction Syntax	Description
setnb(reg); setnb(mem);	Conditional set if (unsigned) not below (Carry=0). See SETA for details.
setnbe(reg); setnbe(mem);	Conditional set if (unsigned) not below or equal to (Carry=0 and Zero=0). See SETA for details.
setnc(reg); setnc(mem);	Conditional set if carry clear (Carry=0). See SETA for details.
setne(reg); setne(mem);	Conditional set if not equal to (Zero=0). See SETA for details.
setng(reg); setng(mem);	Conditional set if (signed) not greater than (Sign<>Overflow or Zero = 1). See SETA for details.
setnge(reg); setnge(mem);	Conditional set if (signed) not greater than (Sign<>Overflow). See SETA for details.
setnl(reg); setnl(mem);	Conditional set if (signed) not less than (Sign=Overflow or Zero=1). See SETA for details.
setnle(reg); setnle(mem);	Conditional set if (signed) not less than or equal to (Sign=Overflow and Zero=0). See SETA for details.
setno(reg); setno(mem);	Conditional set if no overflow (Overflow=0). See SETA for details.
setnp(reg); setnp(mem);	Conditional set if no parity (Parity=0). See SETA for details.
setns(reg); setns(mem);	Conditional set if no sign (Sign=0). See SETA for details.
setnz(reg); setnz(mem);	Conditional set if not zero (Zero=0). See SETA for details.
seto(reg); seto(mem);	Conditional set if overflow (Overflow=1). See SETA for details.
setp(reg); setp(mem);	Conditional set if parity (Parity=1). See SETA for details.
setpe(reg); setpe(mem);	Conditional set if parity even (Parity=1). See SETA for details.
setpo(reg); setpo(mem);	Conditional set if parity odd (Parity=0). See SETA for details.
sets(reg); sets(mem);	Conditional set if sign set (Sign=1). See SETA for details.
setz(reg); setz(mem);	Conditional set if zero (Zero=1). See SETA for details.

shl(imm, reg);
shl(imm, mem);
shl(cl, reg);
shl(cl, mem);
	Shift left. Shifts the destination (second) operand to the left the number of bit positions specified by the first operand. The carry flag contains the value of the last bit shifted out of the second operand. The overflow flag is only defined when the bit shift count is one; this instruction sets overflow flag if the sign changes as a result of this instruction's execution. The sign and zero flags are set according to the result.

Table B-1: 80x86 Integer and Control Instruction Set

Instruction Syntax	Description

shld(imm8, reg, reg);
shld(imm8, reg, mem);
shld(cl, reg, reg);
shld(cl, reg, mem);
	Shift Left Double precision. The first operand is a bit count. The second operand is a source and the third operand is a destination. These operands must be the same size and they must be 16- or 32-bit values (no 8-bit operands). This instruction treats the second and third operands as a double precision value with the second operand being the L.O. word or double word and the third operand being the H.O. word or double word. The instruction shifts this double precision value the specified number of bits and sets the flags in a manner identical to SHL. Note that this instruction does not affect the source (second) operand's value.

shr(imm, reg);
shr(imm, mem);
shr(cl, reg);
shr(cl, mem);
	Shift right. Shifts the destination (second) operand to the right the number of bit positions specified by the first operand. The last bit shifted out goes into the carry flag. The overflow flag is set if the H.O. bit originally contained one. The sign flag is cleared and the zero flag is set if the result is zero.

shrd(imm8, reg, reg);
shrd(imm8, reg, mem);
shrd(cl, reg, reg);
shrd(cl, reg, mem);
	Shift Right Double precision. The first operand is a bit count. The second operand is a source and the third operand is a destination. These operands must be the same size and they must be 16- or 32-bit values (no 8-bit operands). This instruction treats the second and third operands as a double precision value with the second operand being the H.O. word or double word and the third operand being the L.O. word or double word. The instruction shifts this double precision value the specified number of bits and sets the flags in a manner identical to SHR. Note that this instruction does not affect the source (second) operand's value.

stc();	Set Carry. Sets the carry flag to one.
std();	Set Direction. Sets the direction flag to one. If the direction flag is one, the string instructions decrement ESI and/or EDI after each operation.
sti();	Set interrupt enable flag. Generally this instruction is not usable in user (application) mode. In kernel mode it allows the CPU to begin processing interrupts.
stosb(); rep.stosb();	Store String Byte. Stores the value in AL at the location whose address EDI contains. Then it adds ±1 to EDI. If the REP prefix is present, this instruction repeats the number of times specified in the ECX register. This instruction is useful for quickly clearing out byte arrays.
stosw(); rep.stosw();	Store String Word. Stores the value in AX at location [EDI] and then adds ±2 to EDI. See STOSB for details.
stosd(); rep.stosd();	Store String Double Word. Stores the value in EAX at location [EDI] and then adds ±4 to EDI. See STOSB for details.

Table B-1: 80x86 Integer and Control Instruction Set

Instruction Syntax	Description

sub(imm, reg);
sub(imm, mem);
sub(reg, reg);
sub(reg, mem);
sub(mem, reg);
	Subtract. Subtracts the first operand from the second operand and leaves the difference in the destination (second) operand. Sets the zero flag if the two values were equal (which produces a zero result), sets the carry flag if there was unsigned overflow or underflow; sets the overflow if there was signed overflow or underflow; sets the sign flag if the result is negative (H.O. bit is one). Note that SUB sets the flags identically to the CMP instruction, so you can use conditional jump or set instructions after SUB the same way you would use them after a CMP instruction.

test(imm, reg);
test(imm, mem);
test(reg, reg);
test(reg, mem);
test(mem, reg);
	Test operands. Logically ANDs the two operands together and sets the flags but does not store the computed result (i.e., it does not disturb the value in either operand). Always clears the carry and overflow flags. Sets the sign flag if the H.O. bit of the computed result is one. Sets the zero flag if the computed result is zero.

xadd(mem, reg);
xadd(reg, reg);
	Adds the first operand to the second operand and then stores the original value of the second operand into the first operand:
	
	`xadd( source, dest );`
	`temp := dest`
	`dest := dest + source`
	`source := temp`
	
	This instruction sets the flags in a manner identical to the ADD instruction.

xchg(reg, reg);
xchg(reg, mem);
xchg(mem, reg);
	Swaps the values in the two operands, which must be the same size. Does not affect any flags.

xlat();	Translate. Computes AL := [EBX + AL];. That is, it uses the value in AL as an index into a lookup table whose base address is in EBX. It copies the specified byte from this table into AL.

xor(imm, reg);
xor(imm, mem);
xor(reg, reg);
xor(reg, mem);
xor(mem, reg);
	Exclusive-OR. Logically XORs the source operand with the destination operand and leaves the result in the destination. The two operands must be the same size. Clears the carry and overflow flags and sets the sign and zero flags according to the result.

Table B-2: Floating Point Instruction Set

Instruction	Description
f2xm1();	Compute 2^x-1 in ST0, leaving the result in ST0.
fabs();	Computes the absolute value of ST0.

fadd(mem);
fadd(sti, st0);
fadd(st0, sti);
	Add operand to ST0 or add ST0 to destination register (STi, i=0..7). If the operand is a memory operand, it must be a *real32* or *real64* object.

faddp(); faddp(st0, sti);	With no operands, this instruction adds ST0 to ST1 and then pops ST0 off the FPU stack.

Table B-2: Floating Point Instruction Set

Instruction	Description
fbld(mem80);	This instruction loads a ten-byte (80-bit) packed BCD value from memory and converts it to a *real80* object. This instruction does not check for an invalid BCD value. If the BCD number contains illegal digits, the result is undefined.
fbstp(mem80);	This instruction pops the *real80* object off the top of the FPU stack, converts it to an 80-bit BCD value, and stores the result in the specified memory location (tbyte).
fchs();	This instruction negates the floating point value on the top of the stack (ST0).
fclex();	This instruction clears the floating point exception flags.
fcmova(sti, st0);[a]	Floating point conditional move if above. Copies STi to ST0 if c=0 and z=0 (unsigned greater than after a CMP).
fcmovae(sti, st0);	Floating point conditional move if above or equal. Copies STi to ST0 if c=0 (unsigned greater than or equal after a CMP).
fcmovb(sti, st0);	Floating point conditional move if below. Copies STi to ST0 if c=1 (unsigned less than after a CMP).
fcmovbe(sti, st0);	Floating point conditional move if below or equal. Copies STi to ST0 if c=1 or z=1 (unsigned less than or equal after a CMP).
fcmove(sti, st0);	Floating point conditional move if equal. Copies STi to ST0 if z=1 (equal after a CMP).
fcmovna(sti, st0);	Floating point conditional move if not above. Copies STi to ST0 if c=1 or z=1 (unsigned not above after a CMP).
fcmovnae(sti, st0);	Floating point conditional move if not above or equal. Copies STi to ST0 if c=1 (unsigned not above or equal after a CMP).
fcmovnb(sti, st0);	Floating point conditional move if not below. Copies STi to ST0 if c=0 (unsigned not below after a CMP).
fcmovnbe(sti, st0);	Floating point conditional move if not below or equal. Copies STi to ST0 if c=0 and z=0 (unsigned not below or equal after a CMP).
fcmovne(sti, st0);	Floating point conditional move if not equal. Copies STi to ST0 if z=0 (not equal after a CMP).
fcmovnu(sti, st0);	Floating point conditional move if not unordered. Copies STi to ST0 if the last floating point comparison did not produce an unordered result (parity flag = 0).
fcmovu(sti, st0);	Floating point conditional move if not unordered. Copies STi to ST0 if the last floating point comparison produced an unordered result (parity flag = 1).

fcom();
fcom(mem);
fcom(st0, sti);
	Compares the value of ST0 with the operand and sets the floating point condition bits based on the comparison. If the operand is a memory operand, it must be a *real32* or *real64* value. Note that to test the condition codes you will have to copy the floating point status word to the flags register; see Chapter 6 for details on floating point arithmetic.

fcomi(st0, sti);[b]	Compares the value of ST0 with the second operand and sets the appropriate bits in the flags register.
fcomip(st0, sti);	Compares the value of ST0 with the second operand, sets the appropriate bits in the flags register, and then pops ST0 off the FPU stack.

Table B-2: Floating Point Instruction Set

Instruction	Description

fcomp();
fcomp(mem);
fcomp(sti);
	Compares the value of ST0 with the operand, sets the floating point status bits, and then pops ST0 off the floating point stack. With no operands, this instruction compares ST0 to ST1. Memory operands must be *real32* or *real64* objects.

fcompp();	Compares ST0 to ST1 and then pops both values off the stack. Leaves the result of the comparison in the floating point status register.
fcos();	Computes ST0 = cos(ST0).
fdecstp();	Rotates the items on the FPU stack.

fdiv(mem);
fdiv(sti, st0);
fdiv(st0, sti);
	Floating point division. If a memory operand is present, it must be a *real32* or *real64* object; FDIV will divide ST0 by the memory operand and leave the quotient in ST0. If the FDIV operands are registers, FDIV divides the destination (second) operand by the source (first) operand and leaves the result in the destination operand.

fdivp(); fdivp(sti);	Without operands, this instruction replaces ST0 and ST1 with ST1/ST0. With a single register operand, the instruction replaces STi with the quotient STi/ST0 and removes ST0 from the stack.

fdivr(mem);
fdivr(sti, st0);
fdivr(st0, sti);
	Floating point divide with reversed operands. Like FDIV, but computes operand/ST0 rather than ST0/operand.

fdivrp(); fdivrp(sti);	Floating point divide and pop, reversed. Like FDIVP except it computes operand/ST0 rather than ST0/operand.
ffree(sti);	Frees the specified floating point register.
fiadd(mem);	Memory operand must be a 16-bit or 32-bit signed integer. This instruction converts the integer to a real, pushes the value, and then executes FADDP();.
ficom(mem);	Floating point compare to integer. Memory operand must be an *int16* or *int32* object. This instruction converts the memory operand to a *real80* value and compares ST0 to this value and sets the status bits in the floating point status register.
ficomp(mem);	Floating point compare to integer and pop. Memory operand must be an *int16* or *int32* object. This instruction converts the memory operand to a *real80* value and compares ST0 to this value and sets the status bits in the floating point status register. After the comparison, this instruction pops ST0 from the FPU stack.
fidiv(mem);	Floating point divide by integer. Memory operand must be an *int16* or *int32* object. These instructions convert their integer operands to a *real80* value and then divide ST0 by this value, leaving the result in ST0.
fidivr(mem);	Floating point divide by integer, reversed. Like FIDIV above, except this instruction computes mem/ST0 rather than ST0/mem.
fild(mem);	Floating point load integer. Mem operand must be an *int16* or *int32* object. This instruction converts the integer to a *real80* object and pushes it onto the FPU stack.
fimul(mem);	Floating point multiply by integer. Converts *int16* or *int32* operand to a *real80* value and multiplies ST0 by this result. Leaves product in ST0.
fincstp();	Rotates the registers on the FPU stack.
finit();	Initializes the FPU for use.

Table B-2: Floating Point Instruction Set

Instruction	Description
fist(mem);	Converts ST0 to an integer and stores the result in the specified memory operand. Memory operand must be an *int16* or *int32* object.
fistp(mem);	Floating point integer store and pop. Pops ST0 value off the stack, converts it to an integer, and stores the integer in the specified location. Memory operand must be a word, double word, or quad word (64-bit integer) object.
fisub(mem);	Floating point subtract integer. Converts *int16* or *int32* operand to a *real80* value and subtracts it from ST0. Leaves the result in ST0.
fisubr(mem);	Floating point subtract integer, reversed. Like FISUB except this instruction computes mem-ST0 rather than ST0-mem. Still leaves the result in ST0.
fld(mem); fld(sti);	Floating point load. Loads (pushes) the specified operand onto the FPU stack. Memory operands must be *real32*, *real64*, or *real80* objects. Note that FLD(ST0) duplicates the value on the top of the floating point stack.
fld1 ();	Floating point load 1.0. This instruction pushes 1.0 onto the FPU stack.
fldcw(mem16);	Load floating point control word. This instruction copies the word operand into the floating point control register.
fldenv(mem28);	This instruction loads the FPU status from the block of 28 bytes specified by the operand. Generally, only an operating system would use this instruction.
fldl2e();	Floating point load constant. Loads $\log_2(e)$ onto the stack.
fldl2t();	Floating point load constant. Loads $\log_2(10)$ onto the stack.
fldlg2();	Floating point load constant. Loads $\log_{10}(2)$ onto the stack.
fldln2();	Floating point load constant. Loads $\log_e(2)$ onto the stack.
fldpi();	Floating point load constant. Loads the value of pi (π) onto the stack.
fldz();	Floating point load constant. Pushes the value 0.0 onto the stack.
fmul(mem); fmul(sti, st0); fmul(st0, sti);	Floating point multiply. If the operand is a memory operand, it must be a *real32* or *real64* value; in this case, FMUL multiplies the memory operand and ST0, leaving the product in ST0. For the other two forms, the FMUL instruction multiplies the first operand by the second and leaves the result in the second operand.
fmulp(); fmulp(st0, sti);	Floating point multiply and pop. With no operands this instruction computes ST1:=ST0*ST1 and then pops ST0. With two register operands, this instruction computes ST0 times the destination register and then pops ST0.
fnop();	Floating point no-operation.
fpatan();	Floating point partial arctangent. Computes ATAN(ST1/ST0), pops ST0, and then stores the result in the new TOS value (previous ST1 value).
fprem();	Floating point remainder. This instruction is retained for compatibility with older programs. Use the FPREM1 instruction instead.

Table B-2: Floating Point Instruction Set

Instruction	Description
fprem1();	Floating point partial remainder. This instruction computes the remainder obtained by dividing ST0 by ST1, leaving the result in ST0 (it does not pop either operand). If the C2 flag in the FPU status register is set after this instruction, then the computation is not complete; you must repeatedly execute this instruction until C2 is cleared.
fptan();	Floating point partial tangent. This instruction computes TAN(ST0) and replaces the value in ST0 with this result. Then it pushes 1.0 onto the stack. This instruction sets the C2 flag if the input value is outside the acceptable range of $\pm 2^{63}$.
frndint();	Floating point round to integer. This instruction rounds the value in ST0 to an integer using the rounding control bits in the floating point control register. Note that the result left on TOS is still a real value. It simply doesn't have a fractional component. You may use this instruction to round or truncate a floating point value by setting the rounding control bits appropriately. See Chapter 6 for details.
frstor(mem108);	Restores the FPU status from a 108-byte memory block.
fsave(mem108);	Writes the FPU status to a 108-byte memory block.
fscale();	Floating point scale by power of two. ST1 contains a scaling value. This instruction multiplies ST0 by 2^{st1}.
fsin();	Floating point sine. Replaces ST0 with sin(ST0).
fsincos();	Simultaneously computes the sine and cosine values of ST0. Replaces ST0 with the sine of ST0 and then it pushes the cosine of (the original value of) ST0 onto the stack. Original ST0 value must be in the range $\pm 2^{63}$.
fsqrt();	Floating point square root. Replaces ST0 with the square root of ST0.
fst(mem); fst(sti);	Floating point store. Stores a copy of ST0 in the destination operand. Memory operands must be *real32* or *real64* objects. When storing the value to memory, FST converts the value to the smaller format using the rounding control bits in the floating point control register to determine how to convert the *real80* value in ST0 to a *real32* or *real64* value.
fstcw(mem16);	Floating point store control word. Stores a copy of the floating point control word in the specified *word* memory location.
fstenv(mem28);	Floating point store FPU environment. Stores a copy of the 28-byte floating point environment in the specified memory location. Normally, an OS would use this when switching contexts.
fstp(mem); fstp(sti);	Floating point store and pop. Stores ST0 into the destination operand and then pops ST0 off the stack. If the operand is a memory object, it must be a *real32*, *real64*, or *real80* object.
fstsw(ax); fstsw(mem16);	Stores a copy of the 16-bit floating point status register into the specified word operand. Note that this instruction automatically places the C1, C2, C3, and C4 condition bits in appropriate places in AH so that a following SAHF instruction will set the processor flags to allow the use of a conditional jump or conditional set instruction after a floating point comparison. See Chapter 6 for more details.

Table B-2: Floating Point Instruction Set

Instruction	Description

fsub(mem);
fsub(st0, sti);
fsub(sti, st0);
	Floating point subtract. With a single memory operand (which must be a *real32* or *real64* object), this instruction subtracts the memory operand from ST0. With two register operands, this instruction computes *dest := dest - src* (where *src* is the first operand and *dest* is the second operand).

fsubp(); fsubp(st0, sti);	Floating point subtract and pop. With no operands, this instruction computes ST1 := ST0 - ST1 and then pops ST0 off the stack. With two operands, this instruction computes STi := STi - ST0 and then pops ST0 off the stack.

fsubr(mem);
fsubr(st0, sti);
fsubr(sti , st0);
	Floating point subtract, reversed. With a *real32* or *real64* memory operand, this instruction computes ST0 := mem - ST0. For the other two forms, this instruction computes *dest := src - dest* where *src* is the first operand and *dest* is the second operand.

fsubrp(); fsubrp(st0, sti);	Floating point subtract and pop, reversed. With no operands, this instruction computes ST1 := ST0 - ST1 and then pops ST0. With two operands, this instruction computes STi := ST0 - STi and then pops ST0 from the stack.
ftst();	Floating point test against zero. Compares ST0 with 0.0 and sets the floating point condition code bits accordingly.
fucom(sti); fucom();	Floating point unordered comparison. With no operand, this instruction compares ST0 to ST1. With an operand, this instruction compares ST0 to STi and sets floating point status bits accordingly. Unlike FCOM, this instruction will not generate an exception if either of the operands is an illegal floating point value; instead, this sets a special status value in the FPU status register.
fucomi(sti, st0);	Floating point unordered comparison.
fucomp(); fucomp(sti);	Floating point unorder comparison and pop. With no operands, compares ST0 to ST1 using an unordered comparsion (see FUCOM) and then pops ST0 off the stack. With an FPU operand, this instruction compares ST0 to the specified register and then pops ST0 off the stack. See FUCOM for more details.
fucompp(); fucompp(sti);	Floating point unordered compare and double pop. Compares ST0 to ST1, sets the condition code bits (without raising an exception for illegal values; see FUCOM), and then pops both ST0 and ST1.
fwait();	Floating point wait. Waits for current FPU operation to complete. Generally an obsolete instruction. Used back in the days when the FPU was on a different chip than the CPU.
fxam();	Floating point Examine ST0. Checks the value in ST0 and sets the condition code bits according to the type of the value in ST0. See Chapter 6 for details.
fxch (); fxch(sti);	Floating point exchange. With no operands this instruction exchanges ST0 and ST1 on the FPU stack. With a single register operand, this instruction swaps ST0 and STi.
fxtract();	Floating point exponent/mantissa extraction. This instruction breaks the value in ST0 into two pieces. It replaces ST0 with the real representation of the binary exponent (e.g. 2^5 becomes 5.0) and then it pushes the mantissa of the value with an exponent of zero.

Table B-2: Floating Point Instruction Set

Instruction	Description
fyl2x();	Floating point partial logarithm computation. Computes ST1 := ST1 * log$_2$(ST0); and then pops ST0.
fyl2xp1();	Floating point partial logarithm computation. Computes ST1 := ST1 * log$_2$(ST0 + 1.0) and then pops ST0 off the stack. Original ST0 value must be in the range $$(-\left(1 - \frac{\sqrt{2}}{2}\right), \left(1 - \frac{\sqrt{2}}{2}\right))$$

a. Floating point conditional move instructions are only available on Pentium Pro and later processors.
b. FCOMIx instructions are only available on Pentium Pro and later processors.

The following table uses these abbreviations:

reg32	A 32-bit general purpose (integer) register.
mmi	One of the eight MMX registers, MM0..MM7.
imm8	An 8-bit constant value; some instructions have smaller ranges than 0..255. See the particular instruction for details.
mem64	A memory location (using an arbitrary addressing mode) that references a qword value.

NOTE *Most instructions have two operands. Typically the first operand is a source operand and the second operand is a destination operand. For exceptions, see the description of the instruction.*

Table B-3: MMX Instruction Set

Instruction	Description
emms();	Empty MMX State. You must execute this instruction when you are finished using MMX instructions and before any following floating point instructions.

movd(reg32, mmi);
movd(mem32, mmi);
movd(mmi, reg32);
movd(mmi, mem32);
	Moves data between a 32-bit integer register or dword memory location and an MMX register (mm0..mm7). If the destination operand is an MMX register, then the source operand is zero extended to 64 bits during the transfer. If the destination operand is a dword memory location or 32-bit register, this instruction copies only the L.O. 32 bits of the MMX register to the destination.

movq(mem64, mmi);
movq(mmi, mem64);
movq(mmi, mmi);
	This instruction moves 64 bits between an MMX register and a *qword* variable in memory or between two MMX registers.

Table B-3: MMX Instruction Set

Instruction	Description
packssdw(mem64, mm*i*); packssdw(mm*i*, mm*i*);	Pack and saturate two signed double words from source and two signed double words from destination and store result into destination MMX register. This process involves taking these four double words and "saturating" them. This means that if the value is in the range -32768..32768 the value is left unchanged, but if it's greater than 32767 the value is set to 32767 or if it's less than -32768 the value is clipped to -32768. The four double words are packed into a single 64-bit MMX register. The source operand supplies the upper two words and the destination operand supplies the lower two words of the packed 64-bit result. See Chapter 13, "The MMX Instruction Set," for more details.
packsswb(mem64, mm*i*); packsswb(mm*i*, mm*i*);	Pack and saturate four signed words from source and four signed words from destination and store the result as eight signed bytes into the destination MMX register. See Chapter 13 for more details. The bytes obtained from the destination register wind up in the L.O. four bytes of the destination; the bytes computed from the signed saturation of the source register wind up in the H.O. four bytes of the destination register.
packusdw(mem64, mm*i*); packusdw(mm*i*, mm*i*);	Pack and saturate two unsigned double words from source and two unsigned double words from destination and store result into destination MMX register. This process involves taking these four double words and "saturating" them. This means that if the value is in the range 0..65535 the value is left unchanged, but if it's greater than 65535 the value is clipped to 65535. The four double words are packed into a single 64-bit MMX register. The source operand supplies the upper two words and the destination operand supplies the lower two words of the packed 64-bit result. See Chapter 13 for more details.
packuswb(mem64, mm*i*); packuswb(mm*i*, mm*i*);	Pack and saturate four unsigned words from source and four unsigned words from destination and store the result as eight unsigned bytes into the destination MMX register. Word values greater than 255 are clipped to 255 during the saturation operation. See Chapter 13 for more details. The bytes obtained from the destination register wind up in the L.O. four bytes of the destination; the bytes computed from the signed saturation of the source register wind up in the H.O. four bytes of the destination register.
paddb(mem64, mm*i*); paddb(mm*i*, mm*i*);	Packed Add of Bytes. This instruction adds together the individual bytes of the two operands. The addition of each byte is independent of the other eight bytes; there is no carry from byte to byte. If an overflow occurs in any byte, the value simply wraps around to zero with no indication of the overflow. This instruction does not affect any flags.

Table B-3: MMX Instruction Set

Instruction	Description
paddd(mem64, mmi); paddd(mmi, mmi);	Packed Add of Double Words. This instruction adds together the individual dwords of the two operands. The addition of each dword is independent of the other two dwords; there is no carry from dword to dword. If an overflow occurs in any dword, the value simply wraps around to zero with no indication of the overflow. This instruction does not affect any flags.
paddsb(mem64, mmi); paddsb(mmi, mmi);	Packed Add of Bytes, signed saturated. This instruction adds together the individual bytes of the two operands. The addition of each byte is independent of the other eight bytes; there is no carry from byte to byte. If an overflow or underflow occurs in any byte, then the value saturates at -128 or +127. This instruction does not affect any flags.
paddsw(mem64, mmi); paddsw(mmi, mmi);	Packed Add of Words, signed saturated. This instruction adds together the individual words of the two operands. The addition of each word is independent of the other four words; there is no carry from word to word. If an overflow or underflow occurs in any word, the value saturates at either -32768 or +32767. This instruction does not affect any flags.
paddusb(mem64, mmi); paddusb(mmi, mmi);	Packed Add of Bytes, unsigned saturated. This instruction adds together the individual bytes of the two operands. The addition of each byte is independent of the other eight bytes; there is no carry from byte to byte. If an overflow or underflow occurs in any byte, then the value saturates at 0 or 255. This instruction does not affect any flags.
paddusw(mem64, mmi); paddusw(mmi, mmi);	Packed Add of Words, unsigned saturated. This instruction adds together the individual words of the two operands. The addition of each word is independent of the other four words; there is no carry from word to word. If an overflow or underflow occurs in any word, the value saturates at either 0 or 65535. This instruction does not affect any flags.
paddw(mem64, mmi); paddw(mmi, mmi);	Packed Add of Words. This instruction adds together the individual words of the two operands. The addition of each word is independent of the other four words; there is no carry from word to word. If an overflow occurs in any word, the value simply wraps around to zero with no indication of the overflow. This instruction does not affect any flags.
pand(mem64, mmi); pand(mmi, mmi);	Packed AND. This instruction computes the bitwise AND of the source and the destination values, leaving the result in the destination. This instruction does not affect any flags.
pandn(mem64, mmi); pandn(mmi, mmi);	Packed AND NOT. This instruction makes a temporary copy of the first operand and inverts all of the bits in this copy; then it ANDs this value with the destination MMX register. This instruction does not affect any flags.
pavgb(mem64, mmi); pavgb(mmi, mmi);	Packed Average of Bytes. This instruction computes the average of the eight pairs of bytes in the two operands. It leaves the result in the destination (second) operand.
pavgw(mem64, mmi); pavgw(mmi, mmi);	Packed Average of Words. This instruction computes the average of the four pairs of words in the two operands. It leaves the result in the destination (second) operand.

Table B-3: MMX Instruction Set

Instruction	Description
pcmpeqb(mem64, mmi); pcmpeqb(mmi, mmi);	Packed Compare for Equal Bytes. This instruction compares the individual bytes in the two operands. If they are equal this instruction sets the corresponding byte in the destination (second) register to $FF (all ones); if they are not equal, this instruction sets the corresponding byte to zero.
pcmpeqd(mem64, mmi); pcmpeqd(mmi, mmi);	Packed Compare for Equal Double Words. This instruction compares the individual double words in the two operands. If they are equal this instruction sets the corresponding double word in the destination (second) register to $FFFF_FFFF (all ones); if they are not equal, this instruction sets the corresponding dword to zero.
pcmpeqw(mem64, mmi); pcmpeqw(mmi, mmi);	Packed Compare for Equal Words. This instruction compares the individual words in the two operands. If they are equal this instruction sets the corresponding word in the destination (second) register to $FFFF (all ones); if they are not equal, this instruction sets the corresponding word to zero.
pcmpgtb(mem64, mmi); pcmpgtb(mmi, mmi);	Packed Compare for Greater Than, Bytes. This instruction compares the individual bytes in the two operands. If the destination (second) operand byte is greater than the source (first) operand byte, then this instruction sets the corresponding byte in the destination (second) register to $FF (all ones); if they are not equal, this instruction sets the corresponding byte to zero. Note that there is no PCMPLEB instruction. You can simulate this instruction by swapping the operands in the PCMPGTB instruction (i.e., compare in the opposite direction). Also note that these operands are, in a sense, backwards compared with the standard CMP instruction. This instruction compares the second operand to the first rather than the other way around. This was done because the second operand is always the destination operand and, unlike the CMP instruction, this instruction writes data to the destination operand.
pcmpgtd (mem64, mmi); pcmpgtd (mmi, mmi)	Packed Compare for Greater Than, Double Words. This instruction compares the individual dwords in the two operands. If the destination (second) operand dword is greater than the source (first) operand dword, then this instruction sets the corresponding dword in the destination (second) register to $FFFF_FFFF (all ones); if they are not equal, this instruction sets the corresponding dword to zero. Note that there is no PCMPLED instruction. You can simulate this instruction by swapping the operands in the PCMPGTD instruction (i.e., compare in the opposite direction). Also note that these operands are, in a sense, backwards compared with the standard CMP instruction. This instruction compares the second operand to the first rather than the other way around. This was done because the second operand is always the destination operand and, unlike the CMP instruction, this instruction writes data to the destination operand.

Table B-3: MMX Instruction Set

Instruction	Description
pcmpgtw(mem64, mmi); pcmpgtw(mmi, mmi);	Packed Compare for Greater Than, Words. This instruction compares the individual words in the two operands. If the destination (second) operand word is greater than the source (first) operand word, then this instruction sets the corresponding word in the destination (second) register to $FFFF (all ones); if they are not equal, this instruction sets the corresponding dword to zero. Note that there is no PCMPLEW instruction. You can simulate this instruction by swapping the operands in the PCMPGTW instruction (i.e., compare in the opposite direction). Also note that these operands are, in a sense, backwards compared with the standard CMP instruction. This instruction compares the second operand to the first rather than the other way around. This was done because the second operand is always the destination operand and, unlike the CMP instruction, this instruction writes data to the destination operand.
pextrw(imm8, mmi, reg32);	Packed Extraction of a Word. The imm8 value must be a constant in the range 0..3. This instruction copies the specified word from the MMX register into the L.O. word of the destination 32-bit integer register. This instruction zero extends the 16-bit value to 32 bits in the integer register. Note that there are no extraction instructions for bytes or dwords. However, you can easily extract a byte using PEXTRW and an AND or XCHG instruction (depending on whether the byte number is even or odd). You can use MOVD to extract the L.O. dword. To extract the H.O. dword of an MMX register requires a bit more work; either extract the two words and merge them or move the data to memory and grab the dword you're interested in.
pinsw(imm8, reg32, mmi);	Packed Insertion of a Word. The imm8 value must be a constant in the range 0..3. This instruction copies the L.O. word from the 32-bit integer register into the specified word of the destination MMX register. This instruction ignores the H.O. word of the integer register.
pmaddwd(mem64, mmi); pmaddwd(mmi, mmi);	Packed Multiple and Accumulate (Add). This instruction multiplies together the corresponding words in the source and destination operands. Then it adds the two double word products from the multiplication of the two L.O. words and stores this double word sum in the L.O. dword of the destination MMX register. Finally, it adds the two double word products from the multiplication of the H.O. words and stores this double word sum in the H.O. dword of the destination MMX register.
pmaxw(mem64, mmi); pmaxw(mmi, mmi);	Packed Signed Integer Word Maximum. This instruction compares the four words between the two operands and stores the signed maximum of each corresponding word in the destination MMX register.
pmaxub(mem64, mmi); pmaxub(mmi, mmi);	Packed Unsigned Byte Maximum. This instruction compares the eight bytes between the two operands and stores the unsigned maximum of each corresponding byte in the destination MMX register.

Table B-3: MMX Instruction Set

Instruction	Description
pminw(mem64, mm*i*); pminw(mm*i*, mm*i*);	Packed Signed Integer Word Minimum. This instruction compares the four words between the two operands and stores the signed minimum of each corresponding word in the destination MMX register.
pminub(mem64, mm*i*); pminub(mm*i*, mm*i*);	Packed Unsigned Byte Minimum. This instruction compares the eight bytes between the two operands and stores the unsigned minimum of each corresponding byte in the destination MMX register.
pmovmskb(mm*i*, reg32);	Move Byte Mask to Integer. This instruction creates a byte by extracting the H.O. bit of the eight bytes from the MMX source register. It zero extends this value to 32 bits and stores the result in the 32-bit integer register.
pmulhuw(mem64, mm*i*); pmulhuw(mm*i*, mm*i*);	Packed Multiply High, Unsigned Words. This instruction multiplies the four unsigned words of the two operands together and stores the H.O. word of the resulting products into the corresponding word of the destination MMX register.
pmulhw(mem64, mm*i*); pmulhw(mm*i*, mm*i*);	Packed Multiply High, Signed Words. This instruction multiplies the four signed words of the two operands together and stores the H.O. word of the resulting products into the corresponding word of the destination MMX register.
pmullw(mem64, mm*i*); pmullw(mm*i*, mm*i*);	Packed Multiply Low, Signed Words. This instruction multiplies the four signed words of the two operands together and stores the L.O. word of the resulting products into the corresponding word of the destination MMX register.
por(mem64, mm*i*); por(mm*i*, mm*i*);	Packed OR. Computes the bitwise OR of the two operands and stores the result in the destination (second) MMX register.
psadbw(mem64, mm*i*); psadbw(mm*i*, mm*i*);	Packed Sum of Absolute Differences. This instruction computes the absolute value of the difference of each of the unsigned bytes between the two operands. Then it adds these eight results together to form a word sum. Finally, the instruction zero extends this word to 64 bits and stores the result in the destination (second) operand.
pshufw(imm8, mem64, mm*i*);	Packed Shuffle Word. This instruction treats the imm8 value as an array of four two-bit values. These bits specify where the destination (third) operand's words obtain their values. Bits zero and one tell this instruction where to obtain the L.O. word, bits two and three specify where word #1 comes from, bits four and five specify the source for word #2, and bits six and seven specify the source of the H.O. word in the destination operand. Each pair of bytes specifies a word number in the source (second) operand. For example, an immediate value of %00011011 tells this instruction to grab word #3 from the source and place it in the L.O. word of the destination; grab word #2 from the source and place it in word #1 of the destination; grab word #1 from the source and place it in word #2 of the destination; and grab the L.O. word of the source and place it in the H.O. word of the destination (i.e., swap all the words in a manner similar to the BSWAP instruction).

Table B-3: MMX Instruction Set

Instruction	Description

pslld(mem, mm*i*);
pslld(mm*i*, mm*i*);
pslld(imm8, mm*i*);
	Packed Shift Left Logical, Double Words. This instruction shifts the destination (second) operand to the left the number of bits specified by the first operand. Each double word in the destination is treated as an independent entity. Bits are not carried over from the L.O. dword to the H.O. dword. Bits shifted out are lost and this instruction always shifts in zeros.

psllq(mem, mm*i*);
psllq(mm*i*, mm*i*);
psllq(imm8, mm*i*);
	Packed Shift Left Logical, Quad Word. This instruction shifts the destination operand to the left the number of bits specified by the first operand.

psllw(mem, mm*i*);
psllw(mm*i*, mm*i*);
psllw(imm8, mm*i*);
	Packed Shift Left Logical, Words. This instruction shifts the destination (second) operand to the left the number of bits specified by the first operand. Bits shifted out are lost and this instruction always shifts in zeros. Each word in the destination is treated as an independent entity. Bits are not carried over from the L.O. words into the next higher word. Bits shifted out are lost and this instruction always shifts in zeros.

psard(mem, mm*i*);
psard(mm*i*, mm*i*);
psard(imm8, mm*i*);
	Packed Shift Right Arithmetic, Double Word. This instruction treats the two halves of the 64-bit register as two double words and performs separate arithmetic shift rights on them. The bit shifted out of the bottom of the two double words is lost.

psarw(mem, mm*i*);
psarw(mm*i*, mm*i*);
psarw(imm8, mm*i*);
	Packed Shift Right Arithmetic, Word. This instruction operates independently on the four words of the 64-bit destination register and performs separate arithmetic shift rights on them. The bit shifted out of the bottom of the four words is lost.

psrld(mem, mm*i*);
psrld(mm*i*, mm*i*);
psrld(imm8, mm*i*);
	Packed Shift Right Logical, Double Words. This instruction shifts the destination (second) operand to the right the number of bits specified by the first operand. Each double word in the destination is treated as an independent entity. Bits are not carried over from the H.O. dword to the L.O. dword. Bits shifted out are lost and this instruction always shifts in zeros.

pslrq(mem, mm*i*);
pslrq(mm*i*, mm*i*);
pslrq(imm8, mm*i*);
	Packed Shift Right Logical, Quad Word. This instruction shifts the destination operand to the right the number of bits specified by the first operand.

pslrw(mem, mm*i*);
pslrw(mm*i*, mm*i*);
pslrw(imm8, mm*i*);
	Packed Shift Right Logical, Words. This instruction shifts the destination (second) operand to the right the number of bits specified by the first operand. Bits shifted out are lost and this instruction always shifts in zeros. Each word in the destination is treated as an independent entity. Bits are not carried over from the H.O. words into the next lower word. Bits shifted out are lost and this instruction always shifts in zeros.

psubb(mem64, mm*i*); psubb(mm*i*, mm*i*);	Packed Subtract of Bytes. This instruction subtracts the individual bytes of the source (first) operand from the corresponding bytes of the destination (second) operand. The subtraction of each byte is independent of the other eight bytes; there is no borrow from byte to byte. If an overflow or underflow occurs in any byte, the value simply wraps around to zero with no indication of the overflow. This instruction does not affect any flags.

Table B-3: MMX Instruction Set

Instruction	Description
psubd(mem64, mm*i*); psubd(mm*i*, mm*i*);	Packed Subtract of Double Words. This instruction subtracts the individual dwords of the source (first) operand from the corresponding dwords of the destination (second) operand. The subtraction of each dword is independent of the other; there is no borrow from dword to dword. If an overflow or underflow occurs in any dword, the value simply wraps around to zero with no indication of the overflow. This instruction does not affect any flags.
psubsb(mem64, mm*i*); psubsb(mm*i*, mm*i*);	Packed Subtract of Bytes, signed saturated. This instruction subracts the individual bytes of the source operand from the corresponding bytes of the destination operand, saturating to -128 or +127 if overflow or underflow occurs. The subtraction of each byte is independent of the other seven bytes; there is no carry from byte to byte. This instruction does not affect any flags.
psubsw(mem64, mm*i*); psubsw(mm*i*, mm*i*);	Packed Subtract of Words, signed saturated. This instruction subracts the individual words of the source operand from the corresponding words of the destination operand, saturating to -32768 or +32767 if overflow or underflow occurs. The subtraction of each word is independent of the other three words; there is no carry from word to word. This instruction does not affect any flags.
psubusb(mem64, mm*i*); psubusb(mm*i*, mm*i*);	Packed Subtract of Bytes, unsigned saturated. This instruction subracts the individual bytes of the source operand from the corresponding bytes of the destination operand, saturating to 0 if underflow occurs. The subtraction of each byte is independent of the other seven bytes; there is no carry from byte to byte. This instruction does not affect any flags.
psubusw(mem64, mm*i*); psubusw(mm*i*, mm*i*);	Packed Subtract of Words, unsigned saturated. This instruction subracts the individual words of the source operand from the corresponding words of the destination operand, saturating to 0 if underflow occurs. The subtraction of each word is independent of the other three words; there is no carry from word to word. This instruction does not affect any flags.
psubw(mem64, mm*i*); psubw(mm*i*, mm*i*);	Packed Subtract of Words. This instruction subtracts the individual words of the source (first) operand from the corresponding words of the destination (second) operand. The subtraction of each word is independent of the others; there is no borrow from word to word. If an overflow or underflow occurs in any word, the value simply wraps around to zero with no indication of the overflow. This instruction does not affect any flags.
punpckhbw(mem64, mm*i*); punpckhbw(mm*i*, mm*i*);	Unpack high packed data, bytes to words. This instruction unpacks and interleaves the high-order four bytes of the source (first) and destination (second) operands. It places the H.O. four bytes of the destination operand at the even byte positions in the destination and it places the H.O. four bytes of the source operand in the odd byte positions of the destination operand.

Table B-3: MMX Instruction Set

Instruction	Description
punpckhdq(mem64, mm*i*); punpckhdq(mm*i, mm*i*);	Unpack high packed data, dwords to qword. This instruction copies the H.O. dword of the source operand to the H.O. dword of the destination operand and it copies the (original) H.O. dword of the destination operand to the L.O. dword of the destination.
punpckhwd(mem64, mm*i*); punpckhwd(mm*i, mm*i*);	Unpack high packed data, words to dwords. This instruction unpacks and interleaves the high-order two words of the source (first) and destination (second) operands. It places the H.O. two words of the destination operand at the even word positions in the destination and it places the H.O. words of the source operand in the odd word positions of the destination operand.
punpcklbw(mem64, mm*i*); punpcklbw(mm*i, mm*i*);	Unpack low packed data, bytes to words. This instruction unpacks and interleaves the low-order four bytes of the source (first) and destination (second) operands. It places the L.O. four bytes of the destination operand at the even byte positions in the destination and it places the L.O. four bytes of the source operand in the odd byte positions of the destination operand.
punpckldq(mem64, mm*i*); punpckldq(mm*i, mm*i*);	Unpack low packed data, dwords to qword. This instruction copies the L.O. dword of the source operand to the H.O. dword of the destination operand and it copies the (original) L.O. dword of the destination operand to the L.O. dword of the destination (i.e., it doesn't change the L.O. dword of the destination).
punpcklwd(mem64, mm*i*); punpcklwd(mm*i, mm*i*);	Unpack low packed data, words to dwords. This instruction unpacks and interleaves the low-order two words of the source (first) and destination (second) operands. It places the L.O. two words of the destination operand at the even word positions in the destination and it places the L.O. words of the source operand in the odd word positions of the destination operand.
pxor(mem64, mm*i*); pxor(mm*i, mm*i*);	Packed Exclusive-OR. This instruction exclusive-ORs the source operand with the destination operand, leaving the result in the destination operand.

INDEX

Word strings, 689
Words, 59, 62
Wraparound arithmetic, 714

X

XLAT instruction, 593
XOR, 396
XOR instruction, 72, 660
XOR operation, 69, 70

Y

Y2K, 89
YtoX function, 433

Z

Zero divide exception (FPU), 405
Zero extension, 376
Zero flag, 10, 378
Zero terminated strings, 196
Zero terminating byte (in HLA
        strings), 198
Zeroing selected bits, 657

WRITE GREAT CODE
Understanding the Machine

by RANDALL HYDE

Today's programmers are often narrowly trained because the industry moves too fast. This book, from Assembly language guru Randall Hyde, teaches important concepts of machine organization in a language-independent fashion, giving programmers what they need to know to write great code in any language.

2003, 376 PP., $34.95 ($59.95 CDN)
ISBN 1-59327-003-8

HACKING
The Art of Exploitation

by JON ERICKSON

A comprehensive introduction to exploitation techniques and creative problem solving methods known as "hacking." Explains technical aspects of hacking such as stack based overflows, heap based overflows, string exploits, return-into-libc, shellcode, and cryptographic attacks on 802.11b.

2003, 400 PP., $39.95 ($59.95 CDN)
ISBN 1-59327-007-0

HACKING THE XBOX
An Introduction to Reverse Engineering

by ANDREW "BUNNIE" HUANG

A hands-on guide to hardware hacking and reverse engineering using Microsoft's Xbox™ video game console. Covers basic hacking techniques such as reverse engineering and debugging, as well as Xbox security mechanisms and other advanced hacking topics. Includes a chapter written by the Electronic Frontier Foundation (EFF) about the rights and responsibilities of hackers.

2003, 288 PP, $24.99 ($37.95 CDN)
ISBN 1-59327-029-1

HOW NOT TO PROGRAM IN C++

111 Broken Programs and 3 Working Ones, or Why Does 2+2=5986?

by STEVE OUALLINE

Over 100 fun and challenging C++ puzzles that will make you a better programmer. Based on real-world errors, the puzzles range from easy (one wrong character) to mind twisting (errors with multiple threads). Clues help along the way, and answers are provided at the back of the book.

". . . a unique book that is fun to read while still providing valuable information. If you are a C++ programmer and you'd like to hone your skill, this is a great tool to use." — *CodeGuru.com*

2003, 280 PP., $24.95 ($59.95 CDN)
ISBN 1-886411-95-6

CRACKPROOF YOUR SOFTWARE

The Best Ways to Protect Your Software Against Crackers

by PAVOL CERVEN

This essential resource for software developers highlights the weak points in software protection, shows how crackers break common protection schemes, and describes how to defend against them. CD-ROM contains compression and encoding software, debuggers and anti-debugging tricks, and practical protection demonstrations.

"If you develop your own commercial software or computer games, this should be high on your list." — *BookNews*

2002, 272 PP., $34.95 ($52.95 CDN)
ISBN 1-886411-79-4

PHONE:

1 (800) 420-7240 OR
(415) 863-9900
MONDAY THROUGH FRIDAY,
9 A.M. TO 5 P.M. (PST)

FAX:

(415) 863-9950
24 HOURS A DAY,
7 DAYS A WEEK

EMAIL:

SALES@NOSTARCH.COM

WEB:

HTTP://WWW.NOSTARCH.COM

MAIL:

NO STARCH PRESS
555 DE HARO STREET, SUITE 250
SAN FRANCISCO, CA 94107
USA

UPDATES

Visit **http://www.nostarch.com/assembly.htm** for updates, errata, and other information.

CD-ROM LICENSE AGREEMENT FOR
THE ART OF ASSEMBLY LANGUAGE

Read this Agreement before opening the CD package. By opening this package, you agree to be bound by the terms and conditions of this Agreement.

This CD-ROM (the "CD") contains programs and associated documentation and other materials and is distributed with the book entitled *The Art of Assembly Language* to purchasers of the book for their own personal use only. Such programs, documentation, and other materials and their compilation (collectively, the "Collection") are licensed to you subject to the terms and conditions of this Agreement by No Starch Press, Inc., having a place of business at 555 De Haro Street, Suite 250, San Francisco, CA 94107 USA ("Licensor"). In addition to being governed by the terms and conditions of this Agreement, your rights to use the programs and other materials included on the CD may also be governed by separate agreements distributed with those programs and materials (the "Other Agreements"). In the event of any inconsistency between this Agreement and any of the Other Agreements, those Other Agreements shall govern insofar as those programs and materials are concerned. By using the Collection, in whole or in part, you agree to be bound by the terms and conditions of this Agreement. Licensor owns the copyright to the Collection, except insofar as it contains materials that are proprietary to third-party suppliers. All rights to the Collection except those expressly granted to you in this Agreement are reserved to Licensor and such suppliers as their respective interests may appear.

1. Limited License. Licensor grants you a limited, nonexclusive, nontransferable license to use the Collection on a single dedicated computer (excluding network servers). This Agreement and your rights hereunder shall automatically terminate if you fail to comply with any provision of this Agreement or the Other Agreements. Upon such termination, you agree to destroy the CD and all copies of the CD, whether lawful or not, that are in your possession or under your control. Licensor and its suppliers retain all rights not expressly granted herein as their respective interests may appear.

2. Additional Restrictions. (A) You shall not (and shall not permit other persons or entities to) directly or indirectly, by electronic or other means, reproduce (excpet for archival purposes as permitted by law), publish, distribute, rent, lease, sell, sublicense, assign, or otherwise transfer the Collection or any part thereof of this Agreement. Any attempt to do so shall be void and of no effect. (B) You shall not (and shall not permit other persons or entities to) reverse-engineer, decompile, disassemble, merge, modify, create derivative works of, or translate the Collection or use the Collection or any part thereof for any commercial purpose. (C) You shall not (and shall not permit other persons or entities to) remove or obscure Licensor's or its suppliers' or licensors' copyright, trademark, or other proprietary notices or legends from any portion of the Collection or any related materials. (D) You agree and certify that the Collection will not be exported outside the United States except as authorized or permitted by the laws and regulations of the United States. If the Collection has been rightfully obtained outside the United States, you agree that you will not reexport the Collection, except as permitted by the laws and regulations of the jurisdiction in which you obtained the Collection.

3. Disclaimer of Warranty. (A) The Collection and the CD are provided "as is" without warranty of any kind, either expressed or implied, including, without limitation, any warranty of merchantability and fitness for a particular purpose. The entire risk as to the results and performance of the CD and the software and other materials that are part of the Collection is assumed by you, and Licensor and its suppliers and distributors shall have no responsibility for defects in the CD or the accuracy or application of or errors or omissions in the Collection, and do not warrant that the functions contained in the Collection will meet your requirements, or that the operation of the CD or the Collection will be uninterrupted or error-free, or that any defects in the CD or the Collection will be corrected. In no event shall Licensor or its suppliers or distributors be liable for any direct, indirect, special, incidental, or consequential damages arising out of the use of or inability to use the Collection or the CD, even if Licensor or its suppliers or distributors have been advised of the likelihood of such damages occurring. Licensor and its suppliers and distributors shall not be liable for any loss, damages, or costs arising out of, but not limited to, lost profits and revenue; loss of use of the Collection or the CD; loss of data or equipment; costs of recovering software, data, or materials in the collection; cost of substitute software, data, or materials in the Collection; claims by third parties; or similar costs. (B) In no event shall Licensor or its suppliers' distributors' total liability to you for all damages, losses, and causes of action (whether in contract, tort, or otherwise) exceed the amount paid by you for the collection. (C) Some states do not allow exclusion or limiation of implied warranties or limitation of liability for incidental or consequential damages, so the above limitations or exclusions may not apply to you.

4. U.S. Government Restricted Rights. The Collection is licensed subject to RESTRICTED RIGHTS. Use, duplication, or disclosure by the U.S. Government or any person or entity acting on its behalf is subject to restrictions as set forth in subdivision (c)(1)(ii) of the Rights in the Technical Data and Computer Software Clause at DFARS (48 CFR 252.227-7013) for DoD contracts, in paragraphs (c)(1) and (2) of the Commercial Computer Software Restricted Rights clause in the FAR (48 CFR 52.227-19) for civilian agencies, or, in the case of NASA, in clause 18-52.227-86(d) of the NASA Supplement to the FAR, or in other comparable agency clauses. The contractor/manufacturer is No Starch Press, Inc., 555 De Haro Street, Suite 250, San Francisco, CA 94107 USA.

5. General Provisions. Nothing in this Agreement constitutes a waiver of Licensor's or its suppliers' or licensors' rights under U.S. copyright laws or any other federal, state, local, or foreign law. You are responsible for installation, management, and operation of the Collection. This Agreement shall be construed, interpreted, and governed under California law. Copyright © 2003 No Starch Press, Inc. All rights reserved. Reproduction in whole or in part without permission is prohibited.